MAPPING AN EMPIRE

MATTHEW H. EDNEY

MAPPING AN
Empire

THE
GEOGRAPHICAL
CONSTRUCTION OF
BRITISH INDIA,
1765–1843

The University of Chicago Press

Chicago and London

Matthew H. Edney is associate professor of geography-anthropology and American and New England studies and faculty scholar in the Osher Map Library and Smith Center for Cartographic Education at the University of Southern Maine.

The University of Chicago Press, Chicago 60637
The University of Chicago Press, Ltd., London
© 1990, 1997 by The University of Chicago
All rights reserved. Published 1997
Printed in the United States of America

06 05 04 03 02 01 00 99 98 97   1 2 3 4 5

ISBN 0–226–18487–0 (cloth)

Library of Congress Cataloging-in-Publication Data

Edney, Matthew H.
    Mapping an empire : the geographical construction of British
India, 1765–1843 / Matthew H. Edney.
        p.   cm.
    Includes bibliographical references (p. 409) and index.
    ISBN 0-226-18487-0 (cloth : alk. paper).
    1. Cartography—India—History.   2. East India Company—History.
I. Title.
GA1131.E36   1997
912'.54—dc21   96-39703
                                                                      CIP

⊗ The paper used in this publication meets the minimum requirements of the American National Standard for Information Sciences—Permanence of Paper for Printed Library Materials, ANSI Z39.48-1984.

In memory of
John, Brian, and now Josh.

Who knows what other
wonders they would
have given us?

Contents

Illustrations and Maps

TABLES

It is difficult to characterize this study succinctly. My intention has been to write a history of cartography, but my subject matter means that I must necessarily address the history of science and the ideology of British India. The study also has overtones which I hope will interest scholars in cultural studies and cultural history. In trying to address as broad an audience as possible, I have had to explain issues and events which some of my readers will think are too obvious to be mentioned, so I must ask for forbearance in advance. Any errors I have made concerning the history of the East India Company are entirely my own responsibility.

My fundamental topic is the multilayered conflict between the desire and the ability to implement the perfect panopticist survey, between what the British persistently thought they had accomplished and the hybrid cartographic image of India which they actually constructed, and between the ideals and practices of knowledge creation in the later Enlightenment. This book is *not* a detailed explication of all of the East India Company's surveyors and of their work; that has already been accomplished by Reginald Phillimore in his monumental *Historical Records of the Survey of India* (1945–58). This study is chronologically framed by James Rennell's survey of Bengal (1765–71)—the first extensive survey undertaken by the British in India—and by George Everest's retirement from his joint appointment as surveyor general of India and superintendent of the Great Trigonometrical Survey in 1843, by which time a compromise between cartographic ideals and practices had been effected. My approach is both topical and narrative. Parts One and Two examine in detail my protagonist and antagonist: the epistemologies and methodologies of geography and mapmaking in the eighteenth and early nineteenth centuries, on the one hand, and, on the other, the East India Company's institutional structures which led to what might best be described as "cartographic anarchy." Part Three comprises the narrative of how the attempts to create the perfect survey of India were played out and were eventually compromised. Part

Four is the topical resolution to the conflict and explores the significance of the surveys to the British in terms of the representation and self-legitimation of their empire.

I have taken the liberty of updating some of the punctuation of the original quotations in order to clarify them; the original meanings are preserved. I have also used some modern forms of eighteenth- and nineteenth-century terms; for example, for the plural of "surveyor general" I use "surveyor generals," as it is easier on the modern ear than the contemporary plural of "surveyors general."

My primary source has been the East India Company's own archives, now held by the British Library's Oriental and India Office Collections. These archives are incredibly thorough because, prior to 1858, copies of all documents relating to even the smallest decisions made in India were sent to London. Even as the surveyors complained about the number and the length of the reports and letters that they were required to write—and the time it took them to do so—they created a wealth of information covering all aspects of the mapping process. Only a fraction is used here. I have not made use of the archives in India, which include the Survey of India's archives (now in the National Archives of India in New Delhi), for the simple reason that for the time period of this study they duplicate the material in London. Phillimore's *Historical Records* cites very few relevant documents from the Survey of India's archives which I did not also encounter in the Company's regular archival series.

Beyond the Company's own archives, I have used the personal collections of several British administrators and scientists in United Kingdom depositories, notably the British Library (both manuscript and map departments) and the University of Nottingham. Other institutions of great use are listed in the bibliography, to which should be added: the American Geographical Society Collection, Golda Meir Library, University of Wisconsin—Milwaukee; National Register of Archives, London; New York Public Library; Royal Greenwich Observatory, Herstmonceaux (now moved to Cambridge); and the university libraries of University College London, University of London, University of Wisconsin—Madison, State University of New York at Binghamton, and University of Southern Maine. The many librarians, archivists, and curators who have helped me have my heartfelt thanks.

Material support has come from various sources, including the University of Wisconsin—Madison Graduate School, the Wisconsin Alumni Research Foundation, and the College of Arts and Sciences of the University of Southern Maine. The research itself was underwritten by the National Science Foundation under Grant SES 88-01781. The U.S.

Government has certain rights in this material; any opinions, findings, and conclusions or recommendations expressed in this material are mine and do not necessarily reflect the views of the National Science Foundation.

Beyond the archives and libraries, I must acknowledge a number of intellectual debts. David Woodward was first an excellent advisor and has since been an excellent friend. Brian Harley defined for me what the history of cartography should be; we still feel his death keenly, six years later. Robert Frykenberg of the University of Wisconsin History Department provided enthusiastic encouragement and made essential comments on the East India Company. For his immense help with the Company's records and for his generosity in sharing his extensive knowledge of the British mapping of India, I am thoroughly indebted to Andrew Cook. Gordon Bleach deserves a great reward for helping me with art history concepts and for numerous enlightening discussions and explanations in cultural studies. Michael Armstrong, of Active Archives, London, the staff of the *History of Cartography* project in Madison, and Jim Smith all provided odd references and pieces from afar. Don Quaetert, Laura Seltz, and Robert Sweet all read several portions of the manuscript and commented on language, style, and content. Chris Bayly was a most useful commentator. Too many others have commented on parts of this work at various times to be listed here, but they all have my thanks. And, of course, I am especially grateful to all of my family and friends who have tolerated me, distracted me, helped me, and kept me sane for so many years. Special thanks must go to Anne Hedrich, Paul Rogers, Lon Bulgrin, Robert Sweet, Scott Salmon, Tim Lewington, Christi Mitchell, Ros Woodward, my brother Philip, and to my mother.

Note on East India Company Coinage

Before 1818, the currency of account in Madras was the (gold) pagoda, subdivided into forty-two or forty-five (silver) fanams, with one fanam being eighty (copper) cash. Originally a separate coin, the fanam was still occasionally used so, as in the sum of "35 pagodas and 378 fanam" (1807). The pagoda was replaced in 1818 by the (silver) rupee; the official exchange rate was a hundred pagodas to 350 *sonat* rupees.

Bombay and Bengal used the rupee; one rupee contained sixteen anna. Unless otherwise indicated, the rupees cited in the text are *sonat* rupees. However, figures were on occasion given in *sicca* rupees—that is, rupees which were freshly minted and unworn and therefore of higher exchange value. One *sonat* rupee was considered equivalent to fifteen anna *sicca*. A lakh contained ten thousand rupees.

For the sake of comparison, I provide approximate sterling equivalents. Pagodas, being gold, are easily equated to seven shillings, five and one-quarter pence (£0.372). The conversion of rupees, however, depends upon the going rate in London for silver; the accepted range of this rate's fluctuation in the early nineteenth century—"Coins, Weights, and Measures of British India," part one of *Useful Tables, forming an Appendix to the Journal of the Asiatic Society* (Calcutta: Baptist Mission Press, 1834)—gives approximate conversion factors of one shilling, ten pence (£0.092) to a *sonat* rupee, or two shillings (£0.1) to a *sicca* rupee.

One pound sterling contained twenty shillings; one shilling contained twelve pence. It is hard to define present-day sterling equivalents. The index of sterling's commodity value in Douglas Jay's *Sterling: Its Use and Misuse: A Plea for Moderation* (London: Sidgwick and Jackson, 1985), 273–79, indicates, for example, that the purchasing power of the pound more than halved between 1780 and the inflationary peak of 1813; the mean index for the period between 1780 and 1840 suggests that £1 then would buy *approximately* the same as £3 in 1954 or £24 in 1983.

In the text, sums are written as complex numbers separated by slashes. Thus, "20/16" would be twenty pounds and sixteen shillings or twenty pagodas and sixteen fanams.

PLACES MENTIONED IN THE TEXT:
SOUTHERN INDIA AND NORTHERN INDIA

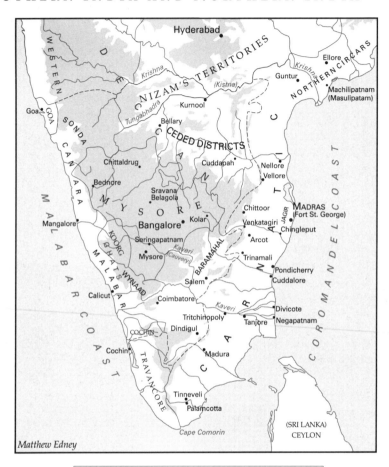

Land above 500m

————— Borders of discrete princely states, if named. The borders in central India were subject to substantial change between 1750 and 1850 and so are not shown here.

- - - - - Border of Mysore in 1792

MYSORE Princely states and general regions

BHONSLE Maratha rajas at height of rule, ca.1800

BARAMAHAL British districts, not named after their principal town

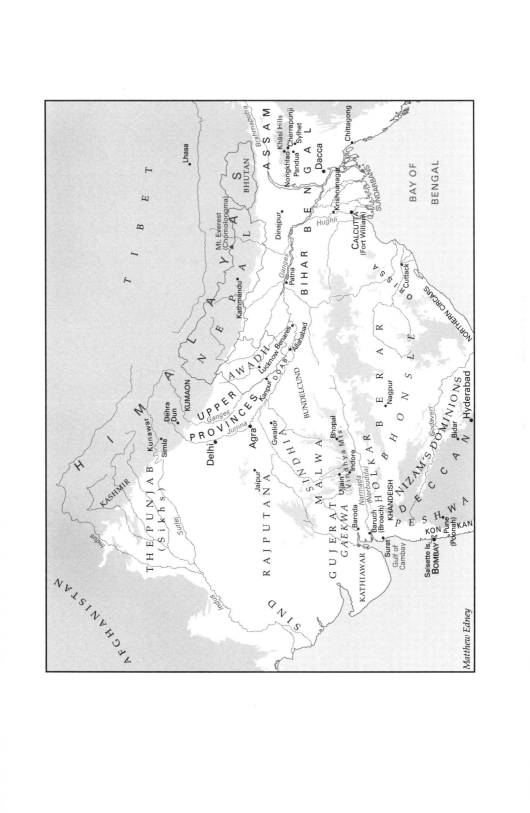

Matthew Edney

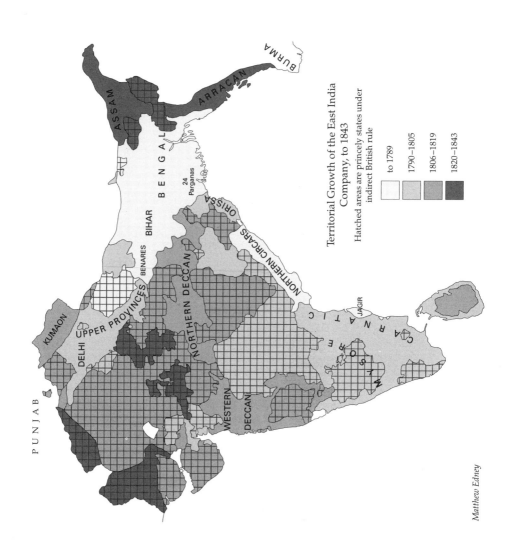

Territorial Growth of the East India
Company, to 1843

Hatched areas are princely states under
indirect British rule

to 1789

1790–1805

1806–1819

1820–1843

Matthew Edney

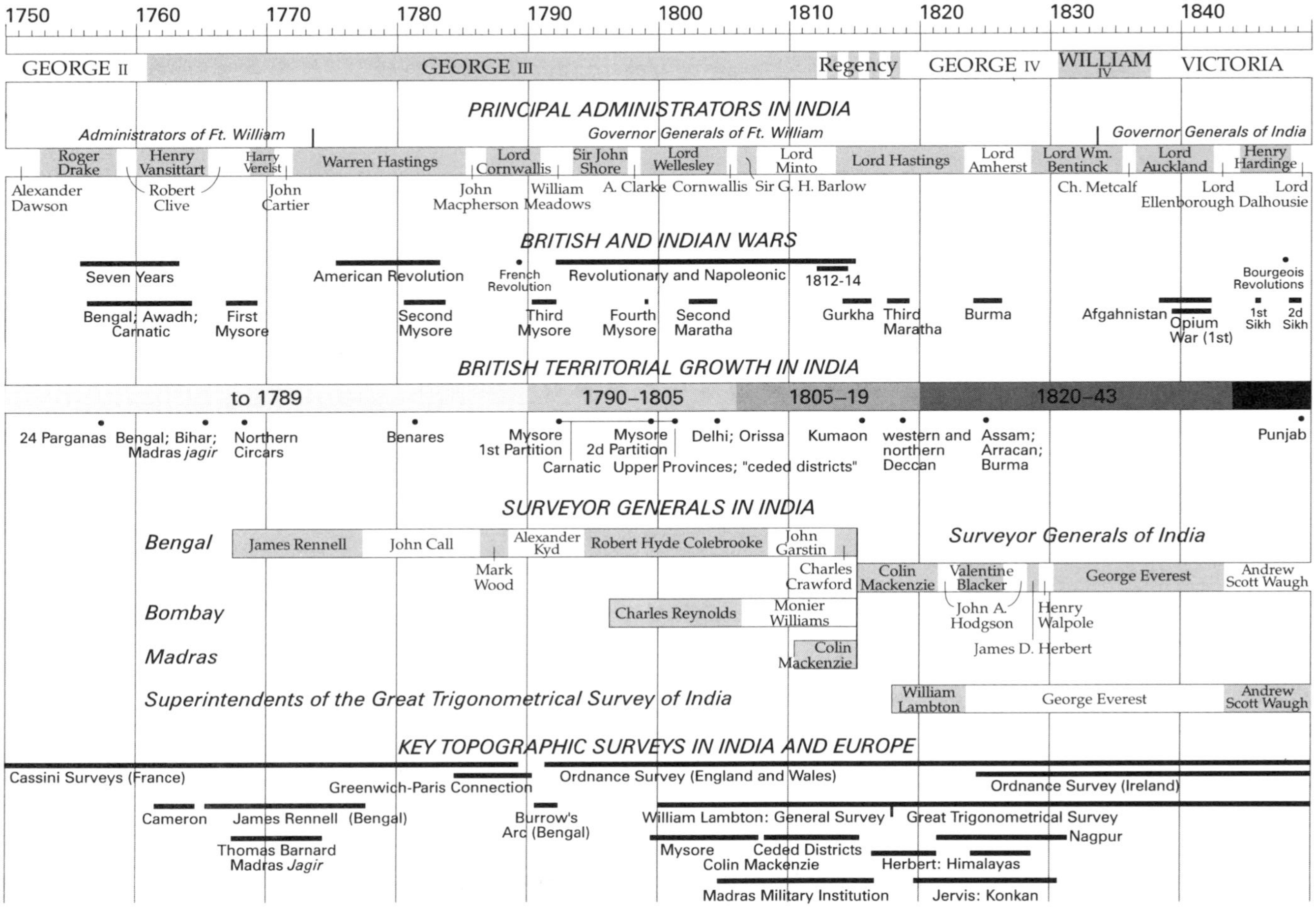

1750
1760
1770
1780
1790
1800
1810
1820
1830
1840
GEORGE II
GEORGE III
Regency
GEORGE IV
WILLIAM IV
VICTORIA
PRINCIPAL ADMINISTRATORS IN INDIA
Administrators of Ft. William
Governor Generals of Ft. William
Governor Generals of India
Roger Drake
Henry Vansittart
Harry Verelst
Warren Hastings
Lord Cornwallis
Sir John Shore
Lord Wellesley
Lord Minto
Lord Hastings
Lord Amherst
Lord Wm. Bentinck
Lord Auckland
Henry Hardinge
Alexander Dawson
Robert Clive
John Cartier
John Macpherson
William Meadows
A. Clarke
Cornwallis
Sir G. H. Barlow
Ch. Metcalf
Lord Ellenborough
Lord Dalhousie
BRITISH AND INDIAN WARS
Seven Years
American Revolution
French Revolution
Revolutionary and Napoleonic
1812-14
Bourgeois Revolutions
Bengal; Awadh; Carnatic
First Mysore
Second Mysore
Third Mysore
Fourth Mysore
Second Maratha
Gurkha
Third Maratha
Burma
Afghanistan
Opium War (1st)
1st Sikh
2d Sikh
BRITISH TERRITORIAL GROWTH IN INDIA
to 1789
1790–1805
1805–19
1820–43
24 Parganas
Bengal; Bihar; Madras jagir
Northern Circars
Benares
Mysore 1st Partition
Carnatic
Mysore 2d Partition
Upper Provinces; "ceded districts"
Delhi; Orissa
Kumaon
western and northern Deccan
Assam; Arracan; Burma
Punjab
SURVEYOR GENERALS IN INDIA
Bengal
James Rennell
John Call
Alexander Kyd
Robert Hyde Colebrooke
John Garstin
Mark Wood
Surveyor Generals of India
Charles Crawford
Colin Mackenzie
Valentine Blacker
George Everest
Andrew Scott Waugh
Bombay
Charles Reynolds
Monier Williams
John A. Hodgson
Henry Walpole
Madras
Colin Mackenzie
James D. Herbert
Superintendents of the Great Trigonometrical Survey of India
William Lambton
George Everest
Andrew Scott Waugh
KEY TOPOGRAPHIC SURVEYS IN INDIA AND EUROPE
Cassini Surveys (France)
Greenwich-Paris Connection
Ordnance Survey (England and Wales)
Ordnance Survey (Ireland)
Cameron
James Rennell (Bengal)
Burrow's Arc (Bengal)
William Lambton: General Survey
Great Trigonometrical Survey
Thomas Barnard Madras Jagir
Mysore
Ceded Districts
Colin Mackenzie
Nagpur
Herbert: Himalayas
Madras Military Institution
Jervis: Konkan

The Ideologies and Practices of Mapping and Imperialism

The activities of the East India Company in sponsoring science are an obvious point of approach to the whole ideology of British rule. The Great Trigonometrical Survey of India shows the workings of British policy better than still another study of Macaulay's education minute.

Susan Faye Cannon, 1978

Imperialism and mapmaking intersect in the most basic manner. Both are fundamentally concerned with territory and knowledge. Their relationship was the subject of Jorge Luis Borges' famous fantasy of an empire so addicted to cartography that its geographers constructed an "unconscionable" map at the same size as the empire itself, coinciding with it point by point.[1] This satire is rooted in an important realization: knowledge of the territory is determined by geographic representations and most especially by the map. Geography and empire are thus intimately and thoroughly interwoven. "In order to set boundaries to their empire and to claim to have reached those that were marked out," Claude Nicolet writes of the Romans, they "needed a certain perception of geographical space, of its dimensions and of the area they occupied." More generally, Nicolet argues, "the ineluctable necessities of conquest and government are to understand (or to believe that one understands) the physical space that one occupies or that one hopes to dominate, to overcome the obstacle of distance and to establish regular contact with the peoples and their territories (by enumerating the former and by measuring the dimensions, the surfaces and the capacities of the latter)."[2] To govern territories, one must know them.

In the case of the British conquest of South Asia in the hundred years after 1750, military and civilian officials of the East India Company undertook a massive intellectual campaign to transform a land of incomprehensible spectacle into an empire of knowledge. At the forefront of this campaign were the geographers who mapped the landscapes and studied the inhabitants, who collected geological and botanical specimens, and who recorded details of economy, society, and culture. More fundamentally than even Susan Cannon recognized, the geographers created and defined the spatial image of the Company's empire. The maps came to define the empire itself, to give it territorial integrity and its basic existence. The empire exists because it can be mapped; the meaning of empire is inscribed into each map.[3]

Imperial British India was far more dependent on maps than early imperial Rome had ever been. The steady expansion of map literacy in Europe since 1450—driven by new print technologies, protocapitalist consumption, and humanist culture—meant that by the eighteenth century the map had become, and has since remained, the dominant vehicle for conveying geographical conceptions. The intellectual process of creating, communicating, and accepting geographical conceptions, whether at an individual or sociocultural level, is thus often referred to as "mapping." It is a process which in the modern world depends heavily on the actual production of maps, which is to say mapmaking *per se*. Just as, in Samuel Johnson's phrase of 1750, "when a book is once in the hands of the public, it is considered as permanent and unalterable; and the reader . . . accommodates his mind to the author's design," so maps shape and manipulate mental geographical images.[4] The mapmaking process and the resulting maps are in turn dependent on aculturated conceptions of space. As with any other form of representation—graphic or textual, artifactual or ephemeral—meaning is invested in all aspects of cartography: in the instrumentation and technologies wielded by the geographer; in the social relations within which maps are made and used; and, in the cultural expectations which define, and which are defined by, the map image.[5]

This study of the surveys and maps which the British made in and of South Asia during the first hundred years of their ascendancy is accordingly a study of the British conceptions of what India should be. It is a study of how the British represented their India. I say "their India" because they did not map the "real" India. They mapped the India that they perceived and that they governed. To the extent that many aspects of India's societies and cultures remained beyond British experience and to the extent that Indians resisted and negotiated with the British, India could never be entirely and perfectly known. The British deluded themselves that their science enabled them to know the "real" India. But what they did map, what they did create, was a *British* India. Wrapped in a scientistic ideology, each survey and geographical investigation was thoroughly implicated in the ideology of the British empire in South Asia.

A Spatial History of "India" to 1780

The creation of British India required the prior acceptance by the British of "India" as signifying a specific region of the earth's surface. Changes in the European involvement with Asia during the seventeenth and eighteenth centuries produced important changes in geographical conceptions, which were in turn more broadly accommodated and disseminated through cartographic representations. The issue here is that unless a region is first conceived of and named, it cannot become the specific subject of a map. Conversely, a mapped region gains prominence in the public eye. For example, there could be no maps of "Southeast Asia" until the Second World War, when the several colonial spheres of interest were replaced by a single theater of war; the distribution of maps of that theater subsequently led to the general acceptance of Southeast Asia as a region sufficiently coherent and meaningful to warrant its own academic discipline.[6] For South Asia, changing economic and political activities led to new geographical conceptions which, by the later eighteenth century, had developed into an image of India that coincided with the territory of the subcontinent and which was given meaning by the commercial and imperial ambitions of the British.

In the fifteenth and sixteenth centuries, Europeans conceived of Asia as an ill-defined series of exotic and fabulously wealthy countries. There was Cathay (China), Cipangu (Japan), and "the Indies." The conception of the Indies derived from Hellenistic Antiquity. It originally signified all the lands east of the Indus, the traditional eastward limit of the Hellenistic world. The Hellenistic image of the Indies was adapted by Renaissance Europe from the geographies of Ptolemy and Strabo and, although the Ptolemaic map was quickly supplanted by new maps constructed by Portuguese navigators, the Hellenistic nomenclature survived. *India intra gangem*—the Indies this side of (within) the Ganges—comprised all the lands lying between the Indus and the mouth of the Ganges and included the peninsula, which Ptolemy seems to have transformed into Taprobana, the oversized Sri Lanka. *India extra gangem*—the Indies beyond (outside of) the Ganges—comprised all the lands further west, specifically Indochina and modern Indonesia. Some

Renaissance geographers carried the name to its logical extension and called China "India superior." Christopher Columbus's conviction that he had indeed reached the Indies in 1492 resulted in the name being transplanted to the New World. The Indies henceforth became the East Indies, or East India. Thus, the London merchants who sought to compete with the Portuguese in the spice trade, and for which they received a monopoly charter from Elizabeth I in 1600, soon acquired the popular name of the "East India Company."

The initial plan of the English merchants was to establish trading centers in what is now Indonesia in order to control the supply of spices. They did so, but were evicted by their Dutch coreligionists in 1623. The English resorted to trading across the whole width of the Indian Ocean, from Arabia and East Africa to the Malay peninsula and further east to southern China. They established several trading centers, known as "factories," of which three on the coast of the subcontinent were dominant by 1700: Madras (Fort St. George), Bombay, and Calcutta (Fort William). The East India Company appointed a council of traders at each of these factories to manage the Company's affairs in each portion of the subcontinent. Each small bureaucracy was known as a "presidency" because its governing council was headed by a president; this name continued to be used even when the three small administrations were transformed into major territorial governments.

The three presidencies were functionally distinct during the initial period of English involvement in South Asia, that is, before the mid-eighteenth century. Administratively, none were responsible for the others. More often than not, they competed rather than cooperated with each other. The principal presidency was Madras. Bombay and Calcutta gave access to the markets and produce of the great Mughal empire, which dominated the north of the subcontinent, but the empire also regulated the English traders. Madras, on the other hand, lay on the southern fringes of Mughal power so that the English there enjoyed much greater economic flexibility. Located at the center of the Indian Ocean trade routes, and set up as an early version of a free-trade zone, Madras flourished. The French Compagnie des Indes sought to emulate the English success when it established its own factory at Pondicherry, just to the south of Madras.

European maps accordingly framed the subcontinent in three distinct ways in this early period. Beginning in the early 1500s, general maps showed the traditional region of the Indies, from the Indus to Indochina. The subcontinent was, of course, a prominent feature of these maps, but it was not their focus. Later in the sixteenth century, Europeans began to produce maps that framed only the peninsula south of the river Krishna, the area of their principal involvement. The third framing developed in the early seventeenth century and focussed on the polity of the Mughal empire. These maps emphasized the seat of Mughal power in the northern plains. They also included the Mughal territories west of the Indus: the Punjab, the Hindu Kush, and on occasion Afghanistan. They omitted the peninsula.[7]

The three framings began to merge in the eighteenth century. In part, this was a manifestation of the Enlightenment's encyclopedic mentality, which produced massive tomes intended to present all available knowledge to their bourgeois readership in a systematic manner. Geographical encyclopedias took the form of huge multivolume texts, which contained many small maps, as well as huge multisheet cartographic extravaganzas. These maps were constructed at such large scales, and were physically so big, that the cartographer could simply copy data directly from survey maps into the expansive graticule of latitude and longitude; he would not have to omit any data to ensure the new map's legibility.[8]

The prominent French cartographer J. B. B. d'Anville published the first such map of the Indies in 1752. He constructed his *Carte de l'Inde* in four sheets at a scale of about 1:3,000,000 (figure 1.1). It comprised almost one square meter of paper, too large to be reproduced here in its entirety. It was framed like all other maps of the Indies, extending from the Indus to the China Sea, with the subcontinent on the left and Indochina on the right. It was not much smaller in scale than maps of the two regional framings, and d'Anville copied data from them directly into the larger frame. The quality of d'Anville's sources was variable. As the region of most European activity, the peninsula was shown in greatest detail; d'Anville used the same sources to construct a somewhat larger-scale map just of the Carnatic, which was published in 1753. For the rest of the Indies, d'Anville's data was so sparse that the map was dominated by substantial areas of white space. D'Anville himself acknowledged that he would never have made this map with such sparse data had not the Compagnie des Indes specifically commissioned him to do so; nor was he reluctant to express his dissatisfaction with the map once it had been published.[9]

More significantly for the idea of India, the southward expansion of Mughal power under Aurungzeb (reigned 1658–1707) in the later seventeenth century led to the merging of the two regional framings in the early eighteenth century. As the empire now encompassed all but the southernmost tip of the subcontinent, in name at least, European cartographers extended their maps of the empire to incorporate the peninsula. Hermann Moll's "The West Part of India, or the Empire of the Great Mogul" (1717) is just one of several maps which equated the subcontinent (the west part of the Indies) with the empire (figure 1.2). The

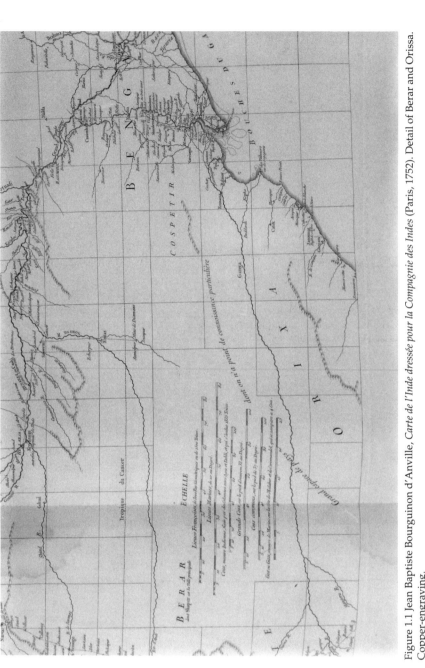

Figure 1.1 Jean Baptiste Bourguinon d'Anville, *Carte de l'Inde dressée pour la Compagnie des Indes* (Paris, 1752). Detail of Berar and Orissa. Copper-engraving.

D'Anville used only information derived from reputable sources, so his data for northern India were sparse; he did, however, borrow from other maps the fictitious Ganga river, shown here passing through the "great extent of country of which there is no particular knowledge." (The Smith Collection, Osher Map Library, University of Southern Maine.)

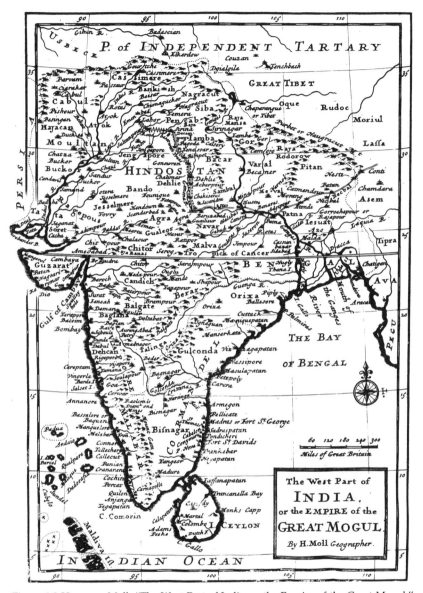

Figure 1.2 Hermann Moll, "The West Part of India, or the Empire of the Great Mogul,"
Atlas Geographicus (London, 1717). Copper-engraving; original size 18 × 25.5 cm.

One of the first maps to show all of South Asia in its modern conception. Previously,
in his *A System of Geography* (1701), Moll had followed the existing convention and had
shown only the Mughal empire. (The Newberry Library.)

map's frame now encompassed the entire region usually considered to be India *per se*, specifically the lands south of the entire circuit of northern mountains and including the lands west of the Indus. Nonetheless, there is still an ambiguity in such maps between the old regional concept of the Indies and the Mughal empire.

It is no coincidence that the early eighteenth century was also the period when the English and the French began to meddle seriously in South Asian politics. The prize was the immense revenue derived from land taxation, revenue which promised to far surpass the profits which could be realized even by monopoly trade. Initially, both European trading companies rented out their regiments to Indian princes; soon they sought to control the princes' finances directly. During the Seven Years' War (1756–1763), the global rivalry between the English and the French spilled over into a struggle for control of the Carnatic. A paradoxical consequence of this conflict was a major shift in English interests away from the south to the north, to Bengal, and to the heart of the Mughal empire. In what might have remained a comparatively minor aspect of the war, a small British army under Robert Clive defeated the Nawab of Bengal at Plassey in 1757, by intrigue as much as by force of arms. The English merchants found themselves in control of one of the richest provinces of the Mughal empire. Clive subsequently negotiated, in 1765, a formal position for the Company as the province's *diwan*, or chief financial and administrative officer. Thereafter the Company steadily eroded the position of the Nawab until they pensioned him off altogether in 1772.

The Company's dramatic territorial growth subsequent to Plassey did not take place in a vacuum. At home, the Company's territorial gains did not please many in Parliament. A series of political arguments over the very existence of the Company culminated in William Pitt's India Act of 1784. The Company's mercantile and territorial functions were separated in order to curb the excesses of the 1760s. As Calcutta was now the most important presidency, its governor was promoted to be governor general of Bengal and given authority in political and military affairs over both the Bombay and Madras presidencies. The governors and the commanders-in-chief of all three presidencies were henceforth to be appointed by the British Crown. And, perhaps most importantly, a parliamentary "Board of Control" was established to oversee, and if necessary to veto, the decisions made by the Company's directors; the board's president became a member of the cabinet. The 1784 act accordingly serves as a useful date for marking the conversion of the Company from a mercantile corporation to a major territorial power. I should also note that the conscious efforts at this time by the

English to incorporate the Scots into the home and colonial governments meant that the English East India Company is henceforth more properly referred to as being British in character.

In South Asia, the British territorial acquisitions were part of the larger process of the Mughal empire's slow disintegration. The forms and rituals of the empire remained, and the mughal himself remained the wellspring of authority. Even so, actual control of Mughal territories increasingly devolved onto the provincial governors and to new territorial powers. The Marathas had long been in conflict with the Mughals in western India and they now established new dynastic states. They also entered into a three-way contest for control of the empire, competing with the Afghans and the Mughals themselves; by the 1780s, the East India Company had replaced the Afghans in the struggle.

It was therefore during the 1760s and 1770s that the two regional framings completely merged to create a conception of India as a region characterized by multiple ambitions to take control of the Mughal empire. That empire had already expanded to cover the entire subcontinent; now British interests followed suit, expanding to encompass the north as well as the south. The new region was mapped as the domain of conflict between the Mughal empire, its successor states, and British interests. It looked as much to Afghanistan and the west as it did to Malaya and the east. Its autonomy was graphically manifested by the repositioning of the center line of the map frame to be coincident with the subcontinent's north-south axis (figure 1.3). Modern India was born.

Rennell and the Framing of India, 1782–88

The new conception of the subcontinent as an actual region in and of itself was most apparent in, and most effectively disseminated by, James Rennell's maps of India and their accompanying geographical memoirs.[10] As surveyor general of Bengal, Rennell had collected together the geographical data acquired by British army columns on campaign. There was now sufficient information that he could compile general maps of the entire subcontinent with much less white space than had plagued d'Anville's maps thirty years before. Admittedly, the detail of some areas remained rather sparse, especially to the northwest. Nonetheless, Rennell's maps provided the definitive image of India for the British and European public. It is in his highly influential maps that we find the establishment of India as a meaningful, if still ambiguous, geographical entity.[11]

The ambiguity of the region is most obvious in the various names

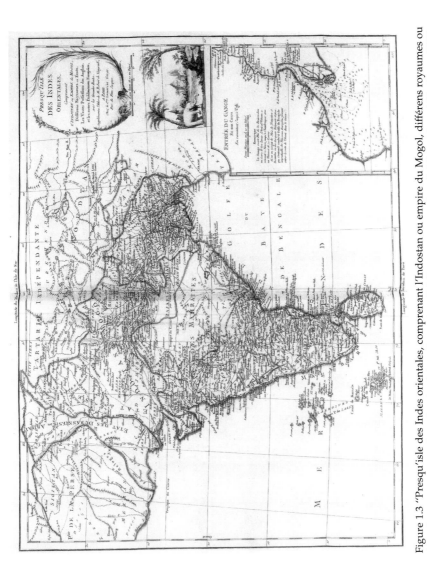

Figure 1.3 "Presqu'isle des Indes orientales, comprenant l'Indostan ou empire du Mogol, différens royaumes ou états, les vastes possessions des Anglais, et les autres établissemens européens," *Atlas universel* (Paris, ca. 1790). Copper-engraving; original size, 62.5 × 47.5 cm.

The original editions of the *Atlas universel* of Gilles and Didier Robert de Vaugondy (first published 1752) contained maps of all the Indies. C. F. Delamarche took over production of the atlas on Didier's death in 1786 and added this map before 1792. (Library of Congress.)

that Rennell used to refer to the region that his maps framed. The titles of the maps and the memoirs all used "Hindustan." But this was not a self-evident region, so Rennell began both of his memoirs with an explanation of its extent. "Hindustan"—land of the Hindus—was originally coined by the early Islamic marauders to refer to the northern plains they conquered. Many Europeans adopted this usage. But the plains were also the historic core of Mughal power, so that "Hindustan" was used by some Europeans as a synonym for the empire. Because Hindus dominate South Asia and, furthermore, because the Mughal empire had by 1700 been extended almost to Cape Comorin, many Europeans took the entire subcontinent to constitute "Hindustan." Rennell did not select one of these three conceptions as being the proper one; instead, he conflated them. The titles of his memoirs explicitly equated Hindustan with the Mughal empire—*Memoir of a Map of Hindoostan; or the Mogul['s] Empire*—whereas the maps themselves were of the entire subcontinent. But within the memoirs themselves, Rennell usually referred to the whole subcontinent as "India." He thus established a conceptual equivalency between the subcontinent, India, and the Mughal empire: they all referred to the same fundamental region which he mapped.

The equivalency was borne out in Rennell's cartographic portrayal of political entities. He decided to subdivide India according to the Mughal subas (provinces) as defined under the emperor Akbar (reigned 1555–1605). Although these divisions did not extend very far south of the Krishna river, Rennell nonetheless thought that the system was "the most permanent one." His knowledge of the old divisions came from the recent translation of an Islamic geography of the empire, the *Ā'īn-i Akbarī* (1598).[12] Rennell showed the names of the subas in regular type on his maps, to distinguish them from contemporary political divisions in a cursive script. The new polities were named after their rulers, such as Nizam Shah or Moodajee Bhonsle (figure 1.4). Rennell explained his decision:

> It must be observed, that since the empire has been dismembered, a new division of its provinces has also taken place . . . These modern divisions are not only distinguished in the map by the names of the present possessors; but the colouring also is entirely employed in facilitating the distinctions between them. So that the modern divisions appear, as it were, in the *fore ground*; and the ancient ones in the *back ground*; one illustrating and explaining the other.[13]

Rennell's failure to identify the East India Company as the contemporary ruler of Bengal implied that Bengal was still a Mughal suba and

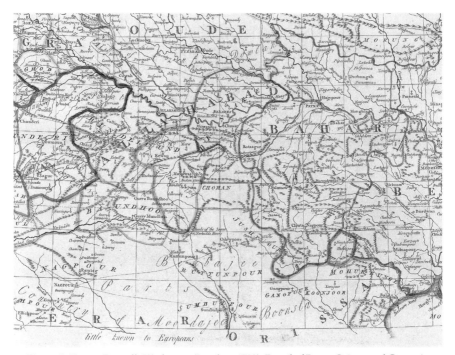

Figure 1.4 James Rennell, *Hindoostan* (London, 1782). Detail of Berar, Orissa, and Gangetic Plains. Copper-engraving.
  Note the variations in type used for the Mughal divisions and the contemporary rulers (in a cursive script; for example, "Country of Moodajee Bhonsle"); also compare the density of Rennell's information with that of d'Anville in figure 1.1. (By permission of the Harvard Map Collection.)

that there had been a legitimate delegation of Mughal authority to the British. Conversely, the mughal himself, Shah Alam (reigned 1759–1807), is identified as actually ruling only the district around Delhi. Rennell thus justified British authority over Bengal as stemming from the sovereign authority of the Mughal empire, even as that empire had itself collapsed into a political anarchy signified through the names of rulers rather than regions. Rennell left the British as the sole representatives of the empire's legitimate and suprapersonal authority.

  Rennell was himself an avid supporter of the East India Company's "splendid territorial aggrandizement." He devoted several paragraphs of his geographical memoirs to the defense of his old patron, Robert Clive, and of others who supported the Company's territorial conquests against critics in London. He was particularly motivated in his 1792 map of southern India to help "explain the present state of the political geography of the Peninsula, together with the advantages that may be derived from our territorial acquisitions."[14] But this is not to say that Rennell possessed any greater idea of a future British empire which would one day cover the whole subcontinent. Instead, the maps of India-as-subcontinent produced by Rennell and copied by other European geographers reflected the continuing potency of the Mughal empire as the sole source of authority in the subcontinent. Contemporary politicians thought that the legitimacy of British power ultimately rested on the Company's adherence to forms of Mughal power and on its claim to rule Bengal as the imperial diwan. That is, the new regional maps embodied the recognition by all political factions that the Company's fortunes had become embroiled with the Mughal empire and its heirs, both *de facto* and *de jure,* almost to the exclusion of its other interests in Asia.

This message also constituted the essence of the remarkable title cartouche for Rennell's first map (figure 1.5). Most eighteenth-century maps were given intricate title cartouches, but very few were as elaborate as this. Rennell gave the following explanation in the memoir:

> *Explanation of the Emblematical Frontispiece to the Map*
> *Brittannia* [sic] receiving into her Protection, the sacred Books of the *Hindoos,* presented by the *Pundits,* or *Learned Bramins:* in Allusion to the humane Interposition of the British Legislature in Favor of the Natives of Bengal, in the Year 1781. *Brittannia* is supported by a Pedestal, on which are engraven the Victories, by means of which the British Nation obtained, and has hitherto upheld, its Influence in India: amongst which, the two recent ones of *Porto Novo* and *Sholingur,* gained by *General [Eyre] Coote,* are particularly pointed out by a Sepoy to his Comrade.[15]

In the background of the image, an East Indiaman is being loaded (the Indian on the beach, beyond the pandit proffering Britannia the sacred texts, can only be dragging his load toward the ship). Britannia's spear rests possessively on a bolt of cotton cloth (then the main Indian export to Europe), next to an artist's palette, mathematical dividers, and the stonemason's mallet and chisels (perhaps alluding to the freemasonry then resurgent in Europe). The iconography develops on that established in the 1730s, as with funerary statuary, in which India was personified according to "notions of place as a function of commerce or as a reference to the Orientalists' enthusiasms."[16] The textual components of British orientalism are emphasized, with the Brahmins handing over their legal texts (*sastras*), but its artistic (the palette), cartographic (the dividers), and architectural (the ziggurat at rear) elements are all included.

Figure 1.5 Title cartouche, E. Edwards *del.* and J. Hall *sc.,* to James Rennell, *Hindoostan* (London, 1 December 1782, 2 sheets). Copper-engraving; original size, 26.7 × 18.4 cm.

The packet being given to Britannia is labeled "shaster," that is, *sastra*, a Hindu religious code or law book. (By permission of The British Library, IOR X/223.)

To these conceptions Rennell added the celebration of empire and of British arms, very much in the Roman mold, complete with mercenary soldiers (the sepoys) and an imperial wreath. The wreath is not made from hallucinogenic laurel, used by oracles for divinely inspired visions, but rather from the opium poppy, the primary cash crop for the China trade. The Roman influence extended to the map itself, as Rennell used Roman sources for fixing places in the northern plains and gave a scale bar for Roman miles in addition to those for geographical [nautical] miles, statute miles, and the coss, a common Indian unit of distance. Rennell thus established India as the site of glorious conquest and territorial aggrandizement.

The continued expansion after 1790 of the Company's territories and of its political power produced an increasing congruence between the old Mughal and the new British empires. The Company's interests, which had grown in 1757 to encompass the eastern seaboard of the subcontinent, expanded still further. By 1818, British military strategy took the entire subcontinent into account even if the British had yet to conquer it all.[17] And with that expansion came new geographical information to be fitted into new editions of old maps or to serve as the basis of entirely new maps of India. The new information was collected and organized according to the new polities shaped and created by British hegemony. The maps of India produced both by the Company's officers in India and by its client cartographers in London increasingly reflected that organization, replacing the Mughal provinces with British districts and creating a geographical entity defined by the extent of British-dominated states and provinces.

Over the course of the nineteenth century, the British mapping of India further consolidated "India" in its modern image. Rennell had to take great care in defining what he understood to be the regions which constituted Hindustan/India. A century or more later, such care was no longer necessary. The geographical rhetoric of British India was so effective that India had become a real entity for both British imperialists and Indian nationalists alike. Both groups held "India" to be a single, coherent, self-referential geographical entity coincident with the bounds of the South Asian subcontinent and the extent of British power but which nonetheless predated British hegemony. Thus, one historian could state in 1902 that the purpose of his account of the empire was "to set before the ordinary reader the story of the steps by which India came gradually to be painted red on the map."[18] The triumph of the British empire, from the imperialist perspective, was its replacement of the multitude of political and cultural components of India with a single all-India state coincident with a cartographically defined geographical whole.

This geographical conception of India was adopted without question in the second half of the nineteenth century by Indian nationalists. They argued that there had historically been a region of cultural unity which coincided with the entire subcontinent. This position is enshrined in the present-day state of India, which has asserted that its northern frontier has run "approximately where it runs now [1959] for nearly three thousand years."[19] India is not unique in this respect. Benedict Anderson has noted that both Thailand and Indonesia have inherited the "colonial imaginings" of coherent geographical entities which supposedly predate the colonial era.[20]

The nineteenth-century consolidation of the idea of India was not a direct outgrowth of the initial framing of the region in the late 1700s. The consolidation depended on the comprehensive mapping of British India. In constructing a uniform and comprehensive archive of India, the British fixed the scope and character of the region's territories. They located and mapped the human landscape of villages, forts, roads, irrigation schemes, and boundaries within the physical landscape of hills, rivers, and forests. They also undertook cadastral surveys, delimiting field boundaries, buildings, and even individual trees, when agriculturally important, at scales sometimes as large as forty feet to an inch (1:480). The British made themselves the intellectual masters of the Indian landscape. And they did so with all the certainty and correctness granted by the Enlightenment's epistemology.

That epistemology, however, was flawed. The archive was certain and truthful only within the rhetoric of the Enlightenment philosophes. "India" does not comprise a pre-existent stage, framed by mountains and oceans, on which the events of history play out. It is not a "theater of its own design," to use Paul Carter's phrase. It is instead a creation of historical events and processes. It is, like all other regions to which we ascribe some meaning, the product of spatial history.[21] To believe otherwise requires intellectual convolutions. B. B. Misra has stated, for example, that although it is "a unified geographical category equipped with national frontiers, the Indian subcontinent has hardly ever been a single, integrated political entity."[22] The geographical unity of India is, in short, a creation of the British mapping of their empire.

The Cartographic Ideal and the
Great Trigonometrical Survey of India

The conceptual potency of James Rennell's framing of India and the subsequent consolidation of that image depended on European culture's unquestioning acceptance of maps as unproblematic and truthful statements of geographical reality. The formation of this cartographic ideal had two stages. First, the Enlightenment philosophes developed an epistemological ideal: correct and certain archives of knowledge could be constructed, they believed, by following rational processes epitomized by mapmaking. In the case of mapmaking, however, the epistemological ideal was undermined by recognized flaws in cartographic technologies. The second stage in the formulation of the cartographic ideal accordingly came with the widespread promulgation of a technological solution—"triangulation"—which promised to perfect geographical knowledge.

In British India, triangulation was represented by the Great Trigonometrical Survey of India (GTS). Because of the GTS, the British could believe that they were indeed constructing a single, complete, truthful, and ordered archive of geographical knowledge for their empire, even though a single, systematic, and coherent survey organization for all of their empire—the Survey of India—was not established until 1878. The literature of the early British surveys in India reflects this belief: the simple presence of the GTS was sufficient to bring all the British mapmaking activities into a single, coherent whole. At the core of this study, however, lies the argument that, in practice, the British could never implement the technological ideal offered by triangulation and were forced to rely on the older epistemological ideal of the eighteenth century. That is, the British could only make their general maps of South Asia by combining multiple surveys within a framework of latitude and longitude. The epistemological ideal is itself open to an extensive critique. More generally, some recent writers on the culture of imperialism have accepted the claims for constructing complete archives of knowledge at face value. As I will further argue, such perfection and total comprehensiveness is impossible *in practice*. The European knowledge of each empire is accordingly far more incomplete and nuanced than has often been recognized.

Rennell provides the starting point for the eighteenth-century style of topographic mapmaking in India. He made the first regional survey in the subcontinent—of Bengal between 1765 and 1771—and he did so with a methodology derived in principle from the techniques of map compilation. Rennell and his assistants measured distances and directions along the roads through Bengal. He also measured the latitude and longitude of key locations—control points—so that he could progressively fit the road surveys into a graticule* of meridians and paral-

* "Graticule" is a neologism, ca. 1875 (Helen Wallis and Arthur H. Robinson, eds., *Cartographical Innovations: An International Handbook of Mapping Terms to 1900* [London: Map Collector Publications for the International Cartographic Association, 1987], 172–74), but

lels and so construct the actual maps (see figure 1.4). This style of survey was fast and relatively easy and it was popular with military surveyors throughout the eighteenth century.[23]

For the eighteenth-century philosophes, mapmaking was the epitome of the ordered and structured creation of a coherent archive of knowledge. All geographical information could be sited and any conflicts reconciled within the map's graticule. The need to evaluate different data sources meant that map compilation was a highly complex and erudite process. Much of the complexity would be removed if the data came from a single source, specifically a regional survey undertaken in a *systematic* manner. Each route would be measured with the same methods and with the same instruments, so that the surveys would be consistent in quality and content, regardless of the skills of the particular surveyors. The survey's organizer would further ensure that all parts of the region were mapped together, without any inefficient duplication or unrealized omissions.

Michel Foucault considered natural history to be the Enlightenment's paradigmatic "Order of Things," but the natural historians themselves consistently employed maps and mapping as the trope for their taxonomic systems. Military reformers of the later 1700s positioned mapping at the core of "military science." Because their basic character lay in the use of instruments to extract meaning from the world, surveying and mapping were major contributors to the visualism and empiricism of later Enlightenment science. Most significantly, the combination of terrestrial and celestial measurements, in a system of knowledge which has recently been termed *mathematical cosmography*, was a fundamental component of the Enlightenment's world order.[24]

The epistemological certainty enjoyed by Enlightenment mapping, however, was substantially undermined by a widely recognized flaw. Both map compilation and the associated regional survey depended upon the astronomical observation of the latitude and longitude of a few important places, and such observations were famously uncertain. Each method of measuring either latitude or longitude was known to contain errors, but those errors could not be quantified. The best that

---

I prefer it to "grid," which has gained currency in the cultural studies' literature regarding maps. Grid implies a regular arrangement of two orthogonal series of equally spaced lines, as in a Cartesian plane, which in turn implies an infinite conception of space. In contrast, graticule embodies the variability of arrangement of parallels and meridians within and between map projections and also suggests the finite space of the earth's surface. Furthermore, twentieth-century topographic maps possess *both* a graticule symbolic of the map projection and a superimposed grid for referencing locations. Contemporary terms such as *réseau, net,* or *mesh* are also too vague.

could be done was to make as many observations as possible on the assumption that the errors would cancel themselves out. The field surveyor, however, rarely had time to make more than just one or two observations at any location. Moreover, each determination of latitude and longitude was independent of all others so that it could not be corrected easily. The result was that the tie between detailed survey and the general map was problematic. The map's theoretical perfection was denied by the imperfections of contemporary technology.

What triangulation offered was a systematic technology whereby geographic information could be made truly certain and comprehensive. Its principles are relatively simple. The surveyor first imagines a series of straight lines joining the tops of hills or tall buildings. The hilltops are selected so that the lines form either a long chain of triangles or a network of interlocking triangles spread out across the landscape (figure 1.6). The surveyor determines the geometry of the triangles by measuring their interior angles. The actual size of the triangles is determined by the very careful measurement on the ground of the length of one side of a triangle; the lengths of all other triangle sides are calculated from this one "baseline" by means of trigonometry. The later Enlightenment term for a triangulation was therefore a *trigonometrical survey*. The result is a rigorous mathematical framework in which all points are defined with respect to each other.

Triangulation's promise of perfection rests on four factors. First, each control point is mathematically bound to its neighbors so that its position is automatically corrected. The triangulation is constructed without reference to any astronomical positions. Some latitudes and longitudes do need to be determined in order to fix the position and orientation of the survey on the earth's surface; the latitude and longitude of each triangle vertex can then be calculated, but these are only secondary calculations and do not affect the survey's structure. Second, the locations of the triangles' vertices are also defined by the configuration of the landscape itself so that the survey's structure is closely congruent with the physical structure of the territory being mapped. Third, the density of triangulated control points—the triangle vertices—is much greater than can be achieved by simple astronomical observations. An extensive triangulation can accordingly support far more detailed and comprehensive district surveys than would otherwise be feasible.

The final factor is triangulation's role in geodesy, the science of determining the size and shape of the earth itself. Triangulation was first used in the sixteenth century for just this task. If a chain of triangles is constructed running north-south along a meridian, then the surveyor

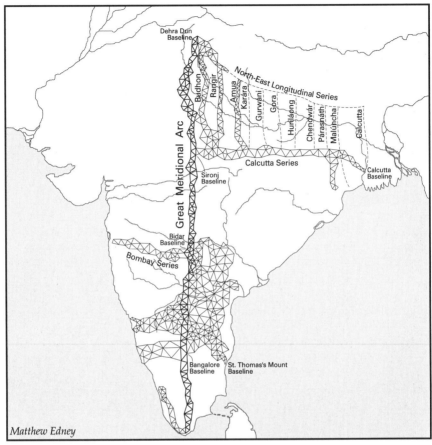

Matthew Edney

Figure 1.6 The extent of William Lambton's initial triangulation in southern India (1799–1817) and the arcs of the Great Trigonometrical Survey of India completed by 1843. Some of Lambton's earlier work, which was not subsequently used by the Great Trigonometrical Survey, is not shown. Note that much of the triangulation shown here was resurveyed or rejected later in the nineteenth century. Based on J. T. Walker, "Index to Great Trigonometrical Survey of India, 1 May 1862," CUL RGO 6/423/10, fol. 152.

can calculate the ground length of that portion—or the arc—of the meridian. The surveyor also measures the difference in latitude between the extremities of the arc. Because these values are measured independently of each other, they can be directly compared, yielding the length of one degree of arc along the earth's circumference. (Similar results can be obtained by measuring an arc of a parallel, but the uncertainty of measuring longitude meant that this was very rare before 1850.) If the earth is assumed to be a sphere, this can be readily converted into the length of the entire circumference, thereby giving the size of the earth's radius. In his *Principia Mathematica* (1687), Isaac Newton demonstrated as a corollary to his theory of gravitation that the earth is in fact flattened at the poles. This realization prompted numerous geodetic arc measurements to prove, or disprove, Newton's theories and to determine the earth's precise shape.[25] The mathematics involved in geodesy are complex and do not concern us here, except to note that they made geodetic triangulations into acts of high science comprehensible by only the select few.

The net result of the greater accuracy of triangulation, of its greater congruence with the land, of its greater degree of control, and of its use in measuring the figure of the earth is that triangulation is held to offer the potential perfection of the map's relationship with the territory mapped. Triangulation defines an exact equivalence between the geographic archive and the world. Triangulation makes it possible to conceive of a map constructed at a scale of 1:1. Not only would this be the same size as the territory it represents, it would *be* the territory. The "technological fix" offered by triangulation has served to intensify the Enlightenment's "cartographic illusion" of the "mimetic map."[26]

Initially, geodetic triangulations in the late eighteenth century did suffer from uncertainties. The increasingly fine discrimination—precision or "exactness" in contemporary usage—of surveying and astronomical instruments through the century meant that repeated measurements of a single angle or length were as varied as observations for latitude and longitude. Unfortunately, both geodetic triangulations and astronomical research entailed extensive repetition of measurements which somehow had to be reduced to single values. Astronomers and geodesists accordingly drove the development of statistical methods, notably "least squares" analysis, for modeling observational uncertainties. Once the intellectually interesting issues of measurement had been solved, geographers and geodesists turned to new questions and left cartography behind as mere technique. In the popular mind, however, mapmaking continued to be imbued with all of the scientism and empiricism of the Enlightenment understanding of science: the world can be mapped exactly, the world can be *known*. In this context, the map's graticule of meridians and parallels signifies the map's scientific, rational, ordered, and systematic foundations. It signifies the map's naturalness: the map *is* the world.[27]

The principal British triangulation of South Asia, and therefore the key to the conceptual consolidation of a pre-existent "India," was the Great Trigonometrical Survey. The GTS had its origins in 1799–1800 when William Lambton, a Crown infantry officer, persuaded the Madras government to fund a triangulation across the peninsula south of the river Krishna. Lambton had two purposes in mind for such a survey. He wanted to contribute to the advances recently made in geodesy by measuring several chains of triangles. In addition to some short chains running along meridians, he also wanted to undertake the highly unusual measurement of an arc of a parallel across the south Indian peninsula. Eventually, Lambton's geodetic efforts focused on a chain of triangles running north from Cape Comorin, an arc which later became known as the Great (or Grand) Meridional Arc of India. The geodetic aspect of the work so dominated Lambton's reports that it precluded almost all reference to the survey's second function, which was to create a rigid framework for controlling detailed topographical and cadastral surveys. Lambton's assistants accordingly covered southern India with a network of triangles; based as it was on the highly accurate Great Arc, this secondary triangulation did not have to be undertaken with the same degree of nicety.

Lambton's survey at first lacked any formal name and was variously referred to as his general, geographical, geodetic, or astronomical survey. (The last name is obviously a misnomer!) The work was also limited to the peninsula south of the Krishna river. All of this changed in 1817 when responsibility for the triangulation was transferred to the Calcutta government and the survey itself was officially entitled the Great Trigonometrical Survey. George Everest, a young artillery officer, was at that time appointed to be Lambton's assistant. Everest became superintendent of the GTS on Lambton's death in 1823 and in 1830 he also became surveyor general of India. Everest completed the Great Arc, carrying it through 21°22′ of latitude, or about 1,400 miles (2,250 km) to Dehra Dun in the foothills of the Himalayas. A truly immense undertaking, as early as 1830 it was recognized in its "length and accuracy, . . . as exceeding . . . all [geodetic] arcs yet measured."[28] Everest's second achievement was to establish a system of triangulation that would eventually be extended across the whole of the subcontinent. Whereas Lambton had opted for a mesh of triangles, Everest advocated the formation of a "gridiron" of chains of triangles which would be easier and therefore cheaper to construct. When he retired in 1843, work on the first cell, covering Bengal, was progressing nicely (see figure 1.6).

The summary histories of the early British surveys in India present the technological fix of the cartographic ideal in all its glory. Their simple, linear sequence begins with Rennell, who began to map all of India in 1765 and who is therefore often called the "Father of Indian

Geography." Lambton put the surveys on a properly scientific footing with his triangulation, once he had overcome the petty objections of some accountants; his measurement in April 1802 of a baseline at St. Thomas's Mount, near Madras, is supposed to have placed *all* of the surveys in India on a "scientific basis." Subsequently, Everest's geodetic work perfected the fit of the triangulation to the actual surface of India. Set against these technological achievements are the conditions in which the surveyors worked and which the surveyors overcame. The result has been to present the history of the surveys in India in the simplest, most stirring, and most romanticized terms. It is all brave and courageous men braving the terrors and prejudices of a harsh environment, narrow-minded bureaucrats, and often hostile natives in order to create useful and essential knowledge of the world itself. It is a history that has been propounded in recent histories of cartography and popularized through a television series.[29]

The longer, more detailed official histories of the British surveys are not as simplistic as the summary accounts, yet they too do not question the underlying assumption that the Great Trigonometrical Survey was instrumental in unifying the surveys of India. Despite all the odd and exceptional surveys, the overall thrust of the British surveys was, they argue, to create a single archive of knowledge. This is the central theme of Andrew Scott Waugh's 1851 report in justification of the GTS's large expenditures in the face of parliamentary questions.[30] Clements Markham's 1871 *Memoir on the Indian Surveys* was imbued with the ideals of the systematic and comprehensive survey even as he united in one archive all of the India Office's geographical materials: geodetic, topographic, geologic, cadastral, marine; graphic and textual.[31] Reginald Phillimore's monumental, four-volume *Historical Records of the Survey of India* (1945–58), covering the period before 1843, was written with the benefit of hindsight—"for professional surveyors now working in India . . . that they might know . . . how the modern system came to be built up"—so that he too was fundamentally committed to the idea that the surveys constituted a coherent intellectual endeavor.[32]

In scope, these accounts fit into the modern perspective on the development of systematic statewide topographic surveys. The cartographic ideal requires that we assume that maps necessarily refer to the physical landscape and that their history is the history of their ever-increasing accuracy and comprehensiveness. From this perspective, triangulation-based surveys are seen as an inevitable and necessary development. The surveys consolidated the "science" of cartography and represent the final rupture from the older, "artistic" forms of mapmaking. In the paradigmatic historical sequence, there were a few precocious triangulation surveys in the sixteenth and seventeenth centuries, but it was not until the eighteenth century and the geodetic and topographic surveys of France that the feasibility of an extensive systematic survey was proven; the other European states soon emulated the French experience with their own triangulation-and-topography territorial surveys. When historians have noticed the institutional circumstances of the new surveys, it has been to cast the surveyors in the role of heroes-of-science who overcame the stupidity of decision-makers who were too narrow-minded to appreciate the need for new and better technologies; the surveyors therefore contributed significantly to human progress.[33]

The epistemological ideal of cartographic perfection has also given rise to the recent critique of maps as paradigmatic tools of modernity's totalizing and all-engulfing culture.[34] It has also carried over into Edward Said's critique of western imperialism's investigations of Oriental cultures and societies. At first, Said employed geographical conquest and hegemony simply as a metaphor for cultural conquest and reconstruction. Subsequently, he has tightened the tie between geographical and cultural domination. He has, for example, argued that Europe's comprehensive observation and codification of the non-European world was done "in so thorough and detailed a manner as to leave no item untouched, no culture unstudied, no people or land unclaimed." Imperialism is "an act of geographical violence through which virtually every space in the world is explored, charted, and finally brought under control. For the native, the history of his or her colonial servitude is inaugurated by the loss to an outsider of the local place . . . "[35] The imperial power thus recreates the empire in its maps, subsuming all individuals and places within the map's totalizing image. Military conquest, geographical conquest, and cultural conquest are functionally equivalent.

In the same vein, we can easily argue that each systematic survey constituted a geographic "panopticon." Jeremy Bentham's ideal prison was characterized by separating the convicts into individual cells for their better control; a system of backlighting would ensure that the convicts could be observed at any time—and they knew that they could be observed—by the invisible, anonymous, and all-seeing/panoptic guard. Foucault used the panopticon as the exemplar for those "instruments of permanent, exhaustive, [and] omnipresent surveillance" which permeate modern society and which fabricate the individual. As mechanisms of the state's discipline, the surveys improved "the exercise of power by making it lighter, more rapid, more effective," and more subtle.[36]

Thus, maps of India—particularly those hung on council-chamber walls—presented to each British official a single and coherent view of South Asia. At one uniform scale, all portions of Indian space became directly comparable and normalized. Knowledge of India was homogenized; particular variations and contingencies were subsumed within a "house of certainty." Each town and district was identified and assigned its own particular location within the fixed and immobile mesh of meridians and parallels. The space of the map was not bounded and limited but was as extensible and as potentially all-encompassing as British power and knowledge could make it. Moreover, that spatial architecture was rooted in non-Indian mathematics and structures; it was a European panopticon. Of course, the analogy of the map with the panopticon is not perfect, if only because the land itself is not sentient and its inhabitants were not necessarily aware of their cartographic representation; the geographic panopticon is not *direct*. The maps of India nonetheless form a disciplinary mechanism, a technology of vision and control, which was integral to British authority in South Asia.

A Flawed Ideal: The Practices of Mapping

The problem with Edward Said's conception of European imperialism is that it is too monolithic; Michel Foucault's understanding of the modern state's surveillant powers is too pessimistic, especially in the context of the nineteenth century.[37] European states and their empires could never be so totalizing. They could never be so effective. Linguistic problems alone meant that the surveyors had to rely extensively upon indigenous assistants, guides, and local informants. Moreover, like all instruments of state power, the surveys were exercises in negotiation, mediation, and contestation between the surveyors and their native contacts, so that the knowledge which they generated was a representation more of the power relations between the conquerors and the conquered than of some topographical reality.[38]

Even if it were epistemologically possible to construct the perfect, totalizing knowledge archive, it would have been institutionally impossible actually to do so. The possibility of constructing a map at 1:1 ignores the reasons why specific institutions make maps in the first place: to stand in for, to represent, the territories they depict in a wide variety of personal, social, and cultural exchanges. Not only would a map at 1:1 be impractical ("the farmers objected: they said it would . . . shut out the sunlight"), it would be quite useless ("so now we use the country itself, as its own map, and I assure you it does nearly as well").[39] It is of course naive to suggest that technological developments were by themselves causal factors in the epistemological shifts of the later Enlightenment. We must also pay attention to social conditions which allow the adoption of new technologies and which seek epistemological change. And because societies are not monolithic, their adoption of new technologies and epistemologies will be variable in character. Ultimately, geographic archives must be incomplete. They are constructed from knowledge circumscribed by the numerous contingencies of knowledge acquisition. The texts and maps did not present truth, nor do the maps constitute panopticons. The British simply believed that they did.

In the present day, such criticism mounts a potent challenge to the cartographic ideal; in the Enlightenment, however, it constituted only an empty threat. Eighteenth-century epistemology acknowledged that the actual measurement and observation of the world would be flawed and it had developed a series of mechanisms to cope. That is, each measurement or observation was construed as possessing a kernel of truth together with some erroneous or flawed aspect; the "rational" comparison and reconciliation of different sources of information would remove the errors and flaws and therefore reveal the truth. Or rather, that was the belief which defined the character of investigations by mapmakers, natural historians, and other scholars. As I will discuss in the following chapters, this epistemology is subject to an extensive critique. The immediate point, however, is that politicians, bureaucrats, and mapmakers in the eighteenth and early nineteenth centuries did not recognize such fundamental flaws.

The experts and decision-makers did, however, recognize the practical limitations of the cartographic ideal's technological fix. Of particular importance was the character of each government and its ability to implement a systematic survey. The colonies and their governing organizations were never coherent, efficient, and singular political entities but instead were characterized by numerous internal divisions. They also suffered from an endemic lack of skilled personnel and money which could only be detrimental for the surveys. A triangulation might be simple in concept, but its implementation has always been difficult. A triangulation is slow. Even the simplest triangulation requires a great deal of planning to identify the hills and buildings to be used as stations. On occasion, towers must be built. Flags and poles have to be erected on hills to provide unambiguous targets for the surveyor; even then, such targets can be obscured by clouds, rain, or heat haze so that the survey's progress is unpredictable. Once the numerous observations have been completed, there are even more complex calculations to be computed. A triangulation is costly. The instruments for measuring horizontal angles (theodolites) are expensive. The principal surveyors have to be skilled and well-educated and so command high salaries. They are, moreover, supported by a large cadre of subordinate surveyors, computers, and laborers whose total payroll can be substantial.

The relationship between a triangulation's extent and its cost is nonlinear. The larger the area to be covered, the greater the care which must be exercised and the greater the accuracy and precision of the instruments to be used. Expenses escalate dramatically. For very large areas, several levels of triangulation will have to be undertaken. A very high-quality, "primary" triangulation is undertaken between widely spaced hills, perhaps as much as sixty miles (96 km) apart, and is computed with respect to the variable curvature of the earth's surface. This serves as the basis for secondary and tertiary triangulations, which provide a sufficient density of points for detailed surveys.

Extensive triangulations could only be undertaken by governments. No single individual had the financial wherewithal to fund them; no commercial entity wielded the necessary authority. The adoption of each and every triangulation-based survey, which is to say each attempt to create a geographic panopticon, was accordingly dependent on the condition of each state. Those which lacked a large and entrenched military-fiscal infrastructure could not muster the long-term resources necessary to support extensive triangulations. When systematic surveys were actually begun, they depended upon the fickle support of individual ministers. The mapping of France by the Académie royale des sciences—the first successful, systematic, statewide survey—was repeatedly interrupted between 1668 and 1740, while the topographic mapping after 1744 featured extensive conflicts between the royal and provincial authorities and within the financial sectors of the French state.[40]

Perhaps the best indicator of the practical infeasibility of the cartographic ideal is the failure by almost every state before 1880 to incorporate a cadastre into their systematic topographic surveys. Conceptually, cadastral surveys were important contributors to the imagined ability to make a map at a scale of $1:1$. The various reconsiderations of cadastral surveys in British India as well as in Europe all proceeded from the expectation that they ought to be based on territorywide triangulations and that they ought to be the primary surveys from which all smaller-scale maps should be derived. But in reality, the survey of each individual village remained unique and separate on its own geometric basis. Cadastral surveys were accordingly significant for the development of cartographic literacy among Europeans in the eighteenth and nineteenth centuries, both in terms of pointing toward the possibility of fulfilling the ideal and in promoting map use. Nonetheless, the cadastral surveys were, in practice, too large-scale, too detailed, and too unwieldy for comprehensive mapping.[41] Their role in this study is accordingly ambiguous. Ideologically influential, they contributed little to the comprehensive mapping of India.

The one attempt to establish a systematic cadastre on a statewide triangulation which succeeded was the Ordnance Survey of Ireland (1824–46). The British mapped their colony at a scale of six inches to a mile (1:10,560), a very large scale for topographic mapping but still rather small for cadastral purposes. Had the British attempted a more suitable larger scale, say one inch to a hundred feet (1:1,200), they would most likely have failed too. On the other hand, the Irish survey's parent organization, the Ordnance Survey of Great Britain, was not so coherent. Dating back to 1791 and a topographical survey of southern England, made in preparation for a possible French invasion, the Ordnance Survey still competed in the 1860s with other state institutions over responsibility and resources for mapping tasks. The Ordnance Survey might today be held to be the epitome of the systematic, statewide survey, yet it is impossible to identify the precise moment when the modern Ordnance Survey was founded.[42] None of the great topographic surveys of the nineteenth and twentieth centuries came into existence fully fledged. Each grew and evolved in conjunction with the expansion of responsibilities and the extension of the power and authority of their respective states.

If we question the precepts of the cartographic ideal, we must question our assumptions about the nature of maps which derive from that ideal, and this in turn requires a reexamination of the history of the systematic surveys promulgated after about 1800. We might follow the lead of the Survey of India's cartographic expert in the early twentieth century, William Coldstream, who referred obliquely to the hollowness of cartographic rhetoric when he asserted that India had never been a "survey utopia where professional survey requirements are paramount."[43] In examining the Indian Survey Committee of 1904–5, whose deliberations were thoroughly imbued with the cartographic ideal, Andrew Cook has demonstrated that the implementation in India of an ideal systematic survey was hampered and constrained by the administrative priorities and bureaucratic structures of the different British governments. Most significantly, priority was always given to cadastral over topographic surveys. And, as already noted, the cadastral surveys were not incorporated into the general mapping program. The progress of the comprehensive mapping of India was therefore quite irregular, so much so that Cook characterized it as being more the result of accident than of design. Deepak Kumar came independently to a similar conclusion in a study of the administration of the several "scientific surveys" established by the British after 1850 to study India's geology, languages, ethnology, and archaeological remains.[44]

The systematic survey of India quickly dissolves into anarchy once these complexities are acknowledged. The perfection offered by the triangulated control of topographic surveys requires that the technology be implemented *in the proper sequence.* If a detailed survey is to take advantage of a mathematically rigorous framework, then it must be founded on triangulated control points right from the start. This in turn implies that the triangulation has to be completely computed and corrected *before* any detailed surveys are begun. If a topographic survey is made first and only then adjusted to fit a triangulation, then its errors are as likely to be increased as to be decreased. That is, not following the proper sequence introduces uncertainties into the surveyed data which are unquantifiable and therefore unremovable.

The British surveys did not follow the proper sequence. It took most of the century for George Everest's gridiron framework of triangles to be completed. On several occasions early in the nineteenth century, the triangulation surveys were awarded scarce resources in preference to the topographic and cadastral surveys. Even so, almost all topographic, and all cadastral, surveys in India were undertaken *before* the general triangulations could reach each respective region. Nor was there ever a single, coherent survey organization that could properly implement a systematic survey. The Great Trigonometrical Survey only emerged victorious in the late 1830s after a long bureaucratic competition over the most appropriate technology for mapping India. Only then did the last advocates of James Rennell's eighteenth-century style of surveying and mapping fall silent and all of the Company's administrators accept the GTS as the provider of structure for their geographic archive. But the acceptance of the GTS did not mean the end of the British dickering over their archive. All British survey activities were (supposedly) unified in 1878 to form the Survey of India, of which the GTS became the "geodetic branch." Subsequently, the Indian Survey Committee was convened in 1904–5 to effect substantial reforms in the various mapping activities. Nonetheless, by the time of Everest's retirement in 1843, the geographical archive's final structure was firmly established. I therefore use 1843 to mark the end of this study.

The role of the Great Trigonometrical Survey in unifying the cartographic image and archive of India rests on an act of cultural confusion. Enlightenment society invested maps with authority because of the manner in which truth was constructed within the space of their graticule. The data which contributed to the maps were indeed the result of measurement and observation, but they could only achieve greater significance and meaning within a graticule of meridians and parallels. In contrast, triangulation provides its own framework whose authority derives entirely from its constitutive acts of measurement and observation. The basis of the map's cultural authority thus shifted from the cartographer in his office to the surveyor in the field. The rhetoric surrounding the GTS in the early nineteenth century, and the assumptions subsequently made by its historians, would have it that the cartographic ideal was indeed implemented. And this is the act of confusion: even with the GTS, the key technologies for constructing the map of India remained in the office. The British achieved a compromise which cloaked the continuing exercise of map compilation in the authority of systematic field observation.

The comprehensive mapping of India was accomplished not through the systematic observation and measurement of the land but through the construction of the cartographic image of the subcontinent. Initial projects to compile a comprehensive map of India were varied and were distributed between London and the three presidencies. The key development in this regard was the establishment, in the 1820s, of a project to compile an *Atlas of India,* at the medium scale of four miles to an inch (1:253,440). In the debates which continued through the 1830s concerning the best way to map India, the very existence of the Great Trigonometrical Survey was tied to the production of the *Atlas.* The *Atlas* would bring together all of the topographic surveys and warp them to fit the GTS in order to create the definitive cartographic representation of India.

It is here that the apparent perfection of the geographical panopticon promised by the Great Trigonometrical Survey is revealed as an empiricist delusion. The chaotic circumstances of British surveying in India are conveniently obscured by a veneer of order and system. The ordered hierarchy of dependence between the surveys did not in fact occur. Whatever order was imposed on the detailed surveys came *after* the fact, when they were incorporated into the general archive. The order did not derive directly from the surveys themselves. What the British implemented was not the ideal, but only the *image* of the ideal.

The Ideologies of Mapmaking and of British India

Modern culture's firmly established conception of cartography envisages the map as a concise statement of facts about geographic reality. Maps are so naturalized within modern culture that their construction and use are rarely remarked upon. Thus, despite the time, labor, money, and general effort invested by the British in mapping India, the topic has rarely been addressed by general historians of South Asia. Only very recently has B. B. Misra recognized the surveys as being "instruments of territorial integration" and has added them to the list of the Company's infrastructural activities deemed worthy of extensive study (revenue administration, judiciary, army, police, schools, censuses).[45]

Increasing sensitivity to epistemological issues has led some historians of South Asia to pay attention to the role of surveyors who were involved in the British endeavor to define their empire intellectually. The surveyors and geographers, notably Francis Buchanan and Colin Mackenzie, have now entered the literature as active agents of imperialism rather than as passive data collectors.[46] Nonetheless, the geographers' specifically cartographic activities remain outside the scope of these studies. The ambiguity of this situation is reflected in David Ludden's recent essay on the changing political contexts of orientalist studies. To characterize the Company's initial gathering of information, Ludden highlights the contributions of three particular officials: James Rennell, the geographer who surveyed Bengal and mapped India; William Jones, the jurist who presided over the translation of Indian legal treatises; and Thomas Munro, the administrator who pioneered the settlement of land rights on individual cultivators. With the consolidation of British rule, Ludden writes, the "pathbreaking discoveries became authoritative wisdom; innovative methods became systems. Jones fathered a discipline [Indology] and Munro an administration."[47] But what did Rennell father? Rennell drops out of the analysis because for Ludden, as for most historians, only Jones and Munro created new intellectual constructs through which to comprehend and govern India. Jones created a systematic code of Hindu law when none had existed before; Munro's idealized conception of rural Indian society as an amalgam of enduring village republics subsequently colored all British policy. But Rennell is seen as having been uncreative, as having merely gathered data from a pre-existent and predefined landscape. Rennell's actions are construed as being necessary for British rule, but not as encompassing intellectual creativity, except perhaps for the overtly artistic title cartouche of his 1782 map (see figure 1.5).

In contrast, this study proceeds on the assumption that technology and knowledge are not neutral and unproblematic phenomena. Neither individuals nor institutions adopt new technologies as a matter of course. Surveyors and cartographers are not bound to make the "best" maps that they can; administrators and bureaucrats are rarely noted for their altruism. In short, the triangulation-based systematic surveys are rooted, like all other modes of cartographic practice, in cultural conceptions of space and in the politics of manipulating spatial representations. Cartography is a human endeavor and is accordingly replete with all of the complexities, ambiguities, and contingencies which characterize any human activity.[48] From this perspective, the British mapping of India takes on an entirely new and vital significance for the character and ideology of the East India Company's curious, hybrid state in South Asia.

The history of the East India Company's mapping activities can be summarized as the history of British attempts to make detailed topographic and cadastral surveys adhere to a systematic standard within a coherent administrative structure, even as the forces of inertia, expediency, and financial strain worked to preserve the almost anarchic conditions of mapmaking in India. Debates within the Company's administrations in London and India over the proper mapping policy to be pursued ran almost continuously through the early nineteenth century. In particular, the bureaucrats and politicians sought a resolution to the three-way contest between the pragmatic need for geographical information, unforgiving fiscal reality, and aspirations to the cartographic ideal. The contest's most revealing aspect for the character of the East India Company is the persistence of the cartographic ideal. Why was it so popular? What is the arena of overlap between the ideology of mapmaking and the ideology of empire?

For the British in India, the measurement and observation inherent to each act of surveying represented *science.* By measuring the land, by imposing European science and rationality on the Indian landscape, the British distinguished themselves from the Indians: they did science, the Indians did not, unless in a limited way and then only at the express request of a British official. Whether or not Indians independently pursued activities which agreed with the European conception of science is beside the point.[49] In the arena of education and knowledge, the surveys were a principal means by which the British held themselves to be superior to the Indians and therefore worthy of the territorial sovereignty which they had acquired. The practicing of cartography—the making of surveys and the compilation of maps—was quintessentially at once a scientific and a British activity.

The precise hierarchy implied by a triangulation-based survey embodied the power-hierarchy of the empire itself. Detailed topographic and cadastral surveys each covered a single pargana or taluk administered by Indian officials; they depended on more extensive triangulations covering one or more of the districts administered by British "collectors" and magistrates; those comprehensive triangulations depended, in turn, upon the geodetic-level triangulation covering all of India, the realm of the provincial governors and the governor general. In both hierarchies, order, policy, and responsibility pass down from top to bottom, while detailed information or money pass upwards. The hierarchies ensured the comprehensive cartographic and political control of all regions. These two aspects of control and knowledge were combined in the hierarchy of labor promoted by the trigonometrical surveys and which became the standard system for all of the scientific, intellectual, or professional agencies within British India: a few expert Europeans engaged in mapping and science and directed several layers of half-caste and Indian laborers, with each subordinate layer being less intellectually autonomous.

The view of science held by the British in the early nineteenth century was a thoroughly bourgeois and genteel conception. The pursuit of science was used as one more means to distinguish members of the European social elites from the lesser classes, although this ideology was by 1800 being contested within British society. By defining themselves as rational and scientific creatures, the British administrators and officials and politicians in India set themselves in opposition not only to the Indians but also to the lower classes of British soldiers, merchants, planters, hangers-on, and all the others who found themselves in India. The British elite created a myth of a bourgeois colonial community comprised only of themselves, which subsequently engendered the greater, more potent, and more ambiguous myths of Raj, of the White Man's Burden, and of the never-setting Sun.

This study therefore extends the work of some South Asianists who critique the cultural and historical knowledge archives which the British constructed for India. Following Edward Said, Ronald Inden has demonstrated that the British constructed an essentialist opposition between the Indians and themselves. Indian thought is characterized as "dreamy imagination," European as "practical reason"; Indian society is characterized as an "imprisoning (but all-providing) caste system," European as being based on the "free (but selfish) individual." India is represented as "simple and unchanging" in contrast to the "relatively complex and shifting" conditions which can be seen to have actually prevailed once the old certainties and polarities are rejected.[50]

A more nuanced perspective, on which this study draws heavily, is offered by C. A. Bayly, who argues that the British representations were enshrined in myths of coherence, order, and rigor. Bayly has indicated that the British derived from their pandits the brahminical perspective of an Indian society hierarchically organized by degree of purity and pollution, which perspective they then mediated through their own

Christian/evangelical, deistic, and rationalist/utilitarian beliefs. The result was a complex construction of Indian society and Hindu religion which enabled the British to rule India and to interact with Indians, yet which effectively obscured from British view the significant changes occurring in South Asian society and culture after 1750.[51] Marika Vicziany accordingly warns modern historians that while Buchanan might indeed have "established a tradition of empirical enquiry into Indian society," it was nonetheless "an empiricism with limits and limitations" which cannot "reveal the underlying realities of life in India at the turn of the nineteenth century."[52]

Thomas Metcalf has argued that the essentialist difference between Indians and Britons was built up by the British to justify the central paradox of their rule: British government was directed by liberal and nationalist ideals at home yet their rule over millions of Indians was clearly despotic. The key to the British self-representation, and therefore of their representation of Indians, lay in their own claims to possess an innate rationality and scientific nature. Unfortunately, Metcalf restricts his discussion of British rationality *per se* to a few observations on the "scientific" manner in which the British studied questions of race, including caste, gender, and history in the period after 1850. That is, Metcalf is concerned with the social phenomena which the British "saw *in* the world."[53] This study effectively takes Metcalf's analysis to its logical conclusion, specifically that the British self-image rested on a perceived difference between how they and Indians saw, and so mapped, the world itself.

Perhaps the most important portion of Claude Nicolet's comments on imperial space quoted at the start of this chapter is the parenthetical phrase, "or to believe that one understands." The British constructed a cartographic archive which they *believed* properly described India. To the British, the cartographic archive and its constituent surveys was indeed a perfect geographic panopticon. But what it described and allowed access to was *British* India, a rational and ordered space that could be managed and governed in a rational and ordered manner, according to "a rigorous tradition of administrative accountancy and . . . an ideology of transcendent law and sovereignty." It was this rationality and certainty which, for Bayly, distinguishes the East India Company's state from other "oriental" states and which marks it most clearly as an *imperial* state.[54]

In seeking knowledge from Indians about features of the South Asian landscapes and societies which could not be directly observed, the British had to negotiate a linguistic and epistemological gap. Company officials relied on the presumed order and system of the archive to absorb and make meaningful the information derived from the numerous Indian informants. The archive thus obscured the basic conceptual gulf between the British and the Indians caused by language and which persisted throughout the period of British rule. But I do not wish to overstate the gulf. Seeing information as a commodity to be purchased from its traditional purveyors, the British adopted the existing intelligence systems of India and added their own systematic archival practices. The fact that the British were able to conquer and control India indicates that much of their political, economic, and strategic knowledge was valid. But that information was not necessarily complete: most obviously, the Mutiny of 1857 caught the British by complete surprise. Ultimately, all British knowledge of the Indian "Other" was "exiguous."[55]

Although the main impulse of this study is to explore the linkages between the ideologies of mapmaking and British India, its examination of the later Enlightenment's cartographic ideal is necessarily relevant for the history of the systematic, statewide surveys generally. The debates on the Great Trigonometrical Survey and the proper manner in which India should be mapped were all rooted in the general British understanding of maps and mapmaking. After 1824, the proponents of the GTS looked to the Ordnance Survey of Ireland as the epitome of what they hoped to achieve in India. Drawing on the concrete example of the Irish survey, they were in the late 1830s finally victorious over the advocates of general surveys made in the style of Rennell.

I cannot, of course, claim that the institutional history of the GTS, the *Atlas of India*, and other mapping activities in India replicates those of the surveys of European states. The general issues which I address—of survey technologies, the epistemology of mapmaking, indigenous resistance and negotiation, administrative structures and internal debates, and the mythic construction of complete territorial archives—do nonetheless apply as much to the European scene as to the Indian. Indeed, the British surveys in India are more European than colonial in their conception. With the exception of the Ordnance Survey in Ireland and the mapping associated with Napoleon's short-lived expedition to Egypt (1798–1801), there were no attempts to establish a systematic, triangulation-based topographic survey for any European colony until the height of economic imperialism after 1870. Before then, colonial cartography was undertaken with the older technologies of the eighteenth century and in an *ad hoc* manner.[56]

One benefit for applying the lessons of the British mapping of India to Europe is to highlight the role of the systematic surveys in the territorial definition of the modern state. Eric Hobsbawm has distinguished the "characteristic modern state" from its early modern precursors by, among other factors, its initial attempts during the later Enlightenment "to impose the same institutional and administrative arrangements and laws all over its territory."[57] A necessary ingredient in this process was the establishment of a sense of territorial uniformity that allowed *all* of a state's territory to be treated in the same manner, regardless of obvious and compelling regional variations. A significant element in the formation of the modern state was, accordingly, the proliferation after 1750 of systematic territorial and statistical surveys. The application of the same techniques and scales of enquiry to each and every district meant that the resultant maps and statistical tables all contained the same sorts of information and were constructed and tabulated in the same manner. They therefore obscured, or denied, local nuances and particular circumstances. The systematic surveys provided the information required by increasingly centralized states and, more fundamentally, they constituted each state's representation of its territorial self.

Such an approach balances the attention usually paid to boundaries as the key elements in defining the state's territory. Borders obviously represent the physical limit of the state's legitimate authority. Modern states have accordingly equated their borders with their sovereignty, so that a breach in the one is a breach of the other. Consideration of the state-territory relationship has thus focused on the role of the border as the line of physical contact and conflict between states and as the delimiter of territory to be filled by the culture and economy of the state's dominant center. Drawing attention back to the rhetorical domination of territory as an active component of the internal negotiations of modern state formation provides an approach to the continuing problem of nationalism and its rhetoric of territorial rootedness.[58]

The present study is therefore more than the history of a particular cartographic institution or a particular manifestation of British imperialism. My concern is with the elite *British* construction of knowledge, with their assumptions and ideologies, as part of the broader goal of understanding the empire they created in India. (I must stress again that I am interested in the construction of knowledge by an *elite*: the scope of knowledge is determined not by some fiction of ethnicity but by society and economics.) I am interested in the cartographic culture transplanted from Europe to India by the British elites. "Cartographic culture" encompasses not material map-artifacts but the understanding of the practices of cartography which a society possesses, the forms of representation employed to experience and explore the world, and the means whereby the social order permeates those representations in order to recast and recreate itself.[59] That is, this is a study of the creation of a legitimating conception of empire, of political and territorial hegemony, mapped out in a scientistic and rational construction of space.

PART ONE

THE ENLIGHTENMENT CONSTRUCTION OF GEOGRAPHICAL KNOWLEDGE

[The Great Trigonometrical Survey] has given us the framework, or anatomy, of India, and on this framework an enormous series of maps, geographical, political, military, and cadastral, has been based. Whatever may be the destiny of India in the future, it must stand as an everlasting testimony to the scientific industry of the British nation. It can never be effaced so long as stone walls can contain the records.

Thomas H. Holdich, 1916

CHAPTER TWO

Observation and Representation

Thomas Holdich, a retired senior officer of the Survey of India, represented the structured assemblage of geographic knowledge as a concrete structure in and of itself. This was not an uncommon strategy. The built environment of the archive and museum has long served as a fundamental metaphor for modern European conceptions of knowledge creation. Data and artifacts can be collected within sturdy walls and there reassembled into meaningful arrangements. Indeed, the walls are overly protective. They physically divorce the collected data and artifacts from the actual contexts of their occurrence and existence. They keep their contents from being harmed and they actively shield them from the confusion and corruption of the world beyond. Within those walls, the archivist or curator constructs an artificial environment within which data and artifacts can be rearranged, manipulated, and controlled. Holdich's conceit, and that of the British more generally, was that the system by which geographical data were arranged within the archive was not artificial but was a true replication of South Asia's actual geography.[1]

Holdich's identification of the Great Trigonometrical Survey as the key contributor to the true representation of India is, historically speaking, a red herring. The survey's geodetic triangulation actually constituted a technological fix for the Enlightenment's older ideal of certainty and truth. That ideal was based on the structural equivalence of the imaginary lines of longitude and latitude on the earth's surface with the same lines as drawn out on a sheet of paper: the structure of the map—the archive—was the same as that of the earth itself. The geographer could mark each measured location at its correct position within the map's graticule of meridians and parallels. The only problem was that contemporary technology could not measure longitude very well. The map was therefore perfect only in principle, not in practice. Triangulation promised a better technology to fix up the Enlightenment ideal—to force practice and principle to coincide—so Holdich attributed the perfection of the geographical archive of India to the Great Trigonometrical Survey. But for a complete understanding of the epistemological basis for the British investigation of India, we must start with the Enlightenment's conceptions of observation and the archive.

The eighteenth-century conception of knowledge placed great significance on the empirical experience of the world. The appropriative character of that knowledge is most clearly demonstrated through the museum. In India, as elsewhere, the British assembled vast collections of mineralogical, botanical, and zoological specimens (some alive). In the human arena, the study of dress, society, tools, and architecture was complemented by the collection of as many artifacts as possible, including manuscripts. Captain James Blunt even attempted to "*collect* a small specimen" of the language of a hill tribe in Ellore, but because his "only method of *acquiring* this [specimen]" was to point to various objects, he was able only to define ten word pairs.[2] The specimen was the fetish of the traveler. The result was the bewildering profusion of animals and birds shot in the hunt, jewelry, insects, paintings, pressed plants, manuscripts, pieces of monuments, and a myriad of other curios which were donated to the Asiatic Society in Calcutta or which found their way to the India Museum in London.[3]

Whether fragmentary or whole, the specimen was taken as representative of the larger entity or population being sampled. Collection necessarily entailed the physical extraction of each specimen from the original, complex contexts of their occurrence, from an ecology or village. Each simplified specimen was then recontextualized within the museum by its arrangement in juxtaposition with other specimens. Within the museum, curators identified relationships between the samples themselves, rather than between each sample and its original environment, thus creating new complexes of knowledge in the form of artificial taxonomies.

Observation and the archive functioned in a manner directly analogous to collection and the museum. Observed facts were considered to be as concrete and as representative as physical specimens. Indeed, collection defined the fundamental stratum for all observational strategies. That is, the empiricism of the later Enlightenment posited a direct, visual link between an entity in the world, the individual's mental perception of that entity, and the individual's inscription of that perception on paper. The inscription could involve any combination of numbers, written statements, or graphic sketches but, regardless of its form, it was assumed to be an "essential" and literal copy of the original entity. The recorded fact would, of course, contain some degree of error—an individual might not draw well, for example—but it would always possess a kernel of truth. The inscribed record of a fact carried away by the geographer was thus directly equivalent to a physical sample or artifact carried away by the geologist or anthropologist. The recorded facts were collected in archives, such as the office of the surveyor general of India, and there related to each other to produce knowledge.[4]

Recent trends in social and cultural studies question the presumption that a representation can constitute an essential copy of reality. Representations of the world—whether numeric, written, or graphic—are bound up both with the acts and conditions of observation and inscription and with the subjective condition of the observer. Indeed, paintings, statistical tables, or written texts are as much representations of those conditions as they are of the reality they purportedly show. Nor can representations stand alone. They all melt together into a vast discursive web which defines *in toto* not what the world is but what it ought to be. From this poststructuralist position, the metaphorical archive constructs itself: there is no pre-existing structure within which to fit and to arrange facts. Instead, the archive stands for the discursive field of knowledge-representations which constitute our understanding of the world. The poststructuralist archive is no longer the coherent and ordered archive as it traditionally has been envisioned: it is fractured, ambiguous, duplicitous, and nuanced. The coherency and order of the archive is an ideological myth.

The British archive for South Asia's geography comprised all the various images, maps, censuses, and textual descriptions which they produced, all of which are embedded in the empire's complex economic, social, and cultural negotiations. In particular, the British representations of their empire were appropriative in character: they commodified the knowledge and aesthetic aspects of the landscape for their own consumption. Indeed, visual representations were generally treated in the eighteenth century as if they were private property. They deny presence—the sharing of time and space by the observer and observed—so that through its representation, the observed is removed, appropriated from its original context, and recast within the archive's discourse.[5]

The Scope of Geography in the Enlightenment

The process of knowledge creation presumes some archive—literal or figurative—to which all new knowledge can be related. In the case of geography, the purpose of the archive is to relate knowledge about particular places to a larger conception of space. Knowledge of South Asia's space was thus essential not only for its pragmatic uses in military and revenue affairs, but also for the structuring of all forms of geographical knowledge spanning all aspects of the physical environment and of human endeavor. Geographers followed a methodical process of comparing the attributes of each new *region* against those of previously defined regions; similarities were noted, differences were explored at length. Geographers observed the physical world and its human occupants with the overt intention of arranging the observed phenomena according to their spatial distribution.

But what is it that defines a region? Is it the inhabitants and their material cultures (density, ethnicity, character, architecture, economy, manufactures, cultural forms, social forms) or is it the physical environment (landforms, rocks, minerals, plants, climate, agriculture)? While some contemporary geographers, like present-day historians of geography, attempted to impose neat boundaries to the scope of their investigations, none succeeded.[6] There could be no disciplinary boundaries in the eighteenth-century's "ferment of knowledge."[7] That is, in examining the geography of India, in transforming India from a land of spectacle into a comprehensible empire, the British examined all aspects of the human and physical environments and distinguished between them as they varied in space.

Geographical discourse was therefore not limited to the map, and geographical observers did not necessarily make cartographic observations. Nonetheless, the map was essential for geographical knowledge, such that the common eighteenth-century conception of the "geographer" was as a mapmaker. Geographers made maps. ("Cartography" was only coined by the viscount de Santarém in 1839.) When, for example, the newly formed Asiatic Society of Bengal in 1799 listed topics which needed to be addressed by its members, it conceived of geography in the narrow sense:

> II. Geography
>
> 1. A catalogue of the names of Towns, Countries, Provinces, Rivers, and Mountains, from the *Shasters* and *Puránas* [Sacred Texts of the Hindus], with their modern names annexed; and a correct list, according to the oriental orthography, of the Towns, &c. mentioned by Major Rennell, and other *European* Geographers. The etymology, as far as practicable, would also be desirable.
>
> 2. What were the geographical and political divisions of the country before the *Musulman* invasion?[8]

Yet these two locational questions were clearly inseparable from those of the vernacular languages and political histories of India. As such, it was impossible to draw hard and fast lines between geography and the other broad categories of knowledge the Asiatic Society propounded: religion, policy, jurisprudence, manners, and customs; biography (historical); commerce, natural history, *materia medica;* medicine and surgery; and, language and literature.

Before the eighteenth century, the scope of geography was defined in terms of the scale of enquiry. Classical scholars distinguished between *geo*-graphy (earth-description) and *choro*-graphy (region-description). Geography entailed the study of the world as a whole and of mapmaking (general or mathematical geography) and the listing of all of the world's constitutive regions, described by their broad physical, demographic, and economic attributes (descriptive or special geography). Chorography was the description of a particular region and its inhabitants without reference to the rest of the world and placed a great deal of its emphasis on history (genealogy, chronology), antiquities, and topography; for very small areas, local folklore was used to distinguish one region from otherwise similar neighbors. On strictly etymological grounds, some geographers denied that chorography was part of geography; others, however, were more open to the apparently intuitive, but actually quite conventional, position that both dealt with the same object of study—the world in its spatial extent—but at different scales.[9]

Lesley Cormack has recently argued that "the three related branches of mathematical, descriptive, and chorographical geography" developed "each with distinct practitioners and different topics of investigation." She nonetheless concluded that geography "in all its guises was forced, *by its very nature,* to employ a methodology of incremental fact gathering," whether those facts were locations by latitude and longitude, social and economic data, or antiquarian-historical information.[10] A point Cormack does not build upon is that each of the three subdisciplines used maps to provide a mental image with which to organize the various observations and to define the limits of study. Chorography might have been the study of particular places without reference to a larger geographical realm, but the provision of a map of the area examined—which was standard after 1677—indicated a spatial ordering of data and the study's ultimate potential for aggregation into the larger geographic realm.[11]

By the end of the seventeenth century, the distinct scales of European cartographic enquiry were becoming so blurred that it was increasingly hard to discern any clear boundary between the two. This merger was effectively complete by 1750: geographic data were held to be conceptually scaleless so that the scale-based distinction between chorography and special geography dissolved.[12] Enlightenment geographers therefore adopted new criteria for classifying the scope of their subject. The

new categories of geographical knowledge reflected the objects of observation—physical as opposed to human features of the landscape—
in accordance with the Cartesian dualism between mind and matter
and the contemporary idea that the natural world is a stage for human
action.[13]

Several times between 1752 and 1762, for example, Philippe Buache
set out his "Idée Générale de la Géographie." This formal analysis of
the purpose and content of geography distinguished between mathematical, physical, and historical geography, which is to say between the
geometrical and astronomical processes of mapmaking (which I follow
Eric Forbes in calling "mathematical cosmography"), the study of the
terraqueous globe, and the study of all of the spatial aspects of human
existence and history.[14] Again, in his eleven-volume *Neue Erdbeschrei-
bung* (1754–92), which was highly popular in English translation, An-
ton Friedrich Büsching distinguished between "civil or political" and
"natural" geography, with the latter comprising "mathematical" and
"physical" geography. Modern historians have tended to give to Büsching's natural geography the name of its principal proponent, Alexander Humboldt, as in the "Humboldtian" project or science. A further
indication of the new classification is Immanuel Kant's separation of
"anthropology" from "physical geography" after 1772.[15]

When the East India Company's highly peripatetic officers examined
South Asia, they accordingly did so with a very broad understanding
of what features and aspects of the landscape ought to be studied. The
clearest example of this breadth is the long list of itemized "heads of
enquiry" issued by Colin Mackenzie to guide his assistants on the survey of Mysore (1800–1807). They encompassed all portions of geographic knowledge: immediately cartographic data (positions of and
distances between towns and rivers); cultural information (languages,
religions); social and economic information (population counts, legal
codes, industries); as well as mineralogical, botanical, and zoological
information (table 2.1). Similarly, Francis Buchanan was instructed to
examine a very broad range of topics in Mysore in 1800–1801 (table 2.2)
and in Bengal between 1807 and 1814 (table 2.3).

Such a wide-ranging scope was not some unattainable ideal. Mackenzie's assistant surveyors were able to gather much of the required
information. On one occasion, Lieutenant John Warren left his survey
of the eastern border of Mysore to follow up a rumor that gold had been
discovered. He found quite extensive areas of gold-bearing earth that
had long been mined by the local inhabitants; his report went into great
detail concerning their methods and tools for mining and separating the
gold, although there proved to be insufficient gold to warrant further

Table 2.1 Categories of Data for Colin Mackenzie's Survey of Mysore, 1800–1807

 1. Modern names of the circar, pargana, taluk, or district to which each village belongs (also provincial designations if beyond Mughal subdivision into circars).
 2. Ancient names of districts.
 3. Names of capitals, cusbas, etc.
 4. Distances in coss or other Indian measures along the road to compare with the measured road distances, so as to form a conversion factor from Indian to British measures.
 5. Computed distances to significant places to either side of the route.
 6. Names of rivers (ancient and modern), their confluences etc.
 7. Names of remarkable hills, tablelands, ghats, passes, etc., plus their forests, minerals, and productions.
 8. Remarkable springs, fountains, lakes, etc., and associated temples.
 9. Most remarkable pagodas, which are especially important for examining revenues and land grants.
10. Languages spoken by the natives.
11. Remains of ancient structures and any local lore about them.
12. Modern history of the country, before and after the Mughal conquest.
13. History of the rajas, poligars, etc.
14. Extent of each pargana or taluk.
15. Districts belonging to hindu rajas.
16. "Productions of the country," including plants and the character of the soil.
17. Minerals, fossils, ores, etc.
18. Manufacturing and the arts.
19. Interior and foreign commerce.
20. System of government and revenue management.
21. Peculiar customs of the natives, and especially any differences of established customs.
22. Books and depositories of native learning.
23. Native legal codes.
24. Alphabets and the characters used.
25. Population of districts by caste, family, villages etc. (tolerable estimate only).
26. Land revenue under Hindus, although too complex for easy examination.
27. Prevailing winds, rains, seasonal changes, etc.
28. Diseases, remedies, medicines, etc.
29. Remarks on the aspect of the country in general, including sketches of the general outline of hills and ridges, with names and computed distances.
30. Animals (wild and tame) peculiar to the area.
31. Principal towns, forts, etc.
32. Positions determined by astronomical observations whenever possible.

Source: Colin Mackenzie, "Hints or Heads of Enquiry for Facilitating our Knowledge of the More Southerly Parts of the Deckan, 1800," ca. 1800, IOR Eur F/128/213 is an 1804 copy.

Table 2.2 Categories of Data for Francis Buchanan, Mysore, 1800–1801

1. Agriculture, "the first great and essential object":
    (a) esculent vegetables: kinds, modes of cultivation, implements of husbandry, manures, irrigation, use of machinery, use as food and fodder;
    (b) cattle and horses: breeds, modes of breeding, species used for draft, potential for improving other breeds;
    (c) farms: extent, tenures, price and payment of labor, as compared with those in Bengal, potential for improvement.
2. Natural productions of the country, "the next immediate object":
    (a) cotton, pepper, sandalwood, cardamoms: cultivation and trade, nature and extent, means of improvements;
    (b) mines, quarries, minerals, and mineral supplies: produce, modes of working, treatment and conditions of labor, potential medicinal qualities of mineral springs.
3. State of the manufactures: exports and imports, labor rates, etc.
4. The climate and seasons of Mysore: prevailing winds, effects of air on human body, areas of salubrity compared with the rest of India.
5. Forests: extent, nature and species of trees, modes of lumbering, etc.
6. "Condition of the inhabitants": food, clothing, habitations; sects, tribes, laws, customs, personal traffic, weights and measures, currency, and "such matters, in respect to their police, as may seem to you to have an immediate or particular tendency towards the protection, security, and comfort of the lower orders of the people."

Source: C. R. Crommelin to Buchanan, 24 Feb 1800, ¶3-8, BPC 14 Mar 1800 §3, IOR P/5/11.

interest.[16] This is, however, a fairly untypical example. The reports and memoirs produced by Buchanan, Mackenzie, and others were generally the result of far more prosaic geographical investigations. They typify the manner in which the British observed languages, economies, historical chronologies, geology, botany, and demography, all within an implicit cartographic framework. That is, geographical observation relied on social conventions and accepted topics for its choice of objects. Geographical observation implicitly constructs new knowledge based on the spatial distribution of phenomena, in which respect it is firmly rooted in the map and mapmaking, but observation itself is part of the larger knowledge discourses constituted by texts, maps, images, and statistical censuses.[17]

Systematic Observation: Vision Directed by Reason

The dominant epistemology of the eighteenth and early nineteenth centuries was strictly visual and mechanistic. By the mid-1600s, the *camera obscura*—the darkened, monocular box which captured images of the world—had been accepted as the dominant model for vision.

Sitting within its darkened interior, the viewer is defined as "isolated, enclosed, . . . autonomous" and "withdrawn from the world." A divide as discrete as the walls of the *camera* is established between the individual and the objectified, "exterior" world. The *camera* explained the functioning of the eye-brain system: vision captures the image and impresses it directly on the viewer's brain, just as images are thrown against the rear wall of the *camera*. Furthermore, the single aperture of the *camera* legitimated and authenticated linear perspective as the dominant concept of vision. The "awkward binocular body of the hu-

Table 2.3 Categories of Data for Francis Buchanan, Bengal, 1807–1814

1. Topographical account of each district: extent, soil, plains, mountains, rivers, harbors, towns, and subdivisions; air and weather; plus "whatever you may discover worthy of remark concerning the *history* and *antiquities* of the country."
2. "The condition of the inhabitants": population, food, clothing, habitations; common diseases and cures; education; poor relief.
3. Religion and customs of each sect or tribe; the emoluments and power enjoyed by priests and chiefs; potential sources of popular discontent.
4. "Natural productions of the country": animal, vegetable, and mineral, especially:
    (a) the fisheries: extent, operation, obstacles to improvement and extension;
    (b) the forests: extent and situation re water conveyance, species, value, improvements;
    (c) the mines and quarries: produce, manner of working, state of employees;
5. Agriculture, especially:
    (a) "the vegetables cultivated for food, forage, medicine, or intoxication, or as raw materials for the arts": modes of cultivation, value, extent, improvements;
    (b) agricultural implements: defects and advantages, potential for improvement;
    (c) manures and irrigation;
    (d) flood control and potential improvements;
    (e) the domestic animals: food, use in labor, value, possible improvements;
    (f) use of fences and their utility;
    (g) "the state of farms": size, expense, rents, wages, condition of laborers, tenures, possible improvements;
    (h) "the state of the landed property" and tenures.
6. "The progress made by the natives in the fine arts, in the common arts, and the state of the manufactures": architecture, sculpture, and painting; different processes and machinery used by workmen; relation of manufactures to locally produced raw materials; possible improvements.
7. Commerce: exports and imports, trade; regulation of money, weights, and measures; transportation of goods by land and water; possible improvements.
8. "In addition to the foregoing objects of inquiry, you will take every opportunity of forwarding to the Company's Botanical garden . . . whatever useful or rare and curious plants and seeds you may be enabled to acquire in the progress of your researches, with such observations as may be necessary for their culture."

Source: Robert Montgomery Martin, *The History, Antiquities, Topography, and Statistics of Eastern India* . . . (London: Wm. H. Allen, 1838, 3 vols.), 1: viii–x.

man subject" was replaced by the *camera* as "a more perfect terminus for [the] cone of vision."[18]

Vision was constrained as a strictly mechanical phenomenon that depended on the pregiven world of independent truth. Jonathan Crary quotes Nietzsche's summary of this epistemology: "the senses deceive, reason corrects the errors; consequently, one concluded, reason is the road to the constant; the least sensual ideas must be closest to the 'true world'."[19] Of all of the senses, sight was the most mechanistic, least sensuous, and hence was closest to truth. Sight's almost exclusive privilege as the means by which to know the world was only reinforced by the use of artificial technologies of vision. In addition to the *camera obscura* itself, telescopes and microscopes underscored the mechanical character of vision by enhancing human faculties and so allowing more of creation to be seen and examined. Vision could also be extended to encompass otherwise intangible and invisible attributes of nature by the use of measuring instruments, such as graduated rulers or thermometers. Measurement became a surrogate for vision and the natural sciences became progressively more instrumentalist after 1750.[20]

Eighteenth- and early nineteenth-century epistemology was thus rooted in a vision which, with its surrogates, established an almost physical distance between the viewer and the viewed, between the subject and the object of vision. That which is viewed is pushed away from the viewer into the external world of objects, an action exaggerated by the use of instruments to see and measure the "true world." Although the *camera obscura* and the mechanistic model of vision rapidly fell victim after 1820 to the more sense- and emotion-oriented issues raised by the Romantics, the Enlightenment's instrumentalist empiricism has remained a strong epistemological force well into the twentieth century.

But vision, while essentially truthful in itself, was inadequate. In discussing eighteenth-century concepts of vision, Crary makes a key distinction between the "spectator" and the "observer." "Spectator" bears the connotation of the passive witness who literally "looks at," in the original Latin meaning of *spectare*. The spectator does not necessarily comprehend his or her visual perceptions; indeed, cultural historians often link the spectacular to the exotic, strange, and unknown. In contrast, and again reflecting Latin etymology, observation (from *observare*) carries the extra connotation of "conforming one's actions to" or of "complying with," in the sense of observing rules, codes, conventions, and practices.[21] Observation is guided vision; the observer looks at the world in a controlled manner.

The Enlightenment's acknowledged guide to vision was "reason."[22]

A loosely defined concept, which accounts for its flexibility and power in Enlightenment thought, reason encompassed both logical procedures and the human mental faculty. It was held to be necessary for making sense of the phenomena an individual viewed. It was the viewer's reason that defined those objects worth noticing and those to be passed over. Guided by reason, the viewer can focus on those aspects of the physical and human environments worthy of remark. With reason, the viewer can make sense of his or her world; without it, the viewer remains mired in savage ignorance. The development of reason was determined by the individual's education: John Locke's arguments that the human mind is a *tabula rasa* waiting to be filled were widely accepted. Accordingly, because sight is a common attribute for all but a few humans, the distinguishing factor between classes and races was the quality of education and of reason (compared with the western European standard). This was of great importance for the British in India and for their understanding of how they differed from the indigenous populations. In particular, it contributed to the denigration of Indian education and mysticism, a topic I discuss in greater detail in Part Four.

Enlightenment thinkers accepted Bernard de Fontenelle's 1699 characterization of rational thought as an *ésprit géometrique*. Denis Diderot and Jean d'Alembert, the editors of the great *Encyclopédie* (1751–65), explained this phrase as meaning "a spirit of computation and of slow and careful arrangement, which examines all parts of an object one after another and compares them among themselves, taking care to omit none."[23] They also used the taxonomic schemes developed by Linnæus (Karl von Linné) and other botanists as the paradigm for geometric reasoning. Modern commentators have followed Diderot and d'Alembert's lead in using natural history as the paradigm of the manner in which a larger description of the world is constructed in an archive through numerous observations of the surficial aspects of natural objects. Perhaps the best known is Michel Foucault, who tied vision and reason together with the aphorism that "the blind man in the eighteenth century can perfectly well be a geometrician, but he cannot be a naturalist."[24]

The goal of natural historians was to identify each plant's structure, which is to say the composition and arrangement of the plant's visible parts. Their debates focused on which of those parts most properly define the character of plants and so allow them to be compared and classified. Most famously, Linnæus used the sexual organs of plants as a limited set of characteristics with which to define and categorize each specimen; this technique was the "System." In contrast, advocates of the "Method" deduced the requisite characteristics for categorization according to the empirical circumstances of each object being observed.

There could be any number of Systems, each artificially restricted to a small and rigid set of characteristics which would delimit observation; there was only one Method, utterly flexible, in which observation of each new object was guided by its character and the results of previous observations. Despite their procedural difference, both approaches required the construction of that larger description in the archive: "the differences of distance [were] factored out" as "one by one the planet's life forms were . . . drawn out of the tangled threads of their life surroundings and rewoven into European-based patterns of global unity and order."[25]

Nonetheless, the eighteenth century possessed a broader understanding of "systematics," in which the observer distinguished degrees of identity and difference between objectified phenomena. Eighteenth-century systematizers carried this classificatory project from the vegetable, animal, and mineral worlds into the realms, for example, of analytical geometry, mechanics, linguistics, and human society.[26] Thus Georg Forster, one of the naturalists on Captain James Cook's 1772–75 circumnavigation, opined that all scientific observers "should have the penetration sufficient to combine different facts and to form a general view from thence, which might in some measure guide him to new discoveries, and point out the proper objects of farther investigation. . . ."[27] The nature of that "general view," and the process of its construction, was explicitly cartographic. Albrecht von Haller, a critic of Linnæus described it thus:

> we perceive with precision from those which we do possess, those things which we lack . . . A theoretician of Nature acts like a land surveyor, who begins a map on which he has determined some locations, but lacks the positions of other places in between. [He] nevertheless makes an outline, and according to half-certain reports, indicates the remaining towns, of which he still has no mathematical knowledge. If he had made absolutely no sketch in which he combined the certain and uncertain [components] in one composition, then his work of determining more exactly the locations and boundaries which still remained would be much more difficult and almost impossible. Indeed, it would not be possible, because [the work] would have no coherence, and would constitute no whole.[28]

The Enlightenment conception of archive-construction was clearly shaped by a cartographic metaphor. Within the abstract space of the archive, each new observation could be located in its proper *place*. Furthermore, "white space" in the archive indicated gaps in knowledge, much as it was assumed to do on maps, and so indicated arenas for future investigation.[29]

Both Linnæan system-ists and the rival method-ists likened their final classifications to maps. Linnæus, for example, referred to his taxonomic system as the *mappa naturae,* the map of nature. Michael Adanson, the Method's initial proponent, used geometrical and cartographic
metaphors for the process of classification, treating vegetable species as
if they were landed property demarcated by sharp boundaries: "find
the most sensible point that establishes the line of separation or of definition between the family of Scabiosa and that of the honeysuckle." [30]
More generally, Ephraim Chambers called his 1728 classification of the
various branches of human inquiry a "map of knowledge," while Diderot and d'Alembert described the *Encyclopédie* as "a kind of world
map." The construction of maps and the prosecution of substantial surveys was thus widely recognized as exercises in the systematic ordering
of observations to create a new knowledge, whether in the office or in
the field.[31]

The reference by von Haller to the manner in which the surveyor, or
systematist, makes half-certain reports certain is of central importance.
The employment of reason was widely acknowledged as the method to
remove the errors which, in practice, affected individual acts of observation. Astronomers and surveyors, for example, recognized that there
was a degree of uncertainty in their measurements of the world, but
they believed themselves able to submerge the uncertainty beneath the
certainty of systematic analysis. The dramatic improvement in measuring instruments over the course of the eighteenth century led to the
increasingly sophisticated mathematical modeling of observations, but
this did not displace the basic assumption that there is a kernel of truth
common to all observations of a phenomenon, and that the truth can be
revealed through the comparison and mutual reconciliation of those
observations.[32] Systematic analysis—reason—was sufficiently flexible
to handle any flaws. The geographer in the field might be unable to
observe a phenomenon or might wish to record information which cannot be actually *seen.* In either case, the geographer then had to rely on
indigenous informants who were treated as if they were themselves
mechanical instruments or self-propelled *camerae obscurae.* The British
prefaced information from a single informant with the same statements
which preface the use of instruments and which affirm the quality and
worth of the instrument. Information from many informants was subjected to a process of corroboration and combination to derive singular
facts.

Without the reasoned combination and comparison of observations,
the communal archive could only remain an incoherent and incomprehensible mass of trivia. There could be no knowledge without reason.

Chapter 3 provides a more detailed analysis of the logical system which underlay the construction of the geographic archive of British India while the remainder of this chapter focuses more on the conventions of observation in the eighteenth and nineteenth centuries and on the presumed autonomy of observed facts.

The conventionality of observation was acknowledged to some degree by the educated elite of the eighteenth and nineteenth centuries. They recognized, with such a highly visual epistemology, that any properly educated individual, who would therefore reason properly, would be able to make trustworthy observations about any subject of interest. Colin Mackenzie, the first surveyor general of India, justified his own historical researches in such terms:

> That science may derive assistance, and knowledge be diffused, in the leisure moments of camps and voyages, is no new discovery; but . . . I am also desirous of proving that, in the vacant moments of an Indian sojourn and campaign in particular (for what is the life of an Indian adventurer but one continued campaign on a more extensive scale), such collected observations may be found useful, at least in directing the observation of those more highly gifted to matters of utility, if not to record facts of importance to philosophy and science.[33]

Mackenzie presented the contemporary conception of knowledge creation as an inherently genteel enterprise. Like other Company officials who came from humble origins, Mackenzie consciously emulated, if not exaggerated, the conventions of his higher-class patrons in order to demonstrate the extent of his learning and therefore his suitability for social and professional advancement. Yet neither Mackenzie nor his colleagues recognized those conventions as being in any way artificial.

When it came to examining the physical and human features of South Asian landscapes, the Company's officials all adhered to a common set of epistemological assumptions and practices. Most particularly, the British believed that their sketches and descriptions were true and correct replications of the environment. But the sketches they drew were not realistic illustrations; the maps they constructed did not mimic the landscape. The British only thought they did. In practice, their examination of the landscape was thoroughly ideological in character. Their very ability to observe and survey was a direct outgrowth of their military, economic, and political power. Each instance of observation was backed by the desire to improve India. The British engineer-surveyor looked at Indian landscapes as a surgeon looks at his patient, as an item to be thoroughly investigated, measured, and prodded so that mala-

dies and imperfections might be identified, understood, adjusted, controlled, and so cured.[34]

Plain Observation: The Scientific Gaze

The manner in which the British looked at the Indian landscape, its features, and its elements was conceptually akin to the way modern states
examine and discipline their populations. The purpose of discipline is
to create order from social chaos through the rigorous partitioning and
hierarchical structuring of society, of time, and of space. The general
manifestation of the disciplinary gaze is the examination—Michel Foucault's "ceremony of objectification"—in which individuals are com-
pulsorily visible to those higher in the power hierarchy; examinations
are generally repeated, continual, and accepted by all concerned as a
basic fact of life. Thus soldiers parade daily before their officers; hospital patients submit themselves to examination by doctors and nurses.
The examination creates an archive of documentation through which
each individual is described. That archive enables and requires individuals to be compared with each other, a process which establishes them
as members of a larger population. Indeed, examination *creates* individuals. It extracts them from the mass one by one and monitors them for
any abnormalities. After examination, and after any deviations from
the norm which might have been identified have been cured, the individual is reinserted into the mass. The mass itself is therefore created by
the sum of all examinations.[35]

The basis of all of the empirical sciences, including geography, is
thus examination and investigation. The analogy between social examinations and investigations of the natural world is not perfect. To begin with, the landscape is not animate and cannot be aware of being
observed. Foucault's concept of discipline requires that awareness to
ensure the subject's obedience and subordination to state power. A
further difference is that the empirical sciences invert the respective
movements of the empowered examiner and examined subject. By and
large, the examiner is stationary as the subjects parade before them. But
to examine the world requires the examiner to move purposefully
through geographic space and the stationary objects of observation. In
1807 and 1816, for example, Alexander Johnstone "made two journies
[*sic*] by land for the express purpose of inquiry *on the spot* into the
history, religion, laws, and customs of the Hindoos in the southern
peninsula of India."[36] Even so, the manner in which the British *looked*
at South Asian geography was as empowered, as privileged, and as
concerned with identifying deviation and abnormality as the discipli-

nary gaze of the doctor or judge. "Gaze" is used to reflect the "prolonged, contemplative" act of observation that regards "the field of vision with a certain aloofness and disengagement," which is characteristic of discipline.[37]

In looking at India, the British employed two principal gazes: the scientific gaze, whose analogous individuals are a wide array of plants, animals, rock outcroppings, whole vistas, and cultural artifacts; and, the aesthetic Picturesque gaze, whose analogous individuals are landscapes. The analogy between the Picturesque and disciplinary gazes is actually quite close: if the view at hand (at eye?) failed to meet the established Picturesque norms, then the observer could alter (that is, cure) the view in its graphic representation until it agreed with those norms. Overall, the various "natural" gazes replicate the power relations inherent in social discipline. The act of observation embodies the observer's physical (military, political, gendered) power over the observed; it also embodies a moral power in that it defines and creates and normalizes the observed.

Barbara Stafford has intensively explored the character of the "scientific aesthetic of discovery"—the scientific gaze—during the period of 1760 to 1840. She explicitly distinguishes it from the aesthetic "concurrently espoused by the followers of the Grand Tour or mere seekers after Picturesque scenery." The scientific gaze was the examination and graphic reproduction of landscape views and of the features of the natural landscape. It was concerned with recording the facts of the external world. It was justified philosophically by two epistemological assumptions: that an exact image of the real world is impressed onto the mind; and, that the viewer cannot help but be "intently engaged by the aggressive identity of a particular object." The scientific gaze dealt not with the general, but with the individual and particular. It did not glide over each object, or the landscape as a whole, but instead was highly focused. The products of the scientific gaze were "plain" and in the same factual style which the scientific report possessed. The graphic products of the scientific gaze were expected to be incorporated into written texts: writing was inherently flawed and one needed to replicate visual observations to complete the presentation of the objects described.[38]

The goal of the scientific gaze is to see, and to record, the world as it is, which of course entails an ontological imposition on the world. The world is considered external to the viewer. The graphic results of the scientific gaze, whether they be of the landscape itself or of a particular object within the landscape, adopt a specific bifurcation of space between foreground and distant panorama. Highly focused images of specific objects stressed the foreground, and often ignored the background altogether (see figure 2.3). This style of graphic was the common form for architectural drawings. Figure 2.1 is a typical example from Colin Mackenzie's collection of drawings: an 1812 rendering of a temple in Java. Alternatively, those images with a larger compass place most emphasis on the distance and play down the foreground. Both forms of representation draw the viewer's attention to the object of study; there is no ambiguity as to what the illustration is about. At the same time, the images serve to hold the viewer at a distance and to keep the viewer separated from the external world represented.[39]

The scientific gaze claims to be a naturalistic gaze which, when the object of the gaze is the landscape, creates "topographical drawings." The ability to make topographical drawings, to portray physical features in a precise and correct manner (with or without the use of instruments like the *camera obscura*), was an ability expected of any well-educated individual of the upper classes. It was a prized skill for army and engineer officers and featured prominently in the military education of the period, where it was closely allied to mapmaking and reconnaissance. The first superintendent of the British Royal Military College (founded in 1799) held that "everything which is put down in writing of necessity takes on some colour from the opinion of the writer. *A sketch map allows of no opinion.*" One reason for a similar academy created at Madras in 1804 was the conviction that it was only by observing and reproducing the landscape that young officers could obtain a proper "knowledge of the ground," which would, in turn, give to their maps "the character of truth" when drawn with "the plainest method and stile [*sic*] . . . equally distant from . . . gaudy coloring and miniature elegance as from undistinct roughness."[40] Indeed, it is the map-like quality of "naturalistic" landscape views—their evident empirical truth and unambiguous representation—which has lead art connoisseurs to lump them together into a single and artificial category of topographical drawing, which can then be derided for lacking creativity and artistic sensibility.[41]

Stafford insists that the topographical drawings produced by the scientific gaze are antithetical to the "artistic" landscape images of the Picturesque. This assertion might be read in part as a reaction to the connoisseurs' cultural elitism. She might also be read as actively denying the ideology that permeates topographic views. The estate view, focused on the manor with home farm and property spread about, was as ubiquitous and as obviously celebratory of landed values as the large-scale estate map. More subtle in its ideology was the British genre of "rustic" landscapes, which have often been derided as "realist," but

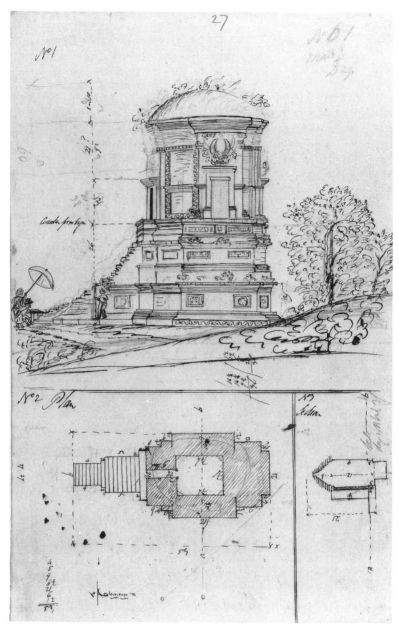

Figure 2.1 Untitled manuscript sketch (ink over pencil) of the east face, floor plan, and vertical section of a temple in Java, 1812, from the Mackenzie collection of drawings. Note the European officer sketching at left, and the pole-bearer in the front providing scale for the officer and making explicit that the various dimensions did indeed come from actual measurement. IOR prints WD 913 is a more polished and less immediate version (partly colored) of the elevation. (By permission of The British Library, IOR prints WD 914.)

which, Ann Bermingham has demonstrated, presented "an illusionary account of the real landscape while alluding to the actual conditions existing in it." Again, Hugh Prince has argued that all of those few landscape views of *named* locations in Britain (excluding estate portraits) which possess identifiable topographic features nonetheless constitute idealized representations of harmonious and ordered rural communities which ignored the economic, social, and technological turmoil that those communities actually experienced. Most fundamentally, the claim to possess a realist and naturalistic view is itself an ideological statement of power.[42]

Landscape Observation: The Picturesque Gaze

Connoisseurs and academic artists at the turn of the eighteenth century recognized how mapping complemented the landscape view, but they considered mapping and topographic views to be "too indelicate a display of power." In contrast, the aesthetic of the Picturesque offered a more refined, subtle, and delicate manipulation of nature through the dominant visual epistemology.[43] The etymology of *picturesque* refers to the idea that a natural scene or object will be more aesthetically pleasing if it deserved to be part of a composed picture, such as the elements of a still-life; such objects were "like a picture." By 1800, Picturesque-with-a-capital-P had come to be almost exclusively applied to landscape and had been codified with a very specific set of rules.[44]

The Picturesque aesthetic blended the themes of Roman pastoral poetry with the style of Italianate landscape art. The former were part of any genteel Englishman's education; the latter was popularized by the aristocrats who embarked on the Grand Tour. Idealized landscapes emulated Claude's Arcadian scenes, halfway between civilization and wilderness, peopled by carefree shepherds and their flocks, as in Virgil's *Eclogues*; or they emulated Poussin's landscapes, improved by the labor of honest rustics guided by gentry in honest retirement from urban life, as in Virgil's *Georgics* and Horace; or they emulated "savage" Rosa's wild scenery. Despite their various subject matter, the Italianate landscapes shared some important compositional characteristics. They were executed in mellow browns, deep greens, and golden yellows and were bathed in a glorious, yet "improbable Italian light." They shared the same structure, derived from the theater stage. In the foreground was the staffage, the idle gypsies and beggars, georgic rustics, shepherds, and so on, who served to enliven the image; the foreground itself was darkened, the result of the shade cast by the trees or ruins which framed the image like the wings of a stage. The result was a *repoussière* effect that forced the eye to focus on the brightly illuminated middle distance wherein is placed a city, castle, church, or other item of interest. Beyond the middle distance is the background, often indistinct and dominated by the golden sky at the horizon. These conventions were steadily augmented through the eighteenth century by more overtly nationalistic elements. The skies became damper and more clearly British; the classical ruins were replaced by ruins of churches and castles from Britain's medieval past; the high perspective of Claude was lowered to bring the viewer into the image, although this eased the strict differentiation between the three grounds; finally, the subject matter became increasingly wild and decreasingly georgic and arcadian.

The intention of the Picturesque was for each landscape to elicit emotional responses from the observer. Medieval ruins (castles and abbeys) were already established in British landscape art for sentimental, antiquarian, moral (*memento mori*), and political-historical reasons; now the Picturesque used them for the "pleasing melancholy" induced by their consideration. Alternatively, wild scenery and mountains could be expected to impress on the beholder the "agreeable horror" of the sublime, especially when mountains were drawn from a low perspective so as to increase their bulk and imposing character. Both ruins and wild scenery were rough, never smooth, so that the artist could employ a free and bold touch in contrasting colors and tones, all to achieve the desired aesthetic effect.

The Picturesque was not limited to the studio artist's creation of idealized landscapes. It required the active application of its precepts to nature: the tourist went in search of Picturesque landscapes. Stimulated by art and directed by detailed guidebooks, the British gentry who could not afford the Grand Tour through Europe instead toured Wales, Scotland, and the English Lake and Peak districts in search of the Picturesque, so that they might appreciate it and draw it for themselves. Yet the Picturesque was an ideal and could only be uncovered by *art*, which is to say by human agency and the active creation of the Picturesque by the observer. Mellow colors could be attained with tinted glass or the Claude Glass, a distorting mirror which brought the foreground into prominence. Guidebooks and maps informed the tourists of the best routes to take so that they might be sure to experience dramatic vistas; the Picturesque was to be appreciated all the more when suddenly impressed on the anticipating mind. The guidebooks gave precise instructions for where to stand and in which direction to look so as to see the most Picturesque view. The guides also instructed the tourist in how to modify that view in their own drawings in order to enhance their aesthetic value: smooth mountains and ridges became

Figure 2.2 Samuel Davis, "Near Tacisudon," 1783. Watercolor.
Michael Aris, *Views of Medieval Bhutan: The Diary and Drawings of Samuel Davis, 1783*
(London: Serindia Publications; Washington, DC: Smithsonian Institution Press, 1982),
p. 11, makes the mistaken assumption that because Davis was a draftsman and surveyor,
his views were accurate and naturally Picturesque: "the tone of his writing is secular and
his art possesses a clear naturalism, neither of which are conducive to false dreams . . .
even behind the reworkings aimed at the nineteenth-century public one senses the sober,
open eye of Davis." (By permission of The British Library, IOR prints WD 3269.)

rugged, and cliffs and ruined walls were foreshortened to tower men-
acingly over the viewer; trees were sharp and angular, smooth buildings were turned into rough ruins.[45]

The British found the Picturesque to be a perfect intellectual tool for
imaging the landscapes of South Asia (figure 2.2). It is true that very
few British tourists went out to India during the Company period. Only
viscount Valentia, accompanied by his secretary and draftsman, Henry
Salt, used India for an aristocratic Grand Tour, in 1803–5. Again, William Hodges and Thomas and William Daniell were the only professional artists to tour the country in order to paint landscapes, doing so
in the late eighteenth century. There was always far more money to be
had painting portraits and historical-dramatic scenes, and that required
the professionals to stay close to their clients in Bombay, Madras, and
especially Calcutta.[46] On the other hand, the duties of many Company's

officials were of a peripatetic nature. Other officials emulated the tours of mountainous Britain by making tours of conquered territories, usually in the northern plains and the foothills of the Himalayas. And as they moved across a strange land, as they observed new sights and landscapes armed with an educated taste for Picturesque scenery, the British recapitulated the Picturesque traveler who sought that elusive view which might be captured before passing on, ultimately to return to the comforts of civilization where those landscapes might be appreciated and remembered at leisure.[47]

In reviewing British travel literature in India, Ketaki Kushari Dyson found innumerable "verbal vignettes celebrating the beauty of mountains and valleys, hills and forests, corn-fields and rivers," and which were couched in the jargon of the Picturesque. These vignettes were in direct opposition to the general disparagement by the British of smooth and unending plains. The inclusion of "corn-fields" in Dyson's list might appear incongruent, except that the picturesque did encompass arcadian and georgic sentiments as well as those of the wild sublime. The naturalist and geographer Francis Buchanan, for example, seemed only to have noticed the landscape through which he passed when it was well-farmed, prosperous, and the epitome of *improved* agriculture.[48]

For the British, India was "naturally" Picturesque. One reason was that the key terms of the Picturesque aesthetic had become hackneyed clichés by 1800. It was *de rigueur* to use "picturesque," "sublime," or "romantic" when describing any landscape, even industrial ones. The realist and Picturesque views merged in India because the subcontinent seemed to possess all of the required elements for properly Picturesque views. The dark, evergreen flora and dusty brown plains eliminated the need for the Claude Glass. The luxuriant, jungle vegetation and lofty, jagged mountains provided wilder and more sublime scenery than any which might be constructed in the increasingly tamed British Isles. Much of the architecture was not smooth and seemed to the British, even when intact, to be crumbling before their very eyes. The ruins were as aesthetically and morally redolent as any ruined church or castle. When published in London, the picturesque views of India appealed to a much broader audience than just the "Anglo-Indians," as when Colonel Charles Forrest's *Picturesque Tour along the Rivers Ganges and Jumna* (London: Ackermann, 1824) was advertised as the companion to the same publisher's *Tours of the Rhine and Seine*.[49]

An example of the aesthetic shared by the British in India is provided by William Lambton, founder of the Great Trigonometrical Survey. Lambton kept a journal of the march in 1799 of a large British army column through newly conquered Mysore. The journal contains several very self-conscious and revealing statements of aesthetic principle which seem to have been intended to impress his noble-born superiors and patrons with the extent of his education and cultural erudition. (The surviving copy of the diary is found in the papers of Lord Wellesley, governor general of India, and elder brother of Lambton's regimental colonel, the Hon. Arthur Wellesley, who also commanded the column; both brothers were Lambton's patrons.) Two comments in particular illustrate a conviction that it was unnecessary to manipulate or even create any landscape features because India was inherently picturesque: "the scenery the whole way is wild and sublime; and to those irregular features of nature, which constitute the picturesque, is added, the ruins of art seldom introduced into landscape painting"; and "the numerous flocks and herds which are scattered in all directions, give a rural sweetness to the face of nature, and the Mysore [country], like antient [sic] Arcadia, both from the mildness of its climate, the variety of its beauties and the simplicity of its native inhabitants (Gentoos), may afford abundant subjects for pastoral poetry."[50]

The Picturesque conventions were slowly naturalized in India. Many people in Britain had already succumbed to the hegemony of visualism, assumed that Picturesque views were *supposed* to be realistic, and so criticized the guidebooks because the illustrations were not true to nature.[51] Their "double desire to be professionally accurate while being artistically conventional" in their landscape images did not pose as much of a problem to the British in India as it did in other parts of the empire.[52] They treated their Picturesque landscapes as possessing the same characteristics of accuracy and objectivity as might be expected of a view made for military or architectural purposes. They "claimed their work to be . . . the communication of facts."[53]

The Indian Picturesque was an imperial Picturesque. No statement expresses India as a site of naturally occurring beauty, to be appropriated and enjoyed by the British, better than this by the Daniells:

> Science has had her adventurers, and philanthropy her achievements: the shores of Asia have been invaded by a race of students with no rapacity but for lettered relics: by naturalists, whose cruelty extends not to one human inhabitant: by philosophers, ambitious only for the extirpation of error, and the diffusion of truth. It remains for the artist to claim his part in these guiltless spoliations, and to transport to Europe the picturesque beauties of these favoured regions.[54]

But the British did not find a naturally Picturesque landscape in India: they created it in line with the highly selective and appropriative nature of the Picturesque aesthetic.

The reverend William Gilpin, the first theorist of the Picturesque, explained the key principal in 1801. "Magnificent nature," he wrote, is the "grand storehouse" of all "picturesque ideas," yet it is the human eye which must add the "little requisites" of artistic forms, such as light and the balance of foreground, which make a scene into a picture. "Nor do we depreciate nature, but exalt her. With an open hand she gives us corn; but she does not condescend to make a loaf." Reacting to the order and structure imposed on nature by European culture, the Picturesque did not hesitate to perform its own improvements and turn the raw ingredients provided by nature into consumable form. The Picturesque gaze was highly selective. It ignored the "succession of high-coloured pictures," which the tourist is normally subjected to, until the "transient glance" suddenly and unexpectantly revealed "a good composition," at which point Gilpin would give "any price to fix and appropriate the scene."[55]

Landscape had become a commodity to be defined, acquired, and consumed by the observer. The Picturesque gaze was, moreover, an inherently elitist and class-based aesthetic; it was an educated taste. Its possession was the hallmark both of gentlepersons, who were confident of their social position and their natural right to own and to shape the land and its products, and of social climbers like Lambton who asserted their right to such status. The Picturesque secured titillating representations of nature that could only be enjoyed by the elite, because only they were properly versed in the conventions. The Picturesque reinforced the elite's comfortable self-perceptions as the owners and controllers even of wildest nature; it brought that nature into their homes and libraries and personalized it. The Picturesque gaze constituted a process of examination, an act of discipline, in which the natural world is viewed, represented, and through that representation is cured and improved.[56]

This was the aesthetic gaze which enabled the British to create Indian landscapes. The smooth and regular geometry of Islamic architecture could be negated by the proper perspective, by the addition of strategically placed trees to break a smooth line, or by the total falsification of a landscape element. When Hodges painted the tomb of emperor Sher Shah (reigned 1540–55), he gave the surrounding rectangular tank an uneven edge in order to redefine the nature of the tomb. No longer isolated and detached from its environment, as intended, the tomb was represented as an integral element of the whole landscape.[57] Mildred Archer has remarked how the many landscapes drawn by British engineers and surveyors in the field all possessed the same elements: their shadows are sepia-washed, while "some interesting feature occupies the middle distance and the foregrounds are enlivened with small figures or animals." Like the Picturesque itself, these drawings have achieved their own formulae and conventions. They are highly selective and manipulative in their content. The frame, the subject matter, the coloring (sepia for that favored mellow brown tint), the composition of three grounds . . . all collude with each other to provide a uniquely British form of description and landscape conceptualization.[58]

Members of the British elite observed an alien land with a common technology, bringing it into comprehensible and personalized forms. In its imperial manifestations, the practitioners of the Picturesque might have thought themselves to have been innocent and "guiltless," but the necessary effect was to draw a divide between the rulers and the ruled, between the rulers and the land, and thus contributed to the developing logic of empire. There was little that was genteel about the gaze in its imperial setting. Most Company officials who engaged in landscape painting were concerned with examining, disciplining, and improving India. They were up-country magistrates, district revenue collectors, army officers on station, engineers building roads, and, especially, officers undertaking cartographic surveys. All these "adventurers" who embarked on "an Indian sojourn and campaign," as Colin Mackenzie expressed it, constructed a particular view of India based on their power over it. "To be a European in the Orient," writes Edward Said, "*always* involves being a consciousness set apart from, and unequal with, its surroundings."[59]

Whatever their claims to naturalism or creativity, British representations of the Indian landscape resulted from an objectifying and appropriative examination. The scientific and Picturesque gazes, and the geographical gaze which depended on both, created power relationships regardless of the political context. Western culture has traditionally drawn an analogy between the inequalities of observation and the gendered inequalities of society. Several commentators, notably Gillian Rose, have remarked on the manner in which nature has been feminized by European culture since the Renaissance. In an imperial setting, the construction of the subordinate Other as feminine is simply all the harder to overlook and ignore.[60] The gaze, or concerted observation, is always appropriative, domineering, and empowered.

Geographical Observation and Narratives

The difference between the scientific and Picturesque gazes is one of conceptual scope. Individual objects that were the focus of examination were represented in the plain style of the scientific aesthetic. Even for the large vistas of topographical drawings, the artist's gaze has a definite focus, be it a mountain, a field or farm, or a manor house. Entire landscapes were constructed through the Picturesque aesthetic. Whereas Stafford might set the two gazes in opposition, they provided basic and complementary tools for the British geographical investigation of the human and physical landscapes of South Asia. Wielding those gazes, a diverse group of Company officers examined different aspects of India and placed their observations in a spatial context. Just as natural historians placed each new plant observation within an artificial space of botanical taxonomy, so geographers placed each observation of the land into the larger spatial framework. Geography requires an *overview* that subsumes and supersedes the individual *view*. That overview is the communal image of space constructed through maps.

It was not necessary for geographical observers to construct maps themselves: observations are spatially recontextualized as long as the observer has a mental image of spatial structures. That mental image comes from two sources. First, it derives from the geographer's cognitive and social reading of maps, which establishes a much broader image of spatial features than direct personal experience can provide. Second, the manner in which geographers move through the landscape means that each observation is automatically placed in a position relative to all other observations. That is, each observation can be tied, in principle, to a specific place on the geographer's route. The route can be fitted into that larger framework, thereby tying each observation into an absolute space. As the gazes themselves are inseparable from the images they produced, so geographical observation is inseparable from the geographers' narratives.

In the following discussion of geographical observation and narratives, I refer extensively to a particular example: the account by Henry Walters of his excursion into the Khāsi Hills in October and November 1828. I use this example because Walters was neither a surveyor nor an explorer of territory hitherto unknown to the British. He nonetheless employed the rhetoric and technologies of the geographer. He was a judge who served in India between 1813 and 1838. In traveling from Dacca to preside over sessions at Sylhet in northeast Bengal, he took advantage of the peaceful relations between the British and the Khāsi rajas to leave the plains and play the tourist. He spent a fortnight in the hills, always on or near the road the British were then building across the hills to link Sylhet with the recently annexed province of Assam. There is no indication that Walters intended to publish his account of his journey: it reads like a personal account sent to a friend and would probably not have been printed in the *Asiatic Researches* were it not for the raja of Nongkhlao taking up arms against the British in April

1829. The Khāsis were still undefeated in 1832 when Walters's account appeared in print as a source of information on this hitherto enigmatic people. Walters's essay accordingly presents the viewpoint of the middle tier of personnel in India.[61]

Walters's account is a geographical narrative, a list of observations structured chronologically and therefore spatially. For each day, Walters lists the routes taken and describes the landscapes he passed through. He mentions the various economic and social activities of the Khāsis, as he saw them. The narrative structure of the account indicates a familial relationship with the hugely popular literary genre of travel and exploration accounts. Indeed, borrowing on that popularity, geographical narratives were preferred over more systematic texts for the popular writing of geography. When, for example, Alexander Gerard sent his hundred-page account of Kunawar—or Kinnaur, the Himalayan valley of the Sutlej River—to a family friend in the late 1830s, he described his manuscript as being "a description of the country, without any narrative; so perhaps it would not interest you." The friend's response was to edit both the account and Gerard's narratives for publication, thereby gaining the best of both worlds.[62]

The relationship between the geographical and other travel narratives was collateral, and not fraternal, in nature.[63] The character of the general travel narratives have recently been examined by Paul Carter. Perhaps their key characteristic is that they are written very much in the first-person. This self-referential quality transforms an erstwhile travel account from the record of traveling into one of stopping places and of the conditions under which writing was possible. The autobiographical character of the travel narrative leads to the inclusion of much personal matter. For British travelers in India, there are descriptions of the writer's British hosts and acquaintances, of their characters, and of the circumstances of their lives in India. Indians are recorded both as individuals and as depersonalized, generalized "natives." Travelers' diaries stress novelties; this is certainly the case with the explorer's account. The quotidian circumstances of travel and exploration, for example, are downplayed; they might be prominent at the start of a narrative, but references to them rapidly disappear from the narrative once the newness of travel wears off. Travel diarists did establish a distance between themselves and the objects and events they recorded, but that distance is permeable and recognized to be so within the narrative itself.[64]

There is much overlap between geographical and travel and exploration narratives. It was impossible to write a purely geographical narrative without being influenced by at least some of the features of the dominant literary form. Accordingly, Walters's account did have some of the character of a general narrative. He included, for example, the funeral description obligatory for all European travelers in India and he accompanied it with similarly stereotypical observations on the Khāsis' "most perfect indifference" to death (27 Oct.).[65] Even so, he couched this description in the objectivity of empirical observation. He did refer to himself in the text, but only in reference to personal acts of seeing and reasoning: "My eyes opened . . ." (1 Nov.); " . . . and I imagine" (3 Nov.); " . . . some of which I collected" (4 Nov.). However, he depersonalized the acts of his traveling with an idiosyncratic syntax which omitted the personal pronoun; the account begins with "Left *Dacca* on the night of the 19th October 1828 . . ." and is riddled with similar statements, such as "After some trouble succeeded in making a start . . ." (27 Oct.), or "Rose by moonlight this morning . . ." (28 Oct.).

Geographical narratives are distinguished from the more common travel and exploration accounts because they reject self-reference. Geographical observation was turned outward from, not in toward, the British self. It was the textual equivalent of the purely mechanistic vision that creates an unassailable distance between the observer and the observed, between (in India) the Company official on the one hand and the Indians and their land on the other. Geographical observation focused on not the new and novel but the everyday and common in order to classify all aspects of a region. The geographer's comprehensive overview of each region had to incorporate all occurrences of even the most mundane features. Geographical observation passed beyond the "primary discoveries" that fill the explorer's account and concentrated instead on the "commonplace, secondary associations." There was a gender difference between the narratives: geographical (and exploration) narratives were universally the products of male writers, whereas a significant portion of the travel literature was written by and for women.[66]

The geographical narrative is characterized by the empiricist rhetoric of observation. Throughout his narrative, Walters matched motion with observation with statements of fact. In doing so, he proclaimed that his statements were correct and trustworthy from being based on actual empirical observation. He had gone into the landscape and had *seen* for himself the facts that he now presented. He made no distinction between the observation of landscape and the observation of material activities. Thus, at the village of *Surarim*:

> passed over a coal region, the coal cropping out of the ground—
> road tolerable so far. Here iron-smelters reside—entered one of the

forges, the bellows are curious, and are worked by women, who stand on the top, and move them with their feet; the furnace is made of clay, hooped with iron: the ore is broken into small pieces, and put into the furnace with charcoal—the iron melts and runs out at the bottom, it is then taken up and cut into large lumps for exportation to the plains. It is very good, and is used for all purposes in this part of India. (30 Oct)

It is reasonable to expect that Walters did indeed glean much of his information *en route* and from single instances of direct observation. Only the more generalized statements seem to depend on a much broader knowledge base, yet they were nonetheless encompassed by Walters's rhetoric of vision so that they too acquire the privileged quality of empirical data. This tension between the representation and process of observation is most acute when Walters turned his attention to Khāsi society and culture:

The *Cásias* are a stout athletic race; fair, as compared with the inhabitants of the plains, and with muscular limbs. They are devoted to chewing *paun* and betel, very fond of spiritous liquor, and eat and drink whatever comes their way. In religion they follow some of the *Hindu* customs. They have no written character, and their language is different from that of the *Garos* and other surrounding tribes; they all appear to be but different dialects of the same original language. Theft is unknown among them, and they are true to their word. In moral character, they tower, like their mountains, over the natives of the plains. They always go armed either with bows and arrows, or long naked iron swords. . . . Their houses are surrounded by yards fenced with neat stone walls; and the villages are usually erected on the side of a hill, the houses rising one above the other. Property descends to the nephew of the occupier, by his sister. They are governed by numerous petty Rajas, who exercise but little control over them. On all occasions of importance, the Queen Mother, and the elders of the tribe, are consulted, and nothing can be done without their consent. Their pigs are a small handsome race, like the Chinese; their cattle large and sleek, and in good condition, the pasturage on the hills being excellent. (27 Oct.)

By recording these statements on diverse topics *en masse* under a single day, Walters implied that they were all based on information derived in a single session of observation. He juxtaposed the observable (the Khāsis go armed, they build walls, they are stout, etc.) with the unobservable (matrilineal inheritance, political structures, religious observances, linguistic relations, etc.). The result was a rhetorical presentation of all information, no matter its source, as being trustworthy and true.

Walters's reliance for knowledge upon local informants was glossed over and submerged beneath the rhetoric of his personal, reliable, singular, and correct observation.

In classifying and categorizing the phenomena encountered, the geographical observer relied very much on their observed, superficial characteristics. As might be expected, this strategy is most apparent in his notes on natural history, in which he constantly identified specific plants and minerals:

> The cinnamon tree grows here wild—the leaves and young branches are exported to the plains for sale. Also a species of holly is found; in fact, here is an ample unexplored field for a Botanist— also for a Mineralogist. I procured some specimens of the coal, and of other rocks. (4 Nov.)

Part of the distinguishing and classifying process involved appeals to what was known. In recording the few occasions when something reminded him of Britain, Walters intimated how *unlike* Britain were the rest of the phenomena he observed.

Walters's urge to classify is also apparent in his antiquarian and ethnographic descriptions. He categorized the many stone funerary monuments erected by the Khāsis, compared them with the megaliths of Britain, and suggested that British cromlechs originally served the same funerary purpose. He allayed his personal unease with such a radical idea with an appeal to epistemology. Are not any doubts concerning the purpose of the British monuments, he asked, "dissipated *by observation*, as to the actual use of similar monuments in this country at the present day?" (3 Nov., emphasis added). Furthermore, the erection of monuments constituted a characteristic by which the Khāsis were to be distinguished from other Indian groups. The equivalence of surficial form with function allowed Walters to equate the hillmen with the ancient occupants of Britain, an equation which served to distinguish yet further the Khāsis from the modern British. (Another contemporary commentator likened the Khāsis to ancient Romans.) [67]

The lengthy ethnographic description quoted above also comprises a litany of classification. The Khāsis were separated from their neighbors in terms of their physiognomy, religion, and language; their essential trait as a fiercely independent people was established. At the same time, Walters was careful to distinguish them from Europeans: they had no writing, and so were barbaric, and their polities approached the anarchic.

The empirical character of Walters's account is reinforced by the extraction of hard data from the environment. As noted above, Walters collected specimens of the plants and rocks he encountered, following the contemporary fetish for collecting rather than any specific scientific plan. He also measured individual objects and whole landforms. Here again he was not as rigorous as other, more dedicated investigators. His own figures were rather vague, such as "the elevation [of Cherrapunji] is about five thousand feet" or "one slab . . . , a circular stone, measured twelve feet in diameter by about two feet thick" (29 Oct.). He did give precise values—for example, "*Lombray* stands at an elevation of 5914 feet" (31 Oct.)—during the short period when he was at Nongkhlao in the company of a surveyor, Captain John Jones, who can be expected to have been equipped with a thermometer and barometer. Jones was probably also responsible for Walters's numeric postscript:

> Latitude of *Nanklow* 25°40′30″ N
> Longitude 91°32′0″ E[68]
> *Range of the Thermometer at Nanklow*
> From 23d to 31st May, thermometer varied from 67°4′ to
> 75°5′
> From 1st to 14th June, thermometer varied from 68°6′ to
> 72°5′

Overall, the scattering of numeric observations reinforce the truthfulness and correctness of the more qualitative observations. The final flourish asserts that, when all is said and done, the text is a collection of similarly unambiguous facts. Other geographers used quantification—and the census—as an efficient means to represent the mundane aspects of their studies. For example, Francis Buchanan and others sampled the density of houses in villages and towns, and estimated the number of people per house, in order to derive values for the population (total and by caste) in each district (see table 2.3).[69]

Graphic Images and the Visualism of Geographic Rhetoric

Henry Walters's account exemplifies the use of graphic images to underscore the empirical truth of the linear narrative. Walters drew, in a plain manner, some examples of artifacts which were all too large to be moved or too complex to be sampled, specifically some of the standing stones and the curious bellows used in smelting iron (figure 2.3). Each item drawn is easily matched with a specific description in the text and so proclaims the visual truth of Walters' statements.

Broadening his gaze to encompass the broader scale of the region, Walters drew a landscape (figure 2.4). The Picturesqueness of this view

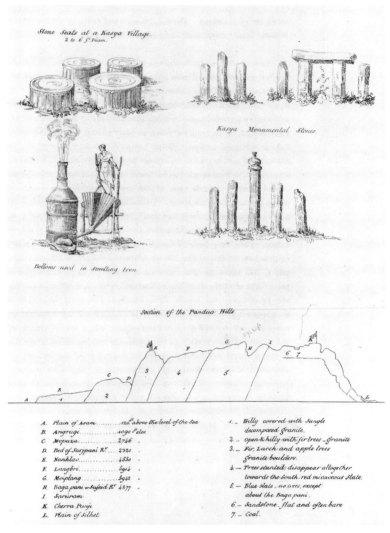

Figure 2.3 Illustrations of funerary monuments and an iron-smelting bellows, original sketches by Henry Walters, 1828. The geological cross-section is not mentioned by Walters and might have been added by an editor in Calcutta. Lithographed by Jean-Baptiste Tassin, Calcutta.

From Henry Walters, "Journey across the Pandua Hills, near Silhet, in Bengal," *Asiatic Researches* 17 (1832): opposite 502.

compliments the aesthetic sentiments repeatedly expressed in Walters's account, concerning sudden vistas, sublime gorges, and rough scenes filled with ruinous monuments. He was self-consciously a tourist in search of the Picturesque. After being diverted from the known road, and although he was worried about the potentially hostile intentions of some Khāsis, he was still able to appreciate a waterfall: "It is a noble fall, and well worth coming out of the way to see" (27 Oct.). In stereotypical contrast, the plains presented Walters with "an uninteresting inundated country" (19 Oct.). The inclusion of a Picturesque view was a natural adjunct to the text.

Significantly, the "View in the Kasya Hills" cannot be matched against any of the particular scenes described in the text. The image is taken to represent the *typical* or *characteristic* landscape of the region, the aesthetic essence of the hills, and the summary of Walters's own

Figure 2.4 "View in the Kasya Hills." In the lower, left-hand corner is the faint note, "Etched by W. Prinsep, 182_"; in the lower, right-hand corner is the same note but with the date 1831.

From Henry Walters, "Journey across the Pandua Hills, near Silhet, in Bengal," *Asiatic Researches* 17 (1832): opposite 506.

Picturesque observations. Walters's Picturesque view is built on geography's ambiguous idea of "landscape." The idea refers first to the single, perspective examination of the land surface and its occupants (either immediate and within the land or indirect through a graphic representation), and second to the more abstract conception of a region's characteristic morphological form, which can only be ascertained by many observations. As a construction for composing the world, landscape is at once personal and social. It is observed by individuals, but the land and its observation are defined by social practices. Landscape is thus "an ideological concept" that constitutes an intermediate position between the observation of the land and the construction of maps.[70] Although socially defined, a landscape is nonetheless constructed as if it had in fact been seen from a specific vantage point.

The modern attitude to the map is similar: although socially defined, the map is the construct of vision. Some commentators persist in the attitude that maps are in some manner perspective images of the world, that they are what the earth looks like when seen from far enough away.[71] A more sophisticated approach has been to draw an analogy with divine omniscience, such that maps are held to provide a "God's eye" or Godlike view.[72] I would like to stress, however, that even this analogy is insufficient as it preserves the idea of viewing, of directly observing the world. Maps are constructs that combine numerous observations into an image of space *without perspective,* although they are then viewed by the individual in lieu of the world.

The impossibility of cartographic vision is suitably demonstrated in the third of Walters's graphics, a map of a cave (figure 2.5). The occasion of his cartographic exercise was his excursion in December 1828, with two other British gentlemen, to explore a deep cave in the limestone hills just to the northeast of Pandua, the account of which is appended to Walters's principal geographical narrative. Guided by a Khāsi, the three men measured distances by pacing and directions by compass, just as if they were on a route march above ground. Walters's map was accompanied in print by a map of different portions of the cave surveyed by John Jones.[73] This itinerary map sits at the cusp between the experience of observation and the general map's cognitive structure. On the one hand, it graphically recapitulates the epistemology of the traveler's observations but, on the other, the entire cave cannot be comprehended except through the compilation of all instances of observation into a single image. A second example of the idea of cognitive mapping is Walters's geological cross-section of the Khāsi Hills in which the strata below ground—unseen to human eye—are deduced from a few observations of minerals and the slope of the strata; interestingly,

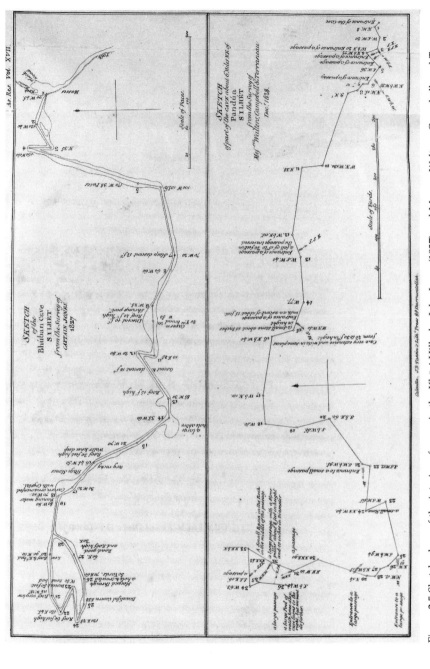

Figure 2.5 Sketch plans of the interior of caves in the Khāsi Hills, by John Jones (1827) and Messrs. Walters, Campbell, and Terreneau (December 1828). Lithographed by Jean-Baptiste Tassin, Calcutta. Jones's map might actually be of a different cave, or it has been inverted at some point.

From Henry Walters, "Journey across the Pandua Hills, near Silhet, in Bengal," *Asiatic Researches* 17 (1832): opposite 512.

it omits the limestone strata in which the caves were formed (see figure 2.3).

I stress these different graphic images created by Walters, and by all geographical observers, in order to reiterate the impersonal character of geographical observation and linear narrative. The geographer looks outwards; he might incidentally insert his presence into his text, but he constituted himself through his rhetoric as an autonomous observing machine. Mechanistic vision and the archive's spatial framework together established a clear-cut relationship between the geographer and the land: the geographer stands in a privileged position outside of the landscape, looking in. The geographer constructs an unassailable barrier between himself and the people, lands, and phenomena he observes. He divorces himself from the landscape. He moves through the landscape but he is never part of it.

Nicholas Dirks is correct to stress the manner in which the Enlightenment linkage of reason and discovery was consolidated within Europe's colonies. The appropriative character of the scientific and Picturesque gazes was most fully articulated in India. In Britain, the implications of the examination of land were somewhat ameliorated by long established cultural overtones, especially the common law rights of the rural masses and topophilic sentiments on the part of landowners. In India, however, those overtones vanished within new environments and new social hierarchies. A key indication of this subtle shift in the character of British aesthetics was the manner in which the emotive elements of the Picturesque slowly disappeared as the British reconfigured India to be naturally Picturesque.[74]

The rhetorical separation of the geographer from the landscape is borne out in the almost total lack of images of the surveyors themselves in the act of surveying and observing the Indian landscape. The archives contain literally thousands of the surveyors' maps and perhaps as many landscape views and plain images of landscape features; there are also a handful of portraits of surveyors, who are often shown posing, rather artificially, with their instruments. For the surveyors to be shown working *within* the landscape would subvert the entire ideology of geographical observation. It is therefore significant that the *one* image I have found of a surveyor *in action* is a caricature of the surveyor set within a parody of Picturesque conventions. The scene is beside a large river in the flat plains of the eastern Punjab; the surveyor is engaged in a project to modify the river to allow irrigation and thus improve the region's productivity. The moss-grown engineer, his servant, and his horse are the passive staffage symbolic of controlled nature and society; the *repoussière* reeds and the telescope direct the viewer's sight to the prominent architectural feature in the middle ground, the indigene's

Figure 2.6 Sir Herbert B. Edwardes, "Lieut. Lake, Engr., ascertaining the capabilities of the Guggur River for irrigation. Herbert Edwardes scratched it," Simla, 1845. Pen and ink. (By permission of The British Library, IOR prints WD 1024.)

shack on stilts; while the vaguely sketched vegetation on the far shore stand in for the more usual distant background relief. The image's parodic elements remove the sting from its critique of the dominant epistemology (figure 2.6). In related circumstances, Godlewska has found that many French officers in Egypt between 1798 and 1801 drew themselves in the act of sketching monumental antiquities—perhaps indicative of the French attempt at self-definition by appropriating ancient Egypt—whereas "this auto-portrait tendency is *entirely absent* from" the images of contemporary Egypt.[75]

Walters, like all geographical observers, presented facts with little analysis. His geographical description is underscored by the observational foundations of his knowledge. The elements of the account—the fundamental structure of the pseudo-diary and its chronological conceit; his idiosyncratic grammar; the consistent referencing of the act of observation; the graphic illustrations—all combine in a powerful rhetoric of vision, empiricism, and presence. Walters *saw* what he recorded and he invited his reader (and, unwittingly, the larger public) to participate in the *same* vision. The immediacy of his vision, underscoring that it was Walters who observed and no one else, is borne out by the rejection of the Khāsis as active participants in the narrative. When Walters did include them, they appear only as guides (as in the caves), laborers (carrying him across rivers), or as stereotypical indigenes (misdirecting him out of caprice). Yet the Khāsis were central to Walters's ability to travel about, to observe, and to understand the hill country. They provided him with knowledge which he appropriated as his own, which he recast as the product of personal observation, and which was thus incorporated into the larger body of British geographical knowledge.

The people and the land were submerged beneath a geographical gaze that claimed to be totalizing and all-consuming. Yet it was not a totally efficient gaze. Traces of local knowledge and of the manner of its acquisition can occasionally be discerned, marked by textual ambiguity or inconsistency. Orthography is a case in point. Walters's account contained three variant spellings for "Khāsi": *Cásia* in Walters's narrative; *Kasya* in the illustrations, probably added by the lithographer; *Kásia* in the separate account of the spelunking expedition. Is the town *Silhet* (most mentions) or *Sylhet* (9 Nov.)? Such variation indicates a subtle linguistic gulf between the British and the Indians which had yet to be closed. In the second half of the nineteenth century, the ethnographic and linguistic surveys of India established firm orthographic rules and conventions which could then be followed (or *observed*) as part of geographical observation. It was those surveys which established the spelling "Khāsi," as used in the present-day *Times Atlas*, Joseph Schwartzberg's *Historical Atlas of South Asia*, and in the official *National Atlas of India*.[76] But in 1828, orthography still depended on the individual ability of the British to capture the sound of placenames.

The ironing out of the uncertainties over the spelling of "Khāsi" indicates the manner in which differences and even outright contradictions among geographical information are ultimately smoothed out within the archive. The individual observations of the narrative are subsumed within the larger geographic space of the archive. Indeed, the narratives were themselves constructed within the context of that more complete body of knowledge. Despite the geographer's claim to timeliness, that each observation was made at the specific point within the journey when it was recorded, even a cursory analysis of the texts reveal that the narratives were, of course, substantially edited before publication. The narratives themselves were significant components of the complex of graphic, cartographic, statistical, and written representations which together constitute the geographical archive. This is certainly the case when spatial locations of objects were being observed: the determination of the location of a particular place must be made, by definition, within the larger concept of space. These issues are explored next.

Surveying and Mapmaking

The geographical narratives used by the officers of the East India Company to record their observations of South Asian landscapes, their physical forms, and the cultures and societies of their human inhabitants were treated as literal representations. The British presumed that their graphic and written descriptions replicated the essential character of the objects that they observed. The narrative's linear form recapitulated the spatial sequence of the geographer's acts of observation. The narratives themselves enjoyed a certain cultural relevance because of their similarities with the hugely popular genres of travel and exploration writing. Even so, they were recognized as being rather incomplete as geographical descriptions.

The problem with geographical narratives was that they ordered their information according to the sequence in which observations were made. References to any given topic, such as agricultural practices or mineral resources, were intermingled with references to all other topics. To obtain a comprehensive conception of one topic would require gleaning the records of individual observations by a thorough reading of the entire narrative. The narrative's lack of topical *system* was seen as a serious drawback. The favored bureaucratic form of geographical writing was therefore the analytical and organized regional description. The production of such systematic texts entailed the careful arrangement and logical ordering of many observations extracted from the geographical narratives and surveys. What the reordered and clearly manipulated geographical accounts lacked in terms of rhetorical immediacy and narrative power, they made up for through their ability to present large amounts of information in a coherent and comprehensible manner. The distinction between observational narratives and archival descriptions was, accordingly, a question of the arrangement and systematization of observed facts.

Consider, for example, the case of the "statistical" survey of Mysore undertaken by Francis Buchanan in 1800–1801. Buchanan kept a chronological narrative of his survey, which was published in three volumes in 1807. He did provide some order to each day's observations when he wrote up his notes in the evening. The first paragraph of each day's entry described the route taken, the condition of the roads, and the broad topographical character of the country. Buchanan rarely engaged in the aesthetic assessment of landscapes but instead sought a more objective assessment of the degree to which the land was farmed and had been "improved" by irrigation; he did not fail to identify improvements that had resulted from the stability provided by the recently imposed British rule. After the initial overview, Buchanan went through his daily observations of culture, society, and material activities, all neatly organized by topic. He did not follow a set sequence, however, because the scope of his observations varied daily.

Buchanan sent a copy of his manuscript journal to London. The Company's librarian was so impressed that he passed it without change to the printer. Buchanan, however, had wanted to systematize the vast amount of information and to give it some structure. But it was too late to do so when he returned on furlough to London in 1806, when he found the work already in press. Buchanan could only make some light revisions and provide a comprehensive index, which he thought would "in some measure supply the want of method." Buchanan's fears were borne out once the work appeared in print: reviewers immediately criticized it for being too laborious and too unsystematic for easy comprehension.[1] Buchanan's subsequent geographical work, on Nepal, was published in a systematic form; his extensive geographical narratives on Bengal remained in manuscript until they were edited and systematized after his death.[2]

Both Buchanan's own concept of his work and that of his critical peers seem to pose a binary opposition between recording observed geographical facts and the collection of those facts in a systematic description. One observes and *then* one brings the observations together within the archive. This polarity relied on the presumption that the recording of observed facts is literal and has the effect of constituting an essential copy of the world. The geographical narrative, however, is constructed within the context of the established archive. The "structure of the travel story," writes Michel de Certeau, is the story of "journeys and actions marked out by the 'citation' of the places that result from them or [that] authorize them."[3] This is evident in the manner in which Buchanan already generalized and arranged his data for each day and in the manner, discussed in the preceding chapter, in which Walters seems to have compounded information from multiple informants into singular statements of fact. It is even more evident in the manner in which the geographical locations observed by travelers were related to the larger framework of geographical space.

System and reason were not simply applied to bring field observations into the geographical archive. The "methodical" practices of
observing the landscape actively related the geographer to the larger
archives of knowledge. Geographical observation was, after all, the observation of the world with the intent of reorganizing the observations
according to their spatial distribution. Accordingly, this chapter starts
with the rhetorical flexibility granted observation by reason before considering the epitome of systematically structured knowledge: the map.

The Failure of Vision and
Use of Indigenous Sources

In his *Journey through Mysore*, Francis Buchanan presents perhaps the
paradigmatic instance of the failure of the rhetorically infallible sight.
Despite his generalization of the daily observations, Buchanan cele-
brates the visual epistemology of his empowered vision: each fact recorded was indeed seen on a specific day, even if the precise time of
observation is obscured. But under the date of 19 May 1801, when
camped near the major Jain temple complex at Sravana Belagola, Buchanan wrote that he could not visit the huge statue of the *bodhisatva* Gomata Raja,

> owing to an inflammation that attacked my eyes the day before,
> and rendered the light almost intolerable. I sent my painter and
> interpreter to inspect the hill. The painter gave me the accompany-
> ing sketch of the image [figure 3.1], for the accuracy of which I can-
> not answer. Its height is seventy feet 3 inches. Sir Arthur Wellesley,
> who has visited the place lately, thinks the drawing rather more
> clumsy than the image.[4]

Without sight, Buchanan is at a loss. His chronology is confused. With
such inflamed eyes, he could not have written this entry in the evening
as he apparently did the rest of his journal. The tense of the passage,
particularly as indicated by the phrase "the day before," is the distant
preterit of a reflective author looking back many days later. And when
did Wellesley visit the site and examine the statue: before Buchanan or
between the time of Buchanan's visit and writing? The certainties exhib-
ited by the rest of the text dissolve into ambiguity and uncertainty.

The rhetoric of geographical narrative was simply that: rhetoric. The
representation of observed facts, of truth portrayed in various graphics
and text, obscured the production of those representations, which is
perhaps the key difference between geographical and travel-explora-
tion narratives. Buchanan, Henry Walters, Alexander Gerard, and all of
the other narrative authors did not produce their journals as they trav-

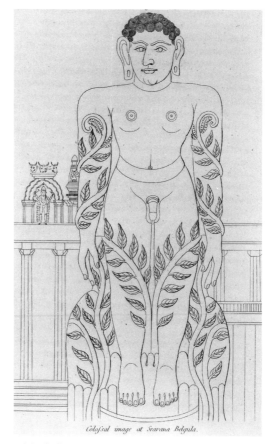

Colossal image at Sravana Belgula.

Figure 3.1 Image of the *bodhisatva* Gomata Raja, from the Jain temple complex at Sravana Belagola, as drawn by Francis Buchanan's "painter" in 1801. Lithograph from Buchanan, *A Journey from Madras through the Countries of Mysore, Canara, and Malabar* . . . (London, 1807), pl. 34, opposite 3:410.

eled on horseback or in a palanquin; instead, they waited until the evening to collect their notes and to reflect, and they waited until their final return to Calcutta, Madras, or Bombay, or even London, to create a more judicious arrangement. Their journals and images were subject to editing and censure at all times.

Geographers did on occasion have to reveal that they were not all-seeing and all-knowing and so exposed the rhetoric of observation. In addition to Buchanan's inflamed eyes, one might point to the political reasons which prevented British officers from entering independent territory or from straying from a road. Surveyors who accompanied an army on the march faced a systemic failure of observation: army col-

umns threw up thick dust clouds, "through which nothing but the experienced eye can at intervals penetrate," and they were restricted from
leaving the column without the special permission of the commanding
officer, so that they could record little beyond the road itself.[5] Surveyors
were at the mercy of atmospheric conditions. Heat haze distorted vision. Fog and low clouds blinded the surveyor altogether and denied
vision's efficacy; they transformed the bold surveyor, who dared to
know and to tame nature, into a lonely and timid man denied sight by
nature's whim.[6]

The reason which guided observation was, however, flexible enough
and sufficiently encompassing to gloss over most of vision's inherent
contradictions. Even on those unavoidable occasions when observation
patently failed and the indigenous informant had to be acknowledged,
that information could still be absorbed into the British archive of factual, observed data. The British achieved this by applying the same
cognitive techniques—which is to say reason—to information from
indigenous informants as were applied to the works of individual geographers to incorporate them into the general geographical archive.
Buchanan, deprived of the power of personal observation, relied first
upon proxy vision, in which respect he did not differ from the established British practice of employing Indian artists to record natural and
social scenes.[7] More important, Buchanan then relied on a second Englishman for an independent account with which to compare that of his
painter, to reconcile the differences, and so extract the kernel of truth
common to both. It was the same system of corroboration and reconciliation that governed the absorption of individual observations into a
systematic and ordered geographic archive.

Indian informants appear frequently in Buchanan's *Journey through
Mysore,* as they do in most narrative and systematic geographical accounts when observation failed the British observer. Indeed, British
maps of areas beyond British control—the body of the subcontinent in
the eighteenth century or Thailand and Tibet in the nineteenth—were
based almost entirely on information from a wide variety of indigenous
sources.[8] Generally, the individual informant is introduced by the same
sort of statement that astronomers and surveyors commonly used to
describe their instruments in order to reassure the reader that the observations taken were indeed of high quality. Buchanan recorded many
such surrogate observers, for example: "the Chief Officer [tasildar] of
Denkina-cotay, a very sensible man, says . . ."; another tasildar was "one
of those native officers who have been brought up under Colonel Read,
and who are much superior to those with whom one usually meets in
India."[9]

Individual Indians are named only when they acted like the British and were responsible for examining areas politically beyond direct British observation. When he was surgeon with the 1802–1803 embassy to Nepal, and restricted to the road to Kathmandu, Buchanan directed his "intelligent Brahman, from Calcutta," Ramajai Batacharji, to obtain information "without alarming a jealous government."[10] Or we might point to Golam Mohammed, "a confidential person" who was sent by Colonel Jacob Camac into the Deccan in 1774 "to gain intelligence concerning the Mahratta powers" and whose measured routes were used by James Rennell in his 1782 map of India.[11] Again, Francis Wilford compiled "a large manuscript map of the Punjáb . . . from the route and compass surveys of a native, Mirza Mogul Beg, *expressly instructed by himself* and employed from 1786 to 1796, in travelling and collecting materials to illustrate an account of Alexander the Great's progress."[12] Throughout the period of British hegemony in India, the only Indians to be fully accredited as field surveyors were the pandits, as they came to be known, who were sent into reclusive Tibet between 1865 and 1885 (see chapter 9).

Information provided by individual informants was subjected to testing and corroboration whenever possible. Rennell used a map of Gujerat which "a Bramin of uncommon genius and knowledge, named *Sadanund*" made at the behest of Charles Malet, the British resident at Pune, and although it had "the appearance of greater accuracy in the outline" than existing information, Rennell still needed to compare it with the *Ā'īn-i Akbarī* (1598), the great geographical description of the Mughal Empire, to "discriminate" the map's "valuable parts."[13] In Nepal, Buchanan supplemented his own limited observations with a great deal of information from a variety of Nepalese and Indian merchants, nobles, diplomats, and Buddhist priests. But this information was, whenever possible, balanced by the reports of other Company officials, especially William Kirkpatrick's earlier account of Nepal and the papers, views, and maps of Charles Crawford, who commanded the embassy's escort. For example, the three maps which Indians drew for Buchanan were,

> as might be expected, very rude, and differ in several points; but they coincide in a great many more, so as to give considerable authority to their general structure; and, by a careful examination of the whole, many differences, apparently considerable, may be reconciled. The general authority of the whole is confirmed by our maps, *as far as they go*, and by the intelligence which Colonel Crawford obtained in Nepal.[14]

Subsequently, when engaged in his statistical survey of Bengal, Buchanan rejected some information because the informant "was a stupid fellow, and no other person [had] heard of such a tradition." Marika Vicziany has noted that Buchanan generally rejected "spectacular stories" as so much "oriental nonsense."[15]

Most often, however, the British simply subsumed Indian informants within factual statements. Indians appear either in a depersonalized, generic form ("A man who had two ploughs would keep 40 oxen . . .") or in aggregate ("On examining the people of the town on this subject . . .").[16] This representation of Indian informants derived from the preferred form of questioning Indians *en masse* so that their evidence might be immediately tested and corroborated, playing off their internal divisions. A detailed description of the manner in which surveyors interacted with local officials is provided by an account of Lieutenant Thomas Arthur's daily activities written by his harkara (messenger, factotum, agent, or spy) to the diwan (chief minister) of Mysore:

> Dassiah Hircarrah (after paying his personal compliments to his excellency) says, I according to my orders am present with Mr. Arthur on the survey, this gentleman arrived at Tonnore on a survey of that district, and placing his glass (*durben*) on the hill there, wrote down by the information of Lingapah Sheristadar, the surrounding hills, tanks, villages & pagodas, from whence he went by Herrode in Astagram Talook to Seringapatam where he remained two days, after which he went to Herrode hill where he noted every thing around & remained at Herrode that night, next day taking Lingapah Tonnore Sheristadar and Astagram Hobly Shambog along with him he surveyed the boundary between these two districts by Begunhilly, Chindre, & Wudderhilly and halted at Jagetmullunhilly from whence he discharges the Astagram Shambog next morning early, taking the Tonnore Sheristadar with him, he ascended Bibi hill where he noted down every thing and then surveyed the boundary between Tannore and Bukenkera by the villages, Mudenhilly, Bopenhilly, Chukurly, Morsenhilly, Cangownhilly, Manchunhilly to Rendikura, next day he went by Bellikury, Chillungeery & Nellunhilly to a hill at the latter place where having made his observations and was descending two bears came before him of which he killed one and brought it on peoples shoulders to Marphilly (½ mile distant) where he remained for the night, and next day went to Mailcottah. Where he will go next I do not know but will hereafter write. Having made all this known, I wait for further orders.[17]

The system did not necessarily function well: one of Arthur's colleagues on the Mysore survey once had to "linger out the day in painful suspense under the shade of an adjoining tree" until the local officials joined him.[18]

Buchanan's daily practice was to tour a district, accompanied by the "leading people of the neighbourhood, whom he questioned on the various points enumerated in his instructions."[19] In another instance, Alexander Read turned to local informants to construct a desperately needed map of the Baramahal (Salem) after its cession from Mysore to the Company in 1792. All of the details and distances for each district "were ascertained by careful inquiries of seldom less than an hundred of the inhabitants," who were all village heads or "other people of local knowledge."[20] The practice of touring a district accompanied by local officials was not unique to an Indian setting—the British followed it in Ireland, too—and seems to have been standard practice for most surveys in which labor was limited or local information was required.

Read's mapmaking raises another point: the British needed to define local itinerary measures so as to be able to adapt distances derived from Indian sources to statute miles. In Read's case, all of the distances he was furnished with were in "gurries," with one gurry being "the distance a man is supposed to travel commonly, in that space of time, which is the Hindoo hour and [which] contains 24 minutes." He accordingly took one gurry to be one and one-half miles.[21] In the eighteenth-century, when most of the European maps of India were derived as much from Indian itineraries as from actual measurements by Europeans, the determination of conversion factors was particularly acute. Rennell, in preparing his 1782 map of India, compared his own information with that recorded by Jean Baptiste Tavernier in the seventeenth century and with that used by the premier French geographer, Jean Baptiste d'Anville, for his *Carte de l'Inde* (1752). Rennell was especially concerned with the variation in the length of the coss, the customary itinerary measure of the northern plains, and included a bar-scale in coss on his maps; the mean coss was about two miles in length.[22] Rennell's conclusions with respect to the length of the coss were applicable only to the northern provinces; in the south, the local measures were still open to interpretation in 1800, so that Colin Mackenzie instructed his assistants on the Mysore survey to record "distances in coss or other Indian measures along the road to compare with the measured road distances, so as to form a conversion factor from Indian to British measures" (see table 2.1, item 4).

The process by which the British accepted and incorporated information from Indian sources was not as simple as using data of higher quality to correct data of lesser quality. The opinion of one informant might have been preferred to that of another, simply because of each individual's reputation. But in a situation in which all sources of information were of equal repute (whether high or low) and all were subject to unquantifiable errors, the British relied on the standard Enlightenment assumption that all observations contained a kernel of truth. That kernel might then be exposed by a process of comparing the various sources with each other, as Buchanan did the three Indian maps of Nepal. He found that the three differed "in several points," but they were in agreement on "a great many more" so that "by a careful examination," many of the apparently significant differences "may be reconciled."[23] Similarly, Mackenzie began to collect as much information as he could about the Deccan plateau when he was appointed in 1792 to be the engineer and surveyor for the army detachment stationed at Hyderabad. This information included information from the "conductors on the great roads," whose information concerning the distances and directions might not have possessed "geometrical accuracy" and was "frequently found obscure and apparently contradictory," yet by "discriminating and selecting, and reconciling these seeming inconsistencies," Mackenzie "obviated these inconveniences, and rendered the information of real use."[24]

In their construction of their geographical archive, the Company's officers consciously relied on "reason" to extend their powers of observation. Their doing so indicates the degree to which observation and compilation were interwoven. Empiricist delusions would have it that the two were separate processes, that the geographer's narrative and his systematic account were distinct. But there can be no such phenomenon as "pure narrative." The rhetoric of observation is made flexible and all-encompassing by the same reason responsible for the construction of knowledge archives. From the time when the geographer put pen to paper to record his day's observations, even before the editing and re-arranging of the text for submission to the government and for eventual publication, each narrative was already a generalized and reasoned account.

Astronomical Observations and Their Correction

The key to the construction of the East India Company's geographical archive in the eighteenth century, and for much of the early nineteenth century, was the determination of locations. If a place's latitude and longitude could be observed, then it could be positioned properly on the map. The use of instruments to measure the positions of the planets and the fixed stars and so derive geographical locations exemplified the period's empiricism in that it entailed the observation of a quite abstract phenomenon to derive concrete, quantified facts. In India, a significant number of the papers published before 1800 in the *Asiatic Researches* comprised short lists by several astronomers, mostly amateurs using their own instruments, of astronomical observations in the northern plains and of the resultant positions.[25] After the turn of the century, these lists were increasingly supplanted by more comprehensive tables in gazetteers and special pamphlets; nonetheless, astronomical observations remained a significant element of most geographical narratives and explorations.[26] The astronomical determination of geographical positions was a fundamental aspect of the East India Company's territorial expansion in India.

Determination of geographical latitude was straightforward. Latitude could be determined easily by simply measuring the angular elevation ("altitude") of Polaris above the horizon. However, Polaris is not situated precisely at the north celestial pole so that this method is rather crude. More precise methods used in the eighteenth century included the observation of the sun's altitude at noon or of the altitudes of a series of stars over several nights. Simple calculations then gave latitude with respect to the fixed celestial pole. In contrast, longitude measurements were highly uncertain. There is no longitudinal equivalent to the celestial pole for providing an unambiguous zero longitude; the definition of the meridian of zero longitude is strictly arbitrary. To determine longitude, the surveyor had to measure the difference in longitude between his location and a place which convention decreed had longitude zero. Unfortunately, in the eighteenth century, the methods of observing longitudinal differences were known to contain many errors.

The basic principle behind the observation of longitudinal differences was the conceptual equivalence of longitude and time. The full equatorial circle of 360 degrees of longitude is equivalent to a temporal variation of twenty-four hours; fifteen degrees are equivalent to one hour of time. If it were determined that the local times of two places differed by one hour, for example, then their longitudinal separation would be fifteen degrees. But how to relate one local time to another? One simple solution, first advanced by Gemma Frisius in 1530, was for the explorer or geographer to take along a timepiece set to the local time of his home base. Local time can be ascertained in the field by observing either the sun or stars, when visible; comparison of this with the clock would give the field location's longitude with respect to the home base. The technique could not be implemented because, until the late 1700s, clocks were just too unwieldy and too inaccurate. In particular, their rates were uneven. The overall trend of a clock might be to slow down, but their speed varied cyclically (and the cyclical variation would also slowly alter . . .). Another method was needed.

Difference in local times could be determined by noting the time at which the same event is witnessed at two locations. Lunar eclipses had been used for this purpose even in classical antiquity, but they were too rare for practical use. In 1610, Galileo Galilei proposed the first workable solution. The moons (satellites) of Jupiter that he had discovered moved in a predictable manner. Astronomers could therefore construct tables of the times when each of the four moons would pass behind (immerse), or pass out from behind (emerse), the body of the planet. Each table (ephemeris), of course, would be expressed in the precise local time of the astronomer's observatory. In the field, a surveyor might note the local time at which he observed an eclipse; a simple comparison with an ephemeris would give the difference in local time and so longitude. By the middle of the eighteenth century, the royal observatories at Paris and Greenwich were regularly publishing tables of the predicted eclipses of Jupiter's satellites. Armed with these, the surveyor could define longitudes east or west of those observatories. This method was the preferred technique during the later eighteenth century. Nonetheless, it was recognized as imperfect. It was difficult to determine the precise moment of eclipse; powerful, and therefore expensive, telescopes were needed to see Jupiter's moons; and, the ephemerides were known to contain unquantifiable and uncorrectable errors.[27]

New techniques for observing longitude were developed in the 1700s to meet the needs of marine navigation. Even were it possible to observe Jupiter's moons from the deck of a heaving ship, their eclipses occurred too infrequently for shipboard navigation. Nevil Maskelyne, the astronomer royal, adapted Tobias Mayer's 1754 lunar tables so that the angular parallax in the moon's position as seen from Greenwich and from a ship would give the longitudinal difference. Lunar observations were made on land by the British in India, but they were held to be less accurate than the observation of Jupiter's moons.[28] The second new marine technique was John Harrison's perfection in 1760 of a chronometer that would keep good time for very long periods; the navigator could then take local Greenwich time with him and calculate longitude whenever he could see the sun or stars to define his local time. Chronometers, however, were still too delicate to withstand the constant shaking of land travel and were too expensive for land surveying. The terrestrial determination of longitude continued to be made primarily by observations of Jupiter's satellites well into the nineteenth century.[29]

The uncertainties of measuring longitude by Jupiter's satellites meant that, even when undertaken by one individual, the observations were guaranteed to produce a wide range of results. For example, Captain James Horsburgh made sixteen observations of Jupiter's moons over three months in 1803 to determine the longitude of Bombay's esplanade with respect to Greenwich (table 3.1). The resultant time differences varied by $2^m11.5^s$, representing a variation in longitude of thirty-three minutes of arc, or thirty-six miles (57.6 km) at Bombay's latitude. Horsburgh had no means to decide on the relative correctness of the different results, so to arrive at a final figure he simply took the mean of all sixteen observations: 72°57′14″.[30]

The surveyor or traveler rarely had the leisure to make many observations. Restricted to Kathmandu for twelve months in 1802–3, Charles Crawford was able to make 180 observations for that town's longitude, but this was truly an exception.[31] Eclipses of Jupiter's satellites were sufficiently infrequent and surveyors traveled too much ever to see more than one eclipse at the same location. Thomas Arthur described a typical longitude observation he had made in Travancore in 1810:

> It was not till very lately that we had it in our power to determine the Longitude by an observation of Jupiter's satellites. Having at length procured a watch that counted seconds, we observed the emersion of his [first] satellite on January 15th 1810, and from thence deduced the Longitude of Bawaddy Kottah to be 76°13′13″ [east of Greenwich] from a single observation.[32]

Not surprisingly, and considering the uncertainties involved, preference was always given to observations for latitude over those for longitude.

There was one location for which British astronomers did establish a very long run of observations for longitude: the Company's Observatory at Madras, which was founded in 1789. One of the tasks of the observatory was to make regular observations of the eclipses of Jupiter's satellites. In 1822, the Company's astronomer, John Goldingham, sought to reconcile over thirty years of observations in a manner which illustrates nicely the convolutions entailed in the systematic combination and reconciliation of data. Like Horsburgh, Crawford, and others, Goldingham used a simple arithmetic mean to define longitudes from small sets of astronomical and chronometric observations.[33] In contrast, the sheer wealth of observations for the observatory's longitude allowed Goldingham to combine the data in a seemingly more sophisticated manner that took their quality into account.

Goldingham had five distinct series of observations, made at various times and with instruments of varying quality. He trusted the more recent observations and weighted them accordingly. The fifth and most reputable series of observations contributed fully one-half of the final value; the other half was contributed by the third and fourth series plus

Table 3.1 James Horsburgh's Determination of the Longitude of Bombay, 1803

		Observed Time of Eclipse of one of Jupiter's moons			Corresponding Greenwich Time (Delambre's Tables)			Time Difference			Longitude w.r.t. Greenwich	
		h	m	s	h	m	s	h	m	s	°	'
23	Jan	14	31	10.5	9	40	2	4	51	8.5	72	47.125
30		16	24	40	11	33	33	4	51	7	72	46.75
1	Feb	10	52	57	6	1	52	4	51	5	72	46.25
8		12	46	34	7	55	26	4	51	8	72	47
11		10	23	35	5	31	48	4	51	47	72	55.75
18		12	57	26	8	5	34	4	51	52	72	58
22		16	33	52	11	42	47	4	51	5	72	46.25
24		11	02	20.5	6	11	16	4	51	4.5	72	46.125
25		15	31	25	10	39	34	4	51	51	72	57.75
4	Mar	18	5	16	13	13	47	4	51	29	72	52.25
26		15	20	07	10	26	51	4	53	16	73	19
28		9	47	39	4	55	22	4	52	17	73	4
2	Apr	7	3	34	2	11	22	4	52	12	73	3
4		11	41	32	6	49	28	4	52	4	73	1
13		8	4	1	3	12	9	4	51	52	72	58
27		11	52	35	7	0	45	4	51	50	72	57.5
		→ maximum			73°19'							
		minimum			72°46'7"							
		range			32'52"			→ mean			72°57'14"	

Source: James Horsburgh to Nevil Maskelyne, 31 May 1804, CUL RGO 4/187/37.

Table 3.2 John Goldingham's Weighting of Longitude Observations (1787–1816) for Madras

Series		Mean	Contribution to Final Value
(a) 1787–1801		$5^h21^m8^s.42$	two contribute 16⅔%
(b) 1794–1801	better telescope	$5^h21^m6^s.35$	so 8⅓ each
(c) mean of (a) and (b)		$5^h21^m7^s.38*$	three together
(d) 1801–2	same as (b)	$5^h21^m7^s.72$	contribute 50%
(e) 1802–15	new telescope, same quality	$5^h21^m5^s.24$	so 16⅔% each
(f) mean of (c), (d), and (e)		$5^h21^m6^s.78$	50% each
(g) 1787–1816	simultaneous observations (Madras & Greenwich)	$5^h21^m11^s.97$	
(h) mean of (f) and (g)		$5^h21^m9^s.4$	
Final Figure		$5^h21^m9^s.4$	⟶ 80°17′21″
Unweighted Mean (20% each)		$5^h21^m7^s.95$	⟶ 80°16′59¼″
Difference	0°0′21¾″	miles, at latitude of Madras	
or	0.4		

*The printed figure for this value is $5^h21^m7^s.77$, a typographic error.

Source: John Goldingham, "Of the Geographical Situation of the Three Presidencies, Calcutta, Madras, and Bombay, in the East Indies," *Philosophical Transactions of the Royal Society* 112 (1822): 423.

the mean of the two oldest series (table 3.2). His result for the observatory's longitude was 80°17′21″ east of Greenwich, or 22″ (0.4 miles; 0.6 km) further east than if he had taken a simple mean of all five series. He followed a similar procedure for the observatory's latitude. Goldingham then compared the computed longitude with the observatory's longitude as derived from eight hundred lunar observations made between 1787 and 1792 by the observatory's founder, William Petrie. He found the lunar observations gave a value 2′55.5″ further east than that calculated. On the assumption that the method of lunar observations was a poorer technique than that of the eclipses of Jupiter's satellites, Goldingham took that difference—without justification—to be standard for *all* lunar observations in India. Accordingly, to calculate Bombay's longitude he took the mean of the results of the 340 lunar observations he had observed in 1791 on his way out to Madras, less the nearly 3′; his own thirty observations of Jupiter's satellites at Bombay; and, his chronometer readings between Bombay and Madras. The result was 72°53′49″ east of Greenwich (cf. table 3.1).[34]

Given all of these difficulties and uncertainties, it should be no surprise that there were few places in the 1700s whose positions were determined by actual measurement. The situation was quite acute in the middle of the century, even in Europe. In his *mappa critica Germaniae* of 1753, Mayer had located two hundred towns, but latitudes had been observed for only thirty-three of these and longitudes for none.[35] By 1800, the situation had improved substantially, in large part because of the availability of astronomical tables and less expensive instruments, but the density of fixed places was still low. The places in between— which is to say the majority of places fitted into the geographical archive's graticule of latitude and longitude—were located not by observation but by estimation and calculation.

If the great-circle distance and direction, with respect to true north, between two places was known, then it was a simple matter of spherical trigonometry to calculate the difference of latitude and longitude between them. These calculations required the earth to be treated as a sphere: even though Isaac Newton had demonstrated in 1687 that the earth is actually a spheroid flattened at the poles, it was not until Carl Friedrich Gauss published his geometry of curved surfaces in 1827 that geodesists had the means of calculating distances across a spheroidal surface. The more fundamental issue, however, was how to determine those distances and directions in the first place. Traditionally, mapmakers were experts in interpreting travelers' accounts to elicit those data for the construction of small-scale maps, such as those illustrated in chapter 1. The construction of medium-scale maps, however, required much more information gathered in the form of surveyed routes.

The Route Survey

Geographical investigations are characterized by the intent to relate all observations to the larger geographical archive. The British traveler, when armed with suitable instruments, was able to situate his distanced, privileged, and disciplined observations according to their geographical relationships. Just as the traveling artist used a *camera obscura* or Claude Glass, so too the geographer carried at least a compass for directions, a timepiece for estimating distances, and—if he was wealthy—perhaps also a sextant or octant for astronomical determinations of location. So armed, the geographer could observe and record the abstract quantities of location as he passed through the land. He could *survey.* The precision of measurement varied with the traveler's purpose. A fast reconnaissance survey *à rue* (that is, without instruments) might at best include times of travel; a detailed and more laborious cartographic survey would include as much information as possible. Yet even the simplest travel and geographical narratives included observations of the distances and directions traveled: the examination of the land became its own object of study.

In its most simple form, the spatial observations of travel comprised the recording of estimated distances and directions between each night's camp. More formally, and of more interest here, the observations took the form of the "route survey," the ubiquitous form of survey in all of Britain's colonial possessions in the eighteenth century. The benefit of the route survey for cartographic purposes was that it was undeniably fast; hence, it remained the basic technique for reconnaissance surveys well into the twentieth century. The route surveyor covered long distances with relative ease. In the vast, flat northern plains of India, route surveys were frequently likened to the maritime technique of "dead [deductive] reckoning," in which a ship's position is defined from its direction of sail and the estimation of distances traveled.

Technically termed a "traverse," a route survey involves the measurement of the distance and direction of each leg of the route traveled. The simplest and most common instances of the route survey measured directions with a compass and distances either with a perambulator, a wheel with a counter attached to record the number of revolutions, or by time-of-travel, with an assumed speed. In the northern plains, route surveys were as often made of rivers as they were of roads. Prominent objects off the course of march were fixed by taking a bearing and estimating the distance to each or, more usually, by taking two or more bearings to each from different points along the march.

The immediate product of this examination was a journal containing the observations recorded. The preferred form was a table of four columns: the middle two columns were for the direction and distance of each segment; the outer columns were for recording observations to objects to either side of the direction of travel. The journal subsequently allowed the draftsman to retrace graphically the surveyor's route, producing long and thin images (figure 3.2). The surveyor's observations of bearing and distance were drawn in the same order as that in which they were recorded: the first direction of travel, the first distance; the next direction, the next distance; and so on. To fix the objects observed away from the line of travel, the draftsman needed only to draw lines

---

Figure 3.2 (*opposite*) Alexander Boileau, [Survey of a Route from Putpurgunj (Delhi) to Allyghur], 1829, 1:126,720, 3 sheets. Ink and watercolor.

Note the variable orientation of each sheet of paper to accommodate the road. (By permission of The British Library, IOR X/1364/1–3.)

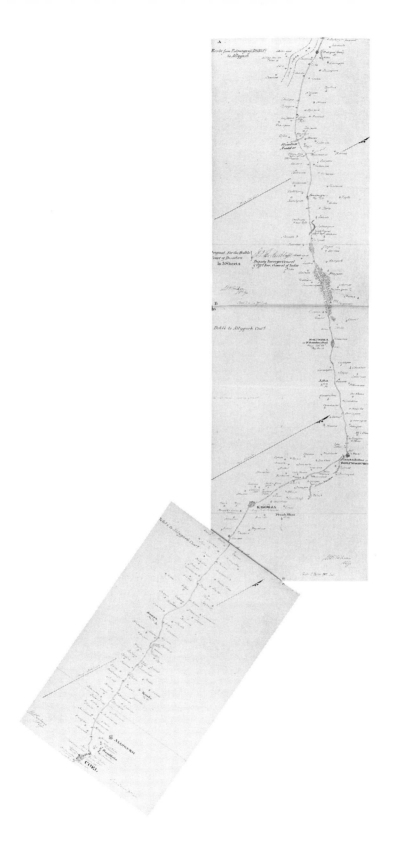

corresponding to the observer's line of sight; the object is located at their intersection. In no other way can use be made of the surveyor's journal. Both the route survey and the resultant map are linear in nature: both reveal a regular unfolding of a narrow band of landscape. The graphic image recapitulates the linearity of geographical observation.

Contemporary surveyors and geographers fully appreciated the several sources of measurement error inherent to any route survey. One surveyor described an error of "five miles in an hundred" as being "not impossible."[36] The instruments used were imprecise. Partly to place his own surveys in a better light, Colonel Robert Kelly suggested in 1784 that the typical route surveyor carried just "a pocket compass and watch," so that "he is allowed to be very accurate in his observations" if "he guesses within half a point of the bearing, and half a mile of the distance, of one village or encampment from another."[37] The increase in precision of larger compasses meant that the effects of local variations in the earth's magnetic field became sensible, thereby introducing another level of subtle error. Also, compasses measured direction with respect to magnetic north and needed to be corrected for true north if that was required.

Conversion from travel-time to distance was inherently subjective, a problem that was not really alleviated by the increased employment of perambulators after 1804 (see chapter 4). A perambulator will always give a reading well over the "true" (direct) distance. There will be a number of twists and turns subsumed under each straight segment. The measured distance is not the required "horizontal" distance as it includes all of the hills and vales the surveyor labored up or coasted down.[38] The largest source of error was that the perambulator operator could not keep a straight line as he traveled but would naturally avoid potholes, mudpatches, and other obstacles.

But how could the surveyors, or the cartographers who used the survey journals, correct for these errors? There were no means to predict the effects of each source of error, so rather arbitrary corrections were the rule. In order to define the "true" distance, cartographers reduced the overall lengths of route surveys by between one-tenth and one-seventh, according to their personal preferences and the character of the terrain over which the survey passed.[39] If some extra information were known, however, then some external correction might be applied. If the survey started and ended at the same location, or if the latitude and longitude of both termini were known, then the survey could be plotted out and the graphic line of the survey could be adjusted until it closed upon itself or terminated at the proper location.[40]

The restriction of the analysis of route surveys to quantifiable errors and the application of quantifiable corrections was integral to surveying's empiricism. Each survey can approach true knowledge of the world as the observational errors are steadily reduced toward zero. No surveyor in the period around 1800, except perhaps the crassest, ever considered it possible to reduce the errors actually to zero, but it was an ideal of perfection to be actively pursued. Stressing the survey as comprising observation and measurement served both to underline the image of the survey as replicating the road's geometry and to turn attention away from the manner in which each survey *defined* the roads through their measurement. As noted, the essential idea of the route survey is that the surveyor breaks down the path of travel into specific, clearly distinct, straight segments. But roads rarely take sharp turns, unless forced to do so by the terrain, and in the premetal era they sprawled out to either side as travelers sought firm footing around potholes and quagmires. The surveyor was ever moving forward, unable to return and retrace his steps, so that the principal points along the road are defined not by some clear idea of the overall shape of the road but by the surveyors' perceptions of the form of the road as seen *in situ.*

That is, each segment will come to an end, and the next segment will start, only when the surveyor's sense of direction and his experiential sense of place tell him that the road has changed. On a road through the plains, the segment might end at a subtle rise in the road where, with a hint of the suddenly revealed Picturesque vista, the surveyor realizes that he can see further than he could just beforehand.[41] Some landmark by the road—a temple, tower, or bridge—might draw the surveyor's attention, causing him to pause and to stop the current segment. The military surveyor especially was on the lookout for items of specific interest, such as possible campgrounds, impediments to artillery trains, river fords, and so on, each of which might establish a bend in the road. In a cursory survey, the surveyor might define each segment as one day's travel, the distance between halts on an infantry march, or that between two villages. Or the surveyor might lose sight of the starting point of his current segment, or he might simply feel at some point along a wide curve that the general trend of the road had sufficiently changed, and so mark off a new segment.

This first instance of the conceptual gap between the surveyor and the surveyed world, between the geographic observer and the observed landscape, might appear to be a rather minor example. Nonetheless, it points to the core of the epistemological dilemma of modern mapping: no matter how accurately and precisely the world's structure is measured, that structure is created through the surveyor's and geographer's experiential perception. This perception is initially personal. Whether we consider the lone surveyor assiduously recording his own observations of a route traveled or the astronomically minded official taking "shots" of the stars, the sun, or the moon for the purposes of defining geographic location, the geographic observer functioned alone and divorced from other observers. Their results, however, were amalgamated into the broader geographical archive through communal acts of cognition.

Systematics and Cartographic Compilation

The field surveyor's technique of first establishing a framework for observation and then handling the particular details of the terrain was central to all scales of mapping. It is the system behind the eighteenth century's organized surveys of extensive regions. The method required the measurement of many interlocking route surveys controlled by a few astronomical observations. Writing in 1827 about Charles Reynolds's surveys in western India in the 1780s, John Jopp described the system as follows:

> In the preparation of [maps], the plan adopted seems to have been to assume as correct the position of some town as Baroche or Baroda where the routes of two or more of [Reynolds's] assistants commenced, and from this point to protract the routes that had been surveyed from it; other assistants were detached to connect the extremities of these routes or to cross them in particular directions.[42]

It is significant that Jopp's description of Reynolds's methodology confused the graphic construction of maps with surveys. The map is made from existing material, gaps are defined, and new surveys undertaken to fill in those gaps. This is the process to which the botanist Albrecht von Haller referred when he likened systematic investigation to mapmaking. The potential of the individual survey cannot be fulfilled until it is brought into the larger cartographical framework of the general map; observed data are not complete until they are reconstituted within the archive of knowledge.

The key to the reconstitution of geographical knowledge within the cartographic archive was the single "language of maps," which allowed all data to be matched, compared, and compiled together. In 1839, William Morison referred to the map's symbology and conventional design as comprising a "language," in the same sense that "map language" is used by present-day cartographers as shorthand for cartography's complex semiotic codes.[43] But in the earlier period, "map language" was more readily understood as the means whereby cartographic data could be related to each other. That is, the language of maps comprehended the mathematical framework of latitude and longitude to which all observations could be fitted. The first step in map construction was to lay out the graticule of meridians and parallels; onto this were then plotted the relatively few places whose locations were well known, and then all other data were fitted in between. (An intriguing reversal of this system was presented ca. 1800 by an emigré French noble in Germany, Joseph de Maimeux, who created tables for a uniform script, in which each word was located by coordinates, specifically analogous to latitude and longitude, each table constituting a "topographic map of the domain of thought."[44])

The projection graticule on a smooth sheet of paper is the cartographic equivalent of the table in a herbarium on which plants can be arranged and rearranged in conceptual knowledge spaces. Within the map's framework, all data are represented in a uniform manner, regardless of the various sources and thus variable quality of the information. It was the map's graticule which promoted all data to one level of quality, allowing otherwise different data to be equated. Such a system enabled cartographers to be very pragmatic and to use any and all available sources to construct their maps with complete justification. Thus, Colonel Gentil, French representative at the court of Awadh in the 1760s, thought it would be possible to use the astronomical calculations of Brahmins in each village to define their latitudes and longitudes "and so construct a correct map of India for military and political purposes."[45] Such a project would require, of course, the conversion of Brahminical longitudes to European longitudes. It was to encourage such conversions that Dr. William Hunter determined the location of Ujjain in the 1790s: "it is considered as the first meridian by the *Hindu* geographers and astronomers, so that its longitude from our *European* observatories is an object of some curiosity." That is, given a translation factor between the two astronomical systems, each might be reduced to the same "language" and the Indian knowledge thereby incorporated into the British archive where it might be tested and corroborated.[46]

The processes of *compilation*, of reconciling different geographical sources and combining various surveys, had achieved the status of a high art by the middle of the eighteenth century. It exemplified the more general geographical process of corroborating and combining observations to provide analyses and more coherent and organized regional descriptions. Anne Godlewska provides a very thorough analysis of cartographic compilation during this period in her study of the

Carte topographique de l'Égypte (Paris, 1825), a forty-seven sheet atlas at 1:100,000 constructed from various materials created during the French occupation of Egypt from 1798 to 1801. A rather sparse framework of astronomically defined locations and a thin triangulation along the Nile brought together plane table surveys of the river and its distributaries, rapid reconnaissance surveys in desert areas, and data derived from older maps and historical materials. Indigenous sources were vital to the entire survey but were barely mentioned by the surveyors in Egypt or the geographers in Paris and were subordinated beneath a visual and graphic rhetoric of cartographic knowledge. The authority of the *Carte* was thus derived not from having been based on rigorously surveyed information but from being combined into a single cartographic archive along regular sheetlines and with a uniform and standardized design.[47]

Cartographers of high repute published memoirs to accompany their larger and more original maps, laying out in minute detail the many sources and the manner of their reconciliation. Indeed, a map's accompaniment by a memoir was a sign of the cartographer's pretension that the map ought to be considered as a cartographic landmark. Through his memoir, a cartographer assured his public that a map was based on the best available sources and he displayed his own conscientiousness and intellectual virtuosity.

James Rennell provides a good example of the logical strategies employed by cartographers to compile their maps. In November 1776, when his health had been failing for some time, he applied to the governor general, Warren Hastings, for a pension to allow him to undertake an ambitious scheme upon his retirement to Britain:

> It is well known that there are deposited in the India House a variety of Maps, Charts, Views of Lands, Sea Journals, and other Geographical and Hydrographical Information of various kinds; all (or most) of which, according to the present System, appear to be laid by to perish. Amongst this vast Collection of Materials much useful Matter might undoubtedly be extracted, was there a proper Person appointed to examine it: whilst in its present confused (I might say chaotic) State, the Good and Bad are blended together and the whole rendered useless either for want of criteria to distinguish their Value, or of Arrangement to convey an Idea of Connection.[48]

Rennell, of course, would be that "proper person." He would undertake the *examination* and *arrangement* of the worthwhile materials, and if the Court of Directors permitted he would also publish the results as a "General Map of all Hindoostan." Rennell had already distinguished himself as the first surveyor general of Bengal (1767–77), in which capacity he had undertaken a survey of the entire province, for which the court granted him an annual pension of £400 and free access to its geographic materials. On his return to London in February 1778, Rennell first worked up his survey materials for publication as *A Bengal Atlas* (1780, 1781) before starting on the general map in early 1781.

Rennell should not, perhaps, have engaged in this project just when the expansion of the Company's territorial and military affairs produced a wealth of new data which required continual updates to his maps. The result was a complex and confusing publication history which needs clarification. Rennell constructed his first map, entitled simply *Hindoostan* (see figure 1.4) and published in December 1782, on two sheets at the relatively small scale of one inch to an equatorial degree (1:4,377,600). He chose the small scale because he was convinced that "the idea of connection and relative position are best preserved, when the matter lies within a moderate compass." Even so, the small size of the map meant that he would have to omit data. Rennell predicted that "I shall incur some censure" because "many people who peruse maps" naively expect to find both "a large extent of the country, and all the minute particular[s] of it, on the same map." To accompany the map, Rennell published the first *Memoir of a Map of Hindoostan* early in 1783. A second state of the *Memoir* was issued with an appendix formed by a reprint of Rennell's 1781 paper on the Ganges and Brahmaputra rivers. This appendix was properly incorporated into the *Memoir's* second edition, published in 1785. The second edition of the *Memoir* should not be taken as indicating a second edition of the map. Rather, Rennell represented his new information on separate maps tipped into the memoir itself; the 1785 edition of the map appears to have been only a reprint.[49]

Rennell's moderation fell before the onslaught of new information. By 1788 he had overcome his concern that there might not be a sufficient commercial market for a new map so soon after the first and so published his second map, in four sheets, at the larger scale of one and one-half inches to an equatorial degree (1:2,918,400): *A New Map of Hindoostan.* He also published a second *Memoir of a Map of Hindoostan,* an entirely new work but distinguished from the first memoir only in its subtitle. Rennell published second editions, with new information, of both the map and the memoir in 1792. A large batch of new data for southern India, produced by the 1790–92 war with Mysore, reached London in 1793. Rennell could have incorporated the new data into a new map of India at an even larger scale, but doing so would make the gaps in coverage for central and western India even more prominent. He therefore published a separate map of the peninsula, with a memoir appended to some copies of a third, repaginated edition of the memoir (1793).[50]

The purpose of the memoirs was to describe in minute detail all of the various sources used for the maps and the criteria by which they were accepted or rejected. Rennell laid out before his public the process whereby he took the good and omitted the bad, in order to produce order and system out of the prevailing confusion and chaos. As such, the memoirs are highly charged texts replete with the rhetoric of science, accuracy, exactness, and precision. Rennell made it quite clear just who was responsible for the work. "The whole construction," he wrote of the first map,

> is entirely new, as will appear at once by comparing it with any of the former maps, the most accurate of which makes the breadth of the *hither* India (or that included between the mouths of the Ganges and Indus) near two degrees and a quarter of longitude *narrower* than it appears in my map, at the same time that it makes the lower part of the Peninsula three quarters of a degree *wider* than mine does.[51]

Rennell's sources included surveyed material and other odd observations, information from Indians in a variety of formats, and any and all works on India that had been published in Europe, including Hellenistic geographies. He might have been dependent on many individuals for their geographical information, but only he brought all of those disparate sources together and welded them into a single, *correct* image. He was the map's author; he was the creator of its knowledge.

Rennell's methodology was first to establish a framework of principal lines, comprising the coastline, in its new and correct proportions, and the main routes through the interior. He then inserted his other data into this fixed frame. Most of the content of his memoirs dealt with the sources for the principal framework, describing them, assessing their quality, and then reconciling them. With that in place, Rennell felt no need to worry about the finer nuances of the lesser details. The complexity of the technique can be illustrated with the section in which Rennell determined the longitude of Cape Comorin, the southernmost tip of the Indian mainland (schematically represented in figure 3.3).

The best-known position in southern India was Madras, which had been the subject of several years' worth of observations. Just to the south, the French port of Pondicherry had also been the site of several astronomical observations for longitude. Rennell nonetheless checked these against its longitude as calculated from Madras through Thomas Barnard's 1767–74 survey of the Company's original land grant about

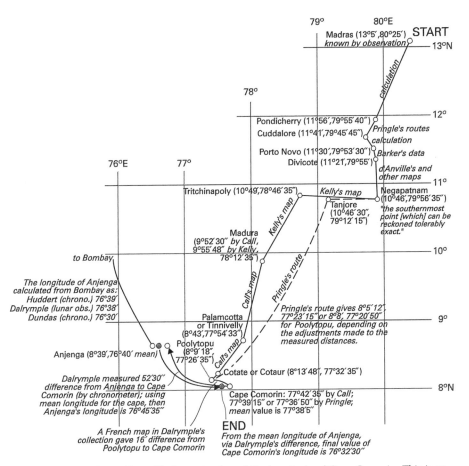

Figure 3.3 James Rennell's determination of the longitude of Cape Comorin. This is an abstract diagram constructed on a square graticule and illustrates Rennell's mathematical procedures, as described in the text. Rennell himself did not draw any figure. See Rennell, *Memoir of a Map of Hindoostan; or the Mogul Empire* (London, 1792, 2d ed.), pp. 13–19.

Fort St. George. From Pondicherry, Rennell used a variety of itineraries and manuscript maps to define the position of Negapatnam (Nagappattinam). Those manuscript maps included one by Jean Baptiste d'Anville, to which Rennell was prepared to award precedence, had it differed from the rest, solely because of d'Anville's reputation. The result was that Negapatnam was "the southmost point, on the eastern side of the peninsula, whose position can be reckoned tolerably exact." From Negapatnam, Rennell followed two routes across the peninsula to "Poolytopu." The manuscript maps of Robert Kelly and John Call, both respected military surveyors, together gave one distance across the peninsula; subtracting either one-eighth or one-ninth of the itinerary distance measured by John Pringle during the Carnatic wars gave Rennell two more direct distances. These three distances produced three different, but close, values for the longitude of Poolytopu. A French map in Alexander Dalrymple's collection placed Poolytopu 16' west of Cape Comorin; Rennell thus had three possible longitudes for the cape, of which he took the mean: 77°38'5" east of Greenwich.[52]

But Rennell did not stop here—not when he had the means to provide further checks. Dalrymple had chronometrically measured the longitudinal difference from the cape to the port of Anjenga, giving Rennell that town's longitude. There were also three other determinations of Anjenga's longitude made with respect to Bombay, one of Rennell's independently fixed locations. Rennell took the mean of all four longitude values and then reapplied Dalrymple's measured difference to get a final value for Cape Comorin's longitude: 77°32'30". Finally, Rennell worked his way back from the cape to Madras, applying small corrections to the positions of each town in-between so "that no distortion of the intermediate parts should take place."[53]

Rennell fits squarely into the genre of regional mapping and map compilation employed by Europeans throughout the eighteenth century, both in European countries and in their colonies. It was used extensively by British military engineers in Scotland (1745–61), Quebec (1760–61), eastern North America (1764–75), Florida (1765–71), and Ireland (1778–90). Rennell himself followed the system in India for his survey of Bengal (1765–71), which, because it was published, is perhaps the most well-known British instance of this style of regional survey.[54] Thereafter, Rennell's example was followed by other surveyor-compilers: Reynolds, who constructed a map of India in 1809; Colin Mackenzie, who in 1796 constructed a large map of the Deccan from his route surveys; and John Hodgson, who conceived of his "Atlas of the North-West of India" (1823; figure 3.4) as an extension to Rennell's *Bengal Atlas*. Rennell's example was followed in London by commercial cartographers, such as Aaron Arrowsmith, who after 1804 compiled several huge maps of India from a variety of surveys and other sources.

Each of these maps might have constituted geographic panopticons—"segmented, immobile, frozen spaces"—created by the application of British discipline to the South Asian landscapes, but they were known to include too many uncertainties. The errors inherent to the route surveys were potentially too great. The density of geographical information was uniformly low: this style of cartography had a very distinctive look, with sparse data strung out along the surveyors' routes, as in the southern portion of figure 3.4. And, despite its appeal

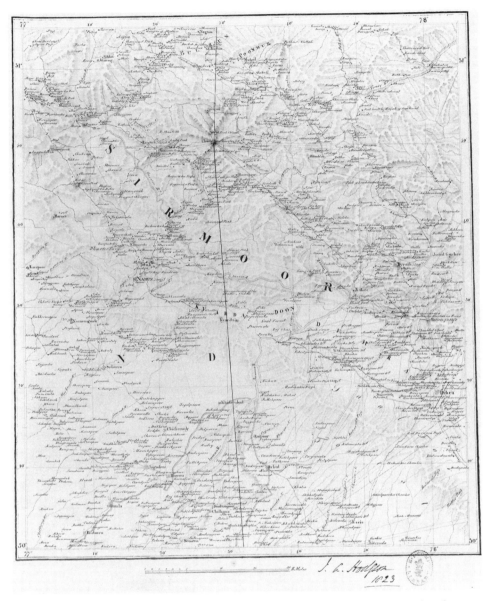

Figure 3.4 John Hodgson, "Atlas of North-West of India . . . ," 1823, 1:253,440. Ink and watercolor.

Sheet 5, showing portions of both the Himalaya mountains and the Gangetic Plains. Note the lines of triangulation in the mountain areas and the low density of information in the plains, defined by route surveys. (By permission of The British Library, IOR X/345/5.)

to Enlightenment sensibilities, the process of map compilation could seem rather forced and spurious to the cynical commentator.

That was the thrust, for example, of an anonymous reviewer's critique of the maps Rennell constructed for the published version of Frederick Hornemann's journal of his travels in the Sahara in 1797 and 1798. The anonymous reviewer added emphasis to a quotation from the publication's preface to cast scorn on Rennell's techniques of map compilation:

> Major Rennell is an adept in this occult science: for he "hath corrected the map of Africa, with a learning and sagacity which *hath converted conjecture into knowledge;* and on experience of those who have explored parts of that great continent, given confidence to each future traveller who may visit its remotest regions."[55]

At root, encyclopedic map compilation was known to be flawed. Even when based on substantial survey records, there was always the possibility that some of the knowledge presented in the maps was still "conjecture." New surveys repeatedly pointed to the need to correct existing geographic data. Doubts about the maps of India were never expressed so baldly as in the last quotation, but they nonetheless underlay the acceptance of other technologies of regional surveying which promised the perfection of the cartographic archive through the execution of large-scale maps of high detail and low error for all of India. The eighteenth-century style of survey steadily declined in use, until the "last deliberate peace-time survey to be based wholly on traverse and astronomical fixings" was made by Alexander Boileau of the country between Agra and Allahabad, in 1827 and 1828.[56]

Topography and Triangulation

Systematic regional surveys in the eighteenth century were derived in concept from the established methods of constructing small-scale maps, in the order of 1:1,000,000 and smaller. I have elsewhere referred to this process as the characteristic technology of the early modern "chorographic" (subsuming geographic) mode of cartographic practice. This was the mode of the intellectual geographer.[57] As the power of European states intensified in the eighteenth century, and as they increasingly sought to exert their control over their territories, those states sought to intensify the coverage and detail of their regional mapping. They continued to use the established methods of regional mapping but applied them at medium scales, in the order of 1:100,000 to 1:1,000,000. James Rennell, for example, surveyed Bengal at a scale of five miles to the inch, or 1:316,800. Unfortunately, the errors and inconsistencies inherent to astronomical observations and route surveys began to show at the larger scales.

Perhaps the most significant drawback for those technologies was their cursory nature. They simply could not support the construction of highly detailed maps. The solution was to extend the techniques of the very large-scale mode of "topography" from the individual estate or village to much larger regions. The result was the apparent merging of the chorographic and topographic modes: both were being used to map large regions at the same, medium scale. They were nonetheless seen as being different, for example, by John Hodgson, surveyor general of India in the 1820s, who described the detailed surveyors of Bombay and Madras as mere "coasters" in comparison with the great "navigators" of the Gangetic Plains. Although Hodgson did not intend to judge the relative merits of the two styles of mapping, his successor in the 1830s did. George Everest repeatedly disparaged the cursory nature of route surveys in a rhetorical effort to promote his own very slow and careful "trigonometrical survey."[58]

The generic meaning of *trigonometrical survey* encompassed any survey technique in which distances on the ground were surveyed indirectly. Those distances were calculated according to some trigonometrical relationship; thus the name. To construct a map, the surveyor first calculated the relative positions of locations and then plotted them, in contrast with the graphic construction of maps directly from the recorded traverse measurements of a route survey. In its simplest manifestation, the trigonometrical survey might entail the determination of the width of a river or, in the classic military problem, the height difference and distance between an artillery piece and a target. Both instances require the determination of a distance which cannot be measured directly. A far more complex, three-dimensional system was proposed by William Webb, in which surveyors in the northern plains might observe horizontal or vertical angles to specific peaks in the Himalayas, whose heights and locations Webb had already determined; basic trigonometry could then be used to "resect" the surveyors' locations.[59] The basic principle of trigonometrical surveying was that the direct measurement of distances was to be avoided: "measurement on the ground is the most difficult task the surveyor has to execute, . . . the most tedious," and, by implication, the most erroneous.[60]

More specifically, however, trigonometrical survey was widely understood to mean the process of triangulation. Triangulation entails spreading a series of interconnecting triangles across a region. The surveyor "occupies" high vantage points, such as hilltops or towers, and measures the angles to other vantage points. (The surveyors' jargon is heavily laden with imperialistic and appropriative connotations.) Each point of observation forms a vertex in the triangulation. The interior angles of each triangle are measured with a theodolite; a "baseline" is measured directly on the ground with a chain and its length iscarried through the entire network by calculation (figure 3.5). The magnitude of each triangle being known, the location of each point can be determined with respect to its neighbors. Astronomical observations at one or two stations will define where the survey is on the earth's surface and will orient the triangulation with respect to true north, so that the latitudes and longitudes of the survey stations can also be calculated, assuming that the size and shape of the earth are known.

Triangulation was initially developed as an aid to geodesy, the science of the size and shape of the earth. A thin chain of triangles is measured north-south along an arc of a meridian and the distance between the ends of the chain is calculated and reduced to sea level. This value is compared against the difference in astronomical latitude between the same ends to give a mean "length of a degree." Two or more results for the lengths of a meridional degree in different latitudes are then combined to determine an approximation to the earth's figure, which is itself quite irregular. Geodetic surveys in the eighteenth and early nineteenth centuries were exercises in high science and epitomized the period's epistemology: with the definition of the meter, observation and measurement turned the world into its own measuring stick.[61] The question of the earth's size was fundamental to supporting the Newtonian, mechanistic, and rational view of the world. Geodesy itself required instruments of the finest accuracy and precision (or "exactness" in contemporary terminology); it required some of the most sophisticated and "cutting-edge" mathematics of the period. Geodesy and its triangulations were fundamental parts of the eighteenth and nineteenth centuries' popular scientism.[62]

Geodetic triangulations were not easily pursued. They needed to be properly designed. Too large or too small internal angles will not cause errors by themselves, but the nature of trigonometrical functions mean that a small error in measuring a very acute or obtuse angle will lead to the propagation of larger errors than would the same size error in a more moderate angle. Everest therefore insisted that all internal angles of the triangles measured for the Great Trigonometrical Survey of India had to be between forty-five and ninety degrees; for Everest, only a properly shaped triangulation in which all of the internal angles had been directly measured could be called a trigonometrical survey.[63] Geodetic surveys required instrumentation of a very high quality and skilled labor, neither of which came cheaply.

The benefit of triangulation was that it created a rigorously structured space. Its observations are always interconnected and are often

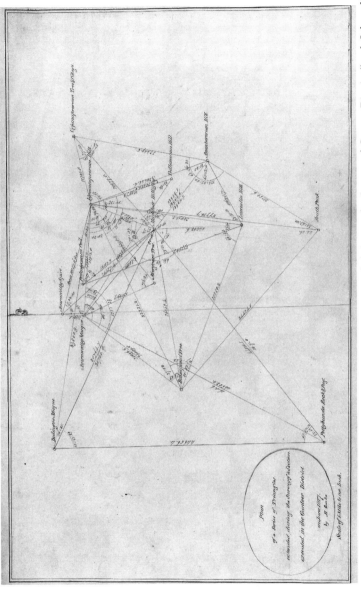

Figure 3.5 Colin Mackenzie, "Plan of a Series of triangles extended during the Survey of Guntur District," n.d. Ink and watercolor. (By permission of The British Library, IOR prints WD 2656.)

redundant, so that errors can be adjusted and reduced by comparing observations against each other. Many triangulations featured the measurement of a second baseline, the "base of verification": the surveyor obtains a measure of the survey's total error by comparing the measured length of the second base with that calculated through the triangulation network from the first; this error can then be distributed throughout the whole network. The result is that a triangulation provides a much more robust and intrinsically accurate series of control points than any series created by astronomical observation. A triangulation still requires some astronomy to fix its position and orientation on the globe, yet even if the global position of its initial point was subsequently revised—as was the case with the longitude of the Madras Observatory[64]—the triangulation still provides a firmly ordered and rigorous framework on which to hang more detailed surveys of the earth's surface.

Control points determined by triangulation are much denser and so provide much better opportunities for controlling detailed topographical surveys than those resulting from astronomical observations. The actual density will depend on the form in which the triangulation is prosecuted. If it is executed as a network, then the points will spread across the countryside; if it is a linear chain, then the fixed points will be limited to bands of country. More generally, triangulations are hierarchically organized: an extensive "primary" triangulation, in which the triangle sides may reach up to sixty miles (96 km), controls a "secondary" triangulation of smaller triangles and so more dense control points, which can in turn control a "tertiary" triangulation. A trigonometrical survey can therefore provide something that astronomical control can never do: a uniform basis extending across a landscape, in which errors are evenly distributed and minimized. Detailed surveys of the actual landscape can then be prosecuted without any danger of accumulating large errors, even if they are undertaken with little care.

The detailed surveys dependent on triangulation control took several forms, all derived from contemporary European land surveying practices codified in numerous texts since the sixteenth century. A technology popular with military surveyors because of its utility for mapping relief was the "plane table." This instrument consists of a wooden board, mounted on a tripod, on which the surveyor spreads a sheet of paper; the surveyor uses an "alidade," a straight edge fitted with a pair of sights, to trace on the paper his sight-lines to other objects. Two sightings are sufficient to locate an object at their intersection, although more are preferred. Once the basic framework of an area is defined, within the triangulated control, the surveyor can then sketch in the topographic relief (figure 3.6). Alternatively, the surveyor measured angles

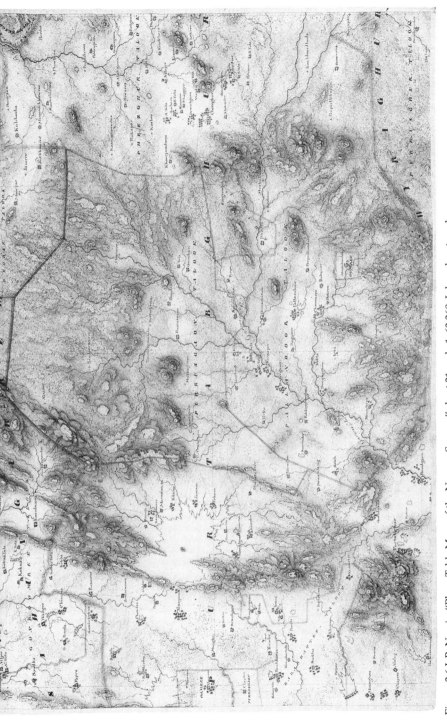

Figure 3.6 J. B. Norris, "Plane Table Maps of the Nagpur Survey," sheet 21, n.d., 1:63,360. Ink and watercolor. The atlas contains a total of sixty-one sheets and an index; the survey itself ran intermittently between 1821 and 1831. (By permission of The British Library, IOR X/1956/21.)

to points of interest at the same time as he observed the sides of the triangles. The position of the point of interest, such as a bend in a river or a building, could then be plotted graphically on the map, or it could be calculated and then plotted.

For very large-scale cadastral mapping, surveyors abandoned the principle of the indirect measurement of distances and returned to the traverse. British cadastral surveys in India were initially rather *ad hoc* so that "every possible method of survey was tried with all description of instruments."[65] A regularized system based on established English practices was introduced in 1822 for the northern plains and was eventually adopted in the Deccan as well. In this, surveyors encompassed the boundaries of each large estate or village with a loop of straight lines; the angles between these lines were measured by a theodolite, their lengths by a "Gunter's chain" sixty-six feet long. Details, especially the defining points of the boundary, were measured by perpendicular "offsets" from the line (figure 3.7). These boundary traverses were used to correct the surveys of individual fields made by Indian surveyors. Those surveyors traditionally measured field edges with wooden poles, although Francis Buchanan thought that they usually only visually estimated each field's area.[66] Nonetheless, a comparison of the total area of fields with the area enclosed within the boundary traverse provided a correction factor for the field surveys, allowing them to be fitted into the village bounds (figure 3.8). This system was revised in 1833 to bring the two parts of the cadastral survey more properly into line with each other.[67]

Trigonometrically controlled surveys were initially undertaken in India within the Madras presidency. In order to provide the basis for a survey of the southeastern coastline of India, Michael Topping and John Goldingham—the Company's astronomer and his then assistant—undertook a triangulation along the coast north of Madras during the period of 1788 to 1794. Inland, the 1792 cession to the Company of the Baramahal from Mysore prompted three surveys, each of which used the principles of triangulation, although to little effect. The first British administrator, Alexander Read, made a hurried reconnaissance survey, in only two months, in which he drew the angles between stations and detail on a plane table; distances were estimated for Read by local village officials. Alexander Allan made another fast survey that featured numerous route surveys combined with a number of bearings taken from hilltop stations, which might have constituted a triangulation.[68] Finally, Read had John Mather make a further survey of the region between 1794 and 1798. Apparently based on triangulation—Mather's account of the survey is confusing—the survey made Mather's

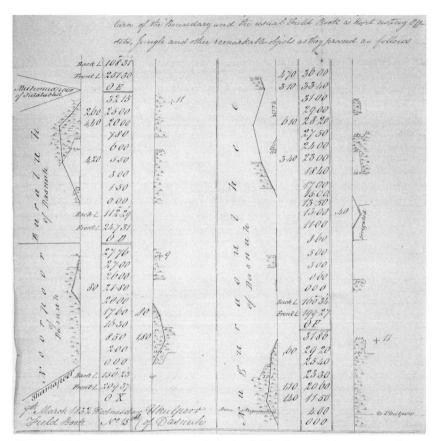

Figure 3.7 Neat copy (ink and watercolor) of a fieldbook entry of part of a village boundary traverse, sent to Governor General Lord William Bentinck. Starting at station (⊙) E, the surveyor measures a back sight (∠, or angle) to ⊙F and a foresight to ⊙D. The surveyor measures distances along the straight line ED (center column) and perpendicular "offsets" (inner columns) to the boundary itself, which is drawn in the outer columns. Some of the figures have been miscopied: the backsight at ⊙E (to ⊙F) should be ~180°, not 108° (transposed?), and the foresight from ⊙E to ⊙D should be ~291°, not 251°.
From William Brown, "Statement of the System . . . ," ¶4, UN Pw Jf 2694/43.

reputation, yet thirty years later it was judged to be worthless. The first regional survey in India definitely based on a "proper" triangulation was Colin Mackenzie's 1799–1807 survey of the rump state of Mysore. Thereafter, a basis of triangulation became standard for all topographic surveys in the Madras presidency. It was also at this time that the plane table began to be used as the favored instrument of the military topo-

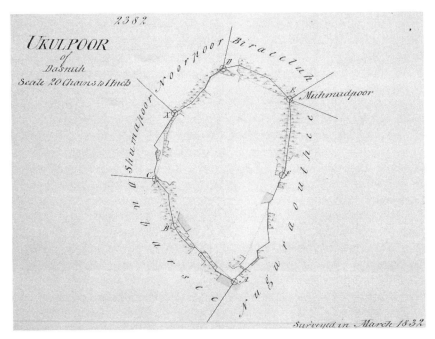

Figure 3.8 Left: map of the boundary traverse shown in figure 3.7, showing ⊙E and ⊙D in their larger context. Right: the same map with the interior detail added. Ink and watercolor.
From William Brown, "Statement of the System . . . ," ¶12 and ¶23, UN Pw Jf 2694/43.

graphical surveyor, introduced through the Military Institution at Madras by its Austrian-born instructor, Anthony Troyer.

Geodetic triangulations also began in southern India in the 1800s. The 1783 challenge by the Académie royale des Sciences to the Royal Society to help measure the longitudinal difference between the royal observatories at Greenwich and Paris prompted an increase in British interest in geodesy. In emulation of that measurement, William Lambton proposed a measure of both latitudinal and longitudinal degrees in the southern peninsula in 1799. This survey became the Great Trigonometrical Survey of India in 1817, whose focus was the Great Meridional Arc, running from Cape Comorin in the far south to Dehra Dun in the foothills of the Himalayas, a distance of some twenty-two degrees of latitude. The Great Trigonometrical Survey eventually acquired responsibility for the basic triangulation for controlling the detailed topographic and cadastral mapping of India: this acquisition is discussed in chapters 6 through 8.

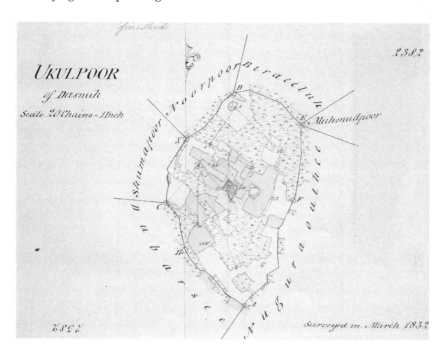

Scientism and the Archive's Technological Fix

Within the precepts of the period's empiricist scientism, trigonometrical surveys were held to create a perfect geographic panopticon.[69] Their skeletal framework allowed a more purely homogenized geographic knowledge. They promoted a high density of segmented information structured according to a system in which even the overall error could be quantified and mathematically corrected. Indeed, triangulation-based surveys made so much information possible at such large scales that even large wall maps could no longer show all of the data. India was broken down into systematic map series, each sheet being of regular size and uniform design; its space was divided and thereby controlled by both blocks of latitude and longitude and by cell-like sheet-lines (figure 3.9).

Such a homogenous division was necessarily imposed on the landscape by the practice of plane-table surveying. James Garling described the manner in which an arbitrary coordinate system is established and the world fitted to it:

> The [plane] table has been prepared, by first drawing [on] it, the
> lines limiting the space destined to be taken by [that is, drawn

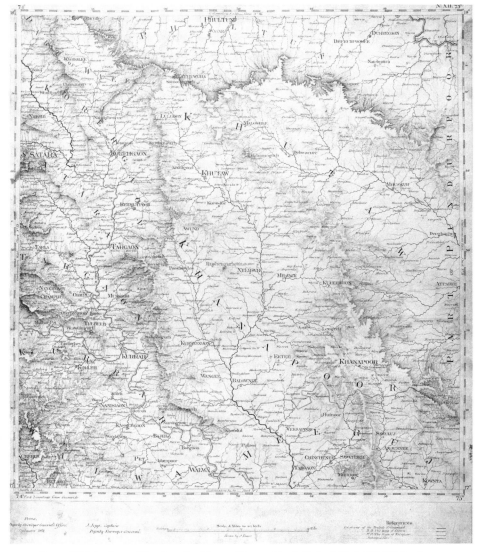

Figure 3.9 John Jopp, "Bombay Presidency: Degree Sheets," sheet 12, 1:253,440, September 1831. Ink and watercolor; original size, 43.8 × 41.7 cm.

One sheet from a regular topographic series intended to have at least sixty sheets, each covering one square degree. Sheet 12 covers 17–18°N, 74–75°E. The IOR set preserves twenty-three of the sheets, dated 1827–33, in two groups: the western Deccan and northern Gujerat. (By permission of The British Library, IOR X/2580/12.)

on] it; these lines are always parallel or perpendicular to the meridian passing through the south end of the [baseline]. The lines
forming the limits being drawn, all points [of the triangulation
framework] falling within then have been protracted in reference
to those lines . . . [70]

Like other surveyors and commercial cartographers, Garling could construct an index to the cartographic archive consisting of a long list of
placenames and their geographical coordinates within this imposed
framework. Colin Mackenzie once suggested that the names of the
smallest villages might be replaced by mathematical coordinates in order to make administration that much more efficient.[71]

The spatial emphasis of triangulation surveys is thus upon a uniform
space, in which all points are treated equally and have the same degree
of certainty and unambiguity. The triangulation's mathematical framework was defined by the very geographical features that were mapped.
As noted in chapter 1, the adoption of triangulation entails a shift in the
source of the epistemological certitude of regional surveys from the office to the field. The Rennell-style of map compilation within the frame
of the graticule was truthful precisely because of the cartographer's
logical processes of comparing and reconciling different data sources;
in principle, the employment of reason could overcome the errors and
uncertainties inherent in data measurement to reveal the kernel of truth
in each observation. In contrast, the office work associated with a comprehensive, systematic, triangulation-based survey is confined only to
working through the myriad computations necessary and plotting the
results, processes which require care, attention, and skill but which are
both mechanical. The truth of the triangulation-based survey rests on
the hierarchical structure of observation and measurement established
by the surveyor in the field. The equivalence between the archive of
geographic data and the real world which is represented depends entirely on the measurement of the world and not on any archival manipulation. And if the surveyor measures enough features with sufficient precision and accuracy, the result will be a corpus of geographical
information at a scale of 1:1. Everything would be included.

Triangulation thus allowed *more* of India to be seen—indirectly—at
a single view. The penetration of British power into the Indian landscape was more effective and more comprehensive. The attention of
Company officials could be turned to ever smaller places. An India-
wide trigonometrical survey promoted the image of the perfect geographical archive constituted by the "painstaking record of infinite
observations"[72] reduced mathematically to replicate the essence of India. It promoted the image of the 1:1 map which exactly replicates the

empire, whose data are housed and protected within the solid walls of the British survey office.

But there were serious flaws in the perfection offered by triangulation. To begin with, and recapping the theme with which this chapter began, the surveyors were not naturally visually empowered. Unlike the geographical traveler and route surveyor who move seemingly unencumbered through the landscape, observing each phenomenon in turn as it presented itself to their gaze, triangulation requires planning. A preliminary reconnaissance, often in the form of a quick route survey,[73] is necessary to lay out the broad configuration of a district and to identify those hills and buildings which form the vertices of well-configured triangles. The actual measurement of angles comes only after extensive preparation and definition of space. Secondary and tertiary triangulations, and detailed topographic surveys, were then to be completed within the existing framework of higher-order surveys.

The surveyors also had to expend much time and energy to ensure that they would indeed be able to see between the chosen hills. It is an exceedingly rare hilltop that possesses clear and unambiguous features which are both visible from all directions and sufficiently precise to serve as targets for observation. Special targets therefore had to be erected to define the "exact" position of each hilltop during the survey (figure 3.10). Lines of sight had to be cleared through any hilltop jungle to allow the surveyor to see his distant targets; paths had to be cleared to the hilltops to allow access for the surveyors. The movements of several observing and target-building parties had to be properly coordinated so that the observers had targets to observe. Geodetic and even lower-level triangulation surveys thus required a huge capital outlay and dedicated institutional support.

In the plains, the surveyors had to deal with the earth's curvature. It is difficult to see very far from ground level: the horizon would be about three miles (4.8 km) away from a person with a stature of six feet (1.8 m), assuming a perfectly smooth earth. Moreover, trees and buildings easily block the surveyor's lines of sight. It was therefore difficult to triangulate in low-lying areas without introducing errors because of all of the extra observations that were necessary. Garling, for example, found that the quality of his 1813–15 survey of Sonda (North Canara) was variable: the small areas of plains were slightly in error whereas the hills were "generally executed with a minute correctness."[74] Triangulations were therefore first undertaken in the upland areas of the Deccan; thus the predominance of such surveys under the Madras government. In the Bengal presidency, trigonometrical networks were used for surveys in the Himalayas in the 1820s by John Hodgson, James Her-

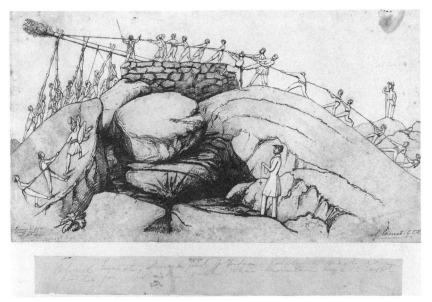

Figure 3.10 Godfrey Thomas Vigne, "Major Everest G.T. Survey of India pulling up Trigon. Mast on top of Chur Mtn," 10 October 1834. Pen and ink.

In his *Travels in Kashmir, Ladak, Iskardo, the Countries adjoining the Mountain-Course of the Indus, and the Himalaya, North of the Panjab* (London: Henry Colburn, 1842, 2 vols.), 1: 34–35, Vigne described his visit: "The camp of our host was pitched as near as possible on the very top, and our chief object was to keep ourselves warm. The tent in which we dined was furnished with a lighted stove, and the entrance carefully closed against air, whilst we drank our wine and talked to a late hour above the clouds. On the huge granite rocks that formed the very apex of the mountain, the labourers in attendance had formed a platform of loose stones, purposely carried thither, and in the center of it they planted a mast, as a mark for the survey. Several that they had previously raised on other summits were visible only by the aid of the theodolite; and a powerful heliotrope (in use at Sahranpur in the plains) might, it was supposed, have reflected the sun's rays towards us from a distance of sixty miles." (By permission of The British Library, IOR prints WD 3114.)

bert, and William Webb, but they were not extended down into the plains (see figure 3.4). Starting in the 1830s, however, the surveyors of the Great Trigonometrical Survey resorted to building towers—artificial hills—in the plains to meet the need for lofty observation stations.

The principal disadvantage to the prosecution of triangulation surveys was thus their cost. The highest quality work of the GTS required the surveyors to spend days, if not weeks, at each station, waiting for the dust and heat haze to clear from the atmosphere in order to have clear observing conditions. Before lamps were introduced by Everest after 1830 to allow observation at night, when the atmosphere is more settled, the best atmospheric conditions in India occurred during the monsoons, which were also the unhealthiest time of year for the British. And there was all of the preparatory work prior to the actual survey. But even the lesser, secondary or tertiary triangulations took more time than the equivalent mesh of route surveys, if only because they generated a higher density of information. Furthermore, the theodolites and chains required for triangulation were expensive and had to be shipped from Europe, whereas the simple compasses and perambulators of the route surveys could be manufactured cheaply in India. Triangulation required extensive and laborious computations and error adjustments; it required skilled and educated surveyors who expected high salaries for their efforts.

In sum, trigonometrical surveys were time-consuming and expensive. Their undertaking required explicit support at the highest political and bureaucratic levels within the East India Company, by individuals who were enamored with the trigonometrical survey's evident status as both a high and practical science, and with the structured, ordered, and hierarchical space which they created. All of the hurdles which I have identified for a survey can conceivably be overcome. With sufficient resources, it is more than feasible to conduct a thorough, high-quality triangulation survey. However, and this is a very big however, the East India Company did not have sufficient resources. The actual prosecution of triangulations and their dependent surveys was shaped by the ability of the Company's directors and administrators to dedicate money, equipment, and personnel to mapping activities. The practical implementation of all surveys depended on several contingent factors.

But the most fundamental issue for the Company's implementation of triangulation surveys in the early nineteenth century was the ability of the Company to support the epistemological shift from the office to the field. Bureaucratic inertia, fueled by the Company's established patronage system, meant that almost all of the offices which were supposed to contribute to the systemizing of the Indian surveys were in fact set up and functioned according to the old eighteenth-century manner. The very flow of information between the levels of the Company's administration in India required the continuation of the archival compilation of geographic data. The epistemological confusion which characterized the relationship of the Great Trigonometrical Survey with the Company's other mapmaking activities in the nineteenth century thus derived from the Company's social institutions and conditions, to which we will now turn.

PART TWO

INSTITUTIONAL STRUCTURES AND CARTOGRAPHIC ANARCHY

We have almost daily experience of the very defective state of our geographical information in many parts of our own territories and of the serious inconveniences and embarrassments arising from this cause in the conduct of ordinary affairs of the administration.

George Dowdeswell, vice-president,
Calcutta Council, April 1818

CHAPTER FOUR

Structural Constraints of the East India Company's Administration

Mapmaking is a practice. As such, the character of any particular instance of mapmaking owes much to the conditions and circumstances within which the mapmakers functioned. In the case of the East India Company's mapping of India, one might point to the imbalance between the administrators' perceived need for maps and the ability of the Company to allocate the necessary resources to gather the required geographical information. This imbalance is clearly expressed in George Dowdeswell's indignation.[1] The dramatic growth of the Company's territories between 1790 and 1820, and the wars preceding that growth, greatly stressed the small bureaucratic system established in the eighteenth century. Moreover, the Company's financial situation was always precarious. As only one of many essential tasks which the Company's territorial administration had to complete, mapmaking often took second place to more urgent activities. With insufficient resources, the British mapping of India proceeded in a crisis-driven and almost anarchic manner.

The lack of resources contributed to and exacerbated several factors that bore directly on the actual implementation of the surveys. Each survey was organized by whomever had both a need for data and available resources. Both requirements were variable. Surveys were accordingly undertaken at the initiative of various administrative levels: the Company's directors and secretariat in London, the central administrations of each of the three presidencies, senior officials in the field, or junior officers acting on their own initiative. Once begun, surveys were disrupted, delayed, or even abandoned because of any of several factors: the ill health of the surveyor, active opposition from Indians, the surveyor having to rejoin his regiment or survey a different territory, the refusal of the directors to sanction the cost, a need to reduce the survey's expenditures, or the surveyor's inadequate skills. Maps were kept in manuscript; with only a small distribution they were easily lost and could not be replaced when damaged by neglect, thereby necessitating new surveys.

The mapping of the northern districts of the Carnatic—the "Northern Circars"—provides an early example of the impediments faced by surveyors. The region was ceded to the Company in 1768 by the Nizam of Hyderabad. Surveys of some of the districts were begun as early as 1769, but they proceeded in a desultory manner. The surveyors were rotated to other military duties or they fell victim to disease. Either way, the surveys lapsed and, "tho' they cost many a pagoda," the few resulting maps had become quite rare by 1807.[2] The region was not comprehensively surveyed until after 1816. More generally, the chaotic character of the British surveys means that in documenting every instance of mapmaking that Reginald Phillimore could identify, his monumental *Historical Records of the Survey of India* (1945–58) could only have been overwhelmingly elaborate, tangled, and—frankly—confusing.[3]

Much of mapmaking's chaotic circumstances stemmed from the character of the Company's bureaucracy. In general, the Company's management of information was based on the Enlightenment's ideal of archival knowledge creation. Data gathered by field officers was sent to the Company's three urban centers of Calcutta (Fort William), Bombay, and Madras (Fort St. George). There, staff officers collected and rationalized those data and then disseminated the resultant knowledge to the governor, the council, and other officers, but only as necessary. The products of the individual surveyors were thus reconciled and compiled into general maps by cartographic staff officers; those maps were kept in manuscript and strict controls were placed on their distribution and use.

This configuration drew a sharp divide between the *ad hoc* field observer and the office archivist, between the surveyor who gathered information as he encountered it and the cartographic staff officer who took the journals and interpolated their contents within the existing archive. The employment of military officers on survey duty was only temporary. The surveyor's autonomous position was maintained by a system of salaries that set the surveyors outside of the regular hierarchy of regimental salary and rank. (Almost all of the surveyors were military officers.) Moreover, the expertise required of the surveyors set them to one side of the regular hierarchy of command. The cartographic staff officers thus acquired the duty of judging the quality of completed surveys and of advising their governors on cartographic matters. But the Company's patronage system prevented those officers from acquiring the power to appoint or dismiss the surveyors themselves. That power remained firmly in the hands of the directors in London; personnel decisions made in India were always subject to ratification by the directors.

The institutional organization of cartographic activities depended to a large extent on the expansion of the Company's territories. Until the 1780s, the territorial administration was limited and comparatively little mapmaking was undertaken, so that the bureaucratic management of mapmaking was loose and informal. The intensification and expansion of territorial control in the 1780s and 1790s led to the regularization and formalization of the manner in which the Company's bureaucrats managed information. Once firmly established, however, that system could not easily accommodate further expansion of the Company's territorial interests.

Thus the chaos. Although their work became increasingly more complex, the surveyors remained separate, autonomous, and so subject to transfer to other, more pressing duties. The workload of the cartographic offices at each presidency steadily increased: the demand for maps rose within the administrations, and each map had to be copied by hand; the flood of new geographical information had to be incorporated into general maps; and the British officers in charge had to write more and more reports on cartographic matters. The Company's almost permanent financial crisis stressed the situation further, as the accountants sought to save as much money as possible.

The Company's politicians and administrators were, of course, well aware of the chaotic circumstances of the mapping of India. If only because of the need to save money, they tried to rationalize the mapping process, eliminate duplication, and so avoid waste. But there was a fundamental disagreement about how to achieve that rationalization, a disagreement which stemmed from the epistemological shift in mapmaking identified in the previous chapters. The first response was based on the existing bureaucratic system and the archival construction of knowledge: the mapping archives ought to be combined into one overall system; for the duration of the fiscal crisis, surveys should be pursued only if absolutely essential. The second response was based on the observational ideal of the triangulation-based, systematic survey: comprehensive surveys would provide a uniform, and permanent, cartographic coverage that would admittedly cost much in the short term but that would pay for itself in the long term. The attempts to undertake comprehensive surveys within the established bureaucracy served only to confuse yet further the circumstances of all of the early surveys. The Company's entrenched system of patronage was especially important as a retarding factor because it could not allow midlevel officials to have the powers of appointment and dismissal necessary for a large survey organization.

I draw on examples from all three presidencies in the following examination of the practical conditions and institutional circumstances of

British mapmaking in India. Chapter 5 focuses on the situation in southern India between 1790 and 1810, when the government in Madras took control and began to map all of the territories south of the Krishna River. Unlike the government in Calcutta, which in the period of 1800 to 1803 took control of the Gangetic Plains—reaching past Delhi, almost to the Sutlej River—surveyors and administrators in Madras attempted to establish a systematic, coherent, and triangulation-based survey of the presidency's entire territory. Those attempts prefigure the flawed development of triangulation-based surveys and the concept of a survey of all India after 1817. (Part Three details the results.) The Madras situation clearly illustrates the tensions and conflicts created within the Company's institutional structures by mapmaking; it demonstrates the various institutional factors which, in different configurations, occurred throughout the rest of Company India.

Territorial Expansion and Map Use

All of the officials of the East India Company were cartographically literate. Even those who did not engage with intellectual issues, like those infantry and cavalry officers who devoted their leisure hours to hunting, had class backgrounds in which they would have been exposed to maps as part of their basic education. They would have been generally aware of the map image and of the graticule of meridians and parallels framing geographic data. Maps were widely adopted as regular tools by the technical military corps of engineers and artillerymen in the seventeenth century. In the eighteenth century, military theorists extended the established geometrical precepts of fortification to encompass strategy and tactics more generally. Mapmaking and map-use were thus prominent components of the curricula of the military academies established throughout Europe after 1750. And although the military academies trained only a minority of officers, they did entrench the map in military culture.[4]

It is, however, a different proposition that a general awareness of maps would lead individuals to go out of their way to use maps in their daily tasks. Institutional inertia has, for example, been identified as a key reason for the slow and differential adoption of maps within early modern European states.[5] Before about 1750, map-use by the British military seems to have been limited to the engineers, to fortress commanders, and to the strategic planners. Commanding officers in the field relied on their outriders for knowledge of the landscapes through which the columns passed. This worked well enough in the Company's wars in Bengal and the Carnatic. But after 1760, the Company came increasingly into conflict with the Marathas and with Haider Ali (reigned 1761–82) and Tipu Sultan (reigned 1782–99) of Mysore. To win against their highly fluid tactics, the Company's armies were forced to tap into the complex and long-established networks of informants, spies, and local guides.[6] They had to know the country in order to succeed; among other informational sources, they realized that they had to make surveys.

The contrast of military sentiment between the 1760s and 1800s is striking. In 1765, Robert Orme, the Company's first official historian, wrote an "Essay on the Art of War" for the benefit of his friends in the Company's armies (although he was not himself a soldier). One of his major themes was that decent maps were essential for all levels of military operations. Orme's argument indicates that maps were rarely used by field officers. Little of the necessary geographic information had been collected, so Orme urged his friends to make surveys.[7] As described below, Orme's urging bore fruit in the form of James Rennell's survey of Bengal and probably other surveys in the northern plains as well.

Forty years later, commanders in chief of the Madras army had no doubts about the need for maps. General James Stuart wrote in 1804 that good geographical information "forms the basis of all military plans":

> It affords the means of concerting those plans upon principles of just combination and of carrying them into execution with precision and due effect. It facilitates that adaptation of the rules of war to the nature of the country which is essential to the success of military operations. Destitute of that knowledge our military measures must be crude and imperfect, inapplicable to the state of the country, dependent for success upon accidental causes, and liable to be counteracted by an enemy acquainted with the country, and to be defeated by circumstances which that knowledge would have enabled us to prevent. An acquaintance with the geography of our territories is necessary in time of peace to determine upon accurate military principles the distribution of the troops and the positions requisite for the defence of the frontiers.[8]

Stuart's successor, Sir John Craddock, was of a like mind: "the necessity of the most minute survey of all the country . . . is so obvious, and I believe universally acknowledged, that it is needless to add any further private opinion."[9]

These and numerous similar comments do possess a self-consciousness which calls into question the extent to which British military officers in India actually felt it necessary to use maps. Stuart and Craddock can be interpreted as being reform-minded officers who were perhaps atypical of the majority of officers. Even so, their arguments give the definite impression that map use, and the awareness that maps ought to be used, was indeed increasing in the Company's military through the period of Company rule. Thus John Hodgson, surveyor general of India, could in 1821 identify a "general taste for geographical research which has within the last fifteen years rapidly increased among the officers of the Indian Army."[10]

Company officials steadily expanded their use of maps for the non-military functions of government. Surveys had in the eighteenth century become essential aspects of any engineering project; in 1806, the Company's directors accordingly took to task a highly regarded officer, Thomas Munro, for initiating reservoir repairs without prior surveys, although Munro argued that the system for funding the surveys was open to fraud.[11] Maps became incorporated into strategic planning. When in November 1824 the British resident at Indore asked the Bombay government to survey the Narmada Valley and its surrounds in order to locate routes used by opium smugglers in defiance of the Company's monopoly and to produce maps "for checking and repressing the disorderly inhabitants of the hills," he wrote that "it is almost needless for me to descant on the utility and importance of possessing on our records such information whether in a political or military, a police or a revenue point of view."[12] Once again, the confidence of the tone reveals the continuing novelty, but increasing acceptance, of maps as tools of daily administration.

The development of cartographic literacy within the Company's civil administration is well illustrated by a story concerning William Lambton's triangulation of southern India, printed in the Asiatic Society's journal, *Gleanings in Science,* for 1830. The tale was that in the early years of the survey, probably 1806, a "leading member of the Finance Committee at Madras" had been unable to understand the survey's implications and had tried to close it down. The accountant argued that "if any traveler wished to proceed to Seringapatam, he need only say so to his head palankeen bearer, [who would vouch] that he would find his way to that place without having recourse to Col. Lambton's map." Although there is no corroboration for the tale, it subsequently became a staple of the heroic historiography of the Indian surveys: look what stupid hurdles the surveyors had to overcome! Of more significance, however, is the story's indication of a contemporary perception that there had been a marked increase in cartographic literacy between 1806 and 1830, from a level just sufficient to counter negative opinion to a much higher level whence that negative opinion might be easily derided.[13]

The expansion of map use within the Company depended on the Company's territorial expansion. Each new conquest or annexation carried with it the obligation on the part of the British to collect geographical information of the territory so that they might govern it. This obligation could function at the most pragmatic level. The partition of Mysore was made in May 1799, for example, by listing the *parganas* (districts) allocated to the Company, the Nizam, and the reinstated raja. It did not take the British long to realize, with no small embarrassment, that they had little knowledge of where the parganas were, let alone of the precise locations of their boundaries! Lieutenant Thomas Sydenham, of the Madras Infantry, was immediately directed to survey the frontier between the rump state and the parganas claimed by the British and the Nizam, but he did little before falling ill. Lord Wellesley, the governor general, then conceived of a more coherent survey of Mysore which would not be "confined to mere military or geographical information," but which would also entail "a statistical account of the whole country."[14] In the end, this was implemented as two overlapping projects: Colin Mackenzie, the most prominent military surveyor in Madras, was given charge of the geographical survey (see table 2.1); Francis Buchanan, one of Wellesley's proteges, made an economic and statistical survey (see table 2.2).

Another example of the pragmatic need for geographic information is provided by the revenue collector of Bombay city and island. A series of urban reforms exposed the complexity of Bombay's land tenures: in 1811 there were no less than nine distinct forms of tenure on the island, whose area was only eighteen square miles. Nor were the Company's own rights as "lord of the land" established; it had leased the island for £10 per annum from the British Crown, which had in turn received it from Portugal as part of Catherine de Braganza's dowry when she married Charles II in 1661. It eventually took Lieutenants Thomas Dickenson and William Tate fifteen years (1812–27) to complete a large-scale cadastral survey, including thorough statistical and historical analyses, to establish the Company's rights.[15]

The relationship between territorial expansion and map use within the East India Company was twofold. If one assumes a constant level of map-use, more territories would entail more surveys and more maps. This is certainly the case with the route surveys undertaken by each army column. Institutional learning means, however, that growth in map-use was not linear. It was cumulative: as Company officials involved with territorial administration became more accustomed to using maps for certain tasks, they gradually extended their use to other tasks. The process of this expansion is still unclear and can be only inferred. Even so, map-use, if not map dependency, was so common by the end of the nineteenth century that a member of the 1904–5 Indian Survey Committee was reported to have exclaimed, "Why, every official in India wants a special map on one sheet, of exactly the size to fit his own writing table and with his own pet area plumb in the center of it."[16]

The different functions of each of the Company's institutions concerned with territorial administration meant that they each required different types of geographical information. Officials responsible for assessing and collecting land revenues wanted maps to define the concept of property and with which to settle the taxes; engineers wanted irrigation and architectural maps; divisional military commanders wanted strategic maps; commanders of army detachments wanted tactical maps; the administrators in India and the directors in London all wanted general maps. These various needs could not be met by just one survey of each district. Mackenzie and his assistants might have constructed exquisite topographic maps of Mysore at scales in the range of one to four inches to the mile (1:63,360 to 1:253,440), but these were unsuitable for the needs of other officials. Two officers of the Madras quartermaster general's department began new surveys in southeastern Mysore in 1815 and the diwan (chief minister) of Mysore proposed a detailed cadastral survey of the state at about the same time.[17] Again, Sir John Malcolm had several of his subordinates survey central and western India, including the valley of the Narmada River, the results of which were collated and published in London by Aaron Arrowsmith in 1823. Yet these were only cursory route surveys, so that the final map was inadequate for close management; the resident at Indore therefore requested in 1824 that a new, detailed survey be made of the region.[18] Overall, the multiple demands for maps led after 1800 to the proliferation of mapmaking activities within the Company's territorial administrations.

The Availability of Field Surveyors: Health and Education

The proliferation of mapmaking activities in British India obviously depended on the availability of skilled surveyors. The issue of the availability of cartographic labor provides a constant backdrop to the institutional character of the British mapping of India; it is so ubiquitous that it is perhaps easy to forget its presence.

There were three broad categories of British surveyors in India. First, there were many officers who together created a huge amount of geographical information but who were nonetheless rather peripheral institutionally. These were the junior officers who were delegated to record the routes taken by an army column. Their cartographic careers were generally limited to recording a few marches; they rarely approached their task with any degree of sophistication, being motivated only by the extra salary that such surveying would earn them. As such, they do not feature prominently in this study. They rarely, if ever, crossed into the second group of "dedicated" cartographic officers. This group comprised those army officers, mostly engineers, who were directed by the councils of each presidency to undertake surveys of specific districts. Several of these officers were repeatedly detached from their corps for survey duty and constituted a central cadre of skilled and experienced surveyors. Finally, several civilians were employed by the Company as surveyors when military officers were not available. The category was not clearly defined, however, because engineer and artillery officers did not always receive commissions in the eighteenth century. The formalization and expansion of the technical corps in the late eighteenth century led to a sufficient supply of military surveyors, so that there were very few nonmilitary surveyors after 1810.

Despite their organizational differences, all field surveyors were affected by several common factors that affected their availability to undertake surveys. I stress this point because, time and again, entire surveys were abandoned when the officers were removed from duty and no replacements could be found.

By the early nineteenth century, there was a sizeable pool of military officers in India who possessed at least a modicum of cartographic skill. In the eighteenth century, the cartographic officers learned the necessary skills as assistants to experienced surveyors. Others, notably William Lambton and Colin Mackenzie, were self-taught. Attempts to regulate military education in the nineteenth century included a Military Institute at Madras (1804–16) to educate infantry ensigns in surveying and mapping and the placement of engineer cadets in the Board of Ordnance's training centers at Woolwich and Chatham. A very few officers received a technical education in British schools. William Webb of the Bengal infantry is perhaps a lone instance. He attended the Royal Mathematical School at Christ's Hospital in London as a child and, when on furlough from 1812 through 1814, spent time at the Royal Observatory and with the Savilian Professor of Astronomy at Oxford.[19]

Possession of cartographic abilities did not mean that an officer was guaranteed to spend his career on survey duty. The surveyor's principal duties *always* lay with his regiment or corps. Of the 280 graduates of the Company's military seminary at Addiscombe between 1809 and 1821,

sixty-five were engineers: forty-four spent a field season with the Ordnance Survey in western Britain to gain practical mapping experience,
but only nineteen appear in Phillimore's *Historical Records* as having
made surveys or maps, and only seven might legitimately be considered as part of a cadre of officers whose careers centered on maps.[20] For
most officers employed on mapping duties, surveying was only an occasional duty, one which was ancillary to their principal military appointments. The status of mapmaking outside of the formal military
hierarchy was reflected in the special salaries and allowances granted
to the officers. Time and again, the surveyors were called back to duty
with their regiments or corps, especially during military or fiscal crises,
and their surveys were abandoned.

The provision of substantial salaries and allowances for surveyors
reflected the considerable hardships involved, hardships which significantly contributed to the smallness of the cadre of "proper" surveyors.
The detrimental effects on the surveyors' health, if not their lives, not
only reduced the number of active surveyors, it discouraged potential
surveyors. Traveling in the interior, slogging up and down mountains
and through jungles, avoiding snakes and sometimes tigers, was hard
work in its own right. Add to this the attacks that were made on surveyors by Indians—which were common enough that the Great Trigonometrical Survey developed its own guard, separate from any of the armies, complete with its own uniform—and the surveyor was clearly in
need of extra recompense.

But the main adversity facing British surveyors in India was disease,
which they blamed on the climate and environment. The British suffered a high mortality rate in India, but the surveyor in the field seems
to have been especially susceptible to "jungle fever." He might have
had servants and porters aplenty to bear the load of heavy labor but
"his hollow eye and cadaverous complexion tell a tale," specifically that
"the surveyor is made to be killed."[21] George Everest wrote of one especially virulent incident in 1819:

> Buoyed up hitherto by the full vigor of youth and a strong consti-
> tution, I had spurned at the thoughts of being attacked by sickness,
> against which I foolishly deemed myself impregnable; but my last
> day's ride through a powerful sun, and over a soil teeming with
> vapor and malaria, had exposed me to all the fatal influence of
> these formidable forests. On the 2d of October, in the evening, I
> found myself laboring under the effects of a violent typhus fever.
> Mr. Voysey [the surgeon] was seized very soon after; within the
> next five days the greater part of my camp (nearly one hundred and
> fifty in number) were laid prostrate; and it seemed indeed as if at

last, the genius of the jungul [*sic*] had risen in his wrath, to chastise
the hardihood of those rash men who had dared to violate the sanc-
tity of his chosen haunt, and brave him in the very season of his
carousal.

The evacuation of the survey party entailed "all of the public elephants
and litters and camels" in Hyderabad; one-tenth of Everest's followers
died.[22] This event severely weakened Everest's constitution. He went on
sick leave, first to the Cape of Good Hope in 1820–21 and then to Europe from 1825 through 1830, where he continued to be "affected with
[an] ulceration on the ilium from which several exfoliations have taken
place" and remained susceptible, he wrote, to "the foul air of the bogs
in Ireland."[23] Back in India as surveyor general, Everest spent as much
time as possible in the salubrious foothills of the Himalayas.

Everest's circumstances were by no means unique: the correspondence between the surveyors and their superiors constitute a continual
series of requests to be allowed to "go to sea" for the fresh air, to go on
furlough, or to quit survey duty altogether. Phillimore's biographical
sketches of the surveyors read as a litany of death and disease. Almost
all of the central cadre of surveyors either died in India—Robert Colebrooke (1808), Mackenzie (1821), Lambton (1823), etc.—or they returned home to Britain as invalids.

The core surveying cadre was always few in number, at most fifteen
officers throughout India in 1800, increasing steadily to a maximum of
perhaps thirty in 1840. These figures are approximate; the idea of the
"proper" surveyor is itself quite vague, so greater precision would be
meaningless. The point to be stressed, however, is that there were very
few British soldiers whose wider regimental duties, whose health, and
whose own ambitions could all combine to dedicate their careers to surveying and mapmaking. The pressing need to acquire geographical information did not lessen, however. The solution was to broaden the labor pool.

Revenue surveyors in the northern plains employed traditional village surveyors for measuring individual fields. Starting as early as 1794,
the Madras government apprenticed local orphans for surveying. Most
of the youths were "Eurasians" or "Anglo-Indians," descended from
Indian mothers and European fathers (traders, soldiers, emigres, missionaries, or local inhabitants of Portuguese descent). A few were the
children of British officers and their wives. The Bombay government
established schools for Eurasians and low-caste Indians in the 1820s,
schools which included a survey curriculum. The Great Trigonometrical Survey and the Madras Observatory also employed a few mathematically educated Brahmins as computers for the complex geodetic

calculations. Semiskilled laborers indigenous to the country came cheaply—with low salaries and few pensions—and were held to be more resilient to the climate than surveyors raised in Britain. Ultimately, it was the Eurasians and poor Europeans who were responsible for the most laborious tasks in surveying and in map construction, copying, and (after 1850) printing. The attitudes toward using Eurasians and Indians are discussed more fully in chapter 9. For now it is sufficient to note that this hierarchy of cartographic labor was to be repeated for all of the scientific and public agencies in India, such as the Geological Survey (founded in 1851), the railroads, and the post office.

Information Management and
the Surveyor Generals of Bengal

At the core of all of the successful states of South Asia was the collection and control of information. In order to maintain their power and to enforce control, the Indian states developed complex arrangements of "newswriters," agents, informants, and spies, all tied together through both public and private communication networks. Chris Bayly has recently advanced a compelling thesis which ties the rise and fall of different states to their ability to control and use information. For example, the archives of the Peshwa, the principal Maratha ruler, contain extensive documents that detail the revenue, political, and social affairs of the Deccan, even at the level of individual villages. Conversely, the decline of the Mughal empire can in part be tied to the atrophy of its information networks. The following discussion owes much to Bayly's argument.[24]

During the eighteenth century, Company officers developed their own information networks. They supplanted the Mughals as patrons of a large network of official "newswriters." They were helped in doing so both by the Company's legal standing (after 1765) as the Mughal diwan of Bengal and, more tangibly, by their financial resources. The better newswriters received large salaries of 300 rupees (£27/12) per month,* the standard monthly rate for senior Company officials. (The equivalence is not complete, however, because before 1784 the British civil officials also received shares in the Company's profits.) The best newswriters could also look forward to receiving large land holdings on their retirement. The Company's penetration of the information networks in the northern plains was aided by the eighteenth-century decline of Mughal patronage and power, which allowed the rise of a

---

*For details of Indian and British coinages, please refer to the "Note on East India Company Coinage" on page xvii.

variety of entrepreneurs and "private traders" whose merchandise included political and commercial intelligence. The flow of information converged on the Bengal government in Calcutta, which steadily sought to systematize its "Persian correspondence" in the second half of the century.[25]

At the same time, the British began to supplement the geographical information obtained from a variety of private and public Indian sources with their own surveys. Like the political and commercial information flowing through the newswriters, residents, and Company agents to Calcutta, the flow of geographical information was one-way, to the center. The basic source of information were the surveys of the routes taken by army columns, supported by astronomical observations made by various travelers. Before the middle of the eighteenth century, most information generated by Europeans pertained to the Carnatic and was produced by the continuing struggle between the British and the French for political domination of the peninsula. The Gangetic Plains were initially known by travelers' sparse reports, such as that of the Père Tieffenthaler, a Jesuit priest who toured northern India from 1743 until his death at Lucknow in 1785; his geographical work was published posthumously, with James Rennell using it for his 1788 map of India.[26] The geographical data collected by the British and French were sent back to Europe and compiled into general maps there.

Before 1757, Europeans still knew very little of Bengal's geography other than the major channels of the Ganges and its distributaries, which also served as the province's major highways. In that year the Company became irreconcilably embroiled in the politics of the Nawab's court. Robert Clive first engineered a military victory over the Nawab at Plassey and then seized political power in a coup. The Company was formally granted the "Twenty-four Parganas" around Calcutta; its merchants used their new political power to advance personal schemes to extract vast fortunes. In addition to mapping the twenty-four parganas, the Calcutta council also commissioned surveys of the navigable river channels to enhance the exploitation of the interior. The surveys themselves were rather hurried and sporadic. The council had a hard time finding qualified personnel who were not already committed to making their personal fortunes. It was no accident that the first official appointment of a "surveyor"—that of Hugh Cameron in 1761 as Surveyor of the New Lands—was given to an artillery officer who had had to leave Bombay because he had been charged (apparently wrongly) with desertion.

Early in January 1767, the Calcutta council appointed Rennell to be the surveyor general *in* Bengal.[27] This is commonly taken as being the origin of the Survey of India; some authors mistakenly refer to Rennell as the surveyor general of India. But too much has been read into this event. Rennell's appointment was quite limited in its institutional scope. It was a position intended primarily for the management of geographical information and for the construction of maps. It was not intended to be the head of a large and coherent survey organization. Nor was it a permanent office; six months passed after Rennell left India in April 1777 before the council found it necessary to revive the position. It was intended, first and foremost, as Clive's reward to Rennell for his past efforts and as an inducement to future labor.

In this respect, Rennell was treated in a manner similar to the news-writers: as surveyor general he received a salary of 300 rupees per month; on his retirement he was able to receive a (then rare) pension from the council as recompense for his loyal pursuit of an often arduous task and he was also permitted to publish his maps for profit. The court subsequently confirmed the pension at £400 per annum. It should be noted that Rennell had given up a marine career and had accepted a commission in the Bengal engineers because he had thought that by doing so he would get a share of the immense wealth then being stripped from Bengal. His expectations were dashed when Clive returned to India in May 1765 and began to curtail the merchants' abuses.[28] It is possible that Rennell's appointment as surveyor general might have had its roots in complaints to Clive about the sudden decline in his fortunes.

The character of Rennell's appointment is clear from the council's explanation to the Court of Directors. Noting that "accurate surveys" were essential both for military and revenue purposes, the council further noted that a survey of Bengal "must ever be imperfect while it is in separate and unconnected plans." The council had therefore appointed "Captain Rennell, a young man of distinguished merit in this branch [of knowledge]" with instructions "to form one general chart from those already made, and [from] such as are now on hand as they can be collected in." The monthly salary was justified in terms of the damage already done to Rennell's health and the future hardships of surveying. The council also noted that Rennell was not barred by this order from undertaking surveys himself and, indeed, shortly thereafter Rennell was given no less than four officers to assist him in the surveys. Nonetheless, the onus of the position was on Rennell's archival construction of the general maps.[29]

Rennell had already defined much of Bengal's geographical structure. As Cameron's successor after April 1764, he had surveyed the Ganges, the Brahmaputra, and several of their distributaries. His work was given a more coherent goal with Clive's order, received in October 1765, "to set about forming a general Map of Bengall with all Expedition."[30] Clive had just forced the Mughal emperor to make the Company the diwan of Bengal and Bihar, thereby formalizing the Company's authority over the provinces. No doubt Clive was motivated by the need for even basic geographical knowledge, but the immediate cause was the request by his old friend Robert Orme to "make me a vast map of Bengal" for use in the second volume of his history of the Company's military victories in India.[31] Rennell was given an assistant for the task: William Richards, an ensign in the Bengal engineers. They worked very hard over the next fifteen months, delayed by Rennell's four-month incapacitation by serious wounds he received in an ambush in February 1766. Even though their river and road surveys were cursory, Rennell and Richards could not completely cover the whole province before they had to construct the final maps in time for Clive's departure for Britain late in January 1767.[32]

As surveyor general, Rennell did take to the field. With the four army officers who were appointed to assist him, he extended, filled-in, and sometimes replaced his earlier work. But his time was increasingly spent in map compilation in Dacca. (He was quite averse to Calcutta, which he found "disagreeable.")[33] His last recorded survey expedition was in February 1771; most of the fieldwork was completed by the end of 1771, although some final areas were surveyed in 1776. In Dacca, Rennell produced numerous maps for the Bengal government and for the directors in London. Although he seriously considered retiring during the period of 1769 to 1771, in the end he persevered in the face of worsening health and did not leave India until April 1777.[34] On his return to Britain, he was able to parley his professional standing into a successful career as a commercial geographer tied very closely to the establishment. Of particular relevance to the following discussion was his publication of his surveys as *A Bengal Atlas* in 1780, with a second edition in 1781.[35]

The Bengal survey can be seen as the first systematic, regional survey in British India. But unlike later surveys, it relied for its coherency on Rennell's compilation of the final maps. His assistant surveyors had varying skill levels and instruments of variable quality such that there was little that was "systematic" about the survey as a whole. In a cover letter to a general map of Bengal and Bihar which Rennell sent to the court in January 1774, he stressed the laborious nature of his work as a cartographic compiler. The map was generated from "500 original surveys," being "the work of 10 different gentlemen." With "so great a diversity of Instruments and Measures, the lines of Bearing and Distance" frequently disagreed "and indeed the Truth is, that the Comparing and Correcting of them employed a large portion of the time."[36] That is, what has usually been treated as a single survey of Bengal should more properly be considered as numerous distinct, linear surveys which owed their certainty and truth to being fitted into the graticule of the geographical map.

The ambiguity of Rennell's position as surveyor general stemmed from the twin factors of a lack of data and a lack of personnel. Rennell had to go into the field to gather the necessary information. Once the basic coverage was completed, Rennell established the epistemological barrier between field surveys and office compilation. When in October 1777 the Calcutta council found it necessary to "revive" the position, they appointed another engineer, Thomas Call. The surveyor general was now construed as an office job. There was no longer the possibility of field surveying as had been entertained when Rennell was appointed surveyor general. Call's orders stipulated that his job was to be "receiving and compiling the Maps and Reports of the Surveyors now on duty." The first regulations for the office, promulgated 5 August 1779, and still in effect in 1817, reinforced the status of the surveyor general as the Bengal government's cartographic expert.[37]

The four positions of "assistants to the surveyor general," which had been created under Rennell, were nominally revived after 1777. One of the four positions was used after 1788 for an officer who managed the cartographic archive in Calcutta. Each surveyor general applied to the council to use the assistants on particular projects, but the council did not always agree. The positions seem instead to have devolved into a means of supporting officers in other activities; by 1801, only the office manager was left. Geographical data continued therefore to be derived from more sporadic sources, such as the route surveys. For example, prodding by Call (as chief engineer) and Mark Wood (surveyor general) led the council to engage Reuben Burrow, a civilian who was then teaching engineer cadets in Calcutta, to establish latitudes *and longitudes* of cities throughout the lower plains; Burrow did so from 1787 to 1789. (Orme's request to Clive that the map of Bengal be based on longitudes was finally implemented.)

The office of surveyor general was not a senior staff position. Call (1777–86), Wood (1786–88), and Alexander Kyd (1788–94) all held the position because of their status as the second most senior engineer. Both Call and Wood resigned from the job when they succeeded to the position of chief engineer. All three, like Rennell before them, served as practicing engineers when necessary. Kyd finally resigned as surveyor general because he had too many other duties as an engineer. Of

Rennell's successors in the eighteenth century, only Call actively constructed new maps, in particular a twenty-sheet "Atlas of India" (see chapter 6).

The field/office distinction was broken once more—by Robert Colebrooke. After his resignation in 1794, Kyd was still the second-ranking engineer, so new criteria were used to select the surveyor general, specifically seniority of rank within the cadre of surveying officers. Francis Wilford, an engineer who had been surveying Benares since 1788, had served longer as an "assistant to the surveyor general," but Colebrooke, an infantry officer, was higher in the army list and so got the job. (Colebrooke did not get the position because he had since 1789 been the officer in charge of the surveyor general's office in Calcutta.) An avid surveyor, Colebrooke took to the field himself to provide geographical information when the Company's territorial expansion in the Gangetic Plains simultaneously caused not only a shortage of survey officers (they were all needed for regimental duty) and a shortfall in revenues, but also an increase in the demand for new data on the region. Colebrooke died on survey duty in 1808; his position was given to, and held simultaneously by, the chief engineer, John Garstin (1808–13) who reestablished the field/office distinction.

Regulating Surveyors and
Geographical Information

One rather surprising point in the very initial period of Bengal surveys was that the surveyor generals did not maintain the archive of maps and survey journals. There seems to have been no clear allocation of responsibility for this task. In order to preserve the maps, and to save the cost of repeat surveys, the Calcutta council directed in June 1768 that all geographical documents ought to be stored in the governor's care; the council's secretary was to maintain a list. It was not until 1787 that those maps were moved to the surveyor general's office, although there was no attempt to recapture all of the maps held by other officers. A request by Mark Wood for an assistant to run the drawing office, essential considering how the surveyor general's time was divided among several jobs, was approved by the court in 1788. Robert Colebrooke was appointed to that position in June 1789.

These last developments were part of the increasing efforts by the Bengal government—especially under Lord Cornwallis (1786–91) and Lord Wellesley (1798–1805)—to control the flow of information to Calcutta and to make their increasingly territorial administrations more efficient and effective. As Bayly makes clear, the British did not simply

tap into the existing intelligence systems. They progressively intensified their control over them; they matched them with their numerous
statistical and geographical surveys. The management of information
was rationalized in Calcutta with the formation in the 1790s of a Persian
department to handle the "Persian correspondence." (The Persian secretaries Neil B. Edmonstone and Henry T. Prinsep will appear in Part
Three as ardent supporters of mapmaking efforts in the nineteenth century.) The British tried to control the information flow physically, by
building up their own postal system, although this did take several decades. The British also formalized their relationship with their newswriters, informants, and subordinate princes; whereas Robert Clive and
Warren Hastings had accepted that information sources would naturally disseminate intelligence to each side in a conflict, Cornwallis and
Wellesley insisted that any communication with an enemy was an act
of treason against the Company. The Company's own officials were in
1799 strictly prohibited against disclosing information to newspapers.
That is, the Company *tried* to emulate the development in Europe of the
information-controlling bureaucracy of the modern state.[38]

The regularization of information flows into Calcutta functioned according to the archival ideal of knowledge construction. The data
would come from *ad hoc* observation and would then be rationalized
within the urban archive. The bureaucrats in Calcutta could not effectively regulate the acts of observation; what they could regulate, however, were the flow of data, once observed, and the observers. This is
clear in the case of the surveys. By 1817, the regulations for the Bengal
"Surveyor General's and Surveying Department" (the title's dichotomy
is itself revealing) totaled fifty-eight paragraphs from twenty-seven
different orders, originally promulgated between 5 August 1779 and
1 May 1815.[39] Those paragraphs fall into four categories: fifteen on survey techniques; sixteen on administrative points; eleven on salaries and
expenses; and the final sixteen on the distribution of survey journals
and maps.

One of the fifteen paragraphs concerning the techniques and duties
of the surveyor in the field was generic and utterly vague: "the
commander-in-chief expects that all officers employed on surveys, in
the several branches of the public service, will consider it [to be] a duty
of the utmost importance, and [will] always exercise the strictest inspection and scrutiny accordingly."[40] The other fourteen paragraphs
specified the manner in which the route taken by each army detachment was to be surveyed. The original standing order, dated 29 September 1788, required each commanding officer to appoint a junior officer
to take note of "the computed distances, the towns, villages and rivers

on their routes, the nature of the roads and places of encampment, or any other observations which they may deem material." It was subsequently modified in January 1804 to define explicitly the form in which the measurements were to be recorded (four columns, not unlike the cadastral traverse of figure 3.7, with horizontal lines marking each place of halt, etc.).[41] Although these regulations sought to ensure the generation of a large quantity of easily comparable geographic information, they could specify neither the skills to be possessed by the survey officers nor the precise quality to which the journals and maps should adhere. The acquisition of geographical knowledge by such means remained haphazard: it depended on where the army detachments happened to march and it led to substantial duplication. Nor could these regulations apply to regional surveys undertaken at the behest of the directors, of one of the presidency councils, or of a field commander.

All of the other regulations were intended to reconcile each new mapmaking activity with the existing hierarchies of discipline (who reported to whom) and authority (rank and pay). In each instance, the field surveyor served at the pleasure of the council; only the council could approve petitions from the surveyors for health leave or for more expenses; only the council could take the officers away from survey duty. The surveyor general was an expert buffer between the council and the officers detached from their regiments for survey duty. He advised the council, when asked; he composed the professional instructions for each survey, at the council's request; and he received and appraised the results of each survey. There was little reflection on how this system of downward flow of orders and upward flow of information was to operate. The regulations were mostly established by the administration's reaction to events and circumstances beyond its immediate control. The issues resolved were varied but one theme stands out: the regulations established the lines and nature of communication between levels in the hierarchy. Surveyors had to send reports to the surveyor general monthly; the surveyor general reported to the military board quarterly, but took his orders from the governor general, to whom he was to submit annual reports; maps and field books had to be submitted in duplicate, one copy for the surveyor general, the other to be sent on to London; and so on. The chain of command was really a chain of communication. For officials to communicate beyond the scope of their authorized correspondents required the explicit, and temporary, permission of each presidency council. Orders passed down the administrative hierarchy from the presidency to the largely autonomous officers in the field; in return, the field officers sent back a vast mass of reports, statistical information, narratives, and maps. For geographical information, the key actors were the officers at each presidency who were charged with storing the data and with compiling maps. Similar configurations are found in other compendia of regulations for all three presidencies.[42]

The *ad hoc* position of the individual surveyors was reinforced in the financial recompense awarded them for their labors. Every officer in the Company's three armies received a salary based on his regimental rank, that rank being determined by strict seniority. Unlike Crown officers, Company officers could not purchase their rank but progressed by strict seniority. Their regimental salaries were augmented by *batta*, gratuities, and tent allowance. *Batta* began as extra, hazard pay during campaigns but by the 1780s, Madras officers received half *batta* and Bengal officers full *batta* even when in garrison and not on active service. The actual levels of pay and allowances were caught between the officers' keenly felt desire to be paid a viable wage and the court's attempts to impose parity across the three armies and the Crown regiments. The expenses of junior officers outstripped their income so that they were heavily in debt when they finally reached "field rank" of major and above. Unless an officer had a personal income, he had two possible solutions: he might actively pursue postings to active campaigns and so receive full *batta*, with the attendant risk to himself, or he might pursue staff or political positions.

Each staff position—such as deputy assistant quartermaster general, adjutant general, and barracks master—carried its own salary and allowances over and above the officer's regimental pay and *batta*. As an officer received recognition and advanced within the staff, he remained on the regimental roster and continued to advance in seniority and rank. A staff officer had to pay his office costs, including the salaries of his Indian clerks and the rental of office space, but these expenses were usually met by separate budget lines. Staff salaries were pure profit, as it were, and could be substantial. James Rennell had begun in 1767 with a monthly salary as surveyor general of 300 rupees (£27/12), as compared with his pay as a captain of engineers of only 120 rupees (£11/1). His monthly staff salary was increased to 500 rupees (£46) in 1776; under Thomas Call it was increased further to 1,000 rupees (£92), but in the retrenchments of 1785 it was cut back to 500 rupees. Thus in 1800, Colebrooke received 630 rupees (£57/19) monthly in regimental pay and *batta*, as a major in the Bengal infantry, plus his 500 rupees in staff salary.

A similar situation prevailed in the Madras and Bombay presidencies. Indeed, the staff salaries were disproportionate in the Bombay army because of its small regimental salaries. For example, in 1807 Monier Williams was a brevet major in the Bombay infantry, for which he received only 296 rupees (£27/5), but his staff salary as surveyor general of Bombay was over twice as much: 702 rupees (£64/12). In Madras, Colin Mackenzie, a major of engineers in 1810, received monthly regimental pay of 525 rupees (£48/6) and a staff salary as surveyor general of another 1,400 rupees (£128/16). Mackenzie lost out in terms of the proportions of regimental to staff salary when simultaneously appointed surveyor general of India in 1815 and promoted to lieutenant colonel; his regimental pay increased to 790 rupees (£72/14) but his staff salary increased only to 1,500 rupees (£138).

Survey duty in the field and managing the map office in one of the three urban centers were also considered to be staff work and were accompanied by extra salaries. In Bengal, surveyors in the field received a salary greater than the surveyor general: 618 rupees (£56/17) per month, or 858 rupees (£78/19) if surveying rivers because of the expense of renting boats. The Bengal surveyors did, however, have to pay for their own instruments, travel, and establishment, but even with those costs, the survey salary would have been a tidy sum for an ensign or lieutenant. Subalterns deputed by their commanding officer to record the route of an army column's march received an extra 100 rupees (£9/4) per month for the duration of the march. Engineer subalterns in Madras received extra salary equivalent to a captain's subsistence and *batta*, or 56/36/60 pagodas (£21/3) per month, plus another 74/22 pagodas (£27/14) in allowances. Bombay surveyors had no extra salary as such and instead drew full *batta* when in the field.[43]

Most of the special and *ad hoc* surveys did not fall into these neat salary categories. Salaries for their officers seem to have been fixed through negotiation by the surveyor and the respective administration, subject of course to approval by the directors in London. Mackenzie, for example, began at a monthly 400 pagodas (£148/16) for the Mysore survey, but this was cut by the court to 200 pagodas (£72/8) because he was still being paid an extra 200 pagodas per month as engineer with the Hyderabad Subsidiary Force.[44] Allowances for exceptional situations were also set by precedent under the Bengal government. For example, James Blunt temporarily ran the surveyor general's office while Colebrooke was surveying in the plains; Blunt's 200 rupees (£18/8) extra salary was accordingly established by official regulation to be the "allowance of an officer of engineers in charge of the surveyor general's office." Similar precedents were set for the allowances for officers surveying army cantonments.[45]

The negotiability of the surveyor's extra allowances distanced him from the formal administrative system of the Company's army. Survey duty was something to be sought out by the able and willing officer. Unless that officer was able to attain an appointment within the office of the surveyor general, or perhaps that of the quartermaster general, survey duty was inherently temporary.

The final set of paragraphs from the 1817 Bengal regulations, numbering sixteen in all, were concerned with limiting, or at the least controlling, the distribution of maps. The Company was faced with a recurring problem, specifically that of surveyors or their commanding officers who treated their maps as private property. Many maps did not find their way to the central administration in Calcutta, nor to the directors in London. Several attempts were therefore made to ensure that surveyors' journals reached the surveyor general's office and that the distribution of the general maps was controlled. Initially, property rights were given as the principal reason for the controls: the directors had funded the collection of the data and the construction of the maps and, from 1768 on, they wanted to ensure that their rights in the matter were preserved.[46]

Most of the first survey regulations of August 1779, still in effect in 1817, dealt with the Company's possession of geographic information. They required all surveyors to give up *all* of their field books and maps upon completion of a survey. Moreover, the surveyor general could "not furnish . . . to any person whatever, copies of any maps or plans of the country, without an order in writing, from the [Military] Board or the commander in chief." If he did, or if he otherwise allowed maps to be distributed, he would be subject to dismissal. Later regulations (1809) required all of the administrators and bureaucrats in Calcutta, even the governor general and the council members, to surrender all of their own maps. If they needed a map, then the surveyor general was to bring it to them; if required to be left overnight, "they are to be secured under lock and key"; maps issued to field officers required a receipt and a "declaration that the papers will be kept secret and no copies taken of them."[47]

Similar regulations were current in Madras and Bombay. But as in Bengal, they seem to have been unevenly enforced. For example, the chief engineer in Madras lost control of his collection of maps and plans in 1776–77, when factional disputes on the council led to the imprisonment of the governor, Lord Pigot. Conversely in 1800, Arthur Wellesley could not order an engineer under his command to give him a copy of a map of the major fortress at Seringapatnam because the engineer had received no order to do so from the Madras council.[48]

The Napoleonic Wars greatly intensified the Company's desire to keep its geographic materials secret. Rennell had been able to publish his *A Bengal Atlas* (1780 and 1781) because his maps were not very large in scale (five miles to the inch, or 1:316,800) and because his profits would constitute a reward for an arduous service. Rennell then went on to publish his maps of India. However, the court stopped sharing geographical data with Rennell "soon after 1788," presumably because the resurgence of the Anglo-French struggle for empire made "the publication of any geographical matter relating to India imprudent."[49] The directors were explicit in their orders of October 1809 that "for reasons which need not be particularly stated . . . our declared enemies or any individual disaffected to our government" should be prevented from "obtaining valuable information touching the Geography of British India, or of any of the Countries belonging to the neighboring Princes or States of Hindostan."[50] Just the hint that Mackenzie might want to publish his 1808 maps of Mysore was sufficient for the directors to dismiss any such project on principle.[51] Until the end of the wars, all but the smallest-scale maps remained in manuscript.

The Company's restrictions were not directed toward hostile Indian states, which were assumed to possess a complete geographical knowledge of their own territories. Instead, the British sought to restrict the information available to other European powers, specifically the French. This rational for the secrecy of geographic information was made explicit by the Board of Control in 1811. The court had relented in its resolve and had given permission to Colebrooke's widow to publish his maps of India for her own benefit, as long as doing so would not be "productive of injury to the Company's interests." The board's objections were strong enough for it to overrule the court. While military maps "may undoubtedly be of use to our own officers," the president wrote, "they may also, at a future period, get into the hands of Europeans [that is, the French] acting in hostility to the Company."[52]

The repeated strictures against the unauthorized dissemination of maps points to the continued distribution of maps and surveyor's journals. The examples of two engineers in Madras demonstrate the existence of a fairly active trade in geographical materials among at least the more serious surveyors. Mackenzie's "general collection" contains documents pertaining to many surveys in southern India; he also broke the Company's correspondence guidelines by sending packets of official documents to his friends in London in order to help them plead his case to the directors.[53] Then again, as the premier cartographer in southern India, Mackenzie is perhaps not typical. Thomas DeHavilland was a less accomplished surveyor, although Mackenzie thought him "an active, enterprizing man" who aspired to "éclat as a Geographer." As an engineer and surveyor on duty since 1797, DeHavilland had by 1810 built up a collection comprising: some fifty-four route maps, dating back to the 1770s; thirty district maps, such as John Mather's of the Baramahal (1798) and Colebrooke's of Awadh (1800); five general maps of the Deccan, including Mackenzie's (1796) and his own (1807); plus nineteen more maps of areas beyond India.[54]

After Napoleon's defeat in 1815, the Company's position with respect to the publication and dissemination of large-scale maps gradually eased. A story seems to have circulated among Company officials in about 1837 which demonstrated the futility of trying to keep geographic information secret. Thomas Jervis wrote that shortly after returning to Europe in 1835, Lord William Bentinck had visited the Depôt de la guerre in Paris, only to find on open display a map which accurately showed the supposedly secret disposition of the Company's troops in India.[55] Certainly, the rhetoric of secrecy had all but disappeared by then. Nonetheless, the directors continued to be jealous of the dissemination of geographical information without proper authorization. The directors made it quite clear that the Company possessed proprietary rights in the information gathered by its officers. In 1822 and 1823 the court actively sought the return of the maps of India constructed by Charles Reynolds and Colebrooke from their respective executors, and in 1828 it specifically prohibited Company officials from treating their maps as private property and publishing them on their own account. (Such had happened, for example, with Sir John Malcolm's map of the Narmada valley, published by Arrowsmith in 1823.)[56]

The Company's institutional aversion to the dissemination of geographic information meant that, before the 1840s, its large-scale mapping was almost entirely manuscript. The aversion was initially self-reinforcing: if maps were not to be published, then copies had to be kept to a minimum in order to minimize errors.[57] There was little problem with publishing relatively small-scale maps of India in London, as long as it was done under the Company's patronage and authority. Through the 1810s and 1820s, the official demand for larger-scale maps steadily grew until it outweighed the ability to make sufficient manuscript copies. This situation led to the slow easing of the Company's restrictions on publishing larger-scale maps that might be of military use. The same period saw the realization both that Britain's competitors for empire were far more capable in their acquisition of sensitive knowledge than had been hitherto thought and that the surveyor generals were less capable than had been thought in keeping their geographic information secret. The result was a steady increase in map publication—both official and private—in London and in India through the rest of the nineteenth century.[58]

Patronage and the Hierarchy
of Cartographic Expertise

The East India Company's official regulation of maps and mapmaking thus focused on two principal topics: the control of the geographic information produced by surveys and the placement of the surveyors within the administrative hierarchy. However, those regulations covered neither the surveys themselves nor the processes of map-compilation. The one exception concerned the sporadic surveys of routes of army detachments which were undertaken by delegated infantry officers who might not have had any survey training. The small cadre of "proper" surveyors undertook the majority of regional surveys without formal regulations. Each member of the cadre was recognized by the administrators as possessing a certain cartographic expertise by dint of his training and experience. And, importantly, the administrators did not possess that expertise.

The issue of expertise means that the bureaucratic position of the surveys was very similar to that of government science in general. Modern bureaucratic hierarchies can be characterized by the progressive increase in knowledge (although not facts), experience, expertise, authority, and responsibility through each level of the hierarchy; at the pinnacle is the ultimate bureaucrat sitting atop an immense dendritic network of information and power. This overly neat characterization is challenged by the specialist, who necessarily possesses greater knowledge than his administrative superiors. Those superiors are incompetent to judge the merits of the specialist's work and so cannot be responsible for it.[59] Time and time again, senior military and political officials in India expressed themselves as being unwilling or unable to understand the work that went into the maps they valued so highly. Lord Amherst told George Everest, for example, that he did not "have the leisure to attend" to explanations of the work of the Great Trigonometrical Survey; even Lord William Bentinck, the most technophilic governor general and Amherst's successor, assured Everest that he "never understood" those explanations despite Everest's "painful efforts to divest them of all obscurities."[60]

Accordingly, the administrators of the three presidencies were unable to promulgate any regulations governing the actual practices of the topographic, revenue, and trigonometrical surveys. They had to rely on the surveyors to regulate themselves within their own separate and informal hierarchy of knowledge and skills. The functioning of this "mini-hierarchy" and its intersection with the Company's predominant hierarchy of political and military control were governed by the established patronage system. Membership of the core cadre of surveyors depended as much on the willingness of officers to serve as surveyors as on their ability to do so; and the willingness to serve depended on their perception of the benefits they would receive. Conversely, entry into and subsequent promotion (increase in staff rank and professional stature) within the mini-hierarchy was controlled by the administrators and politicians who possessed the power to appoint officers to new tasks.

Strictly speaking, *patronage* refers to financial resources which are within the power of an individual or corporation to grant to other individuals. The most common form of patronage in eighteenth- and early nineteenth-century Britain were the "livings" (priesthoods) in the Church of England owned by local landowners and bestowed by them on individuals for a variety of familial, social, and personal reasons. The situation was of course more complex for corporations like the East India Company. Each of the directors possessed personal patronage: they each appointed a certain number of cadets and writers every year.[61] Once within the Company's service, however, individuals were promoted in rank by strict seniority.

Except for the most senior positions, which were controlled by the Crown, the patronage of staff appointments was possessed by the Court of Directors. That is, the appointments were made by the court's chairmen and its powerful secretariat, which enjoyed great leeway in "interpreting the Court's wishes."[62] The court usually ratified the staff appointments made by the councils in India. The administrators in London remained jealous of their powers of appointment and did, on occasion, preempt or overturn appointments made in India. In this respect, the court took a particular interest in the surveyor generals: in 1777 the court wanted James Rennell's assistant William Richards rather than Thomas Call to be surveyor general of Bengal, but Richards retired due to ill-health; it refused to allow the appointment of a surveyor general at Madras until 1810; it appointed Colin Mackenzie surveyor general of India in 1814; it revoked John Hodgson's 1821 appointment in favor of Valentine Blacker; in 1837 it appointed Thomas Best Jervis to succeed Everest. To be appointed to a staff position, an officer therefore had to have the *interest* of key administrators in their presidency, whether councillors themselves or their advisors. To be certain in his appointment, the officer would need interest among the directors in London as well.

The moral economy of corporate patronage was straightforward. The support of surveying gave the Company three essential benefits. First, and most obviously, the surveyors generated and organized information, thereby allowing the Company to exercise power over India. Second, the exercise of patronage was a means to control and to ensure loyalty among the Company's servants. Third, the presence of clearly loyal servants legitimated the Company's sovereignty in the eyes of politicians in Britain, of Indian princes, and of other European states. This last point was particularly relevant to the prestige garnered from the Company's support of surveying and science.[63]

In return, the surveyors would acquire the interest of their superiors. In 1829, for example, Everest identified a "crowd" of surveyors "who possess quite talent sufficient, and *morale* sufficient," and who wished to be "brought forward" to the directors' attention.[64] Such attention translated into professional advancement within the Company. Once granted, a staff position was almost the personal property of an individual officer, from which he could not be removed except by his resignation or promotion. For example, in 1810 the Madras council abolished the position of Company's astronomer, which was then held *pro tem* by John Warren; when John Goldingham returned to Madras in 1812, he took up the position once more. Again, when the court overturned Hodgson's appointment as surveyor general in 1821, the Calcutta council felt obliged to create for him an equivalent position as "revenue surveyor general."

By "doing science" the surveyors would also enhance their social standing, could possibly be elected to scientific societies, and might even attain "genteel" status. Overall, they would achieve financial security. Everest himself was perhaps the most successful of the surveyors in this regard when he returned to Britain. He became a visitor (that is, governor) of the Royal Observatory and a council member of the Royal Geographical Society; after twenty more years of petitions he was knighted. Rennell might have traded his commission for the role of a commercial geographer and the status of "pseudo-gentry," in which he was emulated by Jervis in the 1840s, but Everest built on his family's position in the lesser gentry to become a "true gentleman."[65]

Field surveyors risked much in the name of career advancement. Everest's later career indicates that he had consciously calculated that his self-advancement would outweigh the threat to his health. I have described above how his health deteriorated in the 1820s; it got worse in the 1830s and he decided to retire once he was promoted to lieutenant colonel. When promoted in 1838 he discovered that because of his lengthy furloughs in the 1820s he would not receive a colonel's pension unless he stayed on until 1843. And this he did, despite the risk involved. Everest's actions point to the expectations of all of the surveyors to receive benefit from their service. They might have had other motives—evangelical officers like Jervis were religiously inspired to improve the lot of the "ignorant heathen" in India—but all had a healthy interest for self-advancement.

Undertaking surveys was a potentially difficult approach to advancing one's career. Beyond the Company's formal hierarchy and institutional system of returns, the surveyors were part of informal networks of acquaintance and interest. An aspiring officer expanded his network of interest through his social connections. The ability of junior officers to gain access to the council chambers and to gain the ear of governors and commanders in chief depended on their personal relationships. But by definition, surveying required the officer to be in the field for long periods, when he would be absent from urban society and so denied the possibility of developing his social position. As a result, the officer's chances of advancement would diminish. In return, the surveyors gambled that their work itself would bring them to the attention of councillors and directors; to reinforce their position, the surveyors lost no opportunity to submit petitions explaining at great length the reasons why they deserved their superior's interest. The deployment of interest not only paralleled and reinforced class superiority, it was also a form of investment. Thus William Lambton, who had advanced into a circle of well-connected politicians in Madras, recorded his indebtedness to a friend in England: "I received a letter from Mr. King, and will write him when my eyes are a little better—in the meantime I shall relieve the wants of his son. Heaven is now granting me those favors by which others have had the means of relieving me."[66]

But, as noted, the surveyors' social and political patrons could not define the workings of the surveys or of other scientific enquiries beyond the regular administrative details of authority and discipline. To ensure that the surveyors did not abuse the discretion necessarily awarded them, the administrators had by 1800 formed them into a hierarchy of expert judges. Each surveyor's position in the hierarchy was defined by his level of interest: the more interest, the higher the position, and vice versa. Surveyors close to each administration were charged with the task of certifying that the lesser surveyors had indeed fulfilled their duties properly and so should receive the financial benefits. This hierarchy of observation, and thus of control, was extended to embrace the non-British surveyors so they became the instruments of their military overseers, with their work subject to corroboration and correction. Even if the labor was not British, their surveys still were.

The hierarchy in India was represented by the surveyor general at each presidency (the chief engineer or quartermaster general at Madras before 1810), who was to attest to the accuracy and quality of the maps, records, and journals submitted by the surveyors. The allowance for those officers deputed to measure an army's route was not paid until the surveyor general certified the work, and surveyors' contingent expenses were not paid until all of their work had been received by the surveyor general. Mackenzie evaluated the work of Lambton's Great Trigonometrical Survey as well as Aaron Arrowsmith's *Improved Map of India* (1816). Hodgson assessed Monier William's updated version of Charles Reynolds's map of India.[67] And so on. Most surveyors did produce the required maps and reports, but there were occasional failures. One instance is provided by Alexander Laidlaw, a civilian, who was attached in 1817 to William Webb's survey of the recently conquered district of Kumaon with responsibility for determining the location of metallic ores. Despite his effusive responses to Hodgson's repeated requests for reports, he submitted only bills and was eventually dismissed by the Bengal council in 1818.[68]

The uppermost tier of the hierarchy was situated in London. Rennell was the Company's mapping expert from 1780 until his death in 1830. His judgment seems to have been supplemented in the 1820s by that of Colonel James Salmond, the court's military secretary.[69] When Salmond died in December 1837, the court turned to the cartographer John Walker, until he grew senile in the late 1860s. These men assessed new mapping schemes proposed in either India or Britain and they reported on the quality of the final products. When a particularly exceptional map arrived from India, or when a surveyor petitioned for remuneration over and above his salary, Rennell, Salmond, or Walker first had to approve the work before the court would award large monetary rewards. For example, the court awarded Mackenzie 2,400 pagodas (£900) for his 1796 map of the Deccan, once Rennell had approved it, and it gave Reynolds the huge sum of two lakhs of rupees (£18,400), one lakh for expenses and another as reward. The court approved, probably at Salmond's behest, the 10,300 rupees (£950) granted to Jervis by the Bombay government in 1836 for the survey and census of Konkan.[70]

Despite its reputation for parsimony, the court was more than willing to make or approve these rewards, even as it always ensured that the surveyors' immediate allowances were kept within tight limits. For example, the court had immediately halved Mackenzie's allowances on the Mysore survey, began in 1799; it repeatedly directed that the survey be finished as soon as possible; and it rejected all appeals from the Madras government for an increase in Mackenzie's allowances, until Rennell could judge the final map. Rennell's report was glowing, so the court eventually awarded Mackenzie the sum of 9,000 pagodas (£3,350).[71] By holding out the promise of a lump sum reward for excellent work, the court managed both to control and to entice the surveyors.

The mini-hierarchy of cartographic expertise did not constitute a formal survey organization. The power to move military officers to and from survey duty, together with the right to allocate funds to pay staff salaries and the contingent expenses associated with any survey, remained firmly in the hands of the court and the governing councils, the court's delegated representatives in India. The mini-hierarchy was intertwined with the administrative hierarchy which sought to channel information from the field officers to the central urban bureaucracies. On the other hand, the mini-hierarchy provided a foundation on which the administrative responsibilities of the surveyor generals did eventually build into the Survey of India of the later nineteenth century. The origins of an extensive, detailed India-wide survey, and thus of the regularization of the mini-hierarchy as a formal structure, lie in the Madras presidency in the early nineteenth century and are discussed in the following chapter.

The Working of Interest:
Burrow, Mackenzie, and Lambton

The manner in which interest functioned is best illustrated by contrasting the experiences of Reuben Burrow, William Lambton, and Colin Mackenzie. Born within nine years of each other (between 1747 and 1756), they all came from humble backgrounds in regions distant from Britain's metropolitan centers. Largely self-taught in mathematics, astronomy, and surveying, they became members of the professional and state-supported groups who in the early 1800s challenged the established scientific elites. All three died "in harness" in India. Burrow and Mackenzie also shared orientalist interests. But the three differed considerably in the means of their advancement through the British hierarchies of knowledge and rank and in their ability to undertake new cartographic activities. A comparison of their histories is thus revealing.

Reuben Burrow (or Burrough) was born near Leeds in 1747, the son of a small farmer. Like most other civilian mathematicians, he supported himself as a mathematical teacher and entrepreneur. He worked for the astronomer royal, Nevil Maskelyne, from 1771 to 1774, simultaneously working as a tutor in Greenwich. He founded *The Ladies Diary or Women's Almanac* in 1775 and he continued to publish it when in 1776 he became the mathematics and surveying teacher in the Board of Ordnance's [map] Drawing Room in the Tower of London. His intemperate character alienated his superiors and erstwhile supporters. He quarreled with Maskelyne; he sued Charles Hutton—the son of a Newcastle colliery worker, who was now mathematics master at the Royal Military Academy, Woolwich, thanks to Maskelyne's interest—over Hutton's own almanac. He was obliged to quit the Tower after he talked back to the master general of Ordnance, the duke of Richmond; Burrow recorded that after a rebuke from the duke, he had "looked at [the duke] with all the insolence and blackness of hell, and told him that . . . [he] did not chuse to put up with impertinence from anybody." After Burrow's death, even a supporter could "offer no excuse for Mr. B.'s scurrility and obscenity." [72]

Despite his character, Burrow did acquire the interest of one patron: Henry Watson of the Bengal engineers. While on furlough in London, Watson had recommended Burrow for the job in the Ordnance drawing room.[73] On his resignation in 1782, Burrow took Watson's advice to go out to India and set up shop as a private mathematics teacher in Calcutta. He arrived early in 1783 and entered into the fringes of Calcutta's small intellectual circle, which just then was crystallizing into the Asiatic Society of Bengal. He submitted several papers to the early issues of the society's journal, *Asiatic Researches*, including one on Hindu mathematics. He used Watson's connection to write to Warren Hastings, the governor general and well-known orientalist, on the need for an investigation of Hindu mathematics and astronomy and for extensive observations of latitude and longitude throughout India, in which he ignored James Rennell's work, if he ever knew of it.[74]

The Company's patronage system remained inaccessible to Burrow until 1784 when Watson, as chief engineer, recommended him for the post of mathematical master to the engineer officers at Calcutta (part of yet another attempt to overcome the chronic shortage of trained engineers). Watson left India soon after, but Burrow was able to capitalize on his position. Thomas Call, former surveyor general and now chief engineer, persuaded the Calcutta council to hire Burrow to make astronomical observations for latitude and longitude throughout northern India, to aid the construction of Call's general map. Burrow spent from July 1787 to January 1788 on this task, with a second season from September 1788 to May 1789. Burrow was then selected to measure two geodetic arcs—one each along a parallel and a meridian—which had been suggested in London by William Roy in 1784 (see chapter 5). The court had intended to send out the necessary instruments in 1789, but contractual problems meant that the instruments never arrived. Even so, Burrow measured the two arcs in 1790–91 near Krishnanagar, just north of Calcutta on the Tropic of Cancer; without instruments, he performed the measurement by laying rods directly along the ground. The following field season, Burrow sought to make further corrections to the existing maps of Bengal, but he died at Buxar in June 1792.[75]

Burrow thus represents the lower class of "mathematical practitioners" who survived through their own entrepreneurial efforts as tutors and as authors. There is no doubt that he had the necessary skills for a scientific career, but his antagonistic character prevented him from developing the necessary social connections. It was not until after 1815 that the scientific institutions in London were forced to accept individuals who lacked the proper social background provided by either genteel birth or an official, "covenanted" appointment in the military or civil bureaucracy which conferred pseudo-gentility; in fact, the established societies found it hard to accommodate the new professional scientists who in turn resorted to establishing their own societies organized by intellectual discipline rather than by social connection.[76] Without formal rank in the Company's hierarchy, Burrow and the few others like him had to rely on their own merits and reputations for their *entire* social position. Covenanted officials like Mackenzie could rise that much higher intellectually and professionally.

A few years Burrow's junior, Colin Mackenzie was born in 1754 in Stornoway, the chief port of Lewis in the Outer Hebrides.[77] Mackenzie was doubly indebted to his clan chief, also the Lewis proprietor, for his Indian career. According to his longtime friend, Alexander Johnstone, Mackenzie's mathematical abilities when still "a very young man" had drawn Lord Fortrose's attention. This seems to have led to his appointment, sometime before 1778, to be comptroller of customs for Lewis. Fortrose's son, the earl of Seaforth, employed Mackenzie to write an account of Hindu mathematics for Francis, fifth Lord Napier of Merchiston. Napier had planned, but did not complete, a biography of his seventeenth-century ancestor, John Napier, who had devised logarithms; Mackenzie's hiring was probably motivated by the contemporary idea that decimal digits originated in ancient India.[78] Mackenzie seems to have been strictly self-taught in mathematics; he probably did not attend any university.[79] After Napier's death in 1773, Mackenzie "became very desirous of prosecuting his Oriental researches in India."[80] By 1781, Seaforth had managed to secure a position for his clansman in the Madras infantry. The delay perhaps indicates that Mackenzie took some time to decide whether to join the flood of Highlanders leaving Scotland to seek their fortunes in the new empire, his elder and younger brothers having already emigrated to Canada.

In his third year in India, in 1786, Mackenzie was able to transfer to the engineers. He thereafter automatically climbed the ladder of seniority within that corps and so benefited from progressively higher rank, salary, and prestige. He reached full colonel in August 1819; in 1815 he was awarded the Order of the Bath, the dedicated military order, although only at the junior rank of commander (CB). Mackenzie soon made a name for himself as a courageous siege engineer and as the Company's most capable surveyor. The 1790–92 war with Tipu Sultan of Mysore introduced Mackenzie to Lord Cornwallis, the governor general. After Tipu's surrender, Cornwallis specifically directed that Mackenzie be the engineer and surveyor for the British force attached to the Nizam of Hyderabad. But Mackenzie had little time to survey the Deccan because he was repeatedly detached to engineering tasks: he participated in the siege of Pondicherry in 1793; he took to the field with the Nizam's army against the Marathas in 1795; he was senior engineer on the Ceylon expedition in 1796; he prepared for the abortive Manila expedition in 1797; and, in 1799 he was chief engineer of the Nizam's forces, under Arthur Wellesley's command, during the final campaign against Tipu, in which he played a significant role in the assault on the great fortress of Seringapatnam.

Mackenzie was thereafter employed primarily as a surveyor in Mysore and other regions of southern India (see chapter 5). After fourteen years of petitions and memoranda, he was in October 1810 appointed to be the first surveyor general of Madras. Even so, he continued to serve as an engineer after 1799, most notably with Stamford Raffles' expedition to Java during the years of 1811 to 1814. Upon his return, Mackenzie found himself nominated by the court to be the first surveyor general of India; he spent his last years in Calcutta, fighting the climate, until his death on 8 May 1821 as he sailed up-river in search of more salubrious air.

On his appointment as surveyor general of India, Mackenzie had his portrait taken (figure 4.1). He is surrounded by his pandits who offer him a telescope and a palm-leaf manuscript. Atop distant hills are a "basket-and-pole" survey signal and the giant statue at Sravana Belagola, which Mackenzie measured and sketched after Buchanan's failure (chapter 3). The image demonstrates Mackenzie's situation at the center of "the richest skeins of oriental information and intelligence." He epitomized the "ideal of informed British rule": not only did he collect

Figure 4.1 Thomas Hickey, portrait of Colin Mackenzie, surveyor general of India, Calcutta 1816.

To his left, holding the telescope, is Mackenzie's peon Kistnaji. The old pandit proffering a palm-leaf manuscript is probably "the poor old Jain," Dhurmia. Standing slightly
behind Mackenzie is Kavali Venkata Lakshmaiah, who sought to arrange and translate
Mackenzie's historical collections after his death. (By permission of The British Library,
IOR [Painting] 15.)

geographical information, he employed a large body of pandits to collect—or copy—historical manuscripts and inscriptions; he and his assistants drew hundreds of illustrations of Indian architecture and people.[81] When he died, he had amassed a huge collection of some "3,000 stone and copperplate inscriptions, 1,568 literary manuscripts, 2,070 local tracts, and large portfolios and collections of drawings, plans, images, and antiquities."[82]

Mackenzie had, as noted, gone out to India to pursue his interest in Hindu mathematics. On his arrival, he was soon invited to Madura by the late Lord Napier's favorite daughter, Hester Johnstone, wife of Samuel Johnstone, paymaster at Madura, and mother of Alexander. Mrs. Johnstone had already collected a mass of scientific documents and now wanted Mackenzie to help her organize them; she introduced Mackenzie to scholars from Madura's famous Hindu college; and she prompted his idea of collecting historical and literary manuscripts. But it was not until 1796 that Mackenzie had sufficient time and money to employ pandits to construct his collections.[83] And he set about the task with a vengeance. Official support for his collections was forthcoming after 1805, when the directors awarded him 9,000 pagodas (£3,350) for his previous expenses and allowed him free postage; in 1808 the Madras council gave him the sinecure of barrack master of Mysore to allow him to arrange the collection; the Calcutta council continued to fund his staff after his move to Bengal in 1817.

Mackenzie was widely recognized as being a first-rate surveyor and orientalist. Had he not, he would not have been given financial support for his pandits, nor would he have been appointed surveyor general of India. Yet Mackenzie himself was very ambivalent concerning his reputation. He felt that the Madras council and the Court of Directors had mistreated him. He was especially upset when he compared his own problems with the administration to the undeniably favorable treatment of Lambton.

A Yorkshireman like Burrow, William Lambton was born near Northallerton in 1756, or perhaps 1753 (figure 4.2). Even more than Mackenzie, Lambton's early career reveals all the signs of supportive benefactors: the scholarship to the local grammar school; his 1781 commission as an ensign in a militia regiment; his 1782 transfer to a Crown regiment, HM 33rd Foot, then stationed in North America; and, his appointment in 1785 to the civil position of barracks master for New Brunswick, with a comfortable salary of £400 per annum. Lambton stayed behind when the 33rd returned to Britain. His knowledge of the scientific literature on astronomy and geodesy dates from his leisure reading at this time. His principal patron was Brooke Watson, a York-

Figure 4.2 William Havell, portrait of William Lambton, superintendent of the Great Trigonometrical Survey, Hyderabad 1822. (Royal Asiatic Society, London.)

shireman who had served as commissary general in Canada and who became lord mayor of London; Watson had lobbied in London for Lambton's appointment as barracks master. A 1794 change in army policy meant that Lambton could retain either his military or his civil position, but not both. The 33rd were about to embark for India and Watson was of the opinion "(very common in those times in England) that to go to India, and to acquire a fortune there, were the same thing." So Lambton rejoined his regiment.[84]

Lambton reached Calcutta in 1797, already in debt and with serious reservations about having quit his cushy civil position for a lieutenant's meager salary. His status was quite anomalous: he had not served with his regiment for twelve years; moreover, at the age of 41, his claim to be the oldest subaltern in the British army was more than justified. But he soon received a salaried staff appointment. His age, his administrative experience, the fact that the 33rd were to take part in the campaign planned against Mysore, and most importantly Watson's letter of introduction to the commander in chief in India, Sir Alured Clark, secured for Lambton the staff position of brigade major to the King's Troops stationed within the Madras presidency.

Lambton sailed to Madras in the company of his regimental colonel, Arthur Wellesley, and stayed with him once there (it was a common practice for senior or wealthy officers to provide board and lodging for their juniors). Wellesley unsettled Lambton with his aloofness, but he nonetheless formed a high opinion of the new brigade major. Lambton served well during the campaign against Tipu and played a prominent role in the final assault on Seringapatnam in April 1799. Thereafter he joined the staff of the Grand Army as it toured Mysore under Wellesley's command. It was almost certainly at this time that Lambton conceived of undertaking a geodetic triangulation and geographic survey across southern India.[85] Lambton's survey got off the ground because it was supported by Wellesley, his elder brother the governor general, Lord Wellesley, and their friends within the Madras administration, notably the governor, Lord Clive, and the chief secretary, Josiah Webbe, who was one of Lord Wellesley's principal "creatures."[86]

The extent of Lambton's interest is evident from the first threat to his survey. The court had of course referred both Lambton's and Mackenzie's ideas for surveys of Mysore and southern India to James Rennell's expert judgment. From the fragmentary record, it seems that Rennell did not actually see a copy of Lambton's proposal. Writing in early 1801, he referred to the survey as the "Astronomical Survey on the Mysore Establishment" and described it as constituting only an astronomical (not trigonometrical) framework for Mackenzie's survey. Rennell therefore rejected Lambton's plan as being unnecessary: Mackenzie himself could do the work more cheaply and efficiently.[87] While Lambton excused Rennell for his mistake, he still had to deal with a potentially damning opposition in London. So he appealed to an old friend and creditor, the reverend Samuel Peach. "I wish you could be the means, through some of your scientific friends," Lambton wrote, "of impressing the minds of the Court of Directors with the magnitude and importance of my undertaking."[88] This move did not work. What did work, however, was the support shown by the Madras governor. Clive sent a copy of the misunderstood proposal to his uncle and client: Maskelyne, the astronomer royal. Maskelyne intervened and remonstrated with Rennell, who in turn revised his opinions in favor of Lambton; this event opened a lengthy correspondence between Lambton and Maskelyne. The court acquiesced to its expert cartographer.[89]

Clive was just the first of a number of Company politicians and Crown appointees who were motivated in their support for Lambton's survey by two factors: that the trigonometrical survey constituted a desirable *science* which ought to be supported by the Company and that if Lambton did not undertake it, no one else could. Clive, for example, also wanted to expand Lambton's survey to encompass the measurement of an arc of a meridian in the north of India, as Burrow had been contracted to do.[90]

Clive's successor as governor, Lord William Bentinck, was so strong in his support that Lambton could in 1806 bluntly refuse to cut his expenditures. He openly referred to Bentinck's support in his correspondence with the Finance Committee—"I delayed giving an answer to your letter until I had conversed with His Lordship on the subject"— and blithely asserted that the increase in his expenses represented only a "very trifling augmentation" whereas the figures sent to Lambton for explanation represented a 266 percent increase since 1800. (Lambton's expenditures had actually increased by 454 percent: the committee had mistakenly used the figures for Mackenzie's Mysore survey!) Bentinck also played the card that a similarly qualified officer might never again serve in India. The committee members were forced to acquiesce because, as they admitted, they did "not profess themselves competent" to suggest whether or not the survey ought to be curtailed. They could not put forth a creditable reason why such a survey ought to be cut if the expert (Lambton) said that the costs were necessary and if the governor concurred.[91]

After Bentinck's recall, Lambton received the effusive support of William Petrie, councillor and acting governor.[92] The threat to Lambton's expensive survey by the appointment of the penny-pinching Sir George Barlow as governor was more than offset by the interest shown by the new governor general, Lord Minto. Lambton made it clear to the Madras government that Minto had "entirely acquiesced" to Lambton's opinions in a private conversation; this acquiescence might have been polite response to an importunate officer, but as a fellow of the Royal Society, Minto was one of the few scientifically interested politicians then in India.[93]

Nor was there a lack of promotion and recognition for Lambton, although it was slow at first. He was allowed to keep the staff rank, although not the salary, of brigade major until he was finally promoted through seniority to captain in 1807; he was then able to purchase his majority in 1808, with £3,000 of his own money and £2,000 more from the sale of his captaincy. When the 33rd left India in 1811, Lambton's patrons secured a special dispensation for him to stay in India at the Company's expense, together with the brevet rank of lieutenant colonel.[94] In 1817, Lambton's survey was transferred to the Bengal government and finally given an official name: the Great (or Grand) Trigonometrical Survey of India. In the same year he was elected a corresponding member of the Académie des sciences, through the efforts of Warren, who had returned to restoration France to reclaim his birthright; this prompted a belated recognition from the Royal Society, which elected him a fellow in 1818. (Lambton had been publicly recognized in Britain only once before this, by William Playfair in 1813.)[95] By then over sixty years of age, Lambton had largely retired from the active prosecution of the survey; he died in January 1823 while moving his headquarters from Hyderabad to Nagpur.

In comparison with Lambton, Mackenzie thought himself quite mistreated. He found himself trapped. His career was at the whim of his political overseers; he was appointed to the Mysore survey, to be surveyor general of Madras, and then to be surveyor general of India "without solicitation or any [prior] personal knowledge." Moreover, despite the numerous petitions and memoranda he submitted to the Madras council on the subject of how to make surveys properly, the council failed to give him adequate resources. His surveying work was delayed and made all the more difficult by his being detached for more mundane engineering tasks. And when he sought to leave this difficult situation, he was (in his opinion) denied appointments to more sedate staff positions that were more commensurate with his age and rank. Lambton, however, was veritably showered with money, even as Mackenzie had to prosecute the Mysore survey "under a privation of salary and comfort that," even by 1819 had "never yet been remedied."[96] Phillimore has demonstrated that Mackenzie's *personal* relations with Lambton were quite cordial. Even so, it is clear that Mackenzie's attitude toward Lambton's survey could be hostile. Mackenzie argued that his Mysore survey was the equal of Lambton's and that their difference in quality was "really so small as to make very little difference on the scale of common maps."[97] Subsequently, Mackenzie was particularly aggrieved by the failure in 1817 of the governor general to consult him, in his capacity as surveyor general of India, before transferring Lambton's trigonometrical survey to the Calcutta government.[98]

Mackenzie cast himself as the practical soldier who stood at odds with the political machinations of career bureaucrats and staff officers.

"I have no interest with the managing people at Madras about the Governor and particularly in the Military Department," he wrote in 1801. "Mr. Webbe is the only one I could solicit without repugnance to my own feelings." Eighteen years later, he observed that there were only two officials in Calcutta who were not "*Dandies*" and who were concerned with "the more important branches of government concerns": James Stuart and George Dowdeswell, both council members.[99] Like all of those who see their principles as being fundamentally correct and self-evident, Mackenzie lay the blame for his comparative lack of support on anti-intellectualism and party politics. Once, when particularly depressed and discouraged, Mackenzie asserted, without proof as far as I can tell, that the directors had failed (before 1810) to appoint him surveyor general because of "the stubborn prejudices of old [Alexander] Dalrymple and the more selfish insinuations of others in the dark." In Madras, he admitted that he had indeed "personally" received "uniform attentions" from lords Wellesley and Bentinck, but he lacked support among the Company's bureaucrats. He was particularly critical of General James Stuart, whom he accused of actively stalling his attempts to unify the Madras surveys for the benefit of the quartermaster general.[100] And as for the fulsome statement by Petrie that he had "never passed an opportunity of recording my sincere respect and esteem" for "Major Mackenzie's merits," and that in "labor, assiduity, and zeal, he is inferior to no man," Mackenzie derided it as "a Jesuitical evasion."[101]

Mackenzie possessed a sizable circle of friends drawn from the overlapping communities of military officers and orientalists. He relied on them when he pressed his arguments with his superiors and he requested them to intercede on his behalf with the court in London.[102] His social network seems to have been behind the support given to his historical and literary research, but it failed with respect to his cartographic work. Mackenzie received support from some prominent politicians: Bentinck, who told Mackenzie frankly that his hands were tied by the court's orders; Wellesley; and Cornwallis, who assured Mackenzie of his good opinion before his untimely death in 1805. In fact, circumstances suggest that Wellesley was influenced in his proposal for a comprehensive statistical and geographical survey of Mysore by Mackenzie.[103] But none of these politicians could protect Mackenzie's survey from being pruned back. Mackenzie sent numerous, lengthy memoranda to the council, pleading his case, asking for more resources, but to no avail. In contrast, Lambton was able to avoid reductions in his funding; why was this so?

Institutionally, Lambton was in a better position to pursue a lengthy and laborious survey than perhaps any other cartographically minded officer in India. As a Crown officer with a long history of absence from his regiment, he was not subject to the same external pressures for him to fulfill his regular regimental duties as were Company officers. In this respect, the trigonometrical survey of southern India would probably not have been implemented at the early date that it was, had it been Mackenzie rather than Lambton who had first proposed it. Beyond such a contingent factor, the political support expressed for Lambton was not personal; the disparate treatment meted out to Lambton and Mackenzie was not a function of their respective characters or qualifications, as Mackenzie seems to have imagined. Both surveyors had networks of friends and supporters who appealed informally to the directors at home, and neither network seems to have had much effect. And, despite his complaints to the contrary, Mackenzie did receive political support for his surveys.

But Mackenzie's was nonetheless an ordinary survey and it was accordingly subject to the Company's financial stringencies. Lambton's survey was always held to be superior and qualitatively different; it was always accorded special treatment. The topographic surveys did not have the same cachet of metropolitan science that Lambton's work possessed, no matter the claims to order and system that Mackenzie advanced. Political interest in Lambton's survey was addressed first to the survey and then to Lambton as an educated and "scientific" individual with the necessary expertise to undertake it. For Mackenzie, the political interest was in the surveys themselves; he was treated as a meritorious and zealous surveyor, who had undeniable talents, but who was not engaged in high science. Other officers—Francis Buchanan or Mackenzie's assistants—could no doubt be found to implement the same system. It was not *special*.

The character of British mapmaking in India was defined by a four-way competition between the need for geographical information, the availability of labor to undertake the necessary surveys, the availability of money to pay for the surveys, and the adherence to cultural expectations for making as comprehensive and as accurate maps as possible. None of the four components were static. The appreciation of maps as tools of military and territorial administration increased steadily after 1765. The number of skilled surveyors within the East India Company's army increased through both better officer education and the overall expansion of the engineer corps at each presidency, although the increase was offset by a rise in the noncartographic demands placed upon the engineers and other military surveyors. The Company suffered a chronic shortage of cash that steadily worsened as the Napoleonic Wars dragged on; funding continued to be adversely affected after 1815 by the Maratha and Burmese wars. Finally, the cultural expectations of how maps should be made changed with the advent of triangulation and the supposed shift to the structured observation of the South Asian landscape.

Within this continually evolving give-and-take, the British mapping of India possessed a chaotic, if not anarchic, character. Surveys and maps were made by a host of military and civil officials, some explicitly trained in mapmaking, others working from general knowledge. There was little commitment to seeing a survey through; once started, the survey could be abruptly ended by any of a series of funding, political, personnel, or health problems. The geographical offices in each presidency and in London were thus filled with the products of incidental and organized surveys in various stages of completion. The mapmakers in India and Europe compiled their maps from a widely disparate archive.

The chaos of the surveys tended to obscure the efforts made by bureaucrats and administrators to bring the multifarious mapping activities under control. Those efforts functioned at the interface of two networks of social relations and control. First, the Company's officials were tied together by an intricate web of interest, for which mapmaking was a particularly effective medium. Junior officers could advance their careers by clearly demonstrating their expertise and merit to their superiors; senior officers bolstered their own political positions by expending their interest. The push-and-pull of the patronage system functioned most easily within the context of the formal hierarchy of military rank. The second network was the hierarchy of power and knowledge established to control South Asia and its peoples. The Company organized its territorial officials in a strict and quintessentially bureaucratic pyramid of communication: orders passed down and information passed up. The surveyors worked at the boundary between the uppermost, British portion of the pyramid and the lower foundations staffed by Indians and Eurasians; the cartographers functioned close to the pinnacle of the pyramid, collecting data and disseminating maps downward as necessary.

At the intersection of the two networks there developed a minihierarchy of cartographic expertise. It provided the means whereby the councillors in each presidency could manage the actual geographical surveys. Those surveyors who consistently performed well—in the opinion of other, more experienced surveyors entrusted by the presidency councils—were given new survey tasks and eventually formed a small cadre of known, cartographically skilled officers. But I must stress that this mini-hierarchy was by no means formal. Surveyor generals could be ignored; there was no formula for choosing each new surveyor general or the cartographic expert in London. The informal mini-hierarchy functioned according to the dynamics of the two constitutive networks. It was essentially reactionary; it reacted to each completed survey and had little role in the origination of new surveys. Thus the overall result was the almost anarchic conditions of cartography in British India, with surveys and maps being initiated at all levels of the territorial administration.

The Company's systems of patronage and information management lent themselves naturally to a geographic epistemology based on the archival construction of knowledge. Mapmaking epitomized the several strategies which the British employed to gather and analyze information about their Indian empire. Observation in the field by British officials, or by selected proxies who adhered to British standards and conventions, increasingly supplanted geographical information gathered from traditional Indian sources. As the British expanded their territorial interests, so their surveys expanded in scope and intensified in detail. The East India Company's officials slowly formalized and regularized the various mapmaking activities. The form adopted by the "survey department" in each presidency was organic. There was indeed an internal dynamic to the mapmaking, specifically an epistemology which emphasized the creation of knowledge in the archive. But that dynamic was itself shaped by the Company's larger institutional structures. The net result was that, as implemented in the later eighteenth century, the extent of the Company's mapping policy was to control geographical observers and their information directly. Acts of geographical observation remained largely beyond the scope of administration and were managed only indirectly.

The system of patronage was nonetheless at odds with the competing epistemology of structured field observations based on triangulation. Undertaking a comprehensive survey requires a large institution in which junior surveyors can be hired and fired at will. Yet at the same time, advocacy of that competing epistemology was something of a trump card in the patronage game. Both Mackenzie and Lambton pursued it, and both benefited from it. (Lambton's better institutional position and his more scientific goals meant however that he benefited more than did Mackenzie.)

A clear picture of these competitions, paradoxes, and the resultant chaos is given by the dramatic territorial extension of the Madras presidency in the first decade of the nineteenth century. Some surveyors and administrators sought both to acquire new geographical information and to control the flood of unorganized data by initiating systematic surveys of southern India. The resultant epistemological debate and the institutional debate, between the availability of resources and the means of their deployment, are examined next.

CHAPTER FIVE

Cartographic Anarchy and System in Madras, 1790–1810

A fter 1765, the Bengal government steadily expanded its political interests, and thus its surveys, across the northern plains. Members of the many British army columns and embassies which traveled the plains recorded their routes and some took astronomical observations as well. The annexation or conquest of most of the Gangetic Plains during the period of 1801 through 1803 did not seriously affect the established system of mapping. Dedicated surveys were begun of the new districts when money was available, but even these were conducted as multiple route surveys within the existing administrative division of field surveys and office compilation. Detailed surveys to help with the assessment of land revenues were discouraged by the 1791 "permanent settlement" of Bengal, Bihar, and Orissa. In seeking to stabilize rural society at a time of economic crisis by creating a new, pseudo-British landed gentry independent from the existing elites, the British "settled" property rights for large estates on the zamindars (tax-farmers), in return for which the zamindars managed the collection of land revenues. As Reginald Phillimore summarized the situation for northern India in the early nineteenth century:

> there was no regular plan of survey operations in Bengal. [Surveys] were taken up spasmodically as the need for any particular area became necessary. As a rule it was considered sufficient to send a single surveyor to each task, though occasionally he was given an assistant who was often completely untrained. When a surveyor went sick, or was called away to other duties, the survey was . . . completely abandoned [unless another surveyor could be found]. There was no co-ordination between the different surveyors, and no regular junction between their work . . . Each area was surveyed as a separate entity, and was incorporated into the general map after reaching the surveyor general's office.[1]

The surveyor general therefore relied heavily on the route surveys generated by army columns under the orders of 1788 and 1804.

The Bombay presidency was limited in its territorial extent. Until the

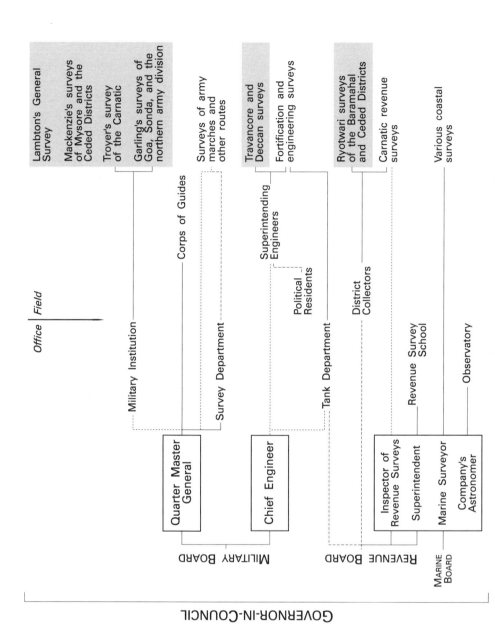

Office | Field

Lambton's General Survey
Mackenzie's surveys of Mysore and the Ceded Districts
Troyer's survey of the Carnatic
Garling's surveys of Goa, Sonda, and the northern army division
Surveys of army marches and other routes

Travancore and Deccan surveys
Fortification and engineering surveys

Ryotwari surveys of the Baramahal and Ceded Districts
Carnatic revenue surveys
Various coastal surveys

Military Institution — Corps of Guides

Survey Department

Superintending Engineers

Political Residents

Tank Department

District Collectors

Inspector of Revenue Surveys — Revenue Survey School

Superintendent

Marine Surveyor

Company's Astronomer — Observatory

Quarter Master General

Chief Engineer

MILITARY BOARD

REVENUE BOARD

MARINE BOARD

GOVERNOR-IN-COUNCIL

cession of extensive territories by the Marathas in 1817–18, Bombay's administration governed only the islands of Bombay itself and Salsette (annexed 1776), Malabar (1792), and the pargana of Broach (1803). The presidency's level of cartographic activity was accordingly low and so does not feature prominently in this study. There was, of course, some mapping, undertaken on the Bengal model. Army officers made many route surveys across the Deccan and northwestern India, which were assembled into general maps in Bombay. Charles Reynolds, of the Bombay infantry, was in 1796 appointed to be an office-bound surveyor general; his appointment overcame the directors' opposition by an administrative sleight of hand that still remains unclear.[2] When Reynolds's successor, Monier Williams, took to the field to make surveys, he did so in his extra capacity as "revenue surveyor" and not as surveyor general.

In contrast to both Bengal and Bombay, the growth of the Madras presidency's territories led to extensive cartographic innovation. In a series of annexations between 1790 and 1801, the British took direct control of the Carnatic; at the same time, war with Mysore (1790–92 and 1799) led ultimately to that state's partition, with the cession of territory to the Company. The governor of Madras presided by 1810 over an almost complete array of cartographic activities for mapping southern India. There were two establishments to educate surveyors, one civilian and one military; three different offices in which maps were copied, stored, or compiled; and a host of officers in both the military and civil services who supervised and conducted the fieldwork. All that was lacking was the engraving and publication of the final maps.

Initially, the mapping activities were structured in a manner similar to Bengal's. On the left in figure 5.1 are the three cartographically related staff positions, each of which kept a repository of maps and engaged in the copying or construction of manuscript maps: the chief engineer, the quartermaster general, and the four posts held by the Company's astronomer. These were tied to the field surveys, at right, by linkages of only weak or nominal control—by links of communication rather than of command. Orders and money passed down the

Figure 5.1 The administrative structure of mapmaking activities in the Madras presidency, 1800–1810. Horizontal differentiation is according to location and political scope: the central administration in Fort St. George (at left); district or regional authorities (center); and actual surveyors in the field (at right). All surveys and map compilation were under the authority of the governor-in-council, some directly (no linkages shown), others through intermediary officials. The hierarchical links of the latter are shown by solid lines (direct control, supervision, or participation), dashed lines (weak control and oversight), and dotted lines (purely nominal control). The text provides a detailed explication.

chain; geographical information, reports, and requests for more resources or health leave all passed upwards. At the top of the figure are the surveys of William Lambton, Colin Mackenzie, and the Military Institution, which together represent the new, triangulation-based configuration of cartography and which could not fit easily into the established field/office dichotomy; they accordingly came under the direct authority of the governor and council.

There was little cohesion among the Madras surveys. There was certainly none to the surveyors as an institutional group. The majority of surveyors were military officers: engineers, who acquired their knowledge of survey techniques from their education and professional experience, and infantrymen and a few cavalrymen, who were educated at the Military Institution or who picked up their survey skills on their own account. Some officers indulged in surveying at their own expense; others taught themselves so as to be able to obtain potentially lucrative survey allowances. The majority of surveyors were only temporarily assigned to mapping duties. Military officers were, after all, creatures of their regiments and corps, to which they owed their rank and basic salary. Only a very few officers were seconded from their regiments to the surveys for a significant portion of their careers. One civilian English surveyor, John Mather, was employed at the same level as the military subalterns; there were also a number of civilian "assistant surveyors" of mixed European and Indian heritage. The surveyors' salaries were highly variable, with engineers receiving higher allowances than other officers and all European officers receiving far more in staff salary alone than the Eurasians received in salary and expenses together. Administrative confusion arose when the larger surveys employed both military officers and civil assistants, so that their superintendents submitted bills to both the military and civil auditor generals.

Once the council decision to go ahead with a survey had been approved by the governor and the council, a surveyor found, and the orders were written, the central administration had little to say with respect to the actual implementation of each survey. Subsequent management of the survey concerned the provision of extra resources and personnel, health leaves, expenses, and sometimes the expansion of its geographical scope. Military surveyors were autonomous with respect to the professional details of their work. They were subordinate neither to the district collectors in British districts nor to the residents in the princely states. They did, of course, adhere to the essential etiquette for all British officials in India of following the correct channels of communication. In the princely states, this meant that a surveyor's correspondence with Madras had to pass through the resident; in general, the surveyors coordinated their activities with the collectors and residents who could then ensure the delivery of necessary supplies and the presence of local district officials to answer the surveyors' questions. Residents and collectors became involved only when the surveyors' actions had political or other local significance, as when Lieutenant Thomas Arthur was briefly suspended from Mackenzie's survey of Mysore in 1804 because his apparent insensitivity to local concerns caused the diwan to protest to the resident.

The bureaucrats in Madras often used the phrase "survey department" as a convenient expression for all of these diverse cartographic activities. But, as will become clear, there was little administrative unity, even when a surveyor general was finally appointed in 1810.

Established Military Mapping Institutions

The observation/archive, or field/office, distinction is clearest in the case of the chief engineer. The officers of the corps of engineers were scattered throughout the Madras territories. They were attached as "superintending engineers" to each army division and to each "subsidiary force" stationed in the princely states; some were posted to the tank (reservoir) department to maintain and extend south India's irrigation network. Superintending engineers did work on general surveys after 1790 but only when they were not engaged in specific projects. For example, the engineers with the Hyderabad subsidiary force, who sequentially pursued what was referred to as the Deccan survey—Colin Mackenzie (1794–1805), who was rarely present, Thomas DeHavilland (1805–7), and John Blair (1807–10)—were all restricted to undertaking a few route surveys when circumstances permitted. The official roster of the survey in 1810 was five officers, but one officer was marking out roads, and the two on loan from the quartermaster general were unable to survey because no guard was available. Similarly, the engineer with the Travancore subsidiary force began a survey of that state in 1805, supposedly at the diwan's request. The survey was accelerated after the 1809 uprising and also had five officers attached in 1810; however, the engineer in charge, Thomas Arthur, was working for the British resident and only one of his four subordinates was actually surveying. Both surveys were therefore closed down in the retrenchments of 1810, to be redone on a systematic plan sometime in the future.[3] Beyond the fact that engineers were just too expensive and too much in demand elsewhere to make efficient surveyors, there was no institutional mechanism to ensure any continuity of support for any officers on survey duty.

The chief engineer himself was responsible only for the finances and general plan of each field project, from reviewing and approving initial estimates to monitoring expenditures in case of cost overruns. The chief engineer also maintained an archive of the reports, plans, and maps generated by the field engineers. Because of their familiarity with maps, the chief engineer's draftsmen were routinely used by the Madras council to copy and compile maps for transmission to London. A bureaucratic rationalization in 1802 required the chief engineer to surrender all activities not explicitly related to engineering to the quartermaster general. Nonetheless, the limited availability of cartographic (or just graphic) skills in Madras meant that the chief engineer's staff continued to be used for copying maps and for compiling new ones from scratch.[4]

The quartermaster general had by 1800 eclipsed the chief engineer as the major cartographic officer in Madras. The quartermaster general's responsibilities embraced "whatever is connected with the movements and positions of armies, the defence of encampments, and the general arrangement of combined operations, as far as these relate to the surface of the ground." To this end, the quartermaster general needed "knowledge of the situation of places; of the roads, passes, mountains, forests, and features of the country; of the positions proper for the encampments of armies and detachments . . . ; of the course and description of rivers and the supplies of water; [and] of the character, resources, and [facilities] of the countries" under British authority.[5] He therefore collected and collated all available geographical materials, principally surveys of the routes taken by army columns. His staff regularly compiled "general preparations," comprising detailed descriptions with sketches and maps of every road in the presidency and the surrounding territories; general maps showed the interconnections of the different routes and were especially useful for planning large troop movements. Because this system entailed the continual collation of new information, the quartermaster general's office made little use of published maps.[6]

The quartermaster general had little control over his sources of information. He was in charge of the guides, some of whom attended the Revenue Survey School; after 1802 the quartermaster general himself "regularly instructed" others in the techniques of "surveying routes, taking bearings and distances, . . . [and of] delineating on paper the local circumstances of the countries which they examine."[7] Nonetheless, surveying was only ancillary to the guides' main duty of blazing trails for army columns. The "survey branch" of the quartermaster general's office was only a shorthand administrative expression for those assistant quartermaster generals who were occasionally detached on survey duty. Also, the quartermaster general officially supervised the Madras Military Institution after December 1807, but this was only a device to bring the institution's students within the regular military hierarchy.[8] The quartermaster general was involved in determining which areas were to be surveyed by the students, but he himself remained an office cartographer. To this end, he had two graduates from the institution posted to his department in 1808 to handle the office work of map storage and compilation.

Mostly, the quartermaster general accepted whatever route surveys were sent to him. In contrast to Bengal, there was no attempt to regulate the surveys of the routes of army columns until February 1800, when the Bengal regulations of 1788 were adapted for southern India. The Bengal regulations of 1804, which defined the content and format of the surveys, were quickly adopted in Madras with important extensions to ensure the surveys' quality: the quartermaster general's supply depots were to supply pedometers and compasses to each army column; furthermore, the officers who kept the survey record would not receive the extra allowance—100 rupees (£9) per month—until the quartermaster general had certified that the journal was of the proper quality and had been lodged in his office.[9] These regulations did not give the quartermaster general control of the surveys themselves.

The pattern of military surveying was clear: surveys were made whenever necessary and the results communicated to the central administration to be compiled into larger maps. Of course, some of the field engineers made their own compilations. Most notably, Mackenzie made several maps of the central Deccan, derived mainly from his own route surveys, while serving as engineer with the Hyderabad subsidiary force after 1792. They were nonetheless sent to Madras for incorporation into the general geographical archive.

Direct Territorial Control and Revenue Surveys

The British followed a different revenue policy in southern India than in Bengal. The failure of the zamindari settlement to achieve its goals, an intellectual desire to construct a system more reflective of the apparent structure of rural India, and the political need to establish the peasantry as a social counter to the elites all meant that, in the Madras districts, land rights were settled and revenues assessed on the *ryots* (individual cultivators). Alexander Read was the first collector to implement a *ryotwari* settlement, in the Baramahal, which had been ceded by Mysore in 1792; it was further developed by his assistant, Thomas Munro, when he settled the revenues of the districts of Bellary, Cuddapah, and Kurnool (known together as the "Ceded Districts" of Mysore; initially granted to the Nizam in 1799, the Company reclaimed them in 1801). The system was subsequently adopted in the Carnatic and in much of the rest of India.[10] The key to ryotwari settlement was the gathering of data concerning all aspects of agricultural productivity, from soil quality and seed type to land tenures. Armed with all of the necessary data, the collector could make annual assessments of the taxes due on each parcel of land. Not surprisingly, the Madras administration began to map their new territories in aid of revenue management, giving rise to the curious combination of four cartographic staff positions held by just one nonmilitary staff officer (see figure 5.1).

The need to increase agricultural production within the Carnatic districts annexed between 1790 and 1792 led the British to begin a program of repairing and expanding the extensive networks of reservoirs and irrigation channels. To manage the prerepair surveys, the council turned to the one skilled surveyor available, Michael Topping. Topping had come to Madras in 1785 to be the marine surveyor; his astronomical skills made him the perfect choice to head the Madras Observatory, founded in 1789 when William Petrie, a member of the council and an amateur astronomer, donated all his instruments to the Company. In 1794, Topping was appointed superintendent of "tank surveys." Surveying all of the reservoirs and canals for repair was clearly a huge task, so Topping persuaded the council to train youths of mixed European-Indian parentage from the Madras Male Asylum (orphanage) as surveyors. They could also make general surveys of the Carnatic for the district collectors. They would work for about one-sixth of a military surveyor's allowances; they would not, Topping thought, need interpreters; and they would not be as susceptible to the climate as individuals raised in Europe.

Topping's assistant, John Goldingham, became superintendent of the new Revenue Survey School. On Topping's death in 1796, a separate "tank department" was set up under the Board of Revenue; Goldingham succeeded Topping as marine surveyor and astronomer and was also appointed to be "inspector of revenue surveys." Goldingham kept these positions until 1805, when he went on furlough and was temporarily replaced by John Warren. The revenue survey positions were abolished in 1810; but on his return in 1812, Goldingham continued to serve as astronomer.

It is hard to distinguish between the four positions. The Observatory and the Revenue Survey School were housed in adjacent buildings and their office staffs were interchangeable. The Observatory also housed the collections of maps produced by the marine and revenue surveys;

the draftsmen and students of the survey school used that archive to construct general maps at the request of various administrators.[11] As marine surveyors, Topping, Goldingham, and Warren undertook the occasional coastal, harbor, or estuarine survey; they also used these as opportunities to make astronomical observations away from Madras. Moreover, the astronomer's principal tasks were oriented to the marine and cartographic issue of longitude determination. The Observatory's staff—mostly Brahmins[12]—defined the periodic pattern at which marine chronometers lost and gained time, so that navigators could apply the necessary corrections to their measurements of longitude; they also made lengthy, although not continuous, series of observations of the eclipses of Jupiter's satellites, so that they could be compared with corresponding observations taken around the Indian Ocean by mariners and at Greenwich in order to define accurate longitudinal differences. In addition, both Goldingham and Warren undertook pendulum experiments to determine the fundamental scientific issue of the figure of the earth.[13]

Most of Goldingham's and Warren's time seems to have been spent in their duties as superintendents of the Revenue Survey School. Their principal task was to educate the young orphans and to train them as surveyors. The school's complement was twenty-four boys, the youngest being ten years of age. Once trained, and at the potentially young age of seventeen, the youths were attached to district collectors throughout the Carnatic to make district surveys; some were attached to the tank department or to military surveys as "assistant surveyors."[14] More generally, the superintendency seems to have subsumed the work of inspector of revenue surveys. In that capacity, Goldingham and Warren were supposed to oversee and check the quality of district surveys made in the Carnatic under the direction of each district collector. But it was a very vaguely defined position; it did not even have a salary or office funds associated with it. In 1806, after a year in the position, Warren complained that he was still "totally uninstructed by any written official document as to [the] nature and extent" of his duties and that he had so far received only one map for inspection.[15]

The position of inspector of revenue surveys would appear to have been a mechanism, however ineffectual, to provide a regular conduit through which the revenue surveyors in the field could communicate their maps to the presidency. Once a youth was placed with a collector, he was removed from Goldingham's and Warren's supervision. Without such a conduit, the survey results would probably have stayed in each district. Not that the youths only made surveys; being literate, the collectors often employed them as general-purpose clerks, who were always in short supply. When the youths did make surveys, the collectors lacked the expertise necessary to overcome the youths' inexperience, so the surveys were of poor quality.[16] Despite their name, the revenue surveys were geographical, not cadastral, in character; and despite their quality, they were to constitute the principal source of general geographical information for the Carnatic until after 1815.[17]

These problems almost led in 1806 to the abolition of all of the revenue surveys. They were saved only because the youths had proven to be very efficient and cost-effective when they were supervised by skilled engineers and surveyors. The hollowness of the inspectorate is demonstrated in that Warren responded to the problem in his capacity as superintendent of the survey school. He implemented new regulations: the surveyors would receive longer training; they would have to gain surveying experience in the tank department for at least two years before being attached to a collector; and they were organized into a clear hierarchy of rank and salary as both incentive and remuneration for "what is generally held to be a laborious line of duty."[18] Even so, those regulations still could not override the collectors' autonomy; they could not prescribe how the collectors were actually to employ the surveyors in the field.

The district collectors' highly localized authority blocked the flow of data to Madras. The gathering of data depended on each collector's large staff of Indian officials, who were drawn from local elites and who jealously guarded their own sources of information as a means to ensure their own position and status. In the Carnatic, the revenue surveys were intended to provide the collectors with information with which to build up an understanding of the general characteristics of the revenue system of each district. The revenue surveyors mapped each district at scales of about one inch to the mile, identifying the lands under cultivation; they did not define property or field boundaries. As such, they could not contribute to the effective British exercise of power by breaking the hold on information of the local elites. David Ludden has analyzed the situation in the southernmost district of Tinnevelly (formally annexed in 1801) and found that "even the best of the early surveys . . . remained useless for assessment and collection for officers outside the village." It was not until the 1860s that the British were in a position to undertake detailed cadastral surveys that included boundary demarcation, field survey, soil classification, revenue assessment, and the recording of rights to the land. Once complete, these surveys formed the ideal tool of the urban bureaucracy; officers in Madras, Bombay, or Calcutta could see for themselves the rights and obligations of each landowner and each field. Until then, those officials relied on the uncertain information provided by the Indian officers.[19]

Read and Munro were able to implement an effective ryotwari administration in those districts ceded from Mysore. Haider Ali and Tipu Sultan had seriously disrupted the local social structures in an effort to cut out the middlemen and so increase their revenues to a level which could sustain a military capable of defeating the British. First, Read trained his own Indian assistants in the Baramahal, who in turn supervised local surveyors in assessing soil qualities and recording property rights; he also had John Mather make a general survey between 1794 and 1798. Munro took the system one large step further when he settled the Ceded Districts by adding a large-scale cadastral survey to the assessment. He began in June 1802 with four Indians who had been trained in land surveying; in two years, they had recruited and trained a further hundred. Both the land measurement and assessment included checks and allowed appeals; even so, with such a large survey staff, the assessment was complete by 1806.[20] The autonomy of the British field officer is clearly demonstrated by the fact that even as Munro conducted this survey on his own initiative, one of his subcollectors undertook his own independent survey.[21]

Mackenzie's Surveys of Mysore, 1799–1815

Concurrent with the various revenue surveys, the military began a number of surveys of both British districts and the princely states in order to define the general topography and geography of southern India for strategic purposes. Without a well-developed system for regional military mapping, the Madras administration was open to implementing the new European trends in mapmaking. When the military surveyors turned their attention to the landscapes of southern India, they did so with the intention of making far more comprehensive surveys than those made in the northern plains. Their goal was complete geographical description—encompassing economic, demographic, cultural, botanical, geological, and locational data—a goal which necessarily had to be accomplished outside of the existing system of sporadic route surveys and archival officers. The epistemological certainty of the comprehensive topographic surveys derived entirely from their field observations. As such, they did not fit into the established mapping bureaucracy with its emphasis on the reasoned truth of archival compilation. The awkward institutional position of the new surveys is indicated by their prominence in figure 5.1.

Colin Mackenzie was directed in September 1799 by the governor general, Lord Wellesley, to undertake a topographic survey of the rump state of Mysore.[22] With Wellesley's encouragement, the survey began with four European assistant surveyors; the survey also had its own surgeon, Dr. Benjamin Heyne, who was also to work on the survey's statistical enquiries. Such a large survey was a tempting target for the accountants in the Company's perpetual drive to save money. Mackenzie was repeatedly told to close the survey; his funds and his own salary were cut, much to his disgust; his assistants were not replaced after they left in poor health or to return to their regiments; Heyne refused to work on the survey. Mackenzie himself was ordered back to his corps several times, but the orders were rescinded by governors who wanted the survey to be finished. By the middle of 1807, Mackenzie's workforce comprised only himself and five "assistant surveyors" trained in the Revenue Survey School.

Despite his funding and staff problems, Mackenzie was able to embark on an ambitious scheme to map much more than just the postpartition state of Mysore. He wanted to make a single, peninsula-wide topographic survey. When he was attached to the Hyderabad Subsidiary Force, he had thought (or so he claimed in 1817) that he might undertake a systematic survey of the Deccan. A survey of the entire peninsula was a major point in his 1796 proposal to be made surveyor general of Madras. Now, very early in 1800, he revealed a personal wish to convert the Mysore Survey into a Peninsula Survey.[23] Although he did not make it explicit until November 1805, Mackenzie's rhetorical strategy was to argue that his real task was to survey not just the rump state of Mysore but, rather, all of "the late Mysore dominions," which constituted a substantial portion of the peninsula.[24]

The larger agenda underlay Mackenzie's unsuccessful proposal late in 1800 to extend his survey to the Ceded Districts of northeastern Mysore; in 1805, Mackenzie directed his assistants to map a portion of the Ceded Districts, which was almost entirely enclosed by Mysore, with the conscious idea that this would be a prelude to the future expansion of the survey.[25] That larger agenda was also responsible for the appointment of two Bombay engineers to survey Canara on Mackenzie's behalf, although they had to return to their corps before the end of 1800 having produced only incomplete maps of Sonda and North Canara.[26] He made political use of the fact that even though he was surveying Mysore, he was still officially attached to the Hyderabad subsidiary force. (This arrangement had been intended only to give him a decent income and remained in effect until the economy drive of 1805.) Mackenzie argued that this dual appointment indicated that the Mysore survey was intended as "a continuation or extended branch on a more detailed plan" of his surveys in the Deccan; it would not take much to extend the more detailed survey back into the Nizam's dominions.[27] He also employed a cartographic rhetoric. He included the Ceded Districts on his 1805 map showing which Mysore territories he had yet to survey.[28] On the 1808 index to his maps he referred to the whole Mysore survey as "the foundation of an atlas of the province dependent upon the Presidency of Fort St. George" (figure 5.2).

Nor was Mackenzie above subterfuge. He described his means of renewing his permission to survey Canara in 1806 as "a *coup de main* (as it were)."[29] He changed a fast and cheap triangulation to correct existing maps, which the council had approved, into a properly systematic survey. He justified this maneuver because by mapping Canara it would be possible "to see an interesting country actually executed on the plan I would suggest for the provincial surveys of the Company's districts, and to show it was practicable."[30] The methodology Mackenzie wanted to demonstrate in Canara was that of a European officer who supervised a large body of Eurasian, or Indian, surveyors.

Mackenzie's surveying system was a hybrid of existing technologies. Each of his subordinate surveyors was assigned a circle of parganas, for which they measured their own bases and triangles (as in figure 3.5). Mackenzie also ran a few primary triangles to link the different parganas together and his assistants observed points common to their neighbors' triangles. Overall, however, there was little sense that the different triangulations would form some larger whole. Topographic detail was acquired in a combination of route surveys, sketches, and intersecting lines of sight from triangulation stations. As the number of his European assistants steadily declined until the last—John Mather—finally resigned in 1806, Mackenzie placed increasing reliance on his assistant surveyors from the Revenue Survey School, whom he formed into efficient survey teams. With the surveyors trained in the same techniques, their work would be all of the same standard. Moreover, they were cheap to employ and were naturally acclimated. As a result, Mackenzie advertised his system as being one of fast, cheap, detailed surveys with none of the discrepancies and errors so common to the work of European surveyors. Mackenzie's system of surveying was based not so much on the idea of a single triangulated framework to control all lesser surveys, but on the idea of a uniform structure of survey parties and of uniform techniques.

In the context of Mackenzie's evident desire for an extensive and systematic survey of southern India, it makes little sense to separate his survey of Mysore (1799–1807) from his survey of the Ceded Districts (1809–15). While they were distinct administratively, cartographically they were part of the same larger scheme. Other than that Mackenzie did not enter the field himself—he stayed in Madras, with the sinecure position of barrack master of Mysore, to arrange his

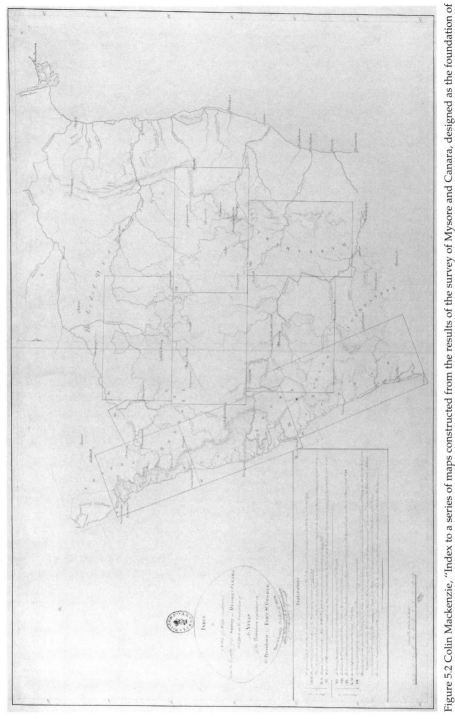

Figure 5.2 Colin Mackenzie, "Index to a series of maps constructed from the results of the survey of Mysore and Canara, designed as the foundation of an atlas of the province dependent upon the Presidency of Fort St. George," 17 October 1808, 1:1,520,640. Ink and watercolor. Note how each sheet is aligned with a principal district. (By permission of The British Library, IOR X/2108/7.)

manuscript collection, also doing some engineering, before serving as superintending engineer on the Java expedition (1810–14)—and that its personnel were all civilian assistants, the second survey was undertaken in the same manner as the first. The maps produced were very similar in form, too, with each survey generating one huge map at four miles to the inch, a set of district maps at two miles to the inch, as well as some maps at one inch to the mile of interesting areas (figure 5.3).[31]

Lambton's General Survey, 1800–1810

Late in 1799, while Colin Mackenzie was organizing the Mysore Survey, William Lambton persuaded the Madras council to allow him to start a trigonometrical survey in emulation of the recent geodetic survey linking the royal observatories of Greenwich and Paris. General William Roy had undertaken the British portion of that work. He had determined the longitudinal difference between the observatories by the novel scheme of measuring the angular convergence of their meridians. In explaining his method to the Royal Society, Roy also referred to a 1784 suggestion by the East India Company's hydrographer, Alexander Dalrymple, that a triangulation along the eastern coast of India would contribute both to coastal charting and, if properly done, to geodetic science. Roy proposed that India, together with Brazil and Russia, had great potential as the site of geodetic measurements; he therefore called on the Company to finance two arcs, one on the eastern coast as Dalrymple had suggested, the other in Bengal.[32] Dalrymple's suggestion led to the appointment of Michael Topping as marine surveyor; in 1791 Topping disregarded political realities and proposed that his coastal triangulation could be extended "throughout India."[33] Roy's suggestion led to Reuben Burrow's inadequate measurement of an arc in Bengal in 1790–91, a measurement that was left unfinished on his death in 1792 (see chapter 4).

In proposing his survey, Lambton seems to have been unaware of both Topping's idea and Burrow's work. Instead, he sought to use Roy's technique to measure the longitudinal width of the peninsula, although he was well aware that southern India lay in "a much more delicate latitude" for the procedure. He planned to measure at least two arcs, one of the meridian through the Carnatic and one of the parallel running west from Madras.[34] It cannot be stressed strongly enough that Lambton himself initially had no intention of undertaking an India-wide triangulation. The political situation did not allow any extension of the survey into the Deccan until 1810; even then, Lambton had no plans to extend the Great Meridional Arc beyond the Deccan and into the northern plains.

Figure 5.3 John Warren, "Map of the Purgunnah of Colar in Mysore according to the Partition of 1799," signed Colin Mackenzie, n.d. (ca. 1802), 1:63,360. Ink and watercolor. Northern half only.

This map shows "the tract impregnated with gold dust," described in chapter 2. It also illustrates the pencil grid used for copying manuscript maps. (By permission of The British Library, IOR X/2136.)

Lambton's proposals began with the fundamental assumption that there was a need for a general map of the peninsula and he justified his two initial arcs as a basis from which to extend his triangles "to an almost unlimited extent in every other direction," as defined by political and physical conditions.[35] Lambton envisaged a single triangulation

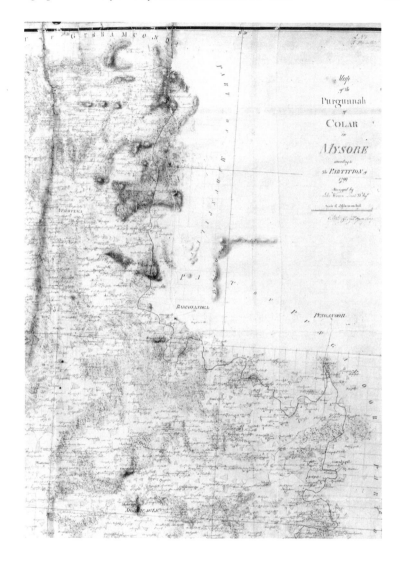

covering all of southern India which would constitute the common referent for combining district surveys made by different surveyors at different times. The principal task of such a triangulation was to define the controlling points with the proper level of accuracy, which required knowledge of the size and shape of the earth, which in turn required the reconciliation of inconsistencies and discrepancies in contemporary geodetic data. Not surprisingly, Lambton's proposals and subsequent reports were dominated by explanations of the complex issues of mathematics, astronomy, and geodesy, all of which obscured the geographic aspects of the survey.

The early history of Lambton's survey demonstrates his dual concern for geography and geodesy. In 1800, he moved the location of his trial survey in order to complement Mackenzie's work in Mysore. In April and May of 1802, he measured a base at St. Thomas's Mount, near Madras, to serve as the origin for both the meridional arc through the Carnatic (1802–3) and the longitudinal arc eastward to Mangalore (1803–5). These arcs he observed with the "Great Theodolite," which arrived from Britain in September 1802. In 1806 he began another meridional arc, running south from Bangalore toward Cape Comorin, which became the Great Arc when carried northwards.[36] At the same time, his first two subordinate officers—John Warren (1802–5) and Henry Kater (1803–6)—surveyed secondary triangles and major topographic features. In fact, Lambton had explicitly requested Kater's appointment to the survey so that he might survey rivers, "the most distinguished outlines in geography," and the "great gun roads."[37]

There was much confusion within the Company's administration concerning the precise character and role of Lambton's survey. Lambton initially called his work a "mathematical and geographical survey," capturing its dual character; subsequently, he usually referred to it as a "general" or "geographical" survey. In contrast, the Madras administration treated it as an adjunct to Mackenzie's survey. Mackenzie later complained about the manner in which Lambton's survey was "huddled together" with his own, but he had only himself to blame. He had in December 1799 described Lambton's proposed work as being astronomical in character (and so perhaps subject to John Goldingham in the Observatory) and as being intended to aid the Mysore survey. Mackenzie also told the Mysore resident that Lambton wanted to survey in the northern peninsula, which would have been impossible given the political jealousies of the Marathas and the Nizam; from his own conversations with Lambton, the resident realized that Mackenzie was wrong.[38]

The result of Mackenzie's judgment was that the Madras council conceived of Lambton's survey as an adjunct to the Mysore survey. The council's request in February 1800 for Mackenzie and Lambton to submit detailed proposals called Lambton's work the "astronomical survey of the southern part of the Peninsula and chiefly [of] those countries which are embraced in the general plan of [Mackenzie's] more detailed survey," which, although restricted to "the purposes of general geography," should nonetheless be made to coincide "to every practicable extent" with Mackenzie's survey "so as to enable him with the greater facility to combine the details of his survey and to verify the positions of the most remarkable stations in the progress of the work."[39] Thereafter, officials in Madras variously described the survey as: "that part of the [Mysore] survey immediately entrusted to" Lambton; the "Astronomical Survey of Mysore"; the "astronomical branch of the Mysore Survey"; "a separate astronomical survey"; or, the "astronomical survey in the Peninsula." Only once have I found a ranking government official refer to it, before 1807, as the "general survey" as Lambton generally did.[40] Even after the completion of the Mysore survey, Lambton's work continued to be referred to as an astronomical survey. The result was a continual misunderstanding on the part of the Madras bureaucrats over the respective accounts of the two surveys.

That Lambton's survey did emerge from underneath Mackenzie's shadow and was progressively restricted to just triangulation was a result of the growing acceptance on the part of the Madras administration of the need for a peninsula-wide topographic survey. In 1804, the governor, Lord William Bentinck, directed that Lambton's subordinates should *not* undertake any topographic mapping, overtly because Kater was duplicating the work of Mackenzie's survey teams, but more fundamentally because Bentinck conceived of a strict and rational division of cartographic labor. Similarly, the quartermaster general was in 1807 denied permission to buy instruments for determining astronomical positions because such observations were Lambton's responsibility.[41] In 1808, William Petrie stated that the topographical surveys were "mechanical" and were "as different in their nature from the survey of Major Lambton, as the measurement of a gentleman's estate in England" was from the Ordnance Survey.[42] Finally, when the office of surveyor general was finally created at Madras in 1810, the council explicitly stated that because Lambton's survey was "of a different nature from that of any of the others" it was not to be subordinate to the new surveyor general.[43]

The separation drawn by the Madras council between Lambton's triangulation and the topographical work of his assistants was made in part because of the foundation in 1804 of the Military Institution, whose students would be responsible for topographic surveys based on Lambton's triangulation framework. In 1807, Lambton was given four graduates of the institution's first class to conduct his secondary triangulation, although Lambton later admitted that he "chiefly employed" them "in a kind of detailed work, which consisted in laying down the roads, rivers, and making topographical sketches of the ranges of mountains."[44] With these officers, and with "assistant surveyors" from the Revenue Survey School, Lambton began a new phase of his survey, building up a net of triangles across the whole peninsula based on the meridional arc through Cape Comorin. The new work was first delayed by damage to the Great Theodolite in 1808 and then by Lambton's active service during the Travancore insurrection of 1809, which also drew off two of his Military Institution graduates. By June 1810, most of the eastern and southern peninsula had been covered with triangles; he now secured the council's permission to extend the new arc north of the Tunghabadra River, into the domain of the Nizam of Hyderabad. The reforms of 1810 meant that he lost his last two institution graduates; Lambton then gave responsibility for the secondary triangulation to Joshua de Penning, one of his assistant surveyors.[45] That is, by 1810, Lambton's survey was strictly trigonometrical in nature.

Troyer and the Military Institution, 1805–17

The Military Institution had its roots in an 1804 minute by Madras Commander in Chief General James Stuart. As a side-issue to the formation of a single map repository, Stuart had suggested that Colin Mackenzie be ordered to survey the Ceded Districts, Canara, and Sonda, with the hint that this would be part of a single survey of the whole peninsula. The governor, Lord William Bentinck, developed the idea further and explicitly called for a complete topographical survey of southern India to be conducted along the same lines as a modern European survey. Mackenzie and William Lambton, he wrote, were "far advanced in a work, which will prove the foundation of every future extension of geographical or topographical pursuits in this country," but they had no hope of being able to fulfill the entire task themselves. Thus the need for more trained surveyors organized in a systematic manner to handle the topographic mapping, but not the triangulation basis, which would remain the province of "men of science."[46]

This was the first acknowledgment by any high official of the East India Company of the character of the trigonometrical survey Lambton had been at such pains to stress in his proposals: it was not just a scientific work, nor just a piece of practical geography, but both. Each side required and dictated the other. Bentinck probably derived his opinions from his client, the Austrian-born Anthony Troyer, who had been trained at the Militär-Akademie and who had accompanied Bentinck to India. Some twenty-five years later, as governor general, Bentinck relied on Troyer for his cartographic policy; there is no reason to suppose that he did not do so as governor of Madras.

The initial plans for the Military Institution called for fifteen or so infantry ensigns to be instructed each year by Troyer. Their course

would cover topography, surveying *"à rue"* (that is, without instruments), and drawing in a moderate style midway between "sparse
scratching" and florid profusion.[47] The students' practical field lessons would also constitute basic surveys in their own right. But stung
by criticism of the education of Madras army officers, Bentinck also
wanted to inculcate "military science" in the Madras army and so reform the army staff.[48] (The Court ultimately rejected the staff reforms as
too expensive and too radical.) With the support of new Commander
in Chief Sir John Craddock, Bentinck expanded the institution's curri
culum to a second year, with classes in field fortifications and trigonometry, even before the first class of twelve ensigns began in April
1805. The careers of the institution's graduates reflect this less overtly
cartographic role. Most of the students from the first few classes were
employed on cartographic duties, many as soon as they left the institution. After the reforms of 1810, far fewer graduates were ever employed on surveys, and of these most were attached to the quartermaster general's staff and had many other duties. A telling statistic is
that a quarter of the fifty pre-1810 graduates went on to spend more
than four years on strictly cartographic duties and so might be considered members of the cadre of "proper" surveyors, compared with only
one-twelfth of the seventy-two post-1810 graduates. Ultimately, the institution was closed because it duplicated the training offered at the
Company's own military seminary for engineer and artillery cadets,
which had been founded at Addiscombe in 1809. The last class graduated in 1817; Troyer returned to regimental duty.[49]

The Madras council cannot be said to have been *committed* after 1804
to the undertaking of a peninsula-wide survey. It was instead simply
open to the idea.[50] The Military Institution's early supporters were
moved more by its role as an educational establishment than as a surveying institution. Many of its early graduates were posted to the quartermaster general's office and to several field surveys, including Lambton's, but financial and military pressures required all of them to return
to regimental duty. On the other hand, Troyer created within the Military Institution itself an organization that might have been effective in
mapping all of southern India, if not the entire subcontinent. In a field
season running from January through April or May, each of the institution's students was required to plane table a predefined square block
of land, their work being controlled by Lambton's triangulation. Troyer's task was to provide a trigonometrical link when necessary between
Lambton's survey and the senior students' plane tables; the assistant
instructor would supervise the junior students. In the "Survey of the
Carnatic," which began with the 1808 field season, each student in the

senior class would be responsible for surveying a 27-square mile rectangle at four miles to an inch in each month of the four-month season.[51] A similar structure was employed by James Garling, Troyer's first assistant instructor, when he undertook surveys of the districts north of Madras and of Goa and Sonda (1810–15): he provided the trigonometrical base (he had acquired at his own expense a theodolite of sufficient accuracy and precision) while institution graduates followed in his wake.[52]

Troyer thus established the only bridge between the central administration in Madras and the surveyors in the field, but the system was by no means perfect. There was no end of confusion when it was realized in mid-1808 that there were not two classes, but *three:* the new junior class; the senior class (the previous year's junior class); and the previous year's senior class, who had yet to draft their neat maps. Also, the students fell foul of the 1809 mutiny by the officers of the Madras army. The subsequent confusion was not ironed out until after 1812, by which time the institution's cartographic emphasis had been softened.

It is significant that Bentinck could not create the desired general survey of southern India as a single cartographic institution. The council could not formally establish the new principle that survey duty should take precedence over regimental duty, at least for a selected few officers; the informal implementation of that policy soon crumbled under pressure from the established institutional framework. Bentinck—perhaps one should say Troyer—might have sought to supplant the archivally based mapping system with one based on systematically structured field observation, but the Military Institution was tangential to the administration's attempts to define cartographic policy. Those attempts were shaped by the field/office division and were motivated by the need to save money. That is, the field operations were to be curtailed until such time as more money was available, when they would again be started up, while the cartographic repositories in Madras would be unified into a single, general office. Instead of a comprehensive survey, the Madras administration pursued a comprehensive map.

Retrenchment, Reform, and a Surveyor General, 1810

It is no exaggeration that the East India Company was perpetually short of money. The need to keep expenditures down, if not to retrench them, is a pervasive theme in the directors' communication with the three governments in India. When the governor of Madras, Lord William Bentinck, suggested that the directors' parsimony was an attribute of the Company's very nature. The vast expenditures occasioned by a large standing army, he wrote, "have been the frequent subject of jealousy and animadversions on the part of the superior authority at home," a superior authority still dominated by the corporate mentality of merchants and bankers.[53] Yet the logic of empire outweighed the logic of finance. The size and cost of the Indian administrations grew inexorably, but the expanding bureaucracies were shaped by the Company's continual rearguard action for economy. There was therefore one fundamental rule in administrative expansion: "all additions [of tasks to existing offices] are far inferior in expense to new institutions."[54]

Several proposals for the formation of an office of surveyor general of Madras were made in the eighteenth century. Those by chief engineer Patrick Ross (1775, 1783) and the surveyor Robert Kelly (1779, 1782) sought to emulate Rennell's appointment in Bengal. Those by Michael Topping (1792) and Colin Mackenzie (1796) proposed an organized, peninsula-wide survey. All were rejected by the directors because their advocates could not demonstrate that the extra costs would be offset by savings. The Court's dismissal of Mackenzie's 1796 proposal was so short and absolute,

> Whenever the expediency of appointing a Surveyor General upon your coast shall come under our consideration, Captain Mackenzie's pretensions and your [Madras council's] recommendation of him for that office will be attended to.[55]

that the council could not thereafter entertain any proposal for a surveyor general. Instead, the administration sought to save money by rationalizing the existing cartographic offices.

The council's deliberations, which led in 1810 to the quartermaster general being given primary cartographic responsibility in Madras, were rather inconsequential in form—they mostly hinged on the allocation to the quartermaster general of just 100 pagodas (£37) for the monthly salaries of four Indian draftsmen—and do not warrant a detailed explanation here.[56] The chief engineer was ordered to transfer all his nonengineering maps to the quartermaster general in 1802. The astronomer first took control of the presidency's geographical archive in November 1804, although the quartermaster general was recalcitrant in transferring his maps.[57] Commander in Chief Sir John Craddock managed to transfer the archive to the quartermaster general's office in November 1806, with the ingenuous argument that because the astronomer was a civilian position dealing with the heavens he did not have the requisite skills for either terrestrial or military mapping.[58] The council reinforced the quartermaster general's role by a general order of November 1807, which compelled the administrative offices, particularly the Board of Revenue, to transfer their maps to him.[59]

This debate dealt only with which office should be the archive for all geographic materials in Madras. The orders did not give *exclusive* cartographic responsibility to either the astronomer or the quartermaster general. The chief engineer and the astronomer continued to supervise the copying and compilation of maps while the 1807 order allowed both officers to keep copies of the maps they transferred to the quartermaster general. The council did not consider the possibility of one of the staff officers actually controlling the field surveys. Nor did the council change the existing flow of information to the staff officers, so newly produced materials were not necessarily sent directly to the principal office. Late in 1809, for example, the quartermaster general complained that he had yet to receive any of Mackenzie's maps of Mysore, copies of which had been sent to the council in 1808, and he now wanted Mackenzie's originals lest they be lost and their expense wasted.[60]

These conditions changed significantly when the directors' response to Craddock's manipulations of 1806 was received in May 1810. (The time delay was caused both by the six-month sea voyage between Britain and India and by the arrears of business in the Company's London secretariat, which in 1813 was still preparing replies to letters on military affairs it had received two years previously.)[61] The Court was very much concerned at this time with the secrecy and accuracy of geographic information, so it ordered the transfer of *all* geographic materials to the quartermaster general; copies were not even to be retained by individual offices. The directors extended that requirement to the products of William Lambton's and Mackenzie's surveys. However, the wording of the council's subsequent order to Lambton and Mackenzie—"the Governor in Council is under the necessity of prohibiting you from retaining any copy of the materials now in your possession"—does indicate some reluctance on the council's part. Finally, the directors took the unprecedented step of requiring Lambton and Mackenzie to adhere to the quartermaster general's orders. Nonetheless, the council interpreted that order literally: the directors had specified Mackenzie's work as "Survey of Mysore," which was no longer officially functional, so the council excluded Mackenzie's survey of the Ceded Districts from the quartermaster general's control.[62]

The quartermaster general now possessed more cartographic power than any other staff officer had yet possessed in India: he had, or would soon have, possession of all maps in Madras; he actually controlled all general military surveys, other than strictly engineering surveys, with the exception of Mackenzie's survey of the Ceded Districts. He did not have control of the revenue surveys: none of the orders could disrupt the district collectors' autonomy in that arena. But this situation did not last long. Just two weeks after those last instructions were sent to Lambton and Mackenzie, the governor initiated a review of the army staff appointments that would culminate before the end of 1810 with Mackenzie's appointment as surveyor general and with the reassertion of the field/office division.

The Company's territorial expansion in India and the long wars with France caused a steady decline in the Company's general finances through the first decade of the nineteenth century. The decline was matched by progressively more severe cuts in expenditures. The perennial interest in minor economies became a drive for major retrenchment after 1806. The expensive surveys presented an obvious target for the accountants. Unfortunately, it is next to impossible to derive precise figures for the surveys' expense for the simple reason that their charges were distributed between several accounts: the salaries and allowances for military surveys were charged to military accounts; Lambton's and Mackenzie's allowances and expenses were charged to the public accounts; the Board of Revenue paid for the "assistant surveyors" no matter if they were employed by the collectors or by military surveyors. Some idea of the magnitude of the sums can be gained by an 1806 report that Mackenzie's and Lambton's monthly expenditures in 1804–5 were respectively 1,130 pagodas (£421) and 919 pagodas (£342), or 4 percent and 3¼ percent of all "public" (that is, nonmilitary) expenditure.[63] Alternatively, the Board of Revenue's cartographic expenses had risen by 1808 to the even larger sum of 18,616 pagodas (£6,925) annually, or 1,551 pagodas (£577) per month (table 5.1).

Political support meant that the first retrenchments did not seriously affect the surveys. For example, the 1807 directive by Sir George Barlow, acting governor general, for the Madras council to cut £250,000 from their annual budget included the explicit suggestion that the Calcutta council had suspended "several very useful surveys" and expected Madras to follow suit. Bentinck fiercely objected to even reducing Lambton's survey; the revenue surveys seem to have survived because of their affiliation with the Observatory, which was jealously protected by Petrie.[64]

When the new governor general, Lord Minto, arrived in late 1807, Barlow was transferred to Madras to replace the recalled Bentinck as governor (Petrie had been acting governor). Once in Madras, Barlow promptly began a new round of cuts. Anthony Troyer, who was already pessimistic, confessed to Bentinck that only Minto's active support had saved the Military Institution from the combined onslaught of Barlow

Table 5.1 Cartographic Expenditures by the Madras Board of Revenue, 1794–1808

fasli		Survey School	Revenue Surveys	Tank Repairs	Mysore Survey	General Survey	Total	Total (£)
1204	1794–95	625					625	232
1205	1795–96	1,800					1,800	670
1206	1796–97	1,830	384				2,214	824
1207	1797–98	1,980	773	452			3,205	1,192
1208	1798–99	1,980	767	135	71		2,954	1,099
1209	1799–1800	1,980	1,411	168	396		3,955	1,471
1210	1800–1801	4,663	890	168	616	150	6,487	2,413
1211	1801–2	2,234	881	168	720	250	4,253	1,582
1212	1802–3	3,026	2,085	233	983	279	6,606	2,457
1213	1803–4	2,416	2,646	371	954	319	6,707	2,495
1214	1804–5	7,008	3,613	533	897	865	12,916	4,805
1215	1805–6	2,767	3,985	1,937	1,352	1,050	11,091	4,126
1216	1806–7	4,694	4,733	2,830	2,483	1,096	15,836	5,891
1217	1807–8	8,381	5,081	1,540	1,306	2,311	18,616	6,925
	TOTAL	45,384	27,251	8,535	9,778	6,321	97,269	
	(£)	16,883	10,137	3,175	3,637	2,351		36,184

Note: All figures are rounded to the nearest pagoda. Figures for *fasli* 1217 are only to 30 April 1808, sixty-one days short of the full year; for comparison, each value in the table has been prorated to provide an estimate for the full-year expenditure. The *fasli* runs from 1 July to 30 June.
Source: MRB 4 Aug 1808, IOR P/289/13, 6486.

and the Finance Committee.[65] Barlow's high-handed manner had alienated the military establishment in Bengal and his reputation had preceded him to Madras. The severity of his retrenchments led in early 1809 to the mutiny of the Madras army's European officers. By August, when Minto took over the Madras government, some 1,300 Company officers had been placed in custody by Crown troops; fewer than 150 had signed the loyalty oath demanded by Barlow.[66]

The "White Mutiny" led in 1810 to an investigation of the state of the Madras army by the commander in chief of India, Sir George Hewett. Barlow's rubric for the inquiry emphasized the organization of the staff: what were their proper duties, responsibilities, and salaries? Barlow drew Hewett's specific attention both to the state of the surveys and to the employment of the Military Institution's graduates. The last, Barlow wrote, enjoyed allowances that exceeded those "of several respectable staff appointments," such as the commissary generals and brigade majors, despite their youth and their failure to serve with their regiments.[67] Hewett's thorough report accordingly identified two reforms of direct importance for the surveys: a surveyor general was needed and the Military Institution's curriculum ought to focus less on mapmaking.[68]

With respect to the surveys as a whole, Hewett adopted the standard position of nonsurveyors with respect to the surveys: he repeatedly disavowed any depth of knowledge on the subject. Even so, he set forth a set of convoluted proposals dominated by the appointment of a surveyor general. He specifically recommended Mackenzie for the job. Hewett's conception of the surveyor general was as the administration's cartographic expert: he would coordinate and facilitate civil surveys, ensuring that there was no more duplication; he would supervise a central depot for storing and for copying, as required, all geographical materials in the government's possession. Hewett would have given all cartographic responsibility to the quartermaster general, except that officer already had too many duties. Hewett reserved for the quartermaster general the responsibility for organizing and supervising military surveys of "routes, passes, and such provinces as have been least explored" (¶248), together with the mandated surveys of the routes of army columns; these surveys would of course be passed on to the surveyor general once all relevant military information had been extracted. The quartermaster general was to remain subordinate to the commander in chief and the Military Board, whereas the surveyor general would answer directly to the governor in council.

Hewett agreed with Bentinck's intent for the Military Institution to improve the education and quality of staff officers, which Hewett found were still demonstrably low. He therefore recommended that all staff officers must first attend the Military Institution but that all of the institution's students must have first served with their corps for at least three years. This last provision would make them better able to appreciate their studies "in the higher walks of military science" (¶233). Both recommendations necessarily required the institution to shift its focus from mapmaking to military science in general.

The creation of the office of surveyor general required Hewett to demonstrate that the reorganization would more than offset the new expenditures. He anticipated that his reductions, all of which he justified as making the staff more effective, would halve the existing cartographic expenditures, before the costs of the new department were added. As implemented through a series of general orders dated 9 October 1810,[69] the savings were actually greater, achieving an overall reduction of about 40 percent from an annual 78,000 pagodas (£29,000) in 1810 to 46,685 pagodas (£17,370) in 1812 (table 5.2).[70] Hewett stopped the Travancore and Deccan surveys because, if officers were to be restricted to their proper tasks, then engineers should be engineering not surveying. Furthermore, only two of the institution's graduates currently on survey duty had served the requisite three years with their regiments; Hewett allowed them to stay on survey, but the rest were

Table 5.2 Savings in Survey Expenditures, Madras, 1810–1812

	Expenditure			
	30 Dec 1810	31 Jan 1812	Increase	Decrease
QMG's Office[a,j]	6,051	3,176		2,875
Lambton, General Survey[b]	12,222	9,607		2,615
Military Institution[c,j]	17,140	9,049		8,091
Travancore Survey[d,j]	5,550	576		4,974
Hyderabad Survey[d,j]	3,618	432		3,186
Goa Survey[e]	9,439	4,428		5,011
Center Division Survey[d]	1,895	0		1,895
Northern Circars Survey[d]	343	0		343
Presidency Surveys[d]	867	0		867
Ile de Bourbon Survey	393	393		0
Surveys in Persia	741	741		0
Observatory and School[f]	8,065	738		7,327
Southern Surveys[g]	6,644	4,266		2,378
Ceded Districts Survey[h]	5,038	3,690		1,348
Surveyor General's Office[i]	0	8,624	8,624	
Eastern Expedition[i]	0	965	965	
TOTALS	78,006	46,685	9,589	40,910
			less	9,589
			Annual Savings	31,321
				(£11,650)

Notes: All figures are the annual costs represented by the then monthly expenditures. All are in pagodas.

[a] Three surveyors removed; only two remained, on reduced allowances.

[b] Four officers (assistants from the Military Institution) removed.

[c] One class on reduced allowance. Field survey reduced from seven to five months.

[d] Abolished.

[e] Five officers struck off.

[f] The appointments of astronomer, inspector of revenue surveys, and superintendent of the survey school all abolished; considerable reduction in the establishment.

[g] Four revenue surveyors removed or struck off; one died and was not replaced.

[h] Office establishment and surveyors' allowances reduced.

[i] No expense under these heads in November 1810.

[j] The original statement of costs as of 31 January 1812 did not include some new costs for the quartermaster general, for Troyer's field expenses, and for administrative adjustments to cover the *batta* of the engineers formerly on the Travancore and Hyderabad surveys.

Source: "Separate Statement shewing the Decrease of Expense in the Surveying Department . . . between the 30th November 1810 and the 31st January 1812," 25 Feb 1812, MMC 11 Feb 1812, IOR F/4/362 9029, 65–66.

returned to regimental duty. The institution's annual field season was transferred to the surveyor general's control and its duration reduced from seven to five months. Hewett reduced allowances. Finally, and most importantly, Hewett adopted the proposals made in 1806 and 1808 to abolish the revenue survey establishment. That placed Warren in an institutionally weak position that subsequently allowed Barlow to abolish the position of Company's astronomer and to place the Observatory under the surveyor general's authority, despite Petrie's 1808 arguments that it was a full-time position.[71]

The abolition of the revenue surveys was the only reform which was not smoothly implemented. Eleven of the forty-two assistant surveyors were allowed to stay under the direction of district collectors because Barlow recognized that to do otherwise would "distress a number of individuals who had been reared in the service of the Public";[72] they continued to work until 1813 on the revenue surveys of Dindigul and Madura, Tinnevelly, and Coimbatore. Of the remainder, those who desired were released from their indentures and the rump were transferred to the surveyor general's control, where they continued to work for both Mackenzie and Lambton.

The relative decreases in the expenditures of each survey are revealing (table 5.3). The Observatory was worst hit, suffering a 90-percent cut. Least affected was Lambton's survey, whose loss of four institution graduates represented a 25-percent reduction. Overall, almost half of the savings came from reductions in the detailed topographical and

Table 5.3 Relative Savings in Survey Expenditures, Madras, 1810–1812

| | Pagodas per Year | | | | Percentage of total savings* |
| | Expenditure | | Decrease | | |
	Nov 1810	Jan 1812	(absolute)	(%)	
Quartermaster General's Office	6,051	3,176	2,875	47.5	7.0
Lambton's General Survey	12,222	9,607	2,615	21.4	6.4
Military Institution	17,140	9,049	8,091	47.2	19.8
Observatory	8,065	738	7,327	90.8	17.9
Topographic Surveys	34,248	14,526	19,722	58.2	48.2

*That is, contribution to the total reduction before the increase of the surveyor general's office is factored in.

Source: "Separate Statement shewing the Decrease of Expense in the Surveying Department . . . between the 30th November 1810 and the 31st January 1812," 25 Feb 1812, MMC 11 Feb 1812, IOR F/4/362 9029, 65–66.

revenue surveys. The very large total retrenchment contributed significantly to the savings effected by all of Hewett's army reforms. One financial summary indicated that the immediate savings totaled 80,616 pagodas (£30,000) per year and another 26,250 pagodas (£9,750) of annual savings would eventually accrue. In other words, just under 40 percent of all of the immediate savings due to military reforms came from the survey department alone.[73]

The institutional result of the reforms was a tripartite division of responsibility. The quartermaster general would control the military surveys as Hewett had anticipated; he was allowed to requisition even the chief engineer's map library. (With the appointment of a surveyor general for all India, in 1815, the quartermaster general's surveying activities became more coherent.) The surveyor general would have the largest responsibility because he would control all other detailed surveys as well as an office establishment devoted to copying and storing all geographical materials, including maps, survey journals, memoirs, route descriptions, and so on. Finally, Lambton's general survey was held to be a distinct and separate entity; Hewett made no mention of it other than in the summary of savings, and he clearly envisioned no change other than the removal of Lambton's institution graduates. Lambton's autonomy, so briefly surrendered to the quartermaster general, was restored.

So, thirty-five years after Patrick Ross had first suggested the appointment of a surveyor general for Madras in 1775, Colin Mackenzie was finally installed in that office. As in Bengal and Bombay, the position was concerned primarily with the maintenance of a geographical archive. A highly significant difference was that the Madras surveyor general would control those surveys which were of a *general* nature. That is, this new position entailed an institutional link between the urban archive and the field survey. However, those surveys continued to exist at the council's discretion. As long as the Company's purse strings remained drawn tight, Mackenzie was in no position to implement a program to finish the general topographical survey of southern India that had long been his goal. As it was, just a few established surveys were permitted to continue: the "assistant surveyors" from the Ceded Districts were redeployed after 1813 in various areas of the Carnatic; the institution's annual field season; and James Garling's survey of Goa. In contrast, those surveys intended for *specific* military or engineering purposes remained beyond the surveyor general's control.

Had Mackenzie stayed at Madras, he might have been able to persuade the council to sanction some new surveys. Yet his position as surveyor general was still subordinate to his duties as one of the senior engineers on the Madras establishment. If nothing else indicates the still problematic status of mapping activities, Mackenzie's posting in April 1811 as chief engineer to the Java Expedition signifies just that. He did not return to Madras until March 1815, when he had already been promoted to be the first surveyor general of India under the Calcutta government. William Morison, who had briefly surveyed with Mackenzie in Mysore, served jointly as commissary general and as surveyor general. He might have been uninterested in the extra office, or he had insufficient time to attend to it, or he lacked Mackenzie's prestige and clout, but whatever the reason, the topographic and revenue surveys stagnated under his control.

When Morison stated in 1839 that the Madras surveys had been systemized in "about 1811,"[74] he missed one very important point. Just because an office of surveyor general had been created at Madras to supervise cartographic activity, it did not mean that mapmaking was magically and instantaneously unified. In the same way, the creation of the office of surveyor general of India in 1815 did not bring the disparate activities at the three presidencies into one grand system. The theme of cartographic anarchy runs throughout Part Three, in which I discuss the development of the Great Trigonometrical Survey; it is apparent in chapter 6, less so in chapters 7 and 8, which principally address policy issues. Despite the attempts by the presidencies to control the collection of data, sporadic surveys continued. The chief engineer of the Army of the Indus, for example, was reported in 1841 as making his own survey, simply because no one else was available. And route surveys were still a requisite for every march by a detachment; the habit of route surveying was so ingrained that even George Everest kept track of his travels for the Great Trigonometrical Survey in that manner.[75] The context for the formation of systematic and efficient cartographic policies by the directors and secretariat in London and by the administrators in India continued to be the continuing collection of geographic information by many different officers.

PART THREE

THE GREAT TRIGONOMETRICAL SURVEY AND CARTOGRAPHIC SYSTEM

There is no other solid basis [than triangulation] on which accurate geography can so well be founded. The primary triangles thus spread over this vast country establish almost beyond error a multitude of points, and the spaces comprehended within these, when filled up by the details of subordinate surveyors, will afford . . . to the world, a map without a parallel, whether in the relation to its accuracy, to its extensiveness, or to the unity of the effort by which it will have been achieved. The importance attached to such works by the economists and statesmen, as well as by the learned of Europe, is proved by the perseverance for so many years of England and France in similar undertakings.

Lord Hastings, governor general
and commander in chief, 1817

CHAPTER SIX

Institutions for Mapping All of British India, 1814–23

It is no coincidence that Lord Hastings should have recorded these sentiments just when the East India Company finally achieved its hegemony over the vast extent of South Asia east of the Punjab. Hastings was then in the field, directing the northern theater of the Company's final war with the Maratha princes of central and western India. The war was the long-anticipated consolidation of British power in the subcontinent after Lord Wellesley's precipitate territorial expansion during the period of 1798 through 1803.[1] Since the 1780s and James Rennell's maps of "Hindustan," the British had possessed a conceptual geography that equated the whole subcontinent with the field of British interest. The political developments of the 1810s intensified that relationship, so that the field of British power coincided with the subcontinent. An integral element of this intensification was the unification of the British geographical archives. The Great Trigonometrical Survey (GTS) played a pivotal role in that unification, but not in the manner that Hastings envisaged. The GTS did provide a new means of structuring and ordering the geographic archive; yet it engendered a compromise in Enlightenment cartography's dichotomy of epistemological certitude between observation in the field and archival compilation.

The Company's development of a coherent geographic archive was defined by changes within the existing institutional structures which governed map production and use in India. The appointment in 1814 of a single surveyor general of India was an attempt by the Court of Directors to control yet further the flow of geographical information. Separate provincial surveyor generals were useful in coordinating the mapping of the three presidencies, but they hindered the construction of maps of all of India. The surveyor generals were not given special permission to correspond with each other, so no one individual could gather together all of the available data. The purpose of a surveyor general of India, at least from the Court's perspective, was to concentrate geographical data from all three presidencies in one site and to distil them for transmission to London.

The concept of a surveyor general of India entailed the construction of a *definitive* map of the subcontinent. There was to be no more duplication and waste. The complete, comprehensive, and encyclopedic geographic archive was to be enshrined in one map of India. The second surveyor general, John Hodgson, did accept this archival understanding of the mapping of India. But his colleagues argued that the only way to make such a definitive map was to ensure that each and every survey was itself to be definitive. Colin Mackenzie, the first surveyor general of India, actively subverted the Court's intentions for his position and advocated a survey of India. Mackenzie's system called for a triangulation of each district to provide the framework for detailed topographic surveys. In contrast, Hastings advocated an India-wide triangulation to define the geometry of the whole subcontinent.

This debate went hand in hand with the development of a policy for disseminating the geographic archive more broadly than in the past. Although the directors sought to preserve the Company's proprietary rights to the geographical archive, they were increasingly open to the publication of a large-scale map of India. The expansion of the geographical scope and responsibilities of the Company's territorial government promoted increased map use to such a level that manuscript copying could barely keep up with demand. At the same time, the steady increase in the number of detailed topographic surveys required the cartographers to increase the scale of their general maps in order to manage all of the information. The European encyclopedic mentality required that *all* data be presented in voluminous texts and multisheet maps. The problem for India remained the highly variable coverage of geographic data: southern and eastern India was far better known than northern and western India, so that any map of India constructed at a scale sufficiently large to incorporate all available data for southern India and Bengal would inevitably have vast expanses of white elsewhere. An alternate method was necessary for organizing and updating the map of India. The directors accordingly reworked their idea of the definitive map. They proposed in 1823 to create an *Atlas of India*. The atlas format was flexible enough that the maps could be updated as necessary without becoming too unwieldy. As each map was engraved and published, it could be disseminated to the Company's officials.

Between those two *cartographic* milestones, Hastings transferred William Lambton's general survey to the Calcutta government and named it the Great Trigonometrical Survey of India. As Hastings assured the Calcutta council, the GTS embodied the ideal of the perfect corpus of geographic data. The formation of the GTS was thus essential for the creation of a single cartographic image of India in that it promoted the idea that the final maps would be definitive. The engraving of the *Atlas* was thus justified as its maps would entail few, if any, subsequent corrections. The tie between the *Atlas* and the Great Trigonometrical Survey was not complete: the surveyors all seem to have thought that to carry the triangulation across the northern plains would be so expensive as to be impractical; in those districts, the *Atlas* would have to be based on astronomical control.

Whatever the form of control, the *Atlas* project was designed to convert the multiple, disorganized topographic surveys into an overall cartographic system. The *Atlas* compromised the principles of trigonometrical surveying and their concern for the uniformity of data in order to promote a uniform image of India derived from multiple data sources of varying quality. Field surveys would be made to be definitive by warping them to fit the triangulation or astronomical framework rather than by prosecuting the surveys in a systematic manner from the start. The *Atlas* continued to systematize the geographical archive rather than geographical observation.

The surveyors in India interpreted the appointment of a single surveyor general of India as implying that the Court recognized the need for a true single survey of the subcontinent. They challenged the epistemological compromises implicit in a single surveyor general and in the *Atlas*. Valentine Blacker, George Everest, and Thomas Best Jervis in particular wished to copy the techniques and institutional organization of the Ordnance Survey of Ireland for a coherent and thoroughly field-based survey of India. Their attempts to establish that survey, discussed in chapters 7 and 8, were unsuccessful. The result of the debates they stimulated was to reinforce the *Atlas of India*'s compromise position.

A Surveyor General of India, 1814:
Controlling the Archive

James Rennell did not make many maps of India after the second edition in 1792 of his *New Map of Hindostan*. An explanation is provided by Lieutenant Colonel James Salmond, formerly of the Bengal infantry, son-in-law of David Scott, a highly influential Company director (chairman, 1796–97), and, after 1809, the Court's secretary for military affairs. Writing in the 1820s, and relying on official lore, Salmond stated that "soon after" 1788 "communications on geographical subjects [had] ceased to be made to Major Rennell." Salmond presumed that this decision was made because the Court "thought the publication of any geographical matter relating to India imprudent."[2] The directors did actually continue to defer to Rennell's opinion on cartographic affairs; they simply did not allow him the use of new maps. The Company's concern to keep maps secret meant that responsibility for constructing and maintaining general maps of India shifted to the various cartographic officers in India.

The Company's insistence that geographic data flow only along the established lines of communication meant that surveyor generals could not gain legitimate access to geographical information collected in other presidencies. This was not always a problem, as when Robert Colebrooke and Charles Reynolds exchanged information after 1804. On the other hand, the Madras council refused in 1808 to allow copies of maps to be sent to Monier Williams in Bombay, to be added to Reynolds's map, and argued that the best place to construct a single map of India was at the center of the information flow: London.[3] Furthermore, by being kept in manuscript, the maps were eventually lost and the money spent on them wasted. In order to avoid these problems, the Court directed in June 1814 that the three provincial surveyor generals should be replaced by a single surveyor general of India.[4]

The Court was very explicit that the reform of the "survey department" was part of the continuing military retrenchments. The orders began with a succinct paragraph: "Having taken into consideration the state of the Department of Survey in India we are particularly struck with the magnitude of the sums which have been expended on it" (¶1, also ¶17). In addition to the Madras surveys, which had consumed "about twenty thousand pounds per annum" over "many years" (¶2), three maps of India were particularly to blame in this regard.

Thomas Call, surveyor general of Bengal, had begun a "general plan" of India in 1779 at the direction of the Calcutta council. His plan was to compile a twenty-sheet atlas at sixteen miles to the inch (1:1,013,760). The numerous additions and corrections caused by each new survey and report meant that the work was still in a "very rough" state when Call resigned in 1786. Nor was it complete: it still needed to have added the results of Reynolds's surveys in western India. Call's successor, Mark Wood, began a neat copy of the map, but found that the paper of the original had significantly deformed and therefore redrew it almost entirely from scratch. Call himself died en route to Britain in 1788, but his "Grand Atlas of India" did reach the Court. Call had initially argued that he could make a better map of India than Rennell because he was "on the spot" and could acquire much more information than Rennell had available to him in London. But Call had been overly optimistic: Rennell's evaluation of the atlas found that his work lacked the recent work by Madras and Bombay surveyors. The London copy of the atlas was lost by 1814, and the Court had no record of how much had been spent on it other than "a considerable sum" (¶4).[5]

Reynolds, surveyor general of Bombay, had obtained the governor general's permission in 1793 to compile a map at twice the scale of Call's atlas (eight miles to an inch, 1:506,880). Constructed on only one sheet, it covered some four hundred square feet (37.16 m²). Reynolds's attempts to gather data for regions beyond Bombay's control were limited by the Court's 1799 order that the map was to include only information which he or his Indian employees had gathered. This curious decision seems to have stemmed from a desire to restrict the flow of geographic information to the proper channels of communication. As a result, the map had weak coverage of the Madras and Bengal presidencies. Three copies of Reynolds's map are known to have been made: Reynolds took one back to London in 1807, where it was hung up in its own room at the India House and was, as a result, eventually destroyed; the original itself was further modified and submitted in 1809 to the governor general by Reynolds's successor, Williams; a third, revised version was submitted to the Bombay government in 1821 but has not survived. In 1814, the directors exclaimed that the map was still unfinished, although its cost had "much exceeded one hundred thousand pounds" (¶2).[6]

Finally, Colebrooke in Bengal made a general map of India at sixteen miles to the inch (1:1,013,760) on his own initiative, probably to keep an up-to-date source from which regional and district maps could be copied whenever requested. Like Reynolds, Colebrooke sought the governor general's permission to acquire the results of the Bombay and Madras surveys. Once again, permission was denied. Colebrooke continued to work on the map until his death in September 1808. His successor, John Garstin, found the map to be barely one-third complete and thought that it would require at least three more years of concerted effort to finish. Garstin, however, had little time to devote to the work and was still adding to it in 1813. By 1819, no copies of the map could be found in Calcutta and no copy seems ever to have been sent to the Court in London. The Court thought that Colebrooke might have "put together with great zeal and assiduity the best materials procurable under the Bengal Presidency" to produce "the most authentic and best performance of his time," yet that map was fundamentally flawed because of the lack of "a considerable portion" of the Bombay and Madras data (¶¶5–6).[7]

Paradoxically, the directors do not seem to have recognized their own role in limiting the transfer of information between the presidencies. The immediate cause of the appointment of a surveyor general of India was not the desire for a cost-efficient mapping system but the Court's perception of rivalries among the surveyors which had blocked the flow of geographical information, even to London. Salmond, who as

military secretary had probably drafted the Court's orders, later recalled that the whole issue of the "geography of India" had been "revived" because the three surveyor generals had "been found to entertain jealousies of each other, and [had been] unwilling to communicate
the geographical information respectively acquired by them, either to
each other or to the Court."[8]

There had indeed been occasions when surveyors had refused even
to transmit their journals and maps to London, and they seem to have
stung the London administration.[9] Referring to Colebrooke's inability
to acquire geographic information from Madras and Bombay, information which had of course been paid for by the Company, the Court
stated:

> ¶7. On every principle of public utility this information ought to
> have been supplied [to Colebrooke], but we apprehend that diffi-
> culties and obstructions might have been experienced in obtaining
> it from the following cause.
>
> ¶8. At each of the other Presidencies there was also a Surveyor
> General carrying on his separate plan. The partiality which these
> officers would feel for their own performances [that is, maps] and
> the prospect which might possibly be entertained of future advan-
> tage from them [namely, their maps] would naturally render them
> averse to furnish information to a rival map. We are not without
> experience of our own orders having failed in procuring informa-
> tion of this nature when we applied for it.

The Court understood that by surrendering a map, a surveyor might
also be surrendering the monetary and rank benefits which were offered to him by the Company's patronage system. What the Court
therefore sought to implement was a system whereby geographical
data were to be collected by just one official in India, thereby eliminat-
ing the prejudices.

The Court's conception of mapmaking was based on the construction
of a uniform archive from data of all types. Only a survey's assimilation
into the larger archive, into "one general Map of India," could "render
it of proper use" (¶9); the "proper object" of geographical information
"ought always to be a general Map of the Country" (¶10); the "main
purpose of the Department of Survey" was the "concentration" of all
data into "one uniform geographical performance" (¶16). The repeated
references to a "department of survey" implied that the archive made
the surveys into a functionally coherent whole even if they did not constitute a single institution. The archive itself was permanent: until a
survey's results were incorporated into the general map, its information
was "liable to become obsolete, . . . lost, or mislaid, or to perish from

vermin, or the effects of the climate" (¶10). The Court did not begrudge the cost of making surveys, but it thought it obvious that the only way to ensure that surveys were properly cost-effective was to concentrate all geographic information in one office. And once concentrated there, it could be distilled and the results sent on to London.

The technological fixation on the archive did not prevent the Court from recognizing that surveys, and thus the information they produced, did vary in quality. The directors asserted that descriptive memoirs were essential for the process of map compilation. Journals kept by the surveyors would allow the surveyor general to gauge the quality of their work and would help in its incorporation into the archive. The surveyor general would in turn keep a memoir that explained that process of compilation and the sources he used and would therefore support the veracity of the final map (¶¶14 and 22). In this, the Court and its advisors—influenced perhaps by fifteen years of the rhetoric of triangulation and complex topographical surveys in Madras—recognized that the most valuable survey was the *definitive* survey which derived its certainty from the methods of observation and not from its subsequent archival compilation. This point is important for the development of the Great Trigonometrical Survey.

The Court therefore ordered that the three provincial surveyor generals be replaced by one surveyor general of India. That officer was "not to conduct Surveys himself." He was "to receive and appreciate the Surveys made by others"; selecting the best of existing and any future materials, he was then charged with "reducing them to a uniform scale, to frame from these materials Maps of Provinces, or of Divisions [that is, regular sheets], comprehending a certain extent in latitude and longitude." The "Separate Maps" would in turn "constitute the foundation" of "a general Map of India . . . reduced to a scale which may confine [it] within manageable limits" (¶19). The surveyor general should regularly transmit copies of his maps to the Court; the Court might in turn publish the maps so as to make them widely useful (¶24).

That is, contrary to the assumption common in the summary histories of the British mapping of India, the presence of a surveyor general was not directed at the creation of uniformity in actual surveying. The new position was an attempt to formalize the interactions between the expert surveyors and their nonexpert superiors by creating a sole expert consultant who was positioned to one side of, not between, the Calcutta council and the surveyors in the formal administrative hierarchy. The Court envisioned that all new surveys would have to be approved by the Calcutta council, regardless of the presidency, with only the advice of the surveyor general. Once done, each survey's journals and maps were to be lodged with the surveyor general, who would then recommend payment (or nonpayment) of the surveyors' allowances (¶22). The chief engineers at Bombay and Madras would revert to their former duties as supervisors of their presidencies' map repositories; they would keep copies of each new survey as completed, but existing and future maps were all to be transferred to Calcutta.

Financially, the Court expected the existing offices of the surveyor general in Bengal and of the chief engineers in Madras and Bombay to accommodate the increased workload with only one or two new draftsmen. It therefore anticipated saving almost the full expense of the offices of surveyor general in the two presidencies which most needed to cut expenditures: £3,000 at Madras and £1,900 at Bombay (¶¶23–25).

Archive or Field? Mackenzie's Redefinition of the Surveyor General's Duties

India's distance from Britain meant that policies set by the Court were not always properly implemented. This was the case with the appointment of a surveyor general of India and the abolition of the three provincial positions. The idea was seen as quite impracticable by the surveyors in India. John Hodgson, one of the senior field surveyors in Bengal, noted its inherent difficulties:

> Surely Lord [Hastings] will see the absurdity of the new arrangements . . . [The Court] might as well order one Superintending Surgeon, or Reviewing General, for the three Presidencies; 'tis not by this sort of economy that the arch-enemy [Napoleon] Buonaparte acted.[10]

The Court's intentions implied an extension of the Calcutta council's authority so as to encompass some of the detailed activities of the Madras and Bombay governments. Yet the Calcutta council could not require the lesser councils to appoint their military officers to (or dismiss them from) staff positions; to do so would have been a radical interference with the interest wielded by those councils. Unless the governor general were to make explicit directives, both Madras and Bombay remained autonomous. And Hastings did not so direct. Instead, he accepted Colin Mackenzie's opinions that local control needed to be wielded over the Madras surveys and so did not force the abolition of the surveyor general's office there. By extension, the Bombay council retained its survey office too. Reiteration of its orders by the Court in 1818 and 1819 had little effect.[11]

Mackenzie was clearly the obvious choice for the new position of surveyor general of India. His duties as chief engineer on the Ceylon and Java expeditions, his highly esteemed work on the survey of Mysore, his historical collections, and his recent appointment to be surveyor general of Madras, all meant that he had a prominent position in the minds of senior officials in both London and India. He was without doubt the preeminent surveyor in India at the time. The directors appointed him to the new position in March 1815; the Calcutta council appointed him as well, in May, well before the Court's decision reached India.[12] Mackenzie had been in Calcutta when the Court's letter of June 1814 arrived the following December, but he had returned to Madras before his new appointment was announced.

Given Mackenzie's commitment to forming a coherent survey organization—most recently expressed in November 1814 when he wrote to the acting surveyor general in Madras about "accelerating [the surveys] and obtaining a more complete knowledge of the Country in an uniform method," as cheaply and as easily as possible[13]—he was bound to oppose the Court's orders. In December 1815, he opposed the abolition of his position in Madras because some officer had to keep the increasing expenditures of the Military Institution and the quartermaster general in check, as well as to supervise the continuing surveys. Indeed, to close these down would be stupid as only about 11 percent of the peninsula remained to be surveyed. Besides, the Eurasian "assistant surveyors" would still have to be supported if the surveys were ended. Furthermore, the office was cheaper than William Lambton's independent trigonometrical survey; because Lambton had not reported any results recently, Mackenzie obliquely hinted that it might be worthwhile to axe the trigonometrical survey rather than the surveyor general's office.[14]

On the other hand, Mackenzie did approve of the rationality of a single cartographic office for India, but he thought that a single *survey* office would be more appropriate. Despite the Court's clear rejection of any such role for the surveyor general of India, Mackenzie asserted that the orders necessarily entailed the active extension of the surveys. "On a mature consideration of those reasons that must have influenced" the Court's decision, which had the "evident view and intention of concentrating the whole under one general System," Mackenzie concluded that the Court did not want to forego "the utility and advantage of extending surveys throughout the whole of the British Possessions in India."[15] In other words, Mackenzie incorrectly ascribed to the directors the same motivations and reasons for giving their orders that he would have had, had he been in their place: if they wanted a uniform map of India, then they must want a uniform system of surveying to create it. (The Court was in actuality set on creating a uniform archival representation.)

The Madras council accepted much of Mackenzie's reasoning. It permitted the continued existence of the survey establishment until the four remaining district surveys and the Deccan survey were completed, but it did not agree to keep the survey office.[16] Mackenzie was reluctant to leave Madras to take up his new position in Calcutta until he received some assurance that the survey office would survive. He repeated his arguments at length and at regular intervals, misrepresenting the Court's orders as necessarily requiring a unified survey system and so dictating the appointment of an assistant surveyor general at Madras. Mackenzie was adamant that *all* surveys should come under the single control of himself, as surveyor general.[17]

The governor general and the council in Calcutta grew increasingly impatient with Mackenzie. Charles Crawford had consented to remain in charge of the office until Mackenzie should replace him, but he retired in December 1815 and left the Calcutta office unsupervised. In April 1817, the Calcutta council directed the Madras council to turn Mackenzie's office over to the chief engineer, whether Mackenzie liked it or not, unless he could provide explicit plans for returning north.[18] The following month, the Calcutta council gave Mackenzie a blunt order—pack up and leave—but softened it with an important concession:

> It seems at least *possible* that the literal execution of the Honorable Court's orders . . . may be a measure of very doubtful utility, and may tend to defeat that projected unity of effort and concentration of geographical and statistical information, which it was the declared object of the Honorable Court of Directors to create, when they placed the whole Indian survey department under a single chief. [original emphasis]

A survey school could also be established in Calcutta with the help of Mackenzie's Eurasian assistants, who would not therefore be thrown off the Company's payrolls. Thus, Hastings was willing to disobey the Court's explicit orders by keeping cartographic establishments at Madras (and by extension at Bombay) and by having the surveyor general control survey activities. But Hastings declined from making any permanent decision until he could talk the matter through personally with Mackenzie, in Calcutta.[19]

With both carrot and stick applied, Mackenzie quickly wrapped up his affairs in the south. The Madras governor acceded to Mackenzie's requests. John Riddell was appointed temporarily in charge of the Madras survey department, his appointment as assistant surveyor general being made permanent in June 1818. Mackenzie left for Calcutta in July 1817. But, once there, he seemed to find little to suit him in his new surroundings, as revealed in his long letters to his old friend Thomas Munro. For a start, Hastings did not prove to be as amenable to making a general survey of India along Mackenzie's lines as Mackenzie had wished. Hastings might have allowed the continuation of the survey offices at Madras and Bombay in order to coordinate the local surveys and to meet local cartographic needs, but he maintained the established distinction in Bengal between the surveyor general and the quartermaster general. Even more to Mackenzie's distaste, Hastings transferred William Lambton's survey to the Calcutta government without consulting Mackenzie.[20] Hastings wished to have a uniform survey, but he wanted Lambton's rather than Mackenzie's system.

The Great Trigonometrical Survey: One Framework for India

The idea that William Lambton's survey should be under the control of the Calcutta government was not new. It had had some currency in 1807, when Lambton was given the services of four graduates of the Military Institution and reported that Lord Minto, the governor general, agreed in principle to a transfer. Lambton was overly optimistic to hope that the Royal Society would resurrect William Roy's proposal for a geodetic arc in Bengal once it received the papers Lambton had sent home with Lord William Bentinck.[21] The possible extension of the survey was taken up again in 1811, when Sir George Barlow, Bentinck's successor as governor of Madras, agreed that Lambton ought to carry his triangles north of the Tunghabadra River and into the territories of the Nizam of Hyderabad, the catch being that the Nizam was officially tied to the Calcutta government.[22]

Neither occasion led to Lambton's transfer, perhaps because the administrators expected a negative reaction from the Court. True to form, the Court wrote to the Madras council in September 1814 that Lambton's survey would soon be completed if it were limited to its "original object." Bearing in mind the confusion over the character of Lambton's survey, it is unclear just what the Court meant by his "original object," but it seems to have taken exception to the steady extension of the survey beyond Mysore and the far south.[23]

In contrast, Lord Hastings had no reservations about either Lambton or his work when he ordered Lambton's transfer in October 1817.[24] His directive made it clear that several institutional barriers had fallen. The commander in chief of the British Army had granted Lambton unlimited leave of absence from his regiment so that he was no longer in any danger of being dragged off to other duties (¶3). Lambton's scientific credentials were now clearly unimpeachable: John Warren's lobbying had led to his election as a corresponding member of the Académie des Sciences in Paris, followed in 1817 by his election as a fellow of the Royal Society in London.[25] Despite Hastings's strenuous refutation of any allegation that he was "vainly seeking to partake [of] the gale of public favor and applause which the labors of Lieut. Colonel Lambton have recently attracted," Lambton's tardy recognition by the most prestigious scientific societies of Europe had significantly bolstered his reputation in India. Third, the "analogous" and "parallel" appointment by the Court of a single surveyor general of India had established the precedent of all-India cartographic institutions. Moreover, since 1814 Lambton had been operating in princely states that were the direct political subordinates of the government of India; placing Lambton under the administration in Bengal would obviate the delays caused by the referral of questions from Madras to Calcutta. Finally, Hastings thought it only logical that a work of such great importance should fall under the principal government in India (¶¶4–5).

Yet these reasons would not have counted for much had Hastings not been an avid supporter of "scientific" surveys. He had had some close contact with the Ordnance Survey in England and Wales when he had been master general of Ordnance (1806–7). His comment that he could therefore speak of the issue "with no ordinary confidence" (¶3) is in marked contrast to the disclaimers usually given by government officials about their lack of even general knowledge of the subject. He waxed lyrical on the fundamental necessity of the survey for the East India Company as an institution with pretensions to sovereign authority:

> This magnificent work was projected and is carried on under [the Court's] particular auspices and munificent patronage, in a manner befitting that dignified body: their perseverance in this grand enterprise is worthy of the splendid original design, and this single public act has raised the name of the English East India Company in the eyes of the scientific world to a level with those of the great sovereigns of Europe, who have been their only rivals in similar undertakings. (¶2)

More practically, in a paragraph used as the epigraph for this Part, Hastings laid down the cartographic facts of life: a geographical survey of any large extent must be based on a triangulation; anything else would simply be inadequate. Hastings accorded to Lambton's survey the essential ingredients of the ideal of systematic surveys based on geodetic triangulations: great accuracy, large extent, and uniformity of process. Only in this manner would truly definitive topographical surveys be made. In contrast, the system of survey advocated by Mackenzie involved many small surveys undertaken with the same processes but only with accuracy *sufficient* for general mapping.

It is possible that Hastings had no other immediate motivation than his personal interest. Certainly, he had already proven himself to be interested in the problems of surveying in India when in 1815 he had written a key memorandum on the Bengal revenue system, which had reasserted the necessity for land surveys as part of the settlement of revenue in the Upper Provinces.[26] But it is more likely that he was stimulated partly by Colin Mackenzie's return to Calcutta[27] and by a letter from Lambton, which is now lost. Lambton was now sixty years old and a lieutenant colonel. Neither factor permitted him to take the field as he ought. He needed to train an assistant, lest the survey lapse for lack of an adequate successor should he die or retire (¶7). If Lambton followed the pattern of his petitions to previous governor generals, this request probably mentioned the prospect of a transfer to the Bengal government.

Hastings set forth a series of resolutions (¶6). As of 1 January 1818, Lambton was to be under the "immediate direction and control" of the Bengal government. His survey was finally given an official name: the Great Trigonometrical Survey of India, in direct imitation of the Ordnance Survey's contemporary title of "Great Trigonometrical Survey of England and Wales." Lambton was to be styled the survey's superintendent. "Out of respect" for Lambton's "rank, talents and eminent services," the GTS was to be separate from the surveyor general; the distinction, however, would be subject to revision once Lambton ceased to be superintendent. Lambton was to receive two more European staff: a chief assistant, and "a person skilled in natural science, and capable of affording medical and surgical aid to the survey establishment" to be both geologist and surgeon. Hastings selected Captain George Everest of the Bengal artillery to be the chief assistant, both because he had been "assured" of Everest's "eminent degree of science as a mathematician" and because Everest had distinguished himself by making surveys in Java and by his work in dredging several hitherto unnavigable rivers (¶7). The first choice for the geologist-surgeon, Dr. John Ross, died in February 1818; Dr. Henry Voysey was subsequently appointed.

The Court agreed to Hasting's decisions with little comment, and it accepted the Great Trigonometrical Survey as a separate and distinct survey. Everest subsequently wrote that this rather surprising acquiescence was because of James Salmond's active support of the triangulation; Salmond's support of definitive, triangulation-based surveys would be made apparent a few years later with the formation of the *Atlas of India*.[28]

The Great Trigonometrical Survey continued to embody the two purposes which had shaped Lambton's work up until that time. It was a work of both geodetic science and general geography. The tension between the two aspects is evident from the third and fourth volumes of Lambton's manuscript general report, which he submitted to the Calcutta council on the first day of his new appointment. Those volumes constituted an extensive record of calculations: first he determined the size and shape of the earth from his own geodetic arcs; given the earth's figure he then derived the latitude and longitude of each survey station in his triangulations. He appended long lists of geographic coordinates to his reports for the benefit of the surveyor general. Lambton was well aware, however, that these lists were not exact. The coordinates would be altered if geodetic arcs measured elsewhere in the world were included in the determination of the earth's figure. Lambton nonetheless asserted that "for the mere purposes of Geography," the latitudes and longitudes were already sufficiently exact and would "never require correction."[29]

Lambton was also torn between geodetic and geographic goals for the operations of his new survey. Continuing the Great Arc to Agra would establish a geodetic connection between the peninsula and the Gangetic Plains. Taking the arc across the northern plains presented formidable technological problems (discussed in chapter 7), and Lambton seems therefore not to have contemplated taking the arc beyond Agra. The extension would be fast, only four years, but it would pass through Maratha territories, which had only just been subjugated. The arc would pass through the territory of Sindhia, one of the Company's Maratha allies, but this did not preclude the possibility of political turmoil and unrest, which would in turn force an indefinite delay in the survey. On the other hand, Lambton thought that he might lay the geographic foundation for a complete survey of the Deccan. That plan would entail a series of longitudinal chains, "branching" out from the Great Arc, which could be extended indefinitely, for example, to Pune, Bombay, and then down the coast to Goa or up the coast to Gujerat. The framework could then be filled up with topographic detail by military surveyors in much the same way as Lambton had employed his assistants until 1811.

But such an ambitious triangulation would require a much larger staff than just Lambton, Everest, and the few remaining civilian assistants (although Lambton had already asked permission to hire more of the last). Lambton therefore proposed that, for the immediate future, he would continue with the Great Arc and Everest would conduct a meridional chain from Hyderabad south to the Ceded Districts.[30] Until his death in 1823, Lambton continued with this plan, working on the Great Arc and a grid of chains of triangles which could then be filled in by the Madras surveyors who were assigned to the Deccan survey. George Everest went to the Cape of Good Hope for his health in October 1820, where he occupied himself remeasuring Nicholas Louis de la Caille's 1752 arc.[31] On his return in February 1822, he started a longitudinal series of chains to connect Bombay to the Great Arc.

Two members of the Calcutta council reacted in April 1818 to Lambton's proposals with lengthy memoranda that reasserted Mackenzie's conception of a survey of India. That James Stuart and George Dowdeswell should have argued against the governor general—who was still in the field, commanding the campaign against the Marathas—by reiterating Mackenzie's position is not surprising, considering that Mackenzie elsewhere recorded that they were his only two friends in the Calcutta administration.[32] Starting with Mackenzie's interpretation of the Court's appointment of one surveyor general, that it required all surveys to be "prosecuted upon one uniform system and under one efficient control," both councillors objected to Lambton's independence. They were forthright concerning the continuing need for geographical information. Stuart wrote that the recent victories over the Marathas had "opened an almost unbounded scope for geographical surveys"; Dowdeswell reflected on the "almost daily experience of the very defective state of our geographical information" and on the "serious inconveniences and embarrassments" that the lack caused "in the conduct of ordinary affairs of the administration."[33] Mackenzie and Lambton had together demonstrated that such surveys were feasible and that their high cost was still much smaller than that of numerous uncoordinated and unsystematic surveys. Stuart and Dowdeswell therefore considered that to retrench the systematic surveys would constitute a false economy.

This did not mean that surveyors were to have a free hand. Given the poor state of the Company's finances and the limited funds available for mapmaking, Stuart concluded that "a vigilant control therefore over the executive conduct of the [survey] department will be the best proofs which Government can give of its solicitude for the extent and success of these beneficial and interesting works." And the very nature of Lambton's "sublime science," of which Stuart acknowledged that he and the rest of the administrators were quite "ignorant," required

Lambton to be supervised.[34] Dowdeswell concurred with Stuart that Mackenzie's role as the government's cartographic consultant should encompass the Great Trigonometrical Survey. It was the surveyor general's responsibility to ensure that costs were not excessive and that the survey work was indeed coherent. The net result was that Mackenzie was requested to prepare a thorough report for the council's information on the history, principles, and progress of the triangulation; Lambton was requested to provide cost estimates for the different chains of triangles he had proposed.[35]

By the middle of 1818, the senior administrators in India had effectively subverted the intent of Salmond and the directors in appointing a surveyor general of India. As Mackenzie had argued, and as the councillors in Calcutta agreed, a single map of India required a single survey of India. The Court's surveyor general would have been a passive consultant and recipient of final maps. In contrast, Mackenzie's surveyor general would actively work in conjunction with the council to initiate surveys; because it was integral to detailed revenue and topographic surveys, the surveyor general would also supervise the GTS. The institutional resilience of the survey offices in Madras and Bombay prevented their abolition, which the Court had explicitly ordered. But given such inertia, it should not really be surprising that neither Mackenzie's nor Lambton's proposed systems for the Indian surveys were actually put into place. The general cartographic practices of British India continued to be anarchic, despite the presence of apparently formal, India-wide cartographic institutions.

Further Fragmenting the Indian Surveys, 1815–23

While William Lambton and Mackenzie repeated their suggestions for a single survey of all of India and a uniform survey establishment,[36] Colin Mackenzie was nonetheless faced by the pragmatic restrictions of cost and the need to undertake "practicable" before "desirable" surveys.[37] Surveys continued to proceed in their haphazard way in all three presidencies as each administration continued to do what was necessary to get geographical information regardless of any official guidelines stating how they should do so. Nor did the rivalries between the three presidencies help. If anything, the appointment of a surveyor general of India made the Company's mapping activities even more confused by adding a layer of generally ineffectual bureaucracy.

Mackenzie's description in December 1817 of the Calcutta survey office indicates that Bengal suffered from a cartographic anarchy similar to that of Madras. "The surveying department I find in a woeful plight," he wrote to his old friend Thomas Munro. Lacking "order" and "regularity,"

> the depôt of materials [is] far inferior to Madras, neglected and deficient altogether as to memoirs. Their surveys are of the itinerary kind. Routes and native information with a few desultory [astronomical] observations compose these maps which at the same time are never sent to the Surveyor General's Office till they have run thro' all hands in the distant provinces. Nor [are] returns made to the office, and no check [made] except copies of very meager field books sent down monthly to insure payment of the allowances, but as the maps do not follow I consider [them] of little use.[38]

Mackenzie was still less than happy with his department in 1820: "the state of the Survey Department in Bengal and the mapping of new provinces I will not attempt to describe to you. More confusion I think prevails than ever . . . "[39]

Mackenzie was unable to break the division between the central and local administrators. After 1824, for example, David Scott made cadastral surveys in Assam that were not unlike those by Munro in the Ceded Districts.[40] Nor could he break the division between surveys done under the surveyor general (civil) and those under the quartermaster general (military). He came into conflict with James Franklin, of the quartermaster general's office, who in 1820 was surveying Bundelcund for the political agent there. According to Mackenzie, the agent thought the survey was for the "exclusive information of his office" and so refused to send a copy to Calcutta. Again, a topographical and statistical survey of Malwa was made in 1818–19 by Frederick Dangerfield of the Bombay infantry at the instigation and benefit of his military commander, Sir John Malcolm. These, Mackenzie held, were symptomatic of the rampant abuse of his position by the local field officers who ordered surveyors to other duties. The Court of Directors was, in response, very critical of the overlapping responsibilities of the surveyor general's and quartermaster general's departments.[41]

Nor was Mackenzie helped by the confused position of both the Calcutta council and the Court as to the proper portion of government to manage the surveys. In 1818, Lord Hastings and his council moved the surveyor general's office, together with the military officers engaged in revenue surveys, into the "public department," because their work was for the benefit of the civil administration of India; the "magnificent . . . Scientific Geographer" (Lambton) clearly belonged on the civil side of administration. The quartermaster general and his specifically military surveys were left in the military department.[42]

The Court's contradictory responses to this policy change demonstrates the directors' reliance on their secretaries to formulate policy. The public secretary, James Harcourt, drafted "public" letters to Bengal in 1820 and 1822 in which he expressed the opinion that because "the principal surveys made in India are for military and political purposes and the Surveyor General as well as the officers employed under him, are usually military men," that officer should be in the military department.[43] At the same time, James Salmond, the Court's military secretary, drafted other letters which the directors duly sent out to Bengal stating that they were "not aware of any material objection" to keeping the surveyor general in the public department![44] The public letters were more strongly worded, so the Calcutta council transferred both the surveyor general's office and the Great Trigonometrical Survey back to the military department, effective 1 January 1823; the entrenchment of the bureaucracy, however, meant that although the revenue surveys were under the surveyor general's authority, they were placed in the territorial department; the quartermaster general maintained control of the military surveys.[45] Although the surveyor general's office and the Great Trigonometrical Survey were henceforth administered as part of the military department, an examination of the military expenditures reveals that all survey costs other than the surveyors' regimental salaries were still met by the public department. It has therefore proven impossible to establish coherent and comprehensive figures for the Company's expenditures on surveys during the early nineteenth century.[46]

The acceptance by the Calcutta council of Mackenzie's argument that the surveyor general should be responsible for all surveys except those of a limited, military or engineering purpose seems to have depended on Mackenzie's personal stature as a surveyor. His ability to control new surveys declined as his health forced him to make repeated journeys away from Calcutta in search of a more hospitable climate. With his death in May 1821, while on just such a trip, the council immediately nominated John Hodgson as his successor. Although an accomplished surveyor, Hodgson lacked Mackenzie's stature and was unable to assert his position. The result was that the council, in the period from 1821 to 1823, established three extensive surveys that did not report to the surveyor general: Thomas Prinsep's survey of the Sundarbans (begun March 1821); Benjamin Blake's river surveys (February 1822); and James Herbert's geological survey in the Himalayas (February 1823). Of these, the first two were under the authority of the territorial (joint finance and revenue) department; the last reported directly to the council. Valentine Blacker, Hodgson's successor in October 1823, could do little better. In one of the stranger administrative decisions made by the Calcutta council, the assistant surveyor on the survey of the Sylhet frontier would report to the territorial department while the senior surveyor was left "floating amongst the several departments" for which he did work (judicial, political, and military).[47] On the other hand, Lambton died in January 1823, and as Hastings had suggested in 1817, the Great Trigonometrical Survey was placed under Hodgson's orders within a fortnight.[48]

The surveyor general's authority was further eroded when the Court did not ratify Hodgson as Mackenzie's successor. It received petitions in June 1822 from Hodgson, Monier Williams, formerly surveyor general of Bombay, and Blacker, once quartermaster general at Madras. Blacker was then in Europe on furlough and was able to meet personally with the directors in London; the Court decided on Blacker.[49] On Blacker's return to India in October 1823, the governor general, Lord Amherst, found a means to satisfy both Blacker's and Hodgson's pretensions. He asserted that the business associated with the nine revenue surveys then in progress in the Upper Provinces—which totaled ten commissioned officers and fourteen uncovenanted civil servants—was equal to that of all the "general geographical surveys" throughout India. Amherst therefore appointed Hodgson to the new position of revenue surveyor general under the territorial department. Blacker and the surveyor general's office remained in the military department.[50]

As the first surveyor generals of India had little control over the surveys in northern India, it should not be surprising that they had little, if any, control over the surveys in the Madras and Bombay presidencies. Mackenzie's personal relationship with the surveyors and administrators in Madras seems to have allowed him to exercise some control in the south, but his successors did not have the same influence. Mackenzie let the assistant surveyor general at Madras take care of both the presidency's map depot and all of the survey details that could not otherwise be handled from Calcutta. In return, Mackenzie frequently received copies of maps from southern India and was able to report frequently to his superiors in Calcutta about the progress of Madras surveys.[51]

The Madras Revenue Board did not feel as constrained as the military surveyors to adhere to the new hierarchy. The Revenue Survey School had been disbanded in 1810, but its rationale persisted: surveyors were still needed for the department of tank repairs. So the board began to train its own. Thomas DeHavilland, superintendent of tank repairs, proposed in May 1821 that his students could make a survey of the town of Madras. Not unnaturally, Francis Mountford, the assistant surveyor general, objected to this on the grounds that his office had been awarded sole responsibility for mapmaking. The ensuing debate led to yet another compromise. The council accepted that DeHavilland had to be able to make surveys and maps to fulfill his duties properly. On the other hand, the assistant surveyor general's office would be the focus of *accurate* mapmaking; Mountford's signature would attest to the quality of each map and prevent other government officials from encroaching upon his preserve.[52]

More generally, the Revenue Board was unhappy with the state of the revenue surveys in the Carnatic districts. Responding in 1816 to queries from the Bengal government after Hastings' minute on the revenue surveys of the Upper Provinces, the board's secretary concluded that "generally speaking [revenue surveys] have not been found [to be] practically useful or fit to be relied on even where executed with most accuracy," which was why the Madras administration had given up on them as official aids to revenue assessment.[53] As governor, Munro initiated in 1821 a review of revenue assessment in the Madras presidency which revealed that many collectors regularly made new measurements of land whenever needed. Several districts nonetheless desperately needed a new survey, most notably Chingleput district about Madras (the *Jagīr*) which had not been remapped since Barnard's survey of 1767–74.[54]

The subsequent formal adoption in 1822 of Munro's detailed form of ryotwari assessment required that the Carnatic districts be resurveyed and their lands classified. The result was the adoption of the cartographic system Munro had used in the Ceded Districts from 1802 through 1807. Each collector was to make new surveys and revisions at the "most convenient" scale that would "admit of each field being readily convertible into acres." The collectors organized their own surveying parties independently of each other and any centralized establishment for revenue surveyors; the only uniformity in the cartographic aspects of the assessment was that the final values for the area of each field would be in acres. Because the ryotwari system did not require minute details to be surveyed beyond field boundaries, the new surveys would not take too much time or money. The Court therefore approved the scheme.[55]

Surveyors and administrators in the Bombay presidency rarely acknowledged the authority of any surveyor general in Calcutta. The Bombay surveys were barely affected by the abolition of the presidency's surveyor general. Williams continued to function as surveyor general, in all but name, and made some thirty-six maps before 1821.[56] The Bombay council appointed James Sutherland to be assistant surveyor general in March 1822. Furthermore, discussions began late in 1821 to establish a school under the chief engineer to train "young men born in the country" both for topographic and revenue surveying; the school was eventually founded in April 1823.[57]

The great majority of the Bombay surveys were made to aid revenue assessments.[58] The acquisition of territory led to several topographic surveys, all of which were begun without prior reference to either the Bengal government or the surveyor general: Khandeish (1821–22), the Deccan (1817–30), South Konkan (1819–30), and Kathiawar (1822–25). The Bombay council did not recognize the surveyor general's control over these surveys until 1825; even then, it explicitly excluded the revenue surveys from that control.[59] Very little, if any, of this activity was reported to the surveyor general. For example, when Munro privately asked Mackenzie for information about the Bombay revenue surveys, Mackenzie had to apologize for being unable to get the information. Mackenzie complained of the situation to the Bengal council; so did Blacker.[60] Hodgson was rather sarcastic when he informed the council in late 1821 that

> From Bombay nothing has been received since the institution of the office of Surveyor General of India so far as I can find after a minute search, except of Kutagram in the Chowrasee Pergunnah of the Surat collectorship and of the village of Umleysar in the Baroach Pergunnah.[61]

The difficulty faced by a surveyor general in Calcutta in controlling the surveyors in Bombay and Madras was exemplified by the change in title of the assistant surveyor generals at the subordinate presidencies. In particular, this event demonstrates the continued division of authority between the three British governments and their armies, all of which dictated against a single cartographic organization. Mountford complained to the Calcutta council in 1823 that neither his salary nor staff position were commensurate with his duties. His staff salary and allowances were less than those of Sutherland at Bombay and of some of the surveyors in Madras who were supposedly Mountford's inferiors. Hodgson and the Calcutta council agreed. No more would the assistant surveyor generals be just the surveyor general's ostensible mouthpieces at Madras and Bombay and otherwise the equal of their colleagues in the field. Mountford was awarded the same staff salary as Sutherland, and both were henceforth designated "deputy surveyor general."[62]

The result was not a perfect hierarchy. The three governments in India, like the Court, were fiercely protective of their rights to patronage, and the subordinate presidencies were jealous of their independence. Orders concerning the technicalities of a survey could, of course, go directly from the surveyor general to his deputies. But if it was a matter of appointing or disbanding a survey, then the surveyor general was obliged to have the Calcutta council request the other government concerned to agree to the measure. Thus, the appointment of Sutherland and Mountford as deputy surveyor generals was made in the form of a request to the Madras and Bombay governments. They were asked, please, to increase Mountford's salary and, please, to call the officers by their new title. The Madras and Bombay governments could—and did—still take the initiative and appoint or transfer surveyors with little reference to Calcutta.

The Court's orders for a single surveyor general of India did not have their desired effect. The reinterpretation of those orders by the surveyors, and the administrators who deferred to their expert opinions, recast the Court's emphasis on maps to an emphasis on surveys. The Court had envisioned a hierarchical flow of information from the field surveyors, through intermediary residents and chief engineers, to the surveyor general in Calcutta. What was created was a hierarchy of authority and responsibility that had to reform the existing bureaucratic structures to be able to function properly. The Bengal, Madras, and Calcutta governments needed something more potent and significant than cartographic policy to force a change in their relationships; the established administrative distinctions between the various officers at each presidency were too inertia-bound to be significantly changed; and, the administrators' need for geographic information was still too pervasive to allow surveying activities to be concentrated in just one organization.

At the same time, the demand steadily increased for *maps* of information that had already been acquired. The Court's second attempt to bring some semblance of order to the Indian surveys again focused on the creation of a single cartographic image of India. The directors now thought in terms of publishing, at quite a large scale, maps constructed from the mixture of trigonometrical and detailed surveys being developed in India: the *Atlas of India.*

Increasing Pressure to Publish after 1815

Two factors underlay the increasing pressure within the East India Company to move from manuscript to printed maps of India. First, there was a growing appreciation that the need for maps outweighed the need for secrecy. This represents not so much a rise in cartographic literacy as a decreasing concern for secrecy due to the defeat of Napoleon and the removal of the French threat to the British overseas empire. Second, the surveyor generals adopted a pragmatic and rather selfish position. Both Colin Mackenzie and John Hodgson found their small staffs laboring under huge arrears of copying both correspondence and maps. The correspondence might not be avoidable, but the map copying could at least be mechanized. In particular, Mackenzie and Hodgson advocated the publication of large-scale atlases.

As surveyor general of India, Mackenzie suffered from a heavy burden of compiling and copying numerous maps; almost every one of Mackenzie's letters to the government at this time describes his arrears at length. Thus, by August 1819, all of his draftsmen were working at capacity and they desperately needed relief. He was far behind in his own correspondence, which was not helped by a natural loquaciousness that produced paragraphs when sentences would have served. He had still to write: general reports on all of the surveys in the three presidencies; a catalog of the Calcutta map depot; a report on the surveying school Lord Hastings had proposed in 1815; and the long overdue report on the Great Trigonometrical Survey, which the Calcutta council had requested eleven times already but which he was never actually to submit.[63] He was furthermore "paralyzed" in his attempts to compile the "general map of India" required by the Court in their orders of June 1814. What data he had—and he was receiving remarkably little new materials—was being used to make maps requisitioned by government officials. He specifically mentioned the superintendents of police "of Bundelcund, of Chittagong, of Cuttack, Benares, etc. etc.," but he was especially annoyed with Thomas DeHavilland, the inspector of tank repairs in Madras, who was engaged in making a map of the peninsula and whose demands for copies of the necessary large-scale maps consumed much of Mackenzie's time.[64]

Mackenzie's solution for his problem was an atlas of India, tied to a systematic survey. He had first implied such a system when he had submitted his 1808 maps of Mysore to the Madras council; he had described those maps as being "designed on the plan of an *Atlas* to comprehend a regular series of maps."[65] The layout of the Mysore atlas— shown in figure 5.2—is typical of the sort of atlas in which each sheet represents one district or perhaps a group of districts. The most obvious example of this type of large-scale atlas was James Rennell's *A Bengal Atlas* (1780–81). Each map is at the same scale, with the district centered on the sheet, surrounded by white space; the orientation of the sheets often varies in order to accommodate their subjects. One problem with such atlases is that the sheets cannot themselves be combined into a large wall-map without being redrawn from scratch; even if great care was taken in cutting away the white space, neighboring districts would probably not match up exactly because of the character of the surveys. Remember that in Mackenzie's survey system, each district was surveyed as a distinct entity.

Mackenzie revived the idea when he sent his atlas of the Ceded Districts of Mysore and several other maps of southern India to the Calcutta council in March 1820. He suggested that a published atlas of India should be at a much larger scale than the nine-sheet *Improved Map of India* recently published at 1:1,013,760 by Aaron Arrowsmith (1816), because the main demand on his time was for maps of particular districts rather than one for all of India. He suggested two miles to the inch (1:126,720), with large provincial wall-maps at four miles to the inch (1:253,440). Mackenzie specified that the atlas should be constructed only from actual, complete, and definitive surveys, lest the cartographers spend all their time updating the maps (the problem faced by Thomas Call forty years before). Completion of the atlas would therefore have to be gradual, but it would preclude the necessity for future resurveys. The definitive surveys should be made by a "permanent arrangement" of staff, which would not be more expensive than the current *ad hoc* organization.[66]

Hodgson again raised the issue of a published atlas. Unlike Mackenzie, Hodgson tended to promote atlases whose sheets were of regular format (size, scale, orientation) and which were compiled without reference to district borders; each sheet would be filled up to the edges. The key to this sort of atlas is that all of the sheets are mapped on the same geographical framework; once their margins are trimmed, the sheets will fit together neatly (assuming that there has been no deformation of the paper). The common framework was originally a graticule of longitude and latitude. For example, Rennell thought that the four sheets of his *New Map of Hindoostan* (1788) might "be joined together for the purposes of bringing the whole [of India] into one point of view"; or they might be bound "in an Atlas";[67] Thomas Call constructed his manuscript "grand atlas" after 1779 on one massive sheet of paper with the intention of then slicing it into twenty-two sheets to form the atlas. This is the conception of an atlas hinted at by the Court when it suggested that the "general map of India" to be maintained by the surveyor general of India could be constructed in "Divisions, [each] comprehending a certain extent in latitude and longitude."[68] This is the system Hodgson advocated. Alternatively, the common geographical framework could be a very extensive triangulation—namely, the Great Trigonometrical Survey—onto which lesser surveys are hung; I will return to this idea below.

The stimulus for Hodgson's proposal for an atlas was the 1821 submission to the Calcutta council of Monier Williams's revision of Charles Reynolds's huge map of India. Mountstuart Elphinstone, governor of

Bombay, had been "struck by the carefulness, distinctness, and beauty of [its] execution" and requested that the governor general remunerate Williams for his effort.[69] To test the map, Hodgson compared it with the recent Arrowsmith map of India, with his own astronomical observations in the Upper Provinces, and with Lambton's triangulation in the south. He found that Arrowsmith's new map—even at sixteen miles to an inch—was far superior in terms of level of content and geometric accuracy to the Reynolds/Williams map, even though the latter was at the larger scale of about seven miles to an inch (~1:440,000). Indeed, Hodgson asserted that Arrowsmith's map was the best published to date as it contained "in the surveyed tracts as many positions as those of some of the civilized countries in Europe."[70] He attributed the difference in quality to the great increase in the amount of geographical information since Reynolds finished his map in 1808. The Bengal government accepted Hodgson's criticisms and reported to both Bombay and London that the Reynolds/Williams map was essentially out of date.[71]

Hodgson used his critique of the Reynolds/Williams map to explain his own ideas for an atlas of India to be compiled from existing documents and which would replace Arrowsmith's large map. Capturing the essence of the eighteenth-century style of compilation, Hodgson took Rennell's *Bengal Atlas* as his role model; he described it as "the foundation of Indian Geography and a proud monument of exact arrangement of materials which could be depended on and of sagacity in making approximation to the truth, from information often contradictory." But Rennell's work suffered from being long out-of-date, being superseded only by Hodgson's own survey of the upper courses of the Ganges and Jumna Rivers. Hodgson was content, however, to accept the bulk of Rennell's information and to add to it the new information gathered by him and others in the Upper Provinces. He had already begun combining all of the new materials into a single map at sixteen miles to an inch and was preparing copies of the originals at four miles to an inch for the Court. It was not his plan, as it had been Mackenzie's, to wait until a district had been thoroughly surveyed before inserting it in the atlas. Rather, he thought in the same terms as the majority of the contemporary cartographers in seeking to make general maps by collecting and reconciling and correcting as much information as possible, whatever its nature.[72]

To this end, Hodgson directed Francis Mountford in Madras to recompile his maps, using Lambton's triangulation as a frame, at both four and sixteen miles to an inch; they were sent to London in December 1822.[73] (Similar orders to James Sutherland in Bombay were ignored, as was a repeated order in 1826.)[74] Hodgson's next batch of maps for London, sent in the following year, included a general map of the peninsula and the manuscripts for his own "Atlas of North-West of India" (see figure 3.4).[75] Hodgson envisioned this atlas as a supplement to Rennell's *Bengal Atlas* and requested that the Court have Arrowsmith or another competent engraver publish them. The Bengal government gave its support to this endeavor and subsequently ordered Valentine Blacker to continue with Hodgson's series of maps even before it had received the Court's sanction for the project.[76]

Finally, Hodgson was responsible for suggesting that maps could be printed in India. He sang the praises of the new lithographic printing technique, which was so much cheaper and easier than copper engraving. Lithography was indeed so inexpensive that it would be easier to print the maps of each revenue survey in the Upper Provinces than to produce the requisite number of copies by hand. He argued further that the lithographic printing could be done in India because it did not need the special skills necessary for copper engraving, which were found only in Europe. In the initial printing trials in 1823, the newly formed Government Lithographic Press printed copies of both revenue surveys and sheets of Hodgson's atlas.[77] It is unclear, however, what effect these and related developments in lithographic printing in India had for the Court's decision to publish a medium-scale topographic atlas of India.

Arrowsmith and an *Atlas of India,* 1823

As so often happened, events in India were overtaken by the Court's own deliberations. In this case, the Court decided to publish an *Atlas of India* in England. It was motivated by the example set by Aaron Arrowsmith's *Atlas of South India* (1822). The Court received copies of this atlas even before it received John Hodgson's first batch of his own atlas maps. Arrowsmith's atlas had eighteen sheets in regular format: a title page, an index map, and sixteen maps at four miles to the inch (figure 6.1). Arrowsmith published at the same time a single-sheet *Sketch of the Outline and Principal Rivers of India* (figure 6.2), which displayed the sheetlines for an atlas of all of India, together with the statement:

> Note. This map is intended to shew how many sheets of this size would be required for a Map of India on a scale of four English Miles to one Inch, any one of which may be engraved independent of another when materials offer, and may be united to the rest by keeping correctly to the lines as drawn on this Map. The sheets as far as No.16 are already engraved on the above scale.[78]

The *Atlas of South India* thus comprised the first sixteen sheets of what Arrowsmith hoped would be an *Atlas of India.*

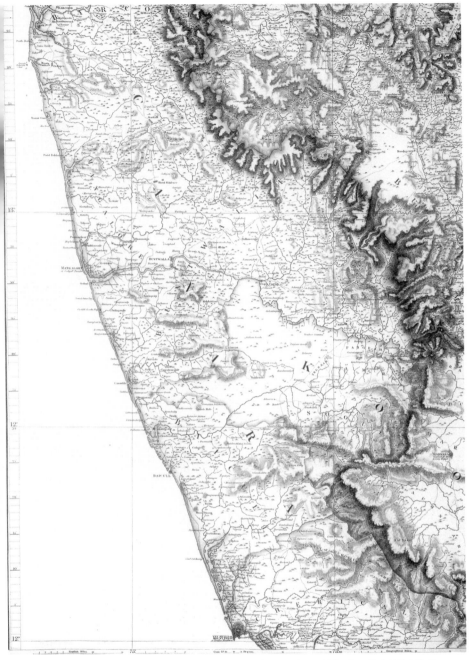

Figure 6.1 Aaron Arrowsmith, *Atlas of South India* (London, 1822), sheet 7, 1:253,440. Copper engraving.

This shows part of the Malabar Coast. Note the difference in the density of detail between Koorg, in the western Ghats, and the surrounding areas which were part of Colin Mackenzie's survey of Mysore (1799–1807). (Library of Congress.)

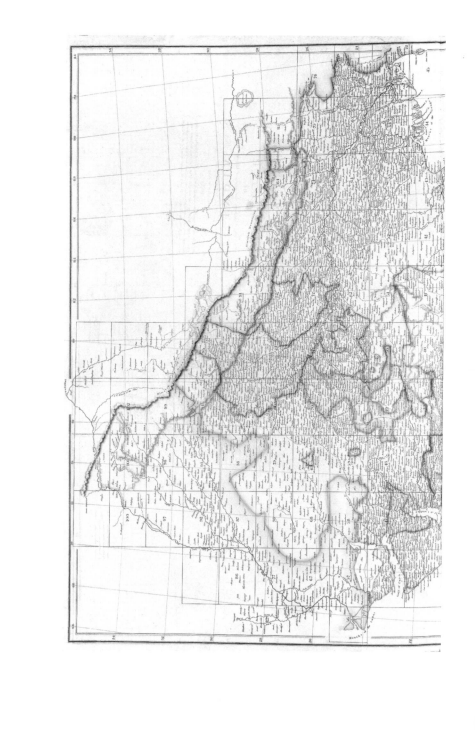

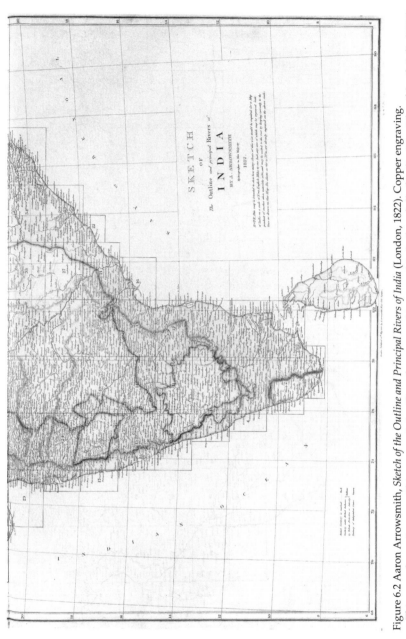

Figure 6.2 Aaron Arrowsmith, *Sketch of the Outline and Principal Rivers of India* (London, 1822). Copper engraving. This map shows Arrowsmith's proposed sheetlines for a general topographical atlas of all of India. His *Atlas of South India* (1822) comprised the first sixteen sheets. Arrowsmith's idea was eventually implemented by John Walker after 1825. (By permission of The British Library, IOR X/344/1/1.)

Arrowsmith was the foremost map publisher in London at the time; he had already made extensive use of the Company's cartographic archives.[79] His reputation rested on the production of huge multisheet maps, which he based only on original source materials and which he regularly updated. He put his 1816 *Improved Map of India*, for example, through three more editions in 1820, 1821, and 1822, each with additional material. Hodgson clearly thought this map to be excellent. Colin Mackenzie, who thought very highly of Arrowsmith's "habits of arrangement and exactness," cited the large map as an example of the utility of publishing maps in order to relieve the problems of extensive copying of manuscripts. He also described it as "useful" for showing the "whole of India in a general view," and he used it to create a standard table of distances to be used in calculating travel allowances in India. Lord Hastings suggested that it be used to plan the general route of a new road.[80]

The 1822 *Atlas of South India* was as thorough in its compilation and as exact in its execution as any of Arrowsmith's other maps. His use of sources is clearly shown by the difference in detail in figure 6.1, between the center-right region of Koo[rg] and the rest of the map, which he derived from Mackenzie's map of Mysore. It is even more apparent in his decision not to include Travancore in his atlas, because no *definitive* information was then available for that state. Arrowsmith's sources defined the scale of the atlas, especially as Mackenzie's maps of Mysore and the Ceded Districts provided about half of his coverage. Arrowsmith also had used four miles to an inch before and found it "adequate to contain all the names and places and other particulars which appear on the several plans and maps which [he had] consulted."[81]

With hindsight, it appears to be suspiciously fortuitous that Arrowsmith submitted his *Atlas of South India* and the *Sketch* to the chairman of the directors, asking permission to dedicate them to the Company, just when the Company's secretariat was preparing a long overdue letter to Bengal on the state of the surveys. The Court had delayed replying to no less than seven letters from Bengal that had dealt with the "survey department" until it had received confirmation that the surveyor general's office had been returned to the military department. With that confirmation, the Court replied all at once to the seven letters, each of which contained details of, or referred to, Mackenzie's and Hodgson's arguments for a single, published map or atlas of India.[82] Just as the directors turned their attention to the mapping of India, they had before them Arrowsmith's implementation of the sort of cartography whose principles had been defined by Mackenzie and Hodgson.

It is clear from the wording of the Court's minutes that the directors had commissioned neither Arrowsmith's *Atlas* nor his *Sketch*.[83]

It is very tempting to suggest that James Salmond was responsible for orchestrating events. Clements Markham claimed several decades later that Salmond had spent upwards of twenty years in correspondence with Mackenzie on the subject of a systematic survey of India. This is probably an exaggeration, as only nine years before, Salmond had been largely responsible for the Court's orders of June 1814 and those had not reflected Mackenzie's ideas. Markham did not substantiate his point. He probably derived it from departmental tradition and perhaps directly from John Walker, who succeeded Arrowsmith as the Company's favored commercial cartographer. Two well-informed, but anonymous, articles in the *Asiatic Journal* do imply, however, that Salmond and the directors were strongly influenced by Mackenzie's ideas. More believable is a second statement by Markham that the Company—that is, Salmond—had "consulted" Arrowsmith in the late 1810s on the possibility of publishing the larger-scale maps then starting to come out of India.[84] Thus, Arrowsmith might well have produced the *Atlas of South India* at Salmond's behest, so that the latter might more easily win over the directors to the idea of publishing large-scale topographic maps of India.

Whoever was behind Arrowsmith's work, the Court was sufficiently compelled to request the advice of James Rennell on the topic of a survey of India. Rennell replied in February 1823. His basic premise was that a proper "military" survey, based on "mensuration, or a series of triangles over the country," would simply take too long and would cost far too much. He therefore advocated the eighteenth-century style of survey, which he himself had used in Bengal, fifty years before (!), and which consisted of route surveys based on time of travel and compass bearings. Control would be provided by a "professed astronomer" who would travel about the country fixing geographical positions by astronomical observation; with only one person making the observations, the inconsistencies so common to such work would be minimized, Rennell argued. It is possible that Rennell's suggestions had no impact on the Court's conception of a systematic survey. Rennell made no provision for any of the work done to date either by Lambton and his assistants or by the topographic and revenue surveyors.[85]

In the end, the Court suggested that an astronomical survey was to be undertaken in the northern plains together with proper ties to Lambton's triangulation in the Deccan; this however was not so much an innovation as an acceptance of the *de facto* survey system already in place in India. One suggestion of Rennell's which might have influenced the Court, or which at least reinforced the message of Arrowsmith's uniform sheetlines, lay in his discussion of the distribution of the astronomical control points. He suggested that India might be subdivided into thirty-five blocks of four square degrees, each of which would have a quincunx of control points. Although he explicitly rejected the idea of apportioning such regular blocks to surveyors in the field, Rennell did imply that the final atlas should be organized as a regular series of sheets, unlike his own *Bengal Atlas*.

With the example of Arrowsmith's *Atlas of South India*, together with Rennell's advice and the lengthy proposals submitted by Mackenzie and Hodgson, the Court wrote new orders for the mapping of India, sent out in October 1823.[86] In the specific context of Hodgson's comments on the Reynolds/Williams map of India, the Court wrote:

> We are extremely desirous of forming and with as little delay as is consistent with accuracy, a complete Indian Atlas upon a scale of 4 miles to an inch, which we consider to be the best suited to general purposes, and which has been adopted by Arrowsmith in a recent publication, of which we transmit [to] you in the packet three copies.
>
> This map would appear to form an useful and judicious basis for a complete geographical delineation of India, and it is our intention to have the several sections into which the sketch map is divided, printed off by some eminent map engraver, as fast as correct and satisfactory materials shall be supplied to us. (¶¶48–49)

The *Atlas of India*, as it came to be known, was to be compiled, engraved, and published in London. Arrowsmith had died in April 1823, so that the project did not get under way until Walker proposed himself for the task in 1825. Walker—who worked under the company name of J. and C. Walker—was already known to the Company's secretariat through his work since 1820 with the Company's favored booksellers, Messrs. Black, Kingsbury, Parbury, and Allen. He began work in June 1825 by establishing his own layout for 177 sheets to cover all of India, Burma, and Malaya. The first six sheets (figure 6.3) were based on a series of maps received from India in 1825; thereafter, almost all of the forty-one sheets and five revisions which Walker listed as having been published by 1851 were of the Madras territories. Most of the sheets were not complete, which is to say they were not filled up right to the margins; areas yet to be properly surveyed remained white, framing the surveyed areas. Only twelve sheets had complete coverage by 1851, of which all were based on Mackenzie's work and seven were mostly

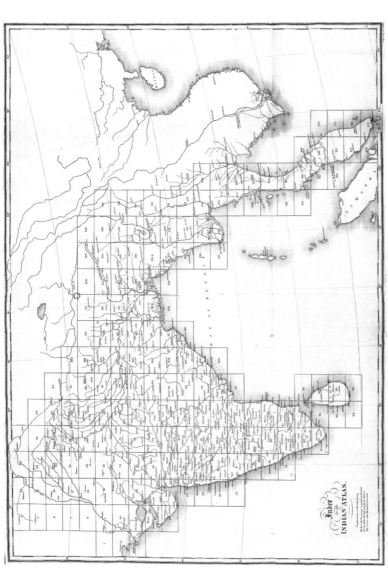

Figure 6.3 John Walker, [Index to the *Atlas of India*] (London, 1825). Copper engraving.
The six sheets shaded (in red pencil) on this copy were the first six published, being based on John Hodgson's and William Webb's work in the Himalayas, and on James Franklin's map of Bundelcund. (By permission of The British Library, BL Maps *52410 (18).)

water. Ultimately, the *Atlas* was to continue as the foremost published map series of British India until the early twentieth century.[87]

An essential aspect of the *Atlas of India's* character was derived from Mackenzie's conception and Arrowsmith's initial implementation of an atlas: its creation was to be progressive in nature.

> Each survey will be printed as soon as received . . . and in this way we may expect within a reasonable time, to obtain a map of India collecting into one view the geographical information which has hitherto been acquired and to serve as a convenient deposit for that which may hereafter be obtained. (¶54)*

Each sheet would be updated, and new sheets published, only as "correct and satisfactory" materials were received (¶53). This, in turn, required that a proper definition be given for the acceptable quality of the mapped data to be included in the atlas. Furthermore, the *Atlas* necessitated the collection of information at a much greater density than was hitherto usual.

The second component of the *Atlas* was the expectation that any new surveys would possess a common "geometrical ground work." In the southern and central uplands, a "more perfect" geometrical basis would be provided by the Great Trigonometrical Survey (¶53). In the northern plains, where triangulation was hard, if not impossible, the surveys would be controlled by an astronomer; the directors therefore sent a copy of Rennell's comments along with the actual orders. The sentiments for a coherent survey were nonetheless rather vague. The most detailed reference to the actual prosecution of new surveys, in a paragraph added by the Board of Control, simply admonished the Bengal government to ensure that "those parts of India should be first surveyed the geographical knowledge of which appears to be most important" (¶24).

The creation of the *Atlas of India* was primarily a cartographic decision. The Court did not hint that they had considered any reform in the existing structure of the surveys in India. Most notably, there was no idea of founding a permanent survey organization as an auxiliary corps parallel to but outside of the formal military hierarchy of fighting units. In its form, the *Atlas* was just like the huge, encyclopedic, multisheet maps of India produced since d'Anville's *Carte de l'Inde* of 1752, only it was larger and had more sheets. Walker acted in the conventional, eighteenth-century mode of map compilation, taking the maps sent to London from India and fitting them into the larger whole.

*The last phrase was modified by the Board; the Court's original wording was " . . . to obtain the long wished for desideratum of a complete map of India."

A significant departure from established practice was that Walker could not construct a map of India in its entirety and then slice it into smaller sheets for engraving and publication. Each sheet of the *Atlas* was a separate publication. But this meant that the *Atlas*'s schema could be expanded indefinitely, with new sheets being added in a regular manner as British interests expanded. This happened twice, once when Walker added six sheets on the western and far northern edges, and again in about 1900 when the eastern sheets were rearranged and re-numbered so as to cover the oceans in the Indian Isles.[88] That there were not more additions reflects the rather generous coverage of Walker's original schema (figure 6.3). Unlike Arrowsmith's suggested sheetlines, which covered India in its restricted and imperial geographical scope, Walker's sheetlines encompassed the classical conception of the Indies. This coverage reflected the recent eastward turn in British interests with the purchases of Singapore (1824) and Malacca (1825) and with Lord Amherst's Burmese War, then in progress (1824–26), for which Walker had already lithographed a "map of the Burman Empire" for the Com-pany.[89] That Walker's schema for the *Atlas* represented an imperial expansion of British India and not a retrograde conception is dem-onstrated by his projection. For the central meridian (which appears straight on the map and along which there would be no distortion), Walker used the meridian of 76°30' east of Greenwich, which runs the length of the peninsula.[90] The further away from the central meridian, the greater the distortion on the map so that, in his schema, the Malay peninsula and Indochina sweep off to the east, away from the map's geometric focus on the subcontinent. Finally, with the exception of the quarter-sheet encompassing Singapore, none of the sheets for Burma and the Malay peninsula were made. (Burma was to get its own quar-ter-inch topographic series after the war of 1885–87.)

The *Atlas of India* and the Great Trigonometrical Survey

Despite its cartographic emphasis, the *Atlas* was essential for the future of the Great Trigonometrical Survey. The directors had been concerned about the cost of the trigonometrical surveys, which they estimated to be more than £6,000 per year. A total of £100,000 had been spent by William Lambton since 1800. In 1823, there was, therefore, a resurgence in the directors' unease over such large expenditures by an officer on a work which was still not completely understood. The directors reiter-ated their requests of 1814 and 1818 that Lambton assure them that his work was both beneficial and destined to end: "we feel that we should

hardly be justified in sanctioning the continuance of so large an expenditure as the survey in question has occasioned and may yet occasion,
unless we have information before us to shew that the objects to be attained are of adequate utility." The Court directed that the Great Trigonometrical Survey be subordinated to the surveyor general, effectively
bringing it back into the control structure of the cartographic mini-
hierarchy. At the same time, the GTS was directed to be tied to the production of the *Atlas* in order to ensure its benefits.[91]

The Great Trigonometrical Survey was clearly essential to the provision of that overall geometrical frame which would allow the ultimate
combination of numerous disparate, but all definitive, maps into *one
image*. Thus, the first maps engraved by John Walker for the *Atlas* were
in fact maps of the current extent of Lambton's triangulation in southern India.[92] Publication in 1830 of George Everest's first memoir on the
Great Arc was sanctioned by the Court because it constituted "part of
the materials for the Atlas of India," and as such copies would be sent
to the same institutions as those to which it had already sent the triangulation maps "already published for the Atlas of India."[93]

Beginning in the 1820s and continuing through the nineteenth and
into the twentieth century, the *Atlas of India* provided the official cartographic image of British India. It solved all of the problems that had
plagued earlier maps of India. It was compiled only from *definitive* surveys, so that each copper plate would only ever be added to and would
never be corrected. Keeping an updated map was no longer a problem.
Nor was the copying and dissemination of geographic information, as
the surveyor general needed only distribute the relevant *Atlas* sheets to
those officers who requested maps. The division of India into regular
sheets provided a balance between the encyclopedic desire to show as
much information as possible and the pragmatic creation of a map that
was not too large to be useful. And, most important, the *Atlas* held out
the idea of a single geometric framework on which a uniform image of
India would be constructed. It was the triangulation framework which
would provide each survey with its definitive character and which
would allow the data to be fitted to the surveys of adjoining districts. It
was the triangulation framework which allowed the map compiler in
London to ignore the arguments of the surveyors that one had to have
field experience in India to be able to manipulate and compile survey
maps correctly. The triangulation framework reduced all geographic
data to a common and universal reference that obviated the need for
any local knowledge.

Although the introduction of lithographic presses eventually allowed the publication in India of provincial topographic map series at

scales larger than four miles to an inch, the *Atlas of India* remained the Company's only large-scale map of all of India. The sheets themselves were never combined into a single map, if only because not all of the sheets were actually published. Provincial maps and atlases were constructed.[94] Even so, the *Atlas* embodied the British view of India in the 1820s: fixed, eternal, imperial, and known (or knowable) to the British through scientific observation. The cartographic image was not as exact, or as scientific, as it might have been. The continuing mix of triangulation and astronomical control jarred the sensibilities of many surveyors and their supporters. As is discussed in the following chapters, the astronomical surveys were soon discarded and triangulation remained, triumphant. Yet that victory depended not on the intrinsic merits of trigonometrical, geodetic-quality surveys for controlling detailed topographical investigations. Rather, it rested on triangulation's provision of a uniform and rational space that could support a uniform cartographic *image* of empire. With the *Atlas*, the British shed their belief that India was defined as the realm of the Mughal empire and recast their conception of India as the realm of British imperial interest in southern Asia.

CHAPTER SEVEN

Triangulation, the Cartographic Panacea, 1825–32

The decision in 1823 by the East India Company's directors to go ahead with the project to create an *Atlas of India* implicitly required the conception of South Asia as a single space structured by a common geometric framework. Only part of that framework was formed by an extensive triangulation; as a whole, the *Atlas* was a cartographic construction based on the long-established graticule of meridians and parallels. The presumed benefit of the Great Trigonometrical Survey in the Deccan, and by other surveys in the Himalayas, was that the triangulation basis would ensure the definitiveness of the lesser topographic surveys. The detailed surveys had to be definitive in order to prevent the *Atlas* from falling out-of-date and needing to be corrected. The *Atlas* was to be *the* map of India. Although the methods of knowledge construction which contributed to the *Atlas* were those of the archive, the triangulation surveys represented a technological fix for the *Atlas* that promised epistemological certitude based on the structured observation of the world. That is, the British transformed the conceptual combination of many actual surveys into an ideological survey of India.

Yet in the 1820s there remained two flaws in the *Atlas*'s technological perfection. The first was that the flat northern plains formed a significant obstacle to the creation of a truly India-wide triangulation. The obstacle could be overcome, but only with the allocation of substantial resources to build towers—artificial mountains—to elevate the surveyors so that they could see long distances. The second flaw was that the surveys themselves did not constitute a coherent system. The manner in which the *Atlas* was to be formed from the GTS and from topographical surveys was not the same as the system that ought to have been followed in making triangulation-based topographical surveys. Each district survey might have been correct, as in the survey system popularized by Colin Mackenzie since 1799, but they should still have been organized as a whole.

Fixing the second flaw, and establishing a systematic and uniform survey organization for mapping all of India, would necessitate the resources to be allocated to fix the first flaw. John Hodgson, surveyor general between 1821 and 1823, did develop a methodology with which he thought he could systematically map the northern plains without triangulation. It was not adopted. His successor, Valentine Blacker (1823–26), promoted the extension of the geodetic skeleton of the Great Trigonometrical Survey into the northern plains, but it was the arguments put forth by George Everest, during his furlough in Europe from 1825 to 1830, which established the Company's acceptance of the GTS as the large institution charged with an India-wide triangulation. Building on the example of the Ordnance Survey of Ireland (1824–46) and aided by the active support of the technophilic governor general, Lord William Bentinck (1828–35), Everest subsequently established the principle of extending subsidiary arcs of the GTS across all of the northern plains. But Everest could not reorganize the topographic and revenue surveys which were supposedly dependent on the triangulation. The apparent system of the British surveys in India now derived solely from the Great Trigonometrical Survey but not from a coherent systematic survey. The final stage in this process, when the directors finally rejected an organized survey of India, in the form of Thomas Best Jervis's proposals of 1837 through 1839, is treated in chapter 8. This chapter addresses the compromises made by Everest and Bentinck to promote geodetic triangulations in India.

Blacker's Advocacy of Triangulation for the Plains, 1823–25

As discussed in chapters 1 and 3, the prosecution of triangulation across a large expanse of flat land presents the surveyor with formidable technological obstacles. For triangulation to provide a proper geometrical framework, the primary triangulation must be constructed from as few triangles as possible; each triangle will then be very large, often forty miles on a side or as much as sixty miles on rare occasions. In flat plains close to sea level, however, the horizon is only three miles (4.8 km) from an observer, assuming that the observer's sight is not blocked by trees, buildings, or subtle rises in the ground. It was standard practice for surveyors on hilltops to fell those trees which were in the line of sight to adjacent stations. To open up three-mile long sightlines in the plains would be quite impractical. It was already common practice in Europe and India for surveyors to build scaffolding atop existing buildings; but where no suitable buildings were properly located, the surveyors would have to construct their own towers, and that cost was too great to be seriously considered. Until about 1824, the British surveyors in India assumed that any geometrical framework for surveys in the plains would have to be formed from astronomical observations.

For example, John Hodgson, the Calcutta council's choice to succeed Colin Mackenzie as surveyor general, suggested in 1821 a method by which Rajputana could be surveyed. Hodgson suggested that the region could be divided into rectangles, each about 34½ by 20 miles (55½ × 32 km). The surveyor would map out the block's geography by tracing out a predefined path around and within each block, defining his position each night.[1] This scheme was not implemented. Two years later, however, Hodgson persuaded the Calcutta council to appoint Alexander Gerard to traverse a circuit formed by direct lines between Agra, Bhopal, Ujjain, and Jaipur. The circuit would form a distorted rectangle approximately four degrees of latitude in height (275 miles, 443 km) and two degrees of longitude in breadth (188 miles, 303 km). Once complete, the frame could be filled in by other surveyors. Gerard began with the north-south leg from Agra to Bhopal. Illness prevented him from continuing beyond Bhopal and the survey lapsed.[2]

It was not that Hodgson was unable to conceive of throwing a triangulation across the plains. He did suggest such a course of action at least once. William Lambton had proposed in April 1822 to extend the Great Arc as far north as Agra, which would take him until 1826. Indeed, Lambton was adamant that he would reach Agra, even though it was clear to George Everest that he was already dying from a lung infection and probably would not live to see the completion of his work. Lambton put Everest to work on the longitudinal series from the Great Arc to Pune and Bombay. The positions of Bombay and Agra would thus eventually be fixed "with geometrical accuracy . . . with respect to the observatory at Madras." In supporting these plans, Hodgson suggested in June 1822—I believe for the first time—that if Lambton's health was to hold out, the Great Arc could be extended even further north, right across the plains and into the Himalayas, to the 32d parallel. Hodgson's problem with the plan was simply its cost.[3]

Hodgson was succeeded by Valentine Blacker in October 1823. Finding that the surveyor general's office in Calcutta contained few good large-scale plans of Bengal, not even a copy of James Rennell's *Bengal Atlas*, Blacker proposed a new provincial topographic survey. Blacker was strongly influenced by his discussions with George Everest, who had just succeeded Lambton, and so argued that the best surveys could only be "final surveys" made "on the most approved principles." The overwhelming urge to do "special surveys" should, Blacker asserted, be resisted. The "only permanent foundation of Indian Geography" was the Great Trigonometrical Survey. Yet Blacker was reluctant even to calculate the number of towers that would be needed for a triangulation of Bengal because he was convinced that neither the council nor the directors would ever approve of the cost. He therefore suggested that John Warren be brought out of retirement at Pondicherry to conduct a thorough astronomical survey.[4] The council disagreed with the need for a new survey. It did however accept Blacker's principled request that astronomical observations be curtailed in districts which would eventually be covered by the GTS, but this restriction would "apply exclusively to those surveyors employed immediately under [Blacker's] authority." Because Blacker actually controlled very few surveys, this was, in practice, a worthless concession.[5]

The Court's letter of 23 October 1823, which included the directives for the *Atlas of India*, reached Calcutta in June 1824. Blacker's response in August became one of the defining statements of the need for a triangulation of all of India. Blacker was especially annoyed at Rennell's idea for a hurried astronomical survey of India as the foundation for the *Atlas*. All of Europe, including Britain, Blacker argued, had recognized the necessity of extensive triangulations as the independent foundation for all detailed surveys. He quoted at length from glowing testimonials to Lambton's work by two prominent mathematicians: Jean Baptiste Delambre and William Playfair. In contrast, Rennell's idea represented a return to "rude expedient" after the Company had for "more than twenty years" supported the Great Trigonometrical Survey, "an operation approved by science." Rennell's plan was quite "unworthy of the character, power, interests, and opportunities enjoyed by the Honorable Company."[6] Instead, Blacker wanted to see the GTS extended as far as possible. He felt the coastal series should be continued from Goa to the Gulf of Cambay on the west coast, and from Masulipatnam to Calcutta on the east coast; the Great Arc should be carried across the plains to the Himalayas. Cost again precluded Blacker from advocating a more extensive triangulation in the plains, so he repeated his request for a well-qualified astronomer to make a very thorough control survey. But, on the principle that astronomical observations were *always* worse than a triangulation, Blacker would rather have the government bite the financial bullet and approve the extension of the triangulation across all of the plains.

Behind Blacker's arguments lay a desire to overcome the exigencies of the Company's bureaucratic system in order to place the Indian surveys on a basis of uniformity: once uniformity of process was ensured, then system and accuracy of results would follow. Implicit within his arguments was the need to expand and formalize the institution of the GTS if its arcs were to be completed in a reasonable amount of time. It would take at least thirteen years for Everest's single survey party to complete the Great Arc and the two coastal arcs. With three survey parties, the results of the three arcs would be made available for controlling other surveys in just four or five years. The plains would need six parties to be covered in seven years. Finally, Blacker also proposed a secondary triangulation of Bombay's territories, which would need more staff, although that plan lapsed with Blacker's death in March 1826 (¶30).[7]

The Calcutta council enthusiastically agreed to the extension of the Great Arc and the coastal series. It is at this point that the full extension of the Great Arc into the Himalayas was explicitly accepted by the Company's administration in India. Blacker's advocacy of the Great Arc rested on the unspoken assumption that it would necessitate the construction of towers, an assumption that the government accepted, assuming, of course, that the councillors were ever aware of it. Even so, the council could not approve any surveys in the plains, whether astronomical or trigonometrical, without first securing the Court's approval of the extra survey parties and their attendant costs. It could only urge the Court not to allow any "relaxation in the completion of a work [that is, the GTS] which must be so interesting to science. Indeed, we are satisfied that such will not be the result under the orders of your Honorable Court."[8]

The council was able to reestablish the principle of the surveyor general's control over the increasingly independent deputy surveyor generals at Madras and Bombay. In doing so, it used Blacker's argument that any "uniformity of principle and practice" can only stem from having "all the instructions proceeding from one source." The current situation featured "no end to the variety of principles, instruments, scales, and practical models employed," none of which could help the general goal of an accurate and *definitive* survey system. Of course, the simple reassertion of the surveyor general's authority did little to bring the other surveys under his real control.[9]

The potential hollowness of Blacker's victory was recognized by other, less sanguine surveyors. Writing in 1829, both Hodgson, who had resumed the position of surveyor general on Blacker's death, and James Herbert, who became acting surveyor general on Hodgson's resignation, were convinced that trigonometrical surveys would be limited to the Deccan and to the Himalayas. (They had themselves collaborated on an extensive triangulation in the northern mountains a decade before.) In between the mountains, they continued to assume that an astronomical survey would have to be prosecuted in the plains.[10] Hodgson and Herbert were, however, left behind by decisions reached by the directors and the Company's secretariat in London. Indeed, Everest himself was left behind by those same decisions. He returned on health leave to Britain in 1826, all set to argue with the Court in defense of the Great Trigonometrical Survey, only to find that the directors were already convinced of its necessity.

The Court's Conversion to the *Ideal* of Triangulation, 1824–27

By 1825, the Great Trigonometrical Survey had reached something of a crisis. The Calcutta council had finally decided that the survey needed to be expanded, but it would not be possible to do so. In the first place, George Everest's continuing health problems served to highlight the smallness of the survey's staff. His work on the Great Arc after William Lambton's death in 1823 had taken him through the northern Deccan, an area of mountains and jungles which the British found quite unhealthy. Everest singled out the Vindhya mountains as being especially malignant.[11] The Calcutta council approved his request to take a second furlough as soon as he had completed the Sironj baseline. During his absence, Everest and Valentine Blacker decided that the one survey party should be entrusted to the GTS's principal civil assistant, Joseph Olliver, who had joined Lambton's survey from the Revenue Survey School at Madras. Olliver would survey a longitudinal chain of triangles from the Sironj baseline to Calcutta. In designing this arc, Everest discarded Lambton's plans for coastal chains of triangulation. The Calcutta series would require the construction of towers near Calcutta, thereby forcing the council to sanction the necessary cost even before the Court's reply—whether affirmative or negative—had been received to Blacker's plans for expanding the GTS.

More fundamentally, the epistemological rationale for the Great Trigonometrical Survey was being undermined by the deteriorated state of its instruments. As Everest subsequently wrote to the Court, the links in Lambton's old measuring chain had worn and the whole chain had lengthened by an indeterminate amount. It now had to be calibrated against the British standards. Moreover, Lambton's Great Theodolite had suffered from the effects of constant use and especially from being dropped from the top of a temple in 1808: "the whole mahogany frame is falling fast to pieces"; the angular divisions on its limb had worn away and the micrometers used to read them were "unsteady and faulty"; the screws used to level the instrument had lost their threads;

and the telescope had developed "a rickety motion in the direction of its axis."[12] Olliver clearly could not use the 36-inch theodolite for the Calcutta series, so Everest gave him the survey's eighteen-inch theodolite. Everest recognized that this instrument would be inadequate to the task, but there was no other available instrument and there was no lesser arc which needed to be surveyed. Blacker and the Calcutta council did not want to delay work by sending any of the instruments home for repair. Instead, they decided to purchase a whole new set.[13]

Everest sailed from Calcutta in November 1825, arriving in London in May 1826. Almost immediately, even before leaving for the healthy sea air of Ramsgate, Everest called on James Salmond, the Court's military secretary, to discuss official business. He especially wished to receive his full salary. Had he gone only as far as the Cape of Good Hope, as he had during 1820 through 1822, he would have been able to draw all of his military salary and five-sixths of his civil allowances, and the period would count toward his retirement; by returning to Britain, however, he had been reduced to half-pay and the time would not count to his retirement. Everest noted that he would actually be engaged in official activities while in Britain. He wanted to supervise the construction of the new instruments approved by the Calcutta council. He also wanted to compute and publish the results of the Great Arc. Lambton had periodically published the results of each section of the arc, as far as the eighteenth parallel (see listing in the Bibliography); Everest now wished to disseminate the results of the next six degrees of the arc. The Court, however, refused to consider him to be on active service. The continuing wrangle colored much of Everest's correspondence with his superiors until, after several extensions of his leave because of continuing ill-health, he sailed again for India in June 1830.[14]

The Court's rejection of his request and Salmond's inability to intercede on his behalf were evidently interpreted by Everest as indicating a lack of appreciation of the character and necessity of the Great Trigonometrical Survey. Following the approach customarily adopted by surveyors when dealing with ignorant politicians, Everest accordingly prepared a very long educational memoir, which he sent to the Court in March 1827.[15] Starting with a comparison of the character and relative quality of surveys based on astronomical positions and triangulations, Everest presented the GTS as the foundation of India's geography. "The trunk and main branches of the system" (¶100) would be the Great Arc and the longitudinal series to Bombay and Calcutta, from which lesser chains would stem. To extend the survey across India required the survey's instruments to be refurbished. It would further require both a large staff comprised of Eurasian civil assistants and the computation and publication of the results of the Great Arc. Everest ended with his claim for salary and remuneration during his furlough.

Everest's rhetoric played upon the Company's honor as a liberal supporter of science and on the directors' desire to be seen as the equal of the truly sovereign rulers of Europe. Indeed, India provided the perfect opportunity to undertake a geodetic triangulation across a "much greater extent than any that can be conducted in Europe" (¶94). All his themes come together in his conclusion:

> Since the year 1800, the rapid strides which have taken place in the practical astronomy, have left our fabrics [that is, instruments] of that period far in the back ground, and it is, I humbly urge, inconsistent with the magnificence of the Honorable Company's Establishments to continue to use this antiquated apparatus whilst other [apparatus] so far superior has been devised. Twenty-five years ago the Government of Fort St. George started in the course of science with an enthusiasm which seemed to vie with all that mankind had ever witnessed; since that time the field for scientific work has been enlarged to an extent that the warmest imagination hardly could have expected. The whole of India is now accessible, the formidable chain of the Vindaya [mountains] which separates the northern from the southern provinces has been crossed and no further obstacle remains to the extension of the Great Meridional Series up to the Himalaya Mountains. This, then assuredly cannot be the time [for the directors] to relax in their offices, when the gaze of all the civilized world has been fixed on their operations and yet it were, I humbly presume, better to relinquish the task at once than to prosecute it on a scale inconsistent with the dignity of the rulers of possessions so vast and important. (¶128)

And should the Court decide to continue with the survey, then there would not, in the long term, be any significant difference in the cost between a survey on a "superb and magnificent scale" and one on a "limited" scale "with inferior apparatus" (¶129).

Once again, Everest's arguments had little direct impact on the Court or, rather, on the few directors and their secretaries who actually ran the Company's affairs. In response, the directors made no mention of either the new instruments or an all-India triangulation, but they did allow Everest one year on full salary to prepare and publish the results of the Great Arc.[16] Everest was now thoroughly perturbed by the Court's seemingly willful ignorance. He bade a director and former Persian secretary, Neil Benjamin Edmondstone, to submit a memoir to the chairmen of the Court, asking why Everest's "luminous and interesting representation" had failed to attract their attention. (Edmondstone's acquaintance with the GTS went back to Lambton's initial proposals, when he had been Lord Wellesley's private secretary.) Edmondstone argued that the directors should take advantage of Everest's presence in India, on his return; they should support him to the fullest extent; and they should provide him with the best instruments available.[17] Yet Edmondstone's memoir produced as little response as Everest's had two months before. Everest's dissatisfaction with the situation seems to have been a factor in his decision to travel to lower Austria and Italy in 1827–28 rather than suffer through an English winter.[18]

The Court's apparent lack of concern for the Great Trigonometrical Survey seems to indicate that the principal directors and their secretariat had already accepted the need for a triangulation of all India. Their response was also defined by bureaucratic procedure. The report by the committee of correspondence on Everest's memoir specifically stated that the committee's concern was for the future advancement of the survey and further noted that the Court had accepted the nature of the Great Trigonometrical Survey in 1823, when it had ordered an India-wide survey as the basis for the *Atlas of India*. Although the committee recognized the survey's need for new instruments, it left the issue out of its report, and so out of the orders to Everest, because the indent for the new instruments had yet to pass the committee of buying.[19]

Three documents from later in 1827 shed light on the Court's conversion to supporting an all-India triangulation. They also indicate that Salmond played a significant role in setting the Court's new cartographic policy. Salmond wrote a memorandum in August to brief the newly appointed governor general, Lord William Bentinck, on the status of a general survey of India. In November, Anthony Troyer reported to Bentinck, his old patron, on the substance of an interview he had had with Salmond to discuss his possible appointment to a staff position, possibly surveyor general, were he to accompany Bentinck back to India. Finally, a September letter on revenue issues, which would not have been drafted by Salmond but he might have been responsible nonetheless, transmitted to the Calcutta council a copy of the parliamentary report that had led to the creation in 1824 of the Ordnance Survey of Ireland. The letter recorded the Court's expectation that the council would find the report to "contain information or suggestions which may be useful in the prosecution of Indian Surveys."[20]

The Court had discarded the original plans for the *Atlas of India*, which had called for a hybrid astronomical and trigonometrical geometric framework, in part because of the pragmatic reason that no one was available for the astronomical component. Edward Sabine, a prominent military engineer and earth scientist, had refused the posi-

tion when asked by the Court. In India, Blacker found only one qualified infantry officer—Peter Grant, who had spent a two-year furlough
at the Cape observatory—but he was needed for regimental duty because of the Burma War.[21] In any case, the parliamentary report had
made it quite clear that the only way to make a systematic survey was
for a strict trigonometrical survey to be undertaken *first;* only then
could detailed, large-scale surveys be made.[22] Blacker's arguments of
August 1824 had only reinforced this position: astronomical control
was simply inadequate for a definitive *Atlas.*[23] The directors were
thus persuaded to allow the Great Trigonometrical Survey, once fully
equipped with new instruments, to be extended across all of Company-
ruled India.

Everest and an Institution for Surveying India, 1829–30

Although the Court of Directors was persuaded that India was to be
completely triangulated, the Company's managers do not seem to have
paid much attention to the Great Trigonometrical Survey's institutional
needs. The directors continued to conceive of the GTS as a small organization. That situation did not change until late 1829 and early 1830,
when George Everest successfully used the example of the Ordnance
Survey of Ireland to convince the Court that the GTS had to grow if it
was not to take far too long in defining a geometrical framework for
India.

For his part, James Salmond fully understood the institutional implications of an organized survey of India based on an all-embracing Great
Trigonometrical Survey. As he wrote to Lord William Bentinck, new
topographic surveys should be undertaken but only once the GTS had
restarted with new instruments. He recognized that such a large formal survey would require a large labor force, just as the Irish survey
did. He therefore supported Bentinck's plan, as described by Anthony
Troyer, "to attempt the establishment of a *permanent system* tending towards obtaining progressively the best knowledge and delineation of
the country."[24] (The only detail of that plan revealed by Troyer was its
liberal employment of Eurasians, but it was likely to have been similar
to the plan advanced by Troyer and Bentinck for a survey of southern
India twenty years earlier.)

On the other hand, Salmond recognized that the formation of such a
survey organization would undoubtedly be subject to the professional
jealousy of the surveying officers in Bengal. He therefore suggested to
Troyer that Bentinck seek the full acquiescence of the Court's chairmen

and the president of the Board of Control. This perhaps indicates the limit of Salmond's authority: he might have been able to push the Court to accept the principle of a high-quality, geodetic survey of India, but a permanent survey institution would have constituted too radical a reform of the Company's institutional structure and the directors' control of their patronage. That is, the Court was more than willing to approve the one-off purchase of new, highly precise and accurate instruments, but it was still reluctant to approve the institutions necessary to wield them.

Consider, for example, the Company's purchase of two sets of state-of-the-art "compensation bars" for baseline measurement. Thomas Colby, superintendent of the Irish survey, had developed the compensation bars between 1826 and 1828. Each bar actually comprised two beams of different metals, with cross-pieces hinged so that as the bars expanded and contracted with changes in temperature—but at different rates because they were different substances—the ends of the cross-pieces would always remain exactly the same distance apart. Compared to the measuring chain, which required lengthy calibration to correct for its thermal expansion and contraction and which also stretched with use, Colby's bars promised instrumental perfection. The first surviving record of the Company's purchase of similar bars was Everest's letter to the Court's chairman in June 1829, which stated that two sets were almost complete, each of three bars.[25]

It is unclear when and why the Court had ordered the bars, but Everest's statement that the bars were to be sent to Bengal and Bombay is significant. Unlike Madras, those two presidencies had yet to be covered by any extensive triangulation. The Court would have received, very early in 1829, notification from the Bombay council that it had approved a proposal by John Jopp, the deputy surveyor general, to resurrect Valentine Blacker's idea for a triangulation of the western Deccan; Robert Shortrede of the Bombay Infantry had been delegated to the task.[26] The prompting of a triangulation of Bombay, the potential for a triangulation of Bengal, and the actuality of the triangulation of Ireland seem to have persuaded the Company's managers to invest in the newest and most precise scientific measuring apparatus available.

Yet the Court purchased the compensation bars without any clear conception of how they were to be used. Although the GTS was the logical institution to receive and employ the bars, they were not purchased with the GTS in mind. Everest addressed the Court on the subject of the bars twice in June 1829, first in reporting on their status and again when he described some flaws he had uncovered when he tested one set of the bars at Greenwich, aided by John Pond, the astronomer royal, and Lieutenant Hastings Murphy of the Ordnance Survey. Everest argued that the bars should indeed be given to the GTS.[27] Everest repeated the argument in early 1830, when the Court asked for his opinions on Jopp's plans for the triangulation of Bombay. Until then, the directors seem to have regarded Shortrede's work as an independent survey. There is no indication of how the directors originally thought the bars destined for Bengal were to be managed. Afterwards, however, the directors acceded to Everest's logic and subordinated Shortrede's triangulation and both sets of compensation bars to the larger program of the GTS.[28] Everest finally tested the modified bars at Lord's cricket ground in April 1830 and took them with him when he returned to India in June.[29]

The initial confusion over the compensation bars and the Bombay triangulation indicates that the directors had been converted to the geographical *ideal* promised by triangulation's technological fix. They were enticed by the exquisite precision and extreme accuracy of the new instrumentation. They would fund these tangible symbols of science and progress, but unlike Salmond they had yet to appreciate the institutional ramifications of an all-India triangulation. The directors' conception of the Great Trigonometrical Survey was broadened by Everest's several memoranda of 1829. These persuaded the directors that the GTS was indeed the sole institution capable of managing the triangulation. Most obviously, Everest acquired the use of the compensation bars.

After his return to Britain from the continent in mid-1828, most of Everest's time was spent working on the results of the Great Arc. He contracted with the Royal Observatory for two computers to do the actual calculations, which were finished by May 1829. At this time, he submitted a memorandum to the Court on the new methods he wanted to introduce for the measurement of the next stages of the Great Arc. Everest submitted the memoir on the Great Arc to the Court in February 1830 and the Court agreed to its publication. The Court gave Everest forty copies to distribute himself, in addition to those it sent to the Royal Society, Royal Astronomical Society, Royal Asiatic Society, Geological Society of London, and British Museum, as part of the materials for the *Atlas of India*.[30]

With the computations of the Great Arc complete, Everest was free to accept Colby's invitation to visit the Irish survey in order to witness for himself the "working of the machinery" of Colby's "beautiful system." He visited with Colby from early July to October 1829, until the "damp and rainy weather" and the "foul air of the bogs" forced a recurrence of his fever. He also consulted with Henry Kater, William Lambton's old assistant, who had since developed close ties to the Ordnance Survey.[31] Everest sent his impressions of the Irish survey, and of those components which would work well in India, to the Court in October 1829. In that memoir and in his subsequent correspondence, Everest concentrated on the *institutional* means whereby the Great Trigonometrical Survey could be extended across India. Most of the memoir discussed the provision of sufficient men and instruments, but with the obvious assumption that the institutions of the GTS had to be expanded and better coordinated.[32]

With respect to personnel, Everest suggested the formation of an organization similar to that created by Colby in Ireland. Military officers, preferably engineers, would, quite naturally, supervise the surveys, although they would need to be enticed to survey work with larger allowances and their appointments would have to be as formal and regular as other staff positions. The detailed work of the Irish survey was managed by sappers and civilian laborers, for whom there were no direct equivalents in India. Enlisted personnel were unsuited to surveying duty: English soldiers "cannot stand the climate, and are besides generally given to drinking and other irregularities" while Indian soldiers were illiterate and thus useless for drawing up field books. Only the Eurasians—"an acute and clever race . . . of whom the great defect is a proneness to falsehood, chiefly attributed to their native education"—could fill the role (¶49). Everest was sure that a group of such Eurasian assistants subject to military discipline and properly educated would quickly demonstrate their appropriateness for survey duties. Obviously, such a corps of surveyors would require a more formally organized survey hierarchy.

Expanding the GTS would place several military officers under Everest's command, although he did not specify precisely how many. The control he would wield over them was exemplified by his proposed regulation of their instruments. Everest proposed that the Company should supply all theodolites, chains, and other instruments for the surveyors. (Everest actually overstated the degree to which surveyors then had to pay for their own instruments; only in Bengal, where the long established dominance of route surveys meant that few expensive theodolites were ever used, did the government not provide high-quality instrumentation.) Everest argued further that the surveyors had to be held responsible for those instruments once they had been issued. Currently, surveyors were not held responsible and so tended to be careless. This had also been the case in Ireland, where surveyors routinely attributed instrument damage to their being blown over by the wind. Colby had directed that the surveyors should be liable for their instruments so that, as it was later described, "if the wind blew down any

more [then] the men should pay for them. Such was the sympathy between the wind and the men that it ceased, and did not blow down any
more."[33] Everest wanted a similar arrangement for the GTS.

Although Everest could not specify how many subordinate officers
he would need, he did specify the instruments. The large 36-inch theodolites were too big to be used on scaffolding atop existing buildings,
so Everest wanted the Company to buy some eighteen-inch theodolites
for primary triangles and smaller instruments (twelve-inch, eight-inch,
and seven-inch) for detailed work. The GTS would still need two 36-
inch theodolites for geodetic work; the new "beautiful" 36-inch theodolite was under construction and Everest thought that Lambton's old
instrument could be refurbished in London for £100, as compared with
the £500 which the new instrument cost; if its repair was infeasible, the
old instrument might be replaced by a 24-inch theodolite. Everest also
wanted a supply of modern lamps, night-lights, and heliotropes similar
to those of the Ordnance Survey to replace the old and inefficient lights
and flags used in India as targets for observation.[34]

The Court bought the new instruments. Its subsequent acceptance of
the increase in the number of the Great Trigonometrical Survey's parties
indicates that the directors had finally realized that the survey had to
grow. Nonetheless, the directors were still not really prepared to make
the GTS a permanent institution. They acceded to Everest's request for
the permanent appointment to the GTS of an artificer to repair the instruments, but they did so grudgingly. Everest first raised the issue in
his October 1829 memoir. He revisited it in December. The usual consequence of severe damage was that the affected instrument "is reported
unserviceable and most likely knocked up for old brass" because it
could not easily be returned to London for repair. The Company had
therefore spent some £5,000 on new instruments over the preceding five
years, a large sum which was more than sufficient to pay the salary and
expenses of an instrument maker. Everest nominated one Henry Barrow for the job. This time, Everest's proposals brought direct results.
His extra theodolites and night-lights were approved, and the Court
agreed to appoint—but only temporarily—Barrow as the survey department's instrument maker and repairer.[35]

The final result of all of Everest's petitions and memoirs was that the
directors decided to appoint Everest to be surveyor general in addition
to his current position as superintendent of the GTS. John Hodgson had
quit India on furlough, and a successor was necessary:

> Resolved by the Ballot, unanimously, that entertaining a high opin-
> ion of the services of Captain George Everest of the Bengal Es-

tablishment, in his office of Superintendent of the Great Trigonometrical Survey, and of his scientific acquirements and general
qualifications for the station of Surveyor General of India, he be
appointed to the said office.[36]

When Everest sailed for India in June 1830, he possessed more political support than any surveyor in India had yet possessed. The Court
was quite adamant that Bengal had to be triangulated and remapped
as part of the contributions to the *Atlas of India*. "We wish," wrote the
directors,

> to impress upon the Surveyor General that the points upon which
> the maps of Bengal Presidency are to be constructed, must have
> triangulation for their basis, being convinced that the *Atlas* can by
> no other method be rendered a permanent and useful work.[37]

Lord Ellenborough, president of the Board of Control, was equally supportive. He was most impressed by Everest's memoir on the application of the Ordnance Survey's techniques to India and by Everest's
published results of the Great Arc, a copy of which was deposited by
Everest in the board's library.[38] Ellenborough wrote to Bentinck that he
looked forward to Everest prosecuting a number of surveys focusing on
the Indus and the Punjab.[39]

There nonetheless remained some ambiguity about the scope of the
Indian surveys. The *Atlas of India* required a complete, triangulation-
based survey of all of British India, but there was still no conception of
a unified hierarchy of surveyors constituting a single survey institution
like the Ordnance Survey of Ireland. Everest's suggestions for a corps
of Eurasian assistant surveyors seem to have fallen on deaf ears. On the
other hand, when he reached India, he found in place a governor general who did think in terms of a unified cartographic organization. Everest then had the opportunity and the political support to create such an
organization, but he was not to succeed because fiscal reality once again
reared its ugly head.

Bentinck, Everest, and the Triumph of
Triangulation, 1830–32

Lord William Bentinck's tenure as governor general (1828–35) was
strongly shaped by his passionate belief in "improvements." As the
member of Parliament for Kings Lynn, he had been instrumental in the
construction of wharves and a new sea canal. He sank huge sums of
money into his Norfolk properties, but he was at the tail end of the
eighteenth-century capitalization of English agriculture and could not

avoid the effects of the agricultural depression that followed the Napoleonic Wars. He accepted the governor generalship as much to be able to pay off his personal debts—which by the mid-1820s had reached £80,000—as to recoup the honor lost when he had been blamed for the Vellore Mutiny and recalled from Madras in 1807. Once he had returned to India, Bentinck described himself as the "chief agent" to "a great estate"; he wanted to drain Calcutta's marshes just like the fens, to create a department of public works, to extend irrigation (for which he cited the example of his elder brother's efforts in Nottinghamshire), and to introduce steam navigation to the Ganges.[40]

Bentinck's improving tendencies were rooted in his evangelical and liberal beliefs. For example, in an 1837 address to Parliament, he announced that

> steam navigation is the great engine of working [India's] moral improvement . . . in proportion as the communication between the two countries shall be facilitated and shortened, so will civilized Europe be approximated, as it were, to these benighted regions; as in no other way can improvement in any large stream be expected to flow in.[41]

The first British steamer on the Ganges, launched in 1834, was not called the "Lord William Bentinck" as a mere sop to the governor general's pride. Bentinck conceived of a regular survey of India, based on the "machinery" of the subdivision of labor, as another great engine designed to improve India, just as Thomas Colby's "machinery" was intended to improve Ireland. Like other improvers and technophiles in the Company's service, Bentinck avidly supported the Great Trigonometrical Survey.

Bentinck's interest in mapping might also have been related to his style of "administrative generalship." He would identify a problem, and then focus all attention on it, gathering as much information as possible, often through personal interviews or through questionnaires sent to officers in the field. The end of each campaign would be a series of long minutes that would form the foundation of policy.[42] It is not so far fetched to suppose that this bias for the active acquisition of information was related to Bentinck's own concerns for the Company's more general acquisition of geographical knowledge. The surveys were themselves the subject of his intense scrutiny from 1829 through 1832, reflected in fourteen substantial memoirs and a host of supporting documents.

Whatever projects Bentinck wanted to implement were nonetheless restricted by the general tenor of his instructions from the Court. The directors ordered Bentinck to make India profitable. The three provincial governments together ran an annual deficit of £3 million between 1823 and 1829. Bentinck's retrenchments led to a surplus of over £1 million for the fiscal year 1829–30. Depression brought the Company to slightly above the break-even point for the next few years; increased revenues again raised the annual surplus to £1 million between 1835 and 1838, until the ruin of the Afghan War plunged the Indian finances back into the red. Bentinck's retrenchments were obviously severe. So intense was the displeasure of the Bengal officers at the abolition of their extra half-*batta*, for example, that Bentinck was still called "The Clipping Dutchman" during the Second World War (the nationalist slur referred to his family's arrival in England with William of Orange in 1688).[43] Any new improvements and reforms Bentinck might have advocated were thus tempered by retrenchments and an all-pervasive drive for economy.

It took six months from his arrival in India before Bentinck turned his attention to the various surveys and to the Court's orders for the creation of an *Atlas of India*. The occasion was John Hodgson's request to return on furlough to England. Bentinck's consideration of who should be the next surveyor general spilled over to encompass general cartographic policy. He made his selection—Major Henry Walpole—by listening to his aide, Anthony Troyer. Walpole had previously been Troyer's assistant instructor at the Madras Military Institution. Bentinck's conceptual debt to Troyer is evinced in his minutes, which repeat Troyer's description of the institution's surveying activities as having constituted an "Ordnance Survey" that comprised a trigonometrical foundation, a military survey based on the triangulation with a "systematical process for ensuring the accuracy and uniformity" of the work, and the production of the final map. Those minutes also reproduced Troyer's mistake of calling William Roy, "Le Roy." Bentinck mimicked Troyer in his vision of a survey based "upon a principle of progressive and systematic execution," just like the Ordnance Survey.[44]

The most complete and thorough of Bentinck's cartographic reports was his "Memorandum Relative to a Military Survey of India" of September 1829. From Troyer, Bentinck picked up the idea of dividing each district into regular blocks, each to be surveyed on a trigonometrical base by plane tables at the large scale of two inches to the mile (1: 31,680), the scale used by the Ordnance Survey since 1791 for its field surveys in England and Wales. Bentinck did not exclude the possibility of taking existing maps and fitting them to the triangulation, as long as they were at that same large scale. He therefore rejected one of the basic premises of the Ordnance Survey, that triangulation had to precede *all* detail surveys, even as he copied one of its basic characteristics. From Salmond, Bentinck took the damning critique that Charles Reynolds's map of India was "not constructed upon those methods which exclusively can afford a permanent value to a work of this nature." "Those methods" were to be those of Lambton, which were, of course, the same as those of the English, French, German, and Swedish surveys, and which had produced the "only really valuable part" of all of the materials sent to London for the *Atlas*. In contrast, Reynolds had relied too much on indigenous information. Nor did Bentinck begrudge the time a detailed survey would necessarily consume, although he was rather uncertain about the area to be mapped and the speed of the proposed technologies. His basic opinion, which drove everything else, was that the best survey would be that which produced the "most correct delineation for all purposes, general and particular, civil and military. The system best conducive to this object will also be ultimately the cheapest." [45]

Walpole, however, had no chance to implement Bentinck's ideas for an India-wide survey. Even though the Court had, as Bentinck pointed out, "expressly sanctioned" the continuation of "geodetical operations," [46] the other members of the Bengal government appear to have objected to the cost that would have been involved in the topographical surveys. Furthermore, the Court's independent decision to appoint Everest to the position of surveyor general overrode Bentinck's authority; Walpole did not take office and James Herbert, the deputy surveyor general, stayed in charge of the office until Everest arrived in Calcutta.

Everest was soon provided with an opportunity for pushing his agenda for a uniform institution. Within a week of his arrival in October 1830, Everest was asked to draft an answer to the Court's letter of 26 May 1830. That letter had presented the Court's intent, prompted by Everest, for Bengal to be triangulated in the same manner as Bombay's territories; the Court also sought information about the state of the topographic survey by Madras officers of the territories of the Nizam of Hyderabad. Everest immediately took the high ground. As surveyor general, he claimed direct control of the Hyderabad survey because the Nizam was tied by subsidiary treaty to the government in Calcutta. (Lord Hastings had used the same argument in 1817 when bringing Lambton under Calcutta's orders.) As superintendent of the Great Trigonometrical Survey, Everest claimed direct control of Robert Shortrede's fledgling Bombay triangulation. He justified himself with the observation that he had to supervise all minor trigonometrical surveys so as to "preserve that uniformity which is desired by the Honorable Court." [47]

At the same time, Everest put forward the scheme that was finally adopted for the Bengal triangulation: several meridional chains of triangles would run from the Calcutta longitudinal series northwards across Bengal (see figure 1.6). The system was flexible. For example, the Karára meridian would pass by Lucknow, capital of Awadh, and a short branch could be run out to Kanpur in the Lower Doab. Alternatively, if the Nawab of Awadh objected to British surveyors in his territories, then the link to Kanpur might be made via the Amua series. Everest especially noted the potential for extending the Párasnáth series southward to tie into Bentley Buxton's triangulation-based topographic survey of Cuttack of the 1810s. Everest wanted this last series to be begun as soon as possible.[48]

After referral to Bentinck, who was then traveling through the Upper Provinces, the Calcutta council agreed to grant Everest control of the Hyderabad and Bombay surveys.[49] No immediate mention was made of his plan to run chains of triangles either to Cuttack or across the Bengal plains, but the idea nonetheless stayed in Bentinck's mind. When Everest requested in early 1831 to have his computing staff increased so as to catch up on the arrears in calculations which had built up, Bentinck reminded the council that it was "incumbent upon us to afford every facility for forwarding and expediting [the] promotion" of the geodetic survey. This in turn required the provision of field parties sufficient for its prosecution, including the appointment to the survey of two engineer subalterns—James Western and Henry Righey—to which the council had already agreed in principal.[50]

Of course, the government still had to find the money to increase the GTS's establishment. The Bombay governor had in 1828 agreed to Shortrede's triangulation of the western Deccan only on the condition that the Gujerat revenue survey be suspended, eight positions in the Bombay revenue surveys having already been axed or left vacant.[51] The Bengal administration followed the same course of action. In this it was justified by Herbert's arguments in 1829 that the revenue surveys in the Upper Provinces were far too ineffective, inaccurate, and expensive. Now, in July 1831, Bentinck suggested that those surveys be ended. The officers should return to regimental duty; the surplus assistant surveyors should be used either on the Great Trigonometrical Survey's field operations or in the office supervising the computing staff.[52]

In the meantime, Bentinck had also discovered the inefficient state of the surveys made by assistant quartermaster generals. Whereas the quartermaster general's surveyors were well organized in Madras, where they made cantonment and route surveys, their colleagues in Bengal were quite unorganized; in particular, they stayed in barracks for most of the field season but continued to draw survey allowances.[53] This prompted yet another lengthy minute, in August 1831, based on the contention that the Court's orders of 1814 and 1823 had failed to achieve the desired goals of a single map of India at a low cost. Bentinck suggested another, cheaper scheme for a military survey of those areas yet to be adequately mapped. His idea was to employ officers from the numerous military garrisons scattered around India who were otherwise idle.[54]

Bentinck reiterated his objections to the inefficiency of the revenue surveys in the Upper Provinces. Anyone who consulted the maps "which are executed with a nicety not to be exceeded in a survey of Regent's Park," he found, "cannot learn from them and their accompanying tables the quantity of land cultivated and paying revenue, its real and rated valuation as to quality, its susceptibility of yielding more rent, nor the quantity culturable but not cultivated nor assessed" (¶13). Moreover, the surveys cost one-fifth of the annual revenues collected from the districts they covered, whereas the much more effective revenue surveys by Thomas Munro had consumed only one-twentieth of the revenues. Bentinck concluded that the revenue surveys might be abandoned with little effect and those surveyors used on geographical surveys.

Finally, Bentinck pointed out that the Court's abolition of the offices of surveyor general at Madras and Bombay had failed: "the only perceptible change [has been] that the designation of Surveyor General at Madras and Bombay is altered to Deputy Surveyor General" (¶17). There were only three topographical surveys underway in the south and all three were winding down; Bombay had only another three. The offices of deputy surveyor general in the two subsidiary presidencies might be abolished without any detrimental effects. It would have been quite unconscionable for the existing deputies at Madras and Bombay to be simply fired, so Bentinck supposed that they should take the field as topographic surveyors, but with the same salaries as they had enjoyed before. He further resurrected the concept of a single survey of India by suggesting that the Madras survey parties be transferred to Bengal or Bombay once the southern districts had been completed.

But the Failure of Topography

Far more than in his earlier discussion papers, Lord William Bentinck's minute of August 1831 expressed most clearly the concept of a military survey which Anthony Troyer had written about in 1827. This survey was not to be an *ad hoc* affair, but a centralized department with no artificial boundaries imposed by the political structures of British India. George Everest tried to build on this vision in his response, but the continuing financial restraints made it impossible to do more than to firmly establish the Great Trigonometrical Survey. He responded to all of Bentinck's ideas in October and November 1831: his plans for the GTS were accepted by the Calcutta council and became the survey's basic policy for the next decade and beyond.[55]

Everest thought that the geodetic core of the GTS—the Great Arc, William Lambton's series from Bangalore to Madras, and the Bombay and Calcutta longitudinal series—would take five years to complete, assuming that Everest was given the requisite staff. He did not, however, go into the expenditures likely to be associated with these operations. At the very least he wanted a second party for the Great Arc. He and another officer would then observe the same stars simultaneously when determining latitude; this would, in turn, allow the removal of hitherto indeterminate but potentially significant errors, especially those due to atmospheric refraction.[56]

The mapping of Bengal would require most of the province to be mapped anew. Everest was adamant that James Rennell's *Bengal Atlas* was insufficiently detailed to be incorporated into new surveys. He did not reject all existing topographic surveys, however; some were of good enough quality to be incorporated into the *Atlas of India* once they had been corrected by the new triangulation. The new mapping would be done by Eurasian laborers working with plane tables. Having lesser expectations of salary and status than army officers, they would still be much cheaper than Bentinck's most recent plan of employing army officers on station. Everest estimated the cost at 1,60,000 rupees (£14,720).

The triangulation framework would comprise ten minor series running north-south at intervals of one degree of longitude, or about sixty miles (97 km); as each chain would only be seventeen or eighteen miles (27–29km) wide, the intervening spaces, each about forty-two miles wide (68 km), would have to be defined by high-quality traverses. The series would be surveyed in order of the importance of the districts that they would traverse. With the exception of the Párasnáth series, none of the series needed to be run to the south of the Calcutta series, into "wild and unprofitable country inhabited by Goands" (¶10). It would take approximately thirty years for the provincial triangulation to be completed by just one survey party of an officer, a civil assistant and apprentice, a fourteen-man guard, sixteen flag coolies, fourteen carriers, two messengers, and one medical assistant. Everest estimated that the staff allowances, salaries, tent allowances, and contingent expenses for the party would total 1,495 rupees (£138) per month; over thirty years, the total would be 5,40,000 rupees (£49,700). Added to this would be the unpredictable costs for constructing towers, most in the "dead flats" of lower Bengal where there were few existing large buildings: an estimated two hundred towers, at 1,500 rupees (£138) each, would cost another 3,00,000 rupees (£27,600) in total.

Everest thus estimated the total cost for mapping Bengal to be ten lakhs of rupees (£92,000). Everest quickly pointed out that the Ordnance Survey of Ireland would cost three times as much were it to cover a region of the same extent. The huge sum "would be expended in a purpose which the wisest of men have always pronounced to be practically useful and nationally honorable" (¶49). Spread over thirty years, the financial impact of the survey would be relatively small. But it was, of course, unthinkable that the survey should take so long; Everest therefore wanted six parties to survey the minor series in just five years, increasing the annual expenditures proportionately.

Everest envisioned his new organization as comprising some eight parties, totaling ten military officers—the superintendent, that is, himself; a chief assistant, as provided for when Lord Hastings had established the GTS in 1817; five first-class assistants; and three second-class assistants—and thirty Eurasian "subassistants." Of course, there were no ready-trained officers or Eurasians to fill any of these positions, but Everest was willing to train them all. James Herbert had already identified several of the revenue surveyors as being well qualified for topographic work, assuming they were able to convert to the new system of surveying. Everest particularly classed perambulator-surveying as being "under the head of knowledge to be unlearned" (¶84). His initial choice of officers, in addition to James Western and Henry Righey, included two revenue surveyors, two topographical surveyors, and two new arrivals in India.

Given the financial situation, Bentinck could not initiate any systematic and coherent survey along the lines envisioned by either himself or Everest. He could allocate funds sufficient for two of the seven new parties Everest desired, one for the Great Arc and one for the southern Párasnáth series.[57] A new topographic survey of Bengal, with all of its institutional costs, would obviously be too big a project to be undertaken without the directors' approval. But even before the Calcutta council referred all the various ideas and plans to London, in March 1832,[58] Bentinck had begun to change his mind. In January, he reversed his stand on the revenue surveys. On "more minute examination" he found them not to be so bad as he had been led to believe. He now rejected any transfer of personnel from the revenue surveys to the GTS; indeed, Bentinck even suggested that the provincial triangulation could be put off in favor of a longitudinal series across the Upper Provinces, which would serve as a partial control for the revenue surveys there. The reprieve for the revenue surveys meant that the council would have to find other sources to fund the expansion of the GTS. Even so, the council allowed Everest to advertise in the Government Gazette for new civil assistants and approved the new costs which were involved.[59]

Bentinck continued to push revenue surveys for the Upper Provinces. His conversion had made him a fanatical advocate of the system. He organized a conference of the revenue surveyors in Allahabad in January 1833. His most important reform was to grant the surveyors greater control over the field surveys made by Indian laborers. Bentinck also disputed the succession of the deputy surveyor general to replace Herbert in Calcutta. Everest wanted Richard Wilcox for the position; Bentinck wanted an officer to be based at Allahabad to supervise an expanded revenue survey program. Needless to say, Bentinck prevailed, although he was eventually overruled by the Court.[60]

The Calcutta council received the Court's response to Bentinck's and Everest's plans for a new Bengal survey, if not for an all-India topographic survey, in May 1833. The directors agreed with all of the proposals for the Great Trigonometrical Survey. They were all too aware of the great expense of an extended triangulation intended to serve as the basis of the *Atlas*, but they were equally aware of the even higher costs of "detached, unscientific and unsatisfactory surveys." The only logical choice was to bite the bullet and sanction the necessary increases. For the same reasons, the directors had absolutely no qualms about abolishing the posts of deputy surveyor general at Madras and Bombay. The continued existence of those positions contravened the directors' orders of 1814 and would impede the progress of the *Atlas*. Setting aside Bentinck's idea of a "revenue" deputy surveyor general, the directors also wanted to abolish Herbert's position in Calcutta as soon as Everest stopped his fieldwork and returned to the office. As for the topography of Bengal, the directors maintained that they wanted to incorporate James Rennell's "accurate delineation" into the *Atlas*. Everest had objected to using Rennell's *Bengal Atlas* because its scale was too small; the directors pointed out in reply that they possessed Rennell's original manuscripts at five miles to the inch (1:316,800), which could easily be slightly enlarged to the *Atlas*'s quarter-inch scale with "a degree of accuracy correspondent with the other parts of the *Atlas*," given sufficient triangulated control points. Finally, the Court reminded the Bengal government that the surveys for the *Atlas* were not to be openended, but were to be completed as soon as possible.[61]

With the Court's approval, the Calcutta council promptly sent out instructions for John Jopp at Bombay and Duncan Montgomerie at Madras to be employed on the GTS. Neither officer was particularly pleased by the sudden change; they both wanted to stay in their own presidencies. Everest sought to have the surplus surveying staff attached either to the detail surveys or to Shortrede's trigonometrical survey. But Bentinck stuck to London's orders: the expenses of the surveys were high enough already; the essential task was the completion of the Great Trigonometrical Survey and the ending of its exorbitant costs. Topographic surveys were suddenly of very minor importance. In the end, neither deputy surveyor general stayed with the surveys; nor would the Calcutta council approve additional personnel for the GTS in their stead. The Court ultimately approved Bentinck's position and approved a drastic drop in the size of the Bombay survey department.[62]

The subordinate surveys at each presidency were transferred to Everest's control in his capacity as surveyor general. It took him some time to obtain actual control of the Bombay surveys. Robert Shortrede's triangulation of Bombay came under Everest's direct supervision in October 1833; Everest promptly requested that an assistant be appointed lest Shortrede fall ill and the survey founder. This was approved, and Lieutenant William Jacob was appointed.[63] Subsequently, in April 1836, Shortrede asked for a temporary leave from the survey in order to examine the progress of the Deccan revenue survey around Pune for the Bombay revenue department. He signed his request—which he made to the Bombay government and not to Everest—as "Superintendent of the Bombay Trigonometrical Survey."[64] Everest had already become uneasy with Shortrede's failure to report on his progress and with his obvious attempt "to revive an *imperium in imperio* under another name and more objectionable form," which is to say to become surveyor general at Bombay in deed if not in name. The Calcutta council agreed with Everest that Shortrede should be either in or out of the trigonometrical survey, but not both. The councillors also agreed to Everest's general proposition that any triangulation "on the Great Scale" was by definition part of the Great Trigonometrical Survey no matter where it might be located, so that all officers employed on such operations had to be trained on the GTS under the direct supervision of its superintendent. Shortrede had not been trained by Everest and was therefore removed from the survey; Jacob was appointed directly to the GTS.[65]

Institutionally, the reforms of May 1833 did not prove to be as productive as Everest had hoped. The abolition of the two deputy surveyor generals simply increased his correspondence load. More generally, he was quite frustrated in his attempts to build a single organization for surveying India. Only the Eurasian subassistants were put on a unified standing, with the same qualifications, pay scales, and governing regulations in all three presidencies. Everest's attempts to establish a similar establishment of "subordinate natives"—which would be independent of the surveyor general and so liable to be unaffected by changes in that office—were rejected by Bentinck because it would form a permanent department. Nor would the council allow Everest the power of summary judgment over inefficient or misbehaving subordinates.[66]

No matter the appreciation of topographic maps held by surveyors and administrators in northern India, new topographical surveys had gotten caught between the trigonometrical and revenue surveys. For the remainder of Everest's joint tenure as surveyor general and superintendent of the Great Trigonometrical Survey, no hard and fast commitment was made, either by the Court of Directors in London or by the Calcutta council, to base all new topographic surveys on prior triangulation. Despite Bentinck's desire for a "military survey," a compromise had to be reached over the cost of *all* of the surveys. Existing topographic surveys were to be used as much as possible for the *Atlas of India*, tied together by a systematic triangulation whose institutional roots were now firmly established. Systematic topographic surveys of all of India continued to be popularized as an ideal to be desired, but they were opposed in practice on the grounds of cost and privilege. I turn to these in the next chapter.

CHAPTER EIGHT

The Final Compromise: Triangulation and Archive, 1831–43

The abolition of the offices of deputy surveyor general in both Madras and Bombay and the continued low level of topographic mapping reflect the financial crises of the 1820s and 1830s. Although both Lord William Bentinck and George Everest sought to create a single "survey of India," they could not do so. If—after all of the reductions, the apparent unification of the geographic institutions in all three presidencies under Everest, and the Court's stated desire to complete the *Atlas of India*—there was one institution which could be interpreted as a single "survey of India," then it was the Great Trigonometrical Survey. But the image of the GTS as an all-India survey relied on William Lambton's mapping in southern India. Under Everest, almost all of the trigonometrical survey's operations were located within territories subordinate to the Calcutta council—Bengal and the Upper Provinces—and the survey was staffed by officers of the Bengal army. There was, of course, Robert Shortrede's and then William Jacob's triangulation of Bombay, but those officers still relied on the Bombay council's permission for raising survey parties.

Everest's tenure as surveyor general was thus marked by an emphasis on the trigonometrical survey—especially the Great Arc, which took most of his energies—and on revenue surveys. Some historians have been ambivalent about Everest's role, at once applauding his scientific zeal yet hinting even so that the decline in topographic surveys stemmed from his lack of interest in them.[1] Such a position is perhaps unfair. Everest clearly wanted to establish a topographic survey organization but was prevented from doing so by the circumstances of the East India Company's territorial empire. Not only did the administration downplay the importance of topographical maps, it also restricted the geodetic character of the triangulation. The Company's administration had accepted an India-wide triangulation only as the basis of the *Atlas* and sought to restrict any extension of its geodetic elements. The new triangulation series were for geographical purposes and were not expected to require the same precision and care as the Great Arc.

The contrast between the progress made in the triangulation and the decline of topographical surveying led to a renewed round of criticism of the survey system in the late 1830s. The principal critique was by Thomas Best Jervis of the Bombay engineers, who sought to establish a large survey organization for all of India. Jervis's plans to emulate the Ordnance Survey of Ireland failed because, once again, the directors refused to surrender their rights of patronage and dismissal. His attempt is nonetheless significant because he made explicit what had hitherto been implicit in the development of the Indian surveys. He enlisted the moral support of the metropolitan scientific institutions and societies in order to argue for the formation of a truly "scientific" survey of India. Indeed, Jervis did succeed in adding the new terrestrial sciences of magnetism and gravimetry to the duties of the British geographers in India. The Court's reaction to his topographical and geodetic proposals indicate both the scientistic image of "science" held by the Company's directors and the inertial strength of the compromise reached in the 1820s between the variant epistemologies represented by the Great Trigonometrical Survey and the *Atlas*.

The Great Trigonometrical Survey, 1831–43

The Great Trigonometrical Survey entered a phase of major growth after 1831. With George Everest's return in October 1830, the GTS surveying staff numbered two officers (Everest and Robert Shortrede in Bombay) and four Eurasian (mostly) civil assistants. Late in 1831, Everest had promised to finish the Great Arc and the Calcutta and Bombay series within five years; that is, by 1837. To do that, and to start on the Bengal subsidiary meridians required a dramatic expansion in the survey's staff. By January 1833, the GTS had grown, almost overnight, to no less than nine officers and twenty-two civil assistants. (To these should be added the numerous Indian laborers, guards, and camp followers.) Although the numbers dipped slightly in the middle of the 1830s, the GTS was back at six officers and twenty-seven civil assistants by 1843. Everest had a permanent instrument maker to repair the GTS's various instruments: Henry Barrow, until 1839, then Mohsin Husain. Everest also developed a large establishment of mathematical computers, most notable of whom was Radhanath Sickdhar, a Calcutta Brahmin, to whom tradition incorrectly describes the computations which established Peak XV in the Himalayas as the world's highest mountain (and which Andrew Waugh named after Everest).[2]

That is, after 1830, the Great Trigonometrical Survey lost its character as a personal institution, which it had had under William Lambton, and

Figure 8.1 James Prinsep's drawing of the measurement of the Calcutta baseline on the Barrackpore Road, 1831. Note the tower marking one end of the base. One of the compensation bars and an old chain—roughly discarded—are in the foreground. A more intricate version of this image was published in Everest's 1847 memoir.

James Prinsep, "Progress of the Indian Trigonometrical Survey." *Journal of the Asiatic Society of Bengal* 1 (1832): 71–72.

was transformed into a proper institution. And, of course, the survey's costs went up accordingly. The summary report by the military auditor general for 1833–34 found that retrenchments across almost the entire military department and army had produced annual savings of over 3,00,000 *sicca* rupees (£27,600). This was offset against increases in a few departments, but "principally from charges on account of the expensive work of the Great Trigonometrical Survey" of about 63,300 *sicca* rupees (£5,825).[3]

The first element of Everest's work on his return was the completion of the Calcutta longitudinal series. Joseph Olliver had by early 1829 carried the series down to the plains near Calcutta. By the time of Everest's return, Olliver had determined where to build the fifteen permanent towers necessary to bring the series into Calcutta. By June 1832, Everest had completed the triangulation and had measured a baseline on the Barrackpore Road in the city's western suburbs with the new compensation bars (figure 8.1).[4]

Under Shortrede, the Bombay triangulation was quite separate from the unfinished Bombay longitudinal series and its quality did not impress Everest. He was not sorry to see Shortrede go in 1834. William

Jacob continued the work, returning to the Bombay series in 1837–38 after spending 1836 with Everest on the Great Arc. Jacob's poor health interrupted progress, but he finally reobserved Everest's work and took part in the remeasurement of the Bider baseline. The series was completed in 1842. Subsequently, the secondary triangulation was reorganized as a series of meridians like those in Bengal.[5]

Work on the Great Arc went well under Everest's direct supervision. Progress was even faster once Waugh, Everest's new assistant, had demonstrated his competence. The Great Arc's route through the plains was examined and an approximate series observed during the field seasons of 1832–33 and 1833–34.[6] The northern terminus of the Great Arc was established in Dehra Dun, a valley in the Himalayan foothills. The engineer corps took their time building the masonry towers across the plains, so Everest was able to spend a great deal of time on the base measurement at Dehra Dun in 1834–35, examining the equipment and discovering that despite their theoretically constant composition, the bars' length still changed slightly with temperature variations. The proper measurement of the Great Arc across the plains was begun in the 1835–36 season; with a second party under Waugh, the work progressed quickly and was completed by the end of the 1836–37 field season. Only two more azimuth observations (to determine precisely the arc's direction) and the astronomical observations for the latitudinal extent of the final section were left to be completed. Everest was not, therefore, too far off his original estimate.

However, Everest found a 3⅓-foot (1 m) discrepancy between the length of the Sironj base as measured in 1824 with Lambton's chains (at the southern end of the final section of the Great Arc) and the same length as calculated through the triangles from the base at Dehra Dun. He therefore obtained the government's permission to remeasure the Sironj base with the compensation bars in 1837–38; the error was found to have been in the 1824 measurement. This then threw into doubt the Bider-Sironj section of the arc. Lambton had then been rather ill and had not observed much of this section himself. Nor had the old three-foot theodolite been used. Accordingly, Everest no longer trusted the angular observations between Bider and Sironj, and he doubted that the Bider base itself was perfect. The observation of the Great Arc was therefore extended. In 1838–39, Everest and Waugh undertook the astronomical observations for the Sironj-Dehra Dun section of the Great Arc, after which Waugh (at Sironj) began to remeasure the triangles southward toward Bider. Lieutenant Thomas Renny had meanwhile begun the remeasurement northwards from Bider. Together, Waugh and Renny completed the Sironj-Bider section. In 1840–41, Everest and

Waugh observed the latitude difference between Bider and Sironj; then in 1841–42, Waugh and Jacob remeasured the Bider base itself, thereby completing the fieldwork of the Great Arc.[7]

The subordinate series through Bengal were affected by a similar set of circumstances as the Bombay triangulation. Illness and inexperience meant that they were prosecuted only slowly and poorly. This is most clearly seen by the first of the series to be undertaken, the South Párasnáth series from the Calcutta series down into Cuttack. James Western began the series in early 1832 but completed little before his dismissal shortly before the 1834–35 field season. His replacement died before he could join the survey. Alexander Boileau worked on the series over the next three seasons (1835–38), but with most of the survey party repeatedly falling ill, little work was completed; Boileau quit the survey altogether in December 1838, leaving it to be finally connected to Bentley Buxton's old work by the senior civil assistant. The subordinate series across the plains were similarly affected. The Budhon series progressed in a desultory fashion under several officers after 1833, and it took no less than three parties to force its completion in 1842–43. The Rangír series began well under Waugh, but it languished when he was transferred to the Great Arc, until it was finally completed in 1842. The Amua series was begun under Renny at the same time as the Rangír series, and despite the time Renny spent on the Great Arc, it was finished in 1839. When Everest quit India in late 1843, work had begun on four more of the subsidiary meridians, including an eleventh which ran through Calcutta (see figure 1.6).

In addition to the subsidiary meridians across Bengal, Everest argued in 1839 that a longitudinal series should be measured along the foothills of the Himalayas. It is unclear whether Everest had ever intended the meridional arcs across the plains to terminate in bases of verification, but he had found some errors in the Calcutta series that made it impossible to trust the subsidiary meridians without some form of verification at their northern end. Individual bases would be too expensive, while another chain run eastward from Dehra Dun along the Himalayan foothills would also permit more points to be determined for the *Atlas*. The Bengal government agreed.[8] The chain of triangles, skirting the politically forbidden territory of Nepal, was eventually christened the North-East Longitudinal Series. It was from observations of the distant Himalayan peaks from this chain that the survey's mathematicians later discovered Peak XV to be the highest mountain in the world.

The Court did not appreciate the necessity for the north-east series, and it asked Everest to justify why a discrepancy of seven feet and eleven inches (2.4 m) between the measured and computed lengths of the Calcutta base—itself a length of nearly six and one-half miles (10 km)—should affect geographical positions for a map at four miles to the inch. Had the Calcutta series been intended, like the Great Arc, to be "for purely scientific purposes," the Court would have understood the problem, but the series had been approved solely for the purposes of the *Atlas*. Given more information, however, the Court did finally accept the opinions of its cartographic experts and it approved the new north-eastern series in 1841.[9]

Neither the Court nor the Calcutta council approved of the delays in the Great Arc and both seriously questioned the need to reobserve the Bider-Sironj section.[10] Throughout 1838 and 1839, the Calcutta council pressured Everest to complete the series and to push on as fast as possible with the subsidiary series in Bengal. So did the Court; it wanted Bengal to be done and Everest to start on some new subsidiary series across the Upper Provinces to the west of the Great Arc in order to allow the incorporation of those regions into the *Atlas of India*. Everest replied that he was willing to undertake the westerly series, but only as long as he was given the means to prosecute them.[11] Neither authority approved Everest's request that the southernmost sections of the Great Arc, between Cape Comorin and Bangalore, be resurveyed to bring them into line with the quality of the northern sections. To do so would be far too expensive and was of questionable necessity: the triangulation was done and maps were already based thereon; the work had served its topographic purpose.[12]

Prinsep's "Geographical Committee," 1839–41

After 1838–39, the Bengal series were accelerated. The Court further directed in September 1841 that it wanted the Great Arc parties devoted to the Bengal series as soon as the scientific work had been finished. To emphasize the relationship of the triangulation to existing topographical materials, the Court also directed that it would not be necessary "that any systematic plan should be adopted" for triangulating between the meridional series. The topographic surveys in the region were complete, despite their age, and could be fitted to the series directly. Any further corrections would be done by means of route surveys that would start and end at triangulation stations. Prompted by its chief secretary, Henry Thoby Prinsep, the Calcutta council therefore ordered that, to accelerate the provision of relevant points for the *Atlas*, the Bengal meridians should be undertaken at intervals of two degrees of longitude rather than the planned interval of one degree.[13]

Prinsep was a strong proponent of the older, compilation style of map creation, with or without the benefits of triangulation. (A conservative Tory, he regularly came into conflict with Bentinck's liberal principles.) Echoing James Herbert from ten years before, Prinsep complained to Thomas Jervis in December 1839 that George Everest,

> like every one of his predecessors . . . since the admirable Rennell has been of no use to Government for purposes of Geography or of practical information of any kind and if by devoting himself to triangulation he has ever made any discoveries in Geognosy or science they are yet wrapped up in his own impenetrable and morose self with no prospect of ever benefitting the Indian or English public.

To exemplify all that was wrong in the surveyor general's office, Prinsep cited the instance of his own planning for the new road to Bombay, which had required fifty separate maps, many in a poor state of repair:

> Now if our Surveyor General[s] had been alive to Geography as old Rennell was, they would have [put] everything new as it came in to be booked [into] maps arranged by degrees so that whenever a map might be wanted of any given tract of country, they would only have to copy for assurance of giving all that was known.[14]

Prinsep does not seem to have been aware that surveyor generals had already tried, and had failed, to implement precisely this sort of map-making.

Prinsep therefore tried to establish a "geographical committee" in Calcutta to be responsible for creating compilations of all worthwhile materials for use by the government. He also wanted to have the deputy surveyor generals reinstated at Madras and Bombay to help in this effort. That is, Prinsep wanted to resurrect the pre-1814 cartographic system. Needless to say, the Court rejected his proposals because they went completely against the principles embodied by the *Atlas of India* and by a single survey office.[15]

The Court also overturned Prinsep's idea of skipping every other subsidiary meridian in Bengal. To do so would reduce the overall accuracy to be imposed on the existing surveys; the series would have to be done sooner or later, and skipping them would thus delay the completion of the *Atlas* sheets for the regions where the omitted meridians would have run. The directors again stated their desire for a uniform triangulation to make definitive surveys: "our objects will not be effectively attained unless the work has a character of perfection and finality which will render altogether unnecessary any future surveys of the same districts for geographical purposes."[16] Moreover, the Court anticipated that when Andrew Waugh succeeded Everest at the end of

1843, he would not have to deal with the Great Arc, so that all of his and his officers' efforts could be centered on the Bengal series, which would therefore be completed that much faster. The Court also wanted subsidiary series to be extended into Bombay and Sind as soon as possible.[17]

With hindsight, Everest's formation of a gridiron of chains of triangles dependent on the accurate backbone of the Great Arc might seem to indicate a coherent view of the future surveying of India. Yet at the same time, it should be clear that the Court was motivated by a desire for "perfection" and "finality" that was not properly thought out. The directors thought the subsidiary arcs across Bengal would be sufficient, even though they could by themselves only correct relatively small bands of territory on existing topographical maps. The intervening gaps, each about forty-two miles (68 km) wide, would remain uncorrected and so unperfected and unfinal. Admittedly, the directors did reject Prinsep's plan to skip alternate series, which would have left bands of territory up to a hundred miles (160 km) without correction: that obviously would have been inadequate. At root, the directors had accepted that the correctness and definitiveness of the topographic surveys derived entirely from the triangulated geometrical framework, regardless of the manner in which the detailed surveys were connected to the triangulation.

The support shown after 1839 by the Court for triangulation and its simultaneous refusal to accept a general topographic survey were not just responses to the Company's financial state and to cartographic activities in India. The Court had also been influenced by the efforts in London between 1837 and 1839 of Jervis, who wanted to adapt Thomas Colby's methodical system for the Irish Survey to India. Jervis failed: the Court was prepared to accept only so much system and expense, and it remained jealous of its rights to appoint and to fire its servants.

Jervis in London, 1836–39

At a time when officers in the Company's service habitually and loudly advertised their service records in an effort to capture the Court's notice and so attain some extra financial reward beyond their salaries and allowances, Thomas Jervis stands out as a particularly shameless self-publicist and propagandist. For example, in 1845 he addressed a number of letters to Lord Aberdeen, then British foreign secretary. He began by sending Aberdeen a copy of a Chinese map of Beijing, which he had lithographed and which was to be presented to Queen Victoria the following day. No sooner had Aberdeen accepted the gift than Jervis sent specimens of his other maps, while expressing the hope that the government would see fit to support his future work. Most egregiously, Jervis claimed that whereas a normal lithographic stone could be used for only three to four thousand impressions, his own could take "a million if requisite."[18]

Before these events, in 1837, Jervis had persuaded the Court to appoint him as the provisional successor to George Everest, should Everest soon retire or die. Jervis then claimed to various politicians and scientific societies that he had actually been appointed surveyor general. This claim underlies his series of proposals for systematic surveys and other scientific activities in India, all of which strike the modern reader as quite proper, once the fervent protestations of faithful and assiduous service are filtered out. These proposals stimulated an intriguing debate which neatly encapsulates the Court's opinions toward triangulation, topography, systematic surveys, and survey institutions in the late 1830s.[19]

Jervis had been born in Ceylon in 1796. His father was a member of the Madras civil service; his mother was the daughter of a royal engineer. It was thus almost inevitable that both he and his older brother George would enter the Company's engineers. He also spent a year with the Ordnance Survey in western England before sailing for Bombay, where he arrived in 1814. Jervis was an ardent evangelical and his desire to convert the Hindus and Moslems of India to Protestant Christianity permeated all of his actions and ideas.[20] His active field career was mostly spent in the southern Konkan, in 1819–20 and from 1823 to 1830. After 1830 he spent his spare time working up a memoir and atlas of the district.[21] Jervis wrote two books on Indian metrology. In the first, he deduced the existence in the distant past of a "Primitive Universal Standard," of which all subsequent standards were corruptions; he sent copies of this to the astronomer John Herschel and to Henry Kater, two specialists on metrology. The second tract argued for the adoption of a single, India-wide system of weights, measures, and coinage based on that universal standard.[22] These two works exemplify Jervis's scientific and intellectual pretensions, pretensions which were to dominate his activities in London when on health furlough from 1836 to 1839. His goal was to change the "deep rooted prejudice" and "indifference to novelties" with which his superiors had met his criticisms of the "total neglect of science" by the British in India, criticisms made when he had been "a very young officer."[23]

Jervis reached London in December 1836, intent on advancing his career and on reforming the surveys of India along "scientific" lines. Both agendas were helped by his assembling a remarkable array of interest from the political and scientific elites in London. Jervis was supported by James Salmond, the Court's powerful military secretary, until the latter's death in December 1837. Outside of the Company, Jervis had two key patrons in Prince Augustus and Sir John Cam Hobhouse. Augustus had been estranged from his father, George III, because of his liberal and intellectual leanings. He was grand master of Freemasons; he had served as president of the Society of Arts in 1816; and he was president of the Royal Society from November 1830 to November 1838. Although he was not himself a practicing scientist, he was nonetheless a most important figure among the educated elite of London.[24] Hobhouse was a Whig politician with radical leanings. As both a fellow of the Royal Society and as president of the Board of Control in Lord Melbourne's second ministry (1835–41), he was clearly of signal importance for Jervis's plans.[25]

The extent and quality of the interest expressed in Jervis's favor is shown by his promotion to major in Queen Victoria's coronation honors list of June 1838. Augustus wrote to Hobhouse in the following month that Charles Grant, former president of the Board of Control (1831–34) was seeking a knighthood for Jervis, together with the honorary title of "Geographer to Her Majesty." Jervis had been brought to Grant's notice by the latter's younger brother, Sir Robert Grant, governor of Bombay (1835–38). The strength and appeal of Jervis's ideas is also demonstrated in a letter written by Lord John Russell, the home secretary and a future prime minister, to Hobhouse in late 1839 on Jervis's behalf requesting that the Great Trigonometrical Survey be extended to the Crown Colony of Ceylon; Hobhouse reluctantly had to decline such a possibility.[26]

Jervis knew that, for his goals to be fulfilled, he had to persuade the directors to appoint him surveyor general of India. To this end, he submitted his topographical and statistical work in the Konkan to the Court, together with a petition couched, even for the period, in excessive hyperbole. "I venture respectfully to affirm," he wrote,

> having personally inspected the whole of the geographical information in your Honble. Court's records in England and in India, that there is no more important and difficult portion of the British Indian Empire so exactly, accurately, and fully completed as the survey of the Konkan, which I have the honor to lay before you, which is from beginning to end entirely new, and was made by myself, I might almost venture to say *single-handed*, as all the natives who filled in the detail were instructed by myself.
>
> It comprises 13,250 square miles, about 5 degrees of latitude of a territory which was hitherto, comparatively speaking, unknown to

us, being throughout one continued series of mountains, forests, and rivers. The whole of this survey is laid down on a minute and careful trigonometrical survey, depending on a base line of 31,003 feet, measured by myself nearly centrally between a base line connecting with the Grand Trigonometrical Survey, south of Goa, measured by Captain Garling, under Colonel Lambton, and another north of Poona, by Lieut. Shortrede under Major Everest. . . . The coincidences of the computations deduced from my own base, with those of the Great Trigonometrical Survey are remarkable, varying only from one, two, and in distances of 75,000 or 90,000 feet, to about 12 feet, an agreement which is so far satisfactory, as it will lead your Honble. Court to see that this survey at least is conclusive for all practical purposes.[27]

(Jervis subsequently claimed—falsely—that his Konkan work constituted "the only and the first census" in British India.)[28] Stretching the truth, Jervis called himself the "senior officer in the Department," which he most definitely was not,[29] and he sought a position accordingly. He bolstered his claims in August 1837 with three "favorable testimonials" from prominent members of each of the political, military, and professional elites in London: Lord Brougham, the Whig grandee; Sir Willoughby Gordon, quartermaster general for British forces; and, James Walker, professor at the Institute of Civil Engineering and engineer to both the Houses of Parliament and the Trinity Board. The Court agreed to Jervis's applications and, in September 1837, appointed him "to succeed to the office of Surveyor General of India upon the death or resignation of Major Everest."[30] Two months later, the Court also awarded him 10,000 *sicca* rupees (£958) for his work in the Konkan, a monetary reward which he had long been promised by the Bombay council.[31]

At the same time as the Court appointed Jervis to be the provisional surveyor general, it also approved his spending the rest of his furlough visiting the Ordnance Survey, universities, and astronomical observatories in order to gain "a perfect knowledge of every late improvement in astronomical and other scientific instruments." With such knowledge, Jervis hoped to reform the British surveys in India. Until the Court finally refused in July 1839 to extend his furlough any longer, Jervis persistently sought permission to transform the British surveys in India into a facsimile of Thomas Colby's Irish survey and to introduce other scientific surveys (geological, magnetic, tidal, marine, statistical) to India under the aegis of the metropolitan scientific institutions in London. As Jervis subsequently explained to the Court's secretary, his efforts at reform had come about because he had in early 1836 persuaded a resident of Bombay to offer his services as an astronomer to the Company without salary, as long as the Company equipped an observatory. In February 1837, the Court asked the recently returned Jervis which instruments would be necessary. On referring to the "scientific bodies in this country," Jervis found that not just astronomy but all of the terrestrial science then popular in Europe could be easily and cheaply undertaken in India by the Company's own engineers, once instruments had been provided. These discussions also led to Jervis's appointment to an Admiralty committee on magnetism, which included such famous military scientists as James Ross, Francis Beaufort, and Edward Sabine.[32]

Jervis secured his support from the members of the London elites on the understanding that he had already been appointed surveyor general. His numerous letters and petitions combined to give the impression that Everest had already resigned and that Jervis was already installed in the office.[33] By doing so, Jervis initiated a very public squabble with Everest. I shall deal with this before I turn to the more significant debate, obscured by the spat between Jervis and Everest, between the Court and the Board of Control over the nature of the British mapping of India.

Confident of a favorable reception for his plans—especially because Everest had stated in a private letter to the Court's secretary that he intended to retire in 1839 and that he approved of Jervis's appointment to succeed him[34]—Jervis sent copies of his various papers and resolutions to Everest. Among those papers was a petition to the Court on behalf of Jervis's pretensions, organized by Augustus and signed by a substantial portion of London's scientific elite. Everest, however, became furious, not so much because of Jervis's presumption but because of the manner in which his own work—and that of William Lambton before him—had been ignored by the metropolitan scientists. Everest's bitter and sarcastic response was published in London in 1839, just after Jervis had left once more for India. Everest wrote his pamphlet as a series of letters addressed to Augustus, chief signatory of the petition. Everest was especially aggrieved that his own status as a fellow of both the Royal Society and the Prince of Wales' Masonic lodge had not protected him from abuse at the hands of his president and grand master.[35]

The metropolitan scientists were merely annoyed by Everest's pamphlet. His conflict with Jervis was quite minor in the bigger scheme of scientific politics. The astronomer royal, George Airy, wrote to John Herschel:

> You have probably seen a pamphlet printed by Lt. Col. Everest (sold by Pickering) in the form of a series of letters addressed to

[Augustus], in which [William] Whewell, [Francis] Baily, and I, are slightly abused, and you come in for a double dose (Heaven knows why). I really began to be a little uneasy—not for fear of the said Everest's pamphlet, but because I thought that Major Jervis must have misrepresented his powers and must have thereby led us to do Everest an injustice.[36]

Herschel agreed with Airy's interpretation, even though he had not seen the pamphlet and now had no desire to do so. He revealed that he had signed Augustus's petition on Jervis's behalf because others had already done so, and not to have done so would have been construed as an insult. Moreover, all of the names on the petition had struck Herschel as "a bolstering up of J[ervis]'s weakness." He concluded that "E[verest] I suppose, like everybody else that comes from India, is bilious and out of sorts—which may be a very good reason for abusing us but none why we should reply to his tirade."[37]

For his part, Everest soon got over his anger. He invited Jervis, on his return to India, to join his party on the Great Arc. Everest's brother Robert, an army chaplain, would be present to form a bridge between Jervis's evangelicalism and Everest's own Deistic mysticism. Everest particularly wanted to gossip about their mutual acquaintances in London society.[38] Jervis sought permission from the Bombay council to make the trip, but he interrupted his plans when Everest's pamphlet reached Bombay in February 1840. Jervis immediately took the moral high ground. He wrote to John Washington, secretary of the Royal Geographical Society, that "we have studied the pulpit with a far more enlarged and philosophic mind than our friend Everest"; he described Everest's pamphlet as "a vicious, venomous piece of writing that can only be dealt with in a court of civil law"; a military court had apparently already rejected the possibility of hearing a libel suit! In the end, the two surveyors never met.[39]

At about the same time as Everest's pamphlet was published in Britain, Jervis's own flaws as a surveyor caught up with him. In April 1838, the Court wrote (rather prematurely) to Bengal that it had received the materials for the Konkan survey and had prepared them for the *Atlas*. But Jervis's elegant maps were not of the level of accuracy he had claimed in 1837 and John Walker could not reconcile their internal discrepancies. Jervis was informed of this problem in November 1838.[40] The following October, the Court passed the problem back to Everest in India, claiming "unforeseen difficulties";[41] it also wrote a sarcastic letter to the Board of Control concerning Jervis's earlier claims for his work.[42] Everest was equally unable to make the maps fit adjoining surveys properly and passed the problem onto Jervis, now back in Bombay. The final blow for Jervis came when Everest discovered that he would have to stay in India until the end of 1843 in order to be eligible for a colonel's pension. Disheartened, Jervis resigned from the Company's service "for health reasons" as of 30 December 1841. The Konkan survey materials caused yet more trouble until being finally corrected upon a new triangulation in 1851 and incorporated into sheets 39–41 of the *Atlas of India*.[43]

Jervis's Plan for a Scientific Survey of India

While he was still riding high in London society, Thomas Jervis had expressed his ideas for restructuring the Indian surveys in a variety of documents and forums. He addressed the Royal Geographical and Astronomical societies in 1837, giving a brief overview of the past surveys and in particular of the differences between the older form of route survey and the more modern trigonometrical surveys. When talking to the geographers, he paid particular attention to the exploration of regions of central Asia and Tibet, which were still largely unknown to the British and which were conceivably of interest to the East India Company.[44] Jervis followed those papers with a lengthy presentation to the 1838 meeting in Newcastle of the British Association for the Advancement of Science. In this, he extended the topic to encompass the other scientific activities which might be pursued in India. Jervis, however, was dissatisfied with the newspaper reports of the association's meeting and so published the paper to publicize his intentions more coherently.[45] He also submitted several lengthy letters and memoranda to the Court, in which he outlined his plans in some detail. Most of his attention in these was given to questions of information and expense.[46]

Finally, Jervis engaged in numerous discussions with the more genteel metropolitan scientists, discussions which led to the petition to the Company jointly submitted by the Royal Society, the Royal Geographical Society, and the Geological Society. Its signatories read like a who's who of metropolitan Humboldtian scientists (table 8.1). Although Augustus was the principal signatory and was certainly intimately involved with the petition, it was actually drafted by Jervis, John Washington, secretary of the Royal Geographical Society, and G. B. Greenough, vice-president of both the RGS and the Geological Society of London. Also, while officially dated 14 July 1838, Augustus sent a copy to Sir John Cam Hobhouse at the Board of Control on 20 July, and Jervis did not formally submit it to the Court until 15 August.[47]

The petition neatly summarizes Jervis's ideas for the prosection of science in India. In addition to the topographical and geological mapping in which they were already engaged, Jervis argued that British

Table 8.1 Signatories to Prince Augustus's Petition to the Court of Directors, 1835

GS	Geological Society of London
RAS	Royal Astronomical Society
RGS	Royal Geographical Society
RS	Royal Society
RSE	Royal Society of Edinburgh

*	Airy, George Biddell	astronomer royal
*	Augustus P[rince]	RS, president
*	Baily, Francis	RS, treasurer and vice-president
*	Beaufort, Francis	hydrographer
	Brewster, David	RSE, vice-president
	Brisbane, Thomas	RSE
	Buckland, William	GS, vice-president
*	Chevsney, F. R.	RS
*	Children, John George	RS, vice-president
*	Christie, S. Hunter	RS, secretary
	Clark, Joseph	RS
	Daubeny, Charles	RS; GS
	de la Beche, M. T.	
*	Faraday, Michael	
*	Greenough, G. B.	GS, vice-president; RGS, vice-president
*	Hamilton, William Rowan	RGS, president
*	Herschel, J. F. W.	
*	Ibbetson, L. F. Boscowen	GS
*	Ivory, James	RS
	Johnson, Ed. J.	RS
	Lloyd, Humphrey	
*	Lubbock, John William	RS
*	Lyell, Charles	GS, vice-president; RS
*	Murchison, Roderick Impey	GS, vice-president; RS
*	Parish, Woodbine	RGS, vice-president
*	Peacock, George	RS
	Philips, John	RS; professor of geology, Kings College London
	Robinson, T. R.	RS; RAS
	Sabine, Edward	
*	Sheepshanks, R.	RS; RAS
	Sidgwick, A.	GS, vice-president
*	Smyth, William H.	RS, foreign secretary
	Stevelly, John [?]	
	Sykes, William H.	RS; Historical Society of London, vice-president
*	Talbot, H. Fox	RS
*	Walker, James	professor, Institute of Civil Engineers
*	Wheatstone, C.	RS
	Whewell, William	GS, president

Note: The signatories are in alphabetical order. Their institutional affiliations and positions of each signatory are as specified on the petition. Names marked with an asterisk appear on the copy of the petition in IOR L/MIL/5/413, fols. 94–97.

surveyors should also undertake observations for tides and for magnetic intensity and variation.[48] Jervis included the very similar ideas proposed by William Lambton in a report of 1822: to combine the Great Trigonometrical Survey's geodetic results with those of the European surveys would require the exact comparison of the Indian standard of length with its European counterparts; to undertake pendulum observations to gauge relative gravity at points along the Great Arc and at the coasts; and to systematically investigate the atmospheric refraction of light rays for correcting survey observations. As these numerous activities would be undertaken by the officers of the surveyor general's department, the only expenditure by the Company would be for instruments, which Jervis estimated as totaling less than £1,684: four pendula; apparatus for three fixed and six traveling magnetic observatories; two "universal instruments" for measuring atmospheric refraction; and, an equatorial for the Bombay astronomical observatory. Expert supervision and aid would be provided by the members of the Royal Society as part of their professional duties. In return, it was expected that the Court would ensure the timely publication of the data gathered.[49]

The opinions expressed by Jervis on the mapping surveys *per se* were not as coherent as those for geophysics. They were, however, all based on his fundamental assumption that those surveys did actually constitute a logical, if somewhat amorphous, whole. Jervis frequently referred to a "Survey of India" which James Rennell, Lambton, Colin Mackenzie, George Everest, and (soon) himself had all directed. Contradicting this assumption, Jervis also railed against both the existence of separate survey departments in each of the three presidencies and the split between the surveyor general's office and the Great Trigonometrical Survey. Like his contemporaries, Jervis routinely conflated the final cartographic images of India with a single empiricist process of mapmaking to create an ideal of a single institutional survey. That single survey flickered in and out of existence as Jervis referred to how the system ought to be versus how the system really was. Jervis clearly believed that Everest's dual appointment represented a more substantial merger of the two principal offices than just the personal combination that it actually was. Jervis saw his own appointment as (provisional) surveyor general of India as encompassing the superintendency of the trigonometrical survey, thereby forming a single Survey of India.

A single survey organization could be realized, Jervis argued, by adopting the *system* Thomas Colby had adopted for the Ordnance Survey of Ireland. Indeed, Jervis admitted that all of his letters and memoranda had been edited by Colby before being submitted to the Court.[50] The essence of that system was its division of cartographic labor. Colby himself described it as a "machine."[51] By setting laborers to repetitive tasks and freeing officers from "drudgery" so as to be able to concentrate on truly "scientific" issues, Jervis argued that the system "reduced" the survey's detailed operations "to the limit of minds of very inferior capacity, by dint of patient instruction and exclusive application to one particular object."[52] The Greenwich and Paris observatories had each organized their computing staff in a similar manner. The system

> anticipates and overrules all the obstacles which human ingenuity may oppose to its progress, absolutely pressing conflicting interests into the service of the public, while it makes it the immediate object of every person engaged, to be honest and diligent, by not exacting or even entrusting the execution of any survey in all its details, to the power, caprice, or capability of any one individual.[53]

It was the cartographic equivalent of the creation and preservation of behavioral norms in a surveillant society, and it should be considered as prefiguring Taylorist "scientific management" and Fordist production. Such a system would, Jervis asserted, be perfect for India, as in his opinion it would obviate the effects of traditional Indian habits such as fraud, dishonesty, collusion, and laziness.

> Such a body [of trained surveyors] would in a singular manner conduce to the easy and unexceptionable introduction of useful science, and industrious habits where they are most wanted: amongst the Natives of India.[54]

The survey would become a major force in removing the iniquities of caste and other social inequalities (excluding, of course, British rule). The use of many laborers to conduct a survey was not a new idea: Jervis cited Thomas Munro's survey of the Ceded Districts at the start of the century and quoted the description of David Scott's similar use of indigenous labor in Assam.[55]

Furthermore, the Irish survey, conducted at a scale of six inches to the mile, was designed for taxation purposes and Jervis saw similar potential for such a survey in India. James Salmond agreed and surmised that if it was advantageous to Ireland where the British government had "only a contingent interest" in improving the country—which is to say that any improvement was the duty of the landlords—then such a survey would be even more useful in India where the British governments were the "immediate proprietors of the soil."[56] The Irish surveyors also produced statistical and historical memoirs of each parish,[57] and Jervis argued that similar memoirs, like Jervis's own of the southern Konkan, would be of immense utility to the Indian government.

Jervis argued that Colby's system would dramatically accelerate the Indian surveys and so substantially reduce their cost. Expensive officers would be employed more efficiently and effectively; the rigorous system of checks would ensure accurate work by the cheap labor. Jervis cited Salmond's estimate that the average annual cost of the geographical surveys had been £10,000 over the seventy-five years since Rennell had started to map Bengal; by 1840, their annual cost was running at about £20,000 per annum. The Great Trigonometrical Survey had cost £110,000 between 1800 and 1824, and another £140,000 in the twelve years since. The total cost of all of the land surveys since 1765, including revenue surveys, was thus estimated at no less than £1,400,000. After the forty years of proper surveying since Lambton and Mackenzie began their surveys—Jervis again lumped the various trigonometrical surveys with the topographical surveys as a single, supposedly systematic whole—materials for the *Atlas* were barely one-third completed, and Jervis envisioned another eighty years to complete the remaining two-thirds, at a commensurate cost. In contrast, the Irish survey cost a mere 2½d per acre, plus 1d per acre for printing; commercial surveyors generally charged one shilling per acre.

The survey of Bombay and Salsette islands (276 square miles; 700 km²), which had taken "many years at great expense and cost of life," Jervis argued, would have been done in a scant twenty-one days by Colby's entire survey establishment, or in fourteen months by one division of seventy-five surveyors, at a total cost of about £3,000. (It is perhaps no coincidence that the Irish survey's labor force was at its largest—about 2,100 officers, sappers, and civilians—between 1835 and 1840.) The whole of India could be surveyed not in the eighty years of high expense that Jervis anticipated but in a mere seven or eight years at a low cost. Jervis was uncertain about this last figure, however, and he later stated that it would take seven to eight years to train a sufficient number of personnel; the survey itself would take longer.[58]

Jervis also wanted to publish the survey maps at a scale much larger than the quarter-inch scale of the *Atlas of India*. He rehearsed the standard arguments that manuscript maps were inefficiently used, that they were subject to damage and loss, and that without publication "no survey can be considered complete, nor indeed have the least pretensions to authenticity."[59] Keeping maps in manuscript to ensure the secrecy of their information was foolhardy and maps should not be restricted in their distribution: if an enemy is sufficiently determined, he argued, it will get hold of "secret" information. As an example, Jervis quoted Lord William Bentinck's recent surprise at finding in the French Depôt de la Guerre a map of India showing current British troop dispositions.[60]

Nor did Jervis like that the *Atlas* was compiled and engraved in London, whereas every European survey compiled, engraved, and published their own maps themselves. The "third party" cartographer in London cannot refer back to the surveyors or to "the ground itself" in order to determine the existence of errors in a survey and, being "utterly unacquainted with the localities and character of the country, cannot possibly compile so faithful a representation of it as the officer who directs the operations."[61] Moreover, production of the *Atlas* was too slow: only 32 of 177 sheets had been completed to date, whereas the Irish survey averaged five to seven sheets per week (but at the very large scale of 1:10,560). Note Jervis's conscious omission of differences in scale and detail level between the two map series, so as to bolster his argument. Jervis wanted all of the survey sheets to be published in India, no matter their scale.

There were, accordingly, three specific proposals Jervis wanted to have implemented. Of paramount importance for Jervis was that Colby had the "entire and complete confidence of Government" and was able to fire and hire staff and to set salaries at will. Jervis quoted the comment by Arthur Wellesley, then master general of Ordnance, which had sealed Colby's authority: "I know Colby; let him have his own way."[62] No complete and systematic survey of India could be accomplished successfully unless the surveyor general had similar powers. Second, Jervis wanted to extend the surveyor general's authority to encompass *all* of the surveys in India, whether geographical, statistical, or marine. He wanted to create the single Survey of India to which he so often referred. Third, there was the issue of manpower: Colby agreed to train about a hundred men and civil assistants, plus officers, for twelve to eighteen months, in the Ordnance Survey way of surveying. In India, these people would then be used to train other staff.[63]

Policy Disagreements between
the Court and the Board

In all of his proposals to the Court of Directors, Thomas Jervis was firmly backed by Sir John Cam Hobhouse and the secretariat of the Board of Control. Hobhouse continued to work with Jervis to promote his ideal of a scientific survey of India in the face of the Court's adamant refusal to accept most of the proposals. The resultant debate between the Court and the Board reveals three common factors behind the Court's reluctance to implement Jervis's proposals: cost, dislike of founding new agencies, and patronage.

The issue of cost is apparent in the Court's negative reaction to Jervis's specific proposal of February 1838 to send exploratory teams into

Central Asia. Considering the state of its finances, the directors were reluctant to engage in any vaguely defined geographical expeditions other than to areas much closer to India. One of the board's secretaries thought that the request might be approved were it resubmitted with a more restricted and specific scope, but no new submission was made. In 1843, Jervis made a similar proposal to the prime minister, with an equal lack of success.[64] It would not be until the 1860s and the rise of imperial tensions with Russia that the British acquired an active interest in mapping central Asia and extended their triangulation into the political gulf between India and Russia.

Cost and the creation of new positions feature in the Court's response to the idea of establishing magnetic observatories in India. In March 1837, when Jervis had been back in England for only a few months, William Denison, RE, wrote to the Royal Society, citing royal approval of a recent proposal "that the Officers of Engineers generally should be employed, under the direction of the Royal Society, in any way by which the interests of science may be forwarded." Posted to permanent stations scattered around the world, Royal Engineer officers were the perfect vehicle for collecting "numerous facts bearing on the natural history, geography, and statistics of the various countries where [they] are located," and to do so continuously. But, as ever, there was the question of funding. For now, Denison just wanted to implement the proposals that Alexander Humboldt had made to the Royal Society with regards to a worldwide chain of magnetic observatories. In particular, Denison wanted the society to provide a complete set of magnetic instruments for the engineer's school at Chatham in order to instruct cadets in their use. Indeed, he went so far as to promise to pay for the instruments himself if the Board of Ordnance refused to fund them. The Royal Society accordingly reappointed the special committee of June 1836 for examining Humboldt's suggestions. This committee's responsibilities were absorbed by the regular Committee on Meteorology, established in July 1838, and to which Jervis was appointed the following December.[65]

In April 1838, the Admiralty's magnetism committee, on which Jervis sat, submitted to the Royal Society a report which specifically credited Jervis with the idea of establishing two, if not three, fixed magnetic and meteorological observatories in India. Augustus forwarded a copy of the report to the Court and assured the directors that both the Crown and the master general of Ordnance would permit Edward Sabine (perhaps at Jervis's suggestion) to supervise the observations in conjunction with the surveyor general.[66] The directors rejected the offer in August because they were "not at present aware that any addition to the Sur-

veyor General's establishment will be requisite for the object in view."
The Board of Control—namely, Hobhouse—argued in opposition that
Sabine's appointment would be necessary to ensure uniformity in the
observations.[67]

The Court's secretary replied in turn that the Company's policy had
always been to add responsibilities to existing departments rather than
to create new establishments with their extra salaries and overhead. In
this case, the surveyor general's office had plenty of educated officers
quite able to make the required observations, especially as James Bedford, deputy surveyor general in Calcutta, had reported in 1834 that
he was quite willing and able to undertake them. Sabine's presence in
India, it was therefore felt, "could only lead to a clashing of authority
without any countervailing advantage." In reply, the board repeated its
belief that the Court was mistaken. But the Court was adamant and, to
prove that their existing servants could make the necessary observations, pointed to a recent article that described the magnetic observations by the Company's astronomer at Madras. Sabine's services were
not accepted.[68]

But this did not mean that Jervis's plans for magnetic observatories
were dead. At the same time that the Court adamantly refused to accept
an extra officer, Jervis submitted the joint petition of the scientific societies to the Court. This was followed in December 1838 by the Royal
Society's committee report on magnetism, which was forwarded to the
Court in April 1839. That report, however, followed Denison's lead and
suggested that engineer officers already on station could handle the
observations.[69] This time, the Court agreed as the plan would not cost
much to implement and it suggested that a magnetic unit be added
to the Madras Observatory with dedicated magnetic observatories at
Bombay and in the Himalayas at Dehra Dun; all were to be under the
direction of the surveyor general. To provide the necessary trained personnel, the Court further directed that engineer officers from each presidency who were then on furlough in Europe should be instructed in the
operation and principles of the relevant instruments. Eventually, Jervis and three other Company engineers were instructed in their use by
Professor Humphrey Lloyd, of Trinity College, Dublin. The Court also
agreed subsequently to expand its meteorological and gravitational
(pendulum) experiments, to move the Dehra Dun station to Simla, and
that at Bombay to Singapore, and to establish a fourth station at Aden.[70]

The rejection of Jervis's plans for the surveys was rather more complex. Jervis was initially successful. Following his letters of December
1837, the Court decided that all future engineer cadets would spend
some time with the Ordnance Survey in Ireland, as would the next

batch of sappers to be sent to India, in much the same way as had been done when Jervis had been a cadet. The Court therefore directed the officer commanding at Chatham, General Charles Pasley, to give the Company's cadets there the same course of instruction as the Royal Engineer cadets received. Pasley agreed, and the Court accepted the extra cost.[71]

Pasley, however, proved to be an opponent of Jervis. As Jervis later wrote to Hobhouse, Pasley and the Court's military secretary Philip Melvill (Salmond's successor) were linked by family ties and they colluded to redirect more of the Company's engineer cadets to Chatham, away from the Company's own military seminary at Addiscombe. Sir Ephraim Stannus, the commandant at Addiscombe, in trying to prevent this, found his opinion "deferred to party considerations." It is not therefore too surprising to find, when Jervis complained to Hobhouse that educating cadets at Chatham was far more expensive than at Addiscombe, that Stannus was one of Jervis's supporters and that Pasley and Melvill were his detractors.[72] Pasley's views were not so much at odds with Jervis's as they were parallel to them. While agreeing with the idea of attaching cadets to the Ordnance Survey, he felt it unnecessary to send sappers and miners as well. He also stole some of Jervis's thunder by asserting that Thomas Colby had never himself educated any of the Ordnance Survey's staff, that task having always fallen to Chatham.[73] Jervis accused Melvill of being "willful" and of being "profoundly ignorant and unconcerned" about military affairs. However, Jervis could cite only one specific instance of Melvill's opposition, when he refused to let Jervis copy a letter from Everest—a letter which Jervis thought would bolster his position—on the grounds that it was a private communication.[74]

Jervis's third principal opponent was John Walker. From their respective comments, their dislike was clearly mutual. Jervis, for example, said Walker was "utterly unable" to manage the engraving of the surveys and he could not understand how the Court could accept Walker's opinion over his own. Walker had as little regard for Jervis's work on the Konkan survey.[75]

The debate was not limited to letters and memoranda. Finding it difficult to deal with all of the directors—"24 men compounded of such perverse and various materials"—Jervis concentrated on the five who were "more accessible to reason" and who were also the most influential: Sir James Rivett Carnac (chairman, 1836–38); John Loch (1829–30, 1833–34); Sir James Lushington (1838–39, 1842–43, 1848–49); Richard Jenkins (1839–40); and, William B. Bayley (1840–41). These five he took in June 1838 to the Ordnance Map Office at the Tower, where Colby,

Francis Beaufort, the Admiralty's hydrographer, and other officers displayed the products of the French, Austrian, Saxon, Russian, and British surveys, comparing them with the maps from India. Jervis informed Hobhouse that he had "succeeded beyond [his] expectations"; Loch in particular had confessed to having had no prior idea of the "wonderfully simple machinery of these great national undertakings." Jervis was therefore directed to address the Court again.[76]

But Jervis had not had as great an effect as he might have thought. On 25 July, after receiving Pasley's comments on Jervis's plans, the Court made its decision. It resolved to ask the master general of Ordnance to allow the Company's engineer cadets to attend the Ordnance Survey in either Scotland or Ireland for three months after leaving Chatham. Furthermore, Pasley was to identify on the Company's behalf those sappers and miners who had completed their training and who were suited for survey duties in India. Finally, the Court recorded its approbation of Jervis's efforts on behalf of the Survey of India. The resolution addressed only one of Jervis's major proposals, and then only partially. Jervis would not be given sole direction of all of the surveys in India; nor would he receive absolute authority over the hiring and firing of personnel; finally, no sappers, let alone any civil assistants, would attend the Ordnance Survey, and the officers would be attached for only three rather than the twelve to eighteen months requested.[77]

Jervis reacted by submitting a further batch of documents to the Court. He was particularly intent on refuting Pasley. He cited George Airy and John Herschel as corroborating his own plans; he cited the (forthcoming) petition from the three scientific societies as evidence for the need for total confidence to be invested in him as surveyor general, and to this end he annexed statements by Colby and Beaufort. His tone reveals a growing panic. He concluded with a memorandum, listing the precise proposals he wished to have implemented, being more of the same: eight officers, seventy sappers, and thirty civilians should be placed under Colby and Jervis for eighteen months to learn topographic surveying and engraving, and Jervis should have complete control of all Indian surveys. Jervis passed a copy of this last document to Hobhouse. He also requested that Hobhouse persuade the Court to award him a "public expression" of its confidence by appointing him "Geographer to the Company," as Rennell had been. Doing so, Jervis thought, "might prevent the secretaries at the India House riding rough shod over the Surveyor General's path." In his postscript he stated his growing frustration.[78]

The debate came to a head in late August 1838. On the 15th, both Jervis and Walker wrote to the Court, Jervis to lay before the Court the petition from the three metropolitan scientific societies and Walker to offer his comments on Jervis's ideas for creating an engraving shop in India (necessary if maps were to published there). Walker was intensely critical of having maps engraved in India. The expense of keeping an establishment of European civilians—the engravers—under pay in India even when there was no work to do would be far too high. In England Walker could hire and fire trained engravers as business dictated. Walker estimated the cost of engraving in India, including shipping the raw plates, would be twice that of engraving in London. Furthermore, the capital investment needed for such an establishment would be equivalent to the cost of producing the remaining sheets of the *Atlas* in London.

Walker's second point was that by insisting that all surveys be sent home to be engraved, the Court could keep track of the progress of the surveys and could therefore exercise control over them. Were the surveys to be engraved in India, then the surveyor general might do as he pleased. And as for Jervis's contention that only people who had surveyed in India were in a position to compile maps of the subcontinent, Walker pointed to the discrepancies he had found in Jervis's own work in the Konkan as indicating that even surveyors are mistaken; what good, then, to blame the compiler? Finally, Walker pointed out that even Colby did not interfere with the surveys made by the quartermaster general in Britain or with the Admiralty's marine surveys, so that Jervis's intention of pulling all surveys in India under one authority had no precedent. Besides, Walker asserted, Colby had direct and easy access to "persons of the first talent" but Walker was convinced that Jervis would not find such an easily available resource in India.[79]

The following day, 16 August, the board replied to the Court's July resolution and requested that the directors accede to Jervis's ideas. It described Colby's system in glowing terms:

> The Board and Court can entertain but one opinion of its expediency as a great moral engine to arrest the progress of that collusion and fraud which have hitherto detracted from the value, and vitiated the results of every revenue survey which has been attempted. The looseness of former systems has hitherto held out a premium upon venality and litigation, as well as shown contempt of our ability to control these evils.

The board also asserted that Jervis's last memorandum had refuted all of Pasley's objections. There should therefore be nothing to stop both engineer cadets and sappers from attending the Ordnance Survey for eighteen months.[80]

In return, the Court was livid that one of its prerogatives had been infringed: how, it asked, did the board see Jervis's latest proposals when the Court had not yet passed them on? It insisted that letters from officers on furlough should go only to the Court. The Court proceeded to remind the board that George Everest was still surveyor general, that he had already examined the Irish survey in the 1820s, and that he was fully competent to suggest innovations for the Indian surveys based on the Ordnance Survey. It restated its opinion that engineer cadets should indeed gain experience by spending three months with the Ordnance Survey before leaving for India, as this would increase the number of officers available to make surveys in India.[81] Similarly, the directors had approved the extension of the curriculum for the sappers and miners to include surveying, so as to provide the surveyor general in India with yet more personnel options. Nor was the Court convinced that a large force of Europeans could undertake the mapping of India. Everest had written that few Europeans could stand the climate and that the only "class of people" adequate to the task were the Eurasians. The Court cited both Walker's and Everest's earlier rejection of having maps engraved in India. To refute the board's low opinion of the revenue surveys, it cited Lord William Bentinck's conversion from disdainful opponent to enthusiastic supporter. And so on. The Court did not, therefore, see fit to change their resolution of July. Finally, the Court adamantly refused to accept Sabine's services for the magnetic observatories.[82]

Jervis tried his luck again in September—even though he admitted that he was "quite dispirited and worn-out with this long protracted and never-ending discussion with the Directors and Pasley and Walker"[83]— and requested that his furlough be extended beyond the following March (1839), when he was due to return to India. The Court refused. He tried again a month later, specifically stating that he wanted yet more time to visit observatories in Europe. The Court denied him again.[84] Thereafter, Jervis spent two days with Carnac, reading to him from the Parliamentary Report that had initially led to the foundation of the Irish survey and received his promise to press Jervis's case once more in October. But nothing apparently came of this.

In November, Jervis requested that Hobhouse intercede for him personally. Until now, communication between the board and Court had been through the secretaries. Jervis was sure that with Hobhouse's own position made clear, the Court would be induced to abandon its position; he thought the whole issue could be cleared up within seven to ten days.[85] It was at about this time that Colby recorded in his diary that Jervis was "violently opposed by all the East India underlings."[86] Hobhouse acquiesced to Jervis's pleas and sent the Court a compromise: instead of eight officers, seventy sappers, and thirty civilians, Hobhouse suggested that six officers, only thirty sappers, and the thirty civilians be attached to the Ordnance Survey, and then only for twelve rather than eighteen months.[87]

The Court, however, remained unswayed; there had been no change in circumstances to admit the acceptance of Jervis's plans. Quite the reverse, in fact: many engineers had been pulled away from their regular stations to join the Army of the Indus in preparation for the assault on Afghanistan, so that the Court felt it essential to replace them with new blood. The Court also repeated its dislike of using civilian surveyors when Eurasians in India would be far more efficacious. Finally, the directors expressed their desire that the best way in which Jervis might serve the Company was to return to India, and that if his private affairs would not allow him to do so, then it would "be encumbent on them to make a different arrangement." That is, Jervis would lose his provisional appointment as surveyor general; the directors' patience had clearly worn thin.[88]

In April 1839, the Court requested to know when Jervis would be free to return to India (in the meantime, Jervis had succeeded in having his leave extended by six months so as to take care of some undefined legal affairs).[89] The Court's draft letter intimated that Jervis might lose his position, but the board deleted the threat.[90] At the same time, Jervis saw the possibility of pressing his claims upon the new chairman (Richard Jenkins) and wrote again to Hobhouse. Jervis cited the board's secretary to the effect that once the Court had accepted the necessity for a "complete territorial survey," then "the necessary machinery must follow in course." He quoted at length a recent, anonymous article in the *Quarterly Review* that had favorably mentioned his own published proposals.[91] But Hobhouse replied to Jervis in a dour tone: "My own opinion is that you had better drop a controversy which experience has shown to be unprofitable. The Court have made up their minds and I have no power to interfere in this matter."[92]

As much as the directors agreed with Jervis's good intentions, and despite the influential support that Jervis was able to marshal, the Court and its secretariat were ultimately unable to approve any of his plans for the surveying of India. The administrative power and scope that Jervis requested was far more than the Court was willing to award to any of its officials in India. The Court took its powers of patronage very seriously indeed and did not want its prerogatives usurped. And, ultimately, there was the question of increased cost and the expansion of the administration in India, two phenomena at which the Court habitually balked.

The directors might perhaps have acquiesced to Jervis, to Hobhouse and the Board, and to the metropolitan scientists, had it not been for their necessary dependence on the established hierarchy of cartographic experts: Everest in India and Walker in London. Everest did little to confound Jervis directly, but he had drawn different conclusions from the Irish Survey and his conclusions demanded more attention because he was currently surveyor general and superintendent of the Great Trigonometrical Survey. Walker made no secret of his displeasure with Jervis and actively opposed him. The result was that the Company's mapping efforts were not dragged into line with the standards set in Europe. The directors were happy to accept the idea of a unified "survey of India"—unified by the Great Trigonometrical Survey, that is—without the accompanying creation of a single institution.

Ideal and Compromise

In the twenty years from William Lambton's death to George Everest's retirement and return to England, the different levels of authority within the East India Company had all acceded to the idea of a single triangulation of all of India. But the emphasis in the rhetoric had also changed. The systematic surveys were no longer as important for the determination of the size and shape of the earth as they had been in the 1800s and 1810s. Triangulation *per se* was losing its cultural attraction; magnetism and the tides had captured the scientific imagination, even as geodesy was relegated from the realm of high intellect to pragmatic fieldwork.[93] Instead, the directors and their secretaries in London, and the councillors and their secretaries in India, all accepted the need for a uniform trigonometrical base to ensure uniformity and consistency in the cartographic image of India, so as to ensure a single picture of the Company's empire. Ultimately, the Great Trigonometrical Survey framed the subcontinent with a network of chains forming great trapezoids which came together at Sironj. Everest did not promote the form the Great Trigonometrical Survey was to take, but he and Lord William Bentinck were instrumental in defining the basic conditions for the survey's eventual expansion.

There remained however a gulf between, on the one hand, the technological fix of cartography's epistemological ideal embodied in a systematic triangulation and, on the other, the actual needs of the various administrations for cartographic information. Bentinck was convinced that a "most correct [cartographic] delineation for all purposes, general and particular, civil and military" could be achieved.[94] At a conceptual level, this statement indicates the empiricism with which mapmaking was already imbued in the early nineteenth century, that the map simply shows the structure of the world, no more and no less, regardless of the purposes of survey from which it was derived. At a more pragmatic level, it indicates the exemplary influence of the Ordnance Survey of Ireland, in which one very large-scale survey could be used for detailed cadastral purposes and, after scale reduction, for military topographical purposes. (As ever, it is beside the point whether the Irish survey actually lived up to its ideal promise.)

But to undertake such a survey required a *permanent* survey organization, with multiple layers in its administrative hierarchy, and with a clear and precise division of labor, all of which required its superintendent to possess uncontested authority over all aspects of operations, from the provision of labor and instruments to the publication of the final maps. The directors seemed to have objected to almost all aspects of such a comprehensive survey. Any portion of the project would simply cost too much, from the engravers and their equipment to the training of the huge establishment which would be necessary. Thomas Jervis found a lingering concern for the sensitivity of geographic information at scales larger than the quarter-inch scale of the *Atlas of India*. A single survey would run across the established political boundaries between the three presidencies and would necessitate new bureaucratic procedures. The superintendent would have more power than any staff officer of an equivalent level elsewhere in India and that was simply unacceptable.

The result was therefore a number of compromises. The Great Trigonometrical Survey attained something like an all-India status because, paradoxically, its operations were now focused on Bengal. It acquired a more formal and rigid hierarchy, which necessarily expanded so that the civil assistants became demoted to subassistants. The officers newly employed as assistants on the GTS after 1831 were almost entirely drawn from the Bengal army, reinforcing its actual provincial character. The Bombay triangulation remained almost completely autonomous. The Madras triangulation was completed and would not be resurveyed; why should it have been, when the whole ideology of the trigonometrical surveys proclaimed that they were exact and *definitive*?

That is, even as the Great Trigonometrical Survey was quite fundamentally recast, the continued currency of its past work meant that the survey's scope was ideologically held to cover all of India. The provincial governments expanded the cadastral ryotwari surveys regardless of other surveys of larger geographical scope. They needed the information to assess and settle the land revenues. The topographic surveys continued in the old *ad hoc* manner, district by district, outside the realm of formal policy. The surveyor general's role as the Company's chief cartographic expert and consultant in India did not change in the 1830s. In this respect, the criticism leveled against Everest for concentrating on the GTS to the near exclusion of the topographic surveys, by Henry Prinsep and by modern historians alike, misses the mark. As GTS superintendent, Everest pursued the *image* of a single systematic survey of India. As surveyor general, he acted according to the existing institutional constraints. Bentinck and Everest, and subsequently Jervis, all tried to create a universal survey, but all three failed.

Bentinck, Everest, and Jervis were in effect victims of their own success. The Company's administrators saw nothing wrong with juxtaposing a brand-new, dense, state-of-the-art, rigorous survey—say that of Nagpur (1823–31)—against James Rennell's antiquated and sparse surveys of the Bengal plains. They could tolerate such a situation because they had learned the lesson of the European surveys, and especially the Ordnance Survey, that the root of cartographic accuracy was a good triangulation. But they had not learned the whole lesson, that a systematic process had to be followed. Instead, they relied on the scientistic faith in observation and archival combination which the Enlightenment had engendered; they were certain that within the scope of a given district, each survey was correct and presented the world's structure. The maps of adjoining districts needed to be fitted into the larger, all-India framework, represented by the *Atlas of India*. That was the task of the Great Trigonometrical Survey, to provide an archival structure to which all data could be fitted, by which any inaccuracies could be *cured*, or fixed like a dog, to stop them from propagating. The Great Trigonometrical Survey was thus constituted as the panacea, the cure-all, for British images of Indian space.

PART FOUR

CARTOGRAPHY, SCIENCE, AND THE REPRESENTATION OF EMPIRE

The munificence and liberality of the Honorable East India Company, in promoting works of science, in the extension of useful knowledge, and in the encouragement of the arts, will remain a lasting monument of their fame, and may be read with pleasure and admiration when the records of conquests, victories, and splendid aggrandizement are consigned to utter oblivion.

William Petrie, October 1807

CHAPTER NINE

Scientific Practice: Incorporating the Rationality of Empire

I n the later Enlightenment, mapmaking was deemed to be a science. It was rooted in the empirical observation and measurement of natural phenomena. It reduced the world's complexity to an ordered mathematical abstraction and did so not through some arbitrary classification but in a "rational" manner, according to the world's own structure. The rhetoric surrounding maps and mapmaking stressed cartography's scientific character. James Gardner, for example, argued in April 1823 that he should replace the recently deceased Aaron Arrowsmith as the East India Company's favored commercial cartographer because his work with the Ordnance Survey in England had made him fully conversant with the "scientific principles" of map construction. As the British acquired more and more territories in India, the Company's directors increasingly ordered that all surveys were to be "scientific and satisfactory"; they called any surveyed (that is, measured) data "scientific" information; and they repeatedly sent orders to India that they wanted "scientifically" trained engineers rather than common infantry officers to conduct the surveys.[1]

Of course, some cartographic activities were deemed to be more scientific than others. In applauding the East India Company's support of the sciences, and of "culture" in general, in 1807, William Petrie was explicitly referring to William Lambton's general survey of southern India.[2] The technological fix of trigonometrical surveying removed the flaws from mapmaking's potential for perfection. With triangulation, the archival practices of mapmaking became even more scientific. Thus, Lambton himself distinguished in 1802 between general, scientific surveys and the "more sublime" work of geodesy; both Colin Mackenzie and John Hodgson discerned between "ordinary" surveys and those based on triangulation, which they called "scientific."[3] It therefore makes sense to interpret the mapping of South Asia in the broader context of other scientific and intellectual practices pursued by the British in their empire.

Mapmaking's shift between epistemological certainties—from the archival structuring of observations to structured observation—was enabled by the adoption of a new methodology and its associated technologies. It would be naive, however, to consider new technologies as driving epistemological change. Part Four examines the ideological factors that promoted and allowed the shift. In particular, the privileging of geodetic surveys points to the significance of scientific practice in the British representations not only of their empire, but also of their imperial Self in opposition to the Indian Other. Following a suggestion by Robert Rundstrom,[4] I consider those representations as falling into two categories: either representations in which meaning (signification) is *incorporated* within the acting out of practices and rituals (this chapter), or those in which meaning is *inscribed* in texts, especially maps (chapter 10). That is, the ambiguities and conflicts between cartographic epistemologies, practices, and institutions are resolved in the realm of ideology.

The Character of British Science in Company India

The standard approach to European intellectual activities in the colonies and empires has been structured, with various degrees of sophistication, around themes of utility, exploitation, and dependence. That is, those activities are understood as having been undertaken in support of the material requirements of the European powers and as having depended upon the provision of specialized advice and personnel by each European metropolis. Historians of science have tended to construe the relationship between each metropolis (core) and its colonies (periphery) rather crudely. They have adopted a simplistic distance-decay function: further away from the metropolis, science becomes less theoretical, more applied, and of lower quality. This core-periphery concept has been enshrined in the two general models—by George Basalla and Roy Macleod—of the dissemination of the Western scientific tradition to areas beyond Europe. Although both models were specifically constructed for colonies of white settlement, respectively the United States and Australia, they have been applied to British India. Both models contain an initial phase of imperial exploration, enumeration, and classification that is directed by and on behalf of the metropolitan scientists, a phase which is especially relevant for the British in India. Geography and geographical surveys are clearly important in this regard.[5]

The themes of utility and exploitation are easily borne out with respect to the East India Company's support of science. The basis of the various histories of British science in India was their utility—if not utter necessity—for the governance and economic exploitation of India.[6] The cartographic surveys were clearly part and parcel of the useful sciences. They provided the fundamental information used by provincial and district officials in their daily work. Sir John Miller, the chair of the Indian Survey Committee of 1904–5, reflected that throughout the nineteenth century there "used to be an idea that a map which was not required for some specific purpose must necessarily be a luxury."[7] That maps were fundamental tools of rule in either Britain itself or in the British Raj cannot be denied. The same applies to the Company's botanical, astronomical, and geological establishments.

The botanical gardens at Calcutta were established in 1787 for the specific purpose of cultivating teak trees for shipbuilding and with the more general, fourfold purpose "of conferring economic benefit to the region, increasing [the] resources in food and plant materials, importing from other parts of the world newer types of plants of economic importance and acclimatizing them here, as well as for extending the interesting science of natural history and particularly botany."[8] Other botanical gardens at Bangalore, Madras, and Bombay were all primarily concerned with the introduction of cash crops into India. When the gardens did not prove particularly successful in this respect, they were subjected to varying degrees of retrenchment; the Bangalore gardens were axed in 1810. Finally, in 1837, the directors objected to the members of the medical corps conducting "agricultural or horticultural experiments" or enquiring into "matters connected with natural history" because doing so would not further the "particular question of the practicability of cultivating the tea-plant with a view to its manufacture as an article of commerce."[9]

The Company's support for astronomical observatories, starting with the Madras Observatory in 1789, reflected the position that astronomy was the "parent and nurse of navigation." Michael Topping, John Goldingham, and John Warren all engaged in a lengthy series of observations at Madras to fix the port's position. Their more immediate duty was to correct and to calibrate the delicate marine chronometers and so make the determination of longitude at sea all the more accurate; major disasters had occurred because of inaccurate chronometers giving incorrect longitudes, as when the frigate Apollo and the 45-ship convoy it escorted were wrecked, or when another convoy was almost wrecked in 1802. Only after these basic tasks were fulfilled could the astronomers' interests turn to other practical, but more involved, issues of determining the coefficients of atmospheric refraction—then a key question for improving the accuracy and precision of astronomical observations—or of correcting the Nautical Almanac. The argument for the utilitarian necessity of astronomy was rehearsed after 1820 by John Curnin, who petitioned for an observatory at Bombay, and by both John Hodgson and Valentine Blacker in their requests for an observatory in Calcutta to be attached to the surveyor general's office.[10]

The Company's official geological investigations were explicitly for economic purposes. Apparently wishing to emulate the geological inquiries attached to the Ordnance Survey in England, Lord Hastings in 1817 appointed geologists to the new Great Trigonometrical Survey and to William Webb's survey of the recently conquered district of Kumaon. Webb ultimately took responsibility for both the geological and topographical aspects of the survey; Frederick Dangerfield and James Herbert made similarly mixed surveys in other areas of the Himalayas throughout the 1820s. The Company's geological work continued in this rather haphazard vein until the appointment in the 1840s of D. H. Williams to survey for coal in Bengal; his work ultimately led to the foundation in 1851 of the Geological Survey of India.[11] The exploitative character of these surveys is shown by the instructions given in 1817 to Alexander Laidlaw, Webb's geologist: he was to "ascertain the existence or otherwise of mineral productions applicable to purposes of public use or available as a source of revenue, and report on the practicability of bringing them to account." Significantly, iron and copper ores were excluded from the scope of Laidlaw's inquiries because the "working of these metals might injuriously affect important articles of British import."[12] India's economy was to be developed for Britain's benefit, not to its detriment.

More generally, Company officials gathered as much information as they could concerning the material state of their territories. The centralized states of Europe had long since recognized the need for information of their provinces upon which to base measures necessary for controlling the populace and augmenting tax revenues. This concept took on a new magnitude with the eighteenth-century development of political economics and fed into the European "era of enthusiasm" for statistics in the second quarter of the nineteenth century. In their attempts to come to grips with their vast and mysterious territories, the British in India preceded the European statistical movement by a couple of decades. Thus, in 1805 Thomas Sydenham reported on the reception in Europe of Alexander Read's materials on the Baramahal district: "the sober political-economists of England were struck dumb at his statistical tables of enormous length and Lord Somerville (the President of the Board of Agriculture and grand encourager of fat sheep) told me that Read was the most tremendous speculator he had ever met with."[13]

Even so, the theme of the dependence of colonial science on metropolitan guidance is not so evident in British India as it might have been in other colonies. There were clear instances when the Company and its officials did follow a metropolitan lead. Chapter 8, for example, demonstrated how members of the Royal Society prompted the Company to sponsor magnetic and tidal research stations; the Company also supported the collection of mineral samples for the benefit of the Royal Institution and of more general information for the Royal Asiatic Society.[14]

It is in this context that we should read the overtly imperialist comments on the intellectual rape of India. Such comments were numerous, from the proclamation by William Roxburgh in 1790,

> "Give me a place to stand on," said the great mathematician [Archimedes], "and I will move the whole earth." Give us time, we may say, for our investigators, and we will transfer to Europe all the sciences, arts, and literature of Asia,

to the Daniells's anticipation in 1810 of the "guiltless spoliations" to be transported from India to Europe (chapter 2), to the exultant thanks in 1829 of two German botanists upon the receipt of thirty barrels of dried plants sent to Europe by Nathaniel Wallich, superintendent of the Calcutta botanical gardens:

> [We] happily received today the costly treasure we owe to your kindness. . . . We are now no simple botanists. We have become as rich as Nabobs and vie with them in treasures. And it is you who made us so rich and glorious. . . . What a new world you have conquered for science and mankind.[15]

The trope of conquest adopted by the natural historians and orientalists is today a dominant theme in the summaries of British science in India and has carried over (but without the core-periphery model) into recent critiques of orientalism and classicism by Edward Said and Martin Bernal. These authors themselves use geography as a metaphor for the scientific and objective attitudes affected by the orientalists and classicists: even as Europeans appropriated the territory of the Orient and of ancient Greece, so too were their culture and history appropriated.[16]

That this is too easy and simple an interpretation for the Company's support of science is indicated by the manner in which the majority of data collected in India were not shipped back to Europe in a raw form. The primary process of classifying and ordering India was undertaken in India, whether that process took the form of map compilation or of fitting botanical specimens into Linnæan categories. And that classification was undertaken for the Company's purposes in India and not for the needs of metropolitan science.

The lack of dependence is evinced in part by the manner in which the trigonometrical surveys were received in London. Before 1818, the only reference to William Lambton's work was William Playfair's 1813 review of Lambton's articles in the *Asiatic Researches*; it was not until Lambton was elected to the Académie des sciences in 1817 that he was elected as a fellow of the Royal Society (1818). Thereafter, Lambton's work was held in high esteem by the metropolitan scientists: Thomas Colby of the Ordnance Survey thought that Lambton's Great Arc was one of the two "best adapted by situation and extent to afford an accurate result" for the earth's size and so used it in his calculations; George Airy thought it "the best [arc] that has ever been surveyed." [17] But the metropolitan scientists did not dictate to the East India Company how the geodetic surveys ought to be prosecuted. When George Everest was in London between 1826 and 1830, he was elected to the Royal Society and he attended the work of the Ordnance Survey in Ireland; even then, no one in Britain told him how to do his work. Ultimately, Everest's anger at Thomas Jervis's plans for a Survey of India and the associated petition by the London scientific societies stemmed from the implication that the science undertaken in India was somehow inherently inferior to that undertaken in London and therefore needed to be supervised by the Royal Society (see chapter 8). In general, the various Company officials who undertook orientalist activities, whether of South Asian culture or environment, were only marginally governed by the wishes of metropolitan science.

Moreover, the scientific work undertaken in India was not necessarily of a lower quality than that in Europe. The perspective that mapmaking and the gathering of data are simply technical handmaidens of creative scientific inquiry developed only in the middle of the nineteenth century. While the cause of this development was apparently the professionalization and increasing disciplinary specialization of the sciences, it also owed much to an increasing globalization of the concerns of natural science. Geologists and geophysicists sought to leave behind the local and particularistic studies of natural history in a drive for global comprehension of physical phenomena. Global studies of the tides, of gravitational and magnetic variation, and rock strata required observations throughout the empires, observations which, of necessity, had to be reduced in a central location, namely, the metropolis. [18] The degree to which the globalization of the natural sciences was engendered, rather than simply enabled, by Europe's imperial and commer-

cial power is still a matter of debate. Certainly, however, that globalization has had a distorting effect on contemporary perceptions of the
character of imperial science before, say, 1840.

David Miller's study of the Royal Society—the archetypal metropolitan scientific society—has the persistent theme that, during the early
nineteenth century, British science was no different in London than in
the provinces or colonies. The British were indeed exploring and enumerating the Indian subcontinent, but like other Europeans they were
still exploring their own natural environment and they were still engaged in ordering and classifying its geology, flora, and fauna. The
scientists in the European empires were not peripheral to metropolitan
society. Or, rather, the core-periphery model should not be construed
so simply as it has been by historians of imperial science.[19]

A further problem with the application of the utilitarian and dependent themes of imperial science to British India is that the Company's
officials supported scientific activities that were neither strictly applied nor directly applicable to an immediate goal. The Madras council
was pleased to sponsor and publish the theoretical work Goldingham
undertook in the Madras observatory (see chapter 5). In London, the
directors routinely set aside money, to the tune of £2,000 per year between 1841 and 1843, to subsidize publications on all aspects of culture, society, history, and environment of the subcontinent. Indeed, the
Court was in this respect such an easy touch that the cartographic firm
of J. and A. Walker (no connection to John Walker of the *Atlas of India*)
requested the Court's patronage of a map of the United States and Canada, although the directors refused because the map was obviously ir-
relevant to their interests.[20]

The Company's support of geodesy and the trigonometrical surveys
is the most obvious case in point. Those surveys do not fit the image of
strictly utilitarian science. The Great Trigonometrical Survey was prosecuted by "scientific servicemen" who, in Britain, were held to epitomize
the pursuit of Baconian science; they worked for a complex mercantile/
territorial, European/Indian hybrid state for which the profit motive
was still the prime mover. But at the fundamental level of the pragmatic
need for information for the administration of India, neither geodesy
nor a general triangulation of India was necessary. As Henry Prinsep
argued in the later 1830s, Rennell's eighteenth-century style of astronomically controlled route surveys would suffice for general purposes.
That recognition lay behind several attempts throughout the early nineteenth century to restrict or even to end the trigonometrical surveys, all
of which failed. Sir George Barlow, whose penny-pinching prompted
the Madras officers to mutiny, seriously threatened Lambton's work

from 1807 through 1809; a year or so later, Barlow nonetheless allowed Lambton to expand his operations northward into the territories of the Nizam of Hyderabad. Again, the directors saw no reason in the later 1830s for the nicety with which Everest was pursuing the Bengal triangulation, yet they too ultimately changed their minds and approved the north-east longitudinal series. Why was the Great Trigonometrical Survey prosecuted with fervor when other scientific and more immediately necessary activities (such as the detailed topographic surveys) were cut back in the name of economy?

The various negotiations within and between the Company's different administrations have been described in the three previous chapters. Those negotiations signified the stresses imposed upon an established bureaucracy by a new technology. New technologies require new practices, new skills and knowledge bases, and they require new staff to be organized along new institutional lines. At this level, the British surveys in India and the gradual acceptance of the Great Trigonometrical Survey constitute an example of the social construction of scientific practices. The form achieved by the surveys was the form allowed by the institutional constraints outlined in Part Two: the Company's finances; its patronage structures and its treatment of individuals with specialized, expert knowledge; steadily rising cartographic literacy; its chronic lack of skilled personnel; internal rivalries within and between the three armies; and the fragmented administrative structure of the three Indian governments and their overseers in London. If nothing else, this study demonstrates the manner in which the technologies wielded by the large, nineteenth-century systematic surveys were defined by their parent institutions.

Such an argument nonetheless assumes that the surveys constituted a neutral technology. Yet at its most fundamental level, cartography is rooted in cultural conceptions of space and in the politics of manipulating spatial representations. In this respect it is no different from any other form of knowledge representation, such as "science," "orientalism," "art," etc. The preceding chapters detail numerous occasions when the senior officers and politicians of the East India Company resorted to a superficially simple argument, although none can match William Petrie's effusive purple prose in the epigraph to this Part. The supporters and advocates of the geodetic triangulations argued that the surveys constituted *science* and should therefore be supported by the Company as a matter of course. A sufficient number of the Company's directors, secretariat, governors, councillors, and other bureaucrats agreed with this fundamental premise. Put simply, it behoved any government to patronize science and so promote progress. That is, the practice of science possessed significance for the British beyond simple utility.

Scientific Practice and British Self-Definition

The attitude that the Company should support science as a matter of course derived from the contemporary assumption that science was an intellectual activity and was accordingly the preserve of the gentility and nobility, of men who had both the leisure and the wherewithal to pursue an unremunerative avocation. Indeed, geodesy, and mathematical cosmography more broadly construed, subtly reinforced the Newtonian worldview of the later Enlightenment elites. One of the corollaries to Newton's theory of gravity, the theory which underpinned the later Enlightenment's faith in lawful and ordered Nature, was that the earth was flattened at the poles. George Airy, later astronomer royal, wrote in 1830 that geodetic measurements continued to be necessary to refine further knowledge of the earth's shape and gravity and so reinforce Newtonian physics. Geodetic surveys were thus fundamental to the reaffirmation of the worldview of the Enlightenment intellectual elite. By reasoning from mechanical principles, the geodesists reduced the world to mathematical equations, to numerical and geometrical abstractions adhering to the Enlightenment's *esprit géometrique*.[21] The act of measuring an arc of meridian was, in and of itself, a statement by members of the elite of their place within a system of universal order and socially constructed space. In this respect, the surveys constitute the Enlightenment's equivalent of cosmological mapping.

A recent discussion of medieval, Christian *mappaemundi* applies equally well to geodetic surveys like the Great Trigonometrical Survey. Those cosmological maps were "emanations of the power of a clerical elite. They [were] . . . representations of a conception of universal order and of a socially constructed worldview, albeit one not requiring the practical terrestrial mapping demanded by an administration, or needed for commerce, or useful in building and maintaining empires."[22] The Enlightenment religion was that of reason and rationality; the clergy comprised the educated intellectuals; as geodesy, the surveys had no direct, practical relevance to the administration of European states or India. The undertaking of a geodetic survey symbolized Educated Man's place within his universe of system and order. (And it was, of course, a universe constructed in masculine terms.) Nor is it coincidence that the practice of geodesy necessitates the combination of terrestrial and celestial phenomena, a combination that is essentially the same as the cosmographical interweaving of secular (earthly) and divine (nonearthly) phenomena. When the Company's directors, administrators, and bureaucrats supported the work of Lambton and Everest, they reaffirmed their superior place in their own society and in their empire.

Science was a class-bound activity. Intellectual circles in London were dominated before 1830 by what Miller has called the Learned Empire: the wealthy gentlemen, the doctors, and the clergymen who practiced a natural history composed of equal parts of philosophy and theology. Educated men examined all sorts of flora, fauna, and geological strata in an effort to understand God's Creation. Their concept of scientific research was closely bound to a social ideology that constructed the gentleman as an amateur; their science constituted another characteristic to distinguish gentlemen from the lesser social orders; their science was a genteel science unfragmented by division into disciplines, a science which merged almost imperceptibly with the study of the classics and with antiquarianism.

Set beside the Learned Empire was a heterogenous collection of individuals who expressed an interest in applied, mathematical, Baconian science. These men were behind the growing subdivision of science into its various disciplines and the associated establishment of specialized societies: the Royal Institution (founded 1799); the Geological Society (1807); and the Royal Astronomical (1820), Zoological (1828), and Geographical (1830) societies. They were spread across the whole spectrum of society, finance, and power. Some were independently wealthy men, but the great majority of such scientists depended on the various forms of patronage controlled by the British government and, to a lesser degree, the East India and other mercantile companies. In particular, they included the "scientific servicemen" of the army and navy who undertook much of the fieldwork of British science.[23]

This principal division of metropolitan scientists was by no means exclusive and rigid. Both groups were dominated by social hierarchies. The generally accepted equation was that science was a genteel avocation; if one pursued science at a sufficiently advanced level, one might be considered to be a gentleman. As discussed in chapter 4, access first to the necessary education and then to opportunities for practicing science was controlled by the prevalent systems of patronage. The debates surrounding the formation of the specialized metropolitan and the many provincial scientific societies, and the debates within the Royal Society after 1815, reflect the increase of wealth in Britain, produced by the agricultural and industrial "revolutions" of the eighteenth century, and the resultant realignment of the British state, including the expansion of its patronage systems. That state nonetheless remained rooted in a class system. The undertaking of any scientific inquiry was as intimately a class position as the aesthetic appreciation of landscape (see chapter 2).[24]

The only significant difference between the intellectual communities in Britain and British India in the early nineteenth century was that of their size. In all other respects, they remained quite similar. Even before the institution of formal systems for their education, the Company's officials had come from mercantile, lesser-gentry, or bourgeois communities, all of which stressed education as a certain route to social and economic advancement. Lord Wellesley founded the College of Fort William in 1800 to educate the youths who were sent out to Bengal as "writers." The curriculum was that of a genteel education modified by the addition of Mughal history, the Indian vernaculars, and the classical languages of Sanskrit, Arabic, and Persian. The college did not pay much attention to science: its single science teacher, James Dinwiddie, returned to England in 1806; nor could Wellesley lure James Rennell back to Calcutta to teach geography.[25] Other candidates for the Company's civil positions passed through the seminary at Haileybury, founded in 1806, which taught the rudiments of mathematics and some science and political economy (instructed by Thomas Malthus) in addition to the traditional curricula. Most of the Company's mathematical talent was drawn from the engineer and artillery officers who passed through the Company's military seminary at Addiscombe, founded in 1809, and, after 1796, the Royal Military Academy at Woolwich and the engineering institution at Chatham. Doctors for the medical corps often came from the medical schools of Scotland and, consequently, reflected the natural history traditions of the Scottish Enlightenment. (However, the largest professional grouping of the British in India, the infantry and cavalry officers, much like their European colleagues, remained remarkably uninterested in intellectual concerns.) The result was a large number of individuals throughout British India who devoted substantial portions of their free time to intellectual inquiry but who were nonetheless far fewer in absolute terms than the equivalent intellectual communities in Britain.

The British were moved to the same broad range of intellectual undertakings in India as they were in Europe. In a manner reflecting the disciplinary concerns of present-day South Asianists, modern historiography has tended to emphasize the linguistic and historical aspects of British "orientalism," especially of the Asiatic Society of Bengal, and has therefore tended to ignore the manner in which the orientalists pursued a broader conception of knowledge, which included natural philosophy and natural history. The twenty volumes of the Asiatic Society's first journal, *Asiatic Researches* (1788–1839), contained 219 articles in the sciences, compared with only 148 in the humanities. The polymath James Prinsep wrote on Indian history, ethnography, geology, chemistry, physics, astronomy, and statistics; Anthony Troyer was secretary to the Calcutta Sanskrit College during his second period in India (1828–35) and published several translations; the second botanist and medical officer on Mackenzie's survey of Mysore, John Leyden, was a noted historian and linguist from the Scottish medical schools and from the Fort William College. The "gentlemanly cult" of knowledge extended to astronomy as well.[26]

The various travelers, officials, and surveyors who applied a geographical gaze to the Indian territories functioned in accordance with the established cultural norms of scientific field practice. They collected, they measured, they observed, and they classified and described. Surveyors and engineers drew the landscapes they mapped and modified. Geologists also studied living phenomena; Henry Voysey expressed an intention to compile a "Fauna Hyderabadiana," listing all of the quadrupeds, birds, reptiles, and insects he found in the Nizam's Dominions. Conversely, Francis Buchanan, the botanist and "greatest of the Anglo-Indian topographers," also left extensive geological collections. The British educated elite in India did not—could not—hold themselves to just one intellectual task each.[27]

The Social and Racial Hierarchy of Scientific Practitioners

For this study, the most significant characteristic of the British intellectual community in India was that it was as hierarchically structured as the British system. A central, "metropolitan" institution was founded in Calcutta in 1784, in the form of the Asiatic Society of Bengal.[28] Although it was dominated by the Calcutta community, the largest British community in India, the society did have members throughout India and was subsequently imitated in a number of provincial literary and scientific societies in Madras and Bombay. The orientalists, with their natural theological and antiquarian interests, represent a small "Learned Empire" transplanted to India. This was offset in the eighteenth century by a number of "mathematical practitioners" (notably James Dinwiddie, Reuben Burrow, Michael Topping, and John Goldingham) who, just like their counterparts in London, taught private pupils and took numerous positions in order to make a decent salary. They thus constituted a lesser social level.[29]

The position of the civilian practitioners declined further with the increase after 1800 of the ranks of the Company's "scientific service-men." This group of mathematically competent officers was always smaller than that of the orientalists; their small numbers meant that by necessity the scientific servicemen had to look back to Europe for professional colleagues; they saw themselves as the intellectual equivalents of the scientific circles in London, from whom they were separated only by the six-month sea voyage.[30] Several became fellows of the Royal Society and other London societies. They knew European publications; William Lambton, for example, had access to the Royal Society's *Philosophical Transactions* in both North America and India. They also published some of their work in Europe, usually at the Company's expense.

With social rank defined by their military rank, and further augmented by the membership of some of their number in European scientific societies, the scientific servicemen formed their own hierarchy, which tied social status to expertise and experience. In describing the type of individual he thought would do well in the astronomical observatories in India, Everest, for example, distinguished between "first-rate mathematicians" and simple technicians as much by their social as by their intellectual pretensions:

> The astronomers must not be fine gentlemen nor need they be first rate mathematicians because the object of such observatories being principally to record facts and observations, a good methodical system, abundance of perseverance and habitual integrity are most likely to advance it; not that I mean to undervalue either literary or scientific or social qualities but when Mr. Goldingham speaks of establishing the place of the Astronomer in Society, I deduce that his arguments are directed against a very different sort of person to what I have in my mind's eye.
>
> To admit the astronomer to the levee of the Governor General on occasions of ceremony is all that could in reason I think be asked, his place in society after this, he must make for himself, but the sort of person whom I should recommend would not be one for whom balls and fetes would hold out much gratification, and we all know that these are the only [social] occasions and that the ladies are the sole sticklers for such questions of precedence.[31]

That is, Everest was more than willing to accept the place in polite society of a good scientist, no matter how low-born (assuming, I suppose, that they behaved themselves properly), but the more tedious jobs required individuals of lesser sensibilities and education.

At the base of the socio-intellectual hierarchy were the semiskilled technicians and laborers. In early nineteenth-century India, the genteel

British made little distinction between the Indian masses and the lower classes of European in India, particularly the soldiers of the Company's "European" and Crown regiments. The agricultural peasantry and burgeoning industrial proletariat in Britain were as foreign to the social and educated elites in Britain as most Indians were to the Company's covenanted servants in India. There is little difference between the complaints of Richard Wilcox that the Assamese were removing his survey markers from either side of the Brahmaputra River "from jealousy, cupidity, or wantonness" and Everest's complaint that he and the astronomer royal, John Pond, were unable to measure a test base with Colby's new compensation bars because every night "the idle people at Greenwich Fair pulled up the . . . marking stones." Nor were Everest's complaints about the poor character of Bengalis with respect to Tamils fundamentally different from his recognition that a staff of Indians would be of greater help in the measurement of the Calcutta baseline than a detachment of European soldiers who might not "be relied on for sobriety during so long a period as three months." And at least one surveyor noted that if Indians were to be used as surveyors, then it would be best not to use any drawn from the elite colleges, as those would certainly have ideas well above the station of the "plodding" surveyor.[32]

British attitudes toward Indian culture in the early nineteenth century had yet to ossify into the institutional racism that prevailed after 1857, yet it is quite clear that British classism and elitism had become grounded in racial differences by the early nineteenth century.[33] Consider the Madras orphanage from which the first assistant surveyors were drawn. Most of the orphans and other state wards were like William Scott, the son of a private from a Crown regiment (HM 52nd Foot) who had left his mistress and illegitimate child behind on returning to England. Benjamin Swain Ward was the exception that proves the rule. He was the son of a lieutenant-colonel who had left no provision for his family after his death. Ward accordingly ended up in the orphanage. He was apprenticed to the revenue survey school, after which he sought an appointment as an infantry officer. In support of his application, he submitted statements by Colin Mackenzie and the acting resident at Mysore, both of which featured the prominent statement: "from the appearance of Mr. Ward there can be no doubt of his being the offspring of European parents." Ward was racially fit to be assumed to be legitimate, to be an officer and a gentleman, to be a scientific serviceman, and not to be a lowly cartographic laborer.[34]

There was a general feeling among the British that Indians did not have the strength of character necessary for surveying. As William Ben-

tinck commented in 1804 on the progress of the district surveys in the
Madras presidency:

> How great would the advantage have been in forming either the
> annual or permanent settlement of our revenue, if the districts had
> been laid down by men of science, precluding the necessity of trust-
> ing to the surveys of natives, equally liable to error from want of
> honesty and from want of knowledge.[35]

When on tour in the Upper Provinces as governor general, Bentinck
damned Indians with faint praise when he noted that "land measuring
is almost universally understood among natives here, but it is indeed
so simple a process that were they ignorant of it, nothing could be
more easily taught them."[36] Similarly, Robert Shortrede recorded that
whereas Marathas were unable to use theodolites, they could nonetheless use chains in much the same manner as their compatriots in the
northern plains used wooden rods—that is, badly—and thereby create
a major source of error. Along with other revenue surveyors, Shortrede
argued that any and all field measurements by Indians had to be corrected to "scientific" surveys based on "European principles."[37]

The British surveys in India accordingly established a hierarchy of
labor and responsibility based on race. Its first official expression was
in 1816, when the Madras government described the ryotwari system
of revenue settlement to the Bengal government.[38] At the top of the
hierarchy were the Company's covenanted officials, who were granted
sole authority for managing any agency within the government. The
middle level of the hierarchy was composed of Eurasians; they could
take on responsibility for mundane operations, but they were denied a
greater role because of their social inadequacy. For example, Mackenzie, who was otherwise a great supporter of the use of Eurasians for
detailed surveying, thought it improper for them to be used on the
Great Trigonometrical Survey. He instead wanted a proper "scale in all
duties, scientific as well as political." Conversely, even though Joseph
Olliver was in charge of the GTS during Everest's absence from 1825
through 1830, Bentinck held that it would be illegal to appoint him to
a covenanted position because he was Eurasian. Thomas Munro, who
was a prominent advocate of "native agency," could not see fit to en-
trust pendulum experiments at the equator to civil assistants.[39]

Nonetheless, for most of the early nineteenth century, the detailed
work of the topographic and the lesser trigonometrical surveys was
delegated to Eurasians. The senior surveyors and administrators wel-
comed their employment because they were cheaper than using mili-

tary officers for the same repetitive and mechanical tasks, they had fewer expectations, they considered India to be their home, they were familiar with the vernaculars from infancy, and they could stand up to the debilitating effects of the climate. Perhaps most important was the British assumption that the Eurasians at least had the potential for improvement through a European-style education.

At the bottom of the hierarchy were the Indians themselves. They were largely employed as laborers, guards, and bearers. It was not until the 1820s that some Indians began to be employed in those positions which had hitherto been the preserve of Eurasians. Their acceptance accelerated with Bentinck's reforms in the 1830s, although Everest's proposals for a permanent "native establishment" were rejected so that the positions of subassistants on the Great Trigonometrical Survey continued to be filled by Eurasians.[40] Everest did, however, begin to employ mathematically educated Indians as computers for the survey, much as Goldingham had employed them in the Madras Observatory (see chapter 5).

This hierarchical division of labor by race, which ultimately became the standard for all of the British scientific and professional institutions in India, ostensibly began as a means to overcome the shortage of British personnel.[41] The British effectively reconstructed their own social division of scientific endeavor—the educated gentleman and philosopher, the skilled craftsman and technician, the unskilled peasant and laborer—with Eurasians and Indians. As an imposition on Indian social systems, it was necessarily simplistic. By privileging their pursuit of science, and of knowledge generally, the British in India consciously declared themselves to constitute a genteel and bourgeois society; that self-definition required the exclusion of lower-class Europeans and especially the common soldiers.[42] At the same time, it required the exclusion of the educated Indian, an exclusion enabled by the general low esteem in which Indian learning, and specifically Indian geographical conceptions, were held.

The institutional dominance of this racial hierarchy of intellectual labor is perhaps best illustrated by the manner in which historians have devoted much attention to the surveys of central Asia by Indian "pandits" in the later nineteenth century. These surveys were remarkable. Denied access for political reasons, the British dispatched numerous Indians into Tibet and China dressed as Buddhist pilgrims. Some of the pandits walked over thousands of miles in the course of their travels, counting their paces with prayer beads; their prayer wheels enclosed compasses. Even so, these surveys constitute a relatively minor episode in the larger scheme of the British mapping of South Asia. The pandits were the last in a long line of Indians employed by the British since the middle of the eighteenth century to survey regions into which British surveyors themselves could not go; the technologies they employed, and the quality of the information they gathered, were also of the eighteenth century.

The pandits' surveys were publicized by one of the most popular descriptions of the British raj: Rudyard Kipling's *Kim* (1901). The intrinsic romance of the surveys also accounts for much of their popularity. The most important reason for the historiographic privileging of the pandits is that throughout the period of British hegemony in India, the pandits were the only Indians ever to be fully accredited by the British as autonomous field surveyors *in their own right*. Their exploits were formally recorded in the Survey of India's annual reports; Kishen Singh received the gold medal of the Royal Geographical Society. Together with the mathematicians who computed the results of the trigonometrical surveys for Everest and Waugh, they have been given a prominent place in the new official survey histories because of the manner in which they promote the presence of Indians in survey activities well before Indians achieved a comparable status in the mapping of India itself. The pandits are thus essential to the self-image of the modern, independent Survey of India.[43]

Converting Indians to European
Conceptions of Space

Underlying the low opinion held by Europeans of the Indians' worth as surveyors were some basic assumptions about the inability of Indians to conceive of space and distance in European terms. The fault lay not with the Indians *per se* but with their education. John Hodgson, for example, took the European standards of length as being perfectly natural and so criticized the Indians for the variable length of their customary units, notably the coss. His assumption was that the use of an indefinite and imprecise measure indicated an indefinite and imprecise conception of space. In this, he conveniently forgot that the standards of length in western Europe were all of recent definition.[44]

Of course, the British had always made maps with substantial amounts of geographical information derived from Indians for those areas to which they themselves could not get access. But the British did not necessarily trust that information. No matter how well it was corroborated and compared within the map's archival framework, information from Indian sources was always discarded as soon as possible. Charles Reynolds, for example, was praised for his exhaustive work in producing his huge 1809 map of India; the map itself was hung in a committee room in East India House. A decade later, John Hodgson compared the map against Lambton's triangulation, at least for the areas common to both, and decided that Indian sources were not as good as actually surveyed material. This, in turn, extended to a statement by James Salmond that "from having been constructed . . . principally on Native information, [Reynolds's map] abounds in errors, which render it unfit for publication, and of little or no utility as a reference." Lord William Bentinck later repeated Salmond's judgment.[45]

Two comments in the early 1830s indicate that at least some British officials remained unconvinced that Indians could understand the concepts of European-style surveying. Charles Metcalfe, when a member of the Calcutta council in 1830, thought that the rulers of Sind and the Punjab would not "comprehend" the proposed survey of the Indus. Between 1821 and 1831, at the insistence of the raja, two Company officers made a survey of Nagpur. When it was completed, there remained the question of what to do with the their instruments; because they had been paid for by the raja, the Court directed in 1832 that they should be returned to him. This decision was made only according to the principles of property. The Court did not think that the instruments would ever be used again because they "can be of no use to a native administration."[46] The British saw themselves as proponents of a system of precise and accurate surveys that had no relevance to either Indian geographical knowledge or the Indian polities.

British attitudes toward Indian conceptions of space were intimately related to questions of religious belief. The British in general reviled the Hindus for their mysticism, which was held to be the fount of the Indians' imprecise and fundamentally erroneous views of the cosmos and the world. Indeed, orientalists have held that the development of geometry in ancient India was related not to land measurement, as it seems to have been in other ancient civilizations, but to the need for designing and laying out alters.[47] The religious views of the Indians were held to encourage despotic political systems. To the general scorn, the British evangelicals added their contempt for Indian depravation and idolatry. European culture, in contrast, was lauded as rational, liberal, precise, and proper.[48] British culture of the period implicitly grouped the liberal state, Christianity, and rational science in a trinity of bourgeois ideology. In his history of astronomy, for example, Adam Smith reasoned that

> The reverence and gratitude, with which some of the appearances of nature inspire [the savage], convince him that they are the proper objects of reverence and gratitude, and therefore proceed from some

> intelligent beings. . . . Hence the origin of Polytheism, and of that
> vulgar superstition which ascribes all the irregular events of nature
> to the favor or displeasure of intelligent, though invisible beings, to
> gods, daemons, witches, genii, fairies.

Smith continued that the establishment of "order and security" through
the rule of "law" will allow the "savage" to indulge his sense of curiosity and inquisitiveness, so that he will be "more desirous to know what
is the chain which links" together nature's "seemingly disjointed phenomena." That single, unifying chain was the singular Judeo-Christian
divinity.[49]

   If a society did not adhere to one aspect of this trinity, it could not
adhere to the others. Indian society was thus by definition despotic,
heathen, and irrational. Conversely, if a society could be made to adhere to one aspect, then it would open itself to the others. Beginning in
the 1820s, British surveyors therefore began to advocate the training of
Indians in surveying and astronomy as one contribution to the British
"civilizing" mission in India. At one level, championed by Everest, the
stereotypical character traits of Eurasians and Indians—their venality,
laziness, unresponsiveness, irresponsibility, and untrustworthiness—
would be overturned if only they were brought up with a European
rather than an Indian education.[50] More fundamentally, the mechanistic
conception of vision required all humans, whether European or Indian,
to see in the same manner. The manifest intellectual difference between
the British and the Indians, or for that matter between social classes,
must therefore have derived from differences in the respective faculties
of reason. It was reason which the British held to guide sight in the
empirical observation of the world, the basic operation in the construction of scientific knowledge. If the Indians could not conceive of the
world in a rational manner, the fault must lie with their misguided
education and religion. Education, and particularly education in geographical phenomena, was thus a central component in the British efforts to correct Indian culture along European lines.

   The conversion of Indians to rational, European thought was thus
an outgrowth of what has been described as the "Enlightenment project." While authors like Max Horkheimer and Theodor Adorno are too
monolithic in their analysis of this project, there can be no doubt that
the most actively pursued goal of Enlightenment intellectuals was the
replacement of myth with reason: "the program of the Enlightenment
was the disenchantment of the world; the dissolution of myths; and the
substitution of knowledge for fancy."[51] Only by freeing the mind from
the fetters of unreasoning belief can an individual or society progress.
The Enlightenment rejection of "myth" did not represent a complete

rejection of faith and religion. The deism and natural theology—plus the continuing religious conservativism—of the eighteenth century led to the evangelical revival of the early 1800s. Thus, the majority of opinions concerning the need for disciplining and reforming mystical Indians might have been expressed by evangelicals, but there were numerous commentators who embody the less ardent Christianity of the 1700s.

George Everest, who was certainly no evangelical, was generally derogatory with respect to the mystical perceptions of Indian villagers. His 1830 account of the Great Arc includes several examples: the "natives of India, whose minds are uninformed and bowed down under the incubus of superstition . . . "; ". . . a circumstance which the wild imaginations of my native followers attributed, as usual, to magic"; ". . . the mountains to the north were rumored far to surpass in unhealthiness of climate and to be invested by a far more malignant race of deo (evil spirits) . . . "; he was himself "the only victim of ill health, offered up to appease the vengeance of the deo of the jungle for his violated rights." In the face of such perceptions of Indian mysticism, Everest was convinced that the teaching of surveying to Bengalis "would be fraught with more real utility than all the metaphysical lore taught at the Hindu College."[52]

In general, the evangelicals took the process one step further and envisioned the active conversion of Indians to Christianity. The subtext to all of Thomas Jervis's work, and those comments written in his support by John Cam Hobhouse at the Board of Control, was the hope that once the mysticism and irrationality of the Indians was swept away by incontrovertible proof that Hindu geographical and other physical conceptions were wrong, then those Indians would be open to conversion.

Early in the 1820s, the Bombay government had established an Engineering Institution, on much the same lines as the old survey school at Madras, to provide the revenue and engineer departments with trained surveyors drawn both from Eurasians and full-blooded Indians. In an 1826 report on the institution, the chief engineer wrote that, with respect to providing an education in astronomy for its students,

> there is probably no knowledge so likely to impress on their minds pure and reasonable notions of religion. In prosecuting this study and in contemplating the structure of the universe and the consequence resulting from it, they can scarcely fail of relieving themselves from a load of prejudice and superstition. They will thus gradually, in proportion as this knowledge is spread (it is reasonable to believe) become better men and better subjects, and less likely ever to be made the tools of any ambitious man or fanatic. The more intelligence exists in a nation, provided the Government

is a liberal one, the less desire there is for a change and whilst society is increasing in wealth and knowledge, they are pleased with themselves, contented and happy. The advantages, therefore, that may reasonably be expected to arise from the Institution, as a branch of education, are great, whether viewed as a question of finance or of policy.

To this end, the institution's instructor, George Jervis (Thomas's elder brother) had already begun translating English texts into the vernacular.[53]

Thomas Jervis and other evangelicals were more extreme in their views than officials like Everest and regarded an education in surveying (and in Western science more generally) as being conducive "in a singular manner to the easy and unexceptionable introduction of useful science, and industrious habits where they are most wanted: amongst the Natives of India," and as being "the least exceptionable of all the methods of introducing to the notice of the people of India generally the advantages of a good education, and habits of order, regularity, industry and moral rectitude." Jervis also called Colby's system for the Ordnance Survey in Ireland—the same system which he hoped to introduce into India—"a sort of Fellenberg School on the grandest scale. . . . Promptitude, regularity, and cheerfulness are the essentials of such [a] system, and here their effects are displayed in every individual of the establishment as in the parts of a steam engine." Philipp Emanuel von Fellenberg (1771–1844) was a Swiss educator whose educational system was intended to elevate lower orders of society and weld them more closely with the higher orders. Agreeing with Jervis, the members of the Board of Control felt that such a system would constitute "a great moral engine" for the improvement of India.[54]

The entire body of such opinions are closely integrated with the general debate during the first four decades of the nineteenth century over the role of education in the Company's India. The older tradition established by the first governor general, Warren Hastings, advocated that the Company's officials should adapt to Indian traditions and culture. This had been overturned as the British acquired political hegemony in India, so that Indians were expected to adapt to Western culture. The Orientalist-Anglicist debate of the 1820s and 1830s, culminating in Thomas Babington Macauley's education minute of 1835, was a debate over the language to be used in the official project of inculcating Western knowledge in India: should it be the Indian vernaculars or English? Both sides accepted implicitly the trinity of liberalism, rationality, and Christianity, and so the inherent superiority of European knowledge: "I have never found [anyone] distinguished by their proficiency in the

Eastern tongues," wrote Macauley in perhaps his most famous passage, "who could deny that a single shelf of a good European library was worth the whole native literature of India and Arabia."[55]

The debate was won by Macauley and the proponents of education in English, but this did not stop the translation of Western knowledge into the vernaculars by Europeans who were unattached to the Company, or even by Company officials acting in a private capacity. The East India Company had traditionally restricted the number of "nonofficial" British (and other Europeans) in its Indian territories; missionary activity had been particularly frowned upon because of the threat it posed to political stability. That had changed with Parliament's renewal of the Company's charter in 1813. The evangelicals in Parliament forced the adoption of the "pious clause," which required the Company to open British territories to any European who sought "the Introduction . . . of useful Knowledge, and of religious and moral improvement" among the Indians. Political compromise meant that the wording did not actually mention missionaries, although they were the intended beneficiaries.[56]

Part of the "useful knowledge" disseminated by the influx of evangelical Anglicans and nonconformists was, of course, geographical. Thus, the French missionary and orientalist G. Herklots published a map of India, written in Persian, in 1826, one of the first maps to be printed in India on the newly introduced lithographic presses (figure 9.1). Similar maps were produced after the official acceptance of English for instruction. Jean-Baptiste Tassin, another French emigre and commercial printer who did some contract work for George Everest and the Calcutta administration, published an *Anglo-Persian Map of India* in 1837, on which place-names were given in both languages. John Bellasis, a revenue surveyor, also made a copy of a small map of India in Persian.[57] It is however significant that these maps are all small-scale and are all in Persian, one of the classical languages of India. This might indicate that they were intended for educated and wealthy Indians who participated in and benefitted from the Company's rule, and who could be expected to appreciate general geographical knowledge, rather than for poorer and less educated Indians.

The dissemination of Western knowledge to the Indians was not a one-sided imposition. The complexity of Indian society and politics had always placed a premium on knowledge as an avenue to power. It was evident to many high-caste and commercial groups in India that at least an acquaintance with Western science was as necessary to participate in and benefit from the British raj as was the knowledge of the English language. The precise form of the response by Indians varied according

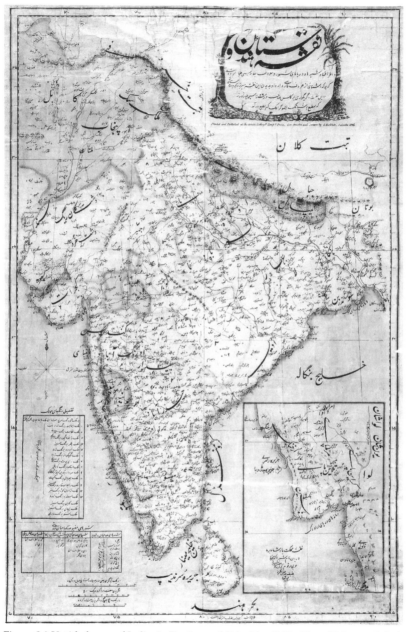

Figure 9.1 Untitled map of India, in Persian, published by G. Herklots (Calcutta: Asiatic Lithographic Press, 1826). Lithograph. (Bodleian Library, University of Oxford, (E) D 10 (228).)

to the specific social formation of each district. In Bengal, Hindus dominated the elites and flocked to the Hindu College in Calcutta, founded in 1817, some at least hoping to learn Western science. In Awadh and the Upper Provinces, the Muslim nobility actively engaged with Western knowledge.[58]

C. A. Bayly has addressed the fine nuances of the interaction between the Europeans, with their cultish support of astronomy, and the Muslim and Hindu astronomers and astrologers. For example, he argues that the 1831 formation of a European-style astronomical observatory by Nasir-ud Din Ahmed, Nawab of Awadh, was part of a political dialogue with the British. The Nawab employed two former deputy surveyor generals from Calcutta—James Herbert (1832–35) and then Richard Wilcox (1835–48)—and began a lithographic press. One of the more intriguing products of this press was a *Sketch of the Solar System for the Use in Schools* published in 1835 (figure 9.2). The copy I have examined has a title and lengthy commentary in English pasted over what I presume was an original text in Persian. The commentary echoes the Bombay chief engineer's argument that astronomical knowledge was a sure path to "pure and reasonable religion":

> Astronomy give[s knowledge] of the works of the Great Invisible Being who created and now sustaineth all things. Thousands and thousands of Suns on all sides at immense distances from each other attended by Ten Thousand time[s] ten thousand worlds all wheeling with aweful velocity in their appointed courses! Yet calm regular and harmonious invariably keeping the paths prescribed to them. . . . The Heavens declare the Glory of God! and the Firmament sheweth the works of His hand! He hangeth the earth upon nothing! By His spirit He hath garnished the Heavens; Lo these are parts of His ways but how small a portion is heard of Him! The fear of God is the beginning of Wisdom . . .

Despite the allusion in the last phrase to Psalm 111, this exhortation to faith does not actually specify any particular religion. As might be expected from a joint Islamic and Christian venture, the Creator to be contemplated might as easily have been Allah as Jehovah. Ultimately, Nasir-ud Din Ahmed's successor used Wilcox's death in 1848 as an excuse to disband the observatory and so remove this "center of printing, cultural liberalism, and covert British influence," all of which he mistrusted.[59]

Representing the Imperial Self

The negotiations within the East India Company's administration concerning the trigonometrical surveys did not just indicate the bureau-

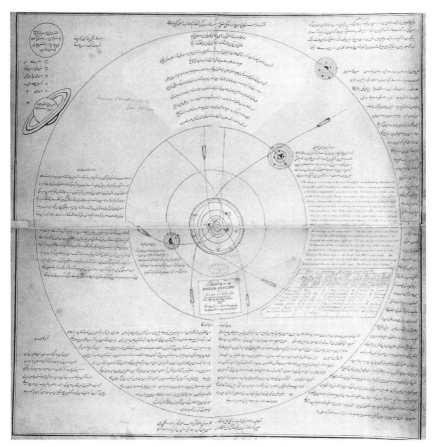

Figure 9.2 *Sketch of the Solar System for the Use in Schools* (Lucknow: Lithographic Press of His Majesty the King of Oude, 1835), perhaps produced under the direction of James Herbert, astronomer to the Nawab of Awadh, 1831–1835. (American Philosophical Society [Philadelphia] 523.2: Sk2s Large.)

cratic stresses resulting from the adoption of new technologies. They were intimately related to the British sense of their imperial Self and the Indian Other. The surveys were part and parcel of the British belief that they pursued a liberal, rational empire as much for the benefit of the Indians as for themselves. The Company's officials ultimately supported all surveys because they were intellectual exercises featuring observation, measurement, and classification. The trigonometrical surveys were privileged because they represented a European science beyond the scope of the Indians themselves. Indians made maps, which were in turn used by the British, but they could not make maps of the quality of those based on European "scientific principles." The Indians could not measure the true size and shape of the earth. They had too many imprecise and mystical geographical conceptions, from uncertain units of length to geographical beliefs featuring seas of treacle and butter (as Macauley disparaged them) and a flat earth seated on the backs of elephants riding on the back of a giant turtle. By pursuing measured surveys, the British proved themselves to be rational and scientific creatures. Each act of surveying thus incorporated the meaning of the British empire, not only as a statement of territorial appropriation and control but also as an expression of the source of their power and legitimacy. The British "did science" intuitively. Indians "did science" only at the express command of the British and, even then, only in a restricted and confined manner. Whether this distinction reflected the actual characters of either the British or the Indians is beside the point; it was the representation that counted.

Moreover, the ontological assumption of vision was that the viewer was active and dominant, whereas the observed was passive and docile. The British were the observers, powerful and cogent. The Indians were observed and reduced in British eyes to a state of passivity; they became little more than objects within the Indian landscape or brief records within the geographical archive. The British reserved the ability to act for themselves. Indians were defined *en masse* as being incapable of independent and autonomous action. Any actions they did undertake could therefore only be for nonindividual reasons. Through British observation, Indians were constituted as an undifferentiated mass motivated only by communal reasons of heathen religion, despotic politics (which seemed to reduce the masses to almost bestial slavery), and unreasoning emotion. Surveying and astronomy, both activities which rely heavily on vision, were thus key to the plans of the evangelical British to educate the lesser classes of Indians. Such an education promised to restore to the Indians the power of observation and that power of individual action and knowledge without which personal Salvation is impossible. Or rather, it promised to impart sufficient autonomy for Salvation but was sufficiently limited and circumscribed to maintain the Indians in a lower social status. Even then, the act of surveying reinforced and justified the superiority of British knowledge, of British reason, and of British rule.

CHAPTER TEN

Cartographic Practice: Inscribing an Imperial Space

It might be argued that the geodetic surveys were not themselves essential to the British representation of themselves as rational, liberal, and Christian rulers. After all, any survey that featured a consistent unit of length and the instrumental observation and measurement of the world could be, and was, construed as scientific and thus inherently European in character. On the other hand, the British easily conceived of training Indians in the lower-level surveying technologies, of giving them *some* of the intellectual skills that were the preserve of European rationality. With proper training, Indians could manage the basic, repetitive, and laborious tasks of the detailed topographic or cadastral survey. But the British kept the higher-level science of geodesy—informed by calculus, complex geometries, and Newtonian mechanics—out of the reach of all but a very few Indians. The imperial significance of the Great Trigonometrical Survey depended in part on the survey's configuration of the British rule of South Asia as being scientific, rational, and liberal, in active opposition to Asian rule, which it stereotyped as being mystical, irrational, and despotic. The meaning of British rule—that the Company-State was not just another Asiatic tyranny—was *incorporated* into the very acts of surveying and observing the South Asian landscape.

The Great Trigonometrical Survey and, indeed, the whole mapping enterprise were significant for the ideological image of geographical space that they created. More than a network of astronomically determined places ever could, the trigonometrical surveys held the promise of a perfect geographical panopticon. Through their agency, the British thought they might reduce India to a rigidly coherent, geometrically accurate, and uniformly precise imperial space, a rational space within which a systematic archive of knowledge about the Indian landscapes and people might be constructed. India, in all of its geographic aspects, would be made knowable to the British. The British accordingly constructed the Great Trigonometrical Survey as a public works which could not be undertaken by the Indians themselves, but which was as concrete and as necessary as irrigation canals and military roads for pulling together, improving, and defining India and its inhabitants. And the spatial significance of the trigonometrical surveys was *inscribed* into the maps the British produced. They defined India.

Triangulation and the Discourse of Imperial Space

In the eighteenth century, commercial cartographers began to advertise their maps as being based on "actual survey," whether or not they really were. They often superimposed spurious graticules of meridians and parallels on large-scale maps. They did so to provide the maps with the same image of correctness and verisimilitude possessed by archivally compiled small-scale maps.[1] By the 1820s it was no longer acceptable for detailed maps to be based on merely "actual surveys"; they had to be based on trigonometrical surveys if they were to be proper and correct. The culmination of this shift in the popular perception of cartographic quality coincides with the final acceptance by the Company's directors and secretariat in London of an all-India triangulation. Whereas in 1823, John Hodgson did not draw a distinction between astronomical or trigonometrical control for his "Atlas of the North-West Provinces"—he would use any surveyed materials available, whatever their character—Valentine Blacker could in 1825 identify a hierarchy of quality for geographic maps. The top of the hierarchy were maps based on trigonometrical frameworks; the two lower levels of maps, lacking that firm geometrical basis, would eventually have to be replaced with surveys of the highest quality. Blacker also specifically implied that an "actual survey" had to have entailed a measured base and a triangulation. A few years later, in 1833, Duncan Montgomerie presented a more precise classification of survey types, which included no less than four distinct forms of trigonometrical survey.[2]

When surveys or archivally compiled maps did not feature a triangulated basis, their makers nonetheless often claimed that they did. For example, an 1831 parliamentary paper contains a list of "trigonometrical surveys" unconnected to the Great Arc: most of those listed for the Bengal presidency did *not* in fact feature any triangulation.[3] A rather harmless instance of rhetoric was the claim of an 1855 small-scale atlas of southern India, lithographed by John Walker, that all the data had been "reduced from the Grand Trigonometrical Survey of India," whereas that survey had provided only the framework and not the detailed information.[4] More blatant was the Royal Geographical Society's 1833 publication of William Monteith's map of the Caucasus. This map's title proclaims its foundation upon trigonometrical surveys; yet in describing his map's construction, Monteith recorded that only a small portion of Azerbaijan was triangulated, the rest of the map being derived from a few astronomical observations and from route information obtained by bribing Persian and Russian officials. Another aspect of this map entails a rhetorical form inherited from the eighteenth century: the manuscript map does not have a graticule, but one has been added to the published version to give it an impression of verisimilitude.[5]

Part of the problem, as discussed in chapter 3, is that "trigonometrical survey" could be understood to encompass any survey in which trigonometrical calculations were necessary to convert the observations to distances. The list of untriangulated trigonometrical surveys in India might accordingly be explained in part by some rather loose conceptions of trigonometrical surveying held by at least two of the Bengal surveyors in the 1820s. When John Hodgson described his method for systematic route surveys in 1821, he thought that the interior of each block of territory might be filled in by an *ad hoc* combination of traverses, astronomical observations, and trigonometrical surveying.[6]

Alexander Gerard, whom Hodgson had recommended to be the principal officer for his systematic survey, began his account of the construction of his map of Kunawur, in the western Himalayas, with the statement that "the survey [1817–18, 1820–22] was strictly trigonometrical with a very few exceptions." Yet those "very few exceptions" were really rather significant. The detail was measured with perambulators between points apparently based on a triangulation, in an advance on the technique then prevalent in the Himalayas of pacing out traverse distances. The triangulation itself was flawed. Because "the measurement of a base was inconvenient and tedious from want of the necessary apparatus," Gerard calculated the lengths of several sides from the astronomically determined positions of their end points and the known size of the earth. These sides then seem to have been used as the basis for several unconnected triangulations. With regards to one stretch of the Sutlej valley through the Himalayas, Gerard specifically noted that it was surveyed "*either* by triangles or by azimuths and latitudes." The result is a curious and inadequate hodgepodge of techniques.[7]

Hodgson's incompatible mixture of astronomical observations and trigonometrical surveys might perhaps reflect a truly loose terminology. Gerard followed the same loose, *ad hoc* mixture of techniques for his surveys but, when he wrote up his account of them, he sought to describe that mixture as being more rigorous than it actually was. It was not necessarily the case that Gerard consciously cheated when he undertook his surveys in the first place. He did not go into the mountains with orders to undertake a triangulation, which he then failed to make, and he did not subsequently seek to hide that failure from the public. Rather, Gerard made his surveys according to the technological standards which then prevailed in the Bengal presidency; it was with hindsight that Gerard realized that what he *ought* to have done (or what he ought to have been able to do) was a proper triangulation in the mountains, as Webb and Herbert succeeded in undertaking. In using the confused language of trigonometrical surveys, Gerard engaged in a newly popular rhetoric that emphasized the great worth of triangulation-based surveys.

That rhetoric—to which Gerard, John Arrowsmith (on behalf of Monteith and the Royal Geographical Society), Walker, and numerous other cartographers all contributed—was grounded in popular conceptions of the scientific nature of the trigonometrical surveys. The trigonometrical surveys promised a technological fix to the geographic panopticon; they promised a coherent structure about which the cartographic archive could be organized. Because the new structure was itself derived from the world and was unremitting in its geometrical rigor, it avoided the errors introduced by the poorer technology and by the human agency that characterized the older, astronomically-based structure. Because the technology was very precise as well as accurate, it promised very detailed and correct results. The end product would be a comprehensive, thorough, detailed, and essentially correct geographical archive for British India.

A specific instance where such an archive was implied as being necessary for the rational, liberal, and Christian rule of India is presented by the several debates over revenue surveys in the 1830s. A recurring theme in the parliamentary hearings for the Company's 1833 charter renewal was the inherent uncertainty of the revenue settlement. The assessment of the portion of each ryot's produce to be paid in tax depended on the personal experience of the assessor in judging the quality of the soil and the crop, the extent of the land, and the abilities of the cultivators. The Company officials who gave evidence to the parliamentary committee on this issue all thought that a precise and accurate survey of boundaries would allow the extent of land cultivated by each ryot to be exactly determined. One source of error and uncertainty would thereby be removed and the assessment would accordingly become that much more certain and thus more equitable.[8] A uniform, detailed map of India was touted as a key element in the establishment of a single, India-wide administration of the revenue and civil justice systems; it would be essential for placing the Company's finances, and indeed its very existence, onto a rigorous and rational footing.[9] John Cam

Hobhouse declared that his support for Thomas Jervis's plans for a survey of India akin to the Ordnance Survey of Ireland derived "from [personal] experience, from a mass of professional evidence altogether independent of Major Jervis' opinions or correspondents, [and] from the soundest and most enlarged views of political economy, of justice, reason, and expediency." [10] William Bentinck explicitly directed his administration toward improving the state of the individual ryot, arguing from the premises of the utilitarian ideal of "happiness" for the common man. He, and many other British in India, believed that making all landholders equal by reducing all land tenures to a common system, and thereby stimulating land ownership and proprietorship, was the chief means of attaining this goal. [11]

Whereas these sentiments were all part of the larger debate over the best manner for the British to govern India, ostensibly for the benefit of the Indians, trigonometrical surveys had been promoted much earlier for their potential benefits to British rule. They constituted the only technology which could combine all surveyed materials into a single and *uniform* archive. When Bentinck had argued for his military survey of southern India in 1804, and when Hastings established the Great Trigonometrical Survey in 1817, they did so not just for the accuracy a trigonometrical base would give to topographical maps but also for the uniformity of information which they would ensure (see Part One). A rigorous mathematical network would, it was assumed, force the lesser, detailed surveys to give up their errors and internal differences and would so produce a single geographic archive, first for each province and ultimately for all India. The directors thought Jervis's survey of the Konkan exemplified the manner in which a "uniform" survey might be prosecuted by different personnel without problems of joining their work together either spatially, where two detailed surveys abutted one another, or chronologically, when one surveyor took over from another. [12]

A uniform geographical archive promoted rational and effective rule. [13] The detailed surveys might have produced a wealth of statistical, revenue, and geographic data useful in the detailed management of a district or region, but on the more extensive scale of an entire presidency or of the whole of India, uniform data allowed the administrators in London, Calcutta, Bombay, or Madras to treat distant areas all in the same manner when they might otherwise be quite distinct. All portions of the territory could be treated in the same way regardless of any special circumstances that might prevail on the ground. Topographical knowledge of all of India would be known for military planning. An all-India infrastructure of roads, railways, telegraphs, and canals might be planned and constructed in as efficient a manner as possible. In this respect, the uniform archive was timeless: it would benefit the future as much as the present.

The whole of India was indexed. Long concordances between place-names and geographical coordinates were drawn up; when published, these indices served to fix and make certain the otherwise highly variable orthographical transcriptions of place-names. Lists of the principal places in southern India, as defined by latitudes and longitudes determined by Lambton, were prominently placed at the front of the *Madras Almanac*, starting in 1803.[14] William Hamilton produced one of the first gazetteers of India in 1820, with the intention "to reduce the Geography of Hindostan to a more systematic form than has yet been attempted," for which purpose he included a similar list of latitudes and longitudes.[15] The Company's favored booksellers in London published two books designed to facilitate the use of general maps of India, both comprising long lists of places and their geographical locations.[16] With these guides and the numerous commercially published gazetteers, the educated British in both India and London could find any place of importance within the confines of the imperial space of Company India. Colin Mackenzie even suggested that if the surveyor took care to match every village in a district against the revenue department's district register, then the individuality of place-names—and the vagaries caused by inconsistent orthography—could be replaced by a location to make the revenue administration that much more efficient.[17]

The trigonometrical surveys allowed the British to *know* India without having to worry about particularities. Perhaps the most telling indicator of this is the Court's insistence on having the *Atlas of India* compiled and engraved in London. The official reason for this was the pragmatic need to minimize the cost of producing the maps: many skilled engravers already worked in London according to a system of piece-work in which they were hired and fired as needed; a similar group of skilled artisans would have to be created in India as permanent employees of the Company and so would have to be paid whether or not there was work for them. Underlying this decision was the more fundamental acceptance that a map compiler in Britain could construct maps of India. Herbert and Jervis both argued that the *Atlas* should be compiled in India where the surveyors might appreciate the uniqueness of place. In contrast, the Court insisted that the Great Trigonometrical Survey established a uniformity and rigor which overrode and which subsumed the unique circumstances of each detailed survey.[18]

The certainty imparted to the geographical archive by the trigonometrical basis was embedded in cartographic images. Legislators in

London could look at the maps of India specially prepared for them by John Walker and could conceive of India as a political entity. They could thus legislate for all of India without thought for particular circumstances.[19] Just as a British prime minister later reminisced about cartographic propaganda in the classroom during the "high imperialism" of the later nineteenth century,

> on the wall at school hung a great map with large portions of it coloured red. It was an intoxicating vision for a small boy. . . . We believed in our great imperial mission[20]

so maps reinforced the imperial mission in India. The maps of provinces and of India which hung on the walls of council chambers and administrators' offices in India and London formed potent symbols of the European creation of a single political entity. Their potency in large part derived from their repeated viewing. Each time they saw a map, each time they read and understood a map, the officials mentally encompassed the territory it represented. Time and again, the surveyors and bureaucrats extolled a map's virtue for bringing an "entire country" into a "single view." And the basic message inscribed in the maps was simple: this is British territory; if it is not, then it could be British territory; this is an imperial space to be governed by us.[21]

Resistance, Language, and a Flawed Geographic Panopticon

But—and this is a very big "but"—the technological fix promised by the trigonometrical surveys was flawed. The surveys of India were political statements of British control of the territory and they were recognized as such by the Indians themselves. The perfection of the geographic panopticon and its archive, which was promised by the use of triangulation, was accordingly subverted by negotiations and contestations between the British and the Indians. Indians were not the passive and docile objects of the potent British vision which the British ontologically assumed them to be. They could and did object in various ways to the British conquest of the subcontinent and the reconstruction of an imperial space. The information acquired by the British did not represent a perfect, empirically known truth, as they thought it did, but instead constituted contested knowledge of a socially constructed reality.

Foucault did not intend the panopticon to be just a metaphor for surveillance and state control; he considered it to be the epitome of the "swarm" of disciplinary mechanisms and technologies of observation and control developed by European states after 1700.[22] Like any technology, it will fail. The archive itself is only as good as its indices and catalogues; the media on which knowledge is stored are not forever permanent but they fade and decay. In India, the quality of record keeping varied; high temperatures and the annual extremes of moisture between the monsoon and dry seasons meant that European inks and papers were not as stable and consistent as they were supposed to be; rats and white ants presented such a danger that, in the Map and Record Issue Office of the Survey of India, the closed cases of original maps were opened and examined daily for infestations and damage, while the stacks of printed maps were kept on open shelves away from the walls; the hanging of manuscript wall maps in the Company's chambers led to their being damaged or even destroyed.[23]

More fundamentally, the East India Company never constituted a monolithic entity. It was instead fractured into several interest groups whose agendas often conflicted with one another. The surveillant control of the power hierarchy was never as complete as Foucault indicated. In British India, there were two important areas of negotiation. First, the objects of surveillance, the Indians, did resist. Second, the linguistic gulf between the British and their Indian subjects meant that British control was not as close and as confined as the panopticon might suggest. I will discuss these two points in turn.

Resistance to British surveying in India crossed all social and economic groups, from rajas to peasants: "the officers employed on the grand trigonometrical survey and other surveys have always experienced, in almost every part of India, the greatest obstructions in the discharge of their duties."[24] The instances are numerous, from the two surveyors attached to the Hyderabad Subsidiary Force who were unable to work because no guard was available to protect against "obstacles arising from the nature of our duty, against which the natives in general are prejudiced," to an 1836 riot in Chittagong, which was prompted by a revenue survey. In the latter, an assistant surveyor had his instruments broken and was severely beaten by fragments of one of his flagstaffs—although the British newspaper report stressed that there "was not the slightest personal feeling in this case"—and the local authorities had to call in the army to quell the unrest.[25] James Garling's survey party in the Northern Circars was met by a group of armed men who called themselves poligars of the Venkatagiri raja. They resented their country being surveyed; to the flagmen, whom they captured and released with threats that they would be killed if they stayed in their current jobs, the poligars expressed the desire to sacrifice the European surveyor in charge. To avoid further confrontation, the Madras government shifted the survey party across the peninsula to Goa.[26] John Hodgson once commented that route surveyors were always being hassled by villagers because they were assumed to be convicted criminals, sentenced to measure roads as punishment; the surveyors therefore provided an easy and apparently legitimate whipping post and focus of anti-British sentiment.[27]

The surveyors' use of flags as signals was particularly significant in stimulating Indian reactions. In Asia and Europe alike, the flag was a common symbol of authority; it announced the presence of a person in whom authority and legitimacy were vested and to whom the flag's blazon was directly linked; or it announced the extension of that authority's control. The British surveyors acknowledged the flag's symbolic importance and were not surprised when they caused rumors of invasion when they flew signal flags from hilltops. The British also understood the concern shown by rajas who knew that signal flags flying from their palace walls—however temporary the installation would have been—would constitute a major affront to their dignity and would undermine their position with respect to their supporters.[28]

The British administrators were well aware of a survey's potential for disturbance and, when there were problems, they redirected the surveys to calmer districts. Metcalfe vehemently objected to a proposed "scheme of surveying the Indus, under the pretence of sending a present" for Ranjit Singh, the Sikh raja. The idea was to map the future battleground between the British and the Russians, but Metcalfe argued that to do so would instead cause a war with the powerful Sikh state.[29] Less caution was necessary within the Company's own territories, yet the British always sought to stop trouble before it could begin by employing only experienced and sensible surveyors and by keeping survey parties as small as possible.[30] Alternatively, the surveyor in the field might head off trouble by making "small presents of turbans, pieces of cloth, bottles of liquor, etc., for information and assistance afforded to the survey."[31]

With respect to this last point, the parties of the Great Trigonometrical Survey formed small armies by themselves. In addition to himself and his assistants, Everest's parties on the Great Arc included 108 Indians to set up flags and heliotropes and to carry instruments and tents. Add to this another thirty or so guards plus all of the various servants and camp followers, and the party could easily contain 200 people. These would be dependent upon the local communities for the purchase of provisions. Surveying the Great Arc also drew on local labor to build roads to hilltops, to clear away trees to open sightlines, to aid in erecting the flags, and so on. Lambton wrote that he often needed some three hundred men drawn from the nearest villages; and while the surveyors paid for such services, the laborers were usually needed in the hills and jungles some distance away from cultivated areas. The trigonometrical survey parties thus put a great strain on the resources of the areas through which they passed. As a result, incidents between the survey followers and locals were not uncommon.[32]

By far the most important reason for the frequent antipathy shown by local Indians toward surveyors was the concern for reducing to a minimum the amount of information falling into Government hands. All Indian states were built on land revenues, and each participant in the state hierarchy—from village headmen through the zamindars and rajas—sought to syphon off as much of that wealth as possible. Thus there was an ingrained passion for secrecy at all levels of Indian society, for hiding actual crop yields from superiors. The majority of Indian objections to the British surveys and the censuses operated at this level.[33]

Anthony Troyer notified the Madras government that many of the headmen in South Arcot had produced "written orders from the Collector (whether true or false it was not in my power to ascertain) enjoining them to withhold [provisions and] information."[34] Lieutenant Peter Conner found himself playing a subtle political game in Koorg, whose raja seemed to treat him "with much personal kindness and respect," but who also "expressly excluded" his subjects from communicating with Conner, so that "all manner of information was denied [him], except what his own ability and ingenuity could collect."[35] In Mysore, Mackenzie found so much resistance to his "general enquiries" that the diwan actively intervened and requested that Mackenzie's assistants not ask questions regarding the female population, to which the Resident acquiesced for the sake of the peace of the country; the diwan then extended the ban to cover both men and women. Mackenzie accordingly directed his subordinates to make

> requisitions [only] for the object of the geometrical survey, or measurement, of the districts, which are few and limited chiefly to the boundaries of the purgunnahs, the roads, [the] list of the villages and waterworks, [and the] facility of getting provision and forage for pay and such aid of guides and village officers as are customary and necessary.[36]

The Resident at Mysore interpreted the diwan's proscription as including all "general enquiries" with the sole exception of historical questions.[37] Mackenzie's pandits also had difficulties collecting or copying historical manuscripts; the efforts in about 1800 by Dr. Strachey to collect Sanskrit manuscripts for Charles Wilkins, one of the Calcutta orientalists, were hindered by Indians who actively purchased those manu-scripts rather than allow them to fall into British hands.[38]

Several of the problems facing the British surveyors seem to have been the result of their dependence on the harkaras of the local British collector (in British territory) or of the local prince (in the princely states). The harkaras formed the interface between the surveyor and the people of each district and were responsible not only for translating between the two sides but also for negotiating for food and labor. It was thus an easily abused position. It seems to have been extensively abused in Mysore early in the nineteenth century, when the diwan sought to control British activities. Mackenzie thought that his har-kara had tried to embroil him in a local altercation: "having chequed his little attempts to tyrannize and establish an improper influence, he [now] seems desirous of creating all the opposition and mischief in his power."[39] The harkara assigned to Thomas Arthur, an assistant on Mackenzie's Mysore survey, sent regular information about Arthur's ac-tivities to the diwan; Arthur himself fell foul of the situation and was briefly suspended from the survey because of his apparent insensitivity to local concerns (see chapter 5). No sooner had Arthur's situation been clarified, when Lambton was accused of keeping a man in confinement for five weeks; it transpired that one of his Indian staff had been respon-sible and that the harkara had not notified Lambton even though Lamb-ton had "so repeatedly requested to inform me in case of any improper conduct in my people towards the inhabitants." One of Henry Kater's *sepoys* was accused of murder.[40]

One of the more intriguing aspects of Indian resistance is the manner in which the British sought to marginalize it by treating it as being the product of religious or irrational beliefs. As such, the British were sure that the resistance would fade or would be replaced by less unscientific or more pragmatic negotiations that might be more easily accommo-dated. This was of course a self-serving process, as it allowed the British to denigrate Indian mysticism even as it promoted their own rational character. For example, one of the surveyors on the Budhon series of the Bengal triangulation recorded that a local official politely refused to have a signal flag fly from his fort, because the fort was sacred to a deota celebrated as a "destructive being" who would certainly kill anyone who might desecrate it.[41] Most of the instances I have encountered de-rive from after 1820, and George Everest seems to have been involved in almost all of them, in some form or another. But it nonetheless seems that by the 1830s it had become common for the British to impose ste-reotypical behavior on the Indians, both peasantry and nobility alike.

Everest had tremendous difficulties in the northern plains when he had to remove trees to clear sightlines. In the hills, his clearances had always been on hilltops, well away from village lands, but now he was suddenly faced by "whole villages . . . in battle array armed with clubs" to protect certain trees which had particular significance as the homes of spirits or as being dedicated to a god. He was finally empowered by the government to pay whatever compensation was asked, even though he did not have the time to investigate local tenures and customs and so could not save himself from being preyed upon by villagers out to swindle the Company by claiming that any old tree was sacred and so obtain monetary compensation.[42] Again, Everest thought that the destruction of survey towers for the Great Arc in Gwalior by large bands of armed villagers, for two years in a row, was tantamount to insurrection against the state, the peasants being in collusion "either with the ruling powers at Gwalior or the subordinate authorities of that state." In response, however, the resident ascribed the problem to Indian polytheistic irrationality when he reported that

> the people inhabiting the wild tract of country in the neighbourhood of Pahargurh took it into their heads that these new platforms were the cause of the failure of the periodical rains. They rose with arms in their hands and in such numbers as to intimidate the police and accomplished the destruction of the platforms.[43]

In both of these cases, Everest argued that the Indians were acting politically or economically, although those actions could be disregarded by other British as simple mysticism.

On the other hand, Everest did himself impute irrational and mystical behavior when it came to the manner in which some Indians treated his own instruments and activities. He wrote that Indians attributed "supernatural and miraculous powers to our instruments and the sites which have been occupied by them"; many traveled for long distances in order to pray before the Great Theodolite to seek a medical cure. At times of natural calamity, the sites occupied by the theodolite became centers of prayer. It was when those prayers were not answered, Everest wrote, that the Indians would set about to destroy the site. Because Everest engraved his station marks into solid rock whenever practicable, the Indians "have been known to proceed in bodies armed with sledgehammers and beat out every vestige of the engraving."[44]

The Company's records hold many more such instances of resistance. I stress them here because they indicate a substantial gulf between the British and the Indians they controlled, or whom they thought they controlled. Whereas Foucault's concept of discipline assumes that the examiner can understand the individual who is examined, the linguistic difference between English and the Indian vernaculars tended to negate that understanding. Bayly has argued that the British acquired a Brahminical view of India from their pandits and translators. More subtly, the pandits were motivated by their own agendas when making their translations. Nicholas Dirks, for example, quotes the start of one of Mackenzie's manuscripts in which the translator admits that he "omitted the tautological and repeated expressions and set aside prolixity but [followed] laconism."[45] Such intervention in the translation process will necessarily change and alter the information absorbed into the British archive.

Perhaps the clearest demonstration of the gulf between the British and the Indians comes from Francis Buchanan's comments on the naming of rivers in the district of Dinajpur. The rivers of Bengal constantly change their course, opening new channels and leaving older channels to become stagnant marshes. The problem was that the local inhabitants continued to call the old channels by their original names:

> This has been a source of great trouble to European geographers, who, endeavouring to trace a great river from where it joins the sea to its most remote source by its principal channel, are astonished to find that it sometimes loses its name altogether; or again, another river, after having for some part lost its original name, is traced further, is found with its former name restored. The geographers of Europe are apt to be enraged, when in tracing a river they find that an inconsiderable stream falling into their grand channel changes its name, and that the source of this smaller stream is obstinately considered by the natives as the source of the river, either having been the first to which they had access, or having at one time been the largest. Geographers are in general very unwilling to admit of these absurdities, and therefore construct their maps according to their own plan, with the same name following the same river from its most remote source to its mouth. It must, however, be confessed, that this improvement, until it shall have been adopted by the inhabitants of the country, is attended with considerable inconvenience to those who wish to use the maps on the spot, and often leads them into most troublesome mistakes.[46]

The British maps of India thus constituted an inherently flawed cognitive panopticon. There were some areas of knowledge that could not be reconciled with the ordered and structured space of the geographical archive. At best, the British could force recalcitrant or inadequate data to fit the framework and they could then promote the results as being *valid* and *true*, but the reapplication of that knowledge on the ground would always display the linguistic, conceptual, and disciplinary gulf. The British created a geographic *myth* of an empire comprising known or knowable territory.

Representing an Imperial India

The geographical investigation and mapping of India, and in particular the prosecution of the trigonometrical surveys, were exercises in self-delusion. The technologies of observation promised a panopticon and the British couched their rhetoric concerning the examination of India accordingly: they saw India in a fragmentary way; in mapping India, they brought those visual fragments together; seeing the maps, they thought to see all of India as the sum of its parts. And just as seeing allowed individual objects and places to be understood, so viewing the map allowed the British to understand India. The administrators in London and India generally supported the triangulation surveys because they promised to perfect that understanding of India. The triangulation and creation of India flourished, despite the practical limitations on the surveys, limitations which were imposed by the political, institutional, and historical circumstances of the East India Company.

British surveyors were aware, to some degree, that their mapping of India constituted a configuration of South Asia's geography. At least, some were aware of the spatial significance of the Great Trigonometrical Survey. It is apparent that they did *not* appreciate the meaning incorporated into their survey practices. John Jopp, the Bombay surveyor, did once evoke the image of a fisherman casting his net to gather fish—or the surveyor gathering in the land—when he wrote that a net of triangulation "might be thrown over the whole country," but this seems to have been a rare instance in the archival record.[47] The rest of the time, the surveyors seem to have thought of their actions in more politically pragmatic terms: surveys were necessary to provide information for British rule and would, of course, be resented and contested by the Indians.

In contrast, there is some indication that a few of the surveyors did appreciate that their cartographic representations of India established the essential character of the subcontinent according to a European conception of space. In 1839, for example, William Morison, a member of the governor general's council and a former surveyor, complained of the manner in which "every [revenue] surveyor apparently draws his plans according to his own fancy, so that these plans, if I may so express it, do not speak the same language, and they might be supposed to represent some part of Europe quite as much as any part of India."[48] Each surveyor's "fancy" was, of course, defined by the existing conventions of cartographic design and structure. Even though they used super-ficially different symbologies—the maps' "language"—their significa-tion of geometrical space was always the same.

The Great Trigonometrical Survey was of central importance in this respect because it replaced the subcontinent's physical geographic structure of mountains, plains, rivers, and deserts with an abstract and mathematical geographic structure of triangles. William Lambton and his supporters repeatedly referred to his trigonometrical surveys as providing the "skeleton" upon which the detailed geography of India might be hung. George Everest took the idea further when he rhetori-cally disparaged the restriction of the Great Trigonometrical Survey to just the Great Arc and the Calcutta series as comprising a "mere skele-ton." Secondary triangulations were necessary, he argued, to extend the new mathematical structure of India in depth and so permeate the sub-continent with mathematical rigor.[49]

The rational, uniform space of the British maps of India was not a neutral, value-free space. Rather, it was a space imbued with power relations, with the fact that the British controlled (or had the power to control) the lands depicted and that they could impose India-wide leg-islation and reforms in a manner impossible for earlier rulers. Imperial space was a space of boundaries. Those boundaries occurred at all geographical scales, from those of princely states and provinces to the fields of individual ryots, but all had been rationalized and fixed by the force of imperial adjudication. In this respect, imperial space used boundaries as a mechanism for equating abstract space with the con-crete reality of territory. In a major conceptual reversal, boundaries were no longer vague axes of dispute (frontiers) between core areas of Indian polities but were configured as the means whereby those core areas were now defined. Political territories were no longer defined with respect to the physical features which characterized them or which bounded them; nor were they defined by the complex "feudal" inter-relationships of their rulers. The British suborned the geographical char-acter of those territories to a mathematical space even as they reduced the political structures to the "rule of law."

The result was, in Paul Carter's phrase, an exercise in "imperial his-tory." India, like Carter's Australia, was not "simply a stage where history occurred"; instead, the British constructed India as the stage upon which historians have placed past events and phenomena in strict chronological sequence. The British created their own interpretations of Indian space as they did the histories and cultures of Asia and ancient Greece.[50]

Wrapped up in their science's epistemological and ontological claims to truth, claims which were integral to the production and very comprehension of their maps, the British could not conceive of their India as anything other than a *natural* entity. The ambiguous geographic entity which was loosely called "India" by Europeans in the early modern era was replaced in about 1800 by the distinct entity "India" defined through the cartographic representation of the extents and potential of British power. As Carter demonstrates, imperial space is inherently expansive. It is able to be extended indefinitely, whether in the form of a graticule of known meridians and parallels or as the field of surveyed triangles. Yet British power could extend (or be thought capable of extending) only so far. Thus India extended only so far: from the oceans by which the British arrived to the northern belt of mountains that so effectively restrained their imperial energies. Eventually, the clash of Britain and Russia in the "Great Game of Empire" led the two European empires to connect their own imperial spaces with a "geodetic connection" carried across the barrier posed by the Himalayas.[51] Other than this one offshoot, the limits to the spread of the survey were defined by politics. None of the Bengal subsidiary series could be extended into Nepal, and the North-East Longitudinal Series was forced to skirt Gurkha territory. The extension of imperial space was contiguous with the empire's political extent. *British* India, which was otherwise a quite arbitrary entity, was naturalized by the British to be a constant, timeless, "natural," uniform geographical entity, political state, and cultural nation.

The British mapping of India was an exercise in discipline: the British surveyed the Indian landscapes in an effort to assess and to improve them. The disciplining of the landscape took place within the scope of the map, within the geographical archive and panopticon. The British sought to bring the landscape into line with their own preconceptions of territorial order. Cadastral surveys were especially rooted in the established British practices of territorial rationalization and agricultural improvement. Although they were even more removed from the Great Trigonometrical Survey than topographical surveys, cadastral surveys defined a key component to the ideology of imperial space. Territory can be mapped at very large scales, as great as 1 : 480 in practice and still greater in theory; the simple prosecution of such surveys demonstrates the archive's potential for perfection. And by being mapped, the territory itself could be improved and made more productive. Thus, revenue surveyors in the western Deccan entered into considerable logical convolutions in order to bring communal agricultural practices into line with the ideological conception of the ryot, the individual cultivator who embodied both the essence of eternal India and the future of a liberal empire. To do so, the British had to break up the communal lands of many villages by "imposing a field assessment." The surveyors set out to repeat the experience of British enclosures and to transform the vestiges of feudal agriculture into a modern, productive, and profitable practice.[52]

The creation of *British* India thus entailed the forced and, at root, ambiguous coincidence of two spatial concepts: "India" and "empire." By mapping the subcontinent, the British defined a conception of a natural and eternal geographical entity called "India." This India was the site of the orientalists' enthusiasms, an India that stood in marked opposition to active and dynamic Britain. Even as the British justified their domination of South Asia in terms of the cultural superiority evident in such an opposition, they sought to improve India; they sought to change the landscape, to make its economies more dynamic and rational. The imperial disciplining of space was thus at odds with the passivity of India's disciplined space. The fundamental contradiction of British India—how can a "liberal democracy" also be an imperial despot?—thus found expression in spatial conceptions. The distance between the two sides of the contradiction steadily widened until the ideology of British India—of rational, disinterested power and cultural superiority—finally cracked and British power in South Asia collapsed in the twentieth century.

Some understanding of the ideological ambiguity presented by the British mapping of India can be reached only through the fact that their maps and texts constituted their geographic archive. Two tensions have been especially important for this study. The first concerned the proper manner of prosecuting triangulations. Established expert cartographic opinion held that primary and secondary triangulations had to be completed before any detailed surveys could be undertaken; only then would the surveyors be certain that a triangulation could severely limit geometrical errors and so attain the geographic perfection it promised. This was the message given, for example, to the 1824 parliamentary committee on reforming Irish taxation by cartographic experts Henry Kater, Thomas Colby, and James Gardner.[53] Set against this technological ideal was the actual implementation of triangulation in India, variously constrained by the Company's institutional structures, in which the Great Trigonometrical Survey generally came after the prosecution of detailed surveys, many of which were themselves based on some dedicated "trigonometrical survey." Even so, Valentine Blacker could state in 1825 that the reconciliation of the different levels of survey in the *Atlas of India* would be made according to "principles that shall stand the test of scientific investigation."[54] Thus, the scientistic rhetoric which enveloped the *Atlas* and the Great Trigonometrical Survey proclaimed the virtues of triangulation even as those virtues were denied and subverted in practice.

The second tension was that between a pragmatic need for geographic information for ruling India and an idealized system to obtain that information. In particular, a very expensive geodetic survey was consistently privileged, occasionally to the detriment of the detailed surveys which, with hindsight, might be thought more obviously necessary to the conquest, consolidation, and exploitation of the subcontinent. The hard-nosed accountants of the Company's administration periodically drew attention to the costly Great Trigonometrical Survey but the survey still prospered. Why was this? Part of the reason for the privileging of the triangulation is embedded in the mechanics of the Company's patronage systems. Yet those mechanisms would not have been functional had those surveys not offered something, however intangible, to the British rule of India.

Both tensions led to rather paradoxical situations because they rest on the assumption that the principal reason for a triangulation is its promotion of locational accuracy. But, for the British mapping of India at least, the principal purpose of the trigonometrical surveys was to impart a greater coherency and cohesion to the mapped spaces than could be attained by the older, astronomical methods for cartographic control. Improved geometrical accuracy was only a secondary benefit. It was the manner in which triangulation promised a *uniform* and *consistent* structure for the geographic archive—no matter how it was employed with respect to detailed surveys—which made the British pursue their trigonometrical surveys across India. The archive itself was still to be constituted in the same manner as it had been in the eighteenth century, which is to say through a process of reconciling, corroborating, and systematically arranging the source materials. But the cartographer's Foucauldian drafting table now featured a rigid and intensive spatial framework which brooked no spatial uncertainty at any cartographic scale. William Bentinck had suggested in 1804 that maps derived from route surveys should all be drawn with a uniform design:

> But although such sketches and remarks [that is, route surveys] must be highly useful where none have before existed, yet it is easy to conceive how imperfect and even unintelligible such works must often be, where no system of drawing and no fixed signs to represent particular objects and features of a country have been established, but where every officer pursues a different mode of expressing the objects which he sees.[55]

Triangulation implicitly created a natural cartographic space to be filled with natural symbols: consistency of representation would derive automatically from consistency in observation and measurement. The triangulation of India promised the perfect geographic panopticon not because its geometry would be better than that of astronomical control but because its geometry would be the same as the world's.

Triangulation appealed to the Enlightened British mentality because it *improved* the archive of geographical knowledge. Indeed, it promised such an improvement that the archive became definitive. The archive could be shipped back to Britain as a symbolic appropriation of the territories and peoples of India. Large wall maps could be hung up in council chambers in London to give India a metaphorical presence in negotiations and debates. The issue of the map as a symbol of appropriation and ownership—so evident in James Rennell's *Hindoostan* (1782)—has run throughout this study. I have not, however, paid it much attention because, in terms of the construction of imperial ideology, it seems to have been largely a red herring. Of more importance was the manner in which the archive, and especially the archive in the form of the *Atlas of India*, could be managed and controlled in London. With its triangulated framework, the production of the *Atlas* could deny the localness and contingency of geographical knowledge. The British geography of South Asia had attained universality and a perfectly nonindexical nature, so that it could be moved and manipulated anywhere. To borrow from Jorge Luis Borges, with whom I began my first chapter, the "Unconscionable Maps" had attained the size of the empire. Denis Wood is, of course, correct when he argues that maps themselves do not grow, but the archive of geographical knowledge which maps constitute does grow and accrete: the British archive of India had become complete and correct in its structure. The Great Trigonometrical Survey formed an abstract map at $1:1$; the triangulation of India *was* India.[56]

The power of this imperial representational system lay in its flexibility. All of the negotiations and flaws inherent to the system—the linguistic gulf between the British surveyors and their Indian aides and informants; the contestation of knowledge between the two sides; and, the structural constraints on the Company's acquisition of information—could and were easily managed. The flaws were not "hidden" by the system; that would imply too conscious a practice of knowledge construction. They were simply subsumed within cartographic representations. Displaying the world's structure, the surveyed map denies the possibility of any error other than the minor geometrical uncertainty inherent to any measurement. The surveyed map proclaims: this *is* the world. Reinforced by the technological and geometrical perfection offered by the trigonometrical surveys, this was a seductive and powerful message.

Obviously, I do not wish to argue that the maps which the British made of India were "lies" or that they constituted "propaganda." Such a position requires the presumption—common among academic cartographers—that the conditions which pertain in the *personal* exchanges of spatial information also pertain at the more complex level of the social exchanges of spatial information. But addressing a few people individually is a manifestly different process to addressing a mass of unknown individuals. At the level of mass culture, lies and propaganda are submerged in a sea of cultural expectations and beliefs; "propaganda maps" are not so much arguments as cultural and social reaffirmations. Maps are one of many means whereby cultures and societies, or segments thereof, redefine and reproduce themselves. Maps are representations of knowledge; as representations, they are constructed according to culturally defined semiotic codes; the knowledge is constructed using various intellectual and instrumental technologies; the knowledge and its representations are both constructed by individuals who work for and within various social institutions, according to cultural expectations. That is, the British did not mis-represent India when they made their maps of the subcontinent; nor did they re-present India, as they claimed. Instead, they created a geographical conception that served them well, within the confines of their imperial system. It is only when we consider the mapping of India from outside of that system that the British self-delusions and the mythic character of their geographical archive become evident.

To move outside of the British imperial system entails more than adopting an anticolonial perspective. It also requires the adoption of critical perspectives toward Modernity's scientism and toward modern cartography's empiricism. In this regard, this work has definite implications for the study of the development of systematic surveys by individual European states in the eighteenth and nineteenth centuries. In particular, it points to the close tie between the conception of the modern state and the Enlightenment's reformulation of space. The reconfiguration of each state's territories was not perhaps so ambiguous as that of British India. The construction of geographical panopticons by European states did entail the improvement and rationalization of territorial space, in order to make state control more efficient and effective. The agents of each state were much closer to the populations which were brought within the state's purview, so that European state formation did not require the same degree of justification as did British rule of India.

Even so, the rationalization of European space was not a simple process. It involved extensive mediation between the state's various social groups, both elite and common, so that each European state experienced a different particular form of spatial reconfiguration through maps and surveys. The implementation of the cartographic shift in epistemological certitude, from archival structuring of observations to structured observation, was different in each state. For the eighteenth and early nineteenth centuries at least, it would appear that all of the European states engaged in the creation of systematic cartographic *images*. Like the British in India, European surveyors were unable to implement the perfect systematic *survey*.

When I began this project about a decade ago, I sought to break away from the incorrect and lazy assumptions that have permeated so much of the study of cartographic history in the twentieth century. I would not treat governments as rational actors; nor would I aspire to the antiintellectual position that mapmaking is an unproblematic and neutral technology employed as a matter of course by all sufficiently advanced cultures (such that if it is not employed, then the respective culture must be at best unsophisticated or at worst intellectually deficient). But I soon found that I had started with at least one unexamined piece of intellectual baggage, in that I drew a sharp distinction between the processes of surveying and of map compilation. I had thought to reject a trait which I had discerned in several histories, in which the survey is confounded with the map. Yet, it is exactly the interwovenness of the survey and the map, of field observation and the archive, which lies at the heart of "systematic" mapping in the later Enlightenment. In the case of British India, the epistemological compromise was enshrined in the formation of a single office of surveyor general for all of India and then in the subordination of the Great Trigonometrical Survey to the *Atlas of India*.

Regardless of the geographer's rhetoric, mapmaking's translation "from the cabinet to the field" is incomplete.[57] The technologies of surveying, which is to say the technologies of observation and measurement, are part and parcel of the graphic representational practices of the map. This linkage is of course denied by those same practices, even as it is perhaps perpetuated by institutional conditions. Modernity's visual rhetoric privileges the observer with a vantage point separate from what is observed; vision's claims to truth conflate the observed with its self-effacing and "naturalistic" representation. One particular expression of that rhetoric is that of the surveyor—one who "watches from above"—and whose actions are as distanced from the "natural" map as from the land itself. Removing and disassembling the barriers between technique and intellect and between data and its representation has led me to a far more nuanced perspective on the British mapping of India than that with which I began.

I am not entirely certain that I have been able to portray adequately all of the subtleties involved in the British mapping of India. The remains and relicts of earlier positions no doubt survive to obscure the nuances. Nonetheless, the broad conclusion is clear: mapmaking was integral to British imperialism in India, not just as a highly effective informational weapon wielded strategically and tactically by directors, governors, military commanders, and field officials, but also as a significant component of the "structures of feeling" which legitimated, justified, and defined that imperialism. The surveys and maps together transformed the subcontinent from an exotic and largely unknown region into a well-defined and knowable geographical entity. The imperial space of India was a space of rhetoric and symbolism, rationality and science, dominance and separation, inclusion and exclusion. Its horizontal spatial boundaries, which enclosed, divided, and so gave political meaning to an otherwise homogenous space, merged imperceptibly with the vertical boundaries of the empire's social hierarchies. The empire might have defined the map's extent, but mapping defined the empire's nature.

BIOGRAPHICAL NOTES

This list is intended to alleviate some of the confusion caused by the proliferation of names throughout this book. It is not a comprehensive list of everyone involved in the British mapping of India, only those discussed in the text. Nor does the list contain all officers who constituted the central cadre of surveyors. Nobles are listed by their titles, as they are referred to in the text.

Airy, George Biddell. 1801–92; knighted, 1872. Astronomer royal, 1835–81.
Allan, Alexander. 1764–1820; cr. baronet, 1819. Madras infantry; captain of Guides, 1792–98; EIC director, 1814–20.
Amherst, Lord [William Pitt Amherst]. 1773–1857; baron Amherst, cr. earl Amherst, 1826. Governor general, 1822–28.
d'Anville, Jean Baptiste Bourguinon. 1697–1782. Parisian commercial cartographer. *Carte de l'Inde* (1752).
Arrowsmith, Aaron. 1750–1823. London commercial cartographer. *Improved Map of India* (1816); *Atlas of South India* (1822).
Arrowsmith, John. 1790–1873. London commercial cartographer, successor to his uncle, Aaron.
Arthur, Thomas. 1779–1817. Madras engineers; assistant, survey of Mysore, 1800–1805; engineer and surveyor, Travancore, 1807–16.
HRH Augustus. 1773–1843; duke of Sussex. Grandmaster of Freemasons, 1811; president, Society of Arts, 1816; president, Royal Society, 1830–38.

Baily, Francis. 1774–1844. Stockbroker and amateur astronomer; founding member, Royal Astronomical Society, 1820.
Barlow, George H. 1762–1846; cr. baronet, 1803. Acting governor general, 1805–7; governor, Madras, 1807–14.
Barnard, Thomas. 1746–1830. Madras engineers (civil); survey of the Madras jagīr (Chingleput district), 1767–74.
Barrow, Henry. 1790/1–1870. Mathematical instrument maker, GTS, 1830–39.
Beaufort, Francis. 1774–1857. RN; Admiralty hydrographer, 1829–55.
Bedford, James. 1788–1871. Bengal infantry; revenue surveyor, 1821–24, 1827–32; deputy surveyor general and superintendent of Bengal revenue surveys, 1832–42.

Bellasis, John Brownrigg. 1806–90. Bombay infantry; revenue survey, Deccan, 1837–39.

Bentinck, Lord William Cavendish. 1774–1839. Governor, Madras, 1803–7; governor general, 1828–35.

Blacker, Valentine. 1778–1826. Madras cavalry; quartermaster general, Madras, 1810–19; surveyor general, 1823–36.

Blair, John. 1774–1812. Madras engineers; engineer and surveyor, Travancore, 1805–7, and Hyderabad, 1807–11.

Blake, Benjamin. 1788–1838. Bengal infantry; river surveys, 1822–24.

Blunt, James T. 1765/6–1834. Bengal engineers; made various surveys, 1787–1807.

Boileau, Alexander. 1807–62. Bengal engineers; surveyor after 1827; assistant, GTS, 1832–38.

Buchanan, Francis. 1762–1829, took name Francis Buchanan Hamilton, 1818. Bengal medical; statistical and geographic surveys of Mysore, 1800–1801, and Bengal, 1807–14.

Burrow, Reuben. 1747–92. Mathematics and surveying teacher to Royal Engineers, 1776–82, and to Bengal engineers, 1784–92; astronomical survey of Upper Provinces, 1787–89; arc measurement, Bengal, 1790–91.

Buxton, Bentley. 1796–1825. Bengal engineers; survey of Orissa, 1818–21.

Call, John. 1732–1801. Madras engineers; chief engineer, Madras, 1760–70.

Call, Thomas. 1749–88. Bengal engineers; surveyor general, Bengal, 1777–86; chief engineer, Bengal, 1786–88.

Camac, Jacob. 1745–84. Bengal infantry; occasional mapmaker.

Cameron, Hugh. ?–1764. Bombay artillery; "surveyor of the New Lands," Bengal, 1761–64.

Clive, Lord [Edward Clive]. 1754–1839; baron Clive, cr. earl of Powis, 1804. Governor, Madras, 1798–1803.

Clive, Robert. 1725–74; cr. baron Clive, 1762. Victor of Plassey, 1757; governor, Bengal, 1758–59 and 1765–67.

Colby, Thomas Frederick. 1784–1852. Royal Engineers; director general, Ordnance Survey, 1820–47.

Colebrooke, Robert Hyde. 1762/3–1808. Bengal infantry; surveyor general of Bengal, 1794–1808.

Conner, Peter Eyre. 1789–1821. Madras infantry; Military Institution, 1807–9; surveys of Koorg, Travancore, and Hyderabad, 1815–21.

Cornwallis, Lord [Charles Cornwallis]. 1738–1805; earl Cornwallis, cr. marquess Cornwallis, 1792. Governor general and commander in chief, India, 1786–93 and 1805.

Craddock, Sir John. 1762–1839. Commander in chief, Madras, 1804–7.

Crawford, Charles. 1760–1836. Bengal infantry; surveyor general, Bengal, 1813–15.

Curnin, John. ?–1849. Astronomer, Bombay, 1822–28.

Dalrymple, Alexander. 1730–1808. Member of Madras council, 1775–77; EIC hydrographer, 1779–1808; Admiralty hydrographer, 1795–1808.

Dangerfield, Frederick. 1789–1828. Bombay infantry; survey of Malwa, 1818–21.

Daniell, Thomas. 1749–1840. Artist; in India, 1786–94.

Daniell, William. 1769–1837. Artist; in India, 1786–94.

DeHavilland, Thomas Fiotte. 1775–1866. Madras engineers; engineer, Hyderabad subsidiary force, 1805–9; superintendent, tank department, Madras.

Delambre, Jean Baptiste. 1749–1822. French astronomer and geodesist.

Denison, William Thomas. 1804–71; knighted 1846. Royal Engineers; governor, Madras, 1861–66; acting governor general, 1863.

de Penning, Joshua. 1784–1845. Revenue Survey School, 1798–1803; civil assistant on Lambton's general survey and GTS, 1803–24.

Dickenson, Thomas. 1783–1861. Bombay engineers; revenue survey, Bombay Island, 1812–21; chief engineer, Bombay.

Dinwiddie, James. 1746–1815. Astronomer on Lord Macartney's embassy to China, 1792–94; mathematics teacher, Calcutta, 1795–1806.

Edmondstone, Neil Benjamin. 1765–1841; baronet. Persian secretary, Bengal, 1794–98; Lord Wellesley's private secretary, 1798–1803; EIC director, 1820–41.

Ellenborough, Lord [Edward Law]. 1790–1871; baron Ellenborough, cr. Earl Ellenborough, 1844. President, Board of Control, 1829–31 and 1834–35; governor general, 1842–44.

Elphinstone, Mountstuart. 1779–1859. Governor, Bombay, 1819–27.

Everest, George. 1790–1866; knighted 1861. Bengal artillery; assistant, GTS, 1818–23; superintendent, GTS, 1823–43; surveyor general of India, 1830–43.

Everest, Rev. Robert. 1798–1870. Bengal chaplain.

Franklin, James. 1783–1834. Bengal cavalry; survey of Bundelcund, 1813–21 (intermittent).

Gardner, James. ?–?. Draftsman, Board of Ordnance [map] Drawing Office; assistant, Ordnance Survey, 1791–1822; agent (map–seller) for OS, 1822.

Garling, James. 1784–1820. Madras infantry; assistant instructor, Military Institution, 1806–8; survey of Goa and Sonda, 1810–15; survey of the Nizam's dominions, 1816–20.

Garstin, John. 1756–1820. Bengal engineers; surveyor general, Bengal, 1808–13; chief engineer, Bengal, 1810–13.

Gentil, Jean Baptiste Joseph. 1726–99. French infantry officer and orientalist; at court of Shuja–ud–daula, Nawab of Awadh, 1760–75.

Gerard, Alexander. 1782–1839. Bengal infantry; revenue surveyor; surveys of Kunawar, 1817–18 and 1821–22; survey of Malwa and Rajputana, 1822–23, 1826.

Goldingham, John. ?–1849. Superintendent, Revenue Survey School, Madras, 1794–1805; Company's astronomer, Madras, 1796–1830.

Grant, Peter Warden. 1794–1828. Bengal infantry; surveyor and agent in Gorakhpur and Nepal frontier, 1817–25.

Greenough, George Bellas. 1778–1855. First president, Geological Society of London, 1811–23, 1833–39; president, Royal Geographical Society, 1839–40; geological map of India, 1854.

Haider Ali. ?–1782. Ruler of Mysore, 1761–82.

Hastings, Lord [Francis Rawdon]. 1754–1836; earl of Moira, cr. marquis of Hastings, 1816. Master general of Ordnance, 1806–7; governor general and commander in chief, India, 1813–23.

Hastings, Warren. 1732–1818. Governor general of India, 1774–85; orientalist.

Herbert, James Dowling. 1791–1835. Bengal infantry; surveys of the Himalaya, 1816–21 and 1824–28; assistant surveyor general, 1821–24, 1828–29; deputy surveyor general, 1829–31; founding editor, *Gleanings in Science,* 1829–31; astronomer to Nawab of Awadh, 1831–35.

Herschel, John Frederick William. 1792–1871; knighted, 1831, cr. baronet, 1838. Astronomer.

Hewett, Sir George. 1750–1840. Commander in chief, India, 1807–11.

Heyne, Benjamin. ?–1819. Madras medical; botanist; assistant, Mysore survey, 1799–1802.

Hobhouse, John Cam. 1786–1869; baronet, cr. baron Broughton, 1851. President, Board of Control, 1835–41 and 1846–52.

Hodges, William. 1744–97. Artist; in India, 1780–83.

Hodgson, John Anthony. 1777–1848. Bengal infantry; surveyor general, 1821–23 and 1826–29; revenue surveyor general, Bengal, 1823–26.

Horsburgh, James. 1762–1836. EIC marine; EIC hydrographer and map publisher, 1810–36.

Humboldt, Alexander [von]. 1769–1859. Prominent geographer.

Hunter, William. 1755–1813. Bengal medical; amateur astronomer and surveyor.

Jacob, William Stephen. 1813–62. Bombay engineers; assistant, Bombay triangulation and GTS, 1833–38, 1840–43; astronomer at Madras, 1849–58.

Jervis, George Ritso. 1794–1852. Bombay engineers.

Jervis, Thomas Best. 1796–1857. Bombay engineers; survey of the Konkan, 1819–30; provisionally appointed surveyor general, 1837.

Johnstone, Alexander. 1775–1849; knighted 1811. Chief justice, Ceylon, 1805–9; president, Ceylon council, 1811–19; founding member, Royal Asiatic Society, 1823.

Jones, John. 1801–75. Bengal infantry; surveys in Assam, 1826–28.

Jones, William. 1746–94; knighted, 1783. Calcutta High Court, 1783–94; founder, Asiatic Society of Bengal, 1784.

Jopp, John. 1792–1861. Bombay engineers; deputy surveyor general, Bombay, 1826–33.

Kater, Henry. 1777–1835. HM 12th Foot; assistant, Lambton's general survey, 1803–6; metrologist.

Kelly, Robert. 1738–90. Madras infantry; avid surveyor, producing an "Atlas of the South Peninsula" in 1781.

Kirkpatrick, William. 1754–1812. Bengal infantry; resident at Hyderabad, 1793–98; orientalist.

Kyd, Alexander. 1754–1826. Bengal engineers; surveyor general, Bengal, 1788–94; chief engineer, Bengal, 1807–10.

Laidlaw, Alexander. ?–1836. Geological assistant, survey of Himalayas, 1817–18.

Lambton, William. 1753/6–1823. HM 33rd Foot; general survey of southern India, 1800–1818; superintendent, GTS, 1818–23.

Leyden, John. 1775–1811. Madras medical; assistant, Mysore survey, 1804–5; linguist.

Lloyd, Rev. Humphrey. 1800–1881. Professor of natural and experimental philosophy, Trinity College Dublin, 1831–62.

Macauley, Thomas Babington. 1800–1859. Legal member, Council of India, 1834–37; historian.

Mackenzie, Colin. 1754–1821. Madras engineers; engineer and surveyor, Nizam's Dominions, 1792–99; survey of Mysore, 1799–1808; surveyor general, Madras, 1810–15; surveyor general, 1815–21.

Malcolm, Sir John. 1769–1833. Bombay infantry and diplomat; governor, Bombay, 1827–30.

Maskelyne, Nevil. 1732–1811. Astronomer royal, 1765–1811.

Mather, John. ?–1808. Civil surveyor; survey of the Baramahal, 1794–98; assistant, survey of Mysore, 1799–1806.

Metcalfe, Charles T. M. 1785–1846; cr. baron Metcalfe, 1845. Acting governor general, 1835–36.

Minto, Lord [Gilbert Elliot]. 1751–1814; baron Minto, cr. earl of Minto, 1813. Governor general, 1807–13.

Mohsin Husain, Syed Mir. ?–1864. Instrument maker, surveyor general's office, 1824–43; GTS mathematical instrument maker, 1843–54.

Monteith, William. 1790–1864. Madras engineers; military observer in Persia, Russia, and Turkey, 1810–29.

Montgomerie, Duncan. 1789–1878. Madras cavalry; Military Institution, 1809–11; deputy surveyor general, Madras, 1824–33; astronomer, Madras, 1827–30.

Morison, William. 1781–1851; knighted 1848. Madras artillery; assistant, survey of Mysore, 1802–4; acting surveyor general of Madras, 1811–15; member, Council of India, 1834–39.

Mountford, Francis. 1790–1824. Madras infantry; Military Institution, 1809–11; assistant and deputy (1823) surveyor general, Madras, 1818–24.

Munro, Thomas. 1761–1827; cr. baronet, 1826. Madras infantry; commissioner, Ceded Districts of Mysore, 1800–1807; governor, Madras, 1820–27.

Olliver, Joseph. 1785/6–?. Revenue Survey School, 1800–1804; civil assistant on Lambton's general survey and GTS, 1804–42.

Orme, Robert. 1728–1801. Madras accountant general, 1757–58; EIC historian, 1768–1801.

Pasley, Charles William. 1780–1861; KCB 1846. Royal Engineers; commandant at Chatham, 1812–41; public examiner, East India College, Addiscombe, 1839–55.

Peach, Rev. Samuel. ?–?. One of Lambton's creditors; certainly related to Samuel Peach of Gloucestershire (1725–1790), EIC director (1773–1781), whose family had ties to some of the London and Cambridge science circles.

Petrie, William. ?–1816. Founder, Company's Observatory at Madras, 1789; acting governor, Madras, 1807.

Playfair, William. 1759–1823. Mathematician.

Pond, John. 1767–1836. Astronomer royal, 1811–35.

Pringle, John. ?–1788. Madras infantry; surveyor; organizer of the corps of Guides, 1777–88.

Prinsep, Henry Thoby. 1793–1878. Persian secretary, Bengal, 1820–40; member, Council of India, 1840–43.

Prinsep, James. 1799–1840. Assay master at Benares, 1820–30, and Calcutta, 1830–38; secretary, Asiatic Society of Bengal, 1832–38; polymath.

Prinsep, Thomas. 1800–1830. Bengal engineers; survey of Sundarbans, 1821–24; canal and river surveys, 1826–30.

Radhanath Sickdhar. 1813–70. Computer and assistant, GTS, 1831–62.

Read, Alexander. 1751–1804. Madras infantry; superintendent of revenue, Baramahal, 1792–99.

Rennell, James. 1742–1830. Bengal engineers; survey of Bengal, 1765–77; surveyor general, Bengal, 1767–77; thereafter London commercial cartographer. *Atlas of Bengal* (1780, 1781); *Hindoostan* (1782); *New Map of Hindoostan* (1788).

Renny[–Tailyour], Thomas. 1812–85. Bengal engineers; assistant, GTS, 1832–54.

Reynolds, Charles. 1756/8–1819. Bombay infantry; surveyor general of Bombay, 1796–1807.

Richards, William. 1745–?. Bengal engineers; assistant, survey of Bengal, 1765–72.

Riddell, John. 1785–1818. Madras infantry; Military Institution, 1806–8; assistant surveyor general, Madras, 1817–18.

Righey, Henry. 1811–81. Bengal engineers; assistant, GTS, 1831.

Ross, James Clark. 1800–1862. RN; arctic explorer.

Ross, Patrick. ca. 1740–1804. Madras engineers; chief engineer, Madras, 1770–1803.

Roxburgh, William. 1751–1815. Madras medical; superintendent, Calcutta Botanical Garden, 1793–1813.

Roy, William. 1726–90. Royal Engineers; military survey of Scotland, 1747–55; geodetic link from Greenwich to Paris, 1784–89.

Russell, Lord John. 1792–1878; cr. earl Russell, 1861. member of Parliament, 1813–61; prime minister, 1846–52 and 1865–66.

Sabine, Edward. 1788–1883. Royal Engineers; geologist.
Salmond, James. ?–1837. Bengal infantry; EIC military secretary, 1809–37.
Salt, Henry. 1780–1827. Artist; in India, 1803–5.
Scott, David. 1786–1831. Governor general's agent for the northeastern frontier, 1823–31.
Scott, William. ca. 1786–1827. Revenue Survey School, 1798–1801; assistant to John Warren, 1801–10.
Shortrede [Shortreed], Robert. 1801–68. Bombay Infantry; trigonometrical survey of Bombay and GTS, 1828–36, 1838–45; Punjab revenue survey, 1851–61.
Stannus, Ephraim Gerrish. 1784–1850; knighted, 1837. Bombay infantry; lieutenant–governor, East India College, Addiscombe, 1834–50.
Stuart, James. 1741–1815. HM 78th Foot; commander in chief, Madras, 1796–1804.
Sutherland, James. 1780/2–1850. Bombay infantry; assistant to surveyor general, Bombay, 1802–8; survey of western Deccan, 1818–22; assistant and deputy (1823) surveyor general, Bombay, 1822–26.
Sydenham, Thomas. ca. 1780–1816. Madras infantry; resident at Pune and Hyderabad, 1804–10.

Tassin, Jean Baptiste. ?–?. French printer in India, 1828–41.
Tate, William Ashmead. 1795–1871. Bombay engineers; revenue survey, Bombay Island, 1821–27; professor of military drawing, Addiscombe, 1849–59.
Tieffenthaler, Père Joseph. 1710–85. SJ; missionary and amateur astronomer.
Tipu Sultan. ?–1799. Ruler of Mysore, 1782–99.
Topping, Michael. ca. 1747–96. Marine surveyor, 1785–96; Company's astronomer, Madras, 1789–96.
Troyer, Anthony Ferdinand. 1775–1865. HM 12th Foot; instructor, Madras Military Institution, 1804–16; secretary, Sanskrit College of Calcutta, 1828–35.

Voysey, Henry Westley. ?–1824. Surgeon with HM 59th, 46th, and 1st Foot; natural historian; assistant, GTS, 1818–24.

Walker, John. 1787–1873. London commercial cartographer, working as "J. & C. Walker"; EIC hydrographer, 1836–58. *Atlas of India*, 1825–68.
Wallich, Nathaniel [né Wulff]. 1756–1854. Bengal medical; superintendent, Calcutta botanical gardens, 1814–42.
Walpole, Henry. 1787–1854. Madras infantry; assistant instructor, Military Institution, 1811–15; nominated to be surveyor general, 1829.
Walters, Henry. ?–?. Judge, Dacca and Sylhet courts, 1813–38; trip to Khāsi Hills, 1828.
Ward, Benjamin Swain. 1786–1835. Madras infantry; Revenue Survey School, 1798–1801; assistant to Colin Mackenzie, 1801–10, when commissioned; on several surveys, 1816–30.

Warren, John [Jean Baptiste François Joseph de]. 1769–1830; comte de Warren, 1816. HM 33rd and 56th Foot; assistant, survey of Mysore, 1799–1802; assistant, Lambton's general survey, 1802–5; acting astronomer, Madras, 1805–10.

Washington, John. 1800–1863. RN; hydrographer; secretary, Royal Geographical Society, 1836–41.

Watson, Brooke. 1735–1807; cr. baronet, 1803. Commissary general in Canada, 1782–83, and Flanders, 1793–95; lord mayor of London, 1796–97.

Watson, Henry. 1737–1786. Bengal engineers; chief engineer, Bengal, 1777–86.

Waugh, Andrew Scott. 1810–78; knighted 1860. Bengal engineers; assistant, GTS, 1832–43; superintendent, GTS, and surveyor general, 1843–61.

Webb, William Spencer. 1784–1865. Bengal infantry; survey of Kumaon, 1815–21.

Webbe, Josiah. 1767–1804. Secretary to Madras council, 1798–1801; resident at Mysore, 1801–4.

Wellesley, Arthur. 1769–1852; cr. duke of Wellington, 1814. Colonel, HM 33rd Foot; prime minister, 1828–30.

Wellesley, Lord [Richard C. Wellesley]. 1760–1842; earl of Mornington, cr. Marquis Wellesley, 1799. Governor general, 1798–1805.

Western, James Roger. 1812–71. Bengal engineers; assistant, GTS, 1831–34.

Whewell, Rev. William. 1794–1866. Mathematician and moral philosopher.

Wilcox, Richard. 1802–48. Bengal infantry; surveys in Assam, 1824–31; assistant, GTS, 1832–35; astronomer to the Nawab of Awadh, 1835–48.

Wilford, Francis. 1750/1–1822. Bengal engineers; in surveyor general's office, 1783–88; survey of Benares, 1788–94; secretary, Benares Sanskrit College, after 1800.

Williams, Monier. 1777–1823. Bombay infantry; surveyor general of Bombay, 1807–15.

Wood, Mark. 1750–1829. Bengal engineers; surveyor general, Bengal, 1786–88; chief engineer, Bengal, 1788–93.

NOTES

To keep the citations short (!) I have omitted references for most details of individual surveys. Readers who want further access to those citations should refer to Reginald Phillimore's *Historical Records of the Survey of India* (Dehra Dun: Survey of India, 1945–58, 4 vols.) and to my original dissertation, "Mapping and Empire: British Trigonometrical Surveys of India and the European Concept of Systematic Survey, 1799–1843" (University of Wisconsin-Madison, 1990; UMI order no. AAC 9027493).

Full references for works cited with short titles can be found earlier in the sequence of notes for each chapter, and (printed materials) in the bibliography as well.

Abbreviations Used in the Notes

I have followed the system of abbreviations for the East India Company's records used by Phillimore in his *Historical Records* in order to allow an easy comparison of sources. The bibliography gives further information on abbreviations for specific record series held in archives marked with an asterisk.

B	Bengal Government
BL	*British Library
BMC	Bengal Military Consultation
Bo	Bombay Government
BoMC	Bombay Military Consultation
BoPC	Bombay Public Consultation
BoRC	Bombay Revenue Consultation
BPC	Bengal Public Consultation
BRC	Bombay Revenue Consultation
CD	Court of Directors of the East India Company
CPL	*Cleveland Public Library
CUL	*Cambridge University Library
EIC	East India Company
GTS	Great Trigonometrical Survey
IMC	India Military Consultation
IPoC	India Political Consultation
IOR	*India Office Records
jud	Judicial Department
M	Madras Government
mil	Military Department
MMC	Madras Military Consultation
MMPoC	Madras Military and Political Consultation

MPC	Madras Public Consultation
MRB	Madras Revenue Board, Proceedings
MRC	Madras Revenue Consultation
nd	not dated
np	not paginated/foliated
pol	Political Department
PRO	*Public Record Office
pub	Public Department
RAS	*Royal Astronomical Society
rev	Revenue Department
RGS	*Royal Geographical Society
RS	*Royal Society
sec	Secret Department
sep	Separate Despatch
UN	*University of Nottingham
US	*University of Southampton

Chapter One

1. Jorge Luis Borges, "Museum: On Rigor in Science," in *Dreamtigers*, translated by Mildred Boyer and Harold Morland (Austin: University of Texas Press, 1964), 90.

2. Claude Nicolet, *Space, Geography, and Politics in the Early Roman Empire*, Jerome Lectures, 19 (Ann Arbor: University of Michigan Press, 1991), 2.

3. Susan Faye Cannon, *Science in Culture: The Early Victorian Period* (New York: Science History Publications, 1978), 251. See John K. Noyes, *Colonial Space: Spatiality in the Discourse of German South West Africa, 1884–1915*, Studies in Anthropology and History, 4 (Chur, Switzerland: Harwood Academic Publishers, 1992).

4. Samuel Johnson in *Rambler* 23, quoted in Alvin Kernan, *Samuel Johnson and the Impact of Print* (Princeton: Princeton University Press, 1987), 18.

5. Matthew H. Edney, "Cartography without 'Progress': Reinterpreting the Nature and Historical Development of Mapmaking," *Cartographica* 30, nos. 2 and 3 (1993): 54–68.

6. Donald K. Emmerson, "'Southeast Asia': What's in a Name?" *Journal of Southeast Asian Studies* 15 (1984): 1–21.

7. This argument is borne out by Donald F. Lach and Edwin J. van Kley, *A Century of Advance: South Asia*, vol. 3.2 of *Asia in the Making of Europe* (Chicago: University of Chicago Press, 1993), annotations to plates 107–11, 134–36; Susan Gole, *Early Maps of India*, foreword by Irfan Habib (New York: Humanities Press; New Delhi: Sanskriti, 1976); Gole, *India within the Ganges* (New Delhi: Jayaprints, 1983); Gole, comp., *A Series of Early Printed Maps of India in Facsimile* (New Delhi: Jayaprints, 1980). On names, see Henry Yule and A. C. Burnell, *Hobson-Jobson: A Glossary of Colloquial Anglo-Indian Words and Phrases, and of Kindred Terms, Etymological, Historical, Geographical and Discursive*, new edition, edited by William Crooke (London, 1903; reprint, Delhi: Munshiram Manoharlal, 1968), 416 ("Hindostan"), 433–37 ("India/Indies").

8. Margarita Bowen, *Empiricism and Geographical Thought from Francis Bacon to Alexander von Humboldt* (Cambridge: Cambridge University Press, 1981), 144–73, on texts; the cartographic aspect of this phenomenon has not been discussed.

9. J. B. B. d'Anville, *Carte de l'Inde dressée pour la Compagnie des Indes* (Paris, 1752); d'Anville, *Eclaircissemens géographiques sur la Carte de l'Inde* (Paris: Imprimerie royale, 1753), vi, re his dissatisfaction; L. Ch. J. Manne and Jean Denis Barbié du Bocage, *Notice des ouvrages de M d'Anville, Premier Géographe du Roi . . .* (Paris, 1802), no. 162. D'Anville,

Coromandel (Paris, 1753); Manne and Barbié du Bocage, no. 165; cf. d'Anville, *Carte des côtes de Malabar et de Coromandel* (Paris, 1737).

10. James Rennell, *Hindoostan* (London, 1782); Rennell, *Memoir of a Map of Hindoostan; or the Mogul's Empire: With an Examination of some Positions in the Former System of Indian Geography* . . . (London, 1783; 2d ed., 1785), cited hereafter as *Memoir I*. Rennell, *A New Map of Hindoostan* (London, 1788); Rennell, *Memoir of a Map of Hindoostan; or the Mogul Empire: with an Introduction, Illustrative of the Geography and Present Division of that Country* . . . (London, 1788; 2d ed., 1792; 3d ed., 1793), cited hereafter as *Memoir II*. See chapter 3 for details of the publication history of both maps and memoirs.

11. Clements R. Markham, *Major James Rennell and the Rise of Modern English Geography* (London: Cassell & Co., 1895), is still the best biography. Several highly derivative essays are listed in the bibliography. Rennell's work was translated into French and German; see reviews in *Monatliche Correspondenz zur Beförderung der Erd- und Himmels-Kunde* 4 (1801): 341–44, and 12 (1805): 250–56.

12. Rennell, *Memoir I* (1st ed.), iv, repeated in *Memoir II* (1st ed.), vi.

13. Rennell, *Memoir I* (1st ed.), 1–2, repeated in *Memoir II* (1st ed.), xix–xx. Original emphasis.

14. James Rennell, *Memoir of a Map of the Peninsula of India* . . . *with Observations on the Political and Military Advantages that may be Derived from the new Cessions* (London, 1793), iii (advertisement, dated 7 Dec 1792). Rennell expressed other pro-empire sentiments in *Memoir I* (1st ed.), 16, and (2d ed.), 19–20; Rennell, *Memoir II* (1st ed.), vii, cv–cvii, and (2d ed.), v.

15. Rennell, *Memoir I* (1st ed.), xii. Two recent essays with different readings of the cartouche suffer from not having seen this explanation: Rosane Rocher, "British Orientalism in the Eighteenth Century: The Dialectics of Knowledge and Government," David Ludden, "Orientalist Empiricism: Transformations of Colonial Knowledge," both in *Orientalism and the Postcolonial Predicament: Perspectives on South Asia*, edited by Carol A. Breckenridge and Peter van der Veer (Philadelphia: University of Pennsylvania Press, 1993), 215–49, esp. 223, and 250–78, esp. 254–55, respectively.

16. Barbara Groseclose, "Imag(in)ing Indians," *Art History* 13 (1990): 488–515, esp. 496. Compare to a 1778 painting, originally in the India House, reproduced by Thomas Metcalf, *Ideologies of the Raj*, vol. 3.4 of *New Cambridge History of India* (Cambridge: Cambridge University Press, 1994), 16.

17. Dirk H. A. Kolff, "End of an *Ancien Régime:* Colonial War in India, 1798–1818," in *Imperialism and War: Essays on Colonial Wars in Asia and Africa*, edited by J. A. de Moor and H. L. Wesseling (Leiden: E. J. Brill, 1989), 22–49.

18. Arthur D. Innes, *A Short History of British India* (London, 1902; reprint, New Delhi: Inter-India, 1985), v; refer also to a similar example quoted in Ronald Inden, *Imagining India* (Oxford: Basil Blackwell, 1990), 9. Yule and Burnell, *Hobson-Jobson*, 433–34, assume an "India Proper," to which all other terms refer inexactly.

19. Ainslee Embree, *Imagining India: Essays on Indian History*, edited by Mark Juergensmeyer (Delhi: Oxford University Press, 1989), 9–27, 67–84, esp. 67, quoting a memorandum, 30 Oct 1959, from the Embassy of India to the Chinese Ministry of Foreign Affairs.

20. Benedict Anderson, *Imagined Communities*, 2d ed. (London: Verso, 1991), 163, 174–78. Thailand was not directly colonized by any European nation; the Thai state nonetheless adopted Western geographical conceptions and incorporated them into its nationalistic rhetoric; see Thongchai Winichakul's excellent study: *Siam Mapped: A History of the Geo-Body of a Nation* (Honolulu: University of Hawaii Press, 1994).

21. Paul Carter, *The Road to Botany Bay: A Spatial History* (London: Faber and Faber,

1987), xv; see John K. Noyes, "The Representation of Spatial History," *Pretexts* 4, no. 2 (1993): 120–27.

22. B. B. Misra, *The Unification and Division of India* (Delhi: Oxford University Press, 1990), introduction.

23. In addition to a considerable dedicated literature, listed in the bibliography, Rennell's survey is featured in *all* of the general works on British mapping in India; Andrew S. Cook, "Major James Rennell and 'A Bengal Atlas' (1780 and 1781)," in *India Office Library and Records Report for the Year 1976* (London: British Library, 1978), 5–42, is essential reading.

24. I discuss these issues in "Cartography without 'Progress'," 61–63; "British Military Education, Mapmaking, and Military 'Map-Mindedness' in the Later Enlightenment," *The Cartographic Journal* 31, no. 1 (1994): 14–20; "Mathematical Cosmography and the Social Ideology of British Cartography, 1780–1820," *Imago Mundi* 46 (1994): 101–16; and, "Cartographic Culture and Nationalism in the Early United States: Benjamin Vaughan and the Choice for a Prime Meridian, 1811," *Journal of Historical Geography* 20, no. 4 (1994): 384–95.

25. George Biddell Airy, "Figure of the Earth," dated 17 Aug 1830, *Encyclopaedia Metropolitana* 5 (1845): 165–*240, esp. 165.

26. J. B. Harley, "Historical Geography and the Cartographic Illusion," *Journal of Historical Geography* 15 (1989): 80–91; Harley, "Deconstructing the Map," *Cartographica* 26, no. 2 (1989): 1–20. Triangulation's technological fix was a key stage in the "time-space compression" which David Harvey, *The Condition of Postmodernity: An Enquiry into the Origins of Cultural Change* (Oxford: Basil Blackwell, 1989), identified as a key element in Enlightenment thought.

27. Stephen M. Stigler, *The History of Statistics: The Measurement of Uncertainty before 1900* (Cambridge, MA: Harvard University Press, 1986), 11–158. On the shift from theory to praxis, see Volker Bialas, *Erdgestalt, Kosmologie und Weltanschauung: Die Geschichte der Geodäsie als Teil der Kulturgeschichte der Menscheit* (Stuttgart: Konrad Winter, 1982); and Anne Godlewska, "Traditions, Crisis, and New Paradigms in the Rise of the Modern French Discipline of Geography, 1760–1850," *Annals of the Association of American Geographers* 79 (1989): 192–213.

28. Airy, "Figure of the Earth," 173.

29. Unless otherwise noted, all of the shorter essays listed in the bibliography fall into this category. Of the earliest essays, the least simplified is William M. Coldstream, "Indian Maps and Surveys," *Journal of the Royal Society of Arts* 74 (1926): 299–320. G. F. Heaney, "Rennell and the Surveyors of India," *Geographical Journal* 134 (1968): 318–27, was the principal source for John Noble Wilford, "Soldiers, Pundits, and the India Survey," in *The Mapmakers: The Story of the Great Pioneers in Cartography from Antiquity to the Space Age* (New York: Random House, 1981), 161–73. Recent histories of cartography have simply copied the Heaney/Wilford sequence, for example, the television essay, "Empire!" part 4 of "The Shape of the World," by Granada TV/WGBH-TV Boston (1991) and the associated text, Simon Berthon and Andrew Robinson, *The Shape of the World: The Mapping and Discovery of the Earth* (London: Granada Television; Chicago: Rand McNally, 1991), 133–49. David N. Livingstone, *The Geographical Tradition: Episodes in the History of a Contested Enterprise* (Oxford: Basil Blackwell, 1992), 242–43, most recently on the St. Thomas's Mount baseline; George Buist, "Proceedings: Geographical Research in 1854–55," *Transactions of the Bombay Geographical Society* 12 (1854–56): lxxiv–xciii, esp. xcii, however, identified 14 Nov 1800, the start of Lambton's trial Bangalore base measurement, as a "red letter day in the annals of Indian geodesy."

30. Andrew Scott Waugh, "Report and Statements of the Operations and Expense of the Trigonometrical Survey of India," *British Parliamentary Papers* 1851 (219) 41: 875–936;

see *Journal of the House of Commons* 105 (15 Feb 1850): 63–64, and "The Great Trigonometrical Survey of India," *The Calcutta Review* 16 (1851): 514–40, for the report's context.

31. Clements R. Markham, *A Memoir on the Indian Surveys*, 2d ed. (London: Allen & Co., 1878; reprint, Amsterdam: Meridian Publishing, 1968). See Donovan Williams, "Clements Robert Markham and the Geographical Department of the India Office, 1867–77," *Geographical Journal* 134 (1968): 343–52; Charles E. D. Black, *A Memoir on the Indian Surveys, 1875–1890* (London, 1891).

32. Reginald H. Phillimore, *Historical Records of the Survey of India* (Dehra Dun: Survey of India, 1945–58, 4 vols.), 1: x.

33. Lloyd A. Brown, *The Story of Maps* (New York: 1949; reprint, New York: Dover, 1979), 241–309, is the paradigmatic statement concerning the adoption of triangulation-based surveys. A succinct expression of Brown's agenda is his "Maps: The Necessary Medium to World Progress," *Surveying and Mapping* 13 (1953): 277–85. Brown's treatment of the surveys in India was quite cursory.

34. Especially J. B. Harley, "Maps, Knowledge and Power," in *The Iconography of Landscape*, edited by Denis Cosgrove and Stephen J. Daniels (Cambridge: Cambridge University Press, 1988), 277–312; Harley, "Deconstructing the Map."

35. Edward W. Said, "Yeats and Decolonization," in *Nationalism, Colonialism, and Literature*, by Terry Eagleton, Frederick Jameson, and Edward W. Said (Minneapolis: University of Minnesota Press, 1990), 69–95, quotes from 72 and 77. Said began this argument in *Orientalism* (New York: Random House, 1978), in which the geography/culture link is strictly metaphorical; it is less so in his *Culture and Imperialism* (New York: Alfred A. Knopf, 1993).

36. Michel Foucault, *Discipline and Punish: The Birth of the Prison*, translated by Alan Sheridan (New York: Random House, 1977), 195 and 201, 195–228, on "panopticism" generally.

37. To be fair, Foucault subsequently acknowledged the overly pessimistic character of *Discipline and Punish*; see Robert Young, *White Mythologies: Writing History and the West* (London: Routledge, 1990), 87.

38. John M. Mackenzie, *Orientalism: History, Theory and the Arts* (Manchester: Manchester University Press, 1995), 1–42, 208–15, provides a succinct critique of Saidean arguments.

39. Lewis Carroll, *Sylvie and Bruno Concluded* (London: Macmillan, 1894), 169, re a supposed map at 1:1. Umberto Eco, "On the Impossibility of Drawing a Map of the Empire on a Scale of 1 to 1," in *How to Travel with a Salmon & Other Essays*, translated by William Weaver (New York: Harcourt Brace, 1994), 95–106; my thanks to Matthew Bampton for this reference. The "uselessness" of such a map is recognized by Borges, "On Rigor in Science."

40. Josef W. Konvitz, *Cartography in France, 1660–1848: Science, Engineering, and Statecraft* (Chicago: University of Chicago Press, 1987), 1–31.

41. Roger J. P. Kain and Elizabeth Baigent, *The Cadastral Map in the Service of the State: A History of Property Mapping* (Chicago: University of Chicago Press, 1992).

42. J. H. Andrews, *A Paper Landscape: The Ordnance Survey in Nineteenth-Century Ireland* (Oxford: Clarendon Press, 1975); Richard Oliver, "The Ordnance Survey in Great Britain, 1835–1870," D.Phil. diss. (University of Sussex, 1986).

43. Coldstream, "Indian Maps and Surveys," 301.

44. Andrew S. Cook, " 'More by Accident than Design': The Development of Topographical Mapping in India in the Nineteenth Century," presented to the Eleventh International Conference on the History of Cartography, Ottawa, 1985; *Report of the Indian Survey Committee, 1904–5*, 3 vols. (Simla: Government Central Printing Office, 1905). Deepak Kumar, "Problems in Science Administration: A Study of the Scientific Surveys in

British India, 1757–1900," in *Science and Empires: Historical Studies about Scientific Development and European Expansion,* edited by Patrick Petitjohn, Catherine Jami, and Anne Marie Moulin (Dordrecht: Kluwer Academic, 1992), 269–80.

45. Misra, *Unification and Division,* 50–57.

46. C. A. Bayly, *Indian Society and the Making of the British Empire,* vol. 2.1 of *The New Cambridge History of India* (Cambridge: Cambridge University Press, 1988), 87–89; Metcalf, *Ideologies of the Raj,* 25–26, 114–16.

47. Ludden, "Orientalist Empiricism," 257–58.

48. Good introductions to the critique of empiricist cartography are J. B. Harley, "Introduction: Texts and Contexts in the Interpretation of Early Maps," in *From Sea Charts to Satellite Images: Interpreting North American History Through Maps,* edited by David Buisseret (Chicago: University of Chicago Press, 1990), 3–15; Denis Wood, *The Power of Maps* (New York: Guilford, 1992).

49. See Roshdi Rashad, "Science as a Western Phenomenon," *Fundamenta Scientiae* 1 (1980): 7–23.

50. Inden, *Imagining India,* 1–4.

51. Bayly, *Indian Society,* 156–59.

52. Marika Vicziany, "Imperialism, Botany and Statistics in early Nineteenth-Century India: The Surveys of Francis Buchanan (1762–1829)," *Modern Asian Studies* 20 (1986): 625–60, esp. 653. This theme runs through a complex reading of Kipling's *Kim* by Thomas Richards: "Archive and Utopia," in *The Imperial Archive: Knowledge and the Fantasy of Empire* (London: Verso, 1993), 11–44, also 1–9 for a succinct summary.

53. Metcalf, *Ideologies of the Raj.*

54. C. A. Bayly, "The British Military-Fiscal State and Indigenous Resistance: India, 1750–1820," in *An Imperial State at War: Britain from 1689 to 1815,* edited by Lawrence Stone (London: Routledge, 1994), 322–54, esp. 324. Refer to Anne Godlewska, "Map, Text, and Image: The Mentality of Enlightened Conquerors: A New Look at the *Description de l'Egypt,*" *Transactions of the Institute of British Geographers* ns 20 (1995): 5–28, esp. 15–16.

55. C. A. Bayly, "Knowing the Country: Empire and Information in India," *Modern Asian Studies* 27 (1993): 3–43, esp. 25, 28, 34–35.

56. See especially Lewis Pyenson, "Astronomy and Imperialism: J. A. C. Oudemans, the Topography of the East Indies, and the Rise of the Utrecht Observatory, 1850–1900," *Historia Scientiarum* 26 (1984): 39–81; Jeffrey C. Stone, "Imperialism, Colonialism and Cartography," *Transactions of the Institute of British Geographers* ns 13 (1988): 57–64.

57. E. J. Hobsbawm, *Nations and Nationalism since 1870: Programme, Myth and Reality* (Cambridge: Cambridge University Press, 1990), 80.

58. Peter Sahlins, *Boundaries: The Making of France and Spain in the Pyrenees* (Berkeley: University of California Press, 1989), 1–9, is a succinct summary of state and boundary issues; Charles Tilley, *Coercion, Capital, and European States, AD 990–1992* (Oxford: Blackwell, 1990), 25–26, re internal negotiations; Edney, "Cartographic Culture and Nationalism," is a preliminary statement.

59. Raymond Williams, *The Sociology of Culture* (New York: Schocken Books, 1982), 13, presents a general meaning of culture as a society's "informing spirit" or essence. Also Ulf Hannerz, *Cultural Complexity: Studies in the Social Organization of Meaning* (New York: Columbia University Press, 1992); Said, *Culture and Imperialism,* xii–xiii.

Chapter Two

1. Thomas H. Holdich, "The Romance of Indian Surveys," *Journal of the Royal Society of Arts* 64 (1916): 173–85, esp. 179.

2. James T. Blunt, "Narrative of a Route from Chunarghur to Yertnagoodum, in the Ellore Circar," *Asiatic Researches* 7 (1801): 57–169, esp. 65 (emphasis added). On collection and philology: Lisa L. Gitelman, "The World Recounted: Science and Narrative in Early Nineteenth-Century Exploration Accounts," Ph.D. diss. (Columbia University, 1991), 124–61.

3. Lists of donations to the Asiatic Society appear in each issue of the *Asiatic Researches;* Ray Desmond, *The India Museum, 1801–1879* (London: HMSO for India Office Library and Records, 1982). The eighteenth- and nineteenth-century fetishization of the specimen, and of jewelry in particular, is the subject of Pauline Lunsingh Scheurleer, "Rich Remains from Social Anthropological Fieldwork in Eighteenth-Century India," *Journal of the History of Collections* 8, no. 1 (1996): 71–91; my thanks to Christian Jacob for this reference.

4. The equivalence of observation and collection is central, for example, to Gitelman's "The World Recounted"; see also Anne Godlewska, "Map, Text, and Image: The Mentality of Enlightened Conquerors: A New Look at the *Description de l'Egypt,*" *Transactions of the Institute of British Geographers,* ns 20 (1995): 5–28, esp. 22–24. Norman Bryson, *Vision and Painting: The Logic of the Gaze* (New Haven: Yale University Press, 1983), gives a complete analysis of the "essential copy" and its philosophical assumptions.

5. Jonathan Crary, *Techniques of the Observer: On Vision and Modernity in the Nineteenth Century* (Cambridge, MA: MIT Press, 1990), 39, citing Jacques Lacan, *The Four Fundamental Concepts of Psycho-Analysis,* translated by Alan Sheridan (New York, 1978), 81, with respect to Bishop Berkeley and others. Johannes Fabian, "Presence and Representation: The Other and Anthropological Writing," *Critical Inquiry* 16 (1990): 753–72; Fabian, *Time and the Other: How Anthropology Makes Its Object* (New York: Columbia University Press, 1983), esp. 105–41. A useful summary of the literature on the themes discussed in Part One, although with an emphasis on the later nineteenth century, is David Spurr, *The Rhetoric of Empire: Colonial Discourse in Journalism, Travel Writing, and Imperial Administration* (Durham, NC: Duke University Press, 1993), 1–26.

6. Two recent examples are Margarita Bowen, *Empiricism and Geographical Thought from Francis Bacon to Alexander von Humboldt* (Cambridge: Cambridge University Press, 1981), and David N. Livingstone, *The Geographical Tradition: Episodes in the History of a Contested Enterprise* (Oxford: Blackwell, 1992).

7. G. S. Rousseau and Roy Porter, eds. *The Ferment of Knowledge: Studies in the Historiography of Eighteenth-Century Science* (Cambridge: Cambridge University Press, 1980), esp. Rousseau's introductory comments about how the contributors were forced to break away from present-day historiographic and disciplinary constructs.

8. "Desiderata," *Asiatic Researches* 6 (1799): iii–vi, esp. iv.

9. On the seventeenth-century English distinction between geography and chorography, see Bowen, *Empiricism and Geographical Thought,* 15–122; Lesley B. Cormack, " 'Good Fences Make Good Neighbours': Geography as Self-Definition in Early Modern England," *Isis* 82 (1991): 639–61, esp. 641–44; Stan Mendyck, *'Speculum Brittaniae': Regional Study, Antiquarianism, and Science in Britain to 1700* (Toronto: University of Toronto Press, 1989), 3–37, esp. 21–25.

10. Cormack, "Geography in Early Modern England," 641 and 661 respectively, emphasis added.

11. Gwyn Walters, "The Antiquary and the Map," *Word & Image* 4 (1988): 529–44, 532.

12. Matthew H. Edney, "Cartography without 'Progress': Reinterpreting the Nature and Historical Development of Mapmaking," *Cartographica* 30, nos. 2 and 3 (1993): 54–68; Edney, "Mathematical Cosmography and the Social Ideology of British Cartography, 1780–1820," *Imago Mundi* 46 (1994): 101–16.

356 Notes to Pages 44–50

13. Stephen Toulmin, *Cosmopolis: The Hidden Agenda of Modernity* (New York: The Free Press, 1990); Clarence J. Glacken, *Traces on the Rhodian Shore: Nature and Culture in Western Thought from Ancient Times to the End of the Eighteenth Century* (Berkeley: University of California Press, 1967); Roy Porter, "The Terraqueous Globe," in *Ferment of Knowledge,* edited by Rousseau and Porter, 285–324.

14. Numa Broc, *La Géographie des philosophes: Géographes et voyageurs français au XVIIIᵉ siècle* (Paris: Editions Ophrys, 1974), 201; Eric G. Forbes, "Mathematical Cosmography," in *Ferment of Knowledge,* edited by Rousseau and Porter, 417–18; Bowen, *Empiricism in Geographical Thought,* 159–60. Charles W. J. Withers, "Geography in Its Time: Geography and Historical Geography in Diderot and d'Alembert's *Encyclopédie*," *Journal of Historical Geography* 19 (1993): 255–64.

15. Bowen, *Empiricism and Geographical Thought,* 154–59, 156 (quotation from Büsching), and 210–59 on the "Age of Humboldt"; Susan F. Cannon, *Science in Culture: The Early Victorian Period* (New York: Dawson and Science History Publications, 1978), 73–110, on "Humboldtian science"; Livingstone, *Geographical Tradition,* 134–38, on the "Humboldtian Project."

16. John Warren, "Observations on the Golden Ore, found in the Eastern provinces of Mysore in the year 1802," *Journal of the Asiatic Society of Bengal* 3 (1834): 463–75, was the first printing of the original account sent to the Asiatic Society in 1802. See figure 5.3.

17. Refer to Felix Driver and Gillian Rose, "Introduction: Towards New Histories of Geographical Knowledge," in *Nature and Science: Essays in the History of Geographical Knowledge,* edited by Driver and Rose, Historical Geography Research Series, 28 (London: London Group of Historical Geographers, 1991), 1–7.

18. Crary, *Techniques of the Observer,* 39 and 53. Barbara Maria Stafford, *Voyage into Substance: Art, Science, Nature, and the Illustrated Travel Account, 1760–1840* (Cambridge, MA: MIT Press, 1984), 226–28 and 426–28, on the use of the *camera obscura* by travelers and its epistemological connotations.

19. Quoted by Crary, *Techniques of the Observer,* 40.

20. Tore Frängsmyr, J. L. Heilbron, and Robin E. Rider, eds., *The Quantifying Spirit in the Eighteenth Century* (Berkeley: University of California Press, 1990).

21. Crary, *Techniques of the Observer,* 5–6.

22. Ibid.; Crary self-consciously argues for a dramatic caesura ca. 1800 between Enlightenment and Romantic theories of vision. The problem is that for the Enlightenment he concentrates only on the conventionality of observation; he picks up the epistemological discussion of "reason" only after 1800. The break/revolution was thus not as dramatic as he makes out.

23. Denis Diderot and Jean Le Rond d'Alembert, eds., *Encyclopédie, ou dictionnaire raisonné des sciences, des arts et des métiers, par une société de gens de lettres* (Paris, 1751–65, 17 vols.), 10: 458, art. "Méthode," quoted and translated by Frängsmyr et al., *Quantifying Spirit,* 2.

24. Michel Foucault, *The Order of Things: An Archaeology of the Human Sciences* (New York: Random House, 1970), 133.

25. Mary Louise Pratt, *Imperial Eyes: Travel Writing and Transculturation* (London: Routledge, 1992), 31. Foucault, *Order of Things,* 138–45, makes the sharp distinction between System and Method.

26. Foucault, *Order of Things,* 125–65; John E. Lesch, "Systematics and the Geometrical Spirit," and Robin E. Rider, "Measure of Ideas, Rule of Language: Mathematics and Language in the 18th Century," both in *Quantifying Spirit,* edited by Frängsmyr et al., 73–111 and 113–40. Stafford, *Voyage into Substance,* 347–96.

27. Quoted by Stafford, *Voyage into Substance,* 426.

28. Albrecht von Haller, "Vorrede," in Georges L. L. Buffon, *Allgemeine Historie der Natur nach allen ihren besondern Theilen abgehandelt; nebst einer Beschreibung der Naturalienkammer Gr. Majestat des Königes von Frankreich* (Hamburg and Leipzig, 1750), 1: ix–xxii, translated with inserts in *From Natural History to the History of Nature: Readings from Buffon and His Critics,* edited by John Lyon and Phillip R. Sloan (Notre Dame: University of Notre Dame Press, 1981), 304.

29. Edney, "Mathematical Cosmography."

30. Michael Adanson, *Familles des plantes,* quoted by Lesch, "Systematics and the Geometrical Spirit," 84, and by Foucault, *Order of Things,* 136. See Giulio Barsanti, "Le immagini della natura: scale, mappa, alberi 1700–1800," *Nuncius* 3 (1988): 55–125.

31. Richard Yeo, "Reading Encyclopaedias: Science and the Organization of Knowledge in British Dictionaries of Arts and Sciences, 1730–1850," *Isis* 82 (1991): 24–49, referring to Ephraim Chambers, *Cyclopaedia; or, An Universal Dictionary of Arts and Sciences* (London, 1728, 2 vols.; 2d ed., 1738). Withers, "Geography in Its Time," 256, quoting Jean d'Alembert's "Discours préliminaire" in *Encyclopédie,* 1: xv.

32. Roger Hahn, "The Laplacean View of Calculation," and J. L. Heilbron, "Introductory Essay," both in *Quantifying Spirit,* edited by Frängsmyr et al., 363–80 and 1–23; Theodore M. Porter, *The Rise of Statistical Thinking, 1820–1900* (Princeton: Princeton University Press, 1986); Stephen M. Stigler, *The History of Statistics: The Measurement of Uncertainty before 1900* (Cambridge: Harvard University Press, 1986).

33. Colin Mackenzie to Sir Alexander Johnstone, 1 Feb 1817, ¶2, in "Biographical Sketch of the Literary Career of the Late Colonel Colin Mackenzie, Surveyor General of India . . ." *Madras Journal of Literature and Science* 2 (1835): 262–91 (see Bibliography for copies).

34. See Nicholas B. Dirks, "Guiltless Spoliations: Picturesque Beauty, Colonial Knowledge, and Colin Mackenzie's Survey of India," in *Perceptions of South Asia's Visual Past,* edited by Catherine B. Asher and Thomas R. Metcalf (New Delhi: Oxford and IBH Publishing for the American Institute of Indian Studies, 1994), 211–32.

35. Michel Foucault, *Discipline and Punish: The Birth of the Prison,* translated by Alan Sheridan (New York: Random House, 1977), 184–92, esp. 187 (quotation) and 225.

36. Alexander Johnstone, Evidence, 19 Jul 1832, "Minutes of Evidence Taken before the Select Committee on the Affairs of the East India Company," vol. 1, "Public," *British Parliamentary Papers* 1831–32 (735.1) 9, ¶1928, emphasis added.

37. Bryson, *Vision and Painting,* 94, contrasting "gaze" with the less engaged and more empathic "glance."

38. Stafford, *Voyage into Substance,* xix and 40 (quotations), 3–7, 31–56, 348–49. Also Livingstone, *Geographical Tradition,* 130–33. On "plain" design, factual statement, and cartography, see Dalia Varanka, "Editorial and Design Principles in the Rise of English World Atlases, 1606–1729," Ph.D. diss. (University of Wisconsin-Madison, 1995).

39. Stafford, *Voyage into Substance,* 17.

40. General Francis Jarry (1733–1807), quoted (my emphasis) in A. R. Goodwin-Austen, *The Staff and Staff College* (London, 1927), 33. [William Bentinck], "Outlines of a Plan of Instruction for the Gentlemen Cadets," nd, MMC 17 Nov 1804, IOR P/255/41, 5534–35 and 5530–31; Jarry had served as "a sort of military mentor" for Bentinck (*Dictionary of National Biography* 10: 691). Also Matthew H. Edney, "British Military Education, Mapmaking, and Military 'Map-Mindedness' in the Later Enlightenment," *The Cartographic Journal* 31, no. 1 (1994): 14–20; Mildred Archer, *British Drawings in the India Office Library* (London: HMSO, 1969, 2 vols.), 1: 4–9.

41. Topographical drawing receives short shrift in connoisseur histories of British landscape art: Kenneth Clarke, *Landscape into Art* (London: Harper and Row, 1949; 2d ed.,

1976); Louis Hawes, *Presences of Nature: British Landscape, 1780–1830* (New Haven: Yale Center for British Art, 1982); Michael Rosenthal, *British Landscape Painting* (Oxford: Phaidon, 1982). Luke Hermann, *British Landscape Painting of the Eighteenth Century* (New York: Oxford University Press, 1974), is more open.

42. Ann Bermingham, *Landscape and Ideology: The English Rustic Tradition, 1740–1860* (Berkeley: University of California Press, 1986), 3; Hugh Prince, "Art and Agrarian Change, 1710–1815," in *The Iconography of Landscape: Essays on the Symbolic Representation, Design and Use of Past Environments*, edited by Denis Cosgrove and Stephen Daniels, Cambridge Studies in Historical Geography, 9 (Cambridge: Cambridge University Press, 1988), 98–118. Also Nicholas Alfrey and Stephen Daniels, eds., *Mapping the Landscape: Essays on Art and Cartography* (Nottingham: University Art Gallery and Castle Museum, 1990); Stephen Daniels, *Fields of Vision: Landscape Imagery and National Identity in England and the United States* (Princeton: Princeton University Press, 1993), 88.

43. Stephen Daniels, "Re-Visioning Britain: Mapping and Landscape Painting, 1750–1820," in Michael Rosenthal et al., *Glorious Nature: British Landscape Painting, 1750–1850* (New York: Hudson Hills Press, 1993), 61–72, esp. 61.

44. This discussion is based largely on Michael Andrews's excellent *The Search for the Picturesque: Landscape Aesthetics and Tourism in Britain, 1760–1800* (Stanford, CA: Stanford University Press, 1989).

45. Of the huge literature on tourism: Andrews, *Search for the Picturesque;* James Buzzard, *The Beaten Track: European Tourism, Literature, and the Ways to Culture, 1800–1918* (Oxford: Clarendon Press, 1993); Stafford, *Voyage into Substance,* discusses the distinction between "traveler" and "tourist."

46. William Foster, "British Artists in India, 1760–1820," *Annual Volume of the Walpole Society* 19 (1930–31): 1–88, is the classic overview of early British art in India. See also, Pratapaditya Pal and Vidya Dehejia, *From Merchants to Emperors: British Artists and India, 1757–1930* (Ithaca, NY: Cornell University Press for the Pierpont Morgan Library, New York, 1986); C. A. Bayly, ed., *Raj: India and the British, 1600–1947* (London: National Portrait Gallery, 1990).

47. Archer, *British Drawings,* 1: 18–23; Mildred Archer and Ronald Lightbown, *India Observed: India as Viewed by British Artists, 1760–1860* (London: Victoria and Albert Museum, 1982), 11, 50–51, 67–68, 87, on Valentia; Ray Desmond, *The European Discovery of the Indian Flora* (Oxford: Oxford University Press for Royal Botanic Gardens, 1992), 173–84; Pal and Dehejia, *From Merchants to Emperors,* 97–129; and, G. H. R. Tillotson, "The Indian Picturesque: Images of India in British Landscape Painting, 1780–1880," in *Raj,* edited by Bayly, 141–51. On Valentia, see also Ketaki Kushari Dyson, *A Various Universe: A Study of the Journals and Memoirs of British Men and Women in the Indian Subcontinent, 1765–1856* (Delhi: Oxford University Press, 1978), 159–62; Pheroza Godrej, "The Travels of Henry Salt and Lord Valentia in India," in *India: A Pageant of Prints,* edited by Pauline Rohatgi and Godrej (Bombay: Marg Publications, 1989), 71–88.

48. Dyson, *Various Universe,* 112. Marika Vicziany, "Imperialism, Botany and Statistics in Early Nineteenth-Century India: The Surveys of Francis Buchanan (1762–1829)," *Modern Asian Studies* 20 (1986): 625–60, esp. 633.

49. Archer and Lightbown, *India Observed,* 86; Forrest drew his artwork while on tour during 1807 and 1808. Daniels, *Fields of Vision,* 57 and 67 re industrial Picturesque.

50. William Lambton, "A Journal [13 Jul to 22 Nov 1799] of the March of the Grand Army from Negamungalum, and of a Tour through the Soondah and Bednore Countries," nd, BL Add MS 13664, fols. 61–113, quotations respectively from fol. 102r (26 Oct), and fol. 63r (16 Jul); this neat copy is not signed, but fol. 60r bears a contemporary annotation that it is by Lambton; its style is very similar to the neat copy of a diary (1804–5) which Lambton sent to Bentinck: UN Pw Jb 79, 156–229.

51. Timothy J. Standring, "Watercolor Landscape Sketching during the Popular Picturesque Era in Britain," in Rosenthal et al., *Glorious Nature*, 73–84, esp. 75.

52. Barbara Belyea, "Captain Franklin in Search of the Picturesque," *Essays on Canadian Writing* 40 (1990): 1–24, esp. 8.

53. G. H. R. Tillotson, "The Paths of Glory: Representations of Sher Shah's Tomb," *Oriental Art*, ns 37 (1991): 4–16, esp. 6, also 14 n. 6.

54. Thomas and William Daniell, *A Picturesque Voyage to India by the Way of China* (London, 1810), quoted by both Mildred Archer, *Early Views of India: The Picturesque Journeys of Thomas and William Daniell, 1786–1794: The Complete Aquatints* (London: Thames and Hudson, 1980), 7, and by Dirks, "Guiltless Spoliations," 211.

55. Quoted by Andrews, *Search for the Picturesque*, 81 and 70, respectively.

56. See W. J. T. Mitchell, "Imperial Landscape," and Ann Bermingham's wonderful "System, Order, and Abstraction: The Politics of English Landscape Drawing around 1795," both in *Landscape and Power*, edited by Mitchell (Chicago: University of Chicago Press, 1994), 5–34, and 77–101.

57. Tillotson, "Paths of Glory," 4 and 8. P. J. Marshall, "Taming the Exotic: The British and India in the Seventeenth and Eighteenth Centuries," in *Exoticism and the Enlightenment*, edited by G. S. Rousseau and Roy Porter (Manchester: Manchester University Press, 1990), 46–65, 62, noted that the British view of India was created by William Hodges and the Daniells.

58. Archer and Lightbown, *India Observed*, 12.

59. Edward W. Said, *Orientalism* (New York: Vintage, 1979), 157.

60. Gillian Rose, *Feminism and Geography: The Limits of Geographical Knowledge* (Minneapolis: University of Minnesota Press, 1993), 86–112; John Berger, *Ways of Seeing* (London: BBC and Penguin, 1972); Rana Kabbani, *Europe's Myths of Orient* (Bloomington: Indiana University Press, 1986); Pratt, *Imperial Eyes*, esp. 201–27, on the "monarch-of-all-I-survey" syndrome; Said, *Orientalism*.

61. Henry Walters, "Journey across the Pandua Hills, near Silhet, in Bengal," *Asiatic Researches* 17 (1832): 499–512. On Walters's career: H. T. Prinsep, ed., *General Register of the Hon'ble East India Company's Civil Servants of the Bengal Establishment from 1790 to 1842* (Calcutta, 1844); "Bengal Civilians, 1740–1858, T–W," fol. 1999b, IOR O/6/2; H. Dodwell, ed., *Alphabetical List of Bengal Civil Servants, 1780–1838* (London, 1839), 552–53; my thanks to Michael Armstrong for this information. On the region and the conflict: Nirode K. Barooah, *David Scott in North-East India, 1802–1831: A Study in British Imperialism* (New Delhi: Munshiram Manoharlal, 1969), 82–84, 191–229; Philip R. T. Gurdon, *The Khasis* (London: D. Nutt, 1907); R. Boileau Pemberton, *Report on the Eastern Frontier of British India* (Calcutta, 1835; reprint, Gauhati: State of Assam, Department of Historical and Antiquarian Studies, 1966), 76–78, 230–69; Adam White, *Memoir of the Late David Scott, Esq., Agent to the Governor General, on the North-East Frontier of Bengal, and Commissioner of Revenue and Circuit in Assam*, edited by Archibald Watson (Calcutta: Baptist Mission Press, 1832), 32–52.

62. Alexander Gerard to George Lloyd, nd, quoted in Gerard, *Account of Koonawur, in the Himalaya, etc. etc. etc.*, edited by Lloyd (London: James Madden, 1841), viii; this text contained the account and narratives of Gerard's 1817–18 survey of Kunawar. The narrative of the 1821–22 survey is vol. 2 of *Narrative of a Journey from Caunpoor to the Barendo Pass in the Himalaya Mountains, via Gwalior, Agra, Delhi, and Sirhind, by Major Sir William Lloyd; and Captain Alexander Gerard's Account of an Attempt to Penetrate by Bekhur to Garoo, and the Lake Manasarowara . . .*, edited by George Lloyd (London: J. Madden, 1840, 2 vols.; 2d ed., 1846). Refer to Gerard, "Memoir of the Construction of a Map of Koonawar in the Hill States of [unclear]," 26 Jul 1825, RGS Library MS. Also, Gerard to Herbert Benson [Bentinck's private military secretary], 28 Aug 1830, UN Pw Jf 2772/4, forwarding Ger-

ard's "Remarks upon that Part of Koonawur, inhabited by Tartars, and some of the adjoining Countries," nd, UN Pw Jf 2772/5–6. On the literary power of narrative: see Gitelman, "The World Recounted," 164–89.

63. Said, *Orientalism*, 157–58.

64. Paul Carter, *The Road to Botany Bay: A Spatial History* (London: Faber and Faber, 1987), esp. 69–98; Gitelman, "The World Recounted," 21–90, specifically on exploration accounts. Andrew Hassam, "'As I Write': Narrative Occasions and the Quest for Self-Presence in the Travel Diary," *Ariel* 21, no. 4 (1990): 33–47; Stafford, *Voyage into Substance*, 399, stated that "the traveller consciously observes himself in a situation and attempts to describe it accurately." Dyson, *Various Universe*; Pratt, *Imperial Eyes*.

65. Dyson, *A Various Universe*, 65–67.

66. Sara Suleri, *The Rhetoric of English India* (Chicago: University of Chicago Press, 1992), 75–110 (the "feminine picturesque" and gender distinction in writing); Stafford, *Voyage into Substance*, 442, re primary-secondary distinction.

67. White, *Memoir*, 34.

68. This is not the same as the values derived for Nongkhlao by Lt. Richard Wilcox, Jones's colleague on the Assam survey: 25°41'50"N, 91°38'0"E, given in Pemberton, *Report on the Eastern Frontier*, table 19, "Table of Latitudes, Longitudes, and Elevations of various places and objects on the Eastern Frontier." Interestingly, the few other places in the Khāsi Hills mentioned in this table have only elevations recorded.

69. Robert Montgomery Martin, *The History, Antiquities, Topography, and Statistics of Eastern India . . .* (London: Wm. H. Allen, 1838, 3 vols.), 1: 35–39 (city of Patna), 1: 110; cf. Vicziany, "Imperialism, Botany and Statistics," 651–54. See also James Prinsep, "Census of the Population of the City of Benares," *Asiatic Researches* 17 (1832): 470–98, which discusses the 1800 census by the kotwal, Zulficar Ali, and Prinsep's census under the aegis of the 1823 Committee of Improvement; Henry Walters, "Census of the City of Dacca," *Asiatic Researches* 17 (1832), 535–58; "Census of the Population of the City and District of Murshedabad, taken in 1829," *Journal of the Asiatic Society of Bengal* 2 (1833): 567–69.

70. Denis Cosgrove, *Social Formation and Symbolic Landscape* (London: Croom Helm, 1984), 9–15, esp. 15; Cosgrove, "Prospect, Perspective and the Evolution of the Landscape Idea," *Transactions of the Institute of British Geographers*, ns 10 (1985): 45–62.

71. The equivalence of mapping and sight was recently reiterated by, for example, Zhilin Li, "Reality in Time-Scale Systems and Cartographic Representation," *The Cartographic Journal* 31 (1994): 50–51. See critiques by Denis Wood, *Power of Maps* (New York: Guilford, 1992), 48–69, and Christian Jacob: *L'Empire des cartes: Approche théorique de la cartographie à travers l'histoire* (Paris: Bibliothèque Albin Michel, 1992), 15–25.

72. For example, Hassam, "Narrative Occasions"; Michel de Certeau, "Spatial Stories," in *The Practice of Everyday Life*, translated by Steven Rendall (Berkeley: University of California Press, 1984), 115–30.

73. Walters, "Journey," 510–12.

74. Dirks, "Guiltless Spoliations."

75. Godlewska, "Map, Text and Image," 20–21, emphasis added.

76. Henry Yule and A. C. Burnell, *Hobson-Jobson: A Glossary of Colloquial Anglo-Indian Words and Phrases, and of Kindred Terms, Etymological, Historical, Geographical and Discursive*, new edition, edited by William Crooke (London, 1903; reprint, Delhi: Munshiram Manoharlal, 1968), 263, "Cossya," states the name to be "more properly" "Kāsia" and also records "Cusseahs" and "Cossyahs."

Chapter Three

1. Francis Buchanan, *A Journey from Madras through the Countries of Mysore, Canara, and Malabar . . .* (London, 1807, 3 vols.; reprint, New Delhi: Asian Educational Services,

1988), 1: viii. See David Prain, "A Sketch of the Life of Francis Hamilton (once Buchanan), sometime Superintendent of the Honourable Company's Botanic Garden at Calcutta," *Annals of the Royal Botanic Gardens, Calcutta* 10, no. 2 (1905): i–lxxv, esp. liv–lv re reviews; Marika Vicziany, "Imperialism, Botany and Statistics in Early Nineteenth-Century India: The Surveys of Francis Buchanan (1762–1829)," *Modern Asian Studies* 20 (1986): 625–60, esp. 627–38, updates Prain's saintly image of Buchanan.

2. Francis Buchanan Hamilton, *An Account of the Kingdom of Nepal and of the Territories annexed to this Dominion by the House of Gorkha* (Edinburgh, 1819; reprint, Bibliotheca Himalayica, ser. 1, vol. 10, New Delhi: Mañjuśrī, 1971). Robert Montgomery Martin, *The History, Antiquities, Topography, and Statistics of Eastern India* . . . (London: Wm. H. Allen, 1838, 3 vols.). Subsequent studies of Buchanan's work deprecate Montgomery Martin's bowdlerizing of the Bengal materials, although most opprobrium stems from his complete failure to acknowledge Buchanan's labors; the most succinct commentary is by George R. Kaye and Edward H. Johnstone, *Minor Collections and Miscellaneous Manuscripts,* vol. 2.2 of *Catalogue of Manuscripts in European Languages in the India Office Library* (London, 1937), 611. A posthumous attempt to publish Buchanan's district journals failed, producing only one: *A Geographical, Statistical, and Historical Description of the District, or Zila, of Dinajpur in the Province, or Soubah, of Bengal,* edited by James D. Herbert and James Prinsep (Calcutta, 1833); several of the journals, listed in the bibliography, were finally published in the twentieth century.

3. Michel de Certeau, "Spatial Stories," in *The Practice of Everyday Life,* translated by Steven Rendall (Berkeley: University of California Press, 1984), 115–30, esp. 120; de Certeau, "Writing the Sea: Jules Verne," in *Heterologies: Discourse on the Other,* Theory and History of Literature, 17, translated by Brian Massumi (Minneapolis: University of Minnesota Press, 1986), 137–49.

4. Buchanan, *Journey through Mysore,* 3: 410. On the statue of Gomata Raja, see John Keay, *India Discovered: The Achievement of the British Raj* (Leicester: Windward, 1981), 238–43. Relevant images in the Mackenzie collection: J. G. Newman, "North View of the Hill of Sravana-Bellagoola, 17 August 1806," drawn April 1816 "from an Original Sketch on the Mysore Survey in 1806 taken by Lieut. Ward," IOR prints WD 576, 592; "View of the Rock of Carcull and the First Appearance of the Gigantic Statue of Goonut Iswar on its summit May 1806," IOR prints WD 576, 783, and 623 (untitled neat version); "Goomut Eswar on a Rock 2 Miles SE of Karcull, May 1806," fol. 181v of "Hindoo Antiquities: A Collection of Drawings of Architecture & Sculpture . . . ," IOR prints WD 1064.

5. John A. Hodgson, "Remarks on the Surveys in India generally, but more especially on those of a combined geographical and military nature, conducted by the officers of the Surveyor General's and the Quarter Master General's departments, . . . ," 21 Nov 1821, ¶7, BPC 7 Dec 1821, §62, IOR F/4/682 18864, 500–525.

6. William Wordsworth, "Written with a slate pencil on a Stone, on the side of the mountain of Black Comb," 1813, in *The Poetical Works of William Wordsworth,* edited by William Knight (Edinburgh: William Patterson, 1883), 4: 269–70.

7. Pratapaditya Pal, "Indian Artists and British Patrons in Calcutta," *Marg* 41, no. 4 (1989): 17–34.

8. Joseph Schwartzberg, "South Asian Cartography," in *Cartography in the Traditional Islamic and South Asian Societies,* edited by J. B. Harley and David Woodward, vol. 2.1 of *The History of Cartography* (Chicago: University of Chicago Press, 1992), 293–509, esp. 324–27 and 427–29 on "hybrid" maps, notes that much of the historic record for South Asian geographical cartography is known from European (mainly British and French) sources. See Susan Gole, *Indian Maps and Plans from Earliest Times to the Advent of European Surveys* (New Delhi: Manohar, 1989). C. A. Bayly, "Knowing the Country: Empire and Information in India," *Modern Asian Studies* 27 (1993): 3–43; Thongchai Winichakul, *Siam*

Mapped: A History of the Geo-Body of a Nation (Honolulu: University of Hawaii Press, 1994), 113–27.

9. Buchanan, *Journey through Mysore,* 3: 433 (13 Jun 1801) and 3: 458 (18 Jun 1801), respectively.

10. [Buchanan] Hamilton, *Account of Nepal,* 1.

11. James Rennell, *Memoir of a Map of Hindoostan; or the Mogul's Empire: With an Examination of some Positions in the Former System of Indian Geography . . .* (London, 1783; 2d ed., 1785), vi; hereafter cited as *Memoir I.* Rennell, *Memoir of a Map of Hindoostan; or the Mogul Empire: with an Introduction, Illustrative of the Geography and Present Division of that Country . . .* (London, 1788; 2d ed., 1792; 3d ed., 1793, reprint, Calcutta: Editions Indian, 1976), (2d ed.) 211, 237–38; cited hereafter as *Memoir II.*

12. James Prinsep, editorial note to M. A. Court, "Extracts Translated from a Memoir on a Map of Pesháwar and the Country Comprised between the Indus and the Hydaspes, the Peucelaotis and Taxila of Ancient Geography," *Journal of the Asiatic Society of Bengal* 5 (1836): 468, emphasis added; Wilford's map was then housed at the Asiatic Society.

13. Rennell, *Memoir II* (2d ed.), 224; the map itself is "A Chart of the Guzurat made by Sudanando, a Bhramin of Cambay," BL Add 8956, fol. 2, reproduced by Gole, *Indian Maps and Plans,* 113. There are several translations of the third volume of Abu al-Fazl's "Institutions of Akbar [Mughal emperor, 1542–1605]," for example, *The Ā'īn-i Akbarī by Abū'l-Fazl 'Allāmī,* Bibliotheca Indica, 61, translated by H. Blochmann, 2d ed. (Calcutta: Asiatic Society of Bengal, 1927, 3 vols.). Before translation, the work had been used as the basis for an atlas of the Mughal empire commissioned by a French officer: Susan Gole, *Maps of Mughal India Drawn by Colonel Jean-Baptiste-Joseph Gentil, Agent for the French Government to the Court of Shuja-ud-daula at Faizabad, in 1770* (London: Kegan Paul International, 1988); see also Pauline Lunsingh Scheurleer, "Rich Remains from Social Anthropological Fieldwork in Eighteenth-Century India," *Journal of the History of Collections* 8, no. 1 (1996): 71–91, esp. 81, on a second album of images commissioned from Faizabad artists by Gentil in 1774, on the manners and customs of the people of India.

14. [Buchanan] Hamilton, *Account of Nepal,* 3, emphasis added. Many of these materials survive in vol. 3 of Buchanan's "Drawings, Maps, and Inscriptions," IOR Eur D/97; Kaye and Johnstone, *Minor Collections and Miscellaneous Manuscripts,* 650–53, §172, describes these and identifies Buchanan's various informants. William Kirkpatrick, *An Account of the Kingdom of Nepaul, being the Substance of Observations made During a Mission to that Country, in the Year 1793* (London: William Miller, 1811; reprint, Bibliotheca Himalayica, ser. 1, vol. 3, New Delhi: Mañjuśrī, 1969).

15. Quoted by V. H. Jackson, "Introduction: The Buchanan Journal and Maps," in *Journal of Francis Buchanan (Afterwards Hamilton) Kept During the Survey of the Districts of Patna and Gaya in 1811–1812,* edited by Jackson (Patna: Superintendent, Government Printing, Bihar and Orissa, 1925), i–xxvi, esp. x. Vicziany, "Imperialism, Botany and Statistics," 646.

16. Buchanan, *Voyage through Mysore,* 2: 108 and 2: 113.

17. "Translation of a Canara Paper marked A, letter from Dassiah Hircarrah to the Dewan of Mysore," enclosure with Thomas Arthur to J. H. Peile [Resident at Mysore], 22 Apr 1803, IOR R/2/1/10, fol. 75. A translation is also provided (fol. 76) of a letter from an amildar to the diwan, re Arthur's actions. It is unclear who made the translations.

18. Mather to Peile, 9 Oct 1803, IOR R/2/1/10, fols. 254–55.

19. Prain, "Francis [Buchanan] Hamilton," xiv.

20. Alexander Read, "Survey," on his "Sketch of the Countries North and East of the Cauvery ceded by Tippoo Sultaun in March 1792 to the Honorable East India Company," nd (ca. June 1792), BL Add 26102a.

21. Read, "Sketch of the Countries North and East of the Cauvery." He plotted the map at two gurries (or three miles) to the inch, or ca. 1:190,000. Henry Yule and A. C. Burnell, *Hobson-Jobson: A Glossary of Colloquial Anglo-Indian Words and Phrases, and of Kindred Terms, Etymological, Historical, Geographical and Discursive,* new edition, edited by William Crooke (London, 1903; reprint, Delhi: Munshiram Manoharlal, 1968), 372–73, define "ghurry" as only a type of water-clock or the Hindu hour of twenty-four minutes.

22. Rennell, *Memoir I* (1st ed.), 17–19; the map was *Hindoostan* (London, 1782) in two sheets. Rennell's discussion of itinerary measures was dramatically expanded in his *Memoir II* (2d ed.), 3–7. Also Guy Deleury, comp., *Les Indes florissantes: Anthologie des voyageurs français (1750–1820)* (Paris: Robert Laffont, 1991), 97–103, quoting Père Cœurdoux (1760) from *Lettres édifantes et curieuses* (Paris, 1841), on Indian itinerary measures. Yule and Burnell, *Hobson-Jobson,* 261–62.

23. [Buchanan] Hamilton, *Account of Nepal,* 3.

24. Colin Mackenzie, "Memoir explanatory of the Materials and Construction of a Map of the Dominions of Nizam Ali Khan Soobadar of the Dekan," 6 Aug 1796, IOR Eur Mackenzie General 60, 59–108, esp. 62.

25. Reuben Burrow, "Observations of some of the Eclipses of Jupiter's Satellites," *Asiatic Researches* 2 (1790): 385–87, gave observed times of immersions between Sep 1787 to Apr 1790, some of the results of which seem to have been included in the 121 places listed in his "Table of Latitudes and Longitudes of Some Principal Places in India, Determined from Astronomical Observations," *Asiatic Researches* 4 (1794): 321–27. Thomas D. Pearse, "Astronomical Observations near Fort William and between Madras and Calcutta," *Asiatic Researches* 1 (1784): 47–109, has both observations and results. William Hunter's several tables are almost all for latitude: "Astronomical Observations made in the Upper Parts of Hindostan and on a Journey thence to Oujein," *Asiatic Researches* 4 (1794): 134–50; "Astronomical Observations," *Asiatic Researches* 4 (1794): 357–60; "Astronomical Observations made in the Upper Provinces of Hindustan," *Asiatic Researches* 5 (1796): 413–22.

26. There were numerous guides to tell the traveler how to determine latitude and longitude, for example, George Everest, "On Instruments and Observations for Longitude for Travellers on Land," *Journal of the Royal Geographical Society* 30 (1860): 315–24, originally published as a pamphlet (London: W. Clowes & Sons, 1859); *The Indian Field Astronomer; or, the Surveyor's Assistant; being a Collection of Problems and Tables to Facilitate the Methods of Ascertaining the Latitude and Longitude of Places on Land between the Parallels of 10 and 35 Degrees North Latitude for the Use of the Officers of the Survey Department* (Calcutta: Government Gazette Press, 1824).

27. "The Great Trigonometrical Survey of India," *Calcutta Review* 38 (1863): 29, cites the late example of the 1845 determination of a point on the U.S.-Canadian boundary; to test the Nautical Almanac, simultaneous observations were made at Greenwich. The difference between the "true" longitude (from the direct comparison of the two sets of observations) and that calculated from the Nautical Almanac was fifteen seconds of time or four miles.

28. Eric G. Forbes, *Tobias Mayer (1723–62): Pioneer of Enlightened Science in Germany,* Niedersächsische Staats- und Universitätsbibliothek Göttingen, Arbeit 17 (Göttingen: Vandenhoeck und Ruprecht, 1980); Derek Howse, *Nevil Maskelyne: The Seaman's Astronomer* (Cambridge: Cambridge University Press, 1989); John Henry Crisp, *On the Methods of Determining Terrestrial Longitudes by the Moon's Right Ascension, as Deduced from Her Altitudes and Culminations* (Calcutta: Baptist Mission Press, 1827), which was the subject of IOR F/4/1050 28957 (1829); Reginald H. Phillimore, *Historical Records of the Survey of India* (Dehra Dun: Survey of India, 1945–58, 4 vols.), 2: 11.

29. Rupert T. Gould, *The Marine Chronometer: Its History and Development* (London: J. D. Potter, 1923); Andrew S. Cook, "Alexander Dalrymple and John Arnold: Chronometers and the Representation of Longitude on East India Company Charts," *Vistas in Astronomy* 28 (1985): 189–95; George Everest, Memoir, 20 Oct 1829, ¶46, UN Pw Jf 2767/1, another copy being IOR L/MIL/5/402 205, fols. 358–406; Hodgson, "Remarks on the Surveys in India," 21 Nov 1821, ¶7.

30. George Buist, "Geology of Bombay," *Transactions of the Bombay Geographical Society* 10 (1850–52): 167–238, esp. 167n, lists other longitudes calculated for Bombay.

31. Phillimore, *Historical Records*, 2: 72.

32. Arthur, Memoir, 18 Jan 1810, quoted in Phillimore, *Historical Records*, 2: 194.

33. John Goldingham, "Of the Difference of Longitudes found by Chronometer, and by Correspondent Eclipses of the Satellites of Jupiter, with some Supplementary Information Relative to Madras, Bombay, and Canton; as also the Latitude and Longitude of Point de Galle and the Friar's Hood," *Philosophical Transactions of the Royal Society* 112 (1822): 431–36.

34. John Goldingham, "Of the Geographical Situation of the Three Presidencies, Calcutta, Madras, and Bombay, in the East Indies," *Philosophical Transactions of the Royal Society* 112 (1822): 408–30.

35. Forbes, *Tobias Mayer,* 63.

36. William S. Webb, "Memoir Relative to a Survey of Kemaon, with some Account of the Principles, upon which it has been Conducted," *Asiatic Researches* 13 (1819): 292–310, esp. 295.

37. Quoted by Phillimore, *Historical Records*, 1: 185.

38. Michael Aris, *Views of Medieval Bhutan: The Diary and Drawings of Samuel Davis, 1783* (London: Serindia Publications, Washington, DC: Smithsonian Institution Press, 1982), pl. 3, "Murichom to Choka," has as staffage a lascar pushing a handheld perambulator up a mountain trail described in the surveyor's journal as running in a "serpentine and exceedingly steep direction" (p. 64).

39. Rennell, *Memoir II* (2d ed.), 5–6, related road conditions to correction factors.

40. J[ohn] G[oldingham], "A Method of Rectifying a Route Protraction," dated 28 Nov 1831, *Journal of the Asiatic Society of Bengal* 1 (1832): 19–20, proposed a method relying on geometrical construction. James D. Herbert, *On the Present System of Survey, by which the Revenue Maps of Villages are Prepared . . .* (Calcutta: Baptist Mission Press, 1830), ¶3, noted that if a large-scale traverse closed, "the proof of the accuracy of the work is considered complete," but gives no sense of how large a misclosure would be necessary before the survey would have to be repeated (¶¶6–8); Herbert did not admit of distributing error about a traverse. Copies of Herbert's work are in India Office Library "Tracts" and UN Pw Jf 2485; manuscript copies are IOR F/4/1313 52280 and UN Pw Jf 2638/10 (early draft, dated 5 Sep 1829); see also UN Pw Jf 2489.

41. Paul Carter, *The Road to Botany Bay: A Spatial History* (London: Faber and Faber, 1987), 48–53, on this phenomenon and its implications for landscape appreciation.

42. Jopp to Hodgson, 19 Dec 1827, ¶5, BoMC 12 Mar 1828, §30, IOR F/4/1116 29943, 33–58.

43. William Morison, "Minute," 15 Jun 1839, ¶10, IMC 30 Sep 1839, §261, IOR F/4/1872 79616, 26–41.

44. Quoted by Robin E. Rider, "Measure of Ideas, Rule of Language: Mathematics and Language in the 18th Century," in *The Quantifying Spirit in the Eighteenth Century,* edited by Tore Frängsmyr, J. L. Heilbron, and Robin E. Rider (Berkeley: University of California Press, 1990), 113–40, esp. 122–24.

45. C. A. Bayly, "Colonial Star Wars: The Politics of the Heavens in India, c. 1780–1880," unpublished manuscript, version of May 1994, in the author's possession; cf. Gole, *Maps of Mughal India.*

46. William Hunter, "Narrative of a Journey from Agra to Oujein," *Asiatic Researches* 6 (1798): 7–76, esp. 35; see *Edinburgh Review* 1, no. 1 (Oct 1802) 27–29. On longitude and the "language of maps," see Matthew H. Edney, "Cartographic Culture and Nationalism in the Early United States: Benjamin Vaughan and the Choice for a Prime Meridian, 1811," *Journal of Historical Geography* 20 (1994): 384–95.

47. Anne Godlewska, "The Napoleonic Survey of Egypt: A Masterpiece of Cartographic Compilation and Early Nineteenth-Century Fieldwork," *Cartographica* 25, nos. 1 and 2 (1988): *Monograph* 38–39; Godlewska, "Napoleon's Geographers (1797–1815): Imperialists and Soldiers of Modernity," in *Geography and Empire,* edited by Godlewska and Neil Smith, Institute of British Geographers, Special Publication 30 (Oxford: Blackwell, 1994), 31–53; Godlewska, "Map, Text, and Image: The Mentality of Enlightened Conquerors: A New Look at the *Description de l'Egypt,*" *Transactions of the Institute of British Geographers,* ns 20 (1995): 5–28. Refer to Matthew H. Edney, "Mathematical Cosmography and the Social Ideology of British Cartography, 1780–1820," *Imago Mundi* 46 (1994): 101–16.

48. Andrew S. Cook, "Major James Rennell and 'A Bengal Atlas' (1780 and 1781)," in *India Office Library and Records Report for the Year 1976* (London: British Library, 1978), 5–42, esp. 15, quoting BPC 5 Dec 1776, IOR P/2/16, 463–64.

49. Rennell, *Memoir I* (1st ed.), i–ii. One copy of the first edition (India Office Library W 4337) has (pp. 100–136) a reprint of his "An Account of the Ganges and Burrampooter Rivers," *Philosophical Transactions of the Royal Society* 71 (1781): 87–114.

50. Rennell, *Memoir II,* iii, re financial reluctance; Rennell, *A New Map of Hindoostan* (London, 1788). Rennell, *A Map of the Peninsula of India from the 19th Degree North Latitude to Cape Comorin* (London: William Faden, 1792); Rennell, *Memoir of a Map of the Peninsula of India; from the Latest Authorities: Exhibiting its Natural, and Political Divisions . . . With Observations on the Political and Military Advantages that may be Derived from the New Cessions: and an Account of the Site and Remains of the Ancient City of Beejanuggur* (London, 1793).

51. Rennell, *Memoir I* (1st ed.), iii–iv.

52. Alexander Allen, "Roads in the Carnatic compiled from actual Surveys, principally made by the late Major John Pringle, of the Corps of Guides in the Years 1786 and 1787," Jan 1790, IOR Eur E/57.

53. Rennell, *Memoir II* (1st and 2d eds.), 13–19.

54. J. B. Harley and Yolande O'Donoghue, "Introduction," in *The Old Series Ordnance Survey Maps of England and Wales, Scale One Inch to One Mile: A Reproduction of the 110 Sheets of the Survey in Early State in 10 Volumes* (Lympne Castle, Kent: Harry Margery, 1975), 1: xi.

55. *"The Journal of Frederick Hornemann's Travels,* from Cairo to Mourzouk, the Capital of the Kingdom of Fezzan, in Africa, in the years 1797–8. London. Nicols. 1802," *Edinburgh Review* 1, no. 1 (Oct 1802): 130–41, esp. 135. This observation is particularly relevant in light of Rennell's creation of a nonexistent mountain chain that persisted for a century; see Thomas J. Bassett and Philip W. Porter, " 'From the Best Authorities': The Mountains of Kong in the Cartography of West Africa," *Journal of African History* 32 (1991): 367–413.

56. Phillimore, *Historical Records,* 3: 26.

57. Matthew H. Edney, "Cartography without 'Progress': Reinterpreting the Nature and Historical Development of Mapmaking," *Cartographica* 30, nos. 2 and 3 (1993): 54–68.

58. Hodgson to William Casement [Bengal military secretary], 24 Jan 1829, BMC 5 Feb 1829, §120, IOR P/33/19. Everest, *Memoir*, 20 Oct 1829, ¶35; Everest, *Memoir*, 21 Apr 1831, BMC 29 Apr 1831, §98, IOR P/34/3; B to CD, mil, 2 Apr 1833, ¶63, IOR F/4/1379 55086, 5–14.

59. Webb, "Memoir Relative to a Survey of Kemaon," 294–96. Also, James Prinsep, "Table for Ascertaining the Heights of Mountains from the Boiling Point of Water," *Journal of the Asiatic Society of Bengal* 2 (1833): 194–200; George Buist, "On the Adaptation of the Aneroid for the Purposes of Surveying in India," *Journal of the Royal Geographical Society* 21 (1851): 42–57; W. H. Sykes, "On the Use of Common Thermometers to Determine Heights," *Transactions of the Bombay Geographical Society* 2, 3 (1838–39): 38–46.

60. Herbert, *Present System of Survey*, ¶8.

61. J. L. Heilbron, "The Measure of Enlightenment," in *Quantifying Spirit*, edited by Frängsmyr et al., 207–42; Witold Kula, *Measures and Men*, translated by R. Szreter (Princeton: Princeton University Press, 1986), 161–64.

62. The basic history of this topic is covered in George Biddell Airy, "Figure of the Earth," *Encyclopaedia Metropolitana* 5 (1845): 165–*240; Volker Bialas, *Erdgestalt, Kosmologie und Weltanschauung: Die Geschichte der Geodäsie als Teil der Kulturgeschichte der Menscheit* (Stuttgart: Konrad Winter, 1982); Isaac Todhunter, *A History of the Mathematical Theories of Attraction and the Figure of the Earth: from the Time of Newton to that of Laplace* (London: Macmillan, 1873, 2 vols.; reprinted in 1 vol., New York: Dover, 1962).

63. Everest to Casement, 10 Nov 1831, ¶9.3, BMC 25 Nov 1831, §145, IOR F/4/1314 52443, 89–99.

64. See Sidney G. Burrard, *On the Values of Longitude Employed in the Maps of the Survey of India*, Professional Paper of the Survey of India no. 7, part 1 (Calcutta, 1903).

65. William Brown, "Statement of the System of Operations Pursued in the Suharunpoor Revenue Survey," 11 Jan 1833, ¶2, UN Pw Jf 2694/43.

66. Montgomery Martin, *Eastern India . . .* , 1: 315; see also 1: 556, 2: 284–85, 2: 576–77, 2: 910–11, 2: 1012–13, 3: 306–7, and 3: 342–43.

67. The calculation of area by the "universal theorem" of George Adams—*Geometrical and Graphical Essays, Containing a Description of the Mathematical Instruments used in Geometry, Civil and Military Surveying, Levelling and Perspective . . .* (London, 1791; 2d ed, 1797), 345–59—was specifically noted by Herbert, *Present System of Survey*, ¶6; Brown, "Statement of the System of Operations," ¶2, ¶13; John H. Simmonds to Bentinck's military secretary, 26 Jul 1832, UN Pw Jf 2694/37.

68. Read, "Survey." Alexander Allan, "Stations in the Barramahl," nd, BL Add 26654a, is a rough sketch of the region showing a core area of route surveys with a periphery comprising several stations on hilltops.

69. Frängsmyr et al., *Quantifying Spirit*; Roger Hahn, "New Considerations on the Physical Sciences of the Enlightenment Era," *Studies on Voltaire and the Eighteenth Century* 264 (1989): 789–96.

70. James Garling, "Soanda Survey: Introductory Observations Illustrative of the Map and Manner in which the Survey has been made," ca. 1815, BL Add 14377, fol. 2r.

71. Ibid., fols. 130–86, listed places determined by his survey in Sonda; Mackenzie to George Strachey [Madras chief secretary], 1 Jun 1817, ¶5, MMC 19 Jun 1817, IOR F/4/636 17424, 239–49.

72. Thomas H. Holdich, "The Romance of Indian Surveys," *Journal of the Royal Society of Arts* 64 (1916): 194–206, esp. 179.

73. Refer to Colin Mackenzie's instructions to his assistants for the Mysore survey (table 2.1, items 4 and 5); John Warren, "Map of the Purgunnah of Colar in Mysore according to the Partition of 1799," 1:63,360, IOR X/2136, notes that "the high roads have

been actually surveyed and the cross roads traced by means of the villages through which they pass."

74. Garling, "Soanda Survey: Introductory Observations," fols. 2v–3r.

Chapter Four

1. George Dowdeswell, Minute, 24 Apr 1818, ¶6, BPC 7 Aug 1818, §20, IOR P/9/44.

2. Mackenzie to Munro, 1 May 1807, IOR Eur F/151/9.

3. Reginald H. Phillimore, *Historical Records of the Survey of India* (Dehra Dun: Survey of India, 1945–58, 4 vols.).

4. Matthew H. Edney, "British Military Education, Mapmaking, and Military 'Map-Mindedness' in the Later Enlightenment," *The Cartographic Journal* 31 (1994): 14–20; J. B. Harley, "The Spread of Cartographical Ideas Between the Revolutionary Armies," in *Mapping the American Revolutionary War*, by Harley, Barbara Bartz Petchenik, and Lawrence W. Towner (Chicago: University of Chicago Press, 1978), 45–78; Gunther E. Rothenberg, *The Art of Warfare in the Age of Napoleon* (Bloomington: Indiana University Press, 1978), 211.

5. David Buisseret, ed., *Monarchs, Ministers, and Maps: The Emergence of Cartography as a Tool of Government in Early Modern Europe* (Chicago: University of Chicago Press, 1992).

6. C. A. Bayly, "Knowing the Country: Empire and Information in India," *Modern Asian Studies* 27 (1993): 3–43.

7. Robert Orme, "Essay on the Art of War," 1765, IOR Eur OV 303, 109–43, esp. 109–11.

8. James Stuart, Minute, 10 Aug 1804, MMC 14 Aug 1804, IOR P/255/38, 3702–16, esp. 3703–4.

9. Craddock to Bentinck, 20 Feb 1805, UN Pw Jb 12.

10. Hodgson to Charles Lushington [Bengal public secretary], 18 Sep 1821, ¶2, BPC 28 Sep 1821, §3, IOR F/4/682 18864, 273–92.

11. "Brigadier General Sir Thomas Munro," 29 Sep 1818, IOR O/6/8, 625. Burton Stein, *Thomas Munro: The Origins of the Colonial State and His Vision of Empire* (Delhi: Oxford University Press, 1989), 111.

12. Resident at Indore to Bombay political secretary, 25 Nov 1824, ¶¶1–5, BMC 8 Sep 1826, §157, IOR F/4/1017 27954, 23–25.

13. First told by John Warren, "Biographical Sketch of the Late Col. Lambton, Superintendent of the Trigonometrical Survey of India," edited by James D. Herbert (from Warren's letters to the *Madras Gazette*), *Gleanings in Science* 15 (Mar 1830): 73–82, esp. 78; then in "The Trigonometrical Survey," *Calcutta Review* 4 (1845): 79–80, whence it has been often repeated, most recently by Deepak Kumar, "Problems in Science Administration: A Study of the Scientific Surveys in British India, 1757–1900," in Patrick Petitjohn et al., eds., *Science and Empires: Historical Studies about Scientific Development and European Expansion*, Boston Studies in the Philosophy of Science, 136 (Dordrecht: Kluwer Academic, 1992), 269–80, esp. 270. See Finance Committee, "Report on Salaries and Establishments in the General Department," 14 Jun 1806, ¶29, MPC 4 Jul 1806, IOR P/243/8, 4829–85.

14. Lord Wellesley, Minute, 4 Sep 1799, MMPoC 4 Sep 1799, IOR P/254/41, 6058–62.

15. Mariam Dossal, "Knowledge for Power: The Significance of the Bombay Revenue Survey, 1811–1827," in *Ports and their Hinterlands in India (1700–1950)*, edited by Indu Banga (Bombay: Manohar, 1992), 227–43; Matthew H. Edney, "Defining a Unique City: Surveying and Mapping Bombay after 1800," in *From Bombay to Mumbai: Changing Perspectives*, edited by Pauline Rohatgi (Bombay: Marg Publications, 1997).

16. William M. Coldstream, "Indian Maps and Surveys," *Journal of the Royal Society of Arts* 74 (1926): 299–320, esp. 300.

17. Madras deputy quartermaster general to Mysore resident, 6 Jul 1815, IOR R/2/1/35, fol. 817; Mysore resident to Madras chief secretary, 10 Nov 1822, IOR R/2/1/202, 318.

18. Aaron Arrowsmith, *Map of Central India, including Malwa and the Adjoining Provinces, Constructed by Order of Major Genl. Sir J. Malcolm, GCB, from the Routes of his Division and the Surveys of Officers under his Command* (London, 5 Apr 1823), 1:1,267,200, BL maps 52450 (23). Resident at Indore to Bombay political secretary, 25 Nov 1824.

19. Webb to Joseph Dart [EIC secretary], 6 Apr 1814, IOR E/1/127, §162.

20. Figures derived from nominal lists are appended to Andrew S. Cook's "The Training of East India Company Surveyors in the Early Nineteenth Century," paper presented at the Tenth International Conference on the History of Cartography, Dublin, September 1983.

21. James Turnbull Thomson, "Extracts from a Journal kept during the Performance of a Reconnoissance [*sic*] Survey of the Southern Districts of the Province of Otago, New Zealand," *Journal of the Royal Geographical Society* 28 (1858): 298–332, esp. 328, in comparing the conditions of colonial surveying in India and New Zealand.

22. George Everest, *An Account of the Measurement of an Arc of the Meridian between the Parallels of 18°3' and 24°7', being a continuation of the Grand Meridional Arc of India* . . . (London: Parbury, Allen, and Co., 1830), 19–20.

23. Sick certificate, 12 Apr 1828, IOR L/MIL/5/402 205, fol. 418; Everest to Peter Auber [CD secretary], 21 Oct 1829, IOR L/MIL/5/402 205, fol. 296.

24. Bayly, "Knowing the Country," 3–24, on Indian states and their information networks.

25. Ibid., 23, 25–29.

26. S. N. Sen, "Tieffenthaler on Latitudes and Longitudes in India: An Eighteenth Century Study of Geographical Coordinates," *Indian Journal of History of Science* 17 (1982): 1–17.

27. BPC 8 Jan 1767, IOR P/1/41, fol. 14v. James Rennell, "The Journals of Major James Rennell, First Surveyor-General of India [*sic*]," edited by T. H. D. LaTouche, *Memoirs of the Asiatic Society of Bengal* 3 (1910): 95–248, esp. 186, records that he was appointed as of 1 Jan 1767.

28. Percival Spear, *The Nabobs: A Study of the Social Life of the English in Eighteenth Century India* (London: Oxford University Press, 1963), 39–40, citing Rennell's letters to his guardian, Rev. Gilbert Burrington, copied in IOR H/765. Phillimore, *Historical Records,* 1:372–73, gives extracts from those letters re Rennell's modest success in "private trade."

29. B to CD, pub, 30 Mar 1767, ¶17, IOR E/4/27.

30. Rennell, "Journals," 151 (10 Oct 1765), recorded the receipt of the orders.

31. Robert Orme to Robert Clive, 21 Nov 1764, IOR Eur OV 222, 114; Clive to Orme, 29 Sep 1765, IOR Eur OV 43, 30, acknowledged. Orme also seems to have been responsible for prompting Colonel Richard Smith, commandant of the British force at Allahabad, to appoint Samuel Showers to survey the Gangetic Plains (1766–69). Refer to Robert Orme, *The History of the Military Transactions of the British Nation in Indostan* . . . (London, 1763 and 1778, 2 vols.), vol. 1 on the Carnatic wars and vol. 2 on Bengal, for maps from a variety of sources. In general, see Asoka SinhaRaja Tammita Delgoda, "Nabob, Historian and Orientalist: The Life and Writings of Robert Orme (1728–1801)," Ph.D. diss. (University of London, 1991), 263–66; Tammita Delgoda, "'Nabob, Historian, and Orientalist': Robert Orme, The Life and Career of an East India Company Servant (1728–1801)," *Journal of the Royal Asiatic Society* 3s 2 (1992): 363–76, esp. 374.

32. Rennell's early surveys (May 1764 to March 1767) are described in his journal (IOR Eur OV 7 is a copy), published as "Journals."

33. Phillimore, *Historical Records*, 1: 372.

34. Spear, *The Nabobs*, 40.

35. Rennell's MS maps and his publication ventures in Britain are thoroughly analyzed, and historiographic confusions clarified, by Andrew S. Cook, "Major James Rennell and *A Bengal Atlas* (1780 and 1781)," in *India Office Library and Records Report for the Year 1976* (London: British Library, 1978), 5–42.

36. James Rennell, "Some Account of the Construction of the Within Maps," 17 Jan 1774, IOR X/995. Rennell's "Set of General and Particular Maps of Bengal, Bahar, etc.," 1773, IOR X/995/32–36, comprise four "particular" maps (~1:726,900) and one "general" map (~1:1,453,750).

37. B to CD, pub, 21 Nov 1777, ¶82, IOR E/4/36. For the regulations of 5 Aug 1779, see *A Code of the Bengal Military Regulations . . . compiled by the Order of Government, Commander-in-Chief's Office, 1st September 1817*, chap. 65, "Surveyor General's and Surveying Department," ¶¶1–9 (Calcutta: Government Gazette Press, 1817). A copy is IOR L/MIL/17/2/440.

38. Bayly, "Knowing the Country," 29–35, esp. 33; Bayly, "The British Military-Fiscal State and Indigenous Resistance: India, 1750–1820," in *An Imperial State at War: Britain from 1689 to 1815*, edited by Lawrence Stone (London: Routledge, 1994), 322–54.

39. *Bengal Military Regulations . . . 1817*, chap. 65, "Surveyor General's and Surveying Department."

40. Ibid., chap. 65, ¶50, 18 Jun 1806.

41. Ibid., chap. 65, ¶35, ¶¶34–47 generally.

42. David Thompson, *Abstract of General Orders from 1817 to 1840* (Delhi: Gazette Press, 1841), 1817: 2–4, 1818: 16, 1819: 54, 1825: 2–3, 1825: 23–25; *General Regulations of the Bengal Army* (Calcutta: Calcutta Gazette, 1855), §58 "Staff," IOR L/MIL/17/2/442; Edward Moor, *A Compilation of all . . . Orders . . . to the 31st July 1801 [re] the Bombay Army* (Bombay: Courier and Gazette Presses, 1801), IOR L/MIL/17/4/545; John W. Aitchison, *A General Code of the Military Regulations in Force under the Presidency of Bombay . . .* (Calcutta: Mission School Press, 1 Jan 1824), §39 "Marches and Routes," §61 "Staff," IOR L/MIL/17/4/546.

43. All of these figures are derived from Phillimore, *Historical Records*, passim.

44. MMC 16 Jun 1807, IOR P/256/10, 5548. For the continuing situation in Madras in the 1820s, see Francis Mountford, "Memorandum of the Amount of Salary granted to Officers Employed in the Surveying Department on the Presidency of Fort St. George," ca. 1822, and "Memorandum shewing the Authority of Government for salaries . . . ," 27 Jan 1823, IOR Eur F/151/95, fol. 43 and fols. 49–50.

45. *Bengal Military Regulations . . . 1817*, chap. 65, ¶22 and ¶¶30–33, 9 Sep 1806.

46. Cook, "Major James Rennell," 11.

47. *Bengal Military Regulations . . . 1817*, chap. 65, respectively ¶¶1–9, quotation from ¶6, and ¶¶10–16, quotations from ¶10 and ¶13.

48. Phillimore, *Historical Records*, 1: 256. On Wellesley: papers in US Well 3/2/1, 31–32, 61–64, and US Well 3/2/2, 20–22; duke of Wellington, *Supplementary Despatches and Memoranda of Field Marshal Arthur Duke of Wellington* (London: John Murray, 1854), 1: 274–75, 282–83, 360–62, 394.

49. James Salmond, "Memorandum respecting a General Survey of India," Aug 1827, UN Pw Jf 2744/5, np. Although unsigned, the memo is clearly by Salmond: this copy is initialed, "JS Aug 1827," and another copy, UN Pw Jf 2744/3, bears an annotation in Bentinck's hand, "1827 Memo from Col. Salmond on general survey."

50. CD to B, mil, 12 Oct 1809, IOR E/4/667.

51. CD to M, pub, 9 Feb 1810, ¶4, IOR E/4/904.

52. CD to B, mil, 10 Jul 1811 (draft), ¶3, IOR F/3/24, 1163–65. Board to CD, 10 Jul

1811, IOR E/2/31, 403–4. The Court's fear that the French would acquire British geographical information no doubt reflected the extensive exchanges between commercial London and Parisian cartographers, some of which have recently been detailed by Mary Pedley, "Maps, War, and Commerce: Business Correspondence with the London Map Firm of Thomas Jefferys and William Faden," *Imago Mundi* 48 (1996): 161–73.

53. James S. Cotton, J. H. R. T. Charpentier, and E. H. Johnston, *The Mackenzie General and Miscellaneous Collections*, vol. 1.2 of *Catalogue of Manuscripts in European Languages Belonging to the Library of the India Office* (London: India Office Library, 1916; new edition, 1992).

54. Phillimore, *Historical Records*, 2: 394, quoting Mackenzie without attribution. Valentine Blacker, "Maps etc. Belonging to Mr. De Havilland," MMC 4 May 1810, IOR P/256/66, 4122–42, esp. 4130–35; the final nineteen included the source materials for, and a copy of, his 1803 map of Egypt.

55. Thomas Best Jervis, *Address Delivered at the Geographical Section of the British Association Descriptive of the State, Progress and Prospects of the Various Surveys and Other Scientific Enquiries Instituted by the . . . East India Company throughout Asia* (Torquay, 1838), 34.

56. Correspondence Committee, Minutes, 16 Oct 1822, IOR D/8, 777–78; CD to B, sep mil, 29 Oct 1823, ¶¶27–32, IOR E/4/679. CD to B, mil, 16 Jan 1828, ¶¶12–13, IOR E/4/721; CD to Bo, mil, 6 Feb 1828, ¶¶4–5, IOR E/4/1049; CD to B, mil, 30 Apr 1828, ¶¶26–28, IOR E/4/721. Arrowsmith, *Map of Central India*.

57. CD to M, mil, 9 Aug 1809, ¶140, IOR E/4/903.

58. Matthew H. Edney, "The *Atlas of India*, 1823–1947: The Natural History of a Topographic Map Series," *Cartographica* 28, no. 4 (1991): 59–91.

59. Stephen P. Turner, "Forms of Patronage," in *Theories of Science in Society*, edited by Susan E. Cozzens and Thomas F. Gieryn (Bloomington: Indiana University Press, 1990), 185–211. Refer to Max Weber, *Economy and Society: An Outline of Interpretive Sociology*, edited by Guenther Roth and Claus Wittich (New York, 1968, 2 vols.; reprint, Berkeley: University of California Press, 1978), 2: 956–1005.

60. Everest to Dart, 21 Jun 1826, ¶7, IOR L/MIL/5/405 205, fols. 321–24. Everest to William Casement [Bengal military secretary], 12 Oct 1831, ¶98, BMC 25 Nov 1831, §143, IOR F/4/1314 52443, 41–75.

61. For the Court's powers of patronage, see C. H. Philips, *The East India Company, 1784–1834* (Manchester: Manchester University Press, 1961, 2d ed.), 14–16, 55–59, 251–54, 295–97.

62. Martin Moir, "The Examiner's Office: The Emergence of an Administrative Elite in East India House (1804–58)," in *India Office Library and Records Report for the Year 1977* (London: HMSO, 1979), 25–42; Moir, "The Examiner's Office and the Drafting of East India Company Despatches," in *East India Company Studies: Papers Presented to Professor Sir Cyril Philips*, edited by Kenneth Ballhatchet and John Harrison (Hong Kong: Asian Research Service, 1986), 125–52.

63. See Matthew H. Edney, "Mathematical Cosmography and the Social Ideology of British Cartography, 1780–1820," *Imago Mundi* 46 (1994): 101–16.

64. Everest to Loch [EIC Chairman], 8 Jun 1829, IOR L/MIL/5/402 205, fols. 352–57, esp. 355r.

65. J. M. Bourne, *Patronage and Society in Nineteenth-Century England* (London: Edward Arnold, 1986), esp. 85–110, on typical goals of clients.

66. Lambton to Peach, 2 Aug 1801, CPL Wq 091.92–L1791.

67. On Mackenzie's and Hodgson's evaluations: Edney, "Atlas of India," 63.

68. The correspondence is in IOR F/4/679 18861. Clements R. Markham, *A Memoir on the Indian Surveys* (London: Allen & Co., 1878, 2d ed.), 207, followed by Kumar, "Problems

in Science Administration," 271, argued incorrectly that Laidlaw was a very able geologist who was hard done by Hodgson.

69. George Everest, *A Series of Letters Addressed to His Royal Highness the Duke of Sussex, as President of the Royal Society, Remonstrating against the Conduct of that Learned Body* (London: Pickering, 1839), 25–26.

70. CD to M, mil, 23 May 1798, ¶19, IOR E/4/884; CD to M, mil, 7 May 1800, ¶175, IOR E/4/886. CD to Bo, mil, 7 Sep 1808, ¶¶8–11, IOR E/4/1023.

71. Rennell to CD, 4 Mar 1809, IOR F/4/280 6426, 209–10; CD to M, pub, 9 Feb 1810, ¶¶1–5, IOR E/4/904.

72. The basic biography is Phillimore, *Historical Records*, 1: 316–20, esp. 1: 317 and 319. See also, Derek Howse, *Nevil Maskelyne: The Seaman's Astronomer* (Cambridge: Cambridge University Press, 1989); Douglas W. Marshall, "Military Maps of the Eighteenth-Century and the Tower of London Drawing Room," *Imago Mundi* 32 (1980): 21–44, esp. 25; E. G. R. Taylor, *Mathematical Practitioners of Hanoverian England, 1740–1840* (Cambridge: Cambridge University Press, 1966), 198–99, has several mistakes.

73. In "Mathematical Cosmography," I mistakenly accorded Burrow's position at the Tower to Hutton.

74. Phillimore, *Historical Records*, 1: 155–57; O. P. Kejariwal, *The Asiatic Society of Bengal and the Discovery of India's Past, 1784–1838* (Delhi: Oxford University Press. 1988), 112–13. See Bibliography for all of Burrow's papers.

75. Phillimore, *Historical Records*, 1: 159–67; W. A. Seymour, ed., *A History of the Ordnance Survey* (Folkestone: Dawson, 1980), 21–22; Isaac Dalby, "A Short Account of the Late Mr. Reuben Burrow's Measurement of a Degree of Longitude; and Another of Latitude, near the Tropic in Bengal, in the Years 1790, 1791," np, RS L&P.X.140.

76. Morris Berman, *Social Change and Scientific Organization: The Royal Institution, 1799–1844* (Ithaca, NY: Cornell University Press, 1978); T. W. Heyck, *The Transformation of Intellectual Life in Victorian England* (London: Croom Helm, 1982); David P. Miller, "The Royal Society of London, 1800–1835: A Study in the Cultural Politics of Scientific Organization," Ph.D. diss. (University of Pennsylvania, 1981).

77. Phillimore, *Historical Records*, 1: 349–52, 2: 419–28, 3: 474–83; W. C. Mackenzie's *Colonel Colin Mackenzie: First Surveyor-General of India* (Edinburgh and London: W. & R. Chambers, 1952) is largely derivative but has much more on Mackenzie's early life. Mackenzie to Johnstone, 1 Feb 1817, in "Biographical Sketch of the Literary Career of the Late Colonel Colin Mackenzie, Surveyor General of India . . . ," *Madras Journal of Literature and Science* 2 (1835): 262–91 (see Bibliography for reprints).

78. Alexander Johnstone, Evidence, 19 Jul 1832, "Minutes of Evidence Taken before the Select Committee on the Affairs of the East India Company, I: Public," *British Parliamentary Papers* 1831–32 (735.1) 9, ¶1930. Mark Napier, *Memoirs of John Napier of Merchiston, his Lineage, Life, and Times, with a History of the Invention of Logarithms* (Edinburgh: W. Blackwood; London: T. Cadell, 1834), ii–viii, on Lord Napier's attempt; David Stewart Erskine (earl of Buchan) and Walter Minto, *An Account of the Life, Writings, and Inventions of John Napier, of Merchiston* (Perth: R. Morison, 1787), 22, on the mathematical tie to India.

79. Mackenzie to Johnstone, 1 Feb 1817, ¶1. Refer to Mackenzie, *Colin Mackenzie*, 7, on the doubtful issue of whether Mackenzie went to a mainland university.

80. Johnstone, Evidence, 19 Jul 1832, ¶1930.

81. Bayly, "Knowing the Country," 34–35. Phillimore, *Historical Records*, 2: pl. 22v, summarizes the debates over the identities of the Indians.

82. Nicholas B. Dirks, "'Guiltless Spoliations': Picturesque Beauty, Colonial Knowledge, and Colin Mackenzie's Survey of India," in *Perceptions of South Asia's Visual Past*, edited by Catherine B. Asher and Thomas R. Metcalf (New Delhi: Oxford and IBH Pub-

lishing for the American Institute of Indian Studies, 1994), 211–32, esp. 214; Dirks, "Colonial Histories and Native Informants: Biography of an Archive," in *Orientalism and the Postcolonial Predicament: Perspectives on South Asia*, edited by Carol A. Breckenridge and Peter van der Veer (Philadelphia: University of Pennsylvania Press, 1993), 279–313. See Mildred Archer, *British Drawings in the India Office Library* (London: HMSO, 1969), 2: 472–552; David M. Blake, "Introduction," in *Mackenzie Collections*, edited by Cotton, Charpentier, and Johnston, new edition, vi–lvii; H. H. Wilson, *A Descriptive Catalogue of the Oriental Manuscripts and other Articles . . . Collected by the late Lieut. Col. Colin Mackenzie* (Calcutta, 1828, 2 vols.; 2d ed., 1882).

83. Mackenzie to Johnstone, 1 Feb 1817, ¶3.

84. Warren, "Biographical Sketch," 75; Phillimore, *Historical Records*, 2: 411–15 and 3: 465–69, adds more details. On Lambton's Yorkshire roots, see C. J. Davison Ingledew, *History and Antiquities of North Allerton in the County of York* (London: Bell and Daldy, 1858), 299; although Phillimore was skeptical that Lambton was from the Northallerton area, Lambton's will (3: 470) indicated that he had relatives near the town.

85. Re the siege: Lambton to Peach, 17 May 1799, CPL Wq 091.92–L1791. Lambton, "A Journal of the March of the Grand Army from Negamungalum, and of a Tour through the Soondah and Bednore Countries," 16 Jul 1799 to 22 Nov 1799, BL Add 13664, fols. 60–113 (see chapter 2 for accreditation); Lambton made no reference in this diary to any ideas for a geodetic survey.

86. Arthur Wellesley to Barry Close [Mysore resident], 3 Jan 1800, US Well 3/2/6, 26–30, and IOR R/2/1/2, fols. 17–18; reprint, *The Dispatches of Field Marshal the Duke of Wellington . . .*, edited by Lt. Col. Gurwood (London: John Murray, 1837), 1: 59. Warren, "Biographical Sketch," 76. Stein, *Thomas Munro*, 93, re Webbe.

87. Rennell's comments are known only through quotations preserved in its transmittal letters to Madras and in Lambton's response: CD to M, pol, 10 Jun 1801, ¶¶18–19, and 9 Sep 1801, ¶1, IOR E/4/888; Lambton to George Keble [Madras public secretary], 17 Mar 1802, IOR P/242/39, 1061–71.

88. Lambton to Peach, 28 Jun 1802, CPL Wq 091.92–L1791. Lambton's letters to Peach—17 May 1799, 27 Jan 1801, 2 Aug 1801, 28 Jun 1802, all in CPL Wq 091.92–L1791—mention a series of mutual acquaintances, including Brooke Watson.

89. Warren, "Biographical Sketch," 77; Everest, *Series of Letters,* 17–18. Maskelyne's papers have none of this correspondence, other than a note that he received a letter from Lambton on 7 Aug 1805: "Maskelyne Notebook, no. 12: Travels and Expenses, 1802–5," CUL RGO 35/148, fol. 14; Lambton to Bentinck, 16 Oct 1806, UN Pw Jb 25, forwarded a copy of a letter to Maskelyne. For the Maskelyne-Clive family connection, see Howse, *Nevil Maskelyne,* 212–13, and 115 on Clive's giving Maskelyne a living in the church.

90. Lambton to Madras Government, 8 Nov 1810, and Petrie, Minute, 10 Nov 1807, MPC 10 Nov 1807, IOR P/243/27, 7423–26.

91. MPC 3 Feb 1807, IOR P/243/15, 475–82, esp. Strachey to Lambton, 24 Jul 1806, which sent the wrong figures, and Lambton to Strachey, 13 Oct 1806 (quotation); Finance Committee, Report, 14 Jun 1806, ¶65 (quotation), gives the figures: the Mysore survey had increased from 5,111 pagodas (£1,900) in 1799–1800 to 13,576 pagodas (£5,050) in 1804–5; Lambton's costs increased from 2,427 pagodas (£900) to 11,029 pagodas (£4,100) over the same period. Lambton to Buchan, 3 Jun 1807, MPC 19 Jun 1807, IOR L/MIL/5/386 96, 22–24; see M to CD, pub no. 1, 21 Oct 1807, ¶¶225–28, IOR E/4/336.

92. Petrie, Minute, 3 Oct 1807, UN Pw Jb 736, 12–14, and IOR P/243/24, 5605–18; repeated *verbatim* in M to CD, pub no. 2, 21 Oct 1807, ¶39, IOR E/4/336. Petrie, "Memorandum respecting the Observatory . . . ," 4 Sep 1808, IOR Eur Mackenzie General 58, 13–

18, esp. 17; Andrew Scott [Puisne Judge on the Madras High Court] to Petrie, 9 Sep 1808, IOR Eur Mackenzie General 58, 11–13; Warren, "Biographical Sketch," 79.

93. Lambton to Madras council, 8 Nov 1807, MPC 10 Nov 1807, IOR P/243/27, 7424–26.

94. Lambton to William Thackery [Madras military secretary], 21 Feb 1811, MMC 5 Mar 1811, IOR P/257/16, 2787–91; Thackery to Lambton, 21 May 1811, MMC 22 May 1811 (diary), IOR P/257/23, 6645–47; M to CD, mil, 29 Feb 1812, ¶¶267–70, IOR E/4/341.

95. [William Playfair], "An Account of a Trigonometrical Survey, and of the Measurement of an Arc of the Meridian in the Peninsula of India, by Major William Lambton, of the 33d Regiment of Foot," *Edinburgh Review* 21 (1813): 310–28. Authorship was attributed to Playfair by Everest, *Series of Letters*, 17, and by William Mudge, superintendent of the Ordnance Survey, in a letter to Thomas Colby, 9 Sep 1813, quoted in Charles Close, *The Early Years of the Ordnance Survey* (Newton Abbot: David and Charles, 1969), 59.

96. Mackenzie to Johnstone, 1 Feb 1817, ¶14, ¶20, ¶26. Mackenzie to Lushington (not sent), 13/15 Dec 1819, ¶2, and Mackenzie, "Cursory Remarks on Lt. Col. Lambton's Letter of 1st January 1818," nd (draft), both BMC 23 Sep 1824, §130, IOR F/4/836 22401, 142–227; Blacker sent these as curios to the Calcutta council.

97. Mackenzie, "Supplementary View of Further Progress to 1st March 1804," 1 Mar 1804, ¶8, IOR Eur F/228/39/2. Phillimore, *Historical Records*, 2: 115–21, refuted Markham's position—*Memoir*, 73—that Mackenzie and Lambton "do not appear to have worked harmoniously."

98. Mackenzie to Munro, 24 Dec 1817, IOR Eur F/151/57.

99. Mackenzie to Kirkpatrick, 14 Oct 1801, IOR Eur F/228/19. Mackenzie to Munro, 1 Jan 1819, IOR Eur F/151/39.

100. Mackenzie to Henry Traill, 2 Aug 1805, IOR Eur F/228/39; also Mackenzie to Kirkpatrick, 16 Nov 1801, IOR Eur F/228/19.

101. Marginal comment to Petrie, Memorandum, 4 Sep 1808, 18, which is identified as being in Mackenzie's handwriting and as dating to before 1810 by James S. Cotton et al., *Mackenzie Collections*.

102. Mackenzie to Read, 23 Mar 1800, IOR Eur E/309/2. Mackenzie to Traill, 30 Jul 1805, asking for help, 2 Aug 1805, on his correspondence with the earl of Seaforth, chief of Clan Kenneth, and his "ancient friend" Sir John Malcolm, and 29 Jan 1806, re Traill's attempts on his behalf, plus Mackenzie to Mark Wilks [Mysore resident], 3 Mar 1807, Wilks to the Madras council, 4 Mar 1807, and Malcolm to Bentinck, 5 Mar 1807, all in IOR Eur F/228/39. This last file also contains three sewn bundles of papers, two being copies of Mackenzie's official reports, the third entitled, "Continuation of Papers and Correspondence relating to Major Mackenzie's Claims and the Survey of Mysore from March 1804 to July 1805 for the Information of Major Mackenzie's Friends," compiled 2 Aug 1805; he told Traill that other copies had been sent to Lord Hobart, governor of Madras in the 1790s, to a Mr. Greville, and "my particular friend Sir Thomas Strange" (a judge). Mackenzie to Grant, 7 Jul 1815, printed in Mackenzie, *Colin Mackenzie*, 223–26. Mackenzie to Munro, 25 Aug 1806 and 1 May 1807, IOR Eur F/151/9.

103. Lord Wellesley to Bentinck, 6 Jul 1804; Bentinck, Minute, ca. Mar 1807; G. Robinson [Cornwallis's secretary] to Mackenzie, 22 Aug 1805; all in IOR Eur F/228/39/3.

Chapter Five

1. Reginald H. Phillimore, *Historical Records of the Survey of India* (Dehra Dun: Survey of India, 1945–58, 4 vols.), 2: 6.

2. Ibid., 1: 265; relevant records have not been found.

3. George Barlow, Minute, 31 Dec 1810, annex, §§4–5, MMC 29 Jan 1811, IOR P/257/14, 1309–10; Mackenzie to William Thackery [Madras military secretary], 18 Feb 1811, MMC 26 Feb 1811, IOR P/257/16, 2311–17. Arthur to John Munro [Madras quartermaster general], 5 Oct 1808, MMC 12 Oct 1808, IOR P/256/39, 10265–66, on working for the resident.

4. I found six references to the copying of maps by the chief engineer's staff in MMC for the years of 1805 and 1806 alone, with many more for the period from 1806 through 1810, although the maps are not identified; also, George Strachey [Madras chief secretary] to Elisha Trapaud [Madras chief engineer], 21 Jan 1805, MMC 21 Jan 1805, IOR P/255/46, 327, requested a general map of southern India be compiled. See Trapaud, "List of Plans, Maps, &c., in the Chief Engineer's Office," 27 Jul 1810, MMC 31 Jul 1810, IOR P/256/72, 7831–41.

5. James Stuart, Minute, 10 Aug 1804, MMC 14 Aug 1804, IOR P/255/38, 3702–16, esp. 3711–12.

6. Blacker [then Madras quartermaster general] to Thackery, 7 Mar 1811, MMC 8 Mar 1811, IOR P/257/17, 2891–95; Blacker to Peile [Madras military secretary], 17 Apr 1811, MMC 23 Apr 1811, IOR P/257/19, 4741–44. See, Blacker's list of maps in quartermaster general's office, 1 Jan 1811, MMC 8 Jan 1811, IOR P/257/13, 279–308.

7. John Craddock, Minute, ca. 9 Aug 1807, UN Pw Jb 736, 147–48. Goldingham to George Buchan [Madras chief secretary], 15 Nov 1804, MPC 30 Nov 1804, IOR P/242/69, 6161–63, on a few Guides attending the Revenue Survey School. C. A. Bayly, "Knowing the Country: Empire and Information in India," *Modern Asian Studies* 27 (1993): 3–43, esp. 29, on the corps' origins in the years from 1780 to 1784.

8. William Petrie, Minute, 18 Dec 1807, MMC 18 Dec 1807, IOR P/256/19, 11289–97; M to CD, mil, 24 Dec 1807, ¶73, IOR E/4/337. The instructor became an assistant quartermaster general.

9. Madras General Order 14 Aug 1804, MMC 14 Aug 1804, IOR P/255/38, 3721–25; modified MMC 28 May 1805, IOR P/255/52, 3390–406, to prevent the duplication of route measurements.

10. C. A. Bayly, *Indian Society and the Making of the British Empire* (Cambridge: Cambridge University Press, 1988), 64–68, 108–10, 129–30.

11. Mackenzie to Thackery, 24 Feb 1811, ¶5, MMC 5 Mar 1811, IOR P/257/16, 2619–26; Warren to Revenue Board, 2 Apr 1809, MRB 11 May 1809, IOR P/289/30, 2747–53, and 30 Nov 1810, MRB 10 Dec 1810, IOR P/289/72, 10749–64. William Scott [school usher] was the principal in compiling a map of the Peninsula for the *Sudr Adalat* (High Court), perhaps Warren's "Map of the Peninsula of India," drawn by Scott, ca. 1810, Bodleian MS D10:7 (3). For Warren's map of John Malcolm's route through Persia, made for Rennell, see Warren to Rennell, 25 Feb 1807, IOR Eur Mackenzie General 58, 7–10. The contents of the Observatory's archive were listed by a "committee of inspection" when they were transferred to the new surveyor general's office: MMC (diary) Apr 1811, IOR P/257/19, 4775–818.

12. John Goldingham, "Observations for Ascertaining the Length of the Pendulum at Madras in the East Indies, Latitude 13°4'19". 1N with the Conclusions Drawn from the Same," *Philosophical Transactions of the Royal Society* 112 (1822): 127–70, esp. 131n, identifies two of his Brahmin assistants; they are represented in pl. 14, the diagram of the apparatus used.

13. William Petrie, "Memorandum respecting the Observatory . . . ," 4 Sep 1808, IOR Eur Mackenzie General 58, 13–18, esp. 14. Goldingham, "Observations"; Goldingham, *Madras Observatory Papers* (Madras: College Press, 1827), contained reprints of articles

from the *Philosophical Transactions* plus previously unpublished work with pendula and chronometers, such as his account of the measurement of the length of the second-pendulum at the equator (MS copy in IOR F/4/760 20656); a copy is IOR Eur G/51/30. John Warren, "An Account of Experiments made at the Observatory near Fort St. George, for Determining the Length of the Simple Pendulum Beating Seconds at that Place; to which are added, Comparisons of the said Experiments, with Others made in Different Parts of the Globe and some Remarks on the Ellipticity of the Earth, as deduced from these Operations," *Asiatic Researches* 11 (1812): 293–308.

14. John Warren, "Draft Regulations for the Revenue Survey School," 1 Dec 1806, §1, MRB 8 Dec 1812, IOR P/288/47, 7510–34; "Copy of Indenture of an Apprentice for seven years in the late Revenue Surveying School, Madras," BPC 1 Jan 1819, §25, IOR F/4/679 18861, 463–68; if the orphan was over fourteen years of age, his indenture would last for seven years, else until he was twenty-one. Phillimore, *Historical Records*, 2: 350–52, is the nominal role of the school's graduates.

15. Warren to Petrie, 1 Dec 1806, MRB 8 Dec 1806, IOR P/288/47, 7506–9.

16. Finance Committee, "Report on Salaries and Establishments in the General Department," 14 Jun 1806, ¶29, MPC 4 Jul 1806, IOR P/243/8, 4829–85.

17. Colin Mackenzie, "Map of the Following Southern Districts under the Company's Management, viz. Tinnevelly, Ramnad, Shevagunga, Madura, and of the District of Tondiman; reduced from original surveys . . . ," Madras, 1 Dec 1815, 1:253,440, IOR X/2310; William Morison, "Plan of the Districts of Tanjore, Trichinopoly, Coimbatoor, and Madura . . . compiled from the Surveys of the late Establishment of Revenue Surveyors, corrected and verified by the Series of Triangles . . . by Major William Lambton," Madras, 14 Oct 1812, 1:253,440, IOR X/2311.

18. Warren, "Draft Regulations," 1 Dec 1806, and Revenue Board's response, MRB 8 Dec 1812, IOR P/288/47, 7534–39 (quotation).

19. David Ludden, *Peasant History in South India* (Princeton: University of Princeton Press, 1985), 107–15, 120–23, esp. 108. See also Robert E. Frykenberg, *Guntur District 1788–1848: A History of Local Influence and Central Authority in South India* (Oxford: Clarendon Press, 1965).

20. T. H. Beaglehole, *Thomas Munro and the Development of Administrative Policy in Madras, 1792–1818: The Origins of "The Munro System"* (Cambridge: Cambridge University Press, 1966), 71–72. Phillimore, *Historical Records*, 2: 180–82, quotes Munro's instructions to the surveyors and his precautions to ensure the work was done properly and consistently. See also Munro's own papers: IOR Eur F/151/18.

21. Reported in Munro to Madras Revenue Board, 16 May 1802, in a copy book created for the Marquess of Tweeddale (Madras governor, 1842–48), now in the possession of Prof. Robert E. Frykenberg, University of Wisconsin-Madison.

22. Lord Wellesley, Minute, 4 Sep 1799, MMPoC 4 Sep 1799, IOR P/254/41, 6058–62; Webbe to Mackenzie, 4 Sep 1799, MMPoC 6 Sep 1799, IOR P/254/42, 6086–89. Mackenzie was first mentioned as the principal surveyor by Arthur Wellesley to Lord Wellesley, 9 Jul 1799, US Well 3/2/2.

23. Mackenzie to Johnstone, 1 Feb 1817, in "Biographical Sketch of the Literary Career of the Late Colonel Colin Mackenzie, Surveyor General of India . . . ," *Madras Journal of Literature and Science* 2 (1835): 262–91 (see Bibliography for reprints). Mackenzie to Lord Hobart, 6 Jul 1796, MMPoC 6 Sep 1796, IOR P/253/64, 3678–83. Mackenzie to Barry Close [Mysore resident], 5 Jan 1800, IOR R/2/1/2, fols. 25–26.

24. Mackenzie to Buchan, 27 Nov 1805, ¶7, MPC 13 Dec 1805, IOR P/242/82, 6051–58.

25. Mackenzie to Close, 23 Dec 1800, IOR R/2/1/7, fol. 2232v. Mackenzie to Thomas Munro, 28 Aug 1805, IOR Eur F/151/8.

26. Colin Mackenzie, "Plan Proposed for the Mysore Survey," Dec 1799, 4n, IOR Eur E/309/2, included both Coimbatore and Canara; Mackenzie, "View of the Progress and Present State of the Mysore Survey from 24th October 1800 to 20th July 1801," 19 Jul 1801, MPC 14 Aug 1801, IOR P/242/33, 3461–62; Mackenzie, "View of the State of the Mysore Survey on 1st October, 1803," 1 Oct 1803, ¶30, IOR Eur F/228/39/2.

27. Mackenzie to Buchan, 29 Jul 1808, ¶3, MPC 16 Aug 1808, IOR F/4/280 6426, 171–85. Re Mackenzie's salary: MMC 15 Apr 1805, IOR P/255/50, 2476–81; CD to M, mil, 7 Sep 1808, ¶¶57–59, IOR E/4/901. Refer Mackenzie to Merrick Shawe [Lord Wellesley's private secretary], 25 Jun 1805, IOR Eur F/228/39/3.

28. Colin Mackenzie, "Continuation of the Progress of the Survey of Mysore to June 1805," 24 Jun 1805, BL Add 13660, fols. 150–59, map fols. 151v–152r.

29. Mackenzie to Munro, 25 Aug 1806, IOR Eur F/151/9.

30. Mackenzie to Munro, 28 Jan 1807, IOR Eur F/151/9.

31. Colin Mackenzie, "A General Map of Mysore comprehending the Territories ceded to the Rajah of Mysore, the Provinces ceded to the Honorable East India Company in Lower Canara and Soonda, and in the Eastern Districts extending from Ponganoor to the Cauvery River . . . ," Henry Hamilton draftsman, 27 Feb 1808, 1:253,440, IOR X/9599; seven district maps at 1:126,720, most dated 1 Oct 1808, with various titles, IOR X/2108/1–7.

Colin Mackenzie, "Geographical and Statistical Map of the North-East Part of the Mysore Dominion or the Ceded Districts . . . ," William Scott draftsman, 1 Nov 1815, 1:253,440, IOR X/2312; Mackenzie, "Atlas of the Provinces Ceded by the Nizam in 1800 to the Honorable East India Company . . . ," 1 Jan 1820, in fifteen sheets (three missing in this copy) at 1:126,720, all originally compiled in 1815, IOR X/2314.

32. Alexander Dalrymple, *Proposition for a Survey of the Coast of Choromandel* (London: George Bigg, 1784), 8; the proposal is signed and dated 13 Dec 1784. William Roy, "An Account of the Mode Proposed to be Followed in Determining the Relative Situation of the Royal Observatories of Greenwich and Paris," *Philosophical Transactions of the Royal Society* 77 (1787): 188–228 and 465–70, esp. 224.

33. Topping to Madras Government, 2 Dec 1791, quoted by Phillimore, *Historical Records*, 1: 190.

34. Lambton to Peach, 27 Jan 1801, CPL Wq 091.92–L1791, re the latitude: the rate at which meridians converge varies from infinity at the poles to zero at the equator, where meridians are parallel to each other; the phenomenon is barely observable close to the equator. This flaw was later noted by [William Playfair], "An Account of a Trigonometrical Survey, and of the Measurement of an Arc of the Meridian in the Peninsula of India, by Major William Lambton, of the 33d Regiment of Foot," *Edinburgh Review* 21 (1813): 310–28, esp. 312 and 317; (see note 95 in chapter 4 for Playfair's authorship). See also William Roy, "An Account of the Trigonometrical Operation, whereby the Distance between the Meridians of the Royal Observatories of Greenwich and Paris has been Determined," *Philosophical Transactions of the Royal Society* 80 (1790): 111–270, 593–614.

William Lambton, "A Plan of a Mathematical and Geographical Survey extending across the Peninsula of India proposed to be carried into Execution by Brigade Major Lambton," 10 Feb 1800, MMPoC 11 Feb 1800, IOR P/254/52, 746–57; Lambton, "An Account of a Method for Extending a Geographical Survey across the Peninsula of India," *Asiatic Researches* 7 (1802): 312–35, esp. 318–19, re Roy and the Ordnance Survey.

35. Lambton, "Account of a Method," 312. Refer Lambton to Close, 29 Dec 1799, IOR R/2/1/4, fol. 438v. Note that no copy has been found of Lambton's first, informal proposal; Mackenzie to Charles Lushington [Bengal public secretary], 15 Oct 1820, ¶8 note, BPC 15 Dec 1820, §36, IOR F/4/681 18863, 508–30, dated it to Dec 1799.

36. William Lambton, "A Memoir containing an Account of the Principal Operations of the Survey carried on in Mysoor in the Year 1801 . . . ," ca. 10 Mar 1802, MPC 26 Mar 1802, IOR P/242/39, 1188–89; also, Lambton to George Keble [Madras public secretary], 22 Sep 1803, MPC 10 Feb 1804, IOR P/242/60, 631–37. Lambton, "An Account of the Trigonometrical Operations carried on in the Carnatic . . . by . . . Lambton assisted by . . . Warren," 22 Sep 1803 (fol. 7v), BL Add 13658, fols. 66v–67r being a map of the triangles; printed as "Account of the Measurement of an Arc on the Meridian on the Coast of Coromandel, and the Length of a Degree deduced therefrom in the Latitude 12°32'," *Asiatic Researches* 8 (1805): 137–93; George Everest, *A Series of Letters Addressed to His Royal Highness the Duke of Sussex, As President of the Royal Society, Remonstrating Against the Conduct of that Learned Body* (London: William Pickering, 1839), 2, noted that this early work was subsequently discarded. Lambton, "An Account of the Trigonometrical Operations in Crossing the Peninsula of India, and connecting Fort St. George with Mangalore," *Asiatic Researches* 10 (1808): 290–384.

37. Lambton to Keble, 29 Jul 1803, MPC 29 Jul 1803, IOR P/242/53, 2761–63, and 22 Sep 1803.

38. Mackenzie to Henry Traill, 29 Jan 1806, IOR Eur F/228/39. Mackenzie to Close, 6 Dec 1799, quoted by Phillimore, *Historical Records*, 2: 115, who omits Mackenzie's description of the intended region of Lambton's survey; that misrepresentation is clear from Close to Mackenzie and to Lambton, 25 Dec 1799, IOR R/2/1/176, 42–44 and 44–48.

39. Webbe to Mackenzie and Lambton, 6 Feb 1800, MMPoC 4 Feb 1800, IOR P/254/52, 593–97 and 597–600.

40. Respectively M to CD, pub, 20 Oct 1802, ¶97, IOR E/4/329, and M to CD, pub, 23 Mar 1804, ¶300, IOR E/4/331; M to CD, pub no. 1, 21 Oct 1807, ¶225, IOR E/4/336; Government response, ¶27, MPC 4 Jul 1806, IOR P/243/8, 4951–64; Lord Clive to Lord Wellesley, 18 Feb 1800, BMC 14 Mar 1800, §9, IOR P/5/11; Webbe to Close, 19 Feb 1800, IOR R/2/1/2, fol. 254. Finance Committee, "Report on Salaries," 14 Jun 1806, ¶¶65–66.

41. William Bentinck, Minute, 21 Oct 1803, MPC 21 Oct 1803, IOR L/MIL/5/386 96, 15–16; Buchan to Lambton, 11 May 1804, MPC 11 May 1804, IOR P/242/63, 2649–51; M to CD, pub, 16 Oct 1804, ¶177, IOR E/4/332; accepted CD to M, pub, 23 Oct 1805, ¶102, IOR E/4/896. MMC 24 Nov 1807, IOR P/256/18, 10557, re instruments.

42. Petrie, Memorandum, 4 Sep 1808, 17–18.

43. Madras General Order, 9 Oct 1810, ¶16, MMC 9 Oct 1810, IOR P/257/3, 10716–24. Also George Barlow, Minute, 9 Oct 1810, IOR L/MIL/5/424, 274.

44. Lambton to Lushington, 1 Jan 1818, ¶7, also ¶8 and ¶13, BPC 7 Aug 1818, §17, IOR P/9/44.

45. See Lambton's several articles in the Bibliography. James Horsburgh, *Plan of the Trigonometrical Operations on the Peninsula of India from the Year 1802 to 1814 inclusive under the Superintendence of Lieut. Col. W. Lambton* (London, 20 Jun 1827), "sculpt. J. & C. Walker."

46. William Bentinck, Minute, 24 Sep 1804, MMC 29 Sep 1804, IOR P/255/39, 4499–509. Stuart, Minute, 10 Aug 1804, 3715–16.

47. "Outlines of a Plan of Instruction for the Gentlemen Cadets," nd, probably by Troyer, MMC 17 Nov 1804, IOR P/255/41, 5530–38.

48. Petrie to Bentinck, 14 Aug 1804, UN Pw Jb 37.

49. Matthew H. Edney, "British Military Education, Mapmaking, and Military 'Map-Mindedness' in the Later Enlightenment," *The Cartographic Journal* 31, no. 1 (1994): 14–20, gives the institution's history. A comparison of Phillimore's nominal role of graduates, in *Historical Records*, 2: 320–21, with his biographical sketches (vols. 2 and 3) gives the following summary figures for graduate employment (columns are: (1) total students;

(2) students who did any surveying at all; (3) students who surveyed for four or more years):

Class	(1)	(2)	(3)	Notable graduates
1807	12	11	8	James Garling; Henry Walpole (nominated SG, 1829)
1808	18	12	3	John Riddell (ASG Madras 1817–18)
1809	20	8	2	
1811	25	7	3	John Crisp (ASG Bengal 1825–27, astronomer 1848+); Duncan Montgomerie (DSG Madras 1824–33, astronomer 1827–30); Francis Mountford (ASG Madras 1818–24)
1814	17	7	0	
1815	9	4	0	
1816	11	2	1	Charles Snell (survey of Northern Circars, 1820–35)
1817	10	5	2	

50. Bentinck's successor, Sir George Barlow, under financial pressure, stated in January 1811 that the Madras Government had no intention of making a general topographic survey: Phillimore, *Historical Records*, 2: 128.

51. MMC 4 Dec 1807, IOR P/256/18, 10893–903 (detailed plan); MMC 1 Jul 1808, IOR P/256/33, 6742–50 (final report).

52. IOR F/4/388 9488 contains the correspondence and details of the Goa survey; also James Garling, "Memoir Descriptive and Illustrative of the Map of the Portuguese Territories dependent on Goa, surveyed in the Years 1811–12," BL Add 14385; "Supplement to the Routes [of Goa]," BL Add 22361–62; BL Add 22361, fly-leaf, is a map of Goa at 1: 253,440. Garling, "Memoir of Soanda," 2 vols. plus appendix, nd, BL Add 14376–78; especially "Soanda Survey: Introductory Observations Illustrative of the Map and the Manner in which the Survey has been made," BL Add 14377, fols. 1–7.

53. William Bentinck, Minute, 24 Feb 1805, MMC 26 Feb 1805, IOR P/255/47, 840.

54. Craddock to Bentinck, 20 Feb 1805, UN Pw Jb 12.

55. CD to M, mil, 23 May 1798, ¶10, IOR E/4/884. John Craddock, Minute, 21 Nov 1806, MMC 29 Nov 1806, IOR P/255/79, 8325–30, assumed that the underlying motive for rejecting Mackenzie was expense.

56. Phillimore, *Historical Records*, 2: 300–301, oversimplified the debate; for details, see chapter 3 of my dissertation.

57. Petrie to Bentinck, 14 Aug 1804. Stuart, Minute, 10 Aug 1804, and council's response, MMC 14 Aug 1804, IOR P/255/38, 3702–27.

58. MMC 16 Aug 1805, IOR P/255/55, 5518–20. John Craddock, Minute, 27 Oct 1806, MMC 27 Oct 1806, IOR P/255/77, 6898–903; Craddock, Minute, 21 Nov 1806, and council's response, MMC 29 Nov 1806, IOR P/255/79, 8325–32.

59. M to CD, mil, 24 Dec 1807, ¶¶69–73, IOR E/4/337. See MRB 20 Dec 1807 (diary), IOR P/288/51, 7–11, re Board of Revenue.

60. John Munro to Buchan, 7 Dec 1809, MMC 12 Dec 1809, IOR P/256/57, 8741–42.

61. C. H. Philips, *The East India Company, 1784–1834* (Manchester: Manchester University Press, 1961, 2d ed.), 17 n. 5; also Martin Moir, "The Examiner's Office: The Emergence of an Administrative Élite in East India House (1804–58)," *India Office Library and Records Annual Report for the Year 1977* (London, 1979), 25–42, esp. 28.

62. CD to M, mil, 9 Aug 1809, ¶¶134–35 and ¶¶139–41, IOR E/4/903. Peile to Lambton and Mackenzie, 4 May 1810, MMC 4 May 1810, IOR P/256/66, 4244–46.

63. Finance Committee, "Report on Salaries," 14 Jun 1806, ¶65.

64. Bentinck's extensive minutes on the retrenchments are found in: MPC 7 Oct 1807, IOR P/243/24 and P/243/25, 5605–6370; IOR P/243/27, 7342–66 and 7518–22; and UN Pw Jb 736. Refer to his Minute H, 20 Sep 1807, UN Pw Jb 736, 441–42, re surveys. Andrew Scott [High Court judge] to Petrie, 9 Sep 1808, IOR Mackenzie General 58, 11–13, and Petrie, Memorandum, 4 Sep 1808, re Lambton and the Observatory.

65. Troyer to Bentinck, 20 Nov 1807 and 17 Oct 1808, UN Pw Jf 2113–14.

66. Stephen P. Cohen, *The Indian Army: Its Contribution to the Development of a Nation* (Berkeley: University of California Press, 1971), 18–20; Alexander G. Cardew, *The White Mutiny: A Forgotten Episode in the History of the Indian Army* (London: Constable & Co., 1929).

67. Barlow, Minute, 19 May 1810, IOR L/MIL/5/424 392, 51–53.

68. George Hewett, Minute, 27 Aug 1810, IOR L/MIL/5/424 392, 61–218. I did not find a copy in the consultations. The quotations in the following paragraphs are from this document.

69. MMC 9 Oct 1810, IOR P/257/3, 10716–28.

70. Colin Mackenzie, Report, 14 Dec 1815, ¶6, IOR F/4/554 13476, 147–249, gave a larger estimate of prereform annual costs than in table 5.2 (85,981 pagodas, or £32,000) with a similar value for postreform expenditures as of 31 Oct 1812 (46,615 pagodas or £17,350), representing a reduction of 45.8 percent.

71. Petrie, Memorandum, 4 Sep 1808, 15. Barlow, Minute, 31 Dec 1810, 1275 re institution graduates, and 1300–1304 re astronomer.

72. Barlow, Minute, 31 Dec 1810, 1293–94, and Minute, 9 Oct 1810, 275.

73. M to CD, sep mil, 29 Feb 1812, ¶¶16–17, IOR E/4/341. 31,321 is 38.85 percent of 80,616.

74. William Morison, Minute, 15 Jun 1839, ¶11, IMC 30 Sep 1839, §261, IOR F/4/1872 79616, 26–41.

75. CD to B, mil, 17 Feb 1841, ¶¶16–17, IOR E/4/765. S. N. Prasad, ed., *Catalogue of the Historical Maps of the Survey of India (1700–1900)* (New Delhi: National Archives of India, 1975), includes several route maps by Everest: F.63/10–16 (1832), F.77/7–8 (1818), F.108/29 (nd).

Chapter Six

1. J. Young [Lord Hastings's military secretary] to John Craigie [Bengal military secretary], 25 Oct 1817, BPC 25 Nov 1817, §111, IOR F/4/679 18861, 385–412, ¶3; reprinted in Andrew Scott Waugh, "Report and Statements of the Operations and Expense of the Trigonometrical Survey of India," *British Parliamentary Papers* 1851 (219) 41: 875–936, esp. 897–98. See C. A. Bayly, *Indian Society and the Making of the British Empire*, New Cambridge History of India, 2.1 (Cambridge: Cambridge University Press, 1988), 80, and Bayly, *Imperial Meridian: The British Empire and the World, 1780–1830* (London: Longman, 1989), 106, re the Maratha wars.

2. James Salmond, "Memorandum respecting a General Survey of India," Aug 1827, UN Pw Jf 2744/5, np (see note 49 in chapter 4 for Salmond's authorship).

3. Reginald H. Phillimore, *Historical Records of the Survey of India* (Dehra Dun: Survey of India, 1945–58, 4 vols.), 2: 286–87.

4. CD to B, sep mil, 3 Jun 1814, IOR E/4/679; detailed citations are given in parentheses in the text.

5. Phillimore, *Historical Records*, 1: 215–17. S. N. Prasad, ed., *Catalogue of the Historical Maps of the Survey of India (1700–1900)* (New Delhi: National Archives of India, 1975), 229,

lists F.95/30–53 "[Old general Map of India]," nd, 1:1,013,760, by Call, which Phillimore, 1:217 n. 4, titles "General Map of India."

6. Phillimore, *Historical Records*, 1: 217–19, 2: 282–85. Salmond, "Memorandum," Aug 1827, marginal annotation re the map being hung in India House; the IOR's "catalogue hall" copy of [Trelawney W. Saunders], *A Catalogue of Manuscript and Printed Reports, Field Books, Memoirs, Maps . . . of the Indian Surveys deposited in the Map Room of the India Office* (London: W. H. Allen, 1878)—see Saunders's obituary in *The Geographical Journal* 37 (1910): 363–65, for attribution of authorship—bears a manuscript notation from the 1920s that the map had been damaged beyond repair by being hung on a roller; other IOR maps show signs of damage from being hung. Prasad, *Catalogue of Historical Maps* records F.94/23–40, "Col. Reynolds' Map of India," 1:506,880, "finished copy by Monier Williams."

7. Phillimore, *Historical Records*, 1: 219–20, 2: 281–82. Refer to Mackenzie to Charles Lushington [Bengal public secretary], 29 Dec 1819, ¶3, BPC 7 Jan 1820, §61, IOR F/4/681 18863, 121–25; Blacker to William Casement [Bengal military secretary], 11 Aug 1824, ¶19, BMC 23 Sep 1824, §126, IOR P/30/60.

8. Salmond, "Memorandum," Aug 1827.

9. For example, CD to M, mil, 23 Jan 1811, ¶200, IOR E/4/906. Bo to CD, mil, 31 Jan 1810, ¶¶33–38, IOR E/4/486, and CD to Bo, mil, 3 Sep 1813, ¶¶18–20, IOR E/4/1024, re a wrangle over surveyors' jurisdiction within an army comprising both Madras and Bombay units and the Court's dissatisfaction.

10. Hodgson to Crawford, 11 Jul 1815, quoted by Phillimore, *Historical Records*, 3: 303.

11. CD to B, mil, 14 Oct 1818, ¶¶47–49, IOR E/4/694; CD to M, mil, 7 Apr 1819, ¶¶155–58, IOR E/4/922.

12. Correspondence Committee, Minutes, 6 Mar 1815, IOR D/4, 983; CD to B, mil, 10 Mar 1815, addendum, IOR E/4/684, 25–26. Bengal General Order 1 May 1815, BMC 5 May 1815, §9, IOR P/27/1.

13. Mackenzie to Morison, 20 Nov 1814, MPC 12 Jan 1816, IOR F/4/554 13476, 250–55.

14. Mackenzie to George Strachey [Madras chief secretary], 14 Dec 1815, ¶¶1–6, ¶¶21–25, ¶¶30–31, MPC 12 Jan 1816, IOR F/4/554 13476, 147–249; ¶30 noted that 30,000 of about 275,000 square miles were still unsurveyed; ¶¶32–41 list the continuing surveys.

15. Mackenzie to Strachey, 14 Dec 1815, ¶21; also ¶27 and ¶¶53–55.

16. D. Hill [Madras public secretary] to Mackenzie, 12 Jan 1816, MPC 12 Jan 1816, IOR F/4/554 13476, 299–300.

17. Mackenzie to Strachey, 18 Apr 1816, ¶¶2–3, MPC 10 May 1816; and also the following letters from Mackenzie to Strachey, 30 Apr 1816, ¶33, MPC 25 May 1816; 1 Aug 1816, ¶¶53–57, MPC 28 Sep 1816; 26 Sep 1816, ¶¶4–7, ¶¶16–28, MPC 11 Nov 1816; 18 Dec 1816, MPC 27 Jan 1817; all in respectively IOR F/4/555 13477, 1–30, 71–121, 143–263, 354–447, and IOR F/4/636 17424, 193–201. Mackenzie to Lushington, 15 Oct 1820, ¶11, BPC 15 Dec 1820, §36, IOR F/4/681 18863, 508–30.

18. Young to B. Wood [Bengal civil auditor], 14 Feb 1817, and Wood to Mackenzie, 15 Apr 1817, MMC 15 Apr 1817, IOR F/4/636 17424, 205–9.

19. Young to Wood, 16 May 1817, ¶3, also ¶¶4–6, MMC 9 Jun 1817, IOR F/4/636 17424, 217–31. On the plan for the survey school, see MPC 17 Apr 1816, IOR F/4/554 13476, 374–419.

20. Mackenzie to Munro, 24 Dec 1817, IOR Eur F/151/57, and 1 Jan 1819, IOR Eur F/151/39.

21. Lambton to Strachey, 8 Nov 1807, MPC 10 Nov 1807, IOR P/243/27, 7424–26; William Petrie, Minute, 10 Nov 1807, MPC 10 Nov 1807, IOR P/243/27, 7423–24. Phillimore,

Historical Records, 2: 386, quoted Colebrooke to Warren, 18 Dec 1806, on extending Lambton's survey to all of India.

22. William Thackery [Madras military secretary] to Lambton, 21 May 1811, MMC 22 May 1811 (diary), IOR P/257/23, 6645–47. See also Troyer to Bentinck, 19 Nov 1811, UN Pw Jf 2115.

23. CD to M, mil, 30 Sep 1814, ¶¶41–43, IOR E/4/914, in reply to M to CD, mil, 29 Feb 1812, ¶¶265–70, IOR E/4/341.

24. Young to Craigie, 25 Oct 1817; parenthetical citations in the following text refer to this letter.

25. For the high esteem in which the Académie des sciences held Lambton, see Jean Baptiste Delambre to Lambton, 30 May 1818, translated by Blacker to Casement, 11 Aug 1824, note to ¶6, reprinted in Waugh, "Report and Statements," 899 n.

26. Lord Hastings (as Lord Moira), Minute, 21 Sep 1815, ¶¶53–66, enclosed with B to CD, sec, 13 Jan 1816, and printed in "Minutes of Evidence Taken Before the Select Committee on the Affairs of the East India Company," vol. 3, "Revenue," *British Parliamentary Papers* 1831–32 (735.3) 11, appendix 9.

27. Phillimore, *Historical Records*, 3: 225, quotes Young's preamble to his letter, as found in BMC 25 Nov 1817, §1, to this effect.

28. George Everest, *A Series of Letters Addressed to His Royal Highness the Duke of Sussex, as President of the Royal Society, Remonstrating Against the Conduct of that Learned Body* (London: Wm. Pickering, 1839), 25–26.

29. Lambton to Lushington, 1 Jan 1818, ¶2, BPC 7 Aug 1818, §17, IOR P/9/44. Lambton's MS reports are listed in [Saunders], *Catalogue of Manuscript and Printed Reports*, but were returned to the Survey of India and are now lodged with the National Archives of India.

30. Lambton to Lushington, 1 Jan 1818, ¶4, ¶¶10–15. Lambton to Lushington, 28 Nov 1817, BPC 7 Aug 1818, §15, IOR P/9/44, re more assistants.

31. George Everest, "On the Triangulation of the Cape of Good Hope," 3 Sep 1821, IOR E/1/145, 186–211; published as *Memoirs of the Astronomical Society of London* 1 (1822): 255–70, and reprinted in C. G. C. Martin, "George Everest on the Triangulation of the Cape of Good Hope," *Colonel Sir George Everest, CB, FRS (1790–1866): A Celebration of the Bicentenary of his Birth, 8 November 1990, at the Royal Geographical Society* (London, 1990), 34–50. Brian Warner, *Charles Piazzi Smyth, Astronomer-Artist: His Cape Years, 1835–1845* (Cape Town: A. A. Balkema, 1983), 27–28.

32. Mackenzie to Munro, 1 Jan 1819.

33. James Stuart, Minute, 24 Apr 1818, ¶1, BPC 7 Aug 1818, §18, IOR P/9/44; this minute was extensively quoted in B to CD, pub, 15 Feb 1821, ¶¶4–23, IOR E/4/106. George Dowdeswell, Minute, 24 Apr 1818, ¶6, BPC 7 Aug 1818, §20, IOR P/9/44.

34. Stuart, Minute, 24 Apr 1818, ¶30.

35. BPC 7 Aug 1818, §19, IOR P/9/44, listed the heads of information wanted from Mackenzie; Lushington to Lambton and Mackenzie, 24 Apr 1818, BPC 7 Aug 1818, §§25–26, IOR P/9/44.

36. Mackenzie to Lushington, 20 Jul 1818, BPC 7 Aug 1818, §70, IOR P/9/44; Mackenzie to Lushington, 7 Mar 1820, ¶18, BPC 10 Mar 1820, §26, IOR F/4/681 18863, 203–48; Mackenzie to Lushington, 15 Oct 1820, ¶11. Lambton to Lushington, 29 Apr 1822, ¶5, BPC 6 Jun 1822, §53, IOR F/4/750 20515, 41–53.

37. Mackenzie to Lushington, 15 Oct 1820, ¶¶14–15.

38. Mackenzie to Munro, 24 Dec 1817.

39. Mackenzie to Munro, 28 Oct 1820, IOR Eur F/151/75.

40. Re Assam, see Adam White, *Memoir of the Late David Scott, Esq., Agent to the Gov-*

ernor General, on the North-East Frontier of Bengal, and Commissioner of Revenue and Circuit in Assam, edited by Archibald Watson (Calcutta: Baptist Mission Press, 1832), 27–28; Nirode K. Barooah, *David Scott in North-East India, 1802–1831: A Study in British Paternalism* (New Delhi: Munshiram Manoharlal, 1969), 97–98.

41. Mackenzie to Lushington, 19 Apr 1820, esp. ¶6, BPC 5 May 1820, §42, IOR F/4/681 18863, 391–407; B to CD, pub, 15 Feb 1821, ¶¶120–24 and ¶¶133–34. CD to B, mil, 14 Oct 1818, ¶50; CD to B, mil, 29 Oct 1823, ¶¶18–21, IOR E/4/709. For the Malwa survey, see BPC 3 Sep 1819, §§12–13, §15, and BPC 19 Nov 1819, §4, respectively IOR F/4/681 18863, 127–30 and 187–91.

42. Hastings to Dowdeswell, 6 Jan 1818, quoted in Phillimore, *Historical Records,* 3: 301–2. Dowdeswell, Resolution, 5 Jun 1818, BPC 5 Jun 1818, §1, IOR F/4/679 18861, 127–31; B to CD, mil, 21 Jul 1818, ¶¶351–55, IOR E/4/99; B to CD, pub, 21 Jul 1818, ¶¶187–90, IOR E/4/99; B to CD, mil, 26 Dec 1818, ¶¶355–56, IOR E/4/100.

43. CD to B, pub, 17 Jul 1822, esp. ¶2, IOR E/4/707; also CD to B, pub, 12 Jul 1820, ¶93, IOR E/4/700.

44. CD to B, mil, 25 Oct 1820, esp. ¶69, IOR E/4/701; also CD to B, mil, 31 Oct 1821, ¶93, IOR E/4/705.

45. BMC 31 Jan 1823, §153, IOR F/4/750 20518, np; Hodgson to Holt Mackenzie, 6 Mar 1823, BMC 11 Apr 1823, §205, IOR F/4/750 20518, np; B to CD, sep mil, 30 Jul 1823, ¶4, IOR E/4/111.

46. IOR L/MIL/8 is the series of annual military accounts. Civil accounts are scattered throughout the proceedings (IOR series P).

47. Casement to Blacker, 29 Jan 1824, ¶2, BMC 29 Jan 1824, §168, IOR F/4/889 23143, 41–45. See Blacker to Casement, 24 Dec 1823, 7 Jan 1824, and 14 Jan 1824, BMC 29 Jan 1824, §§164–66, and 26 Dec 1823, BMC 5 Feb 1824, §137, IOR F/4/889 23143, 27–38 and 47–64.

48. Hodgson to Lushington, 1 Feb 1823, and associated documents, BMC 7 Mar 1823, §§107–12, IOR F/4/750 20518, np.

49. Court Minutes, 31 May 1822, 11 Jun 1822, and 18 Jun 1822, IOR B/175, 154, 186, 207. See Williams's petition of 24 Jul 1821, BPC 20 Sep 1821, §§1–2, IOR F/4/682 18864, 307–15, copied in IOR L/MIL/5/379 35, fols. 71–87; the other two petitions have not been found. Decision: Correspondence Committee, Minutes, 9 Jul 1822, IOR D/8, 607, and Report, §297, 9 Jul 1822, IOR D/66, 444–45; Court Minutes, 10 Jul 1822, IOR B/175, 297. Blacker to Joseph Dart [Court secretary], 12 Dec 1822, IOR E/1/149, 314, acknowledged the appointment.

50. Lord Amherst, Minute, 23 Oct 1823, and Holt Mackenzie to Hodgson, 23 Oct 1823, BRC 23 Oct 1823, §§53–54, IOR P/59/54; BMC 31 Oct 1823, §§162–63, IOR P/30/29. It is likely that Holt Mackenzie was behind this move, as the "territorial department" was his personal fiefdom and Amherst did much as he requested.

51. Mackenzie to Craigie, 25 Apr 1818, BPC 7 Aug 1818, §37, IOR F/4/681 18863, 1–8. Colin Mackenzie, "Memorandum of Heads of Business to be reported on by the Surveyor General . . . ," 1 Aug 1819, ¶3, BPC 1 Oct 1819, §23, IOR F/4/681 18863, 56–79; Mackenzie to Lushington, 7 Mar 1820, BPC 10 Mar 1820, §2; Mackenzie to Lushington, 14 Oct 1820 and 15 Oct 1820, BPC 15 Dec 1820, §31, §36, IOR F/4/681 18863, 491–97, 508–30. See also Phillimore, *Historical Records,* 3: 94–118; Francis Mountford, Memoranda, ca. 1822 and 27 Jan 1823, IOR Eur F/151/95, fol. 43 and fols. 49–50, list the European officers employed on survey.

52. DeHavilland to Munro, 23 May 1821, MPC 29 May 1821, §25, IOR F/4/735 19865, 17–19; Mountford to Madras secretary, 6 Jun 1821, MPC 3 Jul 1821, §16, IOR F/4/735 19865, 25–31. DeHavilland to Revenue Board, 16 Aug 1821, MRB 20 Aug 1821, IOR F/4/

735 19865, 71–84; R. Clarke [Madras Revenue Board secretary] to Madras chief secretary, 20 Aug 1821, MRC 25 Sep 1821, §9, IOR F/4/735 19865, 85–94.

53. Hill to Holt Mackenzie, 17 Apr 1816, MPC 17 Apr 1816, IOR F/4/554 13476, 416–19.

54. Request for info: circular letter by Clarke, 23 Jul 1821, MRB 23 Jul 1821, IOR F/4/750 20509, 21–23; summary of findings, Clarke to Madras chief secretary, 18 Apr 1822, esp. ¶15, MRC 14 May 1822, §1, IOR F/4/750 20509, 25–38.

55. Proposed Circular to Collectors, 18 Apr 1822, ¶5, MRC 14 May 1822, §1, IOR F/4/750 20509, 39–54. See also Munro, Minute, 10 May 1822, MRC 14 May 1822, §2, IOR F/4/750 20509, 55–65, liberally quoted in M to CD, rev, 21 Jun 1822, ¶¶60–67, IOR E/4/352. On implementation: Clarke to Madras chief secretary, 9 May 1822, MRC 17 May 1822, §30, IOR F/4/750 20509, 93–96; Clarke to D. Hill, 30 Sep 1822, MRC 4 Oct 1822, §5, IOR F/4/750 20509, 111–12; M to CD, rev, 14 Jan 1823, ¶55, IOR E/4/353. CD to M, rev, 18 Aug 1824, ¶119, IOR E/4/930; CD to M, rev, 29 Sep 1824, ¶¶119–21, IOR E/4/930.

56. Bo to CD, mil, 26 Aug 1820, ¶¶72–77, IOR E/4/501; Bo to CD, mil, 29 Aug 1821, ¶¶79–84, IOR E/4/503; plus the enclosures to both letters in IOR L/MIL/5/379 35, fols. 54–92.

57. Bo to CD, mil, 17 Sep 1823, ¶¶201–8, IOR E/4/505.

58. Malcolm to Young, 17 May 1818, BPC 3 Sep 1819, §12, IOR F/4/681 18863, 127–30.

59. See BoMC 9 Feb 1825, §§54–57, IOR F/4/928 26090, 21–32.

60. Mackenzie to Munro, 24 Dec 1817. An example of Mackenzie's complaints is in his "Memorandum of Heads of Business," 1 Aug 1819, ¶4. Valentine Blacker, "Statement shewing the Names, Corps, and Extra Allowances of the Officers employed on General Survey under the Three Presidencies," 11 Aug 1824, BMC 23 Sep 1824, §131, IOR P/30/60; Blacker to Casement, 1 Oct 1824, BMC 6 Jan 1825, §181, IOR F/4/928 26090, 5–17.

61. Hodgson to Lushington, 18 Sep 1821, ¶10, BPC 28 Sep 1821, §3, IOR F/4/682 18864, 273–92.

62. Hodgson to Casement, 29 Mar 1823, Mountford to Hodgson, 13 Mar 1823, and Casement to Madras and Bombay military secretaries, 18 Apr 1823, all in BMC 18 Apr 1823, §§145–46, IOR F/4/835 22286, 5–14. B to CD, mil, 31 Jan 1824, ¶¶212–13, IOR E/4/113.

63. Mackenzie to Lushington, 1 Aug 1819, BPC 1 Oct 1819, §20, IOR F/4/681 18863, 27–43. Blacker later found and submitted Mackenzie's draft report on the GTS, in the form of three letters: BMC 23 Sep 1824, §130, IOR F/4/836 22401, 142–227; the first paragraph of the first letter cited the eleven letters he had received from the council before 29 Oct 1819, requesting the report. Mackenzie to Munro, 1 May 1807, IOR Eur F/151/9, drew attention to his reputation for long-windedness: "I shall be glad to hear from you; I do not expect a long letter as I know you are a famous for the laconic, as I am for the prolonged, perhaps."

64. Mackenzie, "Memorandum of Heads of Business," 1 Aug 1819, ¶26. The only detailed references I have found to DeHavilland's project date from a year later: MRC 1 Jun 1821, §11, IOR F/4/735 19865, 21–22; MPC 3 Jul 1821, §§17–18, IOR F/4/735 19865, 31–36; M to CD, rev, 9 Feb 1822, ¶52, IOR E/4/352; CD to M, rev, 18 Aug 1824, ¶133, IOR E/4/930.

65. Mackenzie to Buchan, 18 Oct 1808, ¶¶2–3, MPC 24 Oct 1808, IOR P/243/41, 7571–76.

66. Mackenzie to Lushington, 7 Mar 1820, esp. ¶28. Aaron Arrowsmith, *Improved Map of India Compiled from all the Latest and Most Authentic Materials* (London, 1816, 9 sheets plus small index), BL Maps K.115.17.2. In addition to memoirs and the Ceded District atlas (see chapter 5), the maps were: Mackenzie, "Map of the Province of Dindigul from

the Survey executed in 1815," nd, 1:253,440, IOR X/2429; Garling and Conner, "Map of the Districts of Soanda and Bilgy," 1813–15, 1:126,720, IOR X/2771; Mackenzie, "Sketch of the Grand Traverse of Soanda . . . ," Jul 1817, 1:253,440, IOR X/2773; and, Conner, "Reduction of the Map of the Principality of Kudugu [Coorg] taken in the Years 1815, '16 and '17," 1820, 1:253,440, IOR X/2113.

67. James Rennell, *Memoir of a Map of Hindoostan; or the Mogul Empire: with an Introduction, Illustrative of the Geography and Present Division of that Country . . .* (London, 1788), iv.

68. CD to B, sep mil, 3 Jun 1814, ¶19.

69. J. B. Simson [Bombay public secretary] to Lushington, 26 Jul 1821, BPC 31 Aug 1821, §4, IOR F/4/682 18864, 267–71.

70. John Hodgson, "Remarks on the Surveys in India generally, but more especially on those of a generally combined geographical and military nature, conducted by the officers of the Surveyor General's and the Quarter Master General's departments, . . . ," 21 Nov 1821, ¶2, BPC 7 Dec 1821, §62, IOR F/4/682 18864, 500–525.

71. Hodgson to Lushington, 18 Sep 1821, for the comparison details. Lushington to Bombay chief secretary, 28 Sep 1821, BPC 28 Sep 1821, §5, IOR F/4/682 18864, 302–4; B to CD, pub, 1 Oct 1821, ¶¶179–83, IOR E/4/107.

72. Hodgson to Lushington, 18 Sep 1821, esp. ¶5, ¶¶8–15.

73. Hodgson to Lushington, 26 Dec 1822, IOR F/4/750 20519, 3–12, forwarded the maps. The maps (nos. 29–40 in Hodgson's list) are listed in [Saunders], *Catalogue of Maps,* 85, but are now lost. Hodgson also wanted all surveyors to submit maps to his office at four miles to the inch: Hodgson, "Remarks on the Surveys in India," 21 Nov 1821, ¶46.

74. Hodgson to Sutherland, 18 Nov 1822, and Hodgson to Jopp, 21 Oct 1826, BMC 12 Jan 1827, §237, IOR F/4/976 27498, 38–44.

75. Francis Mountford, "Map of the Peninsula of India reduced from the surveys . . . under the direction of the Surveyor General . . . ," 1823, 1:1,013,760, IOR X/342; John Hodgson, "Atlas of the North-West of India, containing maps of the countries between the latitudes of 28°50' and 32° North, and longitudes of 75°50' and 81°30' East," 1:253,440, in 15 sheets, IOR X/345.

76. Hodgson to Casement, 22 Oct 1823, BMC 7 Nov 1823, §112, IOR P/30/30; B to CD, sep mil, 27 Nov 1823, IOR E/4/112. Casement to Blacker, 11 Dec 1823, BMC 11 Dec 1823, §274, IOR P/30/32; B to CD, mil, 20 Mar 1824, ¶203, IOR E/4/113.

77. Andrew S. Cook, "The Beginning of Lithographic Map Printing in Calcutta," in *India: A Pageant of Prints,* edited by Pauline Rohatgi and Pheroza Godrej (Bombay: Marg Publications, 1989), 125–34, details the period from 1821 through 1825.

78. Three of the copies examined of the *Atlas of South India*—BL Maps 146.e.6, and the duplicates IOR X/344/1–2—have a copy of the *Sketch* bound in; CUL Atlas 1.82.1 (contemporary binding) has no *Sketch;* CUL Maps 360.82.1 is a separate copy of the *Sketch,* with a separate provenance.

79. Matthew H. Edney, "The *Atlas of India,* 1823–1947: The Natural History of a Topographic Map Series," *Cartographica* 28, no. 4 (1991): 59–91, esp. 62–65, summarizes Arrowsmith's work with respect to India. In addition to separate maps, he supervised the production of the maps for publications such as Valentine Blacker's *Memoir of the Operations of the British Army in India, during the Mahratta War of 1817, 1818, & 1819* (London: Black, Kingsbury, Parbury, and Allen, 1821, 2 vols.). Despite his importance for British cartography at the time, little is known about him; see, Coolie Verner, "The Arrowsmith Firm and the Cartography of Canada," *The Canadian Cartographer* 8, no. 1 (1971): 1–7; Coolie Verner and Basil Stuart-Stubbs, *The Northpart of America* (Toronto: Academic Press Canada, 1979), 222–24.

80. Respectively, Mackenzie to Lushington, 29 Dec 1819, ¶3, BPC 7 Jan 1820, §61, IOR F/4/681 18863, 121–25; Mackenzie to Strachey, 11 Jul 1817, ¶5, MPC 3 Jul 1821, §17, IOR F/4/735 19865, 36–50; Mackenzie to Lushington, 1 Aug 1819, ¶3, and to H. Wood, 29 Dec 1818, ¶6, BPC 1 Oct 1819, §20, IOR F/4/681 18863, 27–48. [Hastings], Minute, 4 Dec 1818, BPC 4 Dec 1818, §2, IOR F/4/679 18861, 675–79.

81. Aaron Arrowsmith, *Memoir Relative to the Construction of the Map of Scotland Published by Aaron Arrowsmith in the Year 1807* (London, 1809), 31. Point stressed by "TIM," letter, *Asiatic Journal* 26 (Oct 1828): 430; "J," letter, *Asiatic Journal* 27 (Jan 1829): 56.

82. The actual letters were: B to CD, pub, 21 Jul 1818, ¶¶187–90, IOR E/4/99; B to CD, pub, 15 Feb 1821, ¶¶1–142, IOR E/4/106; B to CD, pub, 2 Apr 1821, ¶¶170–76, IOR E/4/107; B to CD, pub, 2 Jul 1821, ¶¶143–45, IOR E/4/107; B to CD, pub, 1 Oct 1821, ¶¶151–83, IOR E/4/107; B to CD, pub, 27 Nov 1821 (secretary's letter), IOR F/4/679 18861, 111–12; and B to CD, pub, 1 Jan 1822, ¶¶80–94, IOR E/4/108. IOR F/4/679–682 18861–64 are collections of the supporting documents.

83. Court Minutes, 24 May 1822, IOR B/1/175, 132, and Dart to Arrowsmith, 27 May 1822, IOR E/1/258, §1063, accept the dedication of the *Atlas* to the Company; Court Minutes, 4 Sep 1822, IOR B/175, 442, notes that forty copies of the atlas and *Sketch* were bought for £439/18.

84. Clements R. Markham, *A Memoir on the Indian Surveys* (London: Allen & Co., 1878, 2d ed.), 405. "J" [for James Salmond ?], letter, *Asiatic Journal* 27 (Jan 1829): 56; "The *Atlas of India* Published by the East India Company," *Asiatic Journal* 27 (Jun 1829): 723–24.

85. James Rennell, Memoir, 28 Feb 1823, quotations from ¶2, ¶4, also ¶¶8–10, IOR F/4/682 18864(2), np; a copy is UN Pw Jf 2861/5.

86. CD to B, mil, 29 Oct 1823, IOR E/4/709. The parenthetical citations in the following text refer to this work.

87. Edney, "Atlas of India," details Walker's background and the production history of the atlas. I recently encountered another relevant work: James T. Walker, "A Memorandum on the Copper Plates of the Indian Atlas which he has Placed in the Hands of Engravers in London, the Geographical Materials furnished to the Engravers, and the Arrangements for the Final Disposal of the Work; September 1872," in *Abstract of the Reports of the Surveys and of other Geographical Operations in India for 1871–72*, edited by Clements R. Markham (London, 1873), 47–53.

88. Edney, "Atlas of India," 68–69.

89. Correspondence Committee, Minutes, 16 Mar 1825, IOR D/10, recorded that the Court paid Walker £41 8s for the cost of compiling, engraving, printing, and coloring, eighty copies of the map.

90. James T. Walker, "Memorandum on the State of the Arrangements for the Publication of the Sheet[s] of the Indian Atlas in England," in Markham, *Memoir* (2d ed., 1878), 431–39; it was written in 1872, a year before John Walker's death. Arrowsmith had used 78° for the central meridian of his *Atlas of South India*; it passes quite close to Cape Comorin.

91. CD to B, mil, 29 Oct 1823, esp. ¶7, ¶8, ¶10. Refer to CD to M, mil, 30 Sep 1814, ¶¶41–43, IOR E/4/914; CD to M, mil, 4 Nov 1818, ¶¶10–11, IOR E/4/922.

92. *[Section of the Great Meridional Arc from Beder to Takhalkara]*, J. & C. Walker sculpt. (London: Horsburgh, 1 Mar 1827), 1:506,880; *Sketch of the Principal Triangles extending over that Part of the Nizam's Dominions laying to the eastward of Nirmal & Kurnool by Lieut. Col. W. Lambton and Capt. George Everest*, J. & C. Walker sculpt. (London: Horsburgh, 1 Mar 1827), 1:506,880; *Plan of the Trigonometrical Operations in the Nizam's Dominions, Extending from Kurnool to the Godavery by Lieut. Col. Wm. Lambton*, J. & C. Walker sculpt. (London: Horsburgh, 1 Mar 1827), 1:506,880; *Plan of the Trigonometrical Operations on the Peninsula of India*

from the Year 1802 to 1814 inclusive under the Superintendence of Lieut. Col. W. Lambton, J. & C. Walker sculpt. (London: Horsburgh, 20 Jun 1827) in eight sheets. All of these are in IOR X/Plas Newydd purchase; other copies of the last three are BL Maps 52450 (25) and (26), and BL Maps 52415 (25). These maps were sent to India along with CD to B, mil, 11 Jul 1827, ¶53, IOR E/4/719, and CD to Bo, mil, 18 Jul 1827, ¶11, IOR E/4/1048.

93. CD to B, mil, 25 Aug 1830, ¶2, IOR E/4/729. Peter Auber [Court secretary] to Everest, 27 May 1830, IOR E/1/266, §1244; see chapter 7.

94. For example, IOR X/9003 is a set of nine volumes of *Atlas* sheets bound by province, dating largely from the 1880s and early 1890s.

Chapter Seven

1. Hodgson to Charles Lushington [Bengal public secretary], 21 Nov 1821, ¶¶4–5, and Hodgson, "Remarks on the Surveys in India generally, but more especially on those of a generally combined geographical and military nature, conducted by the officers of the Surveyor General's and the Quarter Master General's departments," 21 Nov 1821, ¶¶8–26, BPC 7 Dec 1821, §61 and §62, IOR F/4/682 18864, 493–525.

2. BMC 8 Sep 1826, §§156–57, IOR F/4/1017 27954, 9–100, and B to CD, mil, 31 Jul 1827, ¶¶225–32, IOR E/4/121, on the original correspondence in 1822 and the survey's subsequent history. Alexander Gerard, "Tract from Agra to Bhopal, surveyed . . . 1823," 1:1,013,760, IOR X/1899; Gerard, "Original Maps in 4 Sheets, marked nos. 1, 2, 3, 4," annotated "received from Captain A. Gerard, 18th November 1826," 1:253,440, IOR X/1903, being the route from Agra to Bhopal; Gerard, "Tract from Agra to Bhopal," 1:63,360, copied in 1828, listed in S. N. Prasad, comp., *Catalogue of the Historical Maps of the Survey of India (1700–1900)* (New Delhi: National Archives of India, 1975), F.29/20.

3. Lambton to Everest, 18 Sep 1822, BMC 23 Sep 1824, §129 encl. 4, IOR F/4/836 22401, 139–41. Lambton to Lushington, 29 April 1822, BPC 22 Jun 1822, §53, IOR F/4/750 20515, 41–53; Hodgson to Lushington, 27 Jun 1822, ¶2, BPC 5 Sep 1822, §99, IOR F/4/750 20515, 65–68. George Everest, *An Account of the Measurement of an Arc of the Meridian between the Parallels of 18°3' and 24°7', being a Continuation of the Grand Meridional Arc of India . . .* (London, 1830), 24, on Lambton's death-defying intentions.

4. Blacker to William Casement [Bengal military secretary], 24 Dec 1823, BMC 29 Jan 1824, §164, and 26 Dec 1823, ¶4 and ¶8 (quotations), ¶¶15–16, BMC 5 Feb 1824, §137, IOR F/4/889 23143, 27–28 and 47–64. Reginald H. Phillimore, *Historical Records of the Survey of India* (Dehra Dun: Survey of India, 1945–58, 4 vols.), 3: 240, re Everest and Blacker.

5. Casement to Blacker, 5 Feb 1824, BMC 5 Feb 1824, §138, IOR F/4/889 23143, 65.

6. Blacker to Casement, 11 Aug 1824, ¶23, BMC 23 Sep 1824, §126, IOR P/30/60. IOR F/4/836 22401, 35–231, is a copy with all enclosures; the letter's text was printed as an appendix to Andrew Scott Waugh, "Report and Statements of the Operations and Expense of the Trigonometrical Survey of India," *British Parliamentary Papers* 1851 (219) 41: 875–936, esp. 899–902.

7. Blacker, Memorandum, 22 Oct 1825, BMC 8 Sep 1826, §158, IOR F/4/1017 27954, 83–89; Gerard to Bentinck's military secretary, 10 Jul 1829, UN Pw Jf 2772/2.

8. B to CD, sep mil, 13 Oct 1824, ¶9, IOR E/4/114.

9. Blacker to Casement, 1 Oct 1824, ¶11, and Bengal General Order, forwarded to Bombay and Madras, 6 Jan 1825, BMC 6 Jan 1825, §§181–82, IOR P/31/10. B to CD, mil, 7 Apr 1826, ¶178, IOR E/4/117; B to CD, mil, 26 Apr 1826, ¶178, IOR E/4/118; approved by the Court in CD to Bo, mil, 25 Jan 1828, ¶32, IOR E/4/1049. See also IOR F/4/928 26090.

10. Hodgson to Casement, 24 Jan 1829, BMC 5 Feb 1829, §120, IOR P/33/19; James

Herbert, "On the Construction of the Atlas of India," nd, but annotated as received 27 Apr 1829, UN Pw Jf 2861/6. Refer to John A. Hodgson and James D. Herbert, "An Account of Trigonometrical and Astronomical Operations for Determining the Heights and Positions of the Principal Peaks of the Himalaya Mountains, situated between the latitudes of 31°53'10" and 30°18'30" N and the longitudes of 77°34'04" and 79°57'22" E," *Asiatic Researches* 14 (1822): 182–372.

11. Everest, *Measurement of an Arc of the Meridian*, 4–40, is a very personal account of his service on the GTS.

12. George Everest, "Memoir regarding the Survey Establishment in India and particularly the Great Trigonometrical Survey," nd, but probably Mar 1827, esp. ¶88, also ¶84, IOR L/MIL/5/402 205, fols. 358–406; copies are IOR F/4/1130 30211b (complete) and BL Add 14380, fols. 54v–67v (¶¶10–129 only). This is probably the "various observations and suggestions" recorded as having been received by the Court from Everest in their minutes, 27 Mar 1827, IOR B/179, 740; it was also dated by Neil Benjamin Edmondstone, "Memoir Respecting the Trigonometrical Survey of India," 25 May 1827, IOR L/MIL/5/407 263, fols. 191–200.

13. B to CD, mil, 21 Nov 1825, ¶¶16–20, IOR E/4/116.

14. Phillimore, *Historical Records*, 3: 445–46. The initial correspondence is: Everest to Salmond, 29 May 1826, IOR L/MIL/5/402 205, fols. 319–20; Joseph Dart [Court secretary] to Everest, 15 Jun 1826, IOR F/4/1130 30211a, np; Everest to Dart, 21 Jun 1826, IOR L/MIL/5/402 205, fols. 321–24.

15. Everest, "Memoir regarding the Survey Establishment," Mar 1827, to which the following parenthetical notes in the text refer.

16. Correspondence Committee, Minutes, 15 May 1827, IOR D/12, 127; Court Minutes, 16 May 1827, IOR B/180; Dart to Everest, 18 May 1827, IOR E/1/263, §1129, copy in IOR F/4/1130 30211a.

17. Edmondstone, "Memoir," 25 May 1827, fol. 195v.

18. The motive is imputed to Everest by Troyer to Bentinck, 26 Nov 1827, UN Pw Jf 2127. Everest's travels to Venice, Milan, and Vienna are mentioned by Anthony Hyman, *Charles Babbage: Pioneer of the Computer* (Princeton, NJ: Princeton University Press, 1982), 72 n. 22, because Babbage spent the winter trying to catch up with Everest; see Everest (at Venice) to Babbage, 14 Jun 1828, BL Add 37184, fol. 132r. Everest to Dart, 17 Apr 1828, IOR L/MIL/5/402 205, fols. 417–18, forwarded a sick certificate from Rome.

19. Correspondence Committee, Report, §91, 15 May 1827, IOR D/76, 60–62. Edmondstone, "Memoir," 25 May 1827, fol. 197v, bears a marginal annotation re the status of the indent for the new instruments.

20. James Salmond, "Memorandum respecting a General Survey of India," Aug 1827, UN Pw Jf 2744/5, np (see note 49 in chapter 4 re authorship). CD to B, rev, 26 Sep 1827, ¶¶2–3 (quotation), IOR E/4/720. Troyer to Bentinck, 26 Nov 1827.

21. CD to B, mil, 13 Oct 1824, ¶¶12–13, IOR E/4/712, re Sabine. BMC 3 Jun 1825, §§149–50, IOR F/4/836 22401, 235–40; B to CD, mil, 20 Aug 1825, ¶9, IOR E/4/116, re Grant.

22. "Report of the Select Committee on the Best Mode of Apportioning more equally the Local Burthens collected in Ireland, and to Provide for a General Survey and Valuation of that Part of the United Kingdom," *British Parliamentary Papers* 1824 (445) 8.

23. Blacker to Casement, 11 Aug 1824. See also Everest to Bedford, 1 Jul 1840, ¶¶3–5, IMC 26 Aug 1840, §117, IOR F/4/1917 82333, 42–44.

24. Salmond, "Memorandum," Aug 1827; Troyer to Bentinck, 26 Nov 1827, quotation with original emphasis.

25. Everest to Loch [EIC Chairman], 8 Jun 1829, IOR L/MIL/5/402 205, fols. 352–57. J. H. Andrews, *A Paper Landscape: The Ordnance Survey in Nineteenth-Century Ireland* (Oxford: Clarendon Press, 1975), 45–52, on Colby's bars.

26. BoMC 12 Mar 1828, §§27–32, IOR F/4/1116 29943, 3–69; Bo to CD, mil, 9 Jul 1828, ¶8, IOR E/4/511.

27. Everest to Loch, 8 Jun 1829; Everest to Peter Auber [Court secretary], 25 Jun 1829, IOR L/MIL/5/402 205, fols. 325–28.

28. Everest, Memorandum, nd, but copied Feb 1830, ¶¶1–7, IOR F/4/1116 29943, unpaginated end section; this memoir was sent to India with CD to Bo, mil, 10 Mar 1830, ¶¶8–9, IOR E/4/1052.

29. George Everest, "On the Compensation Measuring Apparatus of the Great Trigonometrical Survey of India," *Asiatic Researches* 19 (1833): 189–214, esp. 208–9, lists the officers in attendance and results of the test at Lord's. See Everest, *An Account of the Measurement of Two Sections of the Meridional Arc of India, bounded by the Parallels of 18°3'15"; 24°7'11"; & 29°30'48"* (London, 1847, 2 vols.); *Account of the Operations of the Great Trigonometrical Survey of India* (Dehra Dun: Survey of India, 1870–1910, 24 vols.), 1: 1–61.

30. Everest to Dart, 29 Nov 1828, and 7 May 1829 (with bills), IOR L/MIL/5/402 205, fols. 419–22, 432–46. George Everest, Memoir (annotated as "Major Everest's Paper on the Measurement of the Meridional Arcs"), nd, but received 27 May 1829 (Court Minutes, 27 May 1829, IOR B/182), IOR L/MIL/5/402 205, fols. 330–36; other copies are BL Add 14380, fols. 68–71, and IOR F/4/1130 30211b. Everest to Auber, 24 Feb 1830, IOR F/4/1130 30211a, np. See also Court Minutes for 3 Dec 1828, 10 Dec 1828, 28 Jan 1829, 13 May 1829, all IOR B/181, and 3 Mar 1830, IOR B/182. Charles F. Close, *The Early Years of the Ordnance Survey* (Newton Abbott: Davis and Charles, 1969), 154, quotes Everest to Colby, 23 Nov 1829, forwarding Everest's final data and requesting Colby to reciprocate. Correspondence Committee, Report, §995, 16 Mar 1830, IOR D/82, 16; Court Minutes, 17 Mar 1830, IOR B/182, and 26 May 1830, IOR B/183; Auber to Everest, 27 May 1830, IOR E/1/266, §1244. Correspondence Committee, Report, §1064, 6 Apr 1830, IOR D/82, 62–67; Court Minutes, 8 Apr 1830, IOR B/182. The final work was Everest's *Measurement of an Arc of the Meridian*.

31. Quotations from Everest to Colby, 27 Jun 1829, in Close, *Early Years*, 154, and Everest to Auber, 21 Oct 1829, IOR L/MIL/5/402 205, fol. 296. Also, Everest to Auber, 25 Jun 1829, ¶9, IOR L/MIL/5/402 205, fols. 325–28. Kater to Herschel, 31 Mar 1830, RS HS.11.14.

32. George Everest, "Memoir Containing an Account of some Leading Features of the Irish Survey, and a Comparison of the Same with the System Pursued in India," 20 Oct 1829, IOR L/MIL/5/402 205, fols. 297–317. Copies are IOR F/4/1130 30211b, np; BL Add 14380, fols. 78–93; and UN Pw Jf 2767/1, np.

33. Andrews, *Paper Landscape*, 63, quoting a comment from 1855.

34. Everest to Auber, 4 Feb 1830, IOR L/MIL/5/402 205, fols. 458–63, for the final indent: two eighteen-inch, seven twelve-inch, twenty-four seven-inch, and seven five-inch theodolites; plus lamps, heliotropes, thermometers, and mountain barometers. Other documents by Everest on instrumentation: all of the collection IOR L/MIL/5/413 302; Everest, Memoir, ca. May 1829; Everest to Pasley, 28 Mar 1829, IOR L/MIL/5/413 312, fols. 250–51. Correspondence Committee, Minutes, 21 Jan 1829 and 24 Jun 1829, IOR D/13, 284 and 648, and Report, §312, 24 Jun 1829, IOR D/79, 367; Court Minutes, 24 Jun 1829, IOR B/182. Jane E. Insley, "'Instruments of a Very Beautiful Class': George Everest in Europe, 1825–1830," in *Colonel Sir George Everest CB FRS: Proceedings of the Bicentenary Conference at the Royal Geographical Society, 8th November 1990* (London: Royal Geographical Society and Royal Institution of Chartered Surveyors, 1990), 23–30.

35. Everest to Auber, 8 Dec 1829, esp. ¶10, IOR L/MIL/5/402 205, fols. 447–53. Correspondence Committee, Report, §767, 15 Dec 1829, and, §951, 17 Feb 1830, IOR D/81, 223–24 and 336; Court Minutes, 22 Dec 1829 and 17 Feb 1830, IOR B/182; Auber to Everest, 18 Feb 1830, IOR E/1/266, §449. Court Minutes, 12 May 1830, IOR B/183. See also CD to B, mil, 10 Feb 1830, ¶¶1–2, IOR E/4/727.

36. Correspondence Committee, Report, §457, 5 Aug 1829, IOR D/81, 26; Court Minutes, 12 Aug 1829, IOR B/182; Court to Everest, 25 Aug 1829, IOR E/1/265, §2054. On Hodgson's and Everest's relative seniority with respect to succeeding Valentine Blacker, see an anonymous memo, IOR L/MIL/5/383 80a, fols. 382–83, dated to 1823 by Anthony Farrington, *Guide to the Records of the India Office Military Department, IOR L/MIL & L/WS* (London: IOLR, 1982), but internal evidence puts it in Jan 1824.

37. CD to B, mil, 20 Jul 1830, ¶¶9–14, esp. ¶11, IOR E/4/732. Very similar sentiments are also in CD to B, mil, 26 May 1830, ¶4, IOR E/4/728; CD to Bo, mil, 22 Apr 1831, ¶¶7–9, IOR E/4/1053; CD to B, mil, 19 Oct 1831, ¶38, IOR E/4/733; CD to Bo, mil, 8 Feb 1832, ¶¶15–17, IOR E/4/1054; CD to B, mil, 18 Jan 1832, ¶6, IOR E/4/734.

38. Lord Ellenborough to Everest, 30 Apr 1830; Everest to Ellenborough, 2 Jun 1830; Ellenborough to Everest, 3 Jun 1830; Everest to Ellenborough, 9 Jun 1830, all in PRO 30/12/20/10 7481.

39. Ellenborough to Bentinck, 22 May 1830, UN Pw Jf 941. For more information on these surveys, see Charles Metcalfe, "Survey of the Indus—Designs of Russia in the East," Oct 1830, in *Selections from the Papers of Lord Metcalfe; late Governor General of India, Governor of Jamaica, and Governor General of Canada,* edited by William Kaye (London: Smith, Elder & Co, 1855), 211–17.

40. John Rosselli, *Lord William Bentinck: The Making of a Liberal Imperialist* (London: Chatto & Windus for Sussex University Press, 1974), 95 and 274, quoting Bentinck to Ellenborough, 5 Nov 1829; Bentinck to Loch, 12 Aug 1828, UN Pw Jf 1202.

41. Unattributed quote by Daniel R. Headrick, *The Tools of Empire: Technology and European Imperialism in the Nineteenth Century* (Oxford: Oxford University Press, 1981), 137, also 22 and 25. See Henry T. Bernstein, *Steamboats on the Ganges: An Exploration in the History of India's Modernization through Science and Technology* (Calcutta: Orient Longman, 1960; reprint, 1987); Rosselli, *Bentinck,* 285–92; Satpal Sangwan, "Technology and Imperialism in the Indian Context: The Case of Steamboats, 1819–1839," in *Science, Medicine and Cultural Imperialism,* edited by Teresa Meade and Mark Walker (New York: St. Martin's Press, 1991), 60–74.

42. Rosselli, *Bentinck,* 316–21.

43. Ibid., 20–21, 317.

44. William Bentinck, Minute, 1 Jan 1829, BMC 9 Jan 1829, §2, IOR P/33/17; Bentinck, Minute, 3 Sep 1829 (quotation); Troyer to Bentinck, 16 Apr 1829; Bentinck, "Memorandum Relative to a Military Survey of India," 3 Sep 1829; respectively BMC 11 Sep 1829, §§45–47, IOR P/33/34. Copies of the minutes are in UN Pw Jf 2904–5. See Phillimore, *Historical Records,* 3: 195–96.

45. Bentinck, "Memorandum Relative to a Military Survey of India," 3 Sep 1829, esp. ¶3 and ¶6; Salmond, "Memorandum," Aug 1827, marginal note. Refer to W. A. Seymour, ed., *A History of the Ordnance Survey* (Folkestone: Dawson, 1980), 58–59; Yolande Hodson, *Ordnance Surveyors' Drawings, 1789–c.1840: The Original Manuscript Maps of the First Ordnance Survey of England and Wales from the British Library Map Library* (London: Research Publications, 1989).

46. Bentinck, "Memorandum Relative to a Military Survey of India," 3 Sep 1829, ¶13.

47. Everest to Casement, 10 Jan 1831, esp. ¶6, BMC 4 Feb 1831, §120, IOR F/4/1314 52437, 5–10, referring to CD to B, mil, 26 May 1830, ¶¶1–5, IOR E/4/728.

48. Everest to Casement, 10 Jan 1831, ¶¶4–5; for Buxton's survey, see the enclosures to Everest to Casement, 17 Nov 1831, BMC 25 Nov 1831, §150, IOR F/4/1314 52444, 5–9.

49. Casement to Everest, 2 Apr 1831, BMC 2 Apr 1831, §§3–4, IOR F/4/1314 52437, 25–27, with copy of letter sent to Madras, 14 Mar 1831. See B to CD, mil, 8 Mar 1832, ¶¶4–7, IOR E/4/138.

50. Bentinck, Minute, 9 Jul 1831, BMC 5 Aug 1831, §196, IOR F/4/1314 52441, 27–31. B to CD, mil, 8 Mar 1832, ¶8, IOR E/4/138, which also (¶¶59–62) summarized Everest's arrears for computing the Bombay and Calcutta series, plus secondary triangles in the Deccan, and for preparing volumes five and six of Lambton's manuscript General Report.

51. See various correspondence, including Malcolm's minute of 7 Mar 1828, in BoMC 12 Mar 1828, §§27–32, IOR F/4/1116 29943, 3–69. Bo to CD, mil, 9 Jul 1828, ¶8, IOR E/4/511, noted that five positions had been cut from the revenue surveys and three left vacant.

52. Herbert to Bentinck's military secretary, 21 Apr 1829, UN Pw Jf 2767/5, forwarded his Memorandum, nd, UN Pw Jf 2767/8; Herbert, "On the Construction of the Atlas of India," ca. Apr 1829; Herbert, *On the Present System of Survey, by which the Revenue Maps of Villages are Prepared* (Calcutta, 1830) (note 40 in chapter 3 lists copies of this work). Bentinck, Minute, 9 Jul 1831; B to CD, mil, 8 Mar 1832, ¶¶59–75, IOR E/4/138.

53. B to CD, mil, 30 Sep 1830, ¶¶176–78, IOR E/4/133, summarizes the Bengal QMG establishment. William Bentinck, Minute, 16 Apr 1831, BMC 6 May 1831, §4, IOR F/4/1314 52439, 17–19; statements on those surveys by Everest and Montgomerie (in Madras) are in BMC 30 Sep 1831, §§17–24, IOR F/4/1314 52439, 23–67. B to CD, mil, 8 Mar 1832, ¶¶12–17, IOR E/4/138.

54. Bentinck, Minute, 8 Aug 1831, BMC 30 Sep 1831, §24, IOR F/4/1314 52439, 53–67; a copy is UN Pw Jf 2906 and it was extensively quoted in B to CD, mil, 8 Mar 1832, ¶¶17–35, IOR E/4/138. Phillimore, *Historical Records,* makes no mention (that I can find) of either version. Most of the minute is published as *The Correspondence of Lord William Cavendish Bentinck, Governor General of India, 1828–1835,* edited by C. H. Philips (Oxford: Oxford University Press, 1977, 2 vols.), §347.

55. Everest to Casement, 12 Oct 1831, 10 Nov 1831, and 17 Nov 1831, with enclosures, BMC 25 Nov 1831, §§143–46, IOR F/4/1314 52443, 41–104, and §150, IOR F/4/1314 52444, 5–9. B to CD, mil, 9 Mar 1832, ¶¶5–6, IOR E/4/138, paraphrases key paragraphs of these essays. The parenthetical references in the following text refer to the letter of 12 Oct 1831.

56. Everest, Memoir, May 1829, was primarily concerned with explaining this procedure.

57. Casement to Everest, 25 Nov 1831, BMC 25 Nov 1831, §152, IOR F/4/1314 52444, 21–22.

58. B to CD, mil, 8, 9, and 10 Mar 1832, IOR E/4/138.

59. William Bentinck, Minute, 16 Jan 1832, BMC 27 Feb 1832, §160, IOR F/4/1338 53055, 75–82. Everest to Casement, 27 Mar 1832, BMC 9 Apr 1822, §152, IOR F/4/1338 53055, 101–2.

60. The conference probably grew out of William Brown, Memorandum, 26 Jul 1832, UN Pw Jf 2694/36, which proposed that a committee should meet to determine what the surveys were to provide and therefore what form they should take. Bentinck, Minutes, 28 May 1832 and 27 Jul 1832, UN Pw Jf 2907.

61. CD to B, mil, 16 Jan 1833, respectively ¶2, ¶8, and ¶10, IOR E/4/736.

62. Casement to Everest, 30 May 1833, BMC 30 May 1833, §2, IOR P/34/42. For Montgomerie's reaction, see BMC 25 Jul 1833, §2, IOR P/34/45, BMC 8 Aug 1833, §8, IOR P/34/45, and BMC 16 Aug 1833, §§13–15, IOR P/34/45. Everest to Casement, 16 and 17 Oct 1833, BMC 15 Nov 1833, §§88–89, IOR P/34/49; B to CD, mil, 10 Apr 1834, ¶¶99–126, IOR

E/4/146. CD to B, mil, 17 Jun 1834, ¶¶8–9, IOR E/4/741; CD to Bo, mil, 24 Apr 1836, ¶5, and CD to Bo, mil, 20 Dec 1836, ¶3, both IOR E/4/1060.

63. Bo to CD, mil, 19 Oct 1833, ¶¶30–31, IOR E/4/520; Everest to Casement, 6 Dec 1833, BMC 19 Dec 1833, §80, IOR P/34/50.

64. Shortrede to Bombay military secretary, 21 Apr 1836, IMC 1 Aug 1836, §11, IOR F/4/1654 66125, 6–7.

65. Everest to Casement, 23 Jun 1836 (quotations), and Casement to Bombay military secretary and to Everest, 1 Aug 1836, IMC 1 Aug 1836, §§12–14, IOR F/4/1654 66125, 11–20, 36–37. B to CD, mil, 12 Jun 1837, ¶¶27–30 and ¶¶51–52, IOR E/4/158.

66. On the subassistants: Everest to Casement, 29 Jul 1833, and enclosures, BMC 22 Aug 1833, §§129–32, IOR P/34/46; Everest to Casement, 28 Oct 1833, BMC 15 Nov 1833, §94, IOR P/34/49; Everest to Stuart, 28 May 1834, BMC 26 Jun 1834, §96, IOR P/34/64; B to CD, mil, 26 Sep 1834, ¶¶33–39, IOR E/4/147. B to CD, mil, 2 Apr 1833, ¶¶98–107, IOR F/4/1379 55089, 1–21. B to CD, mil, 6 Feb 1836, ¶¶28–32, IOR F/4/1556 63557, 1–13.

Chapter Eight

1. G. F. Heaney, "Rennell and the Surveyors of India," *The Geographical Journal* 134 (1968): 318–27, esp. 320; Reginald H. Phillimore, *Historical Records of the Survey of India* (Dehra Dun: Survey of India, 1945–58, 4 vols.), 4: 9–11, 315. Andrew S. Cook, " 'More by Accident than Design': The Development of Topographical Mapping in India in the Nineteenth Century," presented at the eleventh International Conference on the History of Cartography, Ottawa, 1985, is more open about the institutional problems Everest faced.

2. Phillimore, *Historical Records,* 4: 367–68 and 384–85, for GTS nominal roles; 4: 462, re incorrect tradition.

3. B to CD, mil, 3 Apr 1835, IOR E/4/149.

4. Phillimore, *Historical Records,* 3: 261–64, and Walpole to William Casement [Bengal military secretary], 15 Mar 1830, BMC 19 Mar 1830, §131, IOR F/4/1275 51196, 5–9, on the series. UN Pw Jf 2836/2 contains several documents re Everest's problem in locating the baseline: his preferred site would have entailed paying too much compensation for destroying houses, felling trees, and filling tanks, so he was forced to settle for the second best; see also B to CD, mil, 8 Mar 1832, ¶¶36–58, IOR E/4/138.

5. Phillimore, *Historical Records,* 4: 72–75. On the reorganization: Everest to Casement, 26 Sep 1838, IMC 29 Oct 1838, §47, IOR F/4/1821 75186, 125–36; B to CD, mil, 18 Sep 1839, ¶19, IOR E/4/168.

6. Everest to Bentinck, 8 May 1834, UN Pw Jf 2836/4, announced the approximate series' completion. Everest sent Bentinck a lithograph of these triangles: UN Pw Jf 2938.

7. The work on the Great Arc is summarized by George Everest, *An Account of the Measurement of Two Sections of the Meridional Arc of India, bounded by the Parallels of 18°3'15"; 24°7'11"; and 29°30'48"* (London, 1847, 2 vols.), 1: ix–clxxxvii; Phillimore, *Historical Records,* 4: 12–75.

8. Everest to James Stuart [Bengal public secretary], 21 Aug 1839, ¶101, IMC 30 Sep 1839, §57, IOR F/4/1821 75197, 13–89; repeated and approved in Everest to Stuart, 16 Oct 1839, and Stuart to Everest, 25 Oct 1839, IMC 18 Nov 1839, §34, IOR F/4/1872 79615, 7–11. B to CD, mil, 8 Jan 1841, ¶14, IOR E/4/175, recorded that the Bengal Government thought a longitudinal series, on the parallel of Agra, might be carried eastward into Assam.

9. CD to B, mil, 10 Jun 1840, ¶¶20–22, IOR E/4/763. CD to B, mil, 25 May 1841, ¶9, IOR E/4/766.

10. For example, B to CD, mil, 18 Sep 1839, ¶¶7–11, IOR E/4/168, stated the council's

approval of the remeasurement of the Bider Base, but reminded Everest that he had promised that the Great Arc would be finished by 1837. B to CD, mil, 23 Oct 1839, ¶¶1–7, IOR E/4/169, requested the Court's permission for the remeasurement, but noted that it had sanctioned the move only because otherwise Everest would be left hanging and it had no doubt that the Court would approve.

11. CD to B, mil, 20 Nov 1839, ¶¶31–34, IOR E/4/760; CD to B, mil, 29 Jan 1840, ¶¶17–19, IOR E/4/761. B to CD, mil, 8 Jan 1841, ¶¶2–5, IOR E/4/175.

12. B to CD, mil, 27 May 1841, ¶¶1–10, IOR E/4/176; CD to B, mil, 1 Sep 1841, ¶2, IOR E/4/767.

13. CD to B, mil, 1 Sep 1841, ¶3, IOR E/4/767. B to CD, mil, 21 Nov 1842, ¶¶7–9, IOR E/4/182.

14. Prinsep to Jervis, 25 Dec 1839, RGS library MS "Jervis."

15. CD to B, mil, 25 May 1841, ¶¶15–20, IOR E/4/766; CD to B, mil, 4 Aug 1841, ¶¶1–10, IOR E/4/767.

16. CD to B, mil no.1, 26 Sep 1843, esp. ¶30, also ¶¶31–33, IOR E/4/775.

17. CD to B, mil, 2 Aug 1844, ¶¶37–38, IOR E/4/779.

18. Jervis to C. G. A. Dawkins [Lord Aberdeen's private secretary], 4 and 6 Mar 1845, BL Add 43244, fols. 93, 95–96. The map was the *Chinese Plan of the City of Peking* (London: T. B. Jervis, 1 May 1843), at 1:6150, BL Maps 198.f.54; BL Maps 7.aa.23 and 8.c.36 are copies of a variant state, also dated 1843.

19. Unfortunately, the papers of the Court's various committees do not survive from this period; the principal source is therefore a special collection: IOR L/MIL/5/413 306.

20. For biographical details, see Phillimore, *Historical Records,* 3: 463 and 4: 449–51; William Paget Jervis, *Thomas Best Jervis as Christian Soldier, Geographer, and Friend of India, 1796–1857: A Centenary Tribute by his Son* (London: Elliot Stock, 1898); George Wilkins, *The Voice of the Dead: A Funeral Sermon occasioned by the Death of Lieutenant T. B. Jervis* (London, 1857), also published as *Biographical Sketch of T. B. Jervis, being the Substance of a Funeral Sermon* (London, 1857). For his training, see Andrew S. Cook, "The Training of East India Company Surveyors in the Early Nineteenth Century," presented at the Tenth International Conference on the History of Cartography, Dublin, September 1983. Thomas's son William Paget Jervis was such an ardent evangelical, according to his descendent Paola Jervis of Florence, that he left Britain after 1859 rather than occupy the same island as Charles Darwin!

21. Thomas B. Jervis, "Historical and Geographical Account of the Western Coast of India," *Transactions of the Bombay Geographical Society* 4, no. 1 (1840): 1–244. Jervis, "An Atlas Illustrative of a Geographical and Statistical Memoir of the British and Foreign Territories situated in the North-West Coast of peninsular India comprised in that Division of Muharashtra designated in the Ancient Geography of the Hindoos, the Konkun," 1834, MS with some twenty maps and plans, IOR X/2746; Phillimore, *Historical Records,* 3: 463, mistakenly notes that the atlas was published.

22. Thomas B. Jervis, *Records of Ancient Science, Exemplified and Authenticated in the Primitive Universal Standard of Weights and Measures* (Calcutta, 1836); Jervis, *The Expediency and Facility of Establishing the Metrological and Monetary Systems throughout India, on a Scientific and Permanent Basis, Grounded on an Analytical View of the Weights, Measures and Coins of India, and their Relative Quantities with respect to such as Subsist at Present, or have hitherto Subsisted in all past Ages throughout the World* (Bombay: American Mission, 1836). See Jervis to Herschel, 19 Oct 1835, RS HS.10.317.

23. Jervis to CD, 26 Dec 1837, IOR L/MIL/5/413 306, fol. 13.

24. David P. Miller, "The Royal Society of London, 1800–1835: A Study in the Cul-

tural Politics of Scientific Organization," Ph.D. diss. (University of Pennsylvania, 1981), 341–50.

25. Hobhouse's published diaries, *Recollections of a Long Life, with Additional Extracts from his Private Diaries edited by his Daughter, Lady Dorchester* (London: John Murray, 1909–11, 6 vols.), and his biographer, Michael Joyce, *My Friend H: John Cam Hobhouse, Baron Broughton of Broughton de Gyfford* (London: John Murray, 1948), concentrated on his home political career and paid little attention to his scientific, social, or Indian commitments; unfortunately, his diaries held by the British Library start only in 1843. See Jervis to Lloyd, 28 Mar 1839, RS MS.119 (Te 1), §63, and the rather bitter section in Thomas B. Jervis, *India in Relation to Great Britain: Considerations on its Future Administration* (London: John Petheram, 1853), 33–40, esp. 34, also 54–55, for Jervis's debt to Hobhouse.

26. Jervis to Hobhouse, 27 Jun 1838, and Augustus to Hobhouse, 20 Jul 1838, BL Add 36469, fols. 33v, 92. Hobhouse to Lord John Russell, 26 Nov 1839, IOR F/2/12, 402.

27. Jervis to CD, 10 Jul 1837, IOR L/MIL/5/413 306, fols. 3r–4r, original emphasis; see Court Minutes, 12 Jul 1837, IOR B/194, 400–401. His first request, now lost, was apparently that of 2 Jan 1837, referred to by James Cosmo Melvill [EIC secretary] to Jervis, 10 Nov 1837, IOR E/1/273, §2670.

28. Jervis, *India in Relation to Great Britain*, 15.

29. Phillimore, *Historical Records*, 4: 449, notes that James Bedford had served without break since 1821 and had been appointed deputy surveyor general in 1832; other Bengal surveyors had far more years of unbroken service than Jervis, whose appointment as surveyor dated only from 1823 (his period in the Konkan from 1819 to 1821 had been for collecting statistics). Then again, Everest was *the* senior officer!

30. Melvill to Jervis, 10 Nov 1837. Jervis to CD, 5 Aug 1837, IOR L/MIL/5/413 306, fols. 7–9; the testimonials have not survived. Court Minutes, 9, 16, and 23 Aug 1837, IOR B/194, 500, 540, 562–63. J. D. Dickenson [Court's deputy secretary] to Jervis, 9 Sep 1837, IOR L/MIL/5/413 306, fol. 11.

31. Melvill to Jervis, 18 Jan 1838, IOR E/1/274, §154.

32. Melvill to Jervis, 9 Feb 1837, IOR E/1/273, §375; Jervis to Melvill, 15 Aug 1838, IOR L/MIL/5/413 306, fols. 91–93. Jervis to CD, 5 Aug 1837.

33. For example, in two letters to the Royal Astronomical Society, 1 Mar and 4 Jun 1839, RAS Letters 1839, Jervis sought free copies of astronomical works and catalogs from British observatories to be sent to him in India, as surveyor general. The attempt was successful: Jervis to RAS, 13 Sep 1839, RAS Letters 1840. He continued to misrepresent his appointment much later, when he wrote to the British prime minister seeking support for a project of the Royal Geographical Society; Jervis to Sir Robert Peel, 21 Mar 1843, BL Add 40526, fols. 219–20, stated that he had been "appointed in 1837 to the office of Surveyor General of India, once filled by Rennell and Lambton."

34. Jervis to Hobhouse, 16 Nov 1838, BL Add 36469, fol. 188.

35. George Everest, *A Series of Letters Addressed to His Royal Highness the Duke of Sussex, as President of the Royal Society, Remonstrating against the Conduct of that Learned Body* (London: William Pickering, 1839), esp. 4.

36. Airy to Herschel, 3 Oct 1839, and its enclosure, Melvill to Airy, 26 Sep 1839, RS HS.1.82. CUL RGO 6/417/25, fols. 324–32, comprises a copy of the same letters and other documents on the subject.

37. Herschel to Airy, 9 Oct 1839, RS HS.1.83. Similar sentiments (and in a clearer hand) are in Herschel to Baily, nd, RS HS.3.283.

38. Everest to Jervis, 30 Dec 1839, RGS Library MS "Jervis"; Phillimore, *Historical Records*, 4: 438–39, quotes Everest's copy in part. On Everest's religious beliefs, see Everest

to Charles Babbage, 14 Jun 1828, BL Add 37184, fol. 132, and Mary Everest Boole, "The Naming of Mount Everest," in Mary E. Boole, *Collected Works,* edited by E. M. Cobham (London: C. W. Daniel, 1931), 3: 1094–1100. My thanks to Jim Smith for this last reference.

39. Jervis to Washington, 27 Feb 1840, RGS Library MS "Jervis."

40. CD to B, mil, 10 Apr 1838 ¶46, IOR E/4/754. Court Minutes, 21 Nov 1838, IOR B/197, 50; Walker to Melvill, 15 Aug 1838, IOR L/MIL/5/413 306, fol. 109, gives some details.

41. William Cubitt [Bengal military secretary] to Everest, 13 Jan 1840, IMC 13 Jan 1840, §2, IOR F/4/1917 82337, 9–10; also CD to B, mil, 16 Oct 1839, IOR E/4/760.

42. Melvill to William Cabell [Board secretary], 10 Oct 1839, ¶¶2–3, IOR E/2/16, 119–20, §5181.

43. Everest to Cubitt, 25 Feb 1840, and Cubitt to Everest, 18 Mar 1840, IMC 18 Mar 1840, §§165–66, IOR F/4/1917 82337, 11–14; IMC 16 Sep 1840, §§175–78, IOR F/4/1917 82337, 15–19. Phillimore, *Historical Records,* 4: 307–10.

44. Thomas B. Jervis, "Memoir on the Origin, Progress, and Present State of the Surveys of India," *Journal of the Royal Geographical Society* 7 (1837): 127–43, reprinted in *Transactions of the Bombay Geographical Society* 4, no. 2 (1840): 133–53, and in *Madras Journal of Literature and Science* 7 (1838): 424–41; Jervis, "Some Account of the Progress of the Trigonometrical Survey now carrying on in India," *Monthly Notices of the Royal Astronomical Society* 4 (1836–39): 206–10.

45. Thomas B. Jervis, *Address delivered at the Geographical Section of the British Association, Newcastle on Tyne, Descriptive of the State, Progress, and Prospects of the Various Surveys, and Other Scientific Enquiries, Instituted by the Honorable East India Company throughout Asia; with a Prefatory Sketch of the Principles and Requirements of Geography* (Torquay, 1838). Jervis to Washington, 4 Sep 1838, RGS Library MS "Jervis," explained the publication of the *Address:* the *Morning Herald* said that Jervis had superintended the "Survey of India" for thirteen years; the *Newcastle Journal* "put . . . a pack of nonsensical statements into my mouth"; the *Athenaeum [Journal of Literature, Science, and the Fine Arts]* wrote only a few lines on the BAAS meeting and did not mention Jervis's plans. In this last point, Jervis seems to refer specifically to the meeting of Section C (geology) of the BAAS rather than to the whole; the *Athenaeum* had long been an active supporter of the BAAS and gave it extensive coverage and advertising. See Jack Morrell and Arnold Thackery, *Gentlemen of Science: Early Years of the British Association for the Advancement of Science* (Oxford: Oxford University Press, 1981), esp. 286, for the awkward position of geography in the BAAS.

46. Jervis to CD, 26 Dec 1837, enclosing Jervis to Salmond, 13 Oct 1837, and Salmond to Jervis, 23 Oct 1837; Jervis to CD, nd (but received, Court Minutes, 11 Apr 1838, IOR B/195, 909–10), enclosing Jervis, four memoranda, nd, on (1) the provision of instruments, (2) the "annexation of the revenue, statistical and maritime surveys to the Surveyor Generalship," (3) the verification of the Indian standard and the establishment of a "uniform, intelligible and exact system of measures and weights," and (4) publishing all of the Company's geographical materials found in London and Calcutta (a copy is BL Add 14380, fols. 4–17); Jervis to CD, 12 Jun 1838; Jervis to Melvill, 6 Aug 1838, enclosing Jervis, Memorandum, nd, Colby to Jervis, 20 Jun 1838, and Beaufort to Jervis, 22 Jun 1838; Jervis to Melvill, 15 Aug 1838; all in IOR L/MIL/5/413 306, fols. 12–25, 44–67, 76–93. Also, Jervis to Lushington, 16 Jun 1838, BL Add 14380, fols. 18–22.

47. Petition to CD, 14 Jul/15 Aug 1838, included as an appendix to some copies of Jervis, *Address;* for example, BL 10058.c.10. Stand-alone copies are: CUL RGO 6/417/25; CUL RGO 15/48, fols. 93–94; RGS Library MS "Jervis"; BL Add 36469, fols. 38–39 (signed only by Augustus, sent to Hobhouse for his information); and, IOR L/MIL/5/413, fols. 94–97 (incomplete set of signatures). Jervis to Washington, 4 Sep 1838, re authorship.

Augustus to Hobhouse, 16 Jul 1838; Augustus to Lushington, nd (ca. Jul 1838); Augustus to Hobhouse, 20 Jul 1838, all in BL Add 63469, fols. 40–41, 42–43, 92. Submitted: Jervis to Melvill, 15 Aug 1838 (note 32); Court Minutes, 17 Aug 1838, IOR B/196, 452–53. Herschel's diary for 1838–47, RS MS.584, shows that he was in Germany and would not have been able to sign the petition until after his return to England, 4 Aug 1838.

48. See Thomas B. Jervis, "Additional Observations on the Remarkable Tides in the Gulf of Cambay," *Journal of the Royal Geographical Society* 8 (1838): 202–5.

49. The relevant extract from Lambton's report was reprinted as an appendix to Jervis, *Address*; Phillimore, *Historical Records*, 4: 438, does not further identify the source, but it is very similar to Lambton to Charles Lushington [Bengal public secretary], 29 Apr 1822, BPC 6 Jun 1822, §53, IOR F/4/750 20515, 41–53; refer to William Lambton, "Corrections applied to the Great Meridional Arc, extending from Latitude 8°9′38.39″ to Latitude 18°3′23.64″, to reduce it to the Parliamentary Standard," *Philosophical Transactions of the Royal Society* 113 (1823): 27–33. Jervis to Melvill, 15 Aug 1838, re instruments.

50. Jervis to CD, 12 Jun 1838, postscript.

51. Colby to Jervis, 20 Jun 1838.

52. Jervis to Salmond, 13 Oct 1837.

53. Jervis to CD, 12 Jun 1838.

54. Jervis to CD, 26 Dec 1837.

55. Jervis, *Address*, 43–44, extracted Adam White, *Memoir of the late David Scott, Esq., Agent to the Governor General on the North-East Frontier of Bengal, and Commissioner of Revenue and Circuit in Assam, &c. &c. &c.*, edited by Archibald Watson (Calcutta: Baptist Mission Press, 1832), 27–28; BL Add 36469, fol. 354, is a copy which Jervis sent to Hobhouse for his information; see also Tate to Jervis, 12 Sep 1838, appended to Jervis, *Address*.

56. Salmond to Jervis, 23 Oct 1837.

57. For example, H. Richardson, ed., *Ordnance Survey Memoirs for the Parishes of Desertmartin and Kilcronahan, 1836–37* (Ballinascreen Historical Society, 1986). The majority of these memoirs are still in manuscript at the Royal Irish Academy, Dublin. See Morrell and Thackery, *Gentlemen of Science*, 333–34, on the popularity of the OS memoirs ca. 1835.

58. Jervis to Salmond, 13 Oct 1837; Jervis, Memorandum no. 2, Apr 1838; and Jervis to CD, 12 Jun 1838. J. H. Andrews, *A Paper Landscape: The Ordnance Survey in Nineteenth-Century Ireland* (Oxford: Clarendon Press, 1975), 90–91. See chapter 4 for the Bombay survey.

59. Jervis to CD, 12 Jun 1838.

60. Jervis, *Address*, 34.

61. Jervis to CD, 12 Jun 1838.

62. Jervis to Salmond, 13 Oct 1837.

63. Thomas B. Jervis, "Memorandum of the Preliminary Measures, recommended by Major Jervis, to expedite and complete the Great Survey of India," ca. 6 Aug 1838, IOR L/MIL/5/413 306, fols. 84–86.

64. Jervis to CD, 21 Feb 1838, BL Add 36469, fols. 79–81, copy fols. 83–85; Court Minutes, 28 Feb 1838, IOR B/195, 657–58; Jervis to Washington, 26 Feb 1838, RGS Library MS "Jervis," noted the Board's support for this scheme. Melvill to Jervis, [19] Jul 1838, BL Add 36469, fol. 87; Court Minutes, 18 Jul 1838, IOR B/196, 378. Melvill to Cabell, 19 Jul 1838, BL Add 36469, fol. 77, with pencil annotation by Board secretary ("W. L.") on fol. 78v. Jervis to Peel, 21 Mar 1843.

65. Denison to RS secretary, 8 Mar 1837, RS MC.2.243; RS *Council Minutes* 9 Jun 1836, 9 Mar 1837. RS *Council Minutes* 13 Jul 1838, on creating eight permanent committees, including meteorology; RS *Council Minutes* 13 Dec 1838, re Jervis's appointment.

66. Augustus to Lushington, nd, forwarding James C. Ross, "Report of the Magnetic

Committee on the Subject of Magnetic Observations in India," 20 Apr 1838, BL Add 36469, fols. 44–45; received Court Minutes, 18 Jul 1838, IOR B/196, 369. Jervis to Hobhouse, 11 Aug 1838, postscript, BL Add 36469, fol. 122, re Sabine.

67. Court Minutes, 1 Aug 1838, IOR B/196, 421–22. Cabell to Melvill, 6 Aug 1838, IOR F/2/12, 122, copy in IOR E/2/40, 157, §4419.

68. Melvill to Cabell, 17 Aug 1838, IOR E/2/15, §4721; Stark to Melvill, 24 Aug 1838, IOR F/2/12, 134–35, copy in IOR E/2/40, 176–77, §4446; Melvill to Robert Vernon Smith [Board secretary], 30 Aug 1838, IOR E/2/15, 324, §4738. The article was by G. T. Taylor, "Observations of the Magnetic Dip and Intensity at Madras," *Journal of the Asiatic Society of Bengal* 6 (1837): 374–77; see John A. Hodgson and de Blaisville, "Observations on the Inclination and Declination of the Magnetic Needle," *Asiatic Researches* 19 (1833): 1–12.

69. John F. W. Herschel, "Report of a Joint Committee of Physics and Meteorology referred to for an Opinion on the Propriety of Recommending the Establishment of Fixed Magnetic Observatories . . . ," 22 Dec 1838, RS DM.3.2, copy in RS *Council Minutes* 22 Dec 1838, sent to EIC under cover of Lord Northampton [RS president] to Richard Jenkins [EIC chairman], 25 Apr 1839, RS MC.3.20. From Jenkin's reply (RS MC.3.27), it would appear that Herschel also directed a letter to the Court, 30 Apr 1839, which I have not found.

70. Richard Jenkins and William Bayley [EIC chairs] to Northampton, 10 Jun 1839, IOR E/1/275, §1615, copies in RS MC.3.27 and RS *Council Minutes* 13 Jun 1839; RS *Council Minutes* 27 Jun 1839; Melvill to Jervis, 3 Jul 1839, IOR E/1/275, §1859b; Dickenson to Northampton, 9 Jul 1839, IOR E/1/275, §1899, copies in RS MC.3.32 and RS *Council Minutes* 25 Jul 1839. On the training, see Jervis to Lloyd, 28 Mar 1839; RS *Council Minutes* 7 Nov 1839; Melvill to Pasley, 7 Nov 1839, IOR E/1/275, §3051; Melvill to Northampton, 22 Nov 1839, IOR E/1/275, §3161, copies in RS MC.3.54 and RS *Council Minutes* 12 Dec 1839; Melvill to Northampton, 1 Apr 1840 and 19 Jun 1840, RS MC.3.79 and MC.3.100.

71. CD to B, mil, 14 Mar 1838, ¶¶16–17, IOR L/MIL/5/413 306, fol. 26. Dickenson to Pasley, 11 Apr 1838, Pasley to Dickenson, 14 Apr 1838, and Dickenson to Pasley, 21 Apr 1838, IOR L/MIL/5/403 306, fols. 27–29, 39; copies of first and third are IOR E/1/274, §884, §954. Cook, "Training of East India Company Surveyors."

72. Jervis to Hobhouse, 26 Jan 1839 and 21 Mar 1839, BL Add 36470, fols. 65–67, 171–72.

73. The first hint of Pasley's and P. Melvill's opposition is in Jervis to Lushington, 16 Jun 1838. See more particularly, J. C. Melvill to Pasley, 29 Jun 1838, and Pasley to J. C. Melvill, 13 Jun 1838, IOR L/MIL/5/413 306, fols. 68–75. Pasley asserted, strangely, that Colby had wanted to use only civil assistants; Andrews, *A Paper Landscape*, 63–64, shows that this was certainly not the case.

74. Jervis to Hobhouse, 9 Nov 1838, BL Add 63469, fols. 166–68, and 16 Nov 1838.

75. Jervis to Washington, 4 Sep 1838; Walker to Melvill, 15 Aug 1838, IOR L/MIL/5/413 306, fols. 106–11.

76. Jervis to Hobhouse, 27 Jun 1838. Jervis to Lushington, 16 Jun 1838; Jervis to Melvill, 6 Aug 1838. Colby, diary, 5 Jun 1838, quoted by Charles F. Close, *The Early Years of the Ordnance Survey* (Newton Abbott: Davis and Charles, 1969), 93, noted that "Jervis and Loch . . . took my time yesterday at the Tower."

77. Court Minutes, 25 Jul 1838, IOR B/196, 393–94; Melvill to Smith, 28 Jul 1838, IOR L/MIL/5/413 306, fol. 98.

78. Jervis to Melvill, 6 Aug 1838, ¶6; Jervis, Memorandum, nd; Colby to Jervis, 20 Jun 1838; Beaufort to Jervis, 22 Jun 1838. BL Add 36469, fol. 49v, bears a pencil annotation that Colby's and Beaufort's letters to Jervis, and presumably the cover letter and memorandum

as well, had been circulated about the Board of Control for the staff to form their opinions; Jervis to Hobhouse, 11 Aug 1838.

79. Walker to Melvill, 15 Aug 1838.

80. Smith to Melvill, 16 Aug 1838, IOR L/MIL/5/413 306, fol. 102, copy IOR E/2/40, 169–73, §4438.

81. Melvill to Smith, 1 Nov 1838, IOR E/2/15, 371, §4805, noted that two cadets had just graduated from Chatham and wondered whether the Board had any objection to their going to the Ordnance Survey for three months. Cabell to Melvill, 5 Nov 1838, IOR E/2/40, 215, §4521 (received Court Minutes, 7 Nov 1838, IOR B/197, 5), replied that as far as the Board was concerned, the cadets could go for a longer period.

82. Melvill to Smith, 30 Aug 1838, IOR L/MIL/5/413 306, fols. 112–20, copy IOR E/2/15, 325–32, §4739.

83. Jervis to Washington, 4 Sep 1838.

84. Jervis to Melvill, 21 Sep 1838, and Political and Military Committee Minutes, 3 Oct 1838, IOR L/MIL/5/413 306, fol. 30–31; Court Minutes, 3 Oct 1838, IOR B/196, 581 and 584; Melvill to Jervis, 4 Oct 1838, IOR E/1/274, §2512. Jervis to Melvill, 24 Oct 1838, and Political and Military Committee Minutes, 31 Oct 1838, IOR L/MIL/5/413 306, fols. 32–34; Melvill to Jervis, 1 Nov 1838, IOR E/1/274, §2733.

85. Jervis to Hobhouse, 9 Nov 1838, and 15 Nov 1838, BL Add 63469, fols. 82–84. The second letter forwarded the same report to Hobhouse: "Report of the Select Committee on the Best Mode of Apportioning more equally the Local Burthens collected in Ireland, and to Provide for a General Survey and Valuation of that Part of the United Kingdom," *British Parliamentary Papers* 1824 (445) 8. Jervis to Hobhouse, nd, but ca. Nov 1838, BL Add 63469, fols. 186–87, requested Hobhouse's personal intervention.

86. Colby, diary, 5 Dec 1838, quoted by Close, *Early Years*, 93.

87. BL Add 63469, fols. 189 and 352, are untitled and anonymous early drafts. They include the suggestion that the issue be arbitrated by Stannus and Col. Barnewall (Bombay infantry, retired) on one side, as Jervis's friends, and by Carnac and Loch for the Court. The fact that Carnac and Loch were also at least sympathetic toward Jervis is not coincidental! The idea was not included in the eventual letter: Hobhouse to CD, 19 Feb 1839, IOR E/2/40, 283–84, §4651, received Court Minutes, 19 Feb 1839, IOR B/197, 279.

88. CD to Hobhouse, 28 Feb 1839, IOR E/2/15, 465–69, §4940.

89. Jervis to Melvill, 10 Jan 1839, and Jervis to Lushington, 10 Jan 1839, IOR L/MIL/5/413 306, fol. 35–36; Court Minutes, 16 Jan 1839, IOR B/197, 186 and 192.

90. Draft approved, Court Minutes, 10 Apr 1839, IOR B/197, 427; Smith to Melvill, 13 Apr 1839, IOR E/2/40, 322–23, §4717; Melvill to Jervis, 15 Apr 1839, IOR L/MIL/5/413 306, fol. 127, copy is IOR E/1/275, §1067.

91. Jervis to Hobhouse, 12 and 21 Apr 1839, BL Add 63470, fols. 211–12, 274–75. "State and Prospects of Asia," *The Quarterly Review* 63, no. 126 (March 1839): 369–402, extract from 398–99.

92. Hobhouse to Jervis, 23 Apr 1839, BL Add 36470, fol. 276.

93. Volker Bialas, *Erdgestalt, Kosmologie und Weltanschauung: Die Geschichte der Geodäsie als Teil der Kulturgeschichte der Menscheit* (Stuttgart: Konrad Winter, 1982), 197–236, discusses the unification of geodetic "theory" with geodetic "praxis," to the ultimate detriment of the former. Refer to Matthew H. Edney, "Cartography without 'Progress': Reinterpreting the Nature and Historical Development of Mapmaking," *Cartographica* 30, nos. 2 and 3 (1993): 54–68.

94. William Bentinck, "Memorandum Relative to a Military Survey of India," 3 Sep 1829, ¶6, BMC 11 Sep 1829, §47, IOR P/33/34.

Chapter Nine

1. Gardner, Memorial, 29 Apr 1823, IOR E/1/150, 477–79. CD to B, mil, 13 Oct 1824, ¶4 and ¶13, IOR E/4/712; CD to B, mil, 24 May 1826, ¶75, IOR E/4/717; CD to B, mil, 9 Sep 1829, ¶3, IOR E/4/726; CD to B, mil, 17 Feb 1841, ¶16, IOR E/4/765.

2. Petrie, Minute, 3 Oct 1807, IOR P/243/24, 5605–18; M to CD, pub no. 2, 21 Oct 1807, ¶39, IOR E/4/336.

3. Lambton, Memoir, 10 Mar 1802, MPC 26 Mar 1802, IOR P/242/39, 1165–225, 1189. Mackenzie to Charles Lushington [Bengal public secretary], 7 Mar 1820, ¶11, BPC 10 Mar 1820, §26, IOR F/4/681 18863, 203–48; Hodgson to Montgomerie, 31 Nov 1826, ¶2, BMC 12 Jan 1827, §236, IOR F/4/976 27498, 16–34.

4. Robert A. Rundstrom, "Mapping, Postmodernism, Indigenous People, and the Changing Direction of North American Cartography," Cartographica 28, no. 2 (1991): 1–12.

5. George Basalla, "The Spread of Western Science," Science 156 (1967): 611–22; the influence of this paper can still be seen, for example, in Satpal Sangwan's continued re-futations of it, as in his Science, Technology, and Colonisation: An Indian Experience, 1757–1857 (Delhi: Anamika Prakashan, 1991). Roy M. MacLeod, "On Visiting the 'Moving Metropolis': Reflections on the Architecture of Imperial Science," Historical Records of Australian Science 5, no. 3 (1982): 1–16. See the criticism of the core-periphery model by David Wade Chambers, "Period and Process in Colonial and National Science," in Scientific Colonialism, A Cross-Cultural Comparison: Papers from a Conference at Melbourne, Australia, 25–30 May 1981, edited by Nathan Reingold and Marc Rothenberg (Washington, DC: Smithsonian Institution Press, 1987), 297–321, esp. 298–99.

6. S. N. Sen, "The Character of the Introduction of Western Science in India During the Eighteenth and the Nineteenth Centuries," Indian Journal of History of Science 1 (1966): 112–22, set the tone. See the papers by Deepak Kumar and Satpal Sangwan in the bibliography and also Anis Alam's polemical paper, "Imperialism and Science," Social Scientist 6, no. 5 (1977): 3–15.

7. John O. Miller, introducing William Coldstream, "Indian Maps and Surveys," Journal of the Royal Society of Arts 74 (1926): 297–99.

8. B. V. Subbarayappa, "Western Science in India up to the End of the Nineteenth Century AD," in A Concise History of Science in India, edited by D. M. Bose, S. N. Sen, and B. V. Subbarayappa (New Delhi: Indian National Sciences Academy, 1971), 490–97, esp. 492, quoting Joseph Banks on the occasion of the opening of the gardens. Deepak Kumar, "Patterns of Colonial Science in India," Indian Journal of History of Science 15 (1980): 105–13, esp. 107. See Lucile H. Brockway, Science in Colonial Expansion: The Role of the Royal Botanical Society (New York: Academy Press, 1979); Daniel R. Headrick, Tentacles of Progress: Technology Transfer in the Age of Imperialism, 1850–1940 (Oxford: Oxford University Press, 1988), 209–58, on the British biological successes in Asia: chincona (for quinine), hemp (for ship ropes), rubber, tea, plus less successful cash crops, such as potatoes and coffee.

9. CD to B, 23 Aug 1837, IOR E/4/752, quoted by Deepak Kumar, "The Evolution of Colonial Science: Natural History and the East India Company," in Imperialism and the Natural World, edited by J. M. Mackenzie (Manchester: Manchester University Press, 1990), 51–66, esp. 66. On the other gardens, see "Minutes of Evidence Taken before the Select Committee on the Affairs of the East India Company," vol. 1, "Public," British Parliamentary Papers 1831–32 (735.1) 9, 327–34.

10. See chapter 5 on the Madras observatory. Curnin to Court, ca. Apr 1822, IOR E/1/148, 114–16. Hodgson to Lushington, 14 Nov 1822, BPC 22 Nov 1822, §33, IOR F/4/750

20516, 3–13, was prompted by a pamphlet (which I have not seen) by "Copernicus" suggesting the foundation of a Calcutta observatory; B to CD, mil, 31 Mar 1825, ¶¶194–95, IOR E/4/115; Blacker to William Casement [Bengal military secretary], 12 Apr 1825 and associated documents, BMC 15 Apr 1825, §219, IOR P/31/19; B to CD, mil, 9 May 1825, ¶22, IOR E/4/115; CD to B, mil, 4 May 1827, ¶¶86–88, IOR E/4/719.

11. Clements R. Markham, *A Memoir on the Indian Surveys* (London: Allen, 1878, 2d ed.), 207–16; Kumar, "Evolution of Colonial Science," 56–59; also William S. Webb, "Memoir Relative to a Survey in Kemaon, with Some Account of the Principles upon which it has been Conducted," *Asiatic Researches* 13 (1820): 293–310.

12. Holt Mackenzie [Bengal secretary] to Laidlaw, 6 Jun 1817, ¶¶2–3, also Hastings, Minute, 6 Jun 1817, both in BPC 7 Aug 1818, §44, IOR F/4/679 18861, 507–17.

13. Sydenham to Munro, 12 Jan 1805, IOR Eur F/151/8. More generally: Peter Buck, "People Who Counted: Political Arithmetic in the Eighteenth Century," *Isis* 73 (1982): 28–45; Victor L. Hilts, "*Aliis exterendum,* or, the Origins of the Statistical Society of London," *Isis* 69 (1978): 21–43; Theodore M. Porter, *The Rise of Statistical Thinking, 1820–1900* (Princeton: Princeton University Press, 1986), 17–27.

14. Morris Berman, *Social Change and Scientific Organization: The Royal Institution, 1799–1844* (Ithaca, NY: Cornell University Press, 1978), 88–92; CD to M, pub, 22 Aug 1804, ¶11, IOR E/4/893; George Buchan [Madras chief secretary] Buchan to J. P. Auriol, 8 Aug 1805, MPC 8 Aug 1805, IOR P/242/80, 4764–65. James Lushington [Royal Asiatic Society, Madras Auxiliary, secretary] to Mysore Resident, 7 Aug 1828, IOR R/2/1/74, 1087–88, listed the sorts of information desired, in effect no different from those listed in 1800 by Mackenzie and Buchanan (see tables 2.1, 2.2, and 2.3).

15. Roxburgh, IOR Eur D/809, and J. A. and J. H. Schultes to Wallich, 14 Nov 1829, IOR Eur C/280, both quoted by Kumar, "Evolution of Colonial Science," 63 and 53.

16. Edward W. Said, *Orientalism* (New York: Vintage Books, 1979), 65, 79–80, 99–100, 119–20, 123, 159–60, 177, 202, 215–16; Said, *Culture and Imperialism* (New York: Alfred A. Knopf, 1993), 3–14; Martin Bernal, *The Fabrication of Ancient Greece, 1785–1985,* vol. 1 of *Black Athena: The Afroasiatic Roots of Classical Civilization* (London: Free Association Books, 1987).

17. Thomas Colby, Memorandum and "Data for Determining the Longitude of Pendennis Castle," nd, CUL RGO 14/49/11, fols. 260–61. George Airy, "Report on the Progress of Astronomy during the Present Century," *Report of the British Association for the Advancement of Science* 2 (1832): 125–88, esp. 166; Airy, "Figure of the Earth," *Encyclopaedia Metropolitana* 5 (1845): 165–*240, esp. 173.

18. For example, James A. Secord, "King of Siluria: Roderick Murchison and the Imperial Theme in Nineteenth-Century British Geology," *Victorian Studies* 25 (1982): 413–42; Robert A. Stafford, "Geological Surveys, Mineral Discoveries, and British Expansion, 1835–71," *Journal of Imperial and Commonwealth History* 12, no. 3 (1984): 5–32.

19. David P. Miller, "The Royal Society of London 1800–1835: A Study in the Cultural Politics of Scientific Organization," Ph.D. diss. (University of Pennsylvania, 1981). For sophisticated (domestic) implementations of the core-periphery model, see Ian Inkster and Jack Morrell, eds., *Metropolis and Province: Science in British Culture, 1780–1850* (Philadelphia: University of Pennsylvania Press, 1983).

20. Joseph Dart [EIC secretary] to J. and A. Walker, 19 Jun 1827, IOR E/1/263, §1401. Refer to the short notices in IOR L/AG/24/18, an unpaginated collection of miscellaneous materials on the funding of books, maps, and charts.

21. Airy, "Figure of the Earth," 145, 168. See Franklin L. Baumer, *Modern European Thought: Continuity and Change in Ideas, 1600–1950* (New York: Macmillan, 1977), 148; Thomas L. Hankins, *Science and the Enlightenment* (Cambridge: Cambridge University

Press, 1985), 37–41; Stephen Toulmin, *Cosmopolis: The Hidden Agenda of Modernity* (New York: The Free Press, 1990). Matthew H. Edney, "Mathematical Cosmography and the Social Ideology of British Cartography, 1780–1820," *Imago Mundi* 46 (1994): 101–16.

22. J. B. Harley and David Woodward, "Concluding Remarks," in *Cartography in Prehistoric, Ancient, and Medieval Europe and the Mediterranean*, vol. 1 of *The History of Cartography*, edited by Harley and Woodward (Chicago: University of Chicago Press, 1987), 502–9, esp. 507.

23. Miller, "Royal Society," 10–64, 96–142. Berman, *Social Change and Scientific Organization*, xx–xxi; T. W. Heyck, *The Transformation of Intellectual Life in Victorian England* (London: Croom Helm, 1982), esp. 56–64 on creation of disciplines; Toulmin, *Cosmopolis*.

24. Edney, "Mathematical Cosmography."

25. David Kopf, *British Orientalism and the Bengal Renaissance: The Dynamics of Indian Modernization, 1773–1835* (Berkeley: University of California Press, 1969), 45–64. Reginald H. Phillimore, *Historical Records of the Survey of India* (Dehra Dun: Survey of India, 1945–58, 4 vols.), 2: 395–96, on Dinwiddie. For Rennell, see Lord Wellesley to Henry Dundas, 18 Aug 1800, *Two Views of British India: The Private Correspondence of Mr. Dundas and Lord Wellesley: 1798–1801*, edited by Edward Ingram (Bath: Adams and Dart, 1970), 282–83.

26. C. A. Bayly, "Colonial Star Wars: The Politics of the Heavens in India, c.1780–1880," unpublished manuscript, version of May 1994, in the author's possession. Figures taken from the publisher's note to the reprint of *Asiatic Researches* (New Delhi: Cosmo Publications, 1979). O. P. Kejariwal, *The Asiatic Society of Bengal and the Discovery of India's Past, 1784–1838* (Delhi: Oxford University Press, 1988), esp. 129, 170, re Troyer; Kopf, *British Orientalism*, 79, noted the praise awarded Leyden for his linguistic skills.

27. Voysey, report and appendices, 28 Jun 1820, BPC 31 Aug 1821, §§121–22, IOR F/4/682 18864, 149–66. See D. T. Moore, "New Light on the Life and Indian Geological Work of H. W. Voysey (1791–1824)," *Archives of Natural History* 12 (1985): 107–34; K. S. Murty, "Geological Sciences in India in the 18th–19th Centuries," *Indian Journal of History of Science* 17 (1982): 164–78. C. A. Bayly, *Indian Society and the Making of the British Empire* (Cambridge: Cambridge University Press, 1988), 89, re Buchanan.

28. Garland Cannon, "Sir William Jones's Founding and Directing of the Asiatic Society," *India Office Library and Records, Report for 1984–85* (London: British Library Board, 1985), 11–28; S. N. Mukherjee, *Sir William Jones: A Study in Eighteenth-Century British Attitudes to India* (Bombay: Orient Longman, 1987, 2d ed.). Kopf, *British Orientalism*; Kejariwal, *Asiatic Society of Bengal*.

29. S. M. Razaullah Ansari, "The Establishment of Observatories and the Socio-Economic Conditions of Scientific Work in Nineteenth-Century India," *Indian Journal of History of Science* 13 (1978): 62–71, esp. 67–68, has argued that astronomers were very poorly paid throughout the nineteenth century. It is possible that the science instructors at Calcutta's first Hindu and Sanskrit colleges for Indians supported themselves, but their identities and broader intellectual activities are still uncertain: Kopf, *British Orientalism*, 183–85.

30. See Lambton to John Chamier [Madras public secretary], 8 Apr 1802, MPC 9 Apr 1802, IOR P/242/40, 1418–24; Petrie to Bentinck, 14 Aug 1804, UN Pw 37; Petrie to Bentinck, 10 Apr 1807, UN Pw Jb 38; Petrie, Memorandum, 4 Sep 1808, IOR Eur Mackenzie General 58, 14 and 16–17.

31. Everest to Salmond, 17 Nov 1829, IOR L/MIL/5/402 205, fols. 346v–347r.

32. Respectively: Everest to George Swinton [Bombay political secretary], 11 Nov 1830, BoPC 19 Nov 1830, §38, IOR F/4/1357 54158, 25–30; Everest to Peter Auber [Court secretary], 25 Jun 1829, ¶3, IOR L/MIL/5/402 205, 325–28; B to CD, mil, 2 Apr 1833, ¶122,

F/4/1379 55089, 1–21; Everest to Casement, 14 Apr 1831, UN Pw Jf 2836/2; William Brown, "Notes on a Memorandum on the Revenue Surveys," 26 Jul 1832, UN Pw Jf 2694/36.

33. Percival Spear, *The Nabobs: A Study of the Social Life of the English in 18th Century India* (London: Oxford University Press, 1963), 126–45, on the increasing distance between the British and Indian communities throughout the 1700s, not that they were ever close; this theme is picked up by Nicholas B. Dirks, "Castes of Mind," *Representations* 37 (1992): 56–78, re the development of the British construction of caste, and Douglas M. Peers, "'The Habitual Nobility of Being': British Officers and the Social Construction of the Bengal Army in the Early Nineteenth Century," *Modern Asian Studies* 25 (1991): 545–69, on the reorganization of the Bengal army according to the soldiers' race. Michael Adas, *Machines as the Measure of Men: Science, Technology, and Ideologies of Western Dominance* (Ithaca, NY: Cornell University Press, 1989); a caveat: Adas started from the premise that Europeans have traditionally judged other cultures through the level of their scientific and technological achievements, and then searched out such statements. This is not a rigorous attempt to examine all of the ways in which Europeans have examined other cultures. He uses sub-Saharan Africa, China, and India as three examples. Africa and China offer the best grist for his mill, as Europeans maintained a psychological and social distance from their societies; but because Adas is unable to handle more subtle indictments of non-Western society, his treatment of India is flawed. (For example, on p. 103 he strikingly errs in stating that Hindus eagerly entered Company service because they preferred the British to Muslim rulers.) Nor does he distinguish between "science" and the concepts of progress and innovation. Finally, Adas allows the racial denigration of Africans (due to their usual equivalence to slaves) to confuse the issue of the inferiority of Asian societies and cultures.

34. Ward, Memorial, 30 Dec 1806, IOR P/256/2, 111–14. Warren to Morison, 15 May 1811, MMC 28 May 1811, IOR P/257/23, 6944–70, on Scott's parentage. See David Arnold, "European Orphans and Vagrants in India in the Nineteenth Century," *Journal of Imperial and Commonwealth History* 7 (1979): 104–27.

35. Bentinck, Minute, 24 Sep 1804, MMC 29 Sep 1804, IOR P/255/39, 4499–509.

36. Bentinck, Minute, 8 Aug 1831, ¶16, BMC 30 Sep 1831, §24, IOR F/4/1314 52439, 53–67.

37. Bedford to Bentinck, 17 May 1830, UN Pw Jf 2489. Shortrede, "Report on the Revenue Survey and Assessment of the Deckan," 24 Oct 1836, ¶103, BoRC 16 Nov 1836, §6731, IOR F/4/1739 70667, 89–188: " . . . hence if the work was to be carried on entirely by natives, [the] chain was perhaps the only instrument which they could use."

38. Madras secretary to Holt Mackenzie, 17 Apr 1816, MPC 17 Apr 1816, IOR F/4/554 13476, 416–19; M to CD, pub, 26 Sep 1816, ¶176, IOR E/4/346.

39. Colin Mackenzie, "Cursory Remarks," nd, ¶¶10–12 (not sent), BMC 23 Sep 1824, §130.3, IOR F/4/836 22401, 191–227. Bentinck, Minute, 14 May 1832, UN Pw Jf 2907. Munro, Minute, 18 Jan 1822, MPC 22 Jan 1822, IOR F/4/760 20656, 27–29; M to CD, pub, 19 Jul 1822, ¶¶1–6, IOR E/4/352.

40. Bentinck, Minutes, 12 and 14 May 1832, UN Pw Jf 2907, expressed his disappointment that Everest restricted his search for new civil subassistants.

41. Deepak Kumar, "Racial Discrimination and Science in Nineteenth Century India," *The Indian Economic and Social History Review* 19, no. 1 (1982): 63–82; Kumar, "Problems in Science Administration: A Study of the Scientific Surveys in British India, 1757–1900," in *Science and Empires: Historical Studies about Scientific Development and European Expansion,* edited by Patrick Petitjohn, Catherine Jami, and Anne Marie Moulin (Dordrecht: Kluwer Academic, 1992), 269–80. The ideological principles of this racial division of labor

were applied to areas of 'discovery' and 'achievement' beyond science *per se*; see the splendid analysis by Gordon T. Stewart, "Tenzing's Two Wrist-Watches: The Conquest of Everest and Late Imperial culture in Britain, 1921–1953," *Past & Present* 149 (1995): 170–97, of the representation of Tenzing Norgay as no more than Edmund Hillary's assistant on the first successful ascent of Mount Everest (1953).

42. Ann Laura Stoler, "Rethinking Colonial Categories: European Communities and the Boundaries of Rule," *Comparative Studies in Society and History* 31 (1989): 134–61.

43. Kenneth Mason, "Kishen Singh and the Indian Explorers," *Geographical Journal* 62 (1923): 429–40, was the source for G. F. Heaney, "Rennell and the Surveyors of India," *Geographical Journal* 134 (1968): 318–27; Heaney's essay was the principal source for John Noble Wilford, "Soldiers, Pundits, and the India Survey," in *The Mapmakers: The Story of the Great Pioneers in Cartography from Antiquity to the Space Age* (New York: Random House, 1981), 161–73, of which 40 percent discussed the pandits. As the most widely available and easily digestible account, Wilford has influenced most subsequent essays: Thomas Richards, *The Imperial Archive: Knowledge and the Fantasy of Empire* (London: Verso, 1993), 11–44 (an intriguing reading of Kipling's *Kim*); John Goss, *The Mapmaker's Art: An Illustrated History of Cartography* (Chicago: Rand McNally, 1993), 246–53; John Keay, *India Discovered: The Achievement of the British Raj* (Leicester: Windward, 1981; London: Collins, 1988, new edition). Keay was the main advisor for the television essay, "Empire!" part 4 of "The Shape of the World," by Granada TV/ WGBH-TV Boston (1991); Simon Berthon and Andrew Robinson, *The Shape of the World: The Mapping and Discovery of the Earth* (London: Granada Television; Chicago: Rand McNally, 1991), 133–49, is similarly indebted to Wilford. See also S. M. Chadha, *Survey of India Through the Ages* (Dehra Dun: Survey of India, 1990), 12–13; Peter Hopkirk, *Trespassers on the Roof of the World: The Secret Exploration of Tibet* (London: John Murray, 1982; reprint, New York: Kodansha, 1995), 20–54. Henry Yule and A. C. Burnell, *Hobson-Jobson: A Glossary of Colloquial Anglo-Indian Words and Phrases, and of Kindred Terms, Etymological, Historical, Geographical and Discursive*, new edition, edited by William Crooke (London, 1903; reprint, Delhi: Munshiram Manoharlal, 1968), 740–41, "Pundit," re its application to the surveyors.

44. Hodgson to Lushington, 21 Nov 1821, ¶2, BPC 7 Dec 1821, §61, IOR F/4/682 18864, 493–500. Witold Kula, *Measures and Men*, translated by Richard Szreter (Princeton: Princeton University Press, 1986), on the adoption of standards in Europe.

45. Hodgson to Lushington, 18 Sep 1821, ¶5ff, BPC 28 Sep 1821, §3, IOR F/4/682 18864, 273–92; B to CD, pub, 1 Oct 1821, ¶183, IOR E/4/107. Salmond, Memorandum, ca. Aug 1827, marginal note, UN Pw Jf 2744/5. Bentinck, Memorandum, 3 Sep 1829, ¶3, BMC 11 Sep 1829, §47, IOR P/33/34.

46. Charles T. M. Metcalfe, "Survey of the Indus: Designs of Russia in the East," Oct 1830, in *Selections from the Papers of Lord Metcalfe; late Governor General of India, Governor of India, and Governor General of Canada,* edited by John W. Kaye (London: Smith, Elder, & Co., 1855), 211–17, esp. 213. CD to B, pol, 1 Feb 1832, ¶18, IOR E/4/734.

47. See criticism by Rajanikant, "The Origin of Geometry in Ancient India," *Jijñasa* 1 (1974): 51–61.

48. Bernal, *Fabrication of Ancient Greece*, 1: 172–280; Roshdi Rashed, "Science as a Western Phenomenon," *Fundamenta Scientiae* 1 (1980): 7–13.

49. Adam Smith, "The History of Astronomy," in *Essays on Philosophical Subjects* (London, 1795); critical edition by W. P. D. Wightmann, J. C. Bryce, and I. S. Ross, in *Adam Smith*, edited by D. D. Raphael and A. S. Skinner (Oxford: Clarendon, 1980), 3: 33–105; quotations from §III.2–3. See K. C. Cleaver, "Adam Smith on Astronomy," *History of Science* 27 (1989): 211–18.

50. Everest, Memoir, 20 Sep 1829, ¶¶49–51, UN Pw Jf 2767/1; Everest, Memoir, ca. Apr 1827, ¶¶102–3, IOR L/MIL/5/402 205, fols. 358–406.

51. Max Horkeimer and Theodor W. Adorno, *The Dialectic of Enlightenment*, translated by John Cumming (New York: Herder and Herder, 1972; reprint, 1994), 3; also David Harvey, *The Condition of Postmodernity: An Enquiry into the Origins of Cultural Change* (Oxford: Basil Blackwell, 1989). Refer to Anne Godlewska, "Map, Text and Image: The Mentality of Enlightened Conquerors: A New Look at the *Description de l'Egypt*," *Transactions of the Institute of British Geographers*, ns 20 (1995): 5–28.

52. Respectively, George Everest, *An Account of the Measurement of an Arc of the Meridian between the Parallels of 18°3' and 24°7', being a Continuation of the Grand Meridional Arc of India* . . . (London, 1830), 16, 28, 33, 38; and B to CD, mil, 2 Apr 1833, ¶105, IOR F/4/1379 55089, 1–21.

53. Bombay chief engineer to Bombay public secretary, 17 May 1826, BoPC 31 May 1826, §9, IOR F/4/1015 27843, 207–29, esp. 217–18. An appendix by George Jervis, "Return of Boys at the Institution," 6 May 1826, BoPC 31 May 1826, §10, listed a total of eighty-six youths, of which fifty-one were "Maratta," twenty "Guzerati," and fifteen "English." On G. R. Jervis's translations, see the approving comments by Lancelot Wilkinson, "On the Use of the Siddhantas in the Work of Native Education," *Journal of the Asiatic Society of Bengal* 3 (1834): 504–519, esp. 514.

54. Jervis to CD, 26 Dec 1837 and Jervis to Salmond, 13 Oct 1837, both in IOR L/MIL/5/413 306, esp. fols. 14v, 21v, 20r.

55. Concise summaries of the educational debate are John Clive, *Macauley: The Shaping of the Historian* (Cambridge: Harvard University Press, 1987), 342–99; Kopf, *British Orientalism*, 236–52; John Rosselli, *Lord William Bentinck: The Making of a Liberal Imperialist, 1774–1839* (London: Chatto & Windus for Sussex University Press, 1974), 214–25. Macauley's minute, 2 Feb 1835, is reproduced in *Imperialism*, edited by Philip D. Curtin (London: Macmillan, 1971), 179–91, esp. 182. On the precise issue of science and education, see also Michael Adas, "Scientific Standards and Colonial Education in British India and French Senegal," in *Science, Medicine and Cultural Imperialism*, edited by Teresa Meade and Mark Walker (New York: St. Martin's Press, 1991), 4–35; A. Vasantha, "The 'Oriental-Occidental Controversy' of 1839 [*sic*] and its Impact on Indian Science," in *Science and Empires*, edited by Petitjohn, Jami, and Moulin, 49–56.

56. Quoted by Raymond K. Renford, *The Non-Official British in India to 1920* (Delhi: Oxford University Press, 1987), 9.

57. Jean Baptiste Tassin, *Anglo-Persian Map of India* (Calcutta: Oriental Lithographic Press, 1837), BL Maps 52415 (28). Bellasis's map is IOR prints WD 1478/2a.

58. Deepak Kumar, ed., *Science and Empire: Essays in Indian Context* (Delhi: Anamika Prakashan, 1991), esp. the essays by Kapil Raj, "Knowledge, Power and Modern Science: The Brahmins Strike Back," 115–25, and Irfan Habib, "Promoting Science and Its World-View in the Mid-Nineteenth Century India," 139–51; Habib, "Institutional Efforts: Popularization of Science in the mid-19th Century," *Fundamenta Scientiae* 6 (1985): 299–312; Kopf, *British Orientalism*; Ahsan Jan Qaisar, *The Indian Response to European Technology and Culture, AD 1498–1757* (Delhi: Oxford University Press, 1982).

59. Bayly, "Colonial Star Wars." Refer to Ansari, "Establishment of Observatories," 66.

Chapter Ten

1. Paul Laxton, "The Geodetic and Topographical Evaluation of English County Maps, 1740–1840," *The Cartographic Journal* 13 (1976): 37–54.

2. Hodgson to William Casement [Bengal military secretary], 22 Oct 1823, BMC 7 Nov 1823, §112, IOR F/4/832 22115, 11–25. Blacker to Casement, 31 Jan 1825, BMC 4 Feb 1825, §235, IOR P/30/13, and 11 Aug 1824, ¶22, BMC 23 Sep 1824, §126, IOR P/30/60. Montgomerie, Memorandum, 11 Jul 1833, BMC 8 Aug 1833, §8, IOR P/34/45; Montgomerie, "General Descriptive Catalogue of Memoirs, Maps, Geographical and Statistical Materials of Every Description in the Depôt of the Surveyor General's Office, Madras, prepared for the Honorable the Court of Directors, agreeably to Orders dated the 26th June 1827," 22 Dec 1827, IOR X/uncataloged.

3. "Minutes of Evidence Taken before the Select Committee on the Affairs of the East India Company," *British Parliamentary Papers* 1831 (65) 5, 775; the list is signed by James Mill, Nov 1831.

4. *An Atlas of the Southern part of India, including Plans of all the Principal Towns and Cantonments, reduced from the Grand Trigonometrical Survey of India, shewing also the Tenasserim Provinces*, engr. J. & C. Walker (Madras: Pharoah & Co., ca. 1855); while Walker's plates were done in London, the title page seems to have been added separately in Madras.

5. *Parts of Georgia and Armenia, the Persian Provinces, Azerbijan, Talish & Ghilan, from Trigonometrical Surveys by Lieut. Col. W. Monteith, K.L.S. Madras, Eng., made between the Years 1814 and 1828, and the Russian Provinces, with the Caucasus, from Russian Official Documents corrected by his Personal Observations. Engraved at the expense of the Royal Geographical Society* (London: John Arrowsmith, 1833, 4 sheets); the RGS still has the original MS map. William Monteith, Memoir, nd, IOR X/3105; Monteith to Peter Auber [Court secretary], 12 Oct 1830, with enclosure, "Expenses incurred in preparing the Map of the Frontier of Russia and Persia as established in the year 1829; also the general map of Georgia, the Caucuses and Azerbijan," ca. 12 Oct 1830, IOR E/1/174, 34–36, re bribes.

6. John Hodgson, "Remarks on the Surveys in India generally, but more especially on those of a generally combined geographical and military nature, conducted by the officers of the Surveyor General's and the Quarter Master General's departments, . . . ," 21 Nov 1821, ¶¶8–26, BPC 7 Dec 1821, §62, IOR F/4/682 18864, 500–25. See chapter 7.

7. Alexander Gerard, "Memoir of the Construction of a Map of Koonawar . . . ," 26 Jul 1825, ¶1 and ¶6 (emphasis added), RGS Library MS.

8. "Minutes of Evidence Taken before the Select Committee on the Affairs of the East India Company," vol. 3, "Revenue," *British Parliamentary Papers* 1831–32 (735.3) 11, especially the evidence of James Mill, questions 3550ff.

9. "Report of a Police Committee, dated Calcutta, 10th August 1838, with Papers and Evidence; Calcutta 1838–9," *Edinburgh Review* 73 (1841): 425–60, esp. 440–43; "State and Prospects of Asia," *The Quarterly Review* 63, no. 126 (March 1839): 369–402, esp. 398–99.

10. Hobhouse, Memorandum, ca. Nov 1838, BL Add 36469, fol. 189. See also CD to B, mil, 10 Jun 1840, ¶6, IOR E/4/763, and 25 May 1841, ¶19, IOR E/4/766, re a single system of revenue surveys throughout India.

11. John Rosselli, *Lord William Bentinck: The Making of a Liberal Imperialist, 1774–1839* (London: Chatto & Windus for Sussex University Press, 1974) 125–30, 237–71. See, for example, some of the arguments on the proper role of the revenue surveys before Bentinck's Allahabad Conference: Herbert to J. Thomason [Bengal deputy revenue secretary], 18 Jun 1831, IOR F/4/1313 52280, np; Bentinck, Minute, 8 Aug 1831, ¶13, BMC 30 Sep 1831, §24, IOR F/4/1314 52439, 53–67; Everest to Casement, 12 Oct 1831, ¶31 and ¶54ff, BMC 25 Nov 1831, §143, IOR F/4/1314 52443, 41–75. Bentinck, Minute, 27 Jul 1832, Un Pw Jf 2907, explicitly called the revenue surveys "utilitarian."

On the revenue surveys after 1833, see W. Barron, "The Cadastral Survey of India,"

Supplementary Papers of the Royal Geographical Society 1 (1885): 597–618; F. C. Hirst, *Notes on the Old Revenue Surveys of Bengal, Bihar, Orissa, and Assam* (Calcutta: Thacher, Spink & Co., 1912); "A Selection of Papers illustrative of the Character and Results of the Revenue Survey and Assessment which has been Introduced into the North-West Provinces of the Bengal Presidency, since the Year 1833; and Similar Return as to the Presidency of Bombay," 10 Aug 1853, *British Parliamentary Papers* 1852–53 (999) 75.

12. CD to B, mil, 21 Dec 1841, ¶¶20–21, IOR E/4/768.

13. Refer to C. A. Bayly, "The British Military-Fiscal State and Indigenous Resistance: India, 1750–1820," in *An Imperial State at War: Britain from 1689 to 1815*, edited by Lawrence Stone (London: Routledge, 1994), 322–54.

14. The *Madras Almanac* for 1800 does not include such a list, but that for 1803 does; I have not seen the almanacs for 1801 and 1802.

15. William Hamilton, *Geographical, Statistical and Historical Description of Hindostan* (London, 1820), quoted by Bernard S. Cohn, "The Census, Social Structure, and Objectification in South Asia," in *An Anthropologist among the Historians and Other Essays* (Delhi: Oxford University Press, 1987), 224–54, esp. 232.

16. *Index containing the Names and Geographical Positions of all Places in the Maps of India, designed to facilitate the use of those maps and especially that of the Newly Constructed and Extended Map of India, lately published by Kingsbury, Parbury, and Allen, Booksellers to the Hon. East India Company* (London: Kingsbury, Parbury, and Allen, 1826); copy examined was BL 793.c.14; copies of the four-sheet map are BL Maps 52415 (21) [1820 ed.], BL Maps 52415 (23) [1822 ed.], and BL Maps 28.bb.57 [1825 ed.]. Henry Virtue Stephen, *Handbook to the Maps of India* (London: W. H. Allen & Co., 1857).

17. Mackenzie to George Strachey [Madras chief secretary], 1 Jun 1817, ¶5, MMC 19 Jun 1817, IOR F/4/636 17424, 239–49.

18. CD to B, mil, 20 Jul 1831, ¶11, IOR E/4/732; see also chapters 6 and 8.

19. I think here of John Walker's atlases produced for the British government, ca. 1850, showing political, military, and commercial information for all of India and for the North-West Frontier: IOR X/351 and IOR X/352.

20. Clement R. Attlee, *Empire into Commonwealth* (London: Oxford University Press, 1961), 5–6, quoted by John M. Mackenzie, "Introduction," to *Imperialism and Popular Culture*, edited by Mackenzie (London: Manchester University Press, 1986), 6.

21. James Salmond, "Memorandum respecting a General Survey of India," ca. Aug 1827, marginal note, UN Pw Jf 2744/3, notes that Reynolds's large 1809 map was hung up "in a room appropriated for that purpose" (see note 40 in chapter 4 re memorandum). Several of the IOR maps, such as Colin Mackenzie's huge MS map, "A General Map of Mysore, etc.," 1808, 1:253,440, IOR X/9599, show damage from being mounted on rollers. For a map displayed in India, see the portrait of John Mowbray by Thomas Hickey, ca. 1790, reproduced as the frontispiece to C. A. Bayly, *Indian Society and the Making of the British Empire*, vol. 2.1 of *The New Cambridge History of India* (Cambridge: Cambridge University Press, 1988). John Pickles, "Texts, Hermeneutics and Propaganda Maps," in *Writing Worlds: Discourse, Text and Metaphor in the Representation of Landscape*, edited by Trevor J. Barnes and James S. Duncan (London: Routledge, 1992), 193–230, discusses the role of repeated exposure to cartographic images.

22. Michel Foucault, *Discipline and Punish: The Birth of the Prison*, translated by Alan Sheridan (New York: Random House, 1977), 205, 211, 222.

23. Mackenzie to Munro, 24 Dec 1817 and 1 Jan 1819, IOR Eur F/151/57 and /39 respectively, on the "woeful plight" of the survey records in Calcutta. The instability of paper was a common complaint among surveyors and cartographers. On storage prob-

lems, *Report of the Indian Survey Committee, 1904–05* (Simla: Government Central Printing Office, 1905, 3 vols.), 2: 107 n. On destruction caused by hanging the maps from rollers, see chapter 6.

24. Lancelot Wilkinson, "On the Use of the Siddhántas in the Work of Native Education," *Journal of the Asiatic Society of Bengal* 3 (1834): 504–19, esp. 511–12. Wilkinson overcame the hostility of the raja of Kotah to a road survey by quoting a passage concerning the measurement of the size of the earth from an eleventh-century treatise on globes, implying that the road survey was for geodetic purposes and not for knowledge of the raja's territory; see C. A. Bayly, "Colonial Star Wars: The Politics of the Heavens in India, c.1780–1880," unpublished manuscript, version of May 1994, in the author's possession.

25. Lt. J. J. O'Donnoghue to Mackenzie, 4 Jan 1811, MMC 26 Feb 1811, IOR P/257/16, 2315–16. *Asiatic Journal*, ns 23, no. 2 (1837): 103–4 and 194–97, 195.

26. James Garling, "Statement of Circumstances which happened to several public servants attached to the Northern Survey when sent on duty from Tirritumpardee, June 1810," 12 Jul 1810, MMC 27 Jul 1810, IOR P/256/72, 7666–68.

27. Hodgson to Casement, 24 Jan 1829, BMC 5 Feb 1829, §120, IOR P/33/19.

28. Andrew Scott Waugh, "Report and Statements of the Operations and Expense of the Trigonometrical Survey of India," *British Parliamentary Papers* 1851 (219) 41: 877. Reginald H. Phillimore, *Historical Records of the Survey of India* (Dehra Dun: Survey of India, 1945–58, 4 vols.), contains numerous examples of the problems faced by the surveyors.

29. On the scheme, see Ellenborough to Bentinck, 22 May 1830, UN Pw Jf 941. Charles T. M. Metcalfe, "Survey of the Indus: Designs of Russia in the East," Oct 1830, *Selections from the Papers of Lord Metcalfe; late Governor General of India, Governor of India, and Governor General of Canada,* edited by John W. Kaye (London: Smith, Elder, & Co., 1855), 211–17, esp. 211–12.

30. Example comments: Resident of Mysore to Madras military secretary, 5 Nov 1817, IOR R/2/1/195, 304–5; Hodgson to Charles Lushington [Bengal public secretary], 18 Jun 1822, BMC 8 Sep 1826, §157 encl. C, IOR F/4/1017 27954, 89–98.

31. British agent at Nimach to agent in Rajputana, 18 May 1837, ¶5, IMC 24 Jul 1837, §158 (extracted from IPoC 26 Jun 1837), IOR F/4/1774 72929, 8–9.

32. Lambton to Lushington, 28 Nov 1817, BPC 7 Aug 1818, §15, IOR P/9/44.

33. The theme of secrecy of information runs throughout Robert E. Frykenberg, *Guntur District, 1788–1848: A History of Local Influence and Central Authority in South India* (Oxford: Clarendon Press, 1965); Cohn, "Census and Objectification."

34. Troyer to John Munro [Madras quartermaster general], 27 Mar 1807, MMC 10 Apr 1807, IOR P/256/7, 3278–82; also Lt. W. Chevasse to Troyer, 22 Jan 1807, MMC 14 Feb 1807 (diary), IOR P/256/4, 1223–24.

35. Mysore Resident to Madras military secretary, 5 Nov 1817, ¶¶2–3.

36. Mackenzie to J. H. Peile [acting Mysore resident], 15 Sep 1803, IOR R/2/1/10, fol. 229. See Webbe to Mackenzie, 9 Mar 1803, IOR R/2/1/180, 9–10; Peile to Mackenzie, 26 Aug 1803, IOR R/2/1/180, 87.

37. Peile to Mather, 23 Sep 1803, R/2/1/180, 92–93.

38. For example, Nicholas B. Dirks, *The Hollow Crown: Ethnohistory of an Indian Kingdom* (Cambridge: Cambridge University Press, 1987), 16; Mackenzie to Barry Close [Mysore Resident], 23 Dec 1800, IOR R/2/1/7, fols. 2232–33. Bayly, "Colonial Star Wars," re Strachey.

39. Mackenzie to Close, 21 Oct 1800, IOR R/2/1/7, fols. 1979–80.

40. Lambton to Mark Wilks [Mysore resident], 3 Jul 1804, IOR R/2/1/11, fols. 231–32. Wilks to Lambton, 22 Jun 1804, IOR R/2/1/182, 126–27. Lambton to Wilks, 27 May 1805, IOR R/2/1/12, fols. 412–13, re Kater; subsequent papers in IOR R/2/1/12–13 deal with the inquiry.

41. Lt. Roderick Macdonald to Everest, 1 Feb 1834, quoted in Phillimore, *Historical Records*, 4: 62.

42. Everest to Casement, 2 Mar 1835, IMC 6 Apr 1835, §184, IOR F/4/1547 61706, 5–13; associated documents reported in B to CD, mil, 22 Oct 1835, ¶¶33–37, IOR E/4/151.

43. Respectively, Everest to Casement, 4 Nov 1837, and Gwalior resident to officiating secretary, North-West [Upper] Provinces, 14 Dec 1837, ¶3, both in IMC 30 Apr 1838, §§65–66, IOR F/4/1821 75190, 6–11. See also papers in IOR F/4/1654 66137.

44. Everest to RS secretary, 8 Apr 1861, RS MC.6.130. Also, George Everest, *An Account of the Measurement of an Arc of the Meridian between the Parallels of 18°3' and 24°7', being a Continuation of the Grand Meridional Arc of India . . .* (London, 1830), 40; Phillimore, *Historical Records*, 4: 63, more generally.

45. Bayly, *Indian Society*, 156–59; Dirks, *Hollow Crown*, 76 n. 42, quoting IOR Mackenzie General 4.

46. Robert Montgomery Martin, *The History, Antiquities, Topography, and Statistics of Eastern India . . .* (London: Wm. H. Allen, 1838, 3 vols.), 2: 591–92.

47. Jopp to Hodgson, 19 Dec 1827, ¶20, BoMC 12 Mar 1828, §30, IOR F/4/1116 29943, 33–58.

48. William Morison, Minute, 15 Jun 1839, ¶10, IMC 30 Sep 1839, §261, IOR F/4/1872 79616, 26–41.

49. For example, Lambton to Lushington, 1 Jan 1818, ¶16, BPC 7 Aug 1818, §18, IOR P/4/44. Everest to Bentinck, 8 May 1834, UN Pw Jf 2836/4. See also Everest on the reasons for the GTS: Everest to Casement, 12 Oct 1831, ¶¶4–6 and ¶50, BMC 25 Nov 1831, §143, IOR F/4/1314 52443, 41–75; Everest to Casement, 5 May 1838, ¶9, IMC 18 Jun 1838, §38, IOR F/4/1821 75193, 6–14.

50. Paul Carter, *The Road to Botany Bay: An Essay in Spatial History* (London: Faber and Faber, 1987), xiv.

51. Thomas H. Holdich, "A Geodetic Connection between the Surveys of Russia and India," in *Report of the Sixth International Geographical Congress, London 1895* (London: John Murray, 1896), 287–97.

52. H. E. Goldsmid, G. Wingate, and D. Davidson, "The Joint Report, 2 August 1847," ¶¶10–21, in *Papers Relating to the Joint Report of 1847 with the Measurement and Classification Rules of the Deccan, Gujerat, Konkan and Kanara Surveys*, Selections from the Records of the Bombay Government, ns 532 (Bombay, 1917), 1–20.

53. "Report of the Select Committee on the Best Mode of Apportioning more equally the Local Burthens collected in Ireland, and to Provide for a General Survey and Valuation of that Part of the United Kingdom," *British Parliamentary Papers* 1824 (445) 8, 89–90, for Kater's evidence, 25 May 1824; J. H. Andrews, *A Paper Landscape: The Ordnance Survey in Nineteenth-Century Ireland* (Oxford: Clarendon Press, 1975), 26, re Colby and Gardner.

54. Blacker to Casement, 12 Jul 1825, ¶5, BMC 29 Jul 1825, §158, IOR F/4/836 22401; echoed in CD to B, mil, 16 Jan 1833, ¶1, IOR E/4/736.

55. Bentinck, Minute, 24 Sep 1804, MMC 29 Sep 1804, IOR P/255/39, 4499–509.

56. Denis Wood, *The Power of Maps* (New York: Guilford, 1992); David Turnbull, *Maps Are Territories, Science Is an Atlas: A Portfolio of Exhibits* (Chicago: University of Chicago Press, 1993), re Western cartography's claims to nonindexicality.

57. Monique Pelletier, "La France mesurée," *Mappmonde* 86, no. 3 (1986): 26–32, English-language abstract.

ARCHIVAL SOURCES
AND BIBLIOGRAPHY

Unpublished Primary Sources, by Archive

Bodleian Library, Geography and Map Room, University of Oxford
The Bodleian possesses several manuscript and printed maps of India.
[BL] British Library, London
   [BL Add] are the additional manuscripts, of mixed provenance, in the Department of Manuscripts. Specific collections of particular interest are: 12564–3915, papers of Richard Wellesley, earl of Mornington and marquis Wellesley; 14376–85, papers bought from Thomas Best Jervis, July 1843; 36455–83, papers of Sir John Cam Hobhouse, baron Broughton, MP, FRS; and 37182–201, correspondence of Charles Babbage, FRS.
   [BL Maps] indicate printed maps held in the Map Library.
[CPL] Cleveland Public Library, Cleveland, Ohio
   The John G. White Oriental Studies Collection contains a few letters by William Lambton.
[CUL RGO] Cambridge University Library: Royal Greenwich Observatory Archives
   These include the papers of the astronomers royal: group 4, Nevil Maskelyne (AR 1765–1811); 5, John Pond (AR 1811–35); 6, George Biddell Airy (AR 1835–81). Group 14 comprises the archives of the Board of Longitude (1714–1828) and 15, those of the Cape of Good Hope Observatory.
[IOR] British Library, Oriental and India Office Collections, London: India Office Records
   These comprise the official records of the East India Company (1600–1858), the Board of Commissioners for East Indian Affairs (1784–1858), and the India Office (1858–1947). Most important is group P, the approximately 7,600 volumes of "consultations" (or "proceedings") which comprise the written records submitted to and generated by the daily meetings of the council of each of the three Indian governments, and which cover everything from petitions for sick leave to decisions to go to war. Citations to the consultations are by administration, general subject heading, date, and topic number; for example, BMC [Bengal Military Consultations] 15 Apr 1815 §25. Summaries of each council's consultations were sent to London as part of the general correspondence (group E/4); citations to these letters are to the administration, general head, and date; for example, CD to B, pub [public], 14 Apr 1815,

or M to CD, rev [revenue], 1 Jan 1799. "Special collections" were compiled in London of all documents relating to specific topics; those used in this study were made by the Court's military secretaries (subgroup L/MIL/5) and by the Board of Control (subgroup F/4). Both sets of special collections also occasionally contain documents originating in London; these are distinguished in the notes by the absence of any reference to a record series. The one other archival subgroup whose citations are not self-explanatory is R/2/1, papers of the Mysore Residency.

There are also two separate collections of materials collected by the East India Company, the India Office, and their successor institutions.

[IOR Eur] are European-language manuscripts from various personal and institutional collections. Those used are: E/309, Charles Francis Greville (1749–1809); F/128, Sutton Court Collection, containing the papers of the Strachey Family; F/140, Lord Amherst (1773–1857), governor general; F/151, Thomas Munro (1761–1827), governor of Madras; F/181, Waugh Collection, including papers by Andrew Scott Waugh (1810–78), surveyor general; F/228, Kirkpatrick Collection, including papers of Major-General William Kirkpatrick (1754–1812), private secretary to Lord Wellesley; G/51, Madras Observatory Papers, transferred from the Royal Greenwich Observatory in 1963; OV, Orme Various Collection, being miscellaneous papers by Robert Orme (1728–1801); and Mackenzie General Collection, being papers relating to India collected by Colin Mackenzie (1753–1821), surveyor general.

[IOR Print] are the prints, drawings, and photographs. Group WD, "Western Drawings," includes several maps and many other graphic images prepared by surveyors.

[PRO] Public Record Office, Kew
The official depository for the British Government contains one relevant subgroup: 30/12/20/10, correspondence between George Everest, surveyor general, and Lord Ellenborough, president of the Board of Control.

[RAS] Royal Astronomical Society, London
Archives of the society, especially "Letters" to the society and the miscellaneous "Additional" Manuscripts.

[RGS] Royal Geographical Society, London
Archives of the society, especially the "Correspondence" files with the society, the "Journal" manuscripts submitted but not necessarily published, and the miscellaneous "Library" manuscripts.

[RS] Royal Society, London
Archives of the society and other papers. Relevant groups are: DM, "Domestic Miscellaneous" manuscripts; HS, J. F. W. Herschel's papers; L&P, the society's "Letters and Papers"; MC, "Miscellaneous Correspondence"; and MS, other manuscripts.

[UN Pw] University of Nottingham Archives: Portland Collection
Papers of the Cavendish family, dukes of Portland, in particular group J, the papers of Lord William Cavendish Bentinck: Jb, when governor of Madras (1803–7); Jf, when governor general (1828–35).

[US Well] University of Southampton Archives: Wellington Collection
Papers of Arthur Wellesley, first duke of Wellington.

Published Primary Sources

"An Account of the Measurement of two sections of the Meridional Arc of India . . . , conducted under the Orders of the Honourable East India Company by Lieutenant-Colonel Everest . . . and his assistants. London: 1847." *Edinburgh Review* 87 (1848): 392–418.

Account of the Operations of the Great Trigonometrical Survey of India. 22 vols. Dehra Dun: Survey of India, 1870–1910.

Adams, George. *Geometrical and Graphical Essays, containing a Description of the Mathematical Instruments used in Geometry, Civil and Military Surveying, Levelling and Perspective, with many new Problems, illustrative of each Branch.* London, 1791; 2d ed., 1797.

Airy, George Biddell. "Report on the Progress of Astronomy during the Present Century." *Report of the British Association for the Advancement of Science* 2 (1832): 125–88.

Arrowsmith, Aaron. *A Companion to the Map of the World.* London, 1794.

———. *Memoir Relative to the Construction of the Map of Scotland Published by Aaron Arrowsmith in the Year 1807.* London, 1809.

Bentinck, William Cavendish. *The Correspondence of Lord William Cavendish Bentinck.* Edited by C. H. Philips. 2 vols. London: Oxford University Press, 1977.

Blacker, Valentine. *Memoir of the Operations of the British Army in India, during the Mahratta War of 1817, 1818, & 1819.* 2 vols. London: Black, Kingsbury, Parbury, and Allen, 1821.

Blunt, James T. "Narrative of a Route from Chunarghur to Yertnagoodum, in the Ellore Circar." *Asiatic Researches* 7 (1801): 57–169.

Buchanan, Francis. *An Account of Assam, with Some Notices Concerning the Neighbouring Territories.* Edited by S. K. Bhuyan. Gauhati: Department of Historical and Antiquarian Studies, Narayani Handiqui Historical Institute, 1940.

———. *An Account of the Districts of Bihar and Patna in 1811–1812 by Francis Buchanan.* 2 vols. Patna: The Bihar and Orissa Research Society [1936]. Reprint, New Delhi: Usha, 1986.

———. *An Account of the District of Purnea in 1809–10, by Francis Buchanan.* Edited by V. H. Jackson. Patna: The Bihar and Orissa Research Society, 1928.

———. *A Geographical, Statistical, and Historical Description of the District, or Zila, of Dinajpur in the Province, or Soubah, of Bengal.* Edited by James D. Herbert and James Prinsep. Calcutta, 1833.

———. *Journal kept during the Survey of the District of Bhagalpur in 1810–1811.* Edited by C. E. A. W. Oldham. Patna: Bihar and Orissa Government, 1930.

———. *Journal kept during the Survey of the Districts of Patna and Gaya in 1811–1812.* Edited by V. H. Jackson. Patna: Bihar and Orissa Government, 1925.

———. *Journal kept during the Survey of the District of Shahabad in 1812–1813.* Edited by C. E. A. W. Oldham. Patna: Bihar and Orissa Government, 1926.

———. *A Journey from Madras through the Countries of Mysore, Canara, and Mala-bar . . . for the Express Purpose of Investigating the State of Agriculture, Arts and Commerce; the Religion, Manners, and Customs; the History Natural and Civil and Antiquities, in the Dominions of the Rajah of Mysore, and the Countries Acquired by the Honorable East India Company, in the Late and Former Wars, from Tippoo Sultaun.* 3 vols. London, 1807. Reprint, New Delhi: Asian Educational Services, 1988.

Buist, George. "On the Adaptation of the Aneroid for the Purposes of Surveying in India." *Journal of the Royal Geographical Society* 21 (1851): 42–57.

———. "Geology of Bombay." *Transactions of the Bombay Geographical Society* 10 (1850–52): 167–238.

———. "Proceedings: Geographical Research in 1854–55." *Transactions of the Bombay Geographical Society* 12 (1854–56): lxxiv–xciii.

Burrow, Reuben. "Corrections of the Lunar Method of Finding the Longitude." *Asiatic Researches* 1 (1788): 356–57.

———. "Memorandums Concerning an Old Building, in the Hadjipore District, near the Gunduc River, &c." *Asiatic Researches* 2 (1790): 381–84.

———. "Observations of some of the Eclipses of Jupiter's Satellites." *Asiatic Researches* 2 (1790): 385–87.

———. "A Proof that the Hindus had the Binomial Theorem." *Asiatic Researches* 2 (1790): 487–97.

———. "A Synopsis of the Different Cases that may Happen in Deducing the Longitude of One Place from Another by Means of Arnold's Chronometers, and of Finding the Rates when the Difference of Longitude is Given." *Asiatic Researches* 2 (1790): 379–80.

———. "Table of Latitudes and Longitudes of Some Principal Places in India, determined from Astronomical Observations." *Asiatic Researches* 4 (1794): 321–27.

"Census of the Population of the City and District of Murshedabad, taken in 1829." *Journal of the Asiatic Society of Bengal* 2 (1833): 567–69.

A Code of the Bengal Military Regulations including those Relating to the Pay and Audit Departments, to which is Added a Staff Table, with Forms of Returns, Indents, Pay Abstracts, &c, compiled by the Order of Government, Commander in Chief's Office 1st September 1817. Calcutta: Government Gazette Press, 1817.

Colebrooke, H. T. "On the Heights of the Himàlaya Mountains." *Asiatic Researches* 12 (1815): 253–93.

Court, M. A. "Extracts Translated from a Memoir on a Map of Peshàwar and the Country Comprised between the Indus and the Hydaspes, the Peucelaotis and Taxila of Ancient Geography." *Journal of the Asiatic Society of Bengal* 5 (1836): 468–82.

Crisp, John Henry. *On the Methods of Determining Terrestrial Longitudes by the Moon's Right Ascension, as Deduced from her Altitudes and Culminations.* Calcutta: Baptist Mission Press, 1827.

Dalrymple, Alexander. *Proposition for a Survey of the Coast of Choromandel.* London: George Bigg, 1784.

d'Anville, Jean Baptiste Bourguignon. *Eclaircissemens géographiques sur la Carte de l'Inde.* Paris: Imprimerie royale, 1753. Translated by William Herbert as *A Geographical Illustration of the Map of India, translated from the French of Mon^r. d'Anville . . . with some Explanatory Notes and Remarks* (London, 1759).

"Déscription historique et géographique de l'Indostan, par James Rennell, Ingénieur général dans la Bengale: traduite de l'Anglais par J. B. Boucheseiche . . . (1800)." *Monatliche Correspondenz zur Beförderung der Erd- und Himmels-Kunde* 4 (1801): 341–44.

Diderot, Denis, and Jean Le Rond d'Alembert, eds. *Encyclopédie, ou dictionnaire raisonné des sciences, des arts et des métiers, par une société de gens de lettres.* 17 vols. Paris, 1751–65.

Dundas, Henry, and Richard Wellesley. *Two Views of British India: The Private Correspondence of Mr. Dundas and Lord Wellesley: 1798–1801.* Edited by Edward Ingram. Bath: Adams and Dart, 1970.

Everest, George. *An Account of the Measurement of an Arc of the Meridian between the Parallels of 18°3' and 24°7', being a Continuation of the Grand Meridional Arc of India . . .* London, 1830.

———. *An Account of the Measurement of Two Sections of the Meridional Arc of India, bounded by the Parallels of 18°3'15"; 24°7'11"; and 29°30'48".* 2 vols. London, 1847.

———. *On Instruments and Observations for Longitude for Travellers on Land.* London: W. Clowes & Sons, 1859. Reprint, *Journal of the Royal Geographical Society* 30 (1860): 315–24.

———. "On the Compensation Measuring Apparatus of the Great Trigonometrical Survey of India." *Asiatic Researches* 19 (1833): 189–214.

———. "On the Corrections requisite for the Triangles which occur in Geodetic Operations." *Memoirs of the Astronomical Society of London* 2 (1826): 37–44.

———. "On the Formulae for Calculating Azimuth in Trigonometrical Operations." *Asiatic Researches* 19 (1833): 93–106.

———. "On the Geodetical Operations of India." *Report of the British Association for the Advancement of Science* 14, no. 2 (1844): 3–4.

———. "On the Triangulation of the Cape of Good Hope." *Memoirs of the Royal Astronomical Society* 1 (1822): 255–70. Reprinted in C. G. C. Martin, "George Everest on the Triangulation of Good Hope," *Colonel Sir George Everest CB FRS: Proceedings of the Bicentenary Conference at the Royal Geographical Society, 8th November 1990,* 34–50 (London: Royal Geographical Society and Royal Institution of Chartered Surveyors, 1990).

———. "Rectification of Logarithmic Errors in the Measurements of Two Sections of the Meridional Arc of India." *Proceedings of the Royal Society of London* 9 (1857–59): 620–26.

———. *A Series of Letters Addressed to His Royal Highness the Duke of Sussex, As President of the Royal Society, Remonstrating Against the Conduct of that Learned Body.* London: William Pickering, 1839.

Gerard, Alexander. *Account of Koonawur, in the Himalaya . . .* Edited by George Lloyd. London: James Madden, 1841.

G[oldingham], J[ohn]. "A Method of Rectifying a Route Protraction." *Journal of the Asiatic Society of Bengal* 1 (1832): 19–20.

Goldingham, John. *Madras Observatory Papers.* Madras: College Press, 1827.

————. "Observations for Ascertaining the Length of the Pendulum at Madras in the East Indies, Latitude 13°4'19".1 N. with the Conclusions drawn from the Same." *Philosophical Transactions of the Royal Society* 112 (1822): 127–70.

————. "Of the Difference of Longitudes found by Chronometer, and by correspondent Eclipses of the Satellites of Jupiter, with some supplementary Information relative to Madras, Bombay, and Canton; as also the Latitude and Longitude of Point de Galle and the Friar's Hood." *Philosophical Transactions of the Royal Society* 112 (1822): 431–36.

————. "Of the Geographical Situation of the Three Presidencies, Calcutta, Madras, and Bombay, in the East Indies." *Philosophical Transactions of the Royal Society* 112 (1822): 408–30.

Goldsmid, H. E., G. Wingate, and D. Davidson. "The Joint Report, 2 August 1847." In *Papers Relating to the Joint Report of 1847 with the Measurement and Classification Rules of the Deccan, Gujarat, Konkan and Kanara Surveys,* 1–26. Selections from the Records of the Bombay Government, ns 532. Bombay, 1917.

"The Great Trigonometrical Survey of India." *The Calcutta Review* 16 (1851): 514–40.

"The Great Trigonometrical Survey of India." *The Calcutta Review* 38 (1863): 26–62.

Hamilton, Francis Buchanan. *An Account of the Kingdom of Nepal and of the Territories annexed to this Dominion by the House of Gorkha.* Edinburgh, 1819. Reprint, Bibliotheca Himalayica, ser. 1, vol. 10 (New Delhi: Mañjuśrī, 1971).

Hamilton, William. *Geographical, Statistical and Historical Description of Hindostan.* London, 1820.

Herbert, James D. *On the Present System of Survey, by which the Revenue Maps of Villages are Prepared; with an Account of a Preferable Method Proposed to be Substituted for it, as Conducive equally to Superior Accuracy, Economy, and Dispatch.* Calcutta: Baptist Mission Press, 1830.

"Hints for Collecting Geographical Information (Communicated in a Printed Form by the Secretary of the Royal Geographical Society)." *Transactions of the Bombay Geographical Society* 1 (1836–38): 364–70.

Hodgson, John A., and de Blossville. "Observations on the Inclination and Declination of the Magnetic Needle." *Asiatic Researches* 19 (1833): 1–12.

Hodgson, John A., and James D. Herbert. "An Account of Trigonometrical and Astronomical Operations for Determining the Heights and Positions of the Principal Peaks of the Himalaya Mountains, situated between the latitudes of 31°53'10" and 30°18'30" N and the longitudes of 77°34'04" and 79°57'22" E." *Asiatic Researches* 14 (1822): 182–372.

Hunter, William. "Astronomical Observations." *Asiatic Researches* 4 (1794): 357–60.

————. "Astronomical Observations made in the Upper Parts of Hindostan and on a Journey thence to Oujein." *Asiatic Researches* 4 (1794): 134–50.

———. "Astronomical Observations made in the Upper Provinces of Hindustan." *Asiatic Researches* 5 (1796): 413–22.

———. "Narrative of a Journey from Agra to Oujein." *Asiatic Researches* 6 (1798): 7–76.

Index containing the Names and Geographical Positions of all Places in the Maps of India, designed to facilitate the use of those maps and especially that of the newly constructed Extended Map of India lately published by Kingsbury, Parbury, and Allen, Booksellers to the Honorable East India Company. London: Kingsbury, Parbury, and Allen, 1826.

The Indian Field Astronomer; or, Surveyor's Assistant; being a Collection of Problems and Tables to facilitate the Methods of Ascertaining the Latitude and Longitude of Places on Land between the Parallels of 10 and 35 Degrees of North Latitude for the Use of the Officers of the Survey Department. Calcutta: Government Gazette Press, 1824.

Jervis, Thomas Best. "Additional Observations on the Remarkable Tides in the Gulf of Cambay." *Journal of the Royal Geographical Society* 8 (1838): 202–5.

———. *Address delivered at the Geographical Section of the British Association descriptive of the State, Progress and Prospects of the various Surveys and other Scientific Enquiries instituted by the . . . East India Company throughout Asia . . .* Torquay, 1838. Reprint, *Transactions of the Bombay Geographical Society* 4, no. 2 (1840): 155–89.

———. *The Expediency and Facility of Establishing the Metrological and Monetary Systems throughout India, on a Scientific and Permanent Basis, Grounded on an Analytical View of the Weights Measures and Coins of India, and their Relative Quantities with Respect to such as subsist at Present, or have hitherto subsisted in all past Ages throughout the World.* Bombay: American Mission, 1836.

———. "Historical and Geographical Account of the Western Coast of India." *Transactions of the Bombay Geographical Society* 4, no. 1 (1840): 1–244.

———. *India in relation to Great Britain: Considerations of its future Administration.* London, 1853.

———. "Memoir on the Origin, Progress, and Present State of the Surveys in India." *Journal of the Royal Geographical Society* 7 (1837): 127–43. Reprint, *Transactions of the Bombay Geographical Society* 4, no. 2 (1840): 133–53; *Madras Journal of Literature and Science* 7 (1838): 424–41.

———. *Records of Ancient Science, exemplified and authenticated in the Primitive Universal Standard of Weights and Measures.* Calcutta, 1836.

———. "Some Account of the Progress of the Trigonometrical Survey now carrying on in India." *Monthly Notices of the Royal Astronomical Society* 4 (1836–39): 206–10.

Kirkpatrick, William. *An Account of the Kingdom of Nepaul, being the Substance of Observations made During a Mission to that Country, in the Year 1793.* London: William Miller, 1811. Reprint, Bibliotheca Himalayica, ser. 1, vol. 3 (New Delhi: Mañjuśrī, 1969).

Lambton, William. "An Abstract of the Results deduced from the Measurement of an Arc on the Meridian, extending from Latitude 8°9′ 38″.4, to Latitude

18°3′ 23″.6 N., being an amplitude of 9°53′ 45″.2.″ *Philosophical Transactions of the Royal Society* 108 (1818): 486–517.

———. "An Account of a Method for extending a Geographical Survey across the Peninsula of India." *Asiatic Researches* 7 (1801): 312–35.

———. "An Account of the Measurement of an Arc on the Meridian, comprehended between the Latitudes 8°9′33.39″ and 10°59′48.93″ North, being a Continuation of the Grand Meridional Arc commenced in 1804, and Extending to 14°6′19″ North." *Asiatic Researches* 12 (1815): 1–101.

———. "An Account of the Measurement of an Arc on the Meridian extending from Latitude 10°59′49″ to 15°6′0.65″ North." *Asiatic Researches* 12 (1815): 294–359.

———. "An Account of the Measurement of an Arc on the Meridian, extending from Latitude 15°6′0.2″ to Latitude 18°3′45″, being a Further Continuation of the Former Arc commencing in Latitude 8°9′38″." *Asiatic Researches* 13 (1820): 1–127.

———. "An Account of the Measurement of an Arc on the Meridian on the Coast of Coromandel, and the Length of a Degree deduced therefrom in the Latitude 12°32′." *Asiatic Researches* 8 (1805): 137–93.

———. "An Account of the Trigonometrical Operations in Crossing the Peninsula of India, and connecting Fort St. George with Mangalore." *Asiatic Researches* 10 (1808): 290–384.

———. "Corrections applied to the Great Meridional Arc, extending from Latitude 8°9′ 38″.39, to Latitude 18°3′ 23″.64, to reduce it to the Parliamentary Standard." *Philosophical Transactions of the Royal Society* 113 (1823): 27–33.

———. "Extract from the late Colonel Lambton's Notices of Malabar (communicated by Major T. B. Jervis)." *Transactions of the Bombay Geographical Society* 4, no. 2 (1840): 1–9.

Lloyd, William, and Alexander Gerard. *Narrative of a Journey from Caunpoor to the Barendo Pass in the Himalaya Mountains, via Gwalior, Agra, Delhi, and Sirhind, by Major Sir William Lloyd; and Captain Alexander Gerard's Account of an Attempt to Penetrate by Bekhur to Garoo, and the Lake Manasarowara . . .* Edited by George Lloyd. 2 vols. London: J. Madden, 1840; 2d ed., 1846.

Mackenzie, Colin. "Account of the *Jains*, Collected from a Priest of this Sect at *Mudgeri*; Translated by Cavelly Boria, Brahmin, for Major C. Mackenzie." *Asiatic Researches* 9 (1808): 244–86.

———. "Account of the Pagoda at Perwuttum; Extract of a Journal by Captain Colin Mackenzie Communicated by Major Kirkpatrick." *Asiatic Researches* 5 (1796): 303–14.

———. "Biographical Sketch of the Literary Career of the Late Colonel Colin Mackenzie, Surveyor General of India . . ." *Madras Journal of Literature and Science* 2 (1835): 262–91. The core of this is a letter, Colin Mackenzie to Sir Alexander Johnstone, 1 Feb 1817, published in *Asiatic Journal* 13 (Mar–Apr 1822): 242–49 and 313–25; *The East India Military Calendar; containing the Services of General and Field Officers of the Indian Army*, edited by John Philippart, 3: 310–31 (London: Kingsbury, Parbury, and Allen, 1826, 3 vols.); *Journal of the Royal Asiatic Society* 1 (1834): 333–64.

"Manual of Surveying, etc." *The Calcutta Review* 16 (1851): 321–38.

Metcalfe, Charles T. M. *Selections from the Papers of Lord Metcalfe; late Governor General of India, Governor of India, and Governor General of Canada.* Edited by John W. Kaye. London: Smith, Elder, & Co., 1855.

"Minutes of Evidence Taken before the Select Committee on the Affairs of the East India Company." *British Parliamentary Papers* 1831 (65) 5.

"Minutes of Evidence Taken before the Select Committee on the Affairs of the East India Company." 5 vols. *British Parliamentary Papers* 1831–32 (735) 9–13.

Montgomery Martin, Robert. *The History, Antiquities, Topography, and Statistics of Eastern India . . . in relation to their Geology, Mineralogy, Botany, Agriculture, Commerce, Manufactures, Fine Arts, Population, Religion, Education, Statistics, etc.* 3 vols. London: Wm. H. Allen, 1838.

Orme, Robert. *The History of the Military Transactions of the British Nation in Indostan.* 2 vols. London, 1763–78.

Pearse, Thomas D. "Astronomical Observations near Fort William and between Madras and Calcutta." *Asiatic Researches* 1 (1784): 47–109.

Pemberton, R. Boileau. *Report on the Eastern Frontier of British India.* Calcutta, 1835. Reprint, Gauhati: State of Assam, Department of Historical and Antiquarian Studies, 1966.

[Playfair, William]. "An Account of a Trigonometrical Survey, and of the Measurement of an Arc of the Meridian in the Peninsula of India, by Major William Lambton, of the 33d Regiment of Foot." *Edinburgh Review* 21 (1813): 310–28.

Prinsep, James. "Census of the Population of the City of Benares." *Asiatic Researches* 17 (1832): 470–98.

———. "Progress of the Indian Trigonometrical Survey." *Journal of the Asiatic Society of Bengal* 1 (1832): 71–72.

———. "Table for Ascertaining the Heights of Mountains from the Boiling Point of Water." *Journal of the Asiatic Society of Bengal* 2 (1833): 194–200.

Rennell, James. "An Account of the Ganges and Burrampooter Rivers." *Philosophical Transactions of the Royal Society* 71 (1781): 87–114.

———. *A Description of the Roads in Bengal and Bahar . . .* London, 1778.

———. "The Journals of Major James Rennell, First Surveyor-General of India [*sic*]." Edited by T. H. D. LaTouche. *Memoirs of the Asiatic Society of Bengal* 3 (1910): 95–248.

———. *Memoir of a Map of Hindoostan; or the Mogul Empire: With an Introduction, Illustrative of the Geography and Present Division of that Country: And a Map of the Countries Situated between the Head of the Indus, and the Caspian Sea.* London, 1788; 2d ed., 1792; 3d ed., 1793.

———. *Memoir of a Map of Hindoostan; or the Mogul's Empire: With an Examination of some Positions in the Former System of Indian Geography; and some Illustrations of the Present One: And a Complete Index of Names to the Map.* London, 1783; 2d ed., 1785.

———. *Memoir of a Map of the Peninsula of India from the Latest Authorities: Exhibiting its Natural, and Political Divisions: The Latter, Conformable to the Treaty of Seringapatam, in March 1792. With Observations on the Political and Military Ad-*

vantages that may be Derived from the New Cessions: and an Account of the Site and Remains of the Ancient City of Beejanuggar. London, 1793.

"Report of a Police Committee, dated Calcutta, 10th August 1838; with Papers and Evidence." *Edinburgh Review* 73 (1841): 425–60.

"Report of the Select Committee on the Best Mode of Apportioning more equally the Local Burthens collected in Ireland, and to Provide for a General Survey and Valuation of that Part of the United Kingdom." *British Parliamentary Papers* 1824 (445) 8.

Roy, William. "An Account of the Mode Proposed to be Followed in Determining the Relative Situation of the Royal Observatories of Greenwich and Paris." *Philosophical Transactions of the Royal Society* 77 (1787): 188–228, 465–70.

———. "An Account of the Trigonometrical Operation, whereby the Distance between the Meridians of the Royal Observatories of Greenwich and Paris has been Determined." *Philosophical Transactions of the Royal Society* 80 (1790): 111–270, 593–614.

"A Selection of Papers illustrative of the Character and Results of the Revenue Survey and Assessment which has been Introduced into the North-West Provinces of the Bengal Presidency, since the Year 1833; and Similar Return as to the Presidency of Bombay." 10 Aug 1853. *British Parliamentary Papers* 1852–53 (999) 75.

Smith, Adam. "The History of Astronomy." In *Essays on Philosophical Subjects.* London, 1795. Critical edition by W. P. D. Wightmann, J. C. Bryce, and I. S. Ross, in *Adam Smith,* edited by D. D. Raphael and A. S. Skinner, 3: 33–105 (Oxford: Clarendon, 1980).

"State and Prospects of Asia." *The Quarterly Review* 63, no. 126 (March 1839): 369–402.

Stephen, Henry Virtue. *Handbook to the Maps of India.* London: W. H. Allen & Co., 1857.

Sykes, W. H. "On the Use of Common Thermometers to Determine Heights." *Transactions of the Bombay Geographical Society* 2, no. 3 (1838–39): 38–46.

Taylor, G. T. "Observations of the Magnetic Dip and Intensity at Madras." *Journal of the Asiatic Society of Bengal* 6 (1837): 374–77.

Thornton, Edward. *A Gazetteer of the Territories under the Governance of the East India Company.* London, 1854.

"The Trigonometrical Survey." *The Calcutta Review* 4 (1845): 62–95.

Vigne, Godfrey Thomas. *Travels in Kashmir, Ladak, Iskardo, the Countries adjoining the Mountain-Course of the Indus, and the Himalaya, North of the Panjab.* 2 vols. London: Henry Colburn, 1842.

Walters, Henry. "Journey across the Pandua Hills, near Silhet, in Bengal." *Asiatic Researches* 17 (1832): 499–512.

———. "Census of the City of Dacca." *Asiatic Researches* 17 (1832): 535–58.

Ward, B. S., and Peter E. Conner. "Descriptive and Geographical Account of the Province of Malabar (communicated by the Right Honorable Sir F. Adam, Governor of Madras, to Major T. B. Jervis)." *Transactions of the Bombay Geographical Society* 4, no. 2 (1840): 33–124.

Warren, John. "An Account of Experiments made at the Observatory near Fort

St. George, for Determining the Length of the Simple Pendulum Beating Seconds at that Place; to which are added, Comparisons of the said Experiments, with Others made in Different Parts of the Globe and some Remarks on the Ellipticity of the Earth, as deduced from these Operations." *Asiatic Researches* 11 (1812): 293–308.

———. "Biographical Sketch of the Late Col. Lambton, Superintendent of the Trigonometrical Survey of India." Edited by James D. Herbert. *Gleanings in Science* 15 (Mar 1830): 73–82.

———. "Observations on the Golden Ore, Found in the Eastern Provinces of Mysore in the year 1802." *Journal of the Asiatic Society of Bengal* 3 (1834): 463–75.

Waugh, Andrew Scott. "Report and Statements of the Operations and Expense of the Trigonometrical Survey of India." *British Parliamentary Papers* 1851 (219) 41: 875–936.

Webb, William S. "Memoir Relative to a Survey of Kemaon, with some Account of the Principles, upon which it has been Conducted." *Asiatic Researches* 13 (1819): 292–310.

Wellington, 1st Duke [Arthur Wellesley]. *The Dispatches of Field Marshal the Duke of Wellington, K.G. during his various Campaigns in India, Denmark, Portugal, Spain, the Low Countries, and France. From 1799 to 1818.* Edited by John Gurwood. 12 vols. and supplement. New ed. London: J. Murray, 1837–38.

———. *Supplementary Despatches of Field Marshal Arthur Duke of Wellington, K.G.* Edited by the second duke of Wellington. London: John Murray, 1858.

White, Adam. *Memoir of the Late David Scott, Esq., Agent to the Governor General, on the North-East Frontier of Bengal, and Commissioner of Revenue and Circuit in Assam.* Edited by Archibald Watson. Calcutta: Baptist Mission Press, 1832.

Wilcox, Richard. "Memoir of a Survey of Asam and the Neighbouring Countries, Executed in 1825–6–7–8." *Asiatic Researches* 17 (1832): 314–469.

Wilkins, George. *Biographical Sketch of Thomas Best Jervis . . . being the Substance of a Funeral Sermon.* London: Snow, 1857. Also printed as *The Voice of the Dead: a Funeral Sermon occasioned by the Death of Lieutenant Colonel T. B. Jervis.* London, 1857.

Wilkinson, Lancelot. "On the Use of the Siddhántas in the Work of Native Education." *Journal of the Asiatic Society of Bengal* 3 (1834): 504–19.

Williams, Monier. *Memoir on the Zilla of Baroche; being the Result of a Revenue, Statistical, and Topographical Survey of that Collectorate; executed by Order of the Bombay Government.* London, 1825. Reprinted in Selections from the Records of the Bombay Government, 3 (Bombay, 1852).

Secondary Sources Relating to the British Surveys in India

Allen, Charles. "A Forgotten Pioneer of Himalayan Exploration." *Asian Affairs* 11 (1980): 169–77.

Ambashthya, Brahmadeva Praad, ed. *James Rennell's Memoir of a Map of Hindustan or the Mughal Empire and His Bengal Atlas.* Patna: N. V. Publications, ca. 1975.

Baker, J. N. L. "Major James Rennell, 1742–1830, and His Place in the History of Geography." In *The History of Geography*, 130–57. Oxford: Basil Blackwell, 1963.

Barron, W. "The Cadastral Survey of India." *Royal Geographical Society Supplementary Papers* 1 (1885): 597–618.

Berthon, Simon, and Andrew Robinson. "Measuring India." In *The Shape of the World: The Mapping and Discovery of the Earth*, 133–49. (London: Granada Television; Chicago: Rand McNally, 1991).

Black, Charles E. D. *A Memoir on the Indian Surveys, 1875–1890*. London, 1891.

Blake, David M. "Introduction." In *The Mackenzie General and Miscellaneous Collections*, edited by J. S. Cotton, J. H. R. T. Charpentier, and E. H. Johnston, vi–lvii. Vol. 1.2 of *Catalogue of Manuscripts in European Languages belonging to the Library of the India Office*. 2d ed. London, 1992.

Boole, Mary Everest. "The Naming of Mount Everest." In Mary Everest Boole, *Collected Works*, edited by E. M. Cobham, 3: 1094–1100. London: C. W. Daniel, 1931.

Brohier, R. L. *Land, Maps and Surveys: A Review of the Evidence of Land Surveys as Practised in Ceylon from Earliest Known Periods and the Story of the Ceylon Survey Department from 1800 to 1950*. 2 vols. Colombo: Ceylon Government Press, 1950.

Burrard, Sidney G. "An Account of the Operations of the Great Trigonometrical Survey of India under Colonel Lambton." In *Account of the Operations of the Great Trigonometrical Survey of India* 12 (1888): separately paginated appendix.

———. *An Account of the Scientific Work of the Survey of India, and a Comparison of its Progress with that of Foreign Surveys*. Survey of India Professional Paper, 9. Calcutta, 1905.

———. *On the Values of Longitude Employed in the Maps of the Survey of India*. Survey of India Professional Paper, 7 pt. 1. Calcutta, 1903.

Chadha, S. M. *Survey of India Through the Ages*. Dehra Dun: Survey of India, 1990.

Coldstream, William. *Notes on Survey of India Maps and the Modern Development of Indian Cartography*. Records of the Survey of India, 12. Calcutta, 1919.

———. "Indian Maps and Surveys." *Journal of the Royal Society of Arts* 74 (1926): 299–320.

Cook, Andrew S. "Alexander Dalrymple and John Arnold: Chronometers and the Representation of Longitude on East India Company Charts." *Vistas in Astronomy* 28 (1985): 189–95.

———. "The Beginning of Lithographic Map Printing in Calcutta." In *India: A Pageant of Prints*, edited by Pauline Rohatgi and Pheroza Godrej, 125–34. Bombay: Marg Publications, 1989.

———. "Major James Rennell and *A Bengal Atlas* (1780 and 1781)." In *India Office Library and Records Report for the Year 1976*, 5–42. London: British Library, 1978.

———. "Maps." In *South Asian Bibliography: A Handbook and Guide*, edited by J. D. Pearson, 96–107. Hassocks: Harvester Press, 1979.

———. "Maps from a Survey Archive: The India Office Collection." *Map Collector* 28 (1984): 27–32.

———. "'More by Accident than Design': The Development of Topographical

Mapping in India in the Nineteenth Century." Paper presented at the eleventh International Conference on the History of Cartography, Ottawa, 1985.

————. "The Training of East India Company Surveyors in the Early Nineteenth Century." Paper presented at the Tenth International Conference on the History of Cartography, Dublin, September 1983.

[Cook, Andrew S.] "Manuscript Maps by James Rennell." *Geographical Journal* 136 (1970): 161–62.

Crosthwait, H. L. "The Survey of India." *Journal of the Royal Society of Arts* 72 (1924): 194–206.

Dasgupta, Keya. "A City Away from Home: The Mapping of Calcutta." In *Texts of Power: Emerging Disciplines in Colonial Bengal,* edited by Partha Chatterjee, 145–66. Perspectives in Social Sciences Series of the Center for Studies in Social Sciences, Calcutta, India. Minneapolis: University of Minnesota Press, 1995.

Das Gupta, S. P. "Development of Cartography and Thematic Mapping in India." In *Contributions to Indian Geography, I: Concepts and Approaches,* edited by R. P. Misra, 293–313. New Delhi: Heritage, 1980.

Dirks, Nicholas B. "Colonial Histories and Native Informants: Biography of an Archive." In *Orientalism and the Postcolonial Predicament: Perspectives on South Asia,* edited by Carol A. Breckenridge and Peter van der Veer, 279–313. Philadelphia: University of Pennsylvania Press, 1993.

————. "Guiltless Spoliations: Picturesque Beauty, Colonial Knowledge, and Colin Mackenzie's Survey of India." In *Perceptions of South Asia's Visual Past,* edited by Catherine B. Asher and Thomas R. Metcalf, 211–32. New Delhi: Oxford and IBH Publishing for the American Institute of Indian Studies, 1994.

Dossal, Mariam. "Knowledge for Power: The Significance of the Bombay Revenue Survey, 1811–1827." In *Ports and their Hinterlands in India (1700–1950),* edited by Indu Banga, 227–43. Bombay: Manohar, 1992.

Downes, Alan. "James Rennell, 1742–1830." *Geographers: Biobibliographical Studies* 1 (1977): 83–88.

Edney, Matthew H. "The *Atlas of India,* 1823–1947: The Natural History of a Topographic Map Series." *Cartographica* 28, no. 4 (1991): 59–91.

————. "British Military Education, Mapmaking, and Military 'Map-Mindedness' in the Later Enlightenment." *The Cartographic Journal* 31, no. 1 (1994): 14–20.

————. "Defining a Unique City: Surveying and Mapping Bombay after 1800." In *From Bombay to Mumbai: Changing Perspectives,* edited by Pauline Rohatgi. Bombay: Marg Publications, 1997.

————. "Mapping and Empire: British Trigonometrical Surveys in India and the European Concept of Systematic Survey, 1799–1843." Ph.D. diss., University of Wisconsin-Madison, 1990.

————. "The Ordnance Survey and the British Surveys in India." *Sheetlines: The Newsletter of the Charles Close Society* 26 (1989): 3–8 and 27 (1989): 9–10.

————. "The Patronage of Science and the Creation of Imperial Space: The British Mapping of India, 1799–1843." *Cartographica* 30, no. 1 (1993): 61–67.

————. "Systematic Surveys and Mapping Policy in British India, 1757–1830." In *Colonel Sir George Everest CB FRS: Proceedings of the Bicentenary Conference at the Royal Geographical Society, 8th November 1990*, edited by James R. Smith, 1–11. London: Royal Geographical Society and Royal Institution of Chartered Surveyors, 1990.

Gole, Susan. *Early Maps of India*. New York: Humanities Press; New Delhi: Sanskriti, 1976.

————. *India within the Ganges*. New Delhi: Jayaprints, 1983.

————. *Indian Maps and Plans from Earliest Times to the Advent of European Surveys*. New Delhi: Manohar, 1989.

————. *Maps of Mughal India drawn by Colonel Jean-Baptiste-Joseph Gentil, Agent for the French Government to the Court of Shuja-ud-Daula at Faizabad, in 1770*. London: Kegan Paul International, 1988.

————. "When We Get There: Bombay in Early Maps." In *From Bombay to Mumbai: Changing Perspectives*, edited by Pauline Rohatgi. Bombay: Marg Publications, 1997.

Gole, Susan, comp. *A Series of Early Printed Maps of India in Facsimile*. New Delhi: Jayaprints, 1980.

Gordon, R. G. *Part 1: Historical*. Vol. 1 of *The Bombay Survey and Settlement Manual*. 2 vols. 2d ed. Bombay: Government Central Press, 1935.

Gore, St. G. C. *On the Projection for a Map of India and Adjacent Countries on the Scale of 1:1,000,000*. Survey of India, Professional Paper 1. Dehra Dun, 1900; 2d ed., 1903.

Goss, John. "India Surveyed." In *The Mapmaker's Art: An Illustrated History of Cartography*, 246–53. Chicago: Rand McNally, 1993.

Heaney, G. F. "Rennell and the Surveyors of India." *Geographical Journal* 134 (1968): 318–27.

————. "Sir George Everest." *Geographical Journal* 133 (1967): 209–11.

————. *Survey and Mapping Policy*. Survey of India Departmental Paper, 17. Dehra Dun: Survey of India, Geodetic Branch, 1947.

Hirst, Frederick C. *A Companion Atlas to those Published by Major James Rennell in 1779 and 1781*. Calcutta, 1914; 2d ed., 1917.

————. *A Digest of the Original Correspondence upon the Revenue Survey of Jaintia Pargana, District Sylhet, Assam, 1837–40*. Shillong, 1912.

————. *A Memoir upon the Maps of Bengal Constructed from 1764 Onwards by Major James Rennell, FRS*. Calcutta, 1914.

————. *Notes on the Old Revenue Surveys of Bengal, Bihar, Orissa, and Assam*. Calcutta: Thatcher, Spink & Co., 1912.

————. *The Surveys of Bengal by Major James Rennell, FRS, 1764–1777*. Calcutta: Bengal Secretariat Book Depot, 1917.

Hirst, Frederick C., and A. B. Smart. *A Brief History of the Surveys of the Goalpara District*. Shillong, 1917.

Holdich, Thomas H. "A Geodetic Connection between the Surveys of Russia and India." In *Report of the Sixth International Geographical Congress, London 1895*, 287–97. London: John Murray, 1896.

————. "The Romance of Indian Surveys." *Journal of the Royal Society of Arts* 44 (1916): 173–85.

Hopkirk, Peter. *Trespassers on the Roof of the World: The Secret Exploration of Tibet.* London: John Murray, 1982; reprint, New York: Kodansha, 1995.

India. National Archives. *Catalogue of Memoirs of the Survey of India, 1773–1866.* New Delhi: National Archives of India, 1989.

———. *Catalogue of the MRIO-Miscellaneous Maps of the Survey of India.* New Delhi: National Archives of India, 1982.

India. Survey of India. *Report of the Indian Survey Committee, 1904–05.* 3 vols. Simla: Government Central Printing Office, 1905. IOR V/26/420/2–3 are vols. 1 and 2; vol. 3 was only acquired by IOR in 1994 and has yet to be cataloged.

Insley, Jane E. "'Instruments of a Very Beautiful Class': George Everest in Europe, 1825–1830." In *Colonel Sir George Everest CB FRS: Proceedings of the Bicentenary Conference at the Royal Geographical Society, 8th November 1990,* edited by James R. Smith, 23–30. London: Royal Geographical Society and Royal Institution of Chartered Surveyors, 1990.

Jackson, V. H. "Introduction: The Buchanan Journal and Maps." In *Journal of Francis Buchanan (Afterwards Hamilton) Kept During the Survey of the Districts of Patna and Gaya in 1811–1812,* edited by V. H. Jackson, i–xxvi. Patna: Superintendent, Government Printing, Bihar and Orissa, 1925.

Jameson, A. K. "James Rennell: First Surveyor General of India [*sic*]." *Bengal Past and Present* 28, no. 1 (1924): 1–11.

Jervis, William Paget. *Thomas Best Jervis as Christian Soldier, Geographer, and Friend of India, 1796–1857: A Centenary Tribute.* London: Elliot Stock, 1898.

Keay, John. *India Discovered: The Achievement of the British Raj.* Leicester: Windward, 1981. New edition, London: Collins, 1988.

———. *When Men and Mountains Meet: The Explorers of the Western Himalayas, 1820–75.* London: John Murray, 1977; reprint, Karachi: Oxford University Press, 1993.

Kunte, B. G. *Catalogue of Maps in the Bombay Archives.* Many vols. Bombay: Maharashtra Dept. of Archives, 1979– .

———. *Maps of India, 1795–1935.* Bombay: Maharashtra State Archives, 1979.

Mackenzie, William C. *Colonel Colin Mackenzie: First Surveyor-General of India.* Forward by Reginald H. Phillimore. London: W. & R. Chambers, 1952.

Madan, P. L. "Cartographic Records in the National Archives of India." *Imago Mundi* 25 (1971): 79–80.

Markham, Clements R. *A Memoir on the Indian Surveys.* London: Allen & Co., 1871; 2d ed., 1878. Reprint, Amsterdam: Meridian Publishing, 1968.

———. *Major James Rennell and the Rise of Modern English Geography.* London: Cassell & Co., 1895.

Markham, Clements R., ed. *Abstract of the Reports of the Surveys and of other Geographical Operations in India.* 8 vols. London, 1871–79.

Mason, Kenneth. "Kishen Singh and the Indian Explorers." *Geographical Journal* 62 (1923): 429–40.

Phillimore, Reginald H. *Historical Records of the Survey of India.* Dehra Dun: Survey of India, 1945–58, 4 vols. Vol. 1, *18th Century* (1945); vol. 2, *1800 to 1815* (1950); vol. 3, *1815 to 1830* (1954); vol. 4, *1830 to 1843: George Everest* (1958); vol. 5, *1843 to 1861: Andrew Waugh* (1968), was withdrawn shortly after publication but copies exist in the Royal Geographical Society, London, and the Royal Engineers Institution, Chatham.

Prasad, S. N., comp. *Catalogue of the Historical Maps of the Survey of India (1700–1900)*. New Delhi: National Archives of India, 1975.

Rennell Rodd, Lord. "Major James Rennell." *Geographical Journal* 75 (1930): 290–99.

Roy, Rama Deb. "The Great Trigonometrical Survey of India in a Historical Perspective." *Indian Journal of History of Science* 21 (1986): 22–32.

[Saunders, Trelawney W.] *A Catalogue of Manuscript and Printed Reports, Field Books, Memoirs, Maps . . . of the Indian Surveys deposited in the Map Room of the India Office*. London: W. H. Allen & Co., 1878.

Scholberg, Henry. "European Cartography of the West Coast of India." *Indica* 27 (1990): 11–24.

Schwartzberg, Joseph. "South Asian Cartography." In *Cartography in the Traditional Islamic and South Asian Societies*, vol. 2.1 of *The History of Cartography*, edited by J. B. Harley and David Woodward, 293–509. Chicago: University of Chicago Press, 1992.

Sen, S. N. "Tieffenthaler on Latitudes and Longitudes in India: An Eighteenth Century Study of Geographical Coordinates." *Indian Journal of History of Science* 17 (1982): 1–17.

Shaw, T., and A. B. Smart. *A Brief History of the Surveys of the Sylhet*. Shillong, 1917.

Smith, James R. *Everest, the Man, and the Mountain*. Rancho Cordova, CA: Landmark Enterprises, forthcoming.

———. "Sir George Everest, F.R.S. (1790–1866)." *Notes and Records of the Royal Society of London* 46 (1992): 89–102.

Smith, James R., ed. *Colonel Sir George Everest CB FRS: Proceedings of the Bicentenary Conference at the Royal Geographical Society, 8th November 1990*. London: Royal Geographical Society and Royal Institution of Chartered Surveyors, 1990.

Sternstein, Larry. "'Low' Maps of Siam." *Journal of the Siam Society* 73, no. 1 (1985): 132–56.

———. "Low's Description of the Siamese Empire in 1824." *Journal of the Siam Society* 78, no. 1 (1990): 8–34.

———. "Siam and Surrounds in 1830." *Journal of the Siam Society* 78, no. 2 (1990): 90–101.

Styles, Showell. *The Forbidden Frontiers: The Survey of India from 1765–1949*. London: Hamish Hamilton, 1970.

Walckenaer, C. A. "Notice historique sur la vie et les ouvrages de M le Major Rennell." *Mémoires de l'Institut royale de France, Académie des Inscriptions et Belles-Lettres* 14 (1845): 225–43.

Walker, J. T. "An Account of the Operations from the Commencement of the Survey to the Year 1830." In *Account of the Operations of the Great Trigonometrical Survey of India* 1 (1870): xv–xxxv.

———. "A Memorandum on the Copper Plates of the Indian Atlas which he has Placed in the Hands of Engravers in London, the Geographical Materials furnished to the Engravers, and the Arrangements for the Final Disposal of the Work; September 1872." In *Abstract of the Reports of the Surveys and of other Geographical Operations in India for 1871–72*, edited by Clements R. Markham, 47–53. London, 1873.

———. "Memorandum on the State of the Arrangements for the Publication of the Sheet[s] of the Indian Atlas in England." In *A Memoir on the Indian Surveys*, by Clements R. Markham, 431–39. 2d ed. London: Allen & Co., 1878; reprint, Amsterdam: Meridian Publishing, 1968.

Ward, M. P. "Mapping Everest." *The Cartographic Journal* 31 (1994): 33–44.

Wilford, John Noble. "Soldiers, Pundits, and the Indian Survey." In *The Mapmakers: The Story of the Great Pioneers in Cartography from Antiquity to the Space Age* (New York: Random House, 1981), 161–73.

Williams, Donovan. "Clements Robert Markham and the Geographical Department of the India Office, 1867–77." *Geographical Journal* 134 (1968): 343–52.

Principal Secondary Sources

Adas, Michael. *Machines as the Measure of Men: Science, Technology, and Ideologies of Western Dominance*. Ithaca, NY: Cornell University Press, 1989.

———. "Scientific Standards and Colonial Education in British India and French Senegal." In *Science, Medicine and Cultural Imperialism*, edited by Teresa Meade and Mark Walker, 4–35. New York: St. Martin's Press, 1991.

Airy, George Biddell. "Figure of the Earth." *Encyclopaedia Metropolitana* 5 (1845): 165–*240. This essay was dated 17 Aug 1830.

Alam, Anis. "Imperialism and Science." *Social Scientist* 6, no. 5 (1977): 3–15.

Alfrey, Nicholas, and Stephen Daniels, eds. *Mapping the Landscape: Essays on Art and Cartography*. Nottingham: University Art Gallery and Castle Museum, 1990.

Anderson, Benedict. *Imagined Communities: Reflections on the Origin and Spread of Nationalism*. Revised edition. London: Verso, 1991.

Andrews, J. H. *A Paper Landscape: The Ordnance Survey in Nineteenth-Century Ireland*. Oxford: Clarendon Press, 1975.

Andrews, Michael. *The Search for the Picturesque: Landscape Aesthetics and Tourism in Britain, 1760–1800*. Stanford, CA: Stanford University Press, 1989.

Ansari, S. M. Razaullah. "The Establishment of Observatories and the Socio-Economic Conditions of Scientific Work in Nineteenth Century India." *Indian Journal of History of Science* 13 (1978): 62–71.

Appadurai, Arjun. "Number in the Colonial Imagination." In, *Orientalism and the Postcolonial Predicament: Perspectives on South Asia*, edited by Carol A. Breckenridge and Peter van der Veer, 314–39. Philadelphia: University of Pennsylvania Press, 1993.

Archer, Mildred. *British Drawings in the India Office Library*. 2 vols. London: HMSO, 1969.

———. *Early Views of India: The Picturesque Journeys of Thomas and William Daniell, 1786–1794: The Complete Aquatints*. London: Thames and Hudson, 1980.

Archer, Mildred, and Ronald Lightbown. *India Observed: India as Viewed by British Artists, 1760–1860*. London: Victoria and Albert Museum, 1982.

Aris, Michael. *Views of Medieval Bhutan: The Diary and Drawings of Samuel Davis, 1783.* London: Serindia Publications; Washington, DC: Smithsonian Institution Press, 1982.

Arnold, David. "European Orphans and Vagrants in India in the Nineteenth Century." *Journal of Imperial and Commonwealth History* 7, no. 2 (1979): 104–27.

Barooah, Nirode K. *David Scott in North-East India, 1802–31: A Study in British Paternalism.* Bombay: Munshiram Manoharlal, 1969.

Basalla, George. "The Spread of Western Science." *Science* 156 (1967): 611–22.

Bayly, C. A. "The British Military-Fiscal State and Indigenous Resistance: India, 1750–1820." In *An Imperial State at War: Britain from 1689 to 1815,* edited by Lawrence Stone, 322–54. London: Routledge, 1994.

———. "Colonial Star Wars: The Politics of the Heavens in India, c.1780–1880." Unpublished manuscript, version of May 1994. In the author's possession.

———. *Imperial Meridian: The British Empire and the World, 1780–1830.* London: Longman, 1989.

———. *Indian Society and the Making of the British Empire.* Vol. 2.1 of *The New Cambridge History of India.* Cambridge: Cambridge University Press, 1988.

———. "Knowing the Country: Empire and Information in India." *Modern Asian Studies* 27 (1993): 3–43.

Bayly, C. A., ed. *Raj: India and the British, 1600–1947.* London: National Portrait Gallery, 1990.

Beaglehole, T. H. *Thomas Munro and the Development of Administrative Policy in Madras, 1792–1818: The Origins of the 'Munro System.'* Cambridge: Cambridge University Press, 1966.

Bearce, George D. *British Attitudes towards India, 1784–1858.* Oxford: Oxford University Press, 1961.

Berman, Morris. *Social Change and Scientific Organization: The Royal Institution, 1799–1844.* Ithaca, NY: Cornell University Press, 1978.

Bermingham, Ann. *Landscape and Ideology: The English Rustic Tradition, 1740–1860.* Berkeley: University of California Press, 1986.

———. "System, Order, and Abstraction: The Politics of English Landscape Drawing around 1795." In *Landscape and Power,* edited by W. J. T. Mitchell, 77–101. Chicago: University of Chicago Press, 1994.

Bernal, Martin. *The Fabrication of Ancient Greece, 1785–1985.* Vol. 1 of *Black Athena: The Afroasiatic Roots of Classical Civilization.* London: Free Association Books, 1987.

Bernstein, Henry T. *Steamboats on the Ganges: An Exploration in the History of India's Modernization through Science and Technology.* Calcutta: Orient Longman, 1960; reprint 1987.

Bialas, Volker. *Erdgestalt, Kosmologie und Weltanschauung: Die Geschichte der Geodäsie als Teil der Kulturgeschichte der Menscheit.* Stuttgart: Konrad Winter, 1982.

Borges, Jorge Luis. "Museum: On Rigor in Science." In Borges, *Dreamtigers,* translated by Mildred Boyer and Harold Morland, 90. Austin: University of Texas Press, 1964.

Bourne, J. M. *Patronage and Society in Nineteenth-Century England.* London: Edward Arnold, 1986.

Bowen, Margarita. *Empiricism and Geographical Thought from Francis Bacon to Alexander von Humboldt.* Cambridge: Cambridge University Press, 1981.

Broc, Numa. *La Géographie des philosophes: Géographes et voyageurs français au XVIIIᵉ siècle.* Paris: Editions Ophrys, 1974.

Brown, Lloyd A. *The Story of Maps.* New York: 1949. Reprint, New York: Dover, 1979.

Bryson, Norman. *Vision and Painting: The Logic of the Gaze.* New Haven: Yale University Press, 1983.

Buck, Peter. "People Who Counted: Political Arithmetic in the Eighteenth Century." *Isis* 73 (1982): 28–45.

Cannon, Garland. "Sir William Jones's Founding and Directing of the Asiatic Society." In *India Office Library and Records Report for 1984–85,* 11–28. London: British Library, 1985.

Cannon, Susan Faye. *Science in Culture: The Early Victorian Period.* New York: Science History Publications, 1978.

Carter, Paul. *The Road to Botany Bay: A Spatial History.* London and Boston: Faber and Faber, 1987.

Certeau, Michel de. *The Practice of Everyday Life.* Translated by Steven Rendall. Berkeley: University of California Press, 1984.

Chambers, David Wade. "Period and Process in Colonial and National Science." In *Scientific Colonialism, A Cross-Cultural Comparison: Papers from a Conference at Melbourne, Australia, 25–30 May 1981,* edited by Nathan Reingold and Marc Rothenberg, 297–321. Washington, DC: Smithsonian Institution Press, 1987.

Chaudhuri, S. B. *History of the Gazetteers of India.* New Delhi: Ministry of Education, 1965.

Clive, John. *Macauley: The Shaping of the Historian.* Cambridge: Harvard University Press, 1987.

Close, Charles F. *The Early Years of the Ordnance Survey.* Newton Abbott: Davis and Charles, 1969.

Cohn, Bernard S. *An Anthropologist among the Historians and Other Essays.* Delhi: Oxford University Press, 1987.

Cormack, Lesley B. "'Good Fences Make Good Neighbours': Geography as Self-Definition in Early Modern England." *Isis* 82 (1991): 639–61.

Cosgrove, Denis. "Prospect, Perspective and the Evolution of the Landscape Idea." *Transactions of the Institute of British Geographers,* ns 10 (1985): 45–62.

———. *Social Formation and Symbolic Landscape.* London: Croom Helm, 1984.

Cotton, James S., J. H. R. T. Charpentier, and E. H. Johnston. *The Mackenzie General and Miscellaneous Collections.* Vol. 1.2 of *Catalogue of Manuscripts in European Languages Belonging to the Library of the India Office.* London: India Office Library, 1916; 2d ed., 1992.

Crary, Jonathen. *Techniques of the Observer: On Vision and Modernity in the Nineteenth Century.* Cambridge, MA: The MIT Press, 1990.

428 Archival Sources and Bibliography

Daniels, Stephen. *Fields of Vision: Landscape Imagery and National Identity in England and the United States.* Princeton: Princeton University Press, 1993.
———. "Re-Visioning Britain: Mapping and Landscape Painting, 1750–1820." In Michael Rosenthal et al., *Glorious Nature: British Landscape Painting, 1750–1850,* 61–72. New York: Hudson Hills Press, 1993.
Deleury, Guy, comp. *Les Indes florissantes: Anthologie des voyageurs français (1750–1820).* Paris: Robert Laffont, 1991.
Desmond, Ray. *The European Discovery of the Indian Flora.* Oxford: Oxford University Press for Royal Botanic Gardens, Kew, 1992.
———. *The India Museum, 1801–1879.* London: HMSO for the India Office Library and Records, 1982.
Dirks, Nicholas B. "Castes of Mind." *Representations* 37 (1992): 56–78.
———. *The Hollow Crown: Ethnohistory of an Indian Kingdom.* Cambridge: Cambridge University Press, 1987.
Driver, Felix, and Gillian Rose, eds. *Nature and Science: Essays in the History of Geographical Knowledge.* Historical Geography Research Series, 28. London: London Group of Historical Geographers, 1991.
Dyson, Ketaki Kushari. *A Various Universe: A Study of the Journals and Memoirs of British Men and Women in the Indian Subcontinent, 1765–1856.* Delhi: Oxford University Press, 1978.
Edney, Matthew H. "Cartography without 'Progress': Reinterpreting the Nature and Historical Development of Mapmaking." *Cartographica* 30, nos. 2 and 3 (1993): 54–68.
———. "Cartographic Culture and Nationalism in the Early United States: Benjamin Vaughan and the Choice for a Prime Meridian, 1811." *Journal of Historical Geography* 20 (1994): 384–95.
———. "Mathematical Cosmography and the Social Ideology of British Cartography, 1780–1820." *Imago Mundi* 46 (1994): 101–16.
Embree, Ainslie T. *Imagining India: Essays on Indian History.* Edited by Mark Juergensmeyer. Delhi: Oxford University Press, 1989.
Fabian, Johannes. "Presence and Representation: The Other and Anthropological Writing." *Critical Inquiry* 16 (1990): 753–72.
———. *Time and the Other: How Anthropology Makes Its Object.* New York: Columbia University Press, 1983.
Forbes, Eric G. "Mathematical Cosmography." In *The Ferment of Knowledge: Studies in the Historiography of Eighteenth-Century Science.* Edited by G. S. Rousseau and Roy Porter, 417–48. Cambridge: Cambridge University Press, 1980.
Foster, William. "British Artists in India, 1760–1820." *Annual Volume of the Walpole Society* 19 (1930–31): 1–88.
Foucault, Michel. *Discipline and Punish: The Birth of the Prison.* Translated by Alan Sheridan. New York: Random House, 1977.
———. *The Order of Things: An Archaeology of the Human Sciences.* New York: Random House, 1970.
Frängsmyr, Tore, J. L. Heilbron, and Robin E. Rider, eds. *The Quantifying Spirit in the Eighteenth Century.* Berkeley: University of California Press, 1990.

Frykenberg, Robert E. *Guntur District 1788–1848: A History of Local Influence and Central Authority in South India*. Oxford: Clarendon Press, 1965.

Gitelman, Lisa L. "The World Recounted: Science and Narrative in Early Nineteenth-Century Exploration Accounts." Ph.D. diss. Columbia University, 1991.

Glacken, Clarence J. *Traces on the Rhodian Shore: Nature and Culture in Western Thought from Ancient Times to the End of the Eighteenth Century*. Berkeley: University of California Press, 1967.

Godlewska, Anne. "Map, Text, and Image: The Mentality of Enlightened Conquerors: A New Look at the *Description de l'Egypt*." *Transactions of the Institute of British Geographers*, ns 20 (1995): 5–28.

———. "The Napoleonic Survey of Egypt: A Masterpiece of Cartographic Compilation and Early Nineteenth-Century Fieldwork." *Cartographica* 25, nos. 1 and 2 (1988): *Monograph 38–39*.

———. "Napoleon's Geographers (1797–1815): Imperialists and Soldiers of Modernity." In *Geography and Empire*, edited by Anne Godlewska and Neil Smith, 31–53. Institute of British Geographers, Special Publication 30. Oxford: Blackwell, 1994.

———. "Traditions, Crisis, and New Paradigms in the Rise of the Modern French Discipline of Geography, 1760–1850." *Annals of the Association of American Geographers* 79 (1989): 192–213.

Godrej, Pheroza. "The Travels of Henry Salt and Lord Valentia in India." In *India: A Pageant of Prints*, edited by Pauline Rohatgi and Pheroza Godrej, 71–88. Bombay: Marg Publications, 1989.

Groseclose, Barbara. "Imag(in)ing Indians." *Art History* 13 (1990): 488–515.

Habib, Irfan. "Institutional Efforts: Popularization of Science in the mid 19th Century." *Fundamenta Scientiae* 6 (1985): 299–312.

———. "Promoting Science and Its World-View in the Mid-Nineteenth Century India." In *Science and Empire: Essays in Indian Context*, edited by Deepak Kumar, 139–51. Delhi: Anamika Prakashan, 1991.

Hahn, Roger. "New Considerations on the Physical Sciences of the Enlightenment Era." *Studies on Voltaire and the Eighteenth Century* 264 (1989): 789–796.

———. "The Laplacean View of Calculation." In *The Quantifying Spirit in the Eighteenth Century*, edited by Tore Frängsmyr, J. L. Heilbron, and Robin E. Rider, 363–80. Berkeley: University of California Press, 1990.

Hankins, Thomas L. *Science and the Enlightenment*. Cambridge: Cambridge University Press, 1985.

Harley, J. B. "Deconstructing the Map." *Cartographica* 26, no. 2 (1989): 1–20.

———. "Historical Geography and the Cartographic Illusion." *Journal of Historical Geography* 15 (1989): 80–91.

———. "Introduction: Texts and Contexts in the Interpretation of Early Maps." In *From Sea Charts to Satellite Images: Interpreting North American History Through Maps*, edited by David Buisseret, 3–15. Chicago: University of Chicago Press, 1990.

———. "Maps, Knowledge and Power." In *The Iconography of Landscape*, edited by Denis Cosgrove and Stephen J. Daniels, 277–312. Cambridge Studies in Historical Geography, 9. Cambridge: Cambridge University Press, 1988.

Harvey, David. *The Condition of Postmodernity: An Enquiry into the Origins of Cultural Change*. Oxford: Basil Blackwell, 1989.

Hassam, Andrew. "'As I Write': Narrative Occasions and the Quest for Self-Presence in the Travel Diary." *Ariel* 21, no. 4 (1990): 33–47.

Headrick, Daniel R. *The Tentacles of Progress: Technology Transfer in the Age of Imperialism, 1850–1940*. Oxford: Oxford University Press, 1988.

————. *The Tools of Empire: Technology and European Imperialism in the Nineteenth Century*. Oxford: Oxford University Press, 1981.

Heilbron, J. L. "The Measure of Enlightenment." In *The Quantifying Spirit in the Eighteenth Century*, edited by Tore Frängsmyr, J. L. Heilbron, and Robin E. Rider, 207–42. Berkeley: University of California Press, 1990.

Heyck, T. W. *The Transformation of Intellectual Life in Victorian England*. London: Croom Helm, 1982.

Hobsbawm, E. J. *Nations and Nationalism since 1870: Programme, Myth and Reality*. Cambridge: Cambridge University Press, 1990.

Horkheimer, Max, and Theodor W. Adorno. *Dialectic of Enlightenment*. Translated by John Cumming. New York: Herder and Herder, 1972.

Howse, Derek. *Nevil Maskelyne: The Seaman's Astronomer*. Cambridge: Cambridge University Press, 1989.

Inden, Ronald. *Imagining India*. Oxford: Basil Blackwell, 1990.

Inkster, Ian, and Jack Morrell, eds. *Metropolis and Province: Science in British Culture, 1780–1850*. Philadelphia: University of Pennsylvania Press, 1983.

Jacob, Christian. *L'Empire des cartes: Approche théorique de la cartographie à travers l'histoire*. Paris: Bibliothèque Albin Michel, 1992.

Kaye, George R., and Edward H. Johnstone. *Minor Collections and Miscellaneous Manuscripts*. Vol. 2.2 of *Catalogue of Manuscripts in European Languages in the India Office Library*. London, 1937.

Kejariwal, O. P. *The Asiatic Society of Bengal and the Discovery of India's Past, 1784–1838*. Delhi: Oxford University Press, 1988.

Kolff, Dirk H. A. "End of an *Ancien Régime*: Colonial War in India, 1798–1818." In *Imperialism and War: Essays on Colonial Wars in Asia and Africa*, edited by J. A. de Moor and H. L. Wesseling, 22–49. Leiden: E. J. Brill for Universitaire Pers Leiden, 1989.

Konvitz, Josef W. *Cartography in France, 1660–1848: Science, Engineering, and Statecraft*. Chicago: University of Chicago Press, 1987.

————. "The Nation-State, Paris and Cartography in Eighteenth- and Nineteenth-Century France." *Journal of Historical Geography* 16 (1990): 3–16.

Kopf, David. *British Orientalism and the Bengal Renaissance: The Dynamics of Indian Modernization, 1773–1835*. Berkeley: University of California Press, 1969.

Kula, Witold. *Measures and Men*. Translated by Richard Szreter. Princeton: Princeton University Press, 1986.

Kumar, Deepak. "Colonial Science: A Look at the Indian Experience." In *Science and Empire: Essays in Indian Context*, edited by Deepak Kumar, 6–12. Delhi: Anamika Prakashan, 1991.

———. "Economic Compulsions and the Geological Survey of India." *Indian Journal of History of Science* 17 (1982): 289–300.

———. "The Evolution of Colonial Science: Natural History and the East India Company." In *Imperialism and the Natural World*, edited John M. Mackenzie, 51–66. Manchester: Manchester University Press, 1990.

———. "Patterns of Colonial Science in India." *Indian Journal of History of Science* 15 (1980): 105–13.

———. "Problems in Science Administration: A Study of the Scientific Surveys in British India, 1757–1900." In *Science and Empires: Historical Studies about Scientific Development and European Expansion*, edited by Patrick Petitjohn, Catherine Jami, and Anne Marie Moulin, 269–80. Boston Studies in the Philosophy of Science, 136. Dordrecht: Kluwer Academic, 1992.

———. "Racial Discrimination and Science in Nineteenth Century India." *The Indian Economic and Social History Review* 19 (1982): 63–82.

Lesch, John E. "Systematics and the Geometrical Spirit." In *The Quantifying Spirit in the Eighteenth Century*, edited by Tore Frängsmyr, J. L. Heilbron, and Robin E. Rider, 73–111. Berkeley: University of California Press, 1990.

Livingstone, David N. *The Geographical Tradition: Episodes in the History of a Contested Enterprise*. Oxford: Basil Blackwell, 1992.

Ludden, David. "Orientalist Empiricism: Transformations of Colonial Knowledge." In *Orientalism and the Postcolonial Predicament: Perspectives on South Asia*, edited by Carol A. Breckenridge and Peter van der Veer, 250–78. Philadelphia: University of Pennsylvania Press, 1993.

———. *Peasant History in South India*. Princeton: Princeton University Press, 1985.

Mackenzie, John M. *Orientalism: History, Theory and the Arts*. Manchester: Manchester University Press, 1995.

MacLeod, Roy M. "On Visiting the 'Moving Metropolis': Reflections on the Architecture of Imperial Science." *Historical Records of Australian Science* 5, no. 3 (1982): 1–16.

Mahajan, Jagmohan. *The Raj Landscape: British Views of Indian Cities*. New Delhi: Spantech Publishers, 1988.

Marshall, P. J. "Taming the Exotic: The British and India in the Seventeenth and Eighteenth Centuries." In *Exoticism and the Enlightenment*, edited by G. S. Rousseau and Roy Porter, 46–65. Manchester: Manchester University Press, 1990.

Metcalf, Thomas R. *Ideologies of the Raj*. Vol. 3.4 of *The New Cambridge History of India*. Cambridge: Cambridge University Press, 1994.

———. *An Imperial Vision: Indian Architecture and Britain's Raj*. Berkeley: University of California Press, 1989.

Miller, David P. "The Royal Society of London, 1800–1835: A Study in the Cultural Politics of Scientific Organization." Ph.D. diss. University of Pennsylvania, 1981.

Misra, B. B. *The Administrative History of India, 1834–1947: General Administration*. Oxford: Oxford University Press, 1970.

———. *The Central Administration of the East India Company, 1773–1834.* Manchester: Manchester University Press, 1959.

———. *The Unification and Division of India.* Delhi: Oxford University Press, 1990.

Mitchell, W. J. T. "Imperial Landscape." In *Landscape and Power*, edited by W. J. T. Mitchell, 5–34. Chicago: University of Chicago Press, 1994.

Moir, Martin. "The Examiner's Office and the Drafting of East India Company Despatches." In *East India Company Studies: Papers Presented to Professor Sir Cyril Philips*, edited by Kenneth Ballhatchet and John Harrison, 125–52. Hong Kong: Asian Research Service.

———. "The Examiner's Office: The Emergence of an Administrative Élite in East India House (1804–58)." *India Office Library and Records Annual Report for the Year 1977*, 25–42. London, 1979.

Moore, D. T. "New Light on the Life and Indian Geological Work of H. W. Voysey (1791–1824)." *Archives of Natural History* 12 (1985): 107–34.

Morrell, Jack, and Arnold Thackery. *Gentlemen of Science: Early Years of the British Association for the Advancement of Science.* Oxford: Oxford University Press, 1981.

Mukherjee, Soumyendra Nath. *Sir William Jones: A Study in Eighteenth-Century British Attitudes to India.* Cambridge: Cambridge University Press, 1968. Hyderabad: Orient Longman, 1987, 2d ed.

Murty, K. S. "Geological Sciences in India in the 18th–19th Centuries." *Indian Journal of History of Science* 17 (1982): 164–78.

Nicolet, Claude. *Space, Geography, and Politics in the Early Roman Empire.* Jerome Lectures, 19. Ann Arbor: University of Michigan Press, 1991.

Noyes, John K. *Colonial Space: Spatiality in the Discourse of German South West Africa, 1884–1915.* Studies in Anthropology and History, 4. Chur, Switzerland: Harwood Academic Publishers, 1992.

———. "The Representation of Spatial History." *Pretexts* 4, no. 2 (1993): 120–27.

Oliver, Richard. "The Ordnance Survey in Great Britain, 1835–1870." D.Phil. diss. University of Sussex, 1986.

Pal, Pratapaditya. "Indian Artists and British Patrons in Calcutta." *Marg* 41, no. 4 (1989): 17–34.

Pal, Pratapaditya, and Vidya Dehejia. *From Merchants to Emperors: British Artists and India, 1757–1930.* Ithaca, NY: Cornell University Press for the Pierpont Morgan Library, New York, 1986.

Pedley, Mary. "Maps, War, and Commerce: Business Correspondence with the London Map Firm of Thomas Jefferys and William Faden." *Imago Mundi* 48 (1996): 161–73.

Peers, Douglas M. "'The Habitual Nobility of Being': British Officers and the Social Construction of the Bengal Army in the Early Nineteenth Century." *Modern Asian Studies* 25 (1991): 545–69.

Perera, Maharage Christopher Nihal. "Decolonizing Ceylon: Society and Space in Sri Lanka." Ph.D. diss. State University of New York at Binghamton, 1994.

Philips, C. H. *The East India Company, 1784–1834.* 2d ed. Manchester: Manchester University Press, 1961.

Pickles, John. "Texts, Hermeneutics and Propaganda Maps." In *Writing Worlds: Discourse, Text and Metaphor in the Representation of Landscape*, edited by Trevor J. Barnes and James S. Duncan, 193–230. London: Routledge, 1992.

Porter, Roy. "The Terraqueous Globe." In *The Ferment of Knowledge: Studies in the Historiography of Eighteenth-Century Science*, edited by G. S. Rousseau and Roy Porter, 285–324. Cambridge: Cambridge University Press, 1980.

Porter, Theodore M. *The Rise of Statistical Thinking, 1820–1900*. Princeton: Princeton University Press, 1986.

Prain, David. "A Sketch of the Life of Francis Hamilton called Buchanan." In Otto Stapf, *The Aconites of India: A Monograph*, Royal Botanic Gardens, Calcutta, *Annals* 10, no. 2, i–lxxv. Calcutta, 1905.

Pratt, Mary Louise. *Imperial Eyes: Travel Writing and Transculturation*. London: Routledge, 1992.

Pyenson, Lewis. "Astronomy and Imperialism: J. A. C. Oudemans, the Topography of the East Indies, and the Rise of the Utrecht Observatory, 1850–1900." *Historia Scientiarum* 26 (1984): 39–81.

Qaisar, Ahsan Jan. *The Indian Response to European Technology and Culture, AD 1498–1757*. Delhi: Oxford University Press, 1982.

Raj, Kapil. "Knowledge, Power and Modern Science: The Brahmins Strike Back." In *Science and Empire: Essays in Indian Context*, edited by Deepak Kumar, 115–25. Delhi: Anamika Prakashan, 1991.

Rashad, Roshdi. "Science as a Western Phenomenon." *Fundamenta Scientiae* 1 (1980): 7–23.

Renford, Raymond K. *The Non-Official British in India to 1920*. Delhi: Oxford University Press, 1987.

Richards, Thomas. *The Imperial Archive: Knowledge and the Fantasy of Empire*. London: Verso, 1993.

Rider, Robin E. "Measure of Ideas, Rule of Language: Mathematics and Language in the 18th Century." In *The Quantifying Spirit in the Eighteenth Century*, edited by Tore Frängsmyr, J. L. Heilbron, and Robin E. Rider, 113–40. Berkeley: University of California Press, 1990.

Rocher, Rosane. "British Orientalism in the Eighteenth Century: The Dialectics of Knowledge and Government." In *Orientalism and the Postcolonial Predicament: Perspectives on South Asia*, edited by Carol A. Breckenridge and Peter van der Veer, 215–49. Philadelphia: University of Pennsylvania Press, 1993.

Rose, Gillian. *Feminism and Geography: The Limits of Geographical Knowledge*. Minneapolis: University of Minnesota Press, 1993.

Rosselli, John. *Lord William Bentinck: The Making of a Liberal Imperialist, 1774–1839*. London: Chatto & Windus for Sussex University Press, 1974.

Rousseau, G. S., and Roy Porter, eds. *The Ferment of Knowledge: Studies in the Historiography of Eighteenth-Century Science*. Cambridge: Cambridge University Press, 1980.

Rundstrom, Robert A. "Mapping, Postmodernism, Indigenous People, and the Changing Direction of North American Cartography." *Cartographica* 28, no. 2 (1991): 1–12.

Said, Edward W. *Culture and Imperialism.* New York: Alfred A. Knopf, 1993.
———. *Orientalism.* New York: Random House, 1978.
———. "Yeats and Decolonization." In Terry Eagleton, Frederick Jameson, and Edward W. Said, *Nationalism, Colonialism, and Literature,* 69–95. Minneapolis: University of Minnesota Press, 1990.
Sandes, E. W. C. *The Indian Sappers and Miners.* Chatham: The Institution of Royal Engineers, 1948.
———. *The Military Engineer in India.* 2 vols. Chatham: The Institution of Royal Engineers, 1933.
Sangwan, Satpal. "Indian Response to European Science and Technology, 1757–1857." *British Journal for the History of Science* 21 (1988): 211–32.
———. "Natural History in Colonial Context: Profit or Pursuit? British Botanical Enterprise in India, 1778–1820." In *Science and Empires: Historical Studies about Scientific Development and European Expansion,* edited by Patrick Petitjohn, Catherine Jami, and Anne Marie Moulin, 281–98. Boston Studies in the Philosophy of Science, 136. Dordrecht: Kluwer Academic, 1992.
———. "Reordering the Earth: The Emergence of Geology as Scientific Discipline in Colonial India." *Earth Sciences History* 12 (1993): 224–33.
———. *Science, Technology, and Colonisation: An Indian Experience, 1757–1857.* Delhi: Anamika Prakashan, 1991.
———. "Technology and Imperialism in the Indian Context: The Case of Steamboats, 1819–1839." In *Science, Medicine and Cultural Imperialism,* edited by Teresa Meade and Mark Walker, 60–74. New York: St. Martin's Press, 1991.
Scheurleer, Pauline Lunsingh. "Rich Remains from Social Anthropological Fieldwork in Eighteenth-Century India." *Journal of the History of Collections* 8, no. 1 (1996): 71–91.
Scholberg, Henry. *The District Gazetteers of British India: A Bibliography.* Zug: Inter Documentation Company, 1970.
Sen, S. N. "The Character of the Introduction of Western Science in India during the Eighteenth and Nineteenth Centuries." *Indian Journal of History of Science* 1 (1966): 112–22.
Seymour, W. A., ed. *A History of the Ordnance Survey.* Folkestone, Kent: Dawson, 1980.
Spear, Percival. *The Nabobs: A Study of the Social Life of the English in 18th Century India.* London: Oxford University Press, 1963.
Spurr, David. *The Rhetoric of Empire: Colonial Discourse in Journalism, Travel Writing, and Imperial Administration.* Durham, NC: Duke University Press, 1993.
Stafford, Barbara M. *Voyage into Substance: Art, Science, Nature, and the Illustrated Travel Account, 1760–1840.* Cambridge, MA: The MIT Press, 1984.
Standring, Timothy J. "Watercolor Landscape Sketching during the Popular Picturesque Era in Britain." In Michael Rosenthal et al., *Glorious Nature: British Landscape Painting, 1750–1850,* 73–84. New York: Hudson Hills Press, 1993.
Stein, Burton. *Thomas Munro: The Origins of the Colonial State and His Vision of Empire.* Oxford: Oxford University Press, 1989.

Stewart, Gordon T. "Tenzing's Two Wrist-Watches: The Conquest of Everest and Late Imperial Culture in Britain, 1921–1953." *Past & Present* 149 (1995): 170–97.

Stigler, Stephen M. *The History of Statistics: The Measurement of Uncertainty before 1900.* Cambridge, MA: Harvard University Press, 1986.

Stokes, Eric. *The English Utilitarians and India.* Oxford: Clarendon Press, 1959.

Stoler, Ann Laura. "Rethinking Colonial Categories: European Communities and the Boundaries of Rule." *Comparative Studies in Society and History* 31 (1989): 134–61.

Stone, Jeffrey C. "Imperialism, Cartography and Cartography." *Transactions of the Institute of British Geographers,* ns 13 (1988): 57–64.

Subbarayappa, B. V. "Western Science in India up to the End of the Nineteenth Century AD." In *A Concise History of Science in India,* edited by D. M. Bose, S. N. Sen, and B. V. Subbarayappa, 490–97. New Delhi: Indian National Sciences Academy, 1971.

Suleri, Sara. *The Rhetoric of English India.* Chicago: University of Chicago Press, 1992.

Tammita Delgoda, Asoka SinhaRaja. "Nabob, Historian and Orientalist: The Life and Writings of Robert Orme (1728–1801)." Ph.D. diss. University of London, 1991.

———. "'Nabob, Historian, and Orientalist.' Robert Orme: The Life and Career of an East India Company Servant (1728–1801)." *Journal of the Royal Asiatic Society* 3s 2 (1992): 363–76.

Taylor, E. G. R. *The Mathematical Practitioners of Hanoverian England, 1714–1840.* Cambridge: Cambridge University Press for the Institute of Navigation, 1966.

Thongchai Winichakul. *Siam Mapped: A History of the Geo-Body of a Nation.* Honolulu: University of Hawaii Press, 1994.

Tilly, Charles. *Coercion, Capital, and European States, AD 990–1992.* Studies in Social Discontinuity. Oxford: Blackwell, 1990.

Tillotson, G. H. R. "The Paths of Glory: Representations of Sher Shah's Tomb." *Oriental Art,* ns 37 (1991): 4–16.

Toulmin, Stephen. *Cosmopolis: The Hidden Agenda of Modernity.* New York: The Free Press, 1990.

Turner, Stephen P. "Forms of Patronage." In *Theories of Science in Society,* edited by Susan E. Cozzens and Thomas F. Gieryn, 185–211. Bloomington: Indiana University Press, 1990.

Vasantha, A. "The 'Oriental-Occidental Controversy' of 1839 [*sic*] and Its Impact on Indian Science." In *Science and Empires: Historical Studies about Scientific Development and European Expansion,* edited by Patrick Petitjohn, Catherine Jami, and Anne Marie Moulin, 49–56. Boston Studies in the Philosophy of Science, 136. Dordrecht: Kluwer Academic, 1992.

Vicziany, Marika. "Imperialism, Botany and Statistics in Early Nineteenth-Century India: The Surveys of Francis Buchanan (1762–1829)." *Modern Asian Studies* 20 (1986): 625–60.

Walters, Gwyn. "The Antiquary and the Map." *Word & Image* 4 (1988): 529–44.

Weber, Max. *Economy and Society: An Outline of Interpretive Sociology.* Edited by Guenther Roth and Claus Wittich. 2 vols. New York, 1968. Reprint, Berkeley: University of California Press, 1978.

Williams, Raymond. *The Sociology of Culture.* New York: Schocken Books, 1982.

Wilson, H. H. *A Descriptive Catalogue of the Oriental Manuscripts and other Articles . . . Collected by the late Lieut. Col. Colin Mackenzie.* 2 vols. Calcutta, 1828; 2d ed., 1882.

Withers, Charles W. J. "Geography in Its Time: Geography and Historical Geography in Diderot and d'Alembert's *Encyclopédie.*" *Journal of Historical Geography* 19 (1993): 255–64.

Wood, Denis. "Maps and Mapmaking." *Cartographica* 30, no. 1 (1993): 1–9.

————. *The Power of Maps.* New York: Guilford, 1992.

Yeo, Richard. "Reading Encyclopaedias: Science and the Organization of Knowledge in British Dictionaries of Arts and Sciences, 1730–1850." *Isis* 82 (1991): 24–49.

Young, Robert. *White Mythologies: Writing History and the West.* London: Routledge, 1990.

Yule, Henry, and A. C. Burnell, comps. *Hobson-Jobson: A Glossary of Colloquial Anglo-Indian Words and Phrases, and of Kindred Terms, Etymological, Historical, Geographical and Discursive.* New edition, edited by William Crooke. London, 1903; reprint, Delhi: Munshiram Manoharlal, 1968.

INDEX

Boldface page numbers refer to figures in the text.